Lecture Notes in Computer Science

Edited by G. Goos and J. Hartmanis

193

Logics of Programs

Brooklyn, June 17–19, 1985
Proceedings

Edited by Rohit Parikh

Springer-Verlag
Berlin Heidelberg New York Tokyo

Editor

Rohit Parikh
Department of Computer and Information Science, Brooklyn College
Brooklyn, New York 11210, USA

CR Subject Classifications (1985): F.3, D.3.1, D.3.3, D.2.4, F.4.1

ISBN 3-540-15648-8 Springer-Verlag Berlin Heidelberg New York Tokyo
ISBN 0-387-15648-8 Springer-Verlag New York Heidelberg Berlin Tokyo

Printed in Germany

Printing and binding: Beltz Offsetdruck, Hemsbach/Bergstr.
2145/3140-543210

Preface

This volume contains the papers presented at a conference on the Logic of Programs, held at Brooklyn College, June 17-19, 1985. The conference is one of a series of international conferences on Logic of Programs, and the first one to have refereed papers.

The conference was originally to be held in Boston with Dennis Kfoury in charge. However, a Fulbright fellowship took him out of the country, and the job fell on my shoulders with less than a year to prepare for the meeting. I owe Dexter Kozen, Ashok Chandra and Ed Clarke a special debt for helping out with this initial phase.

The program committee consisted of K. Apt, E. Clarke, R. Constable, J. Halpern, D. Kozen, A. Meyer, R. Parikh, R. Statman and J. Tiuryn. I thank the other eight members for their help in the refereeing process as well as with various practical questions. K. McAloon and R. Sigal helped out with local arrangements and Valerie Domfort served as an excellent program secretary.

Financial support for the conference was provided by Brooklyn College, IBM and the National Science Foundation.

We note the sad loss of Irina Bercovici who died before the conference took place. Thanks are due to Albert Meyer for agreeing to prepare her paper for publication and to present it at the meeting.

Rohit Parikh
Larchmont, NY

Table of Contents

*(Demo paper - A live demonstration was arranged)

NONCLAUSAL TEMPORAL DEDUCTION

Martin Abadi
Zohar Manna

Computer Science Department
Stanford University

Abstract

We present a proof system for propositional temporal logic. This system is based on nonclausal resolution; proofs are natural and generally short. Its extension to first-order temporal logic is considered.

Two variants of the system are described. The first one is for a logic with $\Box$ ("always"), $\Diamond$ ("sometime"), and $\bigcirc$ ("next"). The second variant is an extension of the first one to a logic with the additional operators $\mathcal{U}$ ("until") and $\mathcal{P}$ ("precedes"). Each of these variants is proved complete.

1. Introduction

Propositional temporal logic (PTL) is described in [MP]. The language of PTL contains the usual propositional connectives (say, $\wedge$, $\vee$, $\neg$, $\supset$), and modal operators. Time is assumed discrete and linear. In PTL, if u and v range over formulas,

- $\bigcirc u$ means "u is true in the next state";
- $\Box u$ means "u is always true (from now on)";
- $\Diamond u$ means "u is eventually true"; in other words, $\Diamond u \equiv \neg \Box \neg u$;
- $u \,\mathcal{U}\, v$ means "u is true until v is true"; in particular, u is true forever if v is never true (therefore, $\mathcal{U}$ is often called "weak until" or "unless");
- $u \,\mathcal{P}\, v$ means "u precedes v"; in other words, u occurs at least once before v occurs, and u occurs even if v never does, i.e., $(u \,\mathcal{P}\, v) \equiv \neg((\neg u) \,\mathcal{U}\, v)$.

Some other proof systems for PTL have been proposed in the literature. For instance, [GPSS] presents a complete Hilbert-style proof system; this system is theoretically interesting, but not very practical.

Wolper ([W]) discusses the tableau decision procedure for an extended temporal logic (ETL), a proper superset of PTL. The nondeterministic version of this decision procedure is optimal, in the sense that it achieves the worst-case lower bound for the complexity of the ETL decision problem. However, it acts uniformly on all inputs, and may do useless work on irrelevant parts

This research was supported in part by the National Science Foundation under grant MCS-81-11586, by Defense Advanced Research Projects Agency under Contract N00039-84-C-0211, and by the United States Air Force Office of Scientific Research under Contract AFOSR-81-0014.

of them. Moreover, neither the Hilbert-style system of [GPSS] nor the tableaux of [W] seem "liftable" to first-order temporal logic in a natural and efficient way.

Cavalli and Fariñas ([C], [CF]) extended the classical clausal resolution of [R] to PTL. Their approach is more promising than the previous ones in terms of both speed and extensibility. (We believe that their system is complete, but their completeness proof is incorrect.)

In this paper we extend nonclausal resolution ([MW], [M]) to PTL. Nonclausal resolution has the advantage over the classical clausal resolution of not requiring formulas to be in clause form, and thus making them more intelligible. For instance, we can express directly

$$\bigcirc \Box((p \supset \bigcirc q) \wedge (q \supset \bigcirc p)),$$

while in clause form, as defined in [CF], one would have to rewrite this as

$$\Box(\bigcirc \neg p \vee \bigcirc \bigcirc q) \;\wedge\; \Box(\bigcirc \neg q \vee \bigcirc \bigcirc p).$$

Like regular nonclausal resolution proofs, our proofs are generally concise and clear, and do not require guessing clever lemmas. Moreover, some attractive refinements to resolution can easily be incorporated into our system.

In Section 2, we present a version $\mathfrak{R}$ of our system for $\bigcirc$, $\Box$ and $\Diamond$. In Section 4, we extend it to $\mathfrak{R}^+$ to deal also with $\mathcal{U}$ and $\mathcal{P}$. Actually, in the extended system $\mathfrak{R}^+$, we can regard $\Box u$ and $\Diamond u$ as abbreviations for $u \,\mathcal{U}$ *false* and $u \,\mathcal{P}$ *false*, respectively. Both $\mathfrak{R}$ and $\mathfrak{R}^+$ are shown to be complete, in Sections 3 and 5, respectively. In Section 6 we suggest how to lift $\mathfrak{R}$ and $\mathfrak{R}^+$ to first-order temporal logic, despite the intrinsic incompleteness problems involved.

2. $\mathfrak{R}$: The resolution system for $\bigcirc$, $\Box$, $\Diamond$

We write $\vdash w$ to mean that the propositional temporal logic formula w is provable by refutation resolution, i.e., that there is a sequence of formulas $S_0, \ldots, S_n$, such that $S_0 = \neg w$, $S_n = \mathit{false}$, and each S_i is obtained from previous formulas in the sequence by rules of the system. We refer to the S_i's as *proof steps*, and to $S_0, \ldots, S_n$ as a *proof*. For each i, we call $T_i = S_0 \wedge \ldots \wedge S_i$ a *proof trace*.

For our proof notion to be meaningful, we require that rules be sound, i.e., that they maintain satisfiability: T_{j+1} is satisfiable if and only if T_j is satisfiable, for all $j \leq (n-1)$.

While pure refutation systems are sometimes considered counterintuitive, we can easily modify our rules to show directly the validity of a sentence. The modified system we obtain is similar in spirit to the one in [MW].

We distinguish two classes of rules: simplification rules and resolution rules.

(A) Simplification rules

These rules simplify formulas, or put them in forms where the other rules can be applied. They are all of the form

$$G \Rightarrow D.$$

This can be read:

"let u_G be an instance of G, and u_D the corresponding instance of D;
if u_G occurs in the step S_i in T_j, then S_{j+1} is S_i with u_G replaced by u_D."

- *true-false* reduction rules:
  These rules include

$$\Box\, true \Rightarrow true \qquad \Diamond\, true \Rightarrow true \qquad \bigcirc\, true \Rightarrow true$$
$$\Box\, false \Rightarrow false \qquad \Diamond\, false \Rightarrow false \qquad \bigcirc\, false \Rightarrow false$$

  and the regular *true-false* reduction rules in propositional logic, such as $false \wedge u \Rightarrow false$, etc..

- Weakening rules:

$$A \wedge B \Rightarrow A, \qquad A \wedge B \Rightarrow B.$$

  These rules are restricted to positive occurrences of instances of $A \wedge B$ (i.e., to occurrences embedded in an even number, explicit or implicit, of $\neg$'s). This polarity restriction guarantees the soundness of the rules.

- Distribution rules ($\neg$ over modalities):

$$\neg \Box u \Rightarrow \Diamond \neg u, \qquad \neg \Diamond u \Rightarrow \Box \neg u, \qquad \neg \bigcirc u \Rightarrow \bigcirc \neg u.$$

- Distribution rules ($\neg$ over connectives):

$$\neg(u \vee v) \Rightarrow (\neg u \wedge \neg v), \qquad \neg(u \wedge v) \Rightarrow (\neg u \vee \neg v), \qquad \neg\neg u \Rightarrow u.$$

  Similar rules are added for the other connectives.

(B) Resolution rules

We will have a resolution operator R to obtain new formulas from given ones. Our resolution rules will be of the two following forms:

- unary:

$$R[G] \longmapsto D.$$

  This can be read:

  "let u_G be an instance of G, and u_D the corresponding instance of D;
  if u_G occurs in the step S_i in T_j, then S_{j+1} is S_i with u_G replaced by $u_G \wedge u_D$
  (in the special case where $u_G = S_i$, it suffices to take $S_{j+1} = u_D$)."

- binary:

$$R[G_1, G_2] \longmapsto D.$$

  This can be read:

  "let u_{G_1} and u_{G_2} be instances of G_1 and G_2, and u_D the corresponding instance of D;
  if $u_1 \wedge \ldots \wedge u_k$ occurs in the step S_i in T_j, and for some h and h' (possibly $h = h'$),
  $u_{G_1} = u_h$ and $u_{G_2} = u_{h'}$, then S_{j+1} is S_i with $u_1 \wedge \ldots \wedge u_k$ replaced by $u_1 \wedge \ldots \wedge u_k \wedge u_D$;
  if for some h and h' (possibly $h = h'$), $u_{G_1} = S_h$ and $u_{G_2} = S_{h'}$, then we take $S_{j+1} = u_D$."

We will say that the given formulas u_G or u_{G_1}, u_{G_2} are being *resolved upon*, and that the derived sentence u_D is one of their *resolvents*.

Polarity restriction: The rule may be applied only to u_G, u_{G_1}, u_{G_2} which occur with positive polarity (i.e., the given formulas are embedded in an even number, explicit or implicit, of $\neg$'s). Each of our rules has the property that u_D is a logical consequence of u_G or $u_{G_1} \wedge u_{G_2}$. Therefore, with the polarity restriction, the soundness of our rules is guaranteed.

Here are the resolution rules:

The basic rule

The basic nonclausal resolution rule for propositional logic is:

$$R[A\langle u\rangle,\ B\langle u\rangle] \ \longmapsto\ A\langle \mathit{true}\rangle \vee B\langle \mathit{false}\rangle.$$

That is, if the formulas $A\langle u\rangle$ and $B\langle u\rangle$ have a common subsentence u, then we can derive the resolvent $A\langle \mathit{true}\rangle \vee B\langle \mathit{false}\rangle$. This is obtained by replacing certain occurrences of u in $A\langle u\rangle$ with *true*, and certain occurrences of u in $B\langle u\rangle$ with *false*, and taking the disjunction of the results. (Here "certain occurrences" means one or more occurrences.)

This rule does not carry over to PTL. The problem is that while u occurs in both A and B, it need not denote the same truth value in all its occurrences; intuitively, each occurrence of u may refer to different instants of time. In other words, PTL is not compositional. For example, from $\neg u$ and $\diamond u$ we cannot soundly deduce $\neg \mathit{true} \vee \diamond \mathit{false}$, because while the hypotheses are satisfiable (e.g., by the model which makes u false now, but true otherwise), $\neg \mathit{true} \vee \diamond \mathit{false}$ is always false.

The basic rule is sound in PTL under the following restrictions:

The occurrences of u in A or B that are substituted by *true* or *false*, respectively, are all in the scope of the same number of $\bigcirc$'s, and not in the scope of any $\square$ or $\diamond$ in A or B. Intuitively, this means that all the occurrences of u refer to the same instant of time.

For example, consider the formulas

$$A:\ \bigcirc\neg\bigcirc(\square p \vee q)\ \wedge\ \diamond\square p \quad \text{and} \quad B:\ \bigcirc\bigcirc\square p\ \vee\ \bigcirc\square p.$$

Taking u to be $\square p$, the rule allows us to derive the resolvent

$$(\bigcirc\neg\bigcirc(\mathit{true}\ \vee\ q)\ \wedge\ \diamond\square p)\ \vee\ (\bigcirc\bigcirc \mathit{false}\ \vee\ \bigcirc\square p).$$

We only substituted *true* or *false* for those occurrences in the scope of two $\bigcirc$'s. These occurrences are not in the scope of any $\square$ or $\diamond$. We cannot replace the other occurrence of $\square p$ in A by *true*, since it is not in the scope of two $\bigcirc$'s and it is in the scope of a $\diamond$. Also, we cannot replace the other occurrence of $\square p$ in B by *false*, since it is in the scope of only one $\bigcirc$.

This rule is quite general, but does not handle u's in the scope of $\square$'s and $\diamond$'s, and is certainly not complete. To complement this rule, we develop the following additional rules.

Modality rules

These are rules to handle formulas in the scope of $\Box$, $\Diamond$ and $\bigcirc$. They allow us to resolve upon formulas which are otherwise not accessible, because they are in the scope of some modal operator.

- $\Box$ rule:

$$R[\Box u] \longmapsto u \wedge \bigcirc \Box u.$$

- $\Diamond$ rule:

$$R[\Diamond u] \longmapsto u \vee \bigcirc \Diamond u.$$

- $\Box\,\Box$ rule:

$$R[\Box u, \Box v] \longmapsto \Box(\Box u \wedge v).$$

After applying this rule, we we will often attempt to resolve $\Box u$ and v. Thus, we could informally write

$$R[\Box u, \Box v] \longmapsto \Box R[\Box u, v].$$

(Other modality rules can be rephrased similarly, to reflect their intended use.)

- $\Box\,\Diamond$ rule:

$$R[\Box u, \Diamond v] \longmapsto \Diamond(\Box u \wedge v).$$

- $\Diamond\,\Diamond$ rule:

$$R[\Diamond u, \Diamond v] \longmapsto \Diamond(\Diamond u \wedge v) \vee \Diamond(u \wedge \Diamond v).$$

- $\bigcirc\,\bigcirc$ rule:

$$R[\bigcirc u, \bigcirc v] \longmapsto \bigcirc(u \wedge v).$$

Two useful derived rules are:

- $\Box\,\bigcirc$ derived rule (obtained from the $\Box$ and $\bigcirc\,\bigcirc$ rules, with weakening):

$$R[\Box u, \bigcirc v] \longmapsto \bigcirc(\Box u \wedge v).$$

- $\Diamond\,\bigcirc$ derived rule (obtained from the $\Diamond$ and $\bigcirc\,\bigcirc$ rules):

$$R[\Diamond u, \bigcirc v] \longmapsto u \vee \bigcirc(\Diamond u \wedge v).$$

Our powerful induction principle (presented below) makes some of these rules (in fact, all but $\Box$, $\Diamond$, and $\bigcirc\,\bigcirc$) unnecessary for completeness. We include them because they often provide convenient and natural short-cuts in proofs.

The induction rule

The induction rule (μ) is:

if $\vdash \neg(w \wedge u)$, then

$$R[w, \Diamond u] \longmapsto \Diamond(\neg u \wedge \bigcirc(u \wedge \neg w)).$$

A special case of this rule (when $w = \neg u$) is

$$R[\neg u, \Diamond u] \longmapsto \Diamond(\neg u \wedge \bigcirc u).$$

This special case of μ evokes a form of the least number principle: if $\neg\Phi(0)$ and, for some n, $\Phi(n)$, then, for some m, $\neg\Phi(m) \wedge \Phi(m+1)$. However, our rule is more powerful in that it does not require $\neg u$, but simply $\vdash \neg(w \wedge u)$, for some w.

The extra flexibility of having an arbitrary w as hypothesis to μ will be essential for some proofs. The special case of μ will yield those proofs only if we add a special rule to introduce lemmas (intuitively, these lemmas would be useful in guessing inductive sentences). Such a system would depend on clever heuristics to discover good lemmas; of course, this feature is undesirable.

To show that the special case of μ described above is too rudimentary, consider the unsatisfiable sentence S:

$$p \wedge \Box(p \supset \bigcirc p) \wedge (\Diamond \Diamond \neg p).$$

One would like to be able to refute this sentence by induction. The special induction principle must be applied to conjuncts of form $\neg u$ and $\Diamond u$, and, therefore, we must take u to be $\Diamond \neg p$ to resolve upon $\Diamond \Diamond \neg p$. However, since $\neg \Diamond \neg p$ is not one of the conjuncts of S, the special rule cannot be applied. On the other hand, taking w to be $p \wedge \Box(p \supset \bigcirc p)$, the general rule μ can be applied; it requires that

$$\vdash \neg(p \wedge \Box(p \supset \bigcirc p) \wedge \Diamond \neg p),$$

which can easily be proved. Thus we can deduce

$$\Diamond(\neg \Diamond \neg p \wedge \bigcirc(\Diamond \neg p \wedge \neg(p \wedge \Box(p \supset \bigcirc p))))$$

and this leads to a refutation of S in just a few trivial steps.

Distribution rules

Consider the following example. We know that

$$\Box(\neg p \wedge \neg q) \wedge (\Diamond p \vee \Diamond q)$$

is unsatisfiable; we should therefore be able to derive *false* from it. A natural way to do this is to resolve $\Box(\neg p \wedge \neg q)$ with $\Diamond p$ to obtain *false* (by $\Box \Diamond$ and the basic rule), and $\Box(\neg p \wedge \neg q)$ with $\Diamond q$ to obtain *false* (by the same rules), and to form the disjunction of these results. We get *false* $\vee$ *false*, and, then, *false*, concluding the refutation. A key step in this proof was our ability to resolve over $\vee$ in $\Diamond p \vee \Diamond q$.

This motivates the following $\vee$ and $\wedge$ rules:

$$R[u, v \vee w] \longmapsto (u \wedge v) \vee (u \wedge w),$$

$$R[u, v \wedge w] \longmapsto (u \wedge v \wedge w).$$

One can write similar rules for the other propositional connectives, e.g., $\supset$ and *if-then-else*.

An example

Let us prove the validity of the sentence

$$[p \wedge \Box(p \supset \bigcirc \Diamond p)] \supset \Box \Diamond p.$$

In other words, we will refute the sentence

$$[p \wedge \Box(p \supset \bigcirc \Diamond p)] \wedge \neg \Box \Diamond p$$

The refutation is:

1) $[p \wedge \Box(p \supset \bigcirc \Diamond p)] \wedge \neg \Box \Diamond p$	initial assertion
2) p	by weakening (line 1)
3) $\Box(p \supset \bigcirc \Diamond p)$	by weakening (line 1)
4) $\Diamond \neg \Diamond p$	by weakening (line 1), and distributing $\neg$ over $\Diamond$
5) $\Diamond(\neg\neg \Diamond p \wedge \bigcirc(\neg \Diamond p \wedge \neg p))$	by μ (from lines 3 and 4) since $\vdash \neg(p \wedge \neg \Diamond p)$
6) $\Diamond(\Diamond p \wedge \bigcirc \neg \Diamond p)$	by simplifying $\neg\neg \Diamond p$ and weakening
7) $\Diamond((p \vee \bigcirc \Diamond p) \wedge \bigcirc \neg \Diamond p)$	by $\Diamond$
8) $\Diamond((p \wedge \bigcirc \neg \Diamond p) \vee (\bigcirc \Diamond p \wedge \bigcirc \neg \Diamond p))$	by $\vee$ distribution
9) $\Diamond((p \wedge \bigcirc \neg \Diamond p) \vee (\bigcirc \mathit{false} \vee \bigcirc \neg \mathit{true}))$	by the basic rule (on $\Diamond p$) and weakening
10) $\Diamond(p \wedge \bigcirc \neg \Diamond p)$	by simplification
11) $\Diamond((p \wedge \bigcirc \neg \Diamond p) \wedge \Box(p \supset \bigcirc \Diamond p))$	by $\Box \Diamond$ (with line 3)
12) $\Diamond((p \wedge \bigcirc \neg \Diamond p) \wedge (p \supset \bigcirc \Diamond p))$	by $\Box$ and weakening
13) $\Diamond((p \wedge \bigcirc \neg \Diamond p) \wedge ((\mathit{false} \wedge \bigcirc \neg \Diamond p) \vee (\mathit{true} \supset \bigcirc \Diamond p)))$	by the basic rule (on p) and weakening
14) $\Diamond((p \wedge \bigcirc \neg \Diamond p) \wedge \bigcirc \Diamond p)$	by simplification
15) $\Diamond((p \wedge \bigcirc \neg \mathit{true}) \wedge \bigcirc \mathit{false})$	by the basic rule (on $\Diamond p$) and weakening
16) $\Diamond\ \mathit{false}$	by simplification
17) false	by *false* reduction

To justify line 5, we still need to show a refutation for $\neg\neg(p \wedge \neg \Diamond p)$.

1′) $\neg\neg(p \wedge \neg \Diamond p)$	initial assertion
2′) $p \wedge \Box \neg p$	by simplification
3′) $p \wedge \neg p$	by $\Box$ and weakening
4′) false	by the basic rule and weakening

3. Soundness and completeness for $\Re$

We have

Soundness theorem. $\Re$ *is sound.*

and

Completeness theorem. $\Re$ *is complete.*

The proof of the soundness theorem is trivial. We give an outline of the completeness proof.

Proof outline

The tableau decision procedure of [W] is known to be complete. We show that if this decision procedure finds $\neg u$ unsatisfiable, then $\vdash u$. The resolution refutation for $\neg u$ may actually be quite similar to the one found in the tableau.

The tableau decision procedure creates a finite graph with formulas at the nodes. The initial node contains $\neg u$; each node contains formulas derived from those of its parent. Intuitively, children either

- expand what their parent says about the present (for instance, if N contains $\Box u$ then it may have a child with $\Box u$, $\bigcirc \Box u$ and u); or
- summarize what their parent says about tomorrow, by eliminating all formulas not of the form $\bigcirc v$ and erasing $\bigcirc$'s from all others; any node obtained in this way and the initial node are called *pre-states*.

A node is eliminated in the following three cases:

1) Clash: it contains a proposition and its negation;

2) Propagation: all of its descendants have been eliminated;

3) Eventualities: if the node is a pre-state and contains $\Diamond v_1, \ldots, \Diamond v_k$, and on no path from the node do all the v_i's occur.

$\neg u$ is found unsatisfiable if and only if all nodes of the tableau have been eliminated.

Our proof has three main parts; each of them corresponds to one of the ways to eliminate unsatisfiable nodes of the tableau. In each of them, we show that if a node is eliminated, then the formulas it contains can be refuted by $\Re$. They are proved together by induction on the tableau. In this induction, the rank of a node N is smaller than that of another node M if N is not an ancestor of M, and M is an ancestor of N. In particular, all nodes in a cycle have the same rank.

In this proof we will often (informally) identify a node with the set of formulas it contains. Sometimes this set will be identified with the conjunction of the formulas it contains; of course, this is merely for convenience, and involves no special assumptions.

1) Clash: The first case deals with nodes eliminated because they contain some proposition and its negation. Clearly, the formulas in such nodes could just as well be refuted in $\mathfrak{R}$, with the basic rule and the reduction rules for *true* and *false*.

2) Propagation: The second case deals with nodes whose children have all been eliminated. We can assume (by inductive hypothesis) that all those eliminated children could also be refuted in $\mathfrak{R}$, and show that the parent node can be refuted in $\mathfrak{R}$ as well. The proof of this inductive step involves a case analysis, where we consider which tableau rule the children where created by. Two examples of such cases are:

- The parent node contains $u_1, \ldots, u_n, \Box v$, and the child is created by the rule that expands $\Box$'s, i.e., the child contains $u_1, \ldots, u_n, \Box v, v, \bigcirc \Box v$. Assume there is a refutation of $u_1, \ldots, u_n, \Box v, v, \bigcirc \Box v$, to show that there is a refutation of $u_1, \ldots, u_n, \Box v$. This is trivial, by the $\Box$ rule.

- The parent node contains $v_1, \ldots, v_n, \bigcirc u_1, \ldots, \bigcirc u_k$, where the v_i's are not of the form $\bigcirc w$, and the child is created by the rule that erases $\bigcirc$'s, i.e., the child contains $u_1, \ldots, u_k$. Assume there is a refutation of $u_1, \ldots, u_k$, to show that $v_1, \ldots, v_n, \bigcirc u_1, \ldots, \bigcirc u_k$ can also be refuted. The $\bigcirc\bigcirc$ rule will give us a refutation for $\bigcirc u_1, \ldots, \bigcirc u_k$, which can be extended to a refutation for $v_1, \ldots, v_n, \bigcirc u_1, \ldots, \bigcirc u_k$.

3) Eventualities: Finally, the tableau method eliminates pre-states w which contain some unfulfillable eventualities (in other words, $w = v \wedge \Diamond u_1 \wedge \ldots \wedge \Diamond u_k$ and on no path from w do all the u_i's occur). We prove than w can be refuted.

- Since the tableau is finite, some paths from w must cycle back to w, and others may have been stopped further down in the tableau; we will only need to consider those that cycle back to w, and show that all nodes on these cycles can be eliminated (the other paths are dealt with by inductive hypothesis).

- Our goal will be to exploit the finite model property, and derive a formula Φ which expresses that at some point we are in one of the pre-states of the cycles, and at the next moment we are no longer in one. Furthermore, it will be easy to show that Φ can be refuted in $\mathfrak{R}$. The following five lemmas implement this basic idea.

- We will want to construct future pre-states from a given pre-state p_0. More precisely, we get w_i's that describe what the world can be like after i steps: w_i says that one of the pre-states at depth i will be true then. We will call w_i the ith *fringe* of p_0. For instance, if $p_0 = (\Box q \vee \Box r) \wedge \Diamond r$ then $w_0 = p_0$, and

$$w_1 = \bigcirc(\Box q \wedge \Diamond r) \vee \bigcirc\Box q \vee \bigcirc(\Box r \wedge \Diamond r) \vee \bigcirc\Diamond r.$$

While this lemma "normalizes" formulas (roughly, into disjunctions of conjunctions), this does not necessarily correspond to how most proofs work—generally, formulas seem to stay close to their original form.

Lemma 1:
Given a pre-state p_0, $\mathfrak{R}$ can derive formulas w_i built up from the pre-states p_i^l at depth i from p_0 with $\vee$ and $\bigcirc$. Furthermore, each p_i^l occurs in the scope of exactly i $\bigcirc$'s.

Proof:
Let $w_0 = p_0$. For all i, it is easy to obtain w_{i+1} from w_i:
Use the $\Box$ and $\Diamond$ rules to expand p_0, just like in the corresponding tableau. Use the rules for the connectives to push $\neg$'s inwards and to obtain a disjunction of conjunctions. Apply the $\bigcirc\bigcirc$ rule to pull $\bigcirc$'s out of conjunctions. Apply the basic rule whenever both a proposition and its negation appear in a conjunction at depth i. Then, by weakening, throw away all conjuncts at depth i; we are left with those at depth $i+1$.

This lemma does not depend on any inductive hypothesis, and applies to any p_0.

- Lemma 2 uses the inductive hypothesis to eliminate some unsatisfiable pre-states from the w_i's of Lemma 1. In particular, we can eliminate pre-states outside the cycles for w.

Lemma 2:
If in Lemma 1 $p_0 = w$ then the w_i's can be built in such a way that they only include pre-states from the cycles back to w.

Proof:
As soon as we get a pre-state p outside the cycles for w in the construction of Lemma 1, we apply the inductive hypothesis to refute it.

- The following lemma about the tableau decision procedure shows that we only need to worry about one eventuality at a time.

Lemma 3: If w contains the unfulfillable set of eventualities $\{\Diamond u_1, \ldots, \Diamond u_n\}$, then some u_i does not occur on any of the loops back to w.

Proof:
Suppose, on the contrary, that each eventuality is fulfilled on at least one of the loops back to w. Then we can find a path where they are all fulfilled: go through the loop where u_1 occurs, then through the loop where u_2 occurs, ..., then through the loop where u_n occurs. Since this contradicts our hypothesis, there must be one eventuality that is not fulfilled on any of the loops back to w.

Thus, from now on, we will have $w = v \wedge \Diamond u$, where u does not occur on any of the loops back to w.

- The unfulfillable eventuality $\Diamond u$ is blocked at every time in $\mathfrak{R}$.

Lemma 4:
For any i, $\vdash \neg(w_i \wedge \bigcirc^i u)$.

Proof:
Distribute $\bigcirc^i u$ over the pre-states in w_i and eliminate some occurrences of $\Diamond u$ (by weakening), in order to derive w_i' built up from pre-states of the tableau for w with $\vee$ and $\bigcirc$ (and, as usual, all pre-states at the same depth i). Let p be one of these pre-states. p cannot be on the cycles back to w, since it contains u. Hence, we can refute p in $\mathfrak{R}$ (by inductive hypothesis). Therefore, w_i' and $w_i \wedge \bigcirc^i u$ can also be refuted.

- Lemma 5 is the main lemma of the completeness proof.

Lemma 5:
If for all i $\vdash \neg(w_i \wedge \bigcirc^i u)$ then $\vdash \neg w$.

Proof:
$w = w_0$. From w_0 and $\Diamond u$, μ and weakening yield

$$\Diamond \bigcirc(u \wedge \neg w_0)$$

since $\vdash \neg(w_0 \wedge u)$ by hypothesis.
By Lemma 2, we can derive w_1. Furthermore, $\vdash \neg(w_1 \wedge \bigcirc u)$ by hypothesis. Thus, μ yields

$$\Diamond \bigcirc(\bigcirc(u \wedge \neg w_0)) \wedge \neg w_1).$$

In general, we can get all w_i's, and check that $\vdash \neg(w_i \wedge \bigcirc^i u)$, by hypothesis. Successive applications of μ will give

$$\Diamond \bigcirc(\bigcirc(\bigcirc \ldots \bigcirc(u \wedge \neg w_0) \wedge \ldots \wedge \neg w_{t-1}) \wedge \neg w_t)$$

for any t. We weaken this to

$$\Diamond \bigcirc(\bigcirc(\bigcirc \ldots \bigcirc(\neg w_0) \wedge \ldots \wedge \neg w_{t-1}) \wedge \neg w_t).$$

Call this formula Ψ_t, and define also Ω_t by $\Psi_t = \Diamond \Omega_t$. Ψ_t says that at some point we will not be in any of the pre-states in the first $t+1$ fringes of w_0.

The finite model property tells us that there are only finitely many fringes of w_0, up to collapsing. Thus, for some s, Ψ_s says that we are in no pre-state reachable from w_0. (As usual, Lemma 2 tells us that we can limit ourselves to pre-states in the cycles for w.)

$\vdash \neg(w_0 \wedge \Omega_s)$, simply by writing the sth fringe of w_0, and observing that all its pre-states are denied in Ω_s. Thus, we can apply μ (and weakening) once more and get

$$\Diamond(\neg\Omega_s \wedge \bigcirc \Omega_s).$$

Call this formula Φ. Φ says that at some point we are in one of the pre-states reachable from w_0, and that at the next instant we are in none of them. Of course, this cannot be the case; in fact, we can refute $\neg\Omega_s \wedge \bigcirc \Omega_s$: we derive the first fringe of all pre-states in $\neg\Omega_s$, and check that all the pre-states in these fringes were already in $\neg\Omega_s$. Thus, we derived $\Diamond$ *false*, and hence *false*.

Remarks: Note that w contains $\Diamond u$. Let $r = \neg u$. Thus, Lemma 5 connects r being proved at all instants with a proof for $\Box r$. This observation leads us to another formulation of Lemma 5, which makes clear that we could have reduced infinitary systems to $\Re$ (instead of tableaux). Such a reduction is successful only because of the finite model property.

The ω Lemma: If $\vdash v \supset \bigcirc^i r$ for all i then $\vdash v \supset \Box r$.

We will not explore this relation with infinitary logic any further.

- From Lemma 4 and Lemma 5 we obtain that w can be refuted in $\Re$.

4. $\mathfrak{R}^+$: The resolution system for $\bigcirc$, $\mathcal{U}$, $\mathcal{P}$ (and $\square$, $\diamond$)

The resolution system $\mathfrak{R}^+$ for $\bigcirc$, $\mathcal{U}$, and $\mathcal{P}$ is a generalization of $\mathfrak{R}$. In fact, all rules of $\mathfrak{R}$ are natural special cases of rules of $\mathfrak{R}^+$, when we regard $\square u$ and $\diamond u$ as abbreviations for $u\,\mathcal{U}$ *false* and $u\,\mathcal{P}$ *false*, respectively. One important qualification is that $\mathcal{P}$ reverses the polarity of its second argument.

(A) Simplification rules

- *true-false* reduction rules:

$$\begin{array}{lll} false\ \mathcal{U}\ v \Rightarrow v & false\ \mathcal{P}\ v \Rightarrow false & \bigcirc\, false \Rightarrow false \\ true\ \mathcal{U}\ v \Rightarrow true & true\ \mathcal{P}\ v \Rightarrow \neg v & \bigcirc\, true \Rightarrow true \\ u\ \mathcal{U}\ true \Rightarrow true & u\ \mathcal{P}\ true \Rightarrow false & \end{array}$$

  and the regular *true-false* reduction rules in propositional logic.

- Weakening rules: same as for $\mathfrak{R}$.
- Distribution rules ($\neg$ over modalities):

$$\neg(u\,\mathcal{U}\,v) \Rightarrow (\neg u)\,\mathcal{P}\,v, \qquad \neg(u\,\mathcal{P}\,v) \Rightarrow (\neg u)\,\mathcal{U}\,v, \qquad \neg\bigcirc u \Rightarrow \bigcirc\neg u.$$

- Distribution rules ($\neg$ over connectives): same as for $\mathfrak{R}$.

(B) Resolution rules

The basic rule

The basic rule for $\mathfrak{R}^+$ is similar to that for $\mathfrak{R}$. Note, however, that the restriction is now:

> the occurrences of u in A or B that are substituted by *true* or *false*, respectively, are all in the scope of the same number of $\bigcirc$'s, and not in the scope of any $\mathcal{U}$ or $\mathcal{P}$ of A or B.

Modality rules

These are the rules that relate $\bigcirc$, $\mathcal{U}$ and $\mathcal{P}$ by allowing us to resolve formulas in their scope.

- $\mathcal{U}$ rule:

$$R[u\,\mathcal{U}\,v] \longmapsto v \vee (u \wedge \bigcirc(u\,\mathcal{U}\,v)).$$

- $\mathcal{P}$ rule:

$$R[u\,\mathcal{P}\,v] \longmapsto \neg v \wedge (u \vee \bigcirc(u\,\mathcal{P}\,v)).$$

- $\mathcal{U}\mathcal{U}$ rule:

$$R[u\,\mathcal{U}\,v,\ u'\,\mathcal{U}\,v'] \longmapsto v\,\mathcal{P}\,v' \vee (\neg v \wedge (u\,\mathcal{U}\,v) \wedge u')\,\mathcal{U}\,v'.$$

That is, unless $v \mathcal{P} v'$, v does not occur before v', and hence $u \mathcal{U} v$ is true until v', and so are $\neg v$, and, of course, u'.

- $\mathcal{UP}$ rule:

$$R[u \mathcal{U} v,\ u' \mathcal{P} v'] \longmapsto v \mathcal{P} v' \ \vee\ (\neg v \wedge (u \mathcal{U} v) \wedge u') \mathcal{P} v'.$$

That is, unless $v \mathcal{P} v'$, v does not occur before v', and hence $\neg v$ and $u \mathcal{U} v$ are true at the point where u' is true before v'.

- $\mathcal{PP}$ rule:

$$R[u \mathcal{P} v,\ u' \mathcal{P} v'] \longmapsto ((u \wedge u' \mathcal{P} v') \mathcal{P} v) \ \vee\ ((u \mathcal{P} v \wedge u') \mathcal{P} v').$$

That is, if u occurs no later than u', then at some point before v we have u and $u' \mathcal{P} v'$; on the other hand, if u' occurs no later than u, then at some point before v' we have u' and $u \mathcal{P} v$.

- $\bigcirc\bigcirc$ rule: same as for $\mathfrak{R}$.

We also have two useful derived rules:

- $\mathcal{U}\bigcirc$ derived rule (obtained from the $\mathcal{U}$ and $\bigcirc\bigcirc$ rules, with weakening):

$$R[u \mathcal{U} v,\ \bigcirc w] \longmapsto v \vee \bigcirc(u \mathcal{U} v \wedge w).$$

- $\mathcal{P}\bigcirc$ derived rule (obtained from the $\mathcal{P}$ and $\bigcirc\bigcirc$ rules):

$$R[u \mathcal{P} v,\ \bigcirc w] \longmapsto u \vee \bigcirc(u \mathcal{P} v \wedge w).$$

Like in $\mathfrak{R}$, some of these rules are not essential for completeness, and we present them simply because of their usefulness. In fact, of all these modality rules, only $\mathcal{U}$, $\mathcal{P}$, and $\bigcirc\bigcirc$ are indispensable.

The induction rule

The induction rule of $\mathfrak{R}$ was:

if $\vdash \neg(w \wedge u)$, then

$$R[w,\ \Diamond u] \longmapsto \Diamond(\neg u \wedge \bigcirc(u \wedge \neg w)).$$

The μ rule carries over to $\mathfrak{R}^+$, with only minor changes; in $\mathfrak{R}^+$, it has the form:

if $\vdash (w \wedge u) \supset v$, then

$$R[w,\ u \mathcal{P} v] \longmapsto (\neg u \wedge \bigcirc(u \wedge \neg w)) \mathcal{P} (v \vee \bigcirc v).$$

(Notice that in the special case $v = \mathit{false}$ we obtain $\mathfrak{R}$'s μ rule.)

The μ rule in $\mathfrak{R}$ stated that, under the assumption that u and w cannot be true simultaneously, if w is true now, and u is true at some future instant, then eventually u must change from false to true. In other words, at eventually $\neg u \wedge \bigcirc(u \wedge \neg w)$. In $\mathfrak{R}^+$ this is refined to take into account that u must be true before v, and hence $\neg u \wedge \bigcirc(u \wedge \neg w)$ must be true before v and $\bigcirc v$.

Distribution rules

The distribution rules are exactly those for $\mathfrak{R}$.

5. Soundness and completeness for $\mathfrak{R}^+$

We have

Soundness theorem. $\mathfrak{R}^+$ *is sound.*

and

Completeness theorem. $\mathfrak{R}^+$ *is complete.*

The proof of the soundness theorem is trivial. We sketch the proof of the completeness theorem.

Proof sketch

The proof of completeness for $\mathfrak{R}^+$ is a relatively straighforward generalization of that for $\mathfrak{R}$. In particular, $\mathfrak{R}^+$, like $\mathfrak{R}$, is closely related to the tableau decision procedure for the corresponding version of PTL. We prove that any formula that can be shown unsatisfiable by the tableau decision procedure can be refuted by our $\mathfrak{R}^+$ system. The structure of the proof is parallel to that of the completeness proof for $\mathfrak{R}$. However, since there are new ways to create nodes in the tableau, we need to work out some more cases of "propagation." Also, the proof that cycles with unfulfillable eventualities are eliminated is slightly more complex than for $\mathfrak{R}$.

6. Concluding remarks: first-order temporal deduction

We have presented a nonclausal resolution approach to theorem proving in PTL, with modal operators $\bigcirc$, $\Box$, $\Diamond$, and also with the additional modal operators $\mathcal{U}$ and $\mathcal{P}$. Both versions were shown complete. We expect to be able to generalize this approach to get a viable proof system for first-order temporal logic. In particular, we attempt to combine the classical "cut" and "substitution" rules, which are usually expensive in their use of heuristics, into resolution rules with unification.

In the proposed first-order system, the unification would be deferred to the end of the refutation. In this way, we will not need to find unifiers, but just to check that there exist appropriate unifiers for the refutation. Huet ([H72, 75]) discusses some of the benefits of such a "constrained resolution" approach. Another benefit of this approach in temporal logic is that we avoid unsound substitutions into the modal formulas under consideration.

While this lifting is rather natural, it has one major problem: the system we obtain is not complete. A rule to introduce lemmas may prove helpful in enlarging the set of provable sentences. At any rate, there is no hope of constructing a complete system, since arithmetic can be embedded in first-order temporal logic. This makes first-order temporal logic totally undecidable. We expect, however, that most practically useful theorems of first-order temporal logic will have short and elegant proofs in our nonclausal resolution system.

Acknowledgements We are grateful to Gianluigi Bellin, Yoni Malachi, Eric Muller, and Pierre Wolper, for their careful reading of the manuscript and many interesting discussions.

References

[C]

Cavalli, A., "A method of automatic proof for the specification and verification of protocols," *ACM SIGCOMM 84 Symposium*, Montreal, Canada, 1984.

[CF]

Cavalli, A., and L. Fariñas del Cerro, "A decision method for linear temporal logic," *Seventh Conference on Automated Deduction*, Napa, CA, May 1984, pp. 113–127.

[GPSS]

Gabbay, D., A. Pnueli, S. Shelah and J. Stavi, "The temporal analysis of fairness," *Seventh ACM Symposium on Principles of Programming Languages*, Las Vegas, NV, January 1980, pp. 163–173.

[H72]

Huet, G. P., "Constrained resolution: a complete method for higher order logic," Ph.D. Thesis, Case Western University, Jennings Computing Center Report 1117, August 1972.

[H75]

Huet, G. P., "A unification algorithm for typed λ-calculus," *Theoretical Computer Science*, Vol. 1, No. 1, pp. 27–57.

[MP]

Manna, Z. and A. Pnueli, "Verification of concurrent programs: The temporal framework," in *The Correctness Problem in Computer Science* (R.S. Boyer and J S. Moore, eds.), International Lecture Series in Computer Science, Academic Press, London, 1982, pp. 215–273.

[MW]

Manna, Z. and R. Waldinger, "A deductive approach to program synthesis," *ACM Transactions on Programming Languages and Systems*, Vol. 2, No. 1, January 1980, pp. 92–121.

[M]

Murray, N. V., "Completely nonclausal theorem proving," *Artificial Intelligence*, Vol. 18, No. 1, pp. 67–85, January 1982.

[R]

J. A. Robinson, "A machine-oriented logic based on the resolution principle," *Journal of the ACM*, Vol. 12, No. 1, January 1965, pp. 23–41.

[W]

Wolper, P., "Temporal logic can be more expressive," *Proc. 22nd IEEE Symp. on Foundations of Computer Science*, Nashville, 1981, pp. 340–348.

Unsolvable Terms in Typed Lambda Calculus with Fix-Point Operators: Extended Abstract

Irina Bercovici [1]
MIT Laboratory for Computer Science and
CCS Dept., University of Michigan

Abstract. We consider the finitely typed lambda calculus with "fixed-point" combinators Y_σ of each type $(\sigma\to\sigma)\to\sigma$ satisfying the equation

$$Y = \lambda f{:}\sigma\to\sigma.\ f(Yf). \tag{1}$$

This formal system models computations with recursively defined equations. The decision problem for equality of terms of this calculus is open. We present a procedure for deciding when a λ-Y-term is "unsolvable"; this implies decidability of equations between λ-Y-terms and λ-terms without Y's. We also give tight characterizations of unsolvable terms under certain syntactic constraints.

1. Introduction.

The problem of analyzing and optimizing typed recursive declarations in programs leads to a variety of decision questions. For example, the problem of whether two first-order recursive declarations are equivalent "in the limit", i.e., "unwind" to the same Böhm tree, is equivalent to the notorious DPDA equivalence problem (cf. [Cou, Remark 5.7.2]); similar correspondences hold at higher-types.

This paper is motivated by the roughly dual problem of determining when two typed recursive declarations are provably equivalent -- a question raised in the first-order case by Milner [Cou]. Milner, however, considers simultaneous declarations in only "denested" and first-order form, while we consider arbitrary finitely typed functional terms and do not assume additional axioms needed to prove that denesting is possible. (Milner's question and our question of provable equivalence of arbitrary ΛY-terms with only first-order recursion are clearly very close, but we have not yet succeeded in proving that either question definitely reduces to the other.)

---

[1] Irina Bercovici died tragically on February 17, 1985, following childbirth. She left detailed notes for planned revisions and future improvements of the extended abstract she had submitted to the program committee. We hope to eventually carry to completion the improvements she planned, but we felt it appropriate to present here the available record of her written results at the time of her death. The present paper is the extended abstract submitted to the program committee, somewhat revised by us according to Irina's notes. -- A. Meyer and V. Breazu-Tannen, MIT Laboratory for Computer Science.

We present a positive decidability result in the special case when one of the terms has a Y-free normal form. The decision procedure rests on the decidability of when terms are computationally useful, viz., *solvable*, in the technical sense defined below. We also provide some simple characterizations of when denested unsolvable terms are provably equal.

2. Typed lambda-Y-calculus.

Finite types are constructed from a base type, 0, by the function-type constructor $\rightarrow$. ΛY is the finitely typed lambda calculus of [Bar] extended with constants Y_σ satisfying equation (1) for every type σ. Reduction in ΛY is defined by the usual β- and η-reduction rules plus equation (1) directed from left to right, namely the Y-reduction-rule

$$Y \rightarrow \lambda f.f(Yf).$$

It is easy to see ([Bar], p.396) that this set of reduction rules is Church-Rosser. A consequence of normalizability for the pure typed case is that each ΛY-term M has a $\beta\eta$-normal form nf(M).

Let $\Lambda\Omega$ denote the extension of the pure (i.e. constant-free) typed lambda calculus with a constant Ω of base type; similarly for $\Lambda Y\Omega$ and the ΛY-calculus.

Definition 1: A $\Lambda Y\Omega$-term M is *solvable* if there exists a term N of the form

$$\lambda x_1 \ldots \lambda x_k.zN_1 \ldots N_n$$

(where $k \geq 0$, $n \geq 0$) such that $\Lambda Y\Omega \vdash M = N$. The term N is called the *head normal form* of M.

The Church-Rosser property of the reduction system of $\Lambda Y\Omega$ lets us define solvability as a *reduction* to head normal form. An unsolvable term is one that has no head normal form in its equivalence class, hence it can be proven equal only with $\beta\eta$-normal form terms of the form

$$\lambda\vec{x}.Y\vec{N} \quad \text{or} \quad \lambda\vec{x}.\Omega.$$

Notation: Let

$\Omega^0 = \Omega$, $\qquad \Omega^{\sigma\rightarrow\tau} = \lambda x{:}\sigma.\Omega^\tau$,

$Y^{0,\sigma} = Y_\sigma$, $\qquad Y^{k+1,\sigma} = \lambda f{:}\sigma\rightarrow\sigma.f(Y^{k,\sigma}f)$.

For every $\Lambda Y\Omega$-term M, define the $\Lambda\Omega$-term $M_\Omega{}^k$ to be obtained by first replacing every occurrence of Y_σ in M by $Y^{k,\sigma}$ and then replacing in the result every occurrence of Y_σ by $\Omega^{(\sigma\rightarrow\sigma)\rightarrow\sigma}$, for every σ.

The following Lemma is straightforward.

Lemma 2: If $M_\Omega{}^k$ is solvable for some k, then M is solvable.

3. Unsolvability is decidable

In this section we use the semantic model $\mathcal{O}$ (see [P]) consisting of the type frame of all continuous functions on a base domain with two elements $B \leq T$, $B \neq T$. Define inductively on types the generalized notion of bottom and top:

$$B^0 = B,\ B^{\sigma\to\tau} = \lambda d \in \mathcal{O}^\sigma . B^\tau$$
$$T^0 = T,\ T^{\sigma\to\tau} = \lambda d \in \mathcal{O}^\sigma . T^\tau$$

This type frame becomes a model for $\Lambda Y\Omega$ with the usual denotations for lambda terms and with the following interpretations of the constants Ω and Y:

$$[\![\Omega]\!] = B,\ [\![Y_\sigma]\!](f) = \cup_n f^n(B^\sigma)$$

The following continuity property holds: for every environment ρ

$$[\![M]\!]\rho = \cup_k [\![M_\Omega{}^k]\!]\rho$$

All $\mathcal{O}^\sigma$ are finite and the function $h(\sigma)$ producing the length of the longest increasing chain in $\mathcal{O}^\sigma$ is computable straightforwardly as an iterated exponential in the number of $\to$'s in σ. Clearly now $[\![Y_\sigma]\!] = [\![(Y_\sigma)_\Omega{}^{h(\sigma)}]\!]$ and hence, if we denote by $h(M)$ the max of all $h(\sigma)$ for all occurrences of Y_σ in M, we have $[\![M]\!]\rho = [\![M_\Omega{}^{h(M)}]\!]\rho$.

Again, we have straightforwardly:

Lemma 3: If $M:\sigma_1\to\ldots\sigma_n\to 0$ is solvable then $[\![Mx_1\ldots x_n]\!]\rho_T = T$ where $x_i:\sigma_i$ and ρ_T is the environment that assigns to each variable the value T of the corresponding type.

Lemma 4: M is solvable if and only if $M_\Omega{}^{h(M)}$ is solvable.

Proof. The right to left direction follows from Lemma 2. Suppose now that $M:\sigma$ is solvable. Let $N = nf(M_\Omega{}^{h(M)})$. Assume that $M_\Omega{}^{h(M)}$ does not have a hnf, which, since $M_\Omega{}^{h(M)}$ is Y-free, means that $N \equiv \lambda \vec{x}^+ . \Omega$. Then, $[\![N]\!]\rho = B^\sigma$ for any environment ρ. By Lemma 3 we get a contradiction since $[\![N]\!]\rho_T = [\![M]\!]\rho_T \neq B^\sigma$ ∎

Theorem 5: It is decidable whether a $\Lambda Y\Omega$-term is unsolvable.

Proof. To decide if M is unsolvable, compute the normal form of the (Y-free) term $M_\Omega{}^{h(M)}$ and see if it is a head normal form.∎

The running time of this algorithm cannot be better than the computation of $\beta\eta$ normal forms, which is not elementary recursive [Sta].

It is not hard to see that once solvability of ΛY-terms can be decided, one also has:

Theorem 6: It is decidable whether an arbitrary ΛY-term is provably equal to an arbitrary Λ-term (viz. term without Y or Ω).

We note that our proof of Theorem 5 is patterned after the proof in [P] that the problem of whether a $\Lambda Y\Omega$ is provably equal to *some* Λ-term is decidable.

In the remainder of the paper we will restrict our attention to ΛY-terms (without Ω).

4. Syntactic characterization of some unsolvable terms.

A natural reduction method on ΛY-terms consists of a Y reduction followed by a $\beta\eta$ reduction path that reaches again a normal form. Denote such a macro step by R. We claim, but shall not prove here, that every $\beta\eta$-normal form reachable from a term M by a sequence of β, η and Y-reductions is actually reachable from M by a sequence of R-reductions. This makes R a Church-Rosser semi-strategy for ΛY.

Let $\twoheadrightarrow_R$ denote the reflexive and transitive closure of R and $\mathcal{N}(M)=\{M' \mid M\twoheadrightarrow_R M'\}$. Note that all terms in $\mathcal{N}(M)$ other than possibly M itself are in $\beta\eta$-normal form. When M has exactly one Y, R(M) will denote the (necessarily unique) result of one R step on M.

Definition 7: A head normal form is *leading* if it is of the form $\lambda z.\lambda\vec{x}.z\vec{M}$.

Lemma 8: Let M be Y-free. Then, YM is unsolvable if and only if M has a leading hnf.

Proof.(left to right) Suppose YM is unsolvable. We can assume M in nf. Since M is Y-free, M is of the form $\lambda y_1...y_k.zM_1...M_m : \sigma\to\sigma$ If $k=0$ then R(YM) is a hnf, hence $k\geq 1$. Suppose $y_1\neq z$. Then $R(YM)\equiv\lambda y_2...y_k.z(M_1[y_1:=YM])...(M_m[y_1:=YM])$ is again a hnf. It follows that y_1 must equal z. Moreover, from typing constraints we get $m=k-1$ and M_i of the same type as y_{i+1}.

(right to left) Assume M has a leading hnf, hence $R(YM)\equiv\lambda\vec{x}.(YM)\vec{M}$. It is easy to see that further R-reductions preserve this form, hence YM is unsolvable.∎

This last observation actually proves:

Corollary 9: $Y(\lambda z.\lambda \vec{x}.zM)\vec{N}$ is unsolvable.

We now have:

Theorem 10: Let M,N be Λ-terms (Y-free) such that YM is unsolvable. Then, $\Lambda Y \vdash YM = YN$ if and only if $\Lambda \vdash M = N$.

Proof. The right to left direction is trivial. Let now YM be unsolvable. By Lemma 8, $nf(M) \equiv \lambda z \lambda \vec{x}.z\vec{M}$. As YM and YN are provably equal, YN is unsolvable too and by the same result $nf(N) \equiv \lambda z \lambda \vec{y}.z\vec{N}$. Moreover, the proof of Lemma 8 lets us infer

$$\forall T \in \mathcal{N}(YM),\ T \equiv \lambda \vec{x}.(Y\, nf(M))\vec{M}^*$$

$$\forall S \in \mathcal{N}(YN),\ S \equiv \lambda \vec{y}.(Y\, nf(N))\vec{N}^*$$

By the Church-Rosser property, there exist T and S as above that are α equivalent. It follows then that $nf(M) \equiv_\alpha nf(N)$. ∎

Theorem 10 needs its unsolvability hypothesis:

Proposition 11: There exist Y-free terms, M and N such that $\Lambda Y \vdash YM = YN$ but not $\Lambda \vdash M = N$.

Proof. Indeed, let $M = \lambda z{:}(\sigma \to \sigma \to \sigma.\lambda x{:}\sigma \to \sigma.x(z(\lambda w.c))$. We get $R(R(YM)) = \lambda x.xc$. Let now $N = \lambda w{:}(\sigma \to \sigma) \to \sigma.\lambda x{:}\sigma \to \sigma.xc$. Then, $R(YN) = \lambda x.xc$ too. ∎

It is natural to question the restrictions in Lemma 8.

Proposition 12: There exist unsolvable terms of the form YMN such that M is Y-free but does not have a leading hnf.

Proof. Indeed, let $Z = \lambda u{:}\sigma \to \sigma.\lambda z{:}(\sigma \to \sigma) \to \sigma.\lambda x{:}\sigma \to \sigma.x(zu)$. Then taking $M \equiv ZI$ and $N \equiv I$ will do.∎

Proposition 13: There exist unsolvable terms of the form YM where M contains Y such that M does not have a leading hnf.

Proof. Taking $M \equiv Y(\lambda z{:}\sigma.(Y(ZI))(\lambda w{:}\sigma.z))$ where Z is defined in the proof of Proposition 12 will do.[2] ∎

---

[2] The author's two paragraph proof analyzing all possible head R-reductions to prove unsolvability has been omitted here -- A.M. & V.B-T.

A syntactic characterization of unsolvable terms of the form $YM\vec{N}$, without nested Y's can be given when the only recursively defined functions are first-order.

Definition 14:
rank(0)=0,
rank($\sigma\rightarrow\tau$)=max(rank(σ)+1,rank(τ)),
rank(Y_σ)=rank(σ).

Note that for $\sigma=\sigma_1\rightarrow...\sigma_n\rightarrow 0$, rank($\sigma$)=$max_i$(rank($\sigma_i$)+1). The types of rank 1 are of the form 0→..→0. Denote by 0^{k+1} the type of rank 1 that has k+1 0's. This is the type of first-order k-ary functions.

Proposition 15: Let M, $N_1,...,N_m$ be Y-free terms and let rank(Y)=1. Then, $YM\vec{N}$ is unsolvable if and only if M has a leading hnf.

Proof. (left to right) Say $Y:(\sigma\rightarrow\sigma)\rightarrow\sigma$ and $\sigma=0^{k+1}$. Then, $M:0^{k+1}\rightarrow 0^{k+1}$ and $N_i:0$ for $1\leq i\leq m$, $m\leq k$. Assume M is in nf. Using the same argument as in Lemma 8 and type constraints we get:

$$M=\lambda z:0^{k+1}.\lambda x_1:0 \ldots x_n:0.vM_1...M_n \quad \text{where } (vM_1...M_n):0^{k+1-n}.$$

It is easy to see that v cannot be free because YM would have hnf with head variable v and that v cannot be x_i by type constraints. Hence, v=z.

For (right to left) see Corollary 9. ∎

The restriction that M and the N's are Y-free is necessary. Indeed, if $M\equiv\lambda x:0.Y(I_{0^2\rightarrow 0^2})x$ then YM is unsolvable. Even requesting only M to be Y-free and allowing Y in the N's leads to a counterexample. Indeed, if $M\equiv\lambda z:0\rightarrow 0.\lambda x:0.x$ and $N\equiv YIc$ then YMN is unsolvable.

Unfortunately, Proposition 15 does not extend to a simple characterization of equivalence between the unsolvable terms.

Proposition 16: There exist unsolvable terms $P=YMP_1P_2$ and $Q=YMQ_1Q_2$ where M,P_1,P_2,Q_1,Q_2 are Y-free such that $\Lambda Y\vdash P=Q$ but neither $\Lambda\vdash P_1=Q_1$ nor $\Lambda\vdash P_2=Q_2$.

Proof. Indeed, let $M=\lambda z:0\rightarrow 0\rightarrow 0.\lambda x:0.\lambda y:0.zyx$, P_1 the same as Q_2, P_2 the same as Q_1 but P_1 and P_2 not α equivalent. Then R(P)=Q. ∎

References

[Bar] Barendregt, H. The lambda calculus, its syntax and semantics, North-Holland (1981).

[Cou] Courcelle, B. Fundamental properties of infinite trees, *TCS*, **25** (1983), 95-169.

[P] Plotkin, G. A note on functions definable in simple typed lambda calculus, unpublished manuscript, Jan. 1983.

[Sta] Statman, R. The typed lambda calculus is not elementary recursive, *TCS*, **9** (1979), 73-81.

Lambda Calculus with Constrained Types[1]

EXTENDED ABSTRACT

Val Breazu-Tannen

Albert R. Meyer

Massachusetts Institute of Technology[2]

ABSTRACT. Motivated by domain equations, we consider types satisfying arbitrary equational constraints thus generalizing a range of situations with the finitely typed case at one extreme and the type-free case at the other. The abstract model theory of the $\beta\eta$ type-free case is generalized. We investigate the relation between lambda calculus with constrained types and cartesian closed categories (cccs) at proof-theoretic and model-theoretic levels. We find an adjoint equivalence between the category of typed λ-algebras and that of cccs. The subcategories of typed λ-models and concrete cccs correspond to each other under this equivalence. All these results are parameterized by an arbitrary set of higher-order constants and an arbitrary set of higher-order equations.

1. Introduction

For what is usually known as *typed lambda calculus*, types (also called *finite types*) are defined inductively to be either a *base type* or of the form $\sigma \rightarrow \tau$ where σ and τ are previously defined types. The present paper generalizes this, considering the types as elements of a set T equipped with a binary operation $\rightarrow$. For example, types **a** such that $\mathbf{a} \rightarrow (\mathbf{a} \rightarrow \mathbf{a}) = \mathbf{a} \rightarrow \mathbf{a}$ are now possible. We call such types *constrained*, the constraints being the nontrivial identities satisfied in the algebra $(T, \rightarrow)$. The type-free lambda calculus appears as another particular case: the one in which there are so many constraints that we are left with a unique type, $T = \{\mathbf{u}\}$ ($\mathbf{u} \rightarrow \mathbf{u}$ is then forced to equal $\mathbf{u}$). Since the finite types correspond to no constraints at all, our approach applies to a range of situations which has the finitely typed lambda calculus at one extreme and the type-free lambda calculus at the other.

The general motivation for this work is the study of the abstract features of programming languages that allow both higher-order procedure types and recursively defined data types. The denotational semantics of such languages is expressed using *domain equations* which can be seen as constraints on the algebra of types. For practical examples, in addition to $\rightarrow$ one typically also needs operations such as type product, $\times$, type

---

[1]This research was supported in part by NSF Grant MCS80-10707

[2]Authors' address: Laboratory for Computer Science, 545 Technology Sq., Cambridge, MA 02139

sum, +, the-type-with-one-element, 1, while list-of- or tree-of- can be seen as unary operations:

(1) (T, →, ×, 1, +, **tree**, **forest**) where

$$\forall a \in T \quad \mathbf{tree}(a) = a \times \mathbf{forest}(a)$$

$$\forall a \in T \quad \mathbf{forest}(a) = 1 + (\mathbf{tree}(a) \times \mathbf{forest}(a))$$

(2) (T, →, ×, 1, +, **atoms**, **lispobjects**) where

$$\mathbf{lispobjects} = 1 + \mathbf{atoms} + (\mathbf{lispobjects} \times \mathbf{lispobjects}) + (\mathbf{lispobjects} \to \mathbf{lispobjects})$$

Accordingly, we define an *algebra of types* to be a set T equipped with an unspecified collection of operations on types that always contains a distinguished → operation and, for the results related to cartesian closed categories, also contains distinguished × and 1 operations. Note that the constraints embodied in an arbitrary algebra of types are more general that the domain equations that can be solved by Scott's methods ([Scott 72], [Scott 76]).

In order to be of use in such general situations, our approach is *parameterized* in two important ways. First, all concepts are parameterized with an unspecified set of *constants* C. These are intended to model operations that come together with the unspecified operations on types. For example, to use + we need $\mathbf{inleft}_{ab}$:a→a+b, $\mathbf{inright}_{ab}$:b→a+b and $\mathbf{case}_{abc}$:(a→c)→(b→c)→(a+b→c)). Second, it is to be expected that these operations will have some properties that can be expressed as λ-equations and need to be used in the inference process. For example :

$$\mathbf{case}\ f\ g\ (\mathbf{inleft}\ x) = f\ x$$

$$\mathbf{case}\ f\ g\ (\mathbf{inright}\ y) = g\ y$$

$$\mathbf{case}\ (h \circ \mathbf{inleft})\ (h \circ \mathbf{inright})\ z = h\ z$$

To model this, our results are parameterized with an unspecified set of *λ-equations* E.

In Section 2, working with an arbitrary algebra of types (T, →) we define a general T-*lambda calculus.* For this general case we always assume η. We proceed to give common generalizations in the T-lambda calculus to most concepts and results from the abstract model theories of the $\beta\eta$ type-free lambda calculus ([Meyer 82], [Hindley, Longo 80], [Barendregt 84] Chap. 5, [Koymans 84]) and the $\beta\eta$ typed lambda calculus ([Friedman 75], [Halpern, Meyer, Trakhtenbrot 84], [Mitchell 84]). Note however that our life is simplified by considering the $\beta\eta$ case instead of the more general β case.

Section 3 is concerned with the relationship between the general lambda calculus that we define and cartesian closed categories (cccs). As argued in [Scott 80], cartesian closed category theory and typed lambda calculus are both very general theories of *functions* and, on this basis, *philosophically* related. But what, exactly, is the *technical* connection ? This connection is interesting because cccs can be regarded as purely algebraic objects while the lambda calculus features the syntactically convenient but semantically hard to grasp notion of λ-abstraction. In addition, as opposed to combinatory structures, cccs have been developed independently of the lambda calculus and their axioms are quite intuitive (something that cannot be said about combinatory λ-algebras!).

The connection between typed lambda calculus and cccs was discovered by Lambek who studied it in relation to intuitionistic proof theory ([Lambek 72], [Lambek 74], [Lambek 80]). This connection is also studied in [Parsaye-Ghomi 81], [Dybjer 83] and [Curien 83]. One possible technical approach is suggested in [Scott 80]. In [Poigne 84a] and [Poigne 84b] Poigné develops this approach in a context motivated by the study of higher-order algebraic specifications. These two papers introduce types with arbitrary equational constraints but do not point out the syntactic complications that we describe in Section 2. In order to get a good syntactic connection with cccs [Poigne 84b] introduces the so-called lambda calculus with *function types* thus leaving the familiar typed lambda calculus. Our work avoids function types by introducing a better translation, based on Lambek's results, of lambda terms into cartesian closed terms. A similar idea appears in [Lambek, Scott 84] where the existence of an adjoint equivalence between lambda theories and cccs is stated. However, the full details of this correspondence are not given and we were not able to reproduce it. What we establish is a bijection between lambda theories and closed-axiom cartesian closed theories and adjoint equivalences between cccs and λ-algebras and between λ-models and concrete cccs. Thus, we believe that we make progress by presenting the relation between lambda calculus with constrained types and cartesian closed categories as a clear comparison of two logics at proof-theoretic and model-theoretic level (as is done with the relation between the same lambda calculus and combinatory logic).

As remarked before, when the algebra of types consists of just one type we obtain the type-free lambda calculus. More generally, it is to be expected that the type-free lambda calculus can be "embedded" in *any* lambda calculus with constrained types that has a distinguished type **u** such that **u**=**u**→**u**. In Section 4 we report on some work in progress on this issue.

Some notations for what follows: since we use → for functional type construction, we will use →→ for morphisms in cartesian closed categories eg. f:a→→b, and →→→ for ordinary set-theoretic maps eg. φ:A→→→B.

2. Syntax and Semantics of Lambda Calculus with Constrained Types

Fix an arbitrary algebra of types (T, →). A *T-sorted set* is a pair (D,τ) where τ maps D into T, associating to every d∈D its *type*, τ(d).Define D_a={d∈D | τ(d)=a}. Usually, instead of τ(d)=a we will write d∈D_a or, if D is clear from the context, d:a. If D_1 and D_2 are T-sorted sets, a map φ:D_1→→→D_2 is *T-sorted* or *type-preserving* if d:a ⇒ φ(d):a.

Lambda Terms. Fix as a parameter an arbitrary T-sorted set of *constants* C. Fix also a T-sorted set of *variables* X such that each X_a is infinite. The T-sorted set of *lambda terms* Λ is defined inductively by the following *rule schemes* (a and b range over T):

1. $X_a \subset \Lambda_a$

2. $C_a \subset \Lambda_a$

3. if $M:a\to b$ and $N:a$ then $M\bullet_{ab}N:b$ (application)

4. if $x \in X_a$ and $M:b$ then $\lambda_{ab}x.M:a\to b$ (abstraction)

The set of free variables of the term M will be denoted FV(M). As usual terms M with $FV(M)=\emptyset$ are called *closed.*

There is a significant departure here from the classical syntax of the lambda calculus. Conserving that syntax would lead to ambiguities regarding the type of some terms. Indeed, suppose we have $a,b,c\in T$ such that $a\to b=a\to c$, $b\neq c$, then with $M:a\to b(=a\to c)$ and $N:a$ we would construct MN whose type can be b as well as c. This problem does not arise for ordinary finite types because $\sigma\to\tau_1 = \sigma\to\tau_2$ *implies* $\tau_1 = \tau_2$. Therefore, when constructing the term "M applied to N", its syntax should somehow contain its type. Once this was accepted we decided to use more than the minimum necessary "typing information" in the syntax and emphasize the polymorphic nature of the $\bullet$ and λ operators. Among other things, it is clear that we can do induction on lambda terms and how this induction proceeds.

For all practical purposes however, the classical syntax can be used by convention if we are careful to specify unambiguous typing information in the same context. For instance, the β axiom scheme can be written

$$(\lambda x.M)N=[N/x]M \qquad x\in X_a,\ M:b,\ N:a,\ a,b\in T$$

instead of

$$(\lambda_{ab}x.M)\bullet_{ab}N=[N/x]M \qquad x\in X_a,\ M:b,\ N:a,\ a,b\in T$$

In contrast, for some $c\neq b$ such that $a\to c=a\to b$, the "pathological" term $(\lambda_{ab}x.M)\bullet_{ac}N$ is legally constructed but is *not*, by convention, the one meant by $(\lambda x.M)N$ in the context of $x:a$, $M:b$, $N:a$.

Again by convention, the η axiom scheme can be written

$$\lambda x.Mx=M \qquad x\in X_a,\ M:a\to b,\ a,b\in T$$

instead of

$$\lambda_{ab}x.M\bullet_{ab}x=M \qquad x\in X_a,\ M:a\to b,\ a,b\in T$$

Interestingly, if a, b, and c are types such that $a\to b=a\to c$ but $b\neq c$ then both $\lambda_{ab}x.M\bullet_{ab}x=M$ and $\lambda_{ac}x.M\bullet_{ac}x=M$ for some $x\in X_a$ and $M:a\to b(=a\to c)$ are instances of η hence the "pathological" consequence

$$\lambda_{ab}x.M\cdot_{ab}x=\lambda_{ac}x.M\cdot_{ac}x\ !$$

Of course this cannot be expressed in classical syntax. However, such equations do not arise when we generalize results from typed and type-free lambda calculus to arbitrarily constrained types. Rather, such "pathological" terms and equations would appear in results intimately related to the nature of the constraints on types.

Lambda Theories. The formulas concerning us take the form of *equations* between lambda terms. As a parameter, fix a set E of equations between *closed* terms. (This is not a serious restriction since all "useful" situations can be expressed in closed form; the advantage is that *all* our results hold with such a parameter.) We will consider a proof system λ consisting of: usual equational reasoning (i.e. reflexivity,symmetry,transitivity and $\cdot$-congruence); α, β and η axiom schemes and the ξ inference rule scheme (weak extensionality):

$$M=N \vdash \lambda_{ab}x.M=\lambda_{ab}x.N \quad x\in X_a,\ M,N:b,\ a,b\in$$

and all equations in E as axioms.

If F is a set of equations and e a single equation, we will write $F\vdash_\lambda e$ for deduction in the above proof system using additional assumptions from F. A set of equations containing all axioms and closed under all inference rules is called a (C,E)-*lambda theory.*

Environment Models. A *frame* is a tuple $\mathfrak{I}=(D,\ \cdot,\ \gamma)$ where: D is a T-sorted set such that each D_a is non-empty, $\cdot$ is a family of binary operations $\cdot_{ab}:D_{a\to b}\times D_a \to\!\!\to\!\!\to D_b$ and γ is a T-sorted map $\gamma:C\to\!\!\to\!\!\to D$ that interprets constants. A frame is *extensional* if

$$\forall f,g:a\to b\ \ (\forall d:a\ f\cdot_{ab}d=g\cdot_{ab}d)\Rightarrow f=g.$$

Given a frame $\mathfrak{I}$, a map $\varphi:D_a\to\!\!\to\!\!\to D_b$ is *represented* by an element $f\in D_{a\to b}$ (alternatively, f is a *representative* of φ) if $\forall d:a\ \ \varphi(d)=f\cdot_{ab}d$. In an extensional frame, representatives are unique (whenever they exist).

For a frame $\mathfrak{I}$, let D-env be the set of environments (i.e. the T-sorted maps from X to D). A frame is *closed* if it is extensional and the following inductive definition of an assignment of meanings to terms in environments is possible:

$[\![x]\!]\rho=\rho(x) \quad x\in X_a,\ \rho\in D\text{-env}$

$[\![c]\!]\rho=\gamma(c) \quad c\in C_a,\ \rho\in D\text{-env}$

$[\![MN]\!]\rho=[\![M]\!]\rho\cdot_{ab}[\![N]\!]\rho \quad M:a\to b,\ N:a,\ \rho\in D\text{-env}$

$[\![\lambda x.M]\!]\rho$ is the representative of $\varphi:D_a\to\!\!\to\!\!\to D_b \quad x:a,\ M:b,\ \rho\in D\text{-env}$

where $\varphi(d)=[\![M]\!]\rho[d/x] \quad d:a$

Here $\rho[d/x]$ is the "patched" environment that takes the same values as ρ everywhere except in x where it takes the value d.

The delicate step in the inductive definition of $[\![\,]\!]$ above is defining the meaning of abstraction: once $[\![M]\!]\rho$ is defined for *all* environments ρ, the resulting function $\varphi(d)=[\![M]\!]\rho[d/x]$ has to be representable (and this is what is meant by the fact that the inductive definition is possible) and then the meaning $[\![\lambda x.M]\!]\rho$ is defined as its representative (which is unique by extensionality).

An equation $M=N$ is *valid* in a closed frame $\mathcal{I}$, write $\mathcal{I} \models M=N$, if $\forall\ \rho\in$D-env, $[\![M]\!]\rho=[\![N]\!]\rho$. Let **Valid**($\mathcal{I}$) be the set of all equations valid in $\mathcal{I}$. Write $\mathcal{I}\models F$ for $F\subset$**Valid**($\mathcal{I}$). Finally, a (C,E)-*environment model* is a closed frame $\mathcal{I}$ such that $\mathcal{I}\models E$.

There is a bijection between $D_{a\times b}$ and $D_a \times D_b$ given by the map that takes d to $\langle l\,d, r\,d\rangle$ whose inverse is the map that takes $\langle d_1,d_2\rangle$ to $p\,d_1 d_2$. (We will omit the $\bullet$ when its subscripts are clear from the context.) Clearly, D_1 has just one element, s. Finally, there is an injection from $D_{a\to b}$ into Set(D_a,D_b) given by the map that takes f to φ ,where $\varphi(d)=fd$. However, unlike what can be done for finitely typed lambda calculus (see [Halpern, Meyer, Trakhtenbrot 84]), we cannot set $D_{a\times b}=D_a\times D_b$ and $D_{a\to b}\subset$Set(D_a,D_b) again because of possible constraints on types that can make, say, $a_1\times b_1=a_2\times b_2$ while $a_i\neq b_i$, $i=1,2$.

The following theorem confirms the that environment models precisely capture and *justify* the informal intuition behind the general T-lambda calculus.

> **Theorem 1:** (Strong Soundness and Completeness) For any (C,E)-environment model $\mathcal{I}$, **Valid**($\mathcal{I}$) is a (C,E)-lambda theory. For any (C,E)-lambda theory G there exists a (C,E)-environment model $\mathcal{G}$ such that **Valid**($\mathcal{G}$)=G.

Combinatory Models and Combinatory Logic. While environment models have a rather syntactic definition, it is possible to give a class of first-order structures, namely the *combinatory models* that are in 1-1 correspondence with them. We will only briefly survey this connection since it is a straightforward generalization of the treatment for the $\beta\eta$ type-free case (eg. see [Barendregt 84]Sec.5.2 and Sec.7.3).

A *combinatory algebra* is a tuple $\mathcal{I}=(D, \bullet, \gamma, K, S)$ where $(D, \bullet, \gamma)$ is a frame and K and S are families of combinatory constants,

$$K_{ab}:a\to b\to a$$

$$S_{abc}:(a\to b\to c)\to(a\to b)\to a\to c$$

satisfying the well-known combinatory identities:

$$K d_1 d_2 = d_1 \quad d_1{:}a,\ d_2{:}b$$

$$S\,d_1 d_2 d_3 = d_1 d_3 (d_2 d_3) \quad d_1{:}a{\rightarrow}b{\rightarrow}c,\ d_2{:}a{\rightarrow}b,\ d_3{:}a$$

A *combinatory model* is just an extensional combinatory algebra. Combinatory models are many-sorted first-order structures while combinatory algebras are many-sorted algebraic structures, in both cases the set of sorts being T. By *combinatory logic* we understand the many-sorted equational logic associated with the variety of combinatory algebras.

Specifically, let $\mathcal{T}$ be the T-sorted set of *combinatory terms*, constructed from X, C, {K, S} and •. We define effective and type-preserving translations between lambda terms and combinatory terms: $\mathcal{U}:\Lambda{\rightarrow}{\rightarrow}{\rightarrow}\mathcal{T}$ and $\mathcal{L}:\mathcal{T}{\rightarrow}{\rightarrow}{\rightarrow}\Lambda$. We extend these translations to equations and sets of equations. We define (C,E)-*combinatory algebras* and (C,E)-*combinatory models* by additionally requiring the validity of $\mathcal{U}(E)$. We start with a proof system which we will denote cl consisting of reflexivity, symmetry, transitivity, •-congruence, *substitutivity*:

$$M=N \vdash [P/x]M=[P/x]N \quad x\in X_a,\ P{:}a,\ M,N{:}b,$$

the axioms of combinatory algebras and (also as axioms) the equations in $\mathcal{U}(E)$. Let L_λ be the smallest (C,E)-lambda theory i.e. $L_\lambda=\{e \mid \vdash_\lambda e\}=\{e \mid \mathfrak{I}\models e$ for all (C,E)-environment models $\mathfrak{I}\}$. A remarkable fact happens now: $\mathcal{U}(L_\lambda)$ has a finite, pure and closed axiomatization ! That is, there exists a finite set $A_{\beta\eta}$ of equation schemes (each with type variables ranging over T) between pure closed terms (i.e. constructed only from K's and S's) such that $A_{\beta\eta}\vdash_{cl}\mathcal{U}(L_\lambda)$. The untyped version of these equations can be found in [Barendregt 84], page 161.

Therefore, the "good" proof system is $cl\beta\eta=cl+A_{\beta\eta}$. A (C,E)-*combinatory* λ-*algebra* is a (C,E)-combinatory algebra $\mathfrak{I}$ such that $\mathfrak{I}\models A_{\beta\eta}$. From above, it follows that the combinatory λ-algebras can serve as models for the lambda calculus via the translation $\mathcal{U}$ since L_λ will be valid in them. However, only weak soundness holds for these models because **Valid**($\mathfrak{I}$) is not going to be a lambda theory for lack of being closed under the ξ inference rule. This suggests considering extensional combinatory λ-algebras. These turn out to coincide with combinatory models and to be strongly sound and complete models for lambda theories.

A (C,E)-*combinatory* λ-*theory* is a set of combinatory equations containing all the axioms and being closed under all the inference rules of $cl\beta\eta$. Of course, combinatory λ-algebras are strongly sound and complete for combinatory λ-theories. It turns out that the correspondent of lambda theories are the *closed-axiom* combinatory λ-theories i.e. theories G such that there exists a set of closed equations $K\subset G$ such that $K\vdash_{cl\beta\eta}G$. The combinatory models are strongly sound and complete for closed-axiom combinatory λ-theories.

Syntactical λ-Algebras and Weak Lambda Theories. The combinatory models correspond to environment models and the closed-axiom combinatory λ-theories correspond to lambda theories. We will now define the "lambda" concepts that correspond to combinatory λ-algebras and combinatory λ-theories.

A (C,E)-*syntactical* λ-*algebra* is a pair $\mathfrak{I}=(D, [\![\,]\!])$ such that D is a T-sorted set such that each D_a is non-empty, $[\![\,]\!]$ is an assignment of meanings to terms in environments satisfying:

$[\![x]\!]\rho=\rho(x) \quad x{:}a,\ \rho\in D\text{-env}$

$(\rho=\sigma \text{ on } FV(M)) \Rightarrow [\![M]\!]\rho=[\![M]\!]\sigma \quad M{:}a,\ \rho,\sigma\in D\text{-env}$

$[\![\,[N/x]M\,]\!]\rho=[\![M]\!]\rho[\,[\![N]\!]\rho/x\,] \quad N,x{:}a,\ M{:}b,\ \rho\in D\text{-env}$

and such that when we define validity as for environment models we have $\vdash_\lambda e \Rightarrow \mathfrak{I}\models e$ i.e. $L_\lambda\subset$**Valid**$(\mathfrak{I})$.

A syntactical λ-algebra has also a frame structure which we did not include in the definition because it can be derived as follows. Given $f,d\in D$, $f{:}a\to b$, $d{:}a$, choose two variables $x{:}a\to b$ and $y{:}a$ and an environment ρ such that $\rho(x)=f$ and $\rho(y)=d$. Then, define $f\bullet_{ab}d=[\![x\bullet_{ab}y]\!]\rho$. The properties of $[\![\,]\!]$ insure that the definition does not depend on the particular choice of x, y, and ρ. With the same justification, define $\gamma(c)=[\![c]\!]\rho$ for some arbitrary environment ρ. It turns out that (C,E)-environment models are in 1-1 correspondence with extensional (C,E)-syntactical λ-algebras and in the following we will identify them.

We define *homomorphisms* of syntactical λ-algebras $h{:}\mathfrak{I}\to\to\to\mathfrak{I}'$ to be T-sorted maps $h{:}D\to\to\to D'$ such that

$$\forall M\in\Lambda,\ \rho\in D\text{-env} \quad h([\![M]\!]\rho)=[\![M]\!]'h\circ\rho.$$

With these, the (C,E)-syntactical λ-algebras form a category.

A *(C,E)-weak lambda theory* is a set of equations between lambda terms that contains L_λ (and hence E) and is closed under reflexivity, symmetry, transitivity, •-congruence and substitutivity. The (C,E)-syntactical λ-algebras are strongly sound and complete for (C,E)-weak lambda theories. The weak lambda theories are in general not lambda theories because they may be not closed under the inference rule ξ. However:

> **Lemma 2:** Any closed-axiom weak lambda theory is a lambda theory. Conversely, any lambda theory is closed-axiom.

We can now describe the technical contents of the usual claim "lambda calculus and combinatory logic are equivalent". Note the parallelism between the proof-theoretic connection and the model-theoretic connection.

> **Theorem 3:**
> (i) There exists an inclusion-preserving bijection between (C,E)-weak lambda theories and (C,E)-combinatory λ-theories. Under this bijection, the (C,E)-lambda theories correspond to closed-axiom (C,E)-combinatory λ-theories and conversely.
>
> (ii) There exists an isomorphism between the category of (C,E)-syntactical λ-algebras and the category of (C,E)-combinatory λ-algebras such that the full subcategory of (C,E)-environment

models is isomorphic to the full subcategory of (C,E)-combinatory models.

(iii) If the (C,E)-syntactical λ-algebra $\mathfrak{D}$ and the (C,E)-combinatory λ-algebra $\mathcal{E}$ correspond to each other by the isomorphism (ii) then the (C,E)-weak lambda theory **Valid**($\mathfrak{D}$) and the (C,E)-combinatory λ-theory **Valid**($\mathcal{E}$) correspond to each other by the bijection (i).

Term Models. Let G be a (C,E)-weak lambda theory. By regarding equations as pairs of terms, G can be seen as a T-indexed family of binary relations between terms. Since G is closed under equational reasoning these relations are equivalence relations. Let us denote by Λ/G the T-sorted set of equivalence classes modulo G. Let us also denote by $\|M\|$ the equivalence class of the term M. Let M:a and $\rho \in \Lambda/G$-env. Let $FV(M)=\{x_1{:}a_1,\ldots,x_n{:}a_n\}$ and $\rho(x_i)=\|M_i\|$, $M_i{:}a_i, i=1,\ldots,n$. Define:

$$[\![M]\!]\rho=\|[M_1/x_1,\ldots,M_n/x_n]M\|$$

Now, let $\mathcal{G}=(\Lambda/G, [\![\,]\!])$. $\mathcal{G}$ is called the *open term model* of G since it can be checked that $\mathcal{G}$ is a (C,E)-syntactical λ-algebra, that **Valid**($\mathcal{G}$)=G and moreover

Lemma 4: $\mathcal{G}$ is a (C,E)-environment model if and only if G is a (C,E)-lambda theory

If $\mathfrak{D}$ is a syntactical λ-algebra, a *subalgebra* of $\mathfrak{D}$ is a T-sorted subset $S\subset D$ such that each S_a is nonempty and for any $\rho \in D$-env such that $\rho(X)\subset S$, we have $\forall M$, $[\![M]\!]\rho \in S$ (and hence we have a syntactical λ-algebra $\mathcal{S}=(S, [\![\,]\!])$).

If $\mathcal{G}$ is the open term model of a weak lambda theory G then the following subset of Λ/G

$$\Lambda^0/G^0=\{\|M\| \text{ such that M is closed}\}$$

is a subalgebra provided that there are closed terms of every type. If this is true then the syntactical λ-algebra $\mathcal{G}^0=(\Lambda^0/G^0, [\![\,]\!])$ is called the *closed term model* of G. In the following, we will implicitly assume that closed terms of all types exist whenever we mention closed term models.

Are there syntactical λ-algebras that are not environment models i.e. are not extensional ? The answer is "yes" in two important cases. For the type-free lambda calculus with C=E=Ø, Plotkin's ω-incompleteness result states that there exist two closed terms Ξ and Ψ which are not provably equivalent but such that for any closed term M $\beta\eta\vdash \Xi M=\Psi M$ ([Barendregt 84] pp. 455-457) It then follows that the closed term model of the smallest lambda theory, L_λ, is not extensional. The other case is the finitely typed lambda calculus where we let C contain a constant c of base type to insure the existence of closed terms of all types and E=Ø to insure the existence of normal forms. Now, since the only closed normal form of base type is c, (λx.x)M and (λx.c)M are equivalent for any closed M, while λx.x and λx.c are distinct closed normal forms. Hence, the closed term model of the smallest lambda theory is not extensional. We do not know whether such examples can be given for arbitrary algebras of types.

Adjoining Indeterminates. The class of (C,E)-syntactical λ-algebras is closed under taking subalgebras, homomorphic images and products, hence it forms an *equational variety.* The class of (C,E)-environment models is closed under product. However, the subalgebras and the homomorphic images of environment models are, in general, just syntactical λ-algebras (eg. the closed term model is both a subalgebra and a homomorphic image of the open term model). But, remarkably, *every* syntactical λ-algebra is the subalgebra and the homomorphic image (actually, the retract) of some environment model. To show this, we need to explain how to adjoin indeterminates to a syntactical λ-algebra.

Let $\mathfrak{J}$ be a (C,E)-syntactical λ-algebra. $\mathfrak{J}$ can be regarded as a (C∪D,E)-algebra as well ($\forall d \in D, [\![d]\!] = d$). Let H be the set of equations between closed C∪D-lambda terms that are valid in $\mathfrak{J}$. Take the (C∪D,E)-*weak* lambda theory generated by H, H^+, and then the open term model $\mathfrak{H}$ of H^+. $\mathfrak{H}$ can be regarded as a (C,E)-syntactical λ-algebra by restricting $[\![\,]\!]$ to C-lambda terms. The algebra thus obtained is denoted $\mathfrak{J}[X]$ and is said to be obtained by *adjoining the indeterminates X to* $\mathfrak{J}$. There is an injective homomorphism $i:\mathfrak{J} \rightarrowtail\!\to \mathfrak{J}[X]$, $i(d) = \|d\|$, and, by fixing some $\rho \in D\text{-env}$, we get a surjective homomorphism $s:\mathfrak{J}[X] \rightarrowtail\!\to \mathfrak{J}$, $s(\|M\|) = [\![M]\!]\rho$. Moreover, $s \circ i = id$ therefore $\mathfrak{J}$ is a *retract* of $\mathfrak{J}[X]$. But now, H is closed hence H^+ is closed-axiom and therefore a lambda theory so $\mathfrak{J}[X]$ is extensional hence an environment model !

Theorem 5: Any (C,E)-syntactical λ-algebra is the retract of a (C,E)-environment model

3. The Connection with Cartesian Closed Categories

An algebra of types is *cartesian* if in addition to → it also has a specified binary × operation and a specified constant 1. Fix an arbitrary cartesian algebra of types (T, →, ×, 1). The cartesian closed categories that we will consider are all small and have the same set of objects,namely T. In these categories, 1 will be the terminal object, × will define the product of objects and → will define the exponentiation of objects. Therefore we prefer to define these categories as an equational variety of T×T-sorted algebras.

A *cartesian closed category* (ccc) is a tuple

$\mathcal{Q} = (Q, \circ, \textit{id}, \textit{lp}, \textit{rp}, \langle\rangle, \textit{t}, \textit{ev}, \textit{curry})$

where Q is a T×T-sorted set of *morphisms* (write $f{:}a \rightarrowtail\!\to b$ for $f \in Q_{ab}$) such that each Q_{ab} is non-empty, ∘ and ⟨⟩ are families of binary operations, ***curry*** is a family of unary operations and ***id, lp, rp, t, ev*** are families of constants as follows:

(composition) $g \circ_{abc} f{:}a \rightarrowtail\!\to c$ $\qquad$ $f{:}a \rightarrowtail\!\to b,\ g{:}b \rightarrowtail\!\to c$

(identity) $\textit{id}_a{:}a \rightarrowtail\!\to a$

(projections) $\textit{lp}_{ab}{:}a\times b \rightarrowtail\!\to a$, $\textit{rp}_{ab}{:}a\times b \rightarrowtail\!\to b$

(pairing) $\langle f,g\rangle_{abc}:c\rightarrowtail a\times b$ $f:c\rightarrowtail a,\ g:c\rightarrowtail b$

(terminal) $t_a:a\rightarrowtail 1$

(evaluation) $ev_{ab}:(a\to b)\times a\rightarrowtail b$

(currying) $curry_{abc}(f):a\rightarrowtail b\to c$ $f:a\times b\rightarrowtail c$

such that the following identities hold:(we drop the subscripts when they are clear from the context)

$h\circ(g\circ f)=(h\circ g)\circ f$ $f:a\rightarrowtail b,\ g:b\rightarrowtail c,\ h:c\rightarrowtail d$

$f\circ id=f$ $id\circ f=f$ $f:a\rightarrowtail b$

$lp\circ\langle f,g\rangle=f$ $rp\circ\langle f,g\rangle=g$ $f:c\rightarrowtail a,\ g:c\rightarrowtail b$

$\langle lp\circ h, rp\circ h\rangle=h$ $h:c\rightarrowtail a\times b$

$f=t$ $f:a\rightarrowtail 1$

$uncurry(curry(f))=f$ $f:a\times b\rightarrowtail c$

$curry(uncurry(g))=g$ $g:a\rightarrowtail b\to c$

where we have used the auxiliary notation:

$f\times_{abcd}g:a\times b\rightarrowtail c\times d$ $f\times g=\langle f\circ lp, g\circ rp\rangle$ $f:a\rightarrowtail c,\ g:b\rightarrowtail d$

$uncurry_{abc}(g):a\times b\rightarrowtail c$ $uncurry(g)=ev\circ(g\times id)$ $g:a\rightarrowtail b\to c$

The morphisms of the form $p:1\rightarrowtail a$ are called *points.* A ccc is said to have *enough points* or to be *concrete* if

$$\forall f,g:a\rightarrowtail b\quad (\forall p:1\rightarrowtail a\quad f\circ p=g\circ p)\Rightarrow f=g\ .$$

Any concrete ccc is isomorphic with a ccc of sets and functions. This shows that the set-theoretic definition of a cartesian closed type-frame from [Halpern, Meyer, Trakhtenbrot 84] is without loss of generality.

For the connection with cccs we also need to enrich the lambda calculus with some specific constants and some specific axioms. The parameters C and E are said to be *cartesian* if $C=\{\mathbf{l},\mathbf{r},\mathbf{p},\mathbf{s}\}\cup C_r$, and $E=E_{cart}\cup E_r$ where C_r and E_r are an arbitrary T-sorted set of constants and an arbitrary set of closed λ-equations,

$$\mathbf{l}_{ab}:a\times b\to a,\quad \mathbf{r}_{ab}:a\times b\to b,\quad \mathbf{p}_{ab}:a\to b\to a\times b,\quad \mathbf{s}:1\quad a,b\in T$$

are (families of) cartesian constants and E_{cart} are the following cartesian axiom schemes (in closed form):

$$\lambda xy.l_{ab}(p_{ab}xy)=\lambda xy.x \quad x{:}a,\ y{:}b$$
$$\lambda xy.r_{ab}(p_{ab}xy)=\lambda xy.y \quad x{:}a,\ y{:}b$$
$$\lambda z.p_{ab}(l_{ab}z)(r_{ab}z)=\lambda z.z \quad z{:}a\times b$$
$$\lambda u.u=\lambda u.s \quad u{:}1.$$

Fix an arbitrary pair of cartesian parameters, (C,E). By *cartesian closed logic* we understand the many(T×T)-sorted equational logic associated with cccs. Let Γ be the set of C-*cartesian closed terms* constructed from a fixed T×T-sorted set of variables V such that each V_{ab} is infinite, from a T×T-sorted set C^* which is a *copy* of the T-sorted set C_r such that if $c\in(C_r)_a$ then $c^*\in C^*_{1a}$, and from symbols for the constants and operations of cccs. Again, we write $P{:}a\rightarrow\!\!\rightarrow b$ instead of $P\in\Gamma_{ab}$, $a,b\in T$.

We define reciprocal translations between lambda terms and cartesian closed terms:

$\mathcal{C}{:}\Lambda{:}\rightarrow\!\!\rightarrow\!\!\rightarrow\Gamma$ such that $M{:}a \Rightarrow \mathcal{C}(M){:}1\rightarrow\!\!\rightarrow a$

$\mathcal{L}{:}\Gamma{:}\rightarrow\!\!\rightarrow\!\!\rightarrow\Lambda$ such that $P{:}a\rightarrow\!\!\rightarrow b \Rightarrow \mathcal{L}(P){:}a\rightarrow b$

The space does not allow us to give the detailed definitions of these translations but we will make the following remarks: (1) The justification for the typing transformation performed by $\mathcal{C}$ is the bijection $A\simeq\{f \mid f{:}1\rightarrow\!\!\rightarrow\!\!\rightarrow A\}$ where 1 is some one-element set. (2) Because of the different typing, we have used different sets of variables in the definitions of lambda and cartesian closed terms. Therefore, we now have to base our translations on some given reciprocal embeddings of the sets of variables in each other: a 1-1 map $\mathcal{C}{:}X\rightarrow\!\!\rightarrow\!\!\rightarrow V$ such that $\forall a\ \mathcal{C}(X_a)\subset V_{1a}$ and a 1-1 map $\mathcal{L}{:}V\rightarrow\!\!\rightarrow\!\!\rightarrow X$ such that $\forall a,b\ \mathcal{L}(V_{ab})\subset X_{a\rightarrow b}$. To insure the existence of these we will assume that all X_a's and all V_{ab}'s have the same cardinality ($\geq\aleph_0$). In fact, these sets can be assumed countable and the embeddings can be assumed effective which would make the translations effective as well. Modulo these embeddings, both our translations *preserve free variables.* (3) For constants, we set $\mathcal{L}(c^*)=\lambda u.c$, $u{:}1$, $c{:}a$. (4) Our translation of the λ-abstraction is based on the *functional completeness* property of cccs discovered by Lambek.

In contrast, [Poigne 84b], following [Scott 80], translates a lambda term $M{:}b$ with free variables $x_i{:}a_i$, $i=1,n$, into a *variable-free* cc term $M^*{:}a_1\times\ldots\times a_n\rightarrow\!\!\rightarrow b$. This is intuitively attractive, especially since λ-abstraction then corresponds directly to currying of cc terms. However, this translation does not distinguish between terms which are identical except for renaming of *free* variables. This comes in conflict with what is meant by an equation between two lambda terms with free variables in common. Hence the technical complications of [Poigne 84b].

The proof system cc of (C,E)- cartesian closed logic consists of reflexivity, symmetry, transitivity, congruence with regard to the ccc operations, substitutivity, the axioms of cccs and (also as axioms) $\mathcal{C}(E_r)$. We don't need to enrich cc as we did with cl: the role of $A_{\beta\eta}$ is accomplished also by the ccc axioms !

We establish a completely satisfactory correspondence between provability in the two **logics:**

Lemma 6: If L is a set of equations between *closed* lambda terms, M, N are *arbitrary* lambda **terms,** K is a set of equations between *variable-free* cc terms and P, R are *arbitrary* cc terms, **then:**

(i) $L \vdash_{\lambda} M=N$ iff $\mathcal{C}(L) \vdash_{cc} \mathcal{C}(M)=\mathcal{C}(N)$

(ii) $K \vdash_{cc} P=R$ iff $\mathcal{L}(K) \vdash_{\lambda} \mathcal{L}(P)=\mathcal{L}(R)$

(iii) $M=N \vdash_{\lambda} \mathcal{L}(\mathcal{C}(M))=\mathcal{L}(\mathcal{C}(N))$ and $\mathcal{L}(\mathcal{C}(M))=\mathcal{L}(\mathcal{C}(N)) \vdash_{\lambda} M=N$

(iv) $P=R \vdash_{cc} \mathcal{C}(\mathcal{L}(P))=\mathcal{C}(\mathcal{L}(R))$ and $\mathcal{C}(\mathcal{L}(P))=\mathcal{C}(\mathcal{L}(R)) \vdash_{cc} P=R$

A (C,E)-*cc theory* is a set of equations between cc terms which contains all the axioms and is closed under all the inference rules of cc. reasoning. A (C,E)-*ccc* is a ccc in which the equations from $\mathcal{C}(E_r)$ are valid. While the cccs are strongly sound and complete for cc theories, the concrete cccs are strongly sound and complete for closed-axiom cc theories.

From any (C,E)-syntactical λ-algebra $\mathfrak{I}$ we construct a (C,E)-ccc $\mathfrak{I}_{\mathcal{C}}$ such that

$$\mathfrak{I}_{\mathcal{C}} \models P=R \text{ iff } \mathfrak{I} \models \mathcal{L}(P)=\mathcal{L}(R)$$

essentially by showing how to interpret cc terms in $\mathfrak{I}$ via their translation into lambda terms. Similarly, we construct from any (C,E)-ccc $\mathfrak{Q}$ a (C,E)-syntactical λ-algebra $\mathfrak{Q}_{\mathcal{L}}$. These constructions are extended to functors $\mathcal{L}$ and $\mathcal{C}$.

Theorem 7:
(i) There exists an inclusion-preserving bijection between (C,E)-weak lambda theories and (C,E)-cc theories. Under this bijection, the (C,E)-lambda theories correspond to closed-axiom (C,E)-cc theories and conversely.

(ii) $(\mathcal{L}, \mathcal{C})$ is an adjoint equivalence between the category of (C,E)-syntactical λ-algebras and the category of (C,E)-cccs. $\mathcal{C}$ takes (C,E)-environment models into concrete (C,E)-cccs while $\mathcal{L}$ takes concrete (C,E)-cccs into (C,E)-environment models.

(iii) If the (C,E)-syntactical λ-algebra $\mathfrak{I}$ and the (C,E)-ccc $\mathfrak{Q}$ correspond to each other by the adjoint equivalence (ii) (which means either $\mathfrak{I}=\mathfrak{Q}_{\mathcal{L}}$ or $\mathfrak{Q}=\mathfrak{I}_{\mathcal{C}}$) then the (C,E)-weak lambda theory **Valid**($\mathfrak{I}$) and the closed-axiom (C,E)-cc theory **Valid**($\mathfrak{Q}$) correspond to each other by the bijection **(i).**

Adjoint equivalences preserve the universality properties of objects. Using this, it can be shown that if two theories correspond to each other by the bijection (i) above then their open respectively closed term models correspond to each other (up to isomorphism) by the adjoint equivalence (ii) above (we did not describe term models for cc theories here but these are standard algebraic constructions). Hence, it can be argued that the adjoint equivalence tells the whole story, semantically *and* syntactically though, of course, we have obtained the adjoint equivalence essentially via the proof-theoretic connection.

4. The Connection with the Type-Free Lambda Calculus

Let (T, →, **u**) be an algebra of types with a special type **u** such that $\mathbf{u}=\mathbf{u}\to\mathbf{u}$. Every type-free lambda term with variables from $X_{\mathbf{u}}$ can be translated into a T-lambda term M_T:**u** such that $x_T=x$, $(MN)_T=M_T\bullet_{\mathbf{uu}}N_T$ and $(\lambda x..M)_T=\lambda_{\mathbf{uu}}x.x.M_T$. We conjecture the following:

Conjecture 1: The T-lambda calculus is a *conservative extension* of the $\beta\eta$ type-free lambda calculus i.e., for any set E of type-free λ-equations and any two type-free lambda terms M,N

$$E\vdash_{\beta\eta}M=N \quad \text{iff} \quad E_T\vdash_T M_T=N_T$$

It is well-known ([Scott 80], [Koymans 82]) that any ccc with an object $\mathbf{u}=\mathbf{u}\to\mathbf{u}$ determines a (type-free) λ-algebra. But we do not need the cartesian structure for that. Simply, if $\mathfrak{D}=\{D_a\}_{a\in T}$ is a syntactical λ-algebra then $D_{\mathbf{u}}$ can be naturally made into a (type-free) λ-algebra. Moreover, if $\mathfrak{D}$ is an environment model then $D_{\mathbf{u}}$ is a (type-free) λ-model. We conjecture that all (type-free) λ-algebras can (almost) be obtained this way:

Conjecture 2: For any (type-free) λ-algebra $\mathcal{M}$ there exists a syntactical λ-algebra $\mathfrak{D}$ such that $\mathcal{M}$ is a subalgebra of $D_{\mathbf{u}}$. Moreover, if $\mathcal{M}$ is a λ-model then $\mathfrak{D}$ is an environment model.

5. Summary

The following is a picture of the correspondences that we have established:

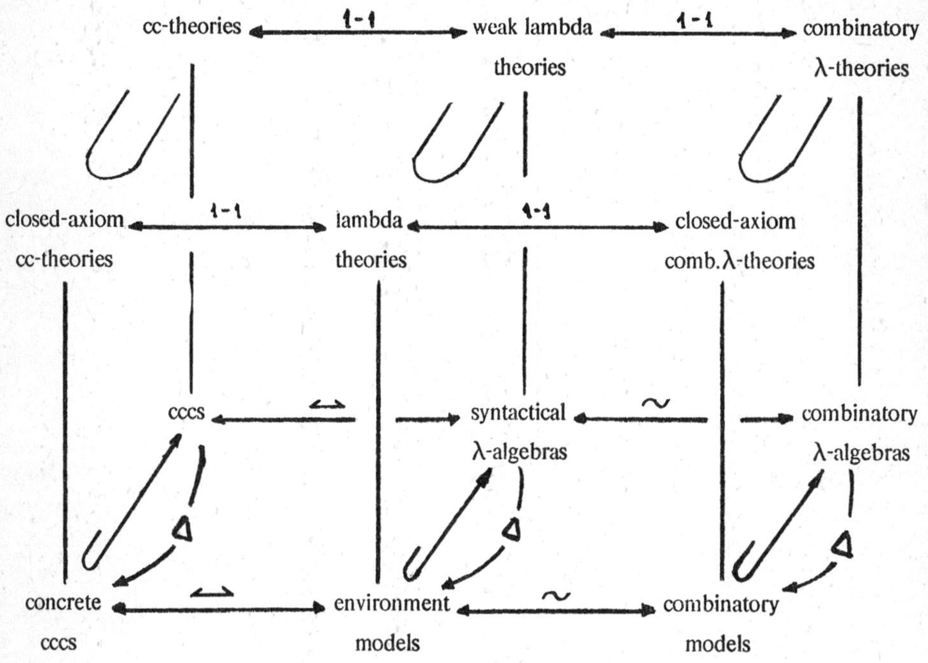

In this picture, 1-1 stands for inclusion-preserving bijection, ~ for isomorphism of categories, ⟷ for adjoint equivalence of categories and ⊂→ for subcategory-of-. The vertical lines mean that the structures on the bottom level are strongly sound and complete for the corresponding theories on the top level. The picture is parameterized by a fixed algebra of types T, a fixed set of constants C and a fixed set of closed λ-equations E. However, note that while the "right cube" exists for any such parameters, the "left cube" exists only for cartesian parameters. With the right interpretation, the two cubes together can be seen as a "commutative diagram". In addition, the ◁ symbols mean that every structure in the back row is the retract of a corresponding structure in the front row obtained by adjoining indeterminates. These operations are also extended to functors and the bottom rectangle with the ◁ functors instead of the ⊂→ ones is also a commutative diagram.

6. Directions for Further Investigation

It seems justified to call the class of (C,E)-environment models a *lambda variety*. The lambda varieties are the higher-type correspondent of the *equational varieties* of algebras. An interesting prospect is that of finding a purely semantical characterization of lambda varieties as Birkhoff's Theorem does for equational varieties (as classes of algebras closed under products, subalgebras and homomorphic images). In view of the results described above, it seems that one should look for a *joint* characterization of the class of models and that of λ-algebras in which a given set of λ-equations holds.

A major problem is proving the existence of non-trivial models. Scott's celebrated results provide models for the type-free lambda calculus while, of course, it is trivial to find models for the finitely typed lambda calculus. (Note however, that most of the techniques used for the deeper results in finitely typed lambda calculus [Statman 82], [Statman 84a], [Statman 84b] are fundamentally dependent on the fact that the types are inductively defined, hence do not directly carry over to our case). For the pure type-free lambda calculus the Church-Rosser theorem implies the existence of a non-trivial model. Therefore, one possibility is to try to generalize this theorem to arbitrarily constrained types. But in this way we obtain syntactically constructed, hence not too interesting models. More meaningful would be to bring in the context of constrained types the techniques used for solving domain equations ([Scott 72], [Scott 76], [Wand 79], [Smyth, Plotkin 82]) and use them to construct models with interesting properties.

Results relating two different algebras of types are also desirable. For example, a homomorphism

$$h : (T, \to) \longrightarrow (T', \to)$$

naturally determines a translation of T-lambda terms into T'-lambda terms. How are the T-λ-models and the T'-λ-models related ? Moreover, the finite types form a free algebra while arbitrary algebras of types can be seen as homomorphic images of such free algebras. Can the categories of models with arbitrarily constrained types be seen in a similar fashion, say, as "quotients" of the category of models for the finitely typed lambda calculus ?

References

[Barendregt 84] Barendregt, Henk P.
Studies in Logic. Volume 103: *The Lambda Calculus: Its Syntax and Semantics.*
North-Holland, 1984.
2nd & revised edition.

[Curien 83] Curien, P-L.
Combinateurs Catégoriques, Algorithmes Séquentiels et Programmation Applicative.
PhD thesis, Université Paris VII, 1983.

[Dybjer 83] Dybjer, P.
Category-Theoretic Logics and Algebras of Programs.
PhD thesis, Chalmers University of Technology, Sweden, 1983.

[Friedman 75] Friedman, H.
Equality between functionals.
In R. Parikh (editor), *LNMath.* Volume 453: *Logic Colloqium, '73*, pages 22-37. Springer-Verlag, 1975.

[Halpern, Meyer, Trakhtenbrot 84]
Halpern, Joseph Y., Albert R. Meyer, and Boris Trakhtenbrot.
The semantics of local storage, or what makes the free-list free?
In *11th ACM Symp. on Principles of Programming Languages*, pages 245-257. , 1984.

[Hindley, Longo 80]
Hindley, R., and G. Longo.
Lambda-calculus models and extensionality.
ZMLGM 26:289-310, 1980.

[Koymans 82] Koymans, Christiaan P.J.
Models of the λ-calculus.
Information and Control 52:306-332, 1982.

[Koymans 84] Koymans, Christiaan P.J.
Models of the Lambda Calculus.
PhD thesis, University of Utrecht, 1984.

[Lambek 72] Lambek, J.
Deductive Systems and Categories III.
In Lawvere, F.W. (editor), *Lecture Notes in Mathematics.* Volume 274: *Toposes, Algebraic Geometry and Logic; Proc. 1971 Dahlhousie Conf.*, pages 57-82. Springer-Verlag, 1972.

[Lambek 74] Lambek, J.
Functional Completeness of Cartesian Categories.
Ann. Math. Logic 6:259-292, 1974.

[Lambek 80] Lambek,J.
From lambda calculus to cartesian closed categories.
In Seldin, J.P. and J.R. Hindley (editors), *To H.B. Curry: Essays on Combinatory Logic, Lambda Calculus and Formalism*, pages 375-402. Academic Press, 1980.

[Lambek, Scott 84]
Lambek, J. and P. J. Scott.
Aspects of Higher-Order Categorical Logic.
Contemporary Mathematics 30:145-174, 1984.

[Meyer 82] Meyer, Albert R.
What is a model of the lambda calculus?
Information and Control 52:87-122, 1982.

[Mitchell 84] Mitchell, John C.
Semantic models for second-order lambda calculus.
In *Proc. 25th IEEE Symp. on Foundations of Computer Science*, pages 289-299. , 1984.

[Parsaye-Ghomi 81]
Parsaye-Ghomi, K.
Higher Order Abstract Data Types.
PhD thesis, University of California, 1981.

[Poigne 84a] Poigné, A.
Higher-Order data Structures-Cartesian Closure Versus λ-Calculus.
In *LNCS*. Volume 166: *Symposium of Theoretical Aspects of Computer Science, Proceedings*, pages 174-185. Springer-Verlag, 1984.

[Poigne 84b] Poigné, A.
On Specifications, Theories and Models with Higher Types.
1984.
to appear *Information and Control.*

[Scott 72] Scott, Dana S.
Continuous Lattices.
In Lawvere, F.W. (editor), *Lecture Notes in Mathematics.* Volume 274: *Toposes, Algebraic Geometry and Logic; Proc. 1971 Dahlhousie Conf.*, pages 97-136. Springer-Verlag, 1972.

[Scott 76] Scott, Dana S.
Data types as lattices.
SIAM J. Computing 5:522-587, 1976.

[Scott 80] Scott, Dana S.
Relating theories of the lambda calculus.
In Seldin, J.P. and J.R. Hindley (editors), *To H.B. Curry: Essays on Combinatory Logic, Lambda Calculus and Formalism*, pages 403-450. Academic Press, 1980.

[Smyth, Plotkin 82]
Smyth, M.B., and Gordon D. Plotkin.
The category-theoretic solution of recursive domain equations.
SIAM J. Computing 11:761-783, 1982.

[Statman 82] Statman, R.
λ-definable functionals and $\beta\eta$ conversion.
Archiv fur Mathematische Logik und Grundlagenforschung 22:1-6, 1982.

[Statman 84a] Statman, R.
Equality between functionals, revisited.
1984.
Friedman Volume, to appear.

[Statman 84b] Statman, R.
Logical relations in the typed lambda-calculus.
1984.
To appear, *Information and Control.*

[Wand 79] Wand, Mitchell.
Fixed-point Constructions in Order-enriched Categories.
Theroretical Computer Science :13-30, 1979.

AN AXIOMATIC TREATMENT OF A PARALLEL PROGRAMMING LANGUAGE

Stephen D. Brookes
Carnegie-Mellon University
Department of Computer Science
Pittsburgh

1. Abstract.

This paper describes a semantically–based axiomatic treatment of a parallel programming language with shared variable concurrency and conditional critical regions, essentially the language discussed by Owicki and Gries [20,21]. We use a structural operational semantics for this language, based on work of Hennessy and Plotkin [22,26], and we use the semantic structure to suggest a class of assertions for expressing properties of commands. We then define syntactic operations on assertions which correspond precisely to syntactic constructs of the programming language; in particular, we define sequential and parallel composition of assertions. This enables us to design a truly compositional proof system for program properties. Our proof system is sound and relatively complete. We examine the relationship between our proof system and the Owicki-Gries proof system. Our assertions are more expressive than Owicki's, and her *proof outlines* correspond roughly to a special subset of our assertion language. Owicki's parallel rule can be thought of as being based on a slightly different form of parallel composition of assertions; our form does not require *interference-freedom*, and our proof system is relatively complete without the need for auxiliary variables. Connections with other work, including the "Generalized Hoare Logic" of Lamport and Schneider [16,17], and with the Transition Logic of Gerth [11], are discussed briefly.

2. A Parallel Programming Language.

We begin with a simple programming language containing the usual sequential constructs (assignment, conditional commands, loops, and sequential composition), together with a simple form of parallel composition, and a "conditional critical region" or *await* construct. Parallel commands interact solely through their effects on shared variables. As usual for imperative languages, we distinguish the syntactic categories of identifiers (**Ide**, with meta-variable I), expressions ($E \in$ **Exp**), boolean expressions ($B \in$ **BExp**), and commands ($\Gamma \in$ **Com**). The abstract syntax for expressions, boolean expressions and identifiers will be taken for granted. For commands we specify:

$$\Gamma ::= \mathbf{skip} \mid I{:=}E \mid \Gamma_1 ; \Gamma_2 \mid [\Gamma_1 \| \Gamma_2] \mid \mathbf{await}\ B\ \mathbf{then}\ \Gamma$$
$$\mid \mathbf{if}\ B\ \mathbf{then}\ \Gamma_1\ \mathbf{else}\ \Gamma_2 \mid \mathbf{while}\ B\ \mathbf{do}\ \Gamma.$$

The notation is fairly standard. The command **skip** is an atomic action having no effect on program variables. An assignment, denoted $I{:=}E$, is also an atomic action; it sets the value of I to the value of E. Sequential composition is represented by $\Gamma_1; \Gamma_2$. A parallel composition $[\Gamma_1 \parallel \Gamma_2]$ is executed by interleaving the atomic actions of the component commands Γ_1 and Γ_2. A command **await** B **do** Γ is a *conditional critical region*; this construct converts Γ into an atomic action, and is executable only when the test expression B evaluates to true. Conditional commands and loops may be given two alternative interpretations: the test is evaluated as a single atomic action, and then either we can allow an interruption point before beginning the selected command or else we can disallow such an interruption; we will discuss both of these alternatives, and clearly the effect of some commands will depend crucially on the interpretation of conditionals. We impose a syntactic constraint: we will not allow nested *await* commands. The use of nested awaits is in any case poor programming style, and this does not significantly restrict the class of programs definable in the language, but slightly simplifies the semantic treatment.

In describing the semantics of this language, we focus mainly on commands. A *state* is a function from identifiers to values:

$$s \in S = [\mathbf{Ide} \to V],$$

where V is some set of expression values (typically containing integers and truth values). We write $s + [I \mapsto v]$ for the state which agrees with s except that it gives identifier I the value v. The value denoted by an expression may depend on the values of its free identifiers. Thus, we assume the existence of a semantic function

$$\mathcal{E} : \mathbf{Exp} \to [S \to V].$$

For boolean expressions we assume a *satisfaction relation* $\models$ on states and booleans; we write $s \models B$ when s satisfies B.

We specify the semantics of commands in the structural operational style [26], and our presentation follows that of [22], where identical program constructs were considered. We define first an abstract machine which specifies the computations of a command. The abstract machine is given by a *labelled transition system*

$$\langle \mathbf{Conf}, \mathbf{Lab}, \to \rangle,$$

where **Conf** is a set of *configurations*, **Lab** is a set of *labels* (ranged over by α, β and γ), and $\to$ is a family

$$\{ \xrightarrow{\alpha} \mid \alpha \in \mathbf{Lab} \}$$

of *transition relations* $\xrightarrow{\alpha} \subseteq \mathbf{Conf} \times \mathbf{Conf}$ indexed by elements of **Lab**. An atomic action is either an assignment, or **skip**, or a test evaluation, or a critical region. We use labels for atomic actions, and assume from now on that all atomic actions of a command have labels: in other words, we deal with *labelled commands*. For precision, we give the following syntax for labelled commands, in which α and β range over **Lab**:

$$\begin{array}{rl} \Gamma ::= & \alpha{:}\mathbf{skip} \mid \alpha{:}I{:=}E \mid \Gamma_1;\Gamma_2 \mid [\Gamma_1 \parallel \Gamma_2] \mid \mathbf{await}\ \beta{:}B\ \mathbf{then}\ \alpha{:}\Gamma \\ & \mid \mathbf{if}\ \beta{:}B\ \mathbf{then}\ \Gamma_1\ \mathbf{else}\ \Gamma_2 \mid \mathbf{while}\ \beta{:}B\ \mathbf{do}\ \Gamma. \end{array}$$

For convenience we introduce a term **null** to represent termination, and we specify (purely for notational convenience) that

$$\begin{aligned} [\mathbf{null} \parallel \Gamma] &= [\Gamma \parallel \mathbf{null}] = \Gamma, \\ \mathbf{null};\Gamma &= \Gamma. \end{aligned}$$

We will use **Com**$'$ for the set containing all labelled commands and **null**. The set of configurations is $\mathbf{Conf} = \mathbf{Com}' \times S$. A configuration of the form $\langle\Gamma, s\rangle$ will represent a stage in a computation at which the remaining command to be executed is Γ, and the current state is s. A configuration of the form $\langle\mathbf{null}, s\rangle$ represents termination in the given state. A *transition* of the form

$$\langle\Gamma, s\rangle \xrightarrow{\alpha} \langle\Gamma', s'\rangle$$

represents a step in a computation in which the state and remaining command change as indicated, and in which the atomic action labelled α occurs. We write $\langle\Gamma, s\rangle \to \langle\Gamma', s'\rangle$ when there is an α for which $\langle\Gamma, s\rangle \xrightarrow{\alpha} \langle\Gamma', s'\rangle$. And we use the notation $\to^*$ for the reflexive transitive closure of this relation. Thus $\langle\Gamma, s\rangle \to^* \langle\Gamma', s'\rangle$ iff there is a sequence of atomic actions from the first configuration to the second.

The transition relations are defined to be the smallest satisfying the axioms and rules of Table 1. This means that a transition is possible if and only if it can be deduced from this table.

In this transition system, we have specified that a parallel composition terminates only when both components have terminated. This is because of our conventions about **null**: we have $\langle[\Gamma_1 \parallel \Gamma_2], s\rangle \xrightarrow{\alpha} \langle\Gamma_2, s'\rangle$ whenever $\langle\Gamma_1, s\rangle \xrightarrow{\alpha} \langle\mathbf{null}, s'\rangle$, for instance.

The transitions from a given initial configuration form a finitely branching (possibly infinite) tree, in which the root node is the initial configuration and the arcs correspond to atomic actions. Such a tree can have two types of leaf node: *successful* leaves corresponding to *termination*, and *unsuccessful* or *stuck* nodes corresponding to await commands in which the test is false. It is important to distinguish between these types of nodes, and we define the following predicates on configurations:

$$\begin{aligned} \mathsf{term}(\langle\Gamma, s\rangle) &\Leftrightarrow \Gamma = \mathbf{null}, \\ \mathsf{stuck}(\langle\Gamma, s\rangle) &\Leftrightarrow \Gamma \neq \mathbf{null}\ \&\ \neg\exists\alpha.(\langle\Gamma, s\rangle \xrightarrow{\alpha}). \end{aligned}$$

TABLE 1: Transition Rules

$$\langle \alpha{:}\mathbf{skip}, s\rangle \xrightarrow{\alpha} \langle \mathbf{null}, s\rangle \tag{A1}$$

$$\langle \alpha{:}I{:=}E, s\rangle \xrightarrow{\alpha} \langle \mathbf{null}, s + [I \mapsto \mathcal{E}[\![E]\!]s]\rangle \tag{A2}$$

$$\frac{\langle \Gamma_1, s\rangle \xrightarrow{\alpha} \langle \Gamma_1', s'\rangle}{\langle \Gamma_1; \Gamma_2, s\rangle \xrightarrow{\alpha} \langle \Gamma_1'; \Gamma_2, s'\rangle} \tag{A3}$$

$$\frac{\langle \Gamma_1, s\rangle \xrightarrow{\alpha} \langle \Gamma_1', s'\rangle \quad s \models B}{\langle \mathbf{if}\ \beta{:}\ B\ \mathbf{then}\ \Gamma_1\ \mathbf{else}\ \Gamma_2, s\rangle \xrightarrow{\alpha} \langle \Gamma_1', s'\rangle} \tag{A4}$$

$$\frac{\langle \Gamma_2, s\rangle \xrightarrow{\alpha} \langle \Gamma_2', s'\rangle \quad s \models \neg B}{\langle \mathbf{if}\ \beta{:}\ B\ \mathbf{then}\ \Gamma_1\ \mathbf{else}\ \Gamma_2, s\rangle \xrightarrow{\alpha} \langle \Gamma_2', s'\rangle} \tag{A5}$$

$$\frac{\langle \Gamma, s\rangle \xrightarrow{\alpha} \langle \Gamma', s'\rangle \quad s \models B}{\langle \mathbf{while}\ \beta{:}\ B\ \mathbf{do}\ \Gamma, s\rangle \xrightarrow{\alpha} \langle \Gamma'; \mathbf{while}\ \beta{:}B\ \mathbf{do}\ \Gamma, s'\rangle} \tag{A6}$$

$$\frac{s \models \neg B}{\langle \mathbf{while}\ \beta{:}\ B\ \mathbf{do}\ \Gamma, s\rangle \xrightarrow{\beta} \langle \mathbf{null}, s\rangle} \tag{A7}$$

$$\frac{\langle \Gamma_1, s\rangle \xrightarrow{\alpha} \langle \Gamma_1', s'\rangle}{\langle [\Gamma_1 \parallel \Gamma_2], s\rangle \xrightarrow{\alpha} \langle [\Gamma_1' \parallel \Gamma_2], s'\rangle} \tag{A8}$$

$$\frac{\langle \Gamma_2, s\rangle \xrightarrow{\alpha} \langle \Gamma_2', s'\rangle}{\langle [\Gamma_1 \parallel \Gamma_2], s\rangle \xrightarrow{\alpha} \langle [\Gamma_1 \parallel \Gamma_2'], s'\rangle} \tag{A9}$$

$$\frac{\langle \Gamma, s\rangle \rightarrow^* \langle \mathbf{null}, s'\rangle \quad s \models B}{\langle \mathbf{await}\ \beta{:}\ B\ \mathbf{then}\ \alpha{:}\Gamma, s\rangle \xrightarrow{\alpha} \langle \mathbf{null}, s'\rangle} \tag{A10}$$

Note that rules (A4)–(A6) specify the "non-interruptible" version of conditionals in which there is no interruption point between evaluation of the test and the beginning of the selected command. To obtain the "interruptible version we merely replace these rules by:

$$\frac{s \models B}{\langle \mathbf{if}\ \beta{:}B\ \mathbf{then}\ \Gamma_1\ \mathbf{else}\ \Gamma_2, s\rangle \xrightarrow{\beta} \langle \Gamma_1, s\rangle} \tag{A4$'$}$$

$$\frac{s \models \neg B}{\langle \mathbf{if}\ \beta{:}B\ \mathbf{then}\ \Gamma_1\ \mathbf{else}\ \Gamma_2, s\rangle \xrightarrow{\beta} \langle \Gamma_2, s\rangle} \tag{A5$'$}$$

$$\frac{s \models B}{\langle \mathbf{while}\ \beta{:}B\ \mathbf{do}\ \Gamma, s\rangle \xrightarrow{\beta} \langle \Gamma; \mathbf{while}\ \beta{:}B\ \mathbf{do}\ \Gamma, s\rangle} \tag{A6$'$}$$

3. Assertion Language.

The tree structure of the transition system suggests a class of assertions with components representing the branch structure of trees. We need to distinguish between successful leaf nodes (arising as the result of termination) and unsuccessful or stuck nodes. We therefore introduce a class of assertions of the form

$$\phi ::= P \sum_{i=1}^{n} \alpha_i P_i \phi_i \mid P\bullet \mid P\circ,$$

where P and the P_i are drawn from some *condition* language, and where the α_i are atomic action labels. The special forms $P\bullet$ and $P\circ$ represent successful and unsuccessful termination respectively. The notation has been chosen to correspond with Milner's linear notation for *synchronization trees* [24]; in addition to labelling the arcs with action labels, we also incorporate conditions at nodes and we have two types ($\bullet$ and $\circ$) of leaves. We make no distinction between assertions which differ only in the order in which their branches are written. A tree representation of such a ϕ will often be preferable to the linear notation; for example, the assertion $P \sum_{i=1}^{n} \alpha_i P_i \phi_i$ may be represented as:

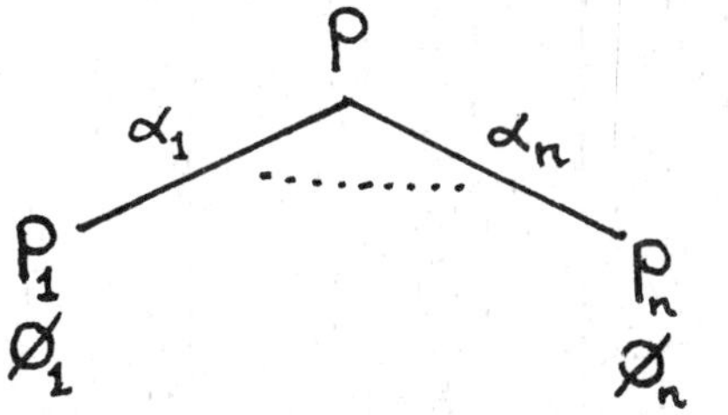

We will feel free to use set braces to delimit conditions as an aid to the eye. Finally, it will be convenient to adopt the convention that $\{P\}\alpha\{Q\}$ (which does not conform to the syntax above) abbreviates the assertion $\{P\}\alpha\{Q\}\{Q\}\bullet$ (which does).

Note that there is an obvious definition of the *depth* of an assertion ϕ, and that all assertions introduced so far have finite depth. Later we will add *recursive assertions* to the assertion language so that we will be able to reason about infinite computation trees.

In order to express the property that a command Γ *satisfies* an assertion ϕ we write a *command assertion*:

$$\Gamma \;\textbf{sat}\; \phi.$$

This type of formal property will be the subject of our proof system.

The interpretation of an assertion of zero depth is obvious:

$$\models \Gamma \;\textbf{sat}\; P\bullet \quad \Leftrightarrow \quad \forall s.[s \models P \Rightarrow \mathrm{term}(\langle \Gamma, s\rangle)],$$
$$\models \Gamma \;\textbf{sat}\; P\circ \quad \Leftrightarrow \quad \forall s.[s \models P \Rightarrow \mathrm{stuck}(\langle \Gamma, s\rangle)].$$

When ϕ is the assertion $P\sum_{i=1}^{n}\alpha_i P_i \phi_i$ we interpret Γ **sat** ϕ in the following way. If the command is started in a state satisfying P, then its initial action must be an α_i drawn from the set of initial labels of the assertion, and these labels are precisely the initial actions possible for the command. If the command starts with an α_i action it reaches a state where P_i is true and where the remaining command satisfies ϕ_i. Specifically, we define .

$$\models \Gamma \,\mathbf{sat}\, P\sum_{i=1}^{n}\alpha_i P_i \phi_i$$

if and only if

$$\forall s \forall \alpha.\,(s \models P \;\&\; \langle \Gamma, s\rangle \xrightarrow{\alpha} \langle \Gamma', s'\rangle \quad \Rightarrow \quad \exists i \le n.\, \alpha = \alpha_i \;\&\; s' \models P_i \;\&\; \Gamma' \models \phi_i), \qquad (1)$$

and

$$\forall s. \forall i.\,(s \models P \;\Rightarrow\; \exists \Gamma_i, s_i.\, \langle \Gamma, s\rangle \xrightarrow{\alpha_i} \langle \Gamma_i, s_i\rangle), \qquad (2)$$

so that all of the actions specified in ϕ are indeed possible for Γ when the initial state satisfies P.

Example 1. The command $[\alpha\!:\!x\!:=\!x+1 \,\|\, \beta\!:\!x\!:=\!x+1]$ satisfies the assertion

$$\begin{aligned}\{x=0\}(&\alpha\{x=1\}\{x=1\}\beta\{x=2\}\\ &+\beta\{x=1\}\{x=1\}\alpha\{x=2\}).\end{aligned}$$

Example 2. The command $[\alpha\!:\!x\!:=\!2 \,\|\, (\beta\!:\!x\!:=\!1; \gamma\!:\!x\!:=\!x+1)]$ satisfies the assertion

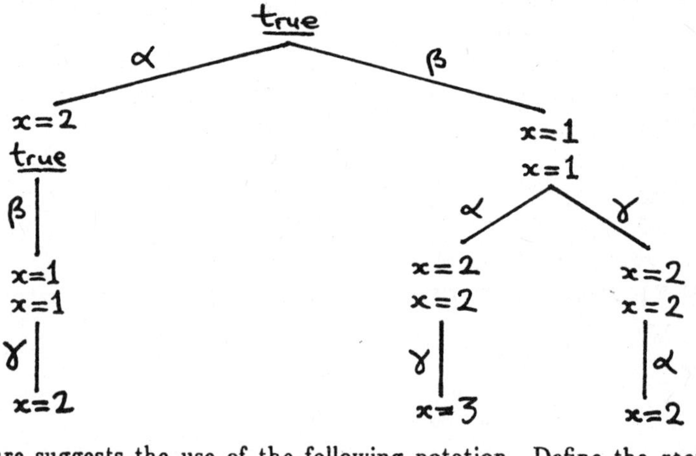

Tree structure suggests the use of the following notation. Define the *root* and *leaf*

conditions for ϕ as follows:

$$\begin{aligned}
\text{root}(P\bullet) = \text{root}(P\circ) &= P, \\
\text{leaf}(P\bullet) &= P, \\
\text{leaf}(P\circ) &= \textbf{false}, \\
\text{root}(P\sum_{i=1}^{n} \alpha_i P_i \phi_i) &= P, \\
\text{leaf}(P\sum_{i=1}^{n} \alpha_i P_i \phi_i) &= \bigvee_{i=1}^{n} \text{leaf}(\phi_i).
\end{aligned}$$

The root condition characterizes the state at the root of a computation tree, and the leaf condition characterizes the successful leaf nodes, being simply the disjunction of the conditions at the successful leaves of the assertion. Note that in the syntactic definition of the class of assertions, we have not required that any logical connection exist between adjacent "intermediate" conditions inside an assertion. Assertions in which such a constraint is satisfied will be called *safe*; they correspond very closely with proof outlines and computation trees. We may formalize this *safe* constraint as follows, by defining the predicate safe(ϕ):

$$\begin{aligned}
\text{safe}(P\bullet) &= \textbf{true}, \\
\text{safe}(P\circ) &= \textbf{false}, \\
\text{safe}(P\sum_{i=1}^{n} \alpha_i P_i \phi_i) &= \bigwedge_{i=1}^{n} (P_i \Rightarrow \text{root}(\phi_i)) \ \& \ \bigwedge_{i=1}^{n} \text{safe}(\phi_i).
\end{aligned}$$

There are good semantic reasons for not making this constraint on the syntax of our assertion language, since assertions satisfying the constraint describe the behaviour of a command in isolation and we know that in general this information is insufficient to characterize the behaviour of a command in all parallel contexts.

4. Proof System.

Atomic assertions.

A terminal assertion $\{P\}\bullet$ represents termination. An *atomic assertion* has the form $\{P\}\alpha\{Q\}\{R\}\bullet$, and the special abbreviated form $\{P\}\alpha\{Q\}$ is thus atomic. Atomic commands satisfy atomic assertions, and the axioms expressing this fact for **skip** and assignment are simple:

$$\alpha{:}\,\textbf{skip}\ \textbf{sat}\ \{P\}\alpha\{P\}\{\textbf{true}\}\bullet \tag{B1}$$

$$\alpha{:}\,I{:=}E\ \textbf{sat}\ \{[E\backslash I]P\}\alpha\{P\}\{\textbf{true}\}\bullet \tag{B2}$$

We use the notation $[E\backslash I]P$ for the result of replacing every free occurrence of I in P by E, with suitable name changes to avoid clashes.

A *conditional critical region* also creates an atomic action out of a command. In order to axiomatize this construct we need to single out a class of assertions which state properties of a command when run in isolation as an indivisible atomic action, since the effect of the critical region construct is to run a command without allowing interruption. This is precisely the class of *safe* assertions, which have the property that at each node of the tree the post-condition established by the previous atomic action implies the root condition of the remaining subtree. When $n = 0$ this is trivially true, and the abbreviated form of atomic assertion $\{P\}\alpha\{Q\}$ is safe. We propose the following rules for critical regions:

$$\frac{\Gamma\ \textbf{sat}\ \phi, \quad \text{safe}(\phi)}{\textbf{await}\ \beta{:}B\ \textbf{then}\ \alpha{:}\Gamma\ \ \textbf{sat}\ \{\text{root}(\phi)\ \&\ B\}\alpha\{\text{leaf}(\phi)\}\{\textbf{true}\}\bullet} \tag{B3}$$

$$\textbf{await}\ \beta{:}B\ \textbf{then}\ \alpha{:}\Gamma\ \ \textbf{sat}\ \{\neg B\}\circ \tag{B4}$$

Rule (B4) expresses the fact that an *await* command is stuck if the test evaluates to false. The soundness of these rules is easy to establish.

Parallel composition.

It is possible to define a parallel composition for assertions. The definition is given inductively. For the base cases we put:

$$\begin{aligned} [P\circ \parallel Q\circ] &= [P\circ \parallel Q\bullet] = [P\bullet \parallel Q\circ] = \{P\ \&\ Q\}\circ, \\ [P\bullet \parallel Q\bullet] &= \{P\ \&\ Q\}\bullet. \end{aligned}$$

For the case when only one of the assertions is terminated, we specify that

$$[P* \parallel Q\sum_{j=1}^{m}\beta_j Q_j \psi_j] = \{P\ \&\ Q\}\sum_{j=1}^{m}\beta_j Q_j [P* \parallel \psi_j],$$

when $*$ is either $\circ$ or $\bullet$ (and a similar symmetric clause). The inductive clause extends the well known *interleaving* operation on synchronization trees [6,24,28] to handle node conditions in an appropriate manner. For assertions $\phi = P(\sum_{i=1}^{n}\alpha_i P_i \phi_i)$ and $\psi = Q(\sum_{j=1}^{m}\beta_j Q_j \psi_j)$ we define

$$[\phi \parallel \psi] = \{P\ \&\ Q\}(\sum_{i=1}^{n}\alpha_i P_i[\phi_i \parallel \psi] + \sum_{j=1}^{m}\beta_j Q_j[\phi \parallel \psi_j]).$$

Of course, this composition is not guaranteed to produce *safe* assertions, even if the component assertions are safe. Nevertheless, the following result shows that parallel composition of assertions does have the correct effect.

Theorem 1. If $\models \Gamma_1$ **sat** ϕ and $\models \Gamma_2$ **sat** ψ then $\models [\Gamma_1 \parallel \Gamma_2]$ **sat** $[\phi \parallel \psi]$. ∎

Thus we are led to the proof rule:

$$\frac{\Gamma_1 \ \mathbf{sat}\ \phi \qquad \Gamma_2 \ \mathbf{sat}\ \psi}{[\Gamma_1 \parallel \Gamma_2]\ \mathbf{sat}\ [\phi \parallel \psi]}. \tag{B5}$$

Sequential composition.

We may also define a sequential composition for assertions. The definition is straightforward, again by induction on depth. The operation grafts ψ on to the successful leaf nodes of the tree corresponding to ϕ. In the base case, we put

$$(P\bullet); Q \sum_{j=1}^{m} \beta_j Q_j \psi_j \ = \ \{P \,\&\, Q\} \sum_{j=1}^{m} \beta_j Q_j \psi_j .$$

When ϕ is $P(\sum_{i=1}^{n} \alpha_i P_i \phi_i)$ and $n > 0$ we put

$$\phi; \psi \ = \ P \sum_{i=1}^{n} \alpha_i P_i (\phi_i; \psi).$$

The special case when $n = 0$ reduces to $P \circ ; \psi \ = \ P \circ$.

Again we can show that the operation has the desired effect.

Theorem 2. If $\models \Gamma_1$ **sat** ϕ and $\models \Gamma_2$ **sat** ψ then $\models (\Gamma_1; \Gamma_2)$ **sat** $(\phi; \psi)$. ∎

This suggests the proof rule:

$$\frac{\Gamma_1 \ \mathbf{sat}\ \phi \qquad \Gamma_2 \ \mathbf{sat}\ \psi}{(\Gamma_1; \Gamma_2)\ \mathbf{sat}\ (\phi; \psi)}. \tag{B6}$$

Conditionals.

The proof rules for conditional commands are simple. The appropriate proof rules for the "non-interruptible" interpretation are:

$$\frac{\Gamma_1 \ \mathbf{sat}\ P \sum_{i=1}^{n} \alpha_i P_i \phi_i}{\mathbf{if}\ \beta{:}B\ \mathbf{do}\ \Gamma_1\ \mathbf{else}\ \Gamma_2\ \mathbf{sat}\ \{P \,\&\, B\} \sum_{i=1}^{n} \alpha_i P_i \phi_i} \tag{B7}$$

$$\frac{\Gamma_2 \ \mathbf{sat}\ P \sum_{i=1}^{n} \alpha_i P_i \phi_i}{\mathbf{if}\ \beta{:}B\ \mathbf{do}\ \Gamma_1\ \mathbf{else}\ \Gamma_2\ \mathbf{sat}\ \{P \,\&\, \neg B\} \sum_{i=1}^{n} \alpha_i P_i \phi_i} \tag{B8}$$

The rules for the interruptible version are:

$$\frac{\Gamma_1 \ \mathbf{sat}\ \phi_1}{\mathbf{if}\ \beta{:}B\ \mathbf{do}\ \Gamma_1\ \mathbf{else}\ \Gamma_2\ \mathbf{sat}\ \{P \,\&\, B\}\beta\{P\}\phi_1} \qquad (B7')$$

$$\frac{\Gamma_2 \ \mathbf{sat}\ \phi_2}{\mathbf{if}\ \beta{:}B\ \mathbf{do}\ \Gamma_1\ \mathbf{else}\ \Gamma_2\ \mathbf{sat}\ \{P \,\&\, \neg B\}\beta\{P\}\phi_2} \qquad (B8')$$

Since (B7) and (B8) correspond to (A4) and (A5), and (B7′) and (B8′) to (A4′) and (A5′), the soundness of these rules is easy to establish.

Loops.

In order to reason about a loop, we use a proof rule which builds an assertion about a loop from a (smaller) assertion already established for the loop and an assertion about the loop body. This means that we will be able to prove in general assertions of arbitrary (but finite) depth for a loop, which is as expected because loops can engage in arbitrarily long computations. For a non-interruptible interpretation we specify the rules:

$$\frac{\mathbf{while}\ \beta{:}B\ \mathbf{do}\ \Gamma\ \mathbf{sat}\ \theta, \quad \Gamma\ \mathbf{sat}\ P\sum_{i=1}^{n}\alpha_i P_i \phi_i}{\mathbf{while}\ \beta{:}B\ \mathbf{do}\ \Gamma\ \mathbf{sat}\ \{P \,\&\, B\}\sum_{i=1}^{n}\alpha_i P_i(\phi_i;\theta)} \qquad (B9)$$

$$\mathbf{while}\ \beta{:}B\ \mathbf{do}\ \Gamma\ \mathbf{sat}\ \{P \,\&\, \neg B\}\beta\{P\}\{\mathbf{true}\}\bullet \qquad (B10)$$

For the interruptible case, we specify instead of (B9):

$$\frac{\mathbf{while}\ \beta{:}B\ \mathbf{do}\ \Gamma\ \mathbf{sat}\ \theta, \quad \Gamma\ \mathbf{sat}\ \phi}{\mathbf{while}\ \beta{:}B\ \mathbf{do}\ \Gamma\ \mathbf{sat}\ \{P \,\&\, B\}\beta\{P\}(\phi;\theta)} \qquad (B9')$$

Again, the obvious connection between (B9), (B10) and (A6), (A7), and between (B9′) and (A6′) shows the soundness of these rules.

The system presented above is sound but not complete. One reason for incompleteness is rather trivial: every command satisfies an assertion ϕ whose root is **false**, but we have no way of proving this from the above rules. One solution is to add a rule to this effect:

$$\frac{\neg\mathrm{root}(\phi)}{\Gamma\ \mathbf{sat}\ \phi} \qquad (B0)$$

Even this does not guarantee completeness by itself. There is no proof from these rules alone that the command

$$[\alpha{:}x{:=}x+1 \;||\; \beta{:}x{:=}x+1]$$

satisfies the assertion

$$\{x=0\}(\alpha\{x=1\}\{x=1\}\beta\{x=2\} \;+\; \beta\{x=1\}\{x=1\}\alpha\{x=2\}).$$

Essentially, the reason for this is that we really need to use *two* assertions about each component command here: we need to be able to say that $x{:=}x+1$ will change the value of x from 0 to 1, and that it will equally well change the value of x from 1 to 2. Of course, in general the number of separate assertions required may be more than two. We will therefore allow *conjunction* of assertions and include a natural rule which expresses an appropriate notion of *implication* for our assertions. For conjunction we simply add to the syntax of our assertion language the clause

$$\phi ::= (\phi_1 \oplus \phi_2).$$

We use $\oplus$ rather than & merely to keep a visual distinction between conjunction at this level and conjunction in the condition language. The interpretation is simple:

$$\models \Gamma\,\mathbf{sat}\,(\phi_1 \oplus \phi_2) \quad \Leftrightarrow \quad \models \Gamma\,\mathbf{sat}\,\phi_1 \quad \& \quad \models \Gamma\,\mathbf{sat}\,\phi_2.$$

Conjunction is clearly associative. We can extend the definitions of our syntactic operations to cover conjunctions. The definition of parallel composition of assertions is a straightforward generalization of the earlier definition. When ϕ and ψ are conjunctions, $[\phi \parallel \psi]$ is defined to be a conjunction: for each conjunct $P\sum_{i=1}^{n} \alpha_i P_i \phi_i$ of ϕ and each conjunct $Q\sum_{j=1}^{m} \beta_j Q_j \psi_j$ of ψ we include in $[\phi \parallel \psi]$ a conjunct of the form:

$$\{P \,\&\, Q\}(\sum_{i=1}^{n} \alpha_i P_i[\phi_i \parallel \psi] + \sum_{j=1}^{m} \beta_j Q_j[\phi \parallel \psi_j]).$$

For sequential composition we merely put $(\phi_1 \oplus \phi_2);\psi = (\phi_1;\psi)\oplus(\phi_2;\psi)$ and similarly when we have a conjunction in the second place: in other words, sequential composition distributes over conjunction. With these additions, the axioms and rules given earlier remain sound. In order to extend the definition of safe(ϕ) to cases when ϕ is a conjunction we define $\mathrm{root}(\phi_1 \oplus \phi_2) = \mathrm{root}(\phi_1) \vee \mathrm{root}(\phi_2)$.

We add rules for conjunction introduction and elimination:

$$\frac{\Gamma\,\mathbf{sat}\,\phi \qquad \Gamma\,\mathbf{sat}\,\psi}{\Gamma\,\mathbf{sat}\,(\phi \oplus \psi)} \tag{C1}$$

$$\frac{\Gamma\,\mathbf{sat}\,(\phi \oplus \psi)}{\Gamma\,\mathbf{sat}\,\phi \qquad \Gamma\,\mathbf{sat}\,\psi} \tag{C2}$$

Implication between assertions is defined as follows for simple assertions without conjunction; the definition extends in the obvious way to conjunctions: we certainly want to have $(\phi \oplus \psi) \Rightarrow \phi$ and $(\phi \oplus \psi) \Rightarrow \psi$ for example. We define

$$\begin{array}{lcl}(P\bullet \Rightarrow Q\bullet) & \Leftrightarrow & (Q \Rightarrow P),\\ (P\circ \Rightarrow Q\circ) & \Leftrightarrow & (Q \Rightarrow P).\end{array}$$

For $\phi = P(\sum_{i=1}^{n} \alpha_i P_i \phi_i)$ and $\psi = Q(\sum_{i=1}^{n} \alpha_i Q_i \psi_i)$, we define

$$(\phi \Rightarrow \psi) \quad \Leftrightarrow \quad (Q \Rightarrow P) \;\&\; \bigwedge_{i=1}^{n} (P_i \Rightarrow Q_i) \;\&\; \bigwedge_{i=1}^{n} (\phi_i \Rightarrow \psi_i).$$

When ϕ is $\{P\}\alpha\{Q\}$ and ψ is $\{P'\}\alpha\{Q'\}$ we have $\phi \Rightarrow \psi$ iff $P' \Rightarrow P$ and $Q \Rightarrow Q'$; this is analogous to the usual Rule of Consequence of conventional Hoare logic [1,12]:

$$\frac{P' \Rightarrow P \quad \{P\}\Gamma\{Q\} \quad Q \Rightarrow Q'}{\{P'\}\Gamma\{Q'\}} \tag{C}$$

Our rule for implication is a form of *modus ponens*:

$$\frac{\Gamma\,\mathbf{sat}\,\phi \quad \phi \Rightarrow \psi}{\Gamma\,\mathbf{sat}\,\psi}. \tag{C3}$$

From the definitions it follows that $\{P\}\alpha\{Q\}\{\mathbf{true}\}\bullet \Rightarrow \{P\}\alpha\{Q\}$. This means that we may derive the following assertion schemas for assignment and skip, by using axioms (B1) and (B2) with (C3):

$$\alpha{:}\mathbf{skip}\;\mathbf{sat}\,\{P\}\alpha\{P\}, \tag{B1'}$$

$$\alpha{:}I{:=}E\;\mathbf{sat}\,\{[E\backslash I]P\}\alpha\{P\}. \tag{B2'}$$

These forms resemble the usual Hoare axioms for these constructs [12].

Example 1. We wish to prove that Γ **sat** θ, where

$$\begin{array}{lcl}\Gamma & = & [\alpha{:}x{:=}x+1 \parallel \beta{:}x{:=}x+1],\\ \theta & = & \{x=0\}(\alpha\{x=1\}\{x=1\}\beta\{x=2\} + \beta\{x=1\}\{x=1\}\alpha\{x=2\}).\end{array}$$

We have the following assertions (by rules B2 and C1):

$$\begin{array}{lcl}\alpha{:}x{:=}x+1\;\mathbf{sat}\,\phi, \quad \phi & = & (\{x=0\}\alpha\{x=1\}\{\mathbf{true}\}\bullet) \oplus (\{x=1\}\alpha\{x=2\}\{\mathbf{true}\}\bullet),\\ \beta{:}x{:=}x+1\;\mathbf{sat}\,\psi, \quad \psi & = & (\{x=0\}\beta\{x=1\}\{\mathbf{true}\}\bullet) \oplus (\{x=1\}\beta\{x=2\}\{\mathbf{true}\}\bullet).\end{array}$$

The parallel composition $[\phi \parallel \psi]$ is a conjunction of four terms, one of which is

$$\{x=0\}(\alpha\{x=1\}[\{\mathbf{true}\}\bullet \parallel \psi] + \beta\{x=1\}[\phi \parallel \{\mathbf{true}\}\bullet).$$

But $[\{\mathbf{true}\}\bullet \parallel \psi] \equiv \psi$ and $\psi \Rightarrow \{x=1\}\beta\{x=2\}$ and (similarly) $\phi \Rightarrow \{x=1\}\alpha\{x=2\}$. The result follows by (B5) and (C3). ∎

Soundness and Completeness.

Although we do not provide a proof in this paper, the proof system formed by (B0)–(B10), (C1)–(C3), is sound: all provable assertions are valid. The system is also relatively complete in the sense of Cook [8]: every true assertion of the form Γ **sat** ϕ is provable, given that we can prove all of the conditions necessary in applications of the critical region rule and of *modus ponens*. Both of these rules require assumptions which take the form of implications between conditions. Let **Th** be the set of valid conditions. Write $\mathbf{Th} \vdash \Gamma\,\mathbf{sat}\,\phi$ if this can be proved using assumptions from **Th**.

Theorem 3. If $\mathbf{Th} \vdash \Gamma\ \mathbf{sat}\ \phi$ then $\models \Gamma\ \mathbf{sat}\ \phi$. ∎

Theorem 4. If $\models \Gamma\ \mathbf{sat}\ \phi$ then $\mathbf{Th} \vdash \Gamma\ \mathbf{sat}\ \phi$. ∎

5. Deriving Owicki's proof rules.

In Owicki's proof system, conventional Hoare-style assertions of the form $\{P\}\Gamma\{Q\}$ are used, although the parallel composition rule requires the use of a *proof outline* above the inference line. A proof outline can be viewed as a command text annotated with conditions, one before and one after each syntactic occurrence of an atomic action, in which adjacent conditions are required to satisfy an implication constraint. At least for sequential commands, *safe* assertions in our assertion language correspond precisely with such proof outlines because computations of sequential commands follow the syntactic structure of the command. The analogy can be extended to parallel commands too, although the syntactic structure of a proof outline is no longer so close to that of the corresponding safe assertion. The following proof rule forms a connection between our proof system and that of Owicki. Above the line, we have a safe assertion of our form, and below we have a Hoare-style partial correctness assertion.

$$\frac{\Gamma\ \mathbf{sat}\ \phi, \qquad \mathrm{safe}(\phi)}{\{\,\mathrm{root}(\phi)\,\}\Gamma\{\,\mathrm{leaf}(\phi)\,\}} \tag{R}$$

Owicki's parallel composition rule corresponds to a slightly different form of parallel composition of assertions, in which pre-conditions are carried through into post-conditions in the obvious way. For the base case we put:

$$\begin{aligned}[P\circ \parallel_O Q\circ] &= [P\bullet \parallel_O Q\circ] = [P\circ \parallel_O Q\bullet] = \{P \,\&\, Q\}\circ,\\ [P\bullet \parallel_O Q\bullet] &= \{P \,\&\, Q\}\bullet.\end{aligned}$$

For $\phi = P\sum_{i=1}^{n}\alpha_i P_i\phi_i$ and $\psi = Q\sum_{j=1}^{m}\beta_j Q_j\psi_j$ we put

$$[\phi \parallel_O \psi] = \{P \,\&\, Q\}(\sum_{i=1}^{n}\alpha_i\{P_i \,\&\, Q\}[\phi_i \parallel_O \psi] + \sum_{j=1}^{m}\beta_j\{P \,\&\, Q_j\}\beta_j[\phi \parallel_O \psi_j]).$$

In the case where one of these is a terminal assertion we put

$$[P* \parallel_O Q \sum_{j=1}^{m} \beta_j Q_j \psi_j] = \{P \,\&\, Q\} \sum_{j=1}^{m} \beta_j \{P \,\&\, Q_j\}[P* \parallel_O \psi_j],$$

where $*$ can be either $\bullet$ or $\circ$.

Unfortunately, this form of composition does not always produce an assertion which correctly describes the behaviour of a parallel composition of commands. We need the notion of *interference-freedom* (due to Owicki) to guarantee this. Define the set atoms(ϕ) of *atomic sub-assertions* of ϕ by induction on depth. An assertion $P\bullet$ or $P\circ$ has no atomic assertions. For the assertion $\phi = P\sum_{i=1}^{n} \alpha_i P_i \phi_i$ we put

$$\text{atoms}(\phi) = \{\{P\}\alpha_i\{P_i\} \mid 1 \leq i \leq n\} \cup \bigcup_{i=1}^{n} \text{atoms}(\phi_i).$$

The interference-free condition is defined as follows:

Definition. Two assertions ϕ and ψ are interference-free, written int-free(ϕ, ψ), iff for every pair of atomic assertions

$$\{p\}\alpha\{p'\} \in \text{atoms}(\phi), \qquad \{q\}\beta\{q'\} \in \text{atoms}(\psi),$$

the assertions $\{p \,\&\, q\}\alpha\{q\}$, $\{p \,\&\, q\}\beta\{p\}$, $\{p \,\&\, q'\}\alpha\{q'\}$, $\{p' \,\&\, q\}\beta\{p'\}$ are valid. ∎

Theorem 5. If ϕ and ψ are interference-free then

$$\models \Gamma_1 \,\textbf{sat}\, \phi, \quad \models \Gamma_2 \,\textbf{sat}\, \psi \quad \Rightarrow \quad \models [\Gamma_1 \parallel \Gamma_2] \,\textbf{sat}\, [\phi \parallel_O \psi]. \ ∎$$

In view of the above theorem we may include the following rule in our system:

$$\frac{\Gamma_1 \,\textbf{sat}\, \phi \quad \Gamma_2 \,\textbf{sat}\, \psi \quad \text{int-free}(\phi, \psi)}{[\Gamma_1 \parallel \Gamma_2] \,\textbf{sat}\, [\phi \parallel_O \psi]}. \tag{B11}$$

Note that this theorem and the proof rule are stated in a form applicable to *all* assertions, not just to safe assertions. This can, therefore, be regarded as a slight extension of Owicki's ideas to encompass a more expressive assertion language. The following result shows that interference-freedom guarantees the preservation of safeness.

Theorem 6. If ϕ and ψ are safe and interference-free, then $[\phi \parallel_O \psi]$ is safe. ∎

The root and leaf conditions of this form of parallel composition satisfy the following logical equivalences:

$$\text{root}(\phi \parallel_O \psi) \equiv \text{root}(\phi) \,\&\, \text{root}(\psi)$$
$$\text{leaf}(\phi \parallel_O \psi) \equiv \text{leaf}(\phi) \,\&\, \text{leaf}(\psi).$$

This may be shown by an inductive argument. The fact that roots and leaves fit together in this way provides us with an obvious link to Owicki's proof rule for parallel composition. This rule, taken from [20], is:

$$\frac{\text{proofs of } \{P_1\}\Gamma_1\{Q_1\},\ \{P_2\}\Gamma_2\{Q_2\} \text{ interference-free}}{\{P_1 \,\&\, P_2\}[\Gamma_1 \parallel \Gamma_2]\{Q_1 \,\&\, Q_2\}} \qquad \text{(O)}$$

Now proof outlines for the Hoare assertions $\{P_i\}\Gamma_i\{Q_i\}$ correspond to safe assertions ϕ_i such that Γ_i sat ϕ_i, with root$(\phi_i) = P_i$ and leaf$(\phi_i) = Q_i$. The interference-freedom of these proof outlines corresponds to interference-freedom of ϕ_1 and ϕ_2. Then $[\phi_1 \parallel_O \phi_2]$ is a safe assertion satisfied by $[\Gamma_1 \parallel \Gamma_2]$, and has root $P_1 \,\&\, P_2$ and leaf $Q_1 \,\&\, Q_2$. Thus, a proof using Owicki's rule can be represented in our system, if we allow the use of (R) and (B11).

Interestingly, the analogy between safe assertions and proof outlines also yields some other connections with conventional Hoare logic. For instance, the sequential composition rule (B6) together with the following property can be used to derive Hoare's rule for sequential composition [12]:

Theorem 7. If ϕ and ψ are safe and (leaf$(\phi) \Rightarrow$ root(ψ)) then $\phi;\psi$ is safe. ∎

Hoare's rule was:

$$\frac{\{P\}\Gamma_1\{Q\} \qquad \{Q\}\Gamma_2\{R\}}{\{P\}\Gamma_1;\Gamma_2\{R\}}.$$

The derivation relies on the facts that for non-trivial and safe ϕ and ψ we have

$$\text{root}(\phi;\psi) \equiv \text{root}(\phi), \qquad \text{leaf}(\phi;\psi) \equiv \text{leaf}(\psi).$$

Auxiliary variables and auxiliary critical regions.

It is well known [20] that a proof system based on (B0)–(B4), (B6)–(B11), (C) and (R) is not complete for partial correctness assertions. As a simple example, it is impossible even to prove the obviously valid assertion

$$\{x = 0\}[x{:=}x+1 \parallel x{:=}x+1]\{x = 2\}$$

using these rules alone. We obtained completeness by introducing conjunctions and implication. This particular assertion, for instance, can be proved by using rule (R) on the assertion discussed in Example 1 earlier. Owicki achieved completeness by adding "auxiliary variables" to programs and adding new proof rules to allow their use. In addition to an Auxiliary Variables rule, the Owicki proof system also requires a rule for eliminating "unnecessary" critical regions and irrelevant atomic actions which have been inserted merely to cope with auxiliary variables. It is arguable whether or not our proof system, which does not require the use of auxiliary variables in proofs, is preferable to Owicki's. The reader might like to compare the styles of proof in the two systems for the example above. Just as it is necessary to exercise skill in the choice and use of auxiliary variables in Owicki's system, our system requires a judicious choice of conjunctions. However, the details of auxiliary variables and reasoning about their values can be ignored in our system. At least we are able to demonstrate that there are alternatives to the earlier proof rules of [20,21] which do not explicitly require the manipulation of variables purely for proof-theoretical purposes and which do not require a notion of interference-freedom to guarantee soundness.

6. Recursive assertions.

The assertions described above are all finite, and thus a single assertion cannot describe the totality of possible computations of a loop. It is clearly possible (as in Milner [24]) to model infinite computations by using recursively defined assertions, perhaps with a version of the μ notation often used for this purpose. Although we do not go into detail here, we give a brief indication of the main idea. Let Θ range over a set of *assertion variables.* We can introduce a syntax for recursive assertions by adding two new clauses to the earlier syntax:

$$\phi ::= \Theta \mid \mu\Theta.\phi.$$

We will only be interested in *closed* and *well guarded* assertions in which no assertion variable occurs free and all recursive calls are guarded by at least one atomic action. For instance, $\mu\Theta.\Theta$ is not well guarded, but $\mu\Theta.\{P\}\alpha\{Q\}\Theta$ is. The interpretation of a closed recursive assertion is:

$$\begin{aligned} \models \Gamma\,\mathbf{sat}\,\mu\Theta.\phi \quad &\Leftrightarrow \quad \forall k \geq 0.\ \models \Gamma\,\mathbf{sat}\,\theta_k, \\ \text{where} \quad \theta_0 \ &= \ \{\mathbf{false}\}\bullet, \\ \theta_{k+1} \ &= \ [\theta_k \backslash \Theta]\phi. \end{aligned}$$

We use the notation $[\theta\backslash\Theta]\phi$ for the result of substituting θ for all free occurrences of Θ in ϕ, with the usual renaming to avoid captures. We specify the root and leaf of a recursive assertion by:

$$\begin{aligned} \text{root}(\mu\Theta.\phi) &= \bigvee_{k=0}^{\infty} \text{root}(\theta_k), \\ \text{leaf}(\mu\Theta.\phi) &= \bigvee_{k=0}^{\infty} \text{leaf}(\theta_k), \end{aligned}$$

where the θ_k are as above. In fact, $\text{root}(\mu\Theta.\phi)$ will collapse to $\text{root}(\theta_1)$ for a guarded assertion.

Using a recursive assertion we may now give a single proof rule for loops. The non-interruptible version is:

$$\frac{\Gamma \text{ sat } P\sum_{i=1}^{n}\alpha_i P_i\phi_i}{\textbf{while } \beta{:}B \textbf{ do } \Gamma \text{ sat } \mu\Theta.[\{P \,\&\, B\}\sum_{i=1}^{n}\alpha_i P_i(\phi_i;\Theta) \oplus \{P \,\&\, \neg B\}\beta\{P\}\{\text{true}\}\bullet]}.$$

For an interruptible version we may use:

$$\frac{\Gamma \text{ sat } \phi}{\textbf{while } \beta{:}B \textbf{ do } \alpha{:}\Gamma \text{ sat } \mu\Theta.[\{P \,\&\, B\}\beta\{P\}(\phi;\Theta) \oplus \{P \,\&\, \neg B\}\beta\{P\}\{\text{true}\}\bullet]}.$$

7. Conclusions.

We have described a syntax-directed proof system for semantic properties of commands in a simple parallel programming language. The assertions were chosen to correspond in form to the semantic structure, which itself was chosen to be powerful enough to allow reasoning about partial correctness properties to be carried out by manipulating assertions in a context-independent manner. We discussed some connections with the Owicki-Gries proof system.

Various proof systems for concurrent languages proposed by Lamport and others can also be related to our work. Lamport [16] uses assertions of the form $\{P\}\Gamma\{Q\}$ with the interpretation that in every execution which starts somewhere inside Γ with P true, P remains true until Γ terminates, when Q will be true. This corresponds to one of our assertions $P\sum_{i=1}^{n}\alpha_i P_i\phi_i$ in which each P_i (and all other intermediate conditions) are identical to P and all leaf conditions are identical to Q. The proof rule for parallel composition given in [16] was:

$$\frac{\{P\}\Gamma_1\{Q\} \quad \{P\}\Gamma_2\{Q\}}{\{P\}[\Gamma_1 \parallel \Gamma_2]\{Q\}}.$$

But our definition of parallel composition of assertions preserves this uniformity property: the parallel composition of (the assertions representing) $\{P\}\Gamma_1\{Q\}$ and $\{P\}\Gamma_2\{Q\}$ will again have leaf Q and each intermediate condition will be P. Thus our rule (B5) suffices to derive Lamport's rule. Lamport suggested using labels λ_i for the control points (or interruption points) of a program, and including in the condition language expressions of the form at(λ), inside(λ), after(λ). Since in a Lamport-style assertion the same P has to represent more than one control point at a time, the conditions can get rather large. Indeed, it can be argued that since the same P is serving a multitude of purposes it is more natural to split it up into its components and to attach these components to the control points at which they are intended to hold; this is more in line with our notation, with control points corresponding to nodes in a tree.

The Generalized Hoare Logic of Lamport and Schneider [17] used a similar type of assertion to those of [16], except that they insisted that the post-condition coincide with the pre-condition: they used invariant assertions $\{P\}\Gamma\{P\}$. The interpretation is as before, that whenever an execution begins somewhere inside Γ with P true, P will remain true until termination. Again, their proof rule for parallel composition is representable in our system. Again, control conditions are used inside invariants, so that an invariant is really serving a multitude of purposes and could profitably be split up and distributed to the separate control points.

The *Transition Logic* of Gerth [11] uses assertions, written $[P]\Gamma[Q]$, which express the property that every transition starting somewhere in Γ from a state satisfying P ends in a state satisfying Q. Gerth's rule for parallel composition is:

$$\frac{[P]\Gamma_1[Q] \quad [P]\Gamma_2[Q]}{[P][\Gamma_1 \parallel \Gamma_2][Q]}.$$

But the assertion $[P]\Gamma[Q]$ can again be rendered in our assertion language as an assertion with a simple structure (alternating P and Q along each branch), and again our parallel composition of assertions has the required effect, producing an assertion representating $[P][\Gamma_1 \parallel \Gamma_2][Q]$ from representations of $[P]\Gamma_1[Q]$ and $[P]\Gamma_2[Q]$.

The proof methodology and program development method advocated by Jones [14] uses *rely* and *guarantee* conditions in addition to pre- and post-conditions. Although we have not yet investigated the connection in any detail, it appears that these ideas are somewhat related to ours; roughly speaking, a rely condition might correspond to a pre-condition assumed by every atomic action in an assertion, and a guarantee condition would then be implied by all post-conditions of atomic actions.

Other authors have proposed compositional proof systems for concurrent programs in which the underlying assertions are temporal in nature. In particular, we refer to [4] and [19]. In contrast to these methods, we have avoided temporal assertions at the expense of using conjunction and implication as operations on more highly structured assertions built from conventional pre- and post-conditions. Our assertions do have some similarity with temporal logic in the sense that an assertion has built into it a specification of the possible atomic actions and the behaviour of the command after each of them, so that one might be able to represent one of our assertions ϕ in a more conventional temporal or dynamic logic.

We can adapt the ideas of this paper to produce an axiomatic treatment of some other forms of parallel programming. In particular, CSP [13] may be axiomatized if we modify the class of assertions to represent the potential for communication. The distributed termination convention of CSP may be handled elegantly in our framework, since we can build it into the definition of parallel composition of assertions. The axiomatization of

CSP will be the subject of a future report. Some connections with earlier work [2,18,27] will become apparent when this is done.

Acknowledgements. The author is grateful for discussions with Eike Best, Ed Clarke, Rob Gerth, Jay Misra, and Glynn Winskel.

8. References. (Some of these are cited only in the expanded version of this paper.)

[1] Apt, K. R., Ten Years of Hoare's Logic: A Survey, ACM TOPLAS, vol. 3 no. 4 (October 1981) 431–483.

[2] Apt, K. R., Francez, N., and de Roever, W. P., A proof system for communicating sequential processes, ACM TOPLAS, vol. 2 no. 3 (July 1980), 359-385.

[3] Ashcroft, E. A., Proving assertions about parallel programs, J. Comput. Syst. Sci. 10 (Jan. 1975), 110-135.

[4] Barringer, H., Kuiper, R., and Pnueli, A., Now You May Compose Temporal Logic Assertions, Proc. 16th ACM Symposium on Theory of Computing, Washington, May 1984.

[5] Best, E., A relational framework for concurrent programs using atomic actions, Proc. IFIP TC2 Conference (1982).

[6] Brookes, S. D., On the Relationship of CCS and CSP, Proc. ICALP 83, Springer LNCS (1983).

[7] Brookes, S. D., A Fully Abstract Semantics and Proof System for An ALGOL-like Language with Sharing, CMU Technical Report (1984).

[8] Cook, S., Soundness and Completeness of an Axiom System for Program Verfification, SIAM J. Comput. vol 7. no. 1 (February 1978) 70–90.

[9] Dijkstra, E. W., Cooperating Sequential Processes, in: Programming Languages, F. Genuys (Ed.), Academic Press, NY (1968) 43-112.

[10] Dijkstra, E. W., A Discipline of Programming, Prentice-Hall, New Jersey (1976).

[11] Gerth, R., Transition Logic, Proc. 16th ACM STOC Conference, 1983.

[12] Hoare, C. A. R., An axiomatic basis for computer programming, CACM 12, 10 (Oct. 1969), 576-580.

[13] Hoare, C. A. R., Communicating Sequential Processes, CACM 21, 8 (Aug. 1978).

[14] Jones, C. B., Tentative Steps Towards a Development Method for Interfering Programs, ACM TOPLAS vol. 5 no. 4, (October 1983) 596–619.

[15] Keller, R. M., Formal verification of parallel programs, CACM 19,7 (July 1976).

[16] Lamport, L., The 'Hoare Logic' of concurrent programs, Acta Inf. 14 (1980).

[17] Lamport, L., and Schneider, F., The "Hoare Logic" of CSP, and All That, ACM TOPLAS 6, 2 (April 1984), 281-296.

[18] Levin, G. M., and Gries, D., A proof technique for communicating sequential processes, Acta Informatica 15 (1981), 281-302.

[19] Manna, Z., and Pnueli, A., Verification of Concurrent Programs: The Temporal Framework, in: "The Correctness Problem in Computer Science", ed. R. S. Boyer and J. S. Moore, Academic Press, London (1982).

[20] Owicki, S. S., and Gries, D., An axiomatic proof technique for parallel programs, Acta Informatica 6 (1976), 319-340.

[21] Owicki, S. S., Axiomatic proof techniques for parallel programs, Ph. D. dissertation, Cornell University (Aug. 1975).

[22] Hennessy, M., and Plotkin, G. D., Full Abstraction for a Simple Parallel Programming Language, Proc. MFCS 1979, Springer LNCS vol. 74, pp. 108–120.

[23] Milner, R., Fully Abstract Models of Typed Lambda-Calculi, Theoretical Computer Science (1977).

[24] Milner, R., A Calculus of Communicating Systems, Springer LNCS vol. 92 (1980).

[25] O' Donnell, M., A Critique of the Foundations of Hoare-Style Programming Logic, CACM vol. 25 no. 12 (December 1982) 927–934.

[26] Plotkin, G. D., A Structural Approach to Operational Semantics, DAIMI Report FN-19, Aarhus University (1981).

[27] Plotkin, G. D., An Operational Semantics for CSP, Proceedings of the W. G. 2.2 Conference, 1982.

[28] Winskel, G., Synchronization Trees, Proc. ICALP 1983, Springer LNCS vol. 154.

RECURSIVE DEFINITIONS IN TYPE THEORY†

R.L. Constable and N.P. Mendler
Computer Science Department
Cornell University
Ithaca, N. Y. 14853

Abstract

We offer a new account of recursive definitions for both types and partial functions. The computational requirements of the theory restrict recursive type definitions involving the *total* function-space constructor (→) to those with only positive occurrences of the defined typed. But we show that arbitrary recursive definitions with respect to the *partial* function-space constructor are sensible. The partial function-space constructor allows us to express reflexive types of Scott's domain theory (as needed to model the lambda calculus) and thereby reconcile parts of domain theory with constructive type theory.

I. Introduction

1.1 Context and Motivation

To understand our reasons for studying recursive definitions in type theory, one should view that theory as an attempt to provide a comprehensive formal logical calculus in which to conduct rigorous programming. We have in mind a language rich enough to precisely specify programming problems and explain their solutions; so the calculus contains a usable programming language as an integral part. From our experience in designing and using logics of this variety, called *programming logics* [12], we have come to believe that type theory is very good for the task. One might find this immediately plausible by observing that the concept of type is to computing practice what the concept of set is to classical mathematical practice. That is, type is one of the central foundational concepts in programming, program is the other.

For us then, type theory is a comprehensive formal theory for expressing computational reasoning. The first type theory, that of *Principia Mathematica*, is such a theory for noncomputational mathematics. Specifically, we are interested in the type theory underlying the programming system Nuprl [11,13,39] but these ideas would apply also to the theories of Martin-Löf [31], Girard [21] and Reynolds [41]. A different approach to these questions was taken in the theory V3 [15]. In all of these theories it is possible to define a sufficiently rich notion of recursive type and recursive function. Nevertheless, none of these theories provides an account which is as convenient and as transparent as the one offered here.

1.2 An Informal Account

Nature of Type Definitions

Every object of concern to us is represented by symbols. Some of these symbols are *canonical,* such as 0,1,2, and some are not, such as 0+1. The canonical terms are those which are irreducible and denote specific objects. The noncanonical can be further reduced, and are said to denote the canonical terms to which they reduce. When

†This work was supported in part by NSF grant MCS81-04018

we specify a new object, we must provide a canonical name for it. Rarely is the name constructed in isolation, but rather we have in mind a *method of constructing a pattern of canonical names*, as with 0, 0′, 0′′, etc. Such methods denote *types*. Sometimes we agree that two canonical names will denote the *same object*, for example 2/4 is the same rational number as 1/2. Thus to completely specify a type, a definition of equality between canonical names is given. A theory of types is concerned with describing the methods of construction and the conditions for equality.

The type theories we consider have constructors for defining the disjoint union of A and B, denoted A | B, the cartesian product, denoted A×B, and the type of all (total computable) functions from A to B, denoted A→B.

Recursive Definitions

Recursive and inductive methods are ways of specifying types. For example, we interpret the definition:

(*) define type T by A | (T×A)

as a method which says:

(**) To construct an element of type T, construct
either an element of A or construct an
element of T and an element of A.

Such definitions are natural when we conceive of the process of construction top-down, that is in a goal oriented manner.

If pairs in A×B are denoted a,b for a in A, b in B; and if inl and inr are the "into the left disjunct" and "into the right disjunct" mappings respectively so that inl(a) and inr(b) are in A|B; then the following are elements of the recursive type in (*):

inl(a)
inr(inl(a),a)
inr(inr(inl(a),a),a)
.
.
.

Such a type has a natural inductive structure. The base case elements are of the form inr(a) for a in A, and the inductive case element, have the form inl(t,a) for t in T and a in A.

Notation

The notation for a recursive type should suggest the rule that elements of the defined type, say T, are built using the pattern of the defining expression. We might write (T:=A | T×A) or use the Algol 68 style, **type** T = A | T×A. Whatever the notation, it is complicated by the possibility that the defined type T may depend on parameters. For example, A might be a regarded as a parameter; to emphasize this, let us use a name that connotes variables, say

define T(y) by y | T(y)×y.

We might also write λy.μT. (y | T(y)×y) following [30] or **type** t(y) = y | T(y)×y. These parameterized definitions do not specify a type until a value is given for the parameter. The parameter may enter in other ways, for example, suppose there is a type of the form [1,n] which denotes the integers 1 up to n. Consider:

define T(n) by [1,n] | T(n+ 1).

We have adopted the notation that rec(t,x. T;a) defines a recursive type parameterized by x and specialized to a. The expression T denotes a type which can use t and x in its formation. We say that t and x are *bound* in

T. Complete binary trees with leaves of type integer are defined by rec(t,x. x | t(x)×t(x);int). This is equivalent to rec(t. int | t×t), which informally we would have written *define* t by int | t×t. A typical element of the type is inr(inr(inl(0),inl(1)),inl(1)).

We prefer this notation to the more common λy.μt.T or to **type** t(y)=T for three reasons. The first two are stylistic, we want to treat rec and fix alike and we think of fix as an operator on functionals (like FIX in LCF [22]), so we would be inclined to write μt.(λy.T) as opposed to λy.μt.T if we were to adopt the mu operator notation. Furthermore, in the case of mutual recursion, say rec(t,x. T;s,y. U) the variables x,y are bound only in T and U respectively whereas t and s are bound in both T and U, so x and y have smaller scope and are written closer to their scopes. The third reason is more technical; we do not in fact treat rec(t,x. T) as a function from some type A into types because the principal use of the notation arises in denoting types, as in rec(t,x. T;a), and treating this as a function application would cause extra steps of reasoning in most uses.

The notation for specifying one of n mutually recursive types is rec(t_1,x_1. T_1;...;t_n,x_n. T_n;t_i;a_i) for i=1,...,n. The t_i have the entire expression as scope and are bound anywhere in the scope, but the x_i has only T_i as scope and is bound only in T_i. Thus in rec(t_1,x_1. int | t_1(x_1);t_2,x_2. t_1(f(x_1,x_2))×t_2(x_2);t_2;a) the occurrence of x_1 in f(x_1,x_2) is free, all other occurrences of x_1 and x_2 are bound.

The approach to recursive types suggested above is by now quite standard, its ancestors can be found at least as far back as Hoare [24] and a detailed rigorous account is given in ML [22] and in Cartwright [7] to name two basic sources. This kind of type definition can be built upon the reference mechanism of Algol 68 or upon the pointer mechanism of Pascal, ADA, etc. The presentation here is simply a manifestation of these basic ideas in the setting of a constructive type theory.

Recursive Definition of Function Spaces

The concept of a recursive type involving the function space constructor is far more delicate than the above case and is not treated in Hoare or Cartwright for example, although Algol 68 does provide a mechanism to represent such types as

mode t = proc(t)t

where proc(A)B is the mode of all (partial) functions from mode A to mode B (see McGettrich [34]), and ML [22] provides such types, written absrectype t = t→t.

There have been numerous approaches to recursive type definitions involving the function space. The best known are probably Scott's use of lattices and domain theory because they provided the first lambda calculus models [44]. This approach is intimately connected with partial functions and will be discussed later. Another approach based on partial functions is MacQueen and Sethi [30] where types are treated as ideals. Function spaces also arise in accounts of generalized inductive definitions, both classically as in Feferman [20] and constructively as in Kriesel [27] and Martin-Löf [32]. These accounts are based on total functions and are close to the one given here, so it might be more suggestive to call these *inductive types*. But we will see that the computer science terminology is justified once we introduce the partial function type A~>B.

When one first approaches recursive types defined over the function spaces, such as rec(t. t→t) or rec(t. t→A), it appears that these notations do provide a prescription for building objects and that the lambda expressions provide the required canonical objects. In fact, naively thinking of rec(t,x. T) as a prescription for building objects appears to make sense regardless of the form of T as long as it is defined under the assumption that t is a type and x belongs to some type. But let us examine the simple special case rec(t. t→A) where A is any type.

Let T = rec(t. t→A), then to build an object of type T, we must build one of type T→A. This is a function type, so we assume x:T and build an element of A. This assumption amounts to x:T→A. To use x we must build an element of T. But x itself is such an element, thus $\lambda x.x(x)$ belongs to T. Now then, $(\lambda x.x(x))(\lambda x.x(x))$ belongs to A.

If A is void, then the above derivation shows an inconsistency. But even if A is inhabited, the element $(\lambda x.x(x))(\lambda x.x(x))$ yields a nonterminating computation. So $\lambda x.x(x)$ is not a total function as is required to be an element of a function space such as rec(t. t→A) → A.

Analysis of the Function Case

Why does the example rec(t. t→A) cause problems? One answer is that the rule for function introduction and the rule for recursive type introduction combine in such a way as to produce a vicious circle. To see this, consider the function rule in this top down form:

> To build an element of A→B,
> assume x is in A and build an
> element b of B. The element
> of A→B is then $\lambda x.b$.

Now the rule for rec(t. t→A) says, assume x is in rec(t. t→A) and build a term b in rec(t. t→A). But by assuming x:rec(t. t→A) we are already assuming that we know rec(t. t→A), the type we are trying to build. This is similar to the situation underlying Russell's paradox, and indeed the term $\{x \mid \neg x(x)\}$ is similar to $\lambda x.x(x)$. We see here a genuine and instructive parallel because the rule for recursive types is a rule to determine the existence of functions which is an issue of the same force as determining the existence of sets.

Mendler has shown that whenever t is not positive in T, then rec(t. T) contains terms whose computations fail to terminate. For example t is negative in t→t, in t→A, in A→(t→B) and in general whenever t is in an odd number of antecedents. This suggests that rec(t. T) might be sensible only when t does not occur negatively in T. So far we have only been able to show that whenever t does not occur as an antecedent to an implication, then the definition is reasonable, at least in the sense that the function elements of the recursive type are total. So in terms such as A→t, A→(B→t), etc. t occurs in a safe way. In section III we say that t occurs positively in T under these conditions, but not all nonnegative occurrences, such as (t→A)→B are positive.

If one begins with the concept of a partial function, as in [29,30,43], recursive types are analyzed in a very different way. The element $(\lambda x.x(x))(\lambda\ x.x(x))$ is assigned a value, say $\perp$, and the analysis above shows that $\perp$ must occur in every type. Such a conclusion is at variance with the propositions-as-types principle used in organizing AUTOMATH [18], Martin-Löf type theories [31] and Nuprl [11,13,39]. Moreover, in constructive logic the concept of a total computable function is more basic than that of a partial function and is indeed needed to define it, as will be suggested in this paper. So it is interesting to first clarify the concept of recursive definitions involving the total function spaces.

Significance of Partial Functions

We would like to have a convenient and natural account of partial functions in type theory in as far as they facilitate programming in it and in order to explain ordinary programming. We intend that our type theories provide not only a *logically adequate* foundation for computing but a *practically adequate* foundation as well in the sense that the formal theory can be used as a real programming language. This requires that the execution facilities be efficient and that the means of expression be natural.

Partial Functions in Type Theory

We think that there is a direct way to treat partial functions in type theory. An example of this method appears in [12]. The idea is that with every partial function f on A into B we associate a domain condition, dom(f). The dom (f) condition is a recursive type of the theory. Here is an example of dom(f) for a simple recursive function written in a neutral notation:

f(x): = *if* b(x) *then* g(x) *else* h(f(e(x)))*fi*

dom(f)(x) = rec(d,x. dom(b)(x) &
(b(x) = true ⇒ dom(g)(x))
&(b(x) = false ⇒ dom(e)(x) & d(e(x)) & dom(h)(f(e(x)))))(x)

(The actual definition given in III.2 uses a conditional-and in place of ⇒.)

In this setting we think of an algorithm as simultaneously specifying a domain and a function. But the algorithm is present directly and can perhaps be executed for elements about which we have no information that dom(f). In these cases we cannot guarantee the properties of the algorithm.

We want our notation for algorithms to be natural, at least as natural as function definitions in algol-like or lisp-like programming languages. To this end we adopt a style similar to ML[22]. A *partial recursive function*, or algorithm, is written as fix(f,x. F) where F is an expression. The computation rule for fix(f,x. F) is typeless, namely for any expression a fix(f,x. F)[a] = F(a/x,fix(f,x. F)/f).

Concept of a Partial Function Type

We want the partial functions from A to B to form a type, but we cannot define such a type with the existing constructors. So we introduce a new type A~>B which could be used to define A → B by the condition A → B = {f:A~>B | ∀x:A. dom (f)(x)}.† Once this new type is available, we can use it in recursive definitions to give a coherent account of rec(t. t~>t). This sort of type allows us to treat reflexive types in the sense of Scott [43].

II. Recursive Types

1. Syntax

The Recursive Form

We introduce a new syntactic form to denote mutually recursive types. The simplest special case is rec(t. T) as in rec(t. int|(t#t)). For parameterized types we use rec(t,x. T;a) as in rec(t,x. x|(t#t);int). In full generality we use the notation rec(t_1,x_1. T_1;...;t_n,x_n. T_n; t_i;a) for i in {1,...,n}. This represents the mutually recursive definition of $t_1(x_1)$,...,$t_n(x_n)$. Any of the x_i parameters can be omitted. The t_i are bound in T_1,...,T_n but x_i is bound only in T_i. Here is a scheme for three mutually recursive types rec(v. A|A#v; t,x. v|t(x)#f(g(x)); f,y.B#t(h(y))|c#f(y); t;a).

†We do not in fact use this definition in Nuprl because the total function space constructor, →, is needed to define the meaning of logical operations such as ∀x:A. dom(f)(x).

Nonrecursive Forms

In order to precisely define the syntax of recursive types, we must specify the underlying type expressions. We use Nuprl for this [13,39] but the account given here is reasonably self contained. The base types are int and void. The type constructors are |, #, →, list, // and {}, but the last three constructors, for lists, quotients and sets do not introduce a new complexity into the definition, so only the first three are used here.[†] The rules for defining these types are presented in the Nuprl style in terms of <u>sequents</u>.

H >> T in U_1

where H is a list of typings, of the form $x_1{:}A_1, x_2{:}A_2(x_1), \ldots, x_n{:}A_n(x_1, \ldots, x_{n-1})$, T is a type and U_1 is a universe. For our purposes a universe can be considered as a type whose elements are types, and we will only use one universe, U_1. This sequent means that T is a type in the U_1 under the assumptions in H. Here we are using the notation $A(x_1, \ldots, x_n)$ to indicate that the free variables $x_1, \ldots, x_n$ may occur among the free variables of A. We will write A(t/x) to denote the substitution of t for all free occurrences of x. A formation rule is presented in this form

H >> A|B in U_1
  1. H >> A in U_1
  2. H >> B in U_1

This rule is read, A|B is a type in U_i under assumptions H, if A is in U_j under assumptions H, and B is in U_k under assumptions H. Here are the rules for type formation.

1. disjoint union

    H >> A|B in U_1 by intro
    1. H >> A in U_1
    2. H >> B in U_1

2. dependent product

    H >> x:A#B(x) in U_1 by intro
    1. H >> A in U_1
    2. H, x:A >> B(x) in U_1

3. function space

    H >> x:A→B(x) in U_1 by intro
    1. H >> A in U_1
    2. H, x:A >> B(x) in U_1

In the expressions x:A#B(x) and x:A→B(x), occurrences of x in B are bound.

With the disjoint union, the dependent product, and with integers there are compound expressions used in the introduction and elimination rules. They are inl(a), inr(b), decide(d;u.t_1;v.t_2), <a,b>, spread(p;u,v.t) and ind(e;b;u,v.h). These forms satisfy the following computation rules.

1. decide(inl(a);u.t_1;v.t_2) = t_1(a/u)
   decide(inr(b);u.t_1;v.t_2) = t_2(b/v)

2. spread(<a,b>;u,v.t) = t(a/u,b/v)

3. ind(0;b;u,v.h) = b
   ind(x+ 1;b;u,v.h) = h(x/u,ind(x;b;u,v.h)/h)

The expressions inl(e), inr(e) are used to inject e into the left or right sides respectively of a disjoint union, and <a,b> is used to build a pair in a dependent product.

[†]In section 1 we used × as the operator for cartesian product rather than #, but now that the account is rigorous, we want to use the notation from the implemented Nuprl theory [39].

Restrictions on Recursive Forms

In forming rec(t. T) and other recursive types, it is necessary to ensure that t occurs only positively in T, for reasons discussed in the introduction. The basic restriction is that t not occur as the domain type of a function space, as in t→int. We can prevent this by saying t is positive in T provided: if T is $T_1 | T_2$, then t is positive in T_1 and in T_2; if T is x:T_1#T_2, then t is positive in T_1 and T_2; if T is x:T_1→T_2 then t does not occur in T_1 and is positive in T_2. But this definition is complicated by the mutually recursive form and by the presence of the elimination forms, decide, spread and ind. Here is the general definition.

Definition: The recursive definition form rec(t_1,x_1.T_1;...;t_n,x_n.T_n;t_i;a) is *positive* in t_1,...,t_n provided the t_k occur only positively in the T_j. Say that t occurs positively in T (or say for short t *is positive in* T) under these conditions. If

1. T is int or void or a type variable,
2. T is A|B, and t is positive in A and in B,
3. T is x:A#B(x), and t is positive in A and in B(x),
4. T is x:A→B(x), and t does not occur in A and is positive in B(x),
5. T is rec(s_1,y_1. S_1;...;s_m,y_m. S_m;s_j;b) and t is positive in S_k for k=1,...,m.
6. T is decide(d;u.e_1,v.e_2), and t is positive in d,e_1,e_2 and if t occurs in d, then u,v are positive in e_1,e_2 respectively,
7. T is spread(p;u,v.q), and t is positive in p and q and if t occurs in p, then u,v are positive in q,
8. T is ind(e;b;u,v.h), and t is positive in e,b and h, and if t occurs in b, then v is positive in h,
9. T is f(a), and if f is a variable, then t does not occur in a; otherwise if f is λx.b, then t is positive in a and b, and x is positive in b. If f is noncanonical, then t is positive f and a.

We also need to say when t occurs positively in introduction forms involving types such as inl(t→A) or <t,A>. (In M-L [31] one would also have to consider such forms as (t→A)′ where ′ is the successor operation.) We say that t is positive in T′, inl(T), inr(T), <T_1,T_2> provided it is positive in T, T_1, T_2.

2. Proof Rules

General

The proof rules for recursive types are organized, as nearly all rules are, into the categories of formation, introduction, and elimination. But the category of elimination is subdivided into ordinary elimination and induction. In every rule *it must be the case that the recursive type expression is positive.* This is checked during parsing. Optional parts of a rule are enclosed in []. We assume that all hypotheses are numbered but we do not display the number.

Formation Rules

1. H >> rec(t_1,x_1. T_1;...;t_n,x_n. T_n; t_i;a) in U_k
   by intro using A_1,...,A_n at U_k [new x,y_1,...,y_n]
   0. H >> a in A_i
   1. H >> A_1 in U_k
   2. H >> A_2 in U_k
   ⋮

$n.H >> A_n$ in U_k
$n+1.H, t_1:A_1 \rightarrow U_k, x_1:A_1, \ldots,$
$t_n:A_n \rightarrow U_k, >> T_1$ in U_k

$\vdots$

$n+n.H, t_1:A_1 \rightarrow U_k, \ldots, t_n:A_n \rightarrow U_k, x_n:A_n >> T_n$ in U_k

The new y_i are used to rename x_i if H already contains a declaration of x_i.

The hypotheses $t_i:A_i \rightarrow U_k$, need not be named because they are used only in eliminations in which case their number is a sufficient reference. When the x_i do not appear, then "using A_i" need not occur either. A very simple special case of this rule is:

H >> rec(t. T) in U_i by intro at U_i
H, t:U_i >> T in U_i

Here are simple examples of these rules:

ex1-F: >> rec(t. t) in U_1 by intro at U_1
t:U_1 >> t in U_1

ex2-F: >> rec(t,x. t(x);5) in U_1 by intro using int at U_1 new z
>> 5 in int
t:int→ U_1, x:int >> t(x) in U_1

ex3-F: >> rec(t,x. x|x#t(x);int) in U_1 by intro using U_1 at U_1 new z
>> int in U_1
t:U_1→U_1, x:U_1 >> x|x#t(x) in U_1

We can think of rec(t,x. x|x#t(x);A) as the type list(A).

ex4-F: >> rec(t. A|t#f;f. B|f#t;t) in U_1 by intro at U_1
t:U_1, f:U_1 >> A|t#f in U_1
t:U_1, f:U_1 >> B|f#t in U_1

Introduction Rules

2. H >> rec(t_1,x_1. T_1;...;t_n,x_n. T_n;t_i;a) by intro
H >> T_i(rec(–;t_j)/t_j, a/x_i)

The expression rec(–;t_j) abbreviates rec(t_1,x_1. T_1;...;t_n,x_n. T_n;t_j) throughout.

Here are examples of the application of this rule:

ex1-I: >> rec(t. t) by intro
>> rec(t. t)

One can see from one application that it will be impossible to build an element of either rec(t.t) or rec(t,x.t(x);5).

ex2-I: >> rec(t,x. t(x);5) by intro
>> rec(t,x. t(x);5)

ex3-I: >> rec(t,x. x|x#t(x);int) by intro
>> int|int#rec(t,x. x|x#t(x);int)

Elimination Rules

3. $H, y{:}rec(t_1,x_1.T_1;\ldots;t_n,x_n.T_n;t_i;a), H' >> T$ by elim y
$H, y{:}T_i(rec(-;t_j)/t_j,\ a/x_i), H' >> T$

Here are examples of the simple elimination rule:

ex1-E: y:rec(t. t) >> int by elim y
y:rec(t. t) >> int

So the elimination rule makes no progress in this case.

ex2-E: y:rec(t,x. x|x#t(x);int) >> int by elim y
y:int|int#rec(t,x. x|x#t(x);int) >> int

One might try to build an integer for the goal by another elimination on y. In the subcase y:int >> int the method succeeds, but in the case y:int#rec(-) >> int it would not be possible to continue using elimination on the recursive type indefinitely; eventually another rule such as explicit introduction would be necessary.

Induction

The most general form of elimination on a recursive type is an induction rule. The induction is on the process of building terms and makes sense because a term can be constructed in rec(-) only by a finite number of applications of the introduction rules. Here is the rule for the simple case of a parameter free recursive type.

$H, x{:}rec(t.\ T) >> G$ by ind on x at U_l new $X{:}U_l$,h,y
$H, X{:}U_l, h{:}(y{:}X \rightarrow G), x{:}T(X/t) >> G$

The new type X represents a completely unknown type of the right level which is used to indicate an appeal to the induction hypothesis in the decomposition of T(X/t). The induction hypothesis is h:(x:X→G).

Notice that while we can prove nothing by simple elimination on rec(t. t), we can prove <u>anything</u> by induction on that type. For instance

x:rec(t. t) >> void by ind x at U_1 new X,h,y
$X{:}U_1$,h:y:X→void, x:X >> void

To finish the proof, perform an elimination on h with x; so h(x) belongs to void. This happens because rec(t. t) is empty and induction performs a structural analysis on an arbitrary element. But elimination only gives an analysis of some specific element whose pattern can be displayed by applications of the elimination rule.

The computational form extracted from this rule is a recursive procedure where h represents a recursive call of the procedure. (The procedure is fix(f,x. f(x)) as we will see in part III.)

Instead of presenting the complete rule, we examine another special case which illustrates the treatment of parameters and includes all of the essential information.

H, w:rec(t,x. T;a) >> G(a/g)
by ind w over A using g.G at U_l new X,h

$H, X{:}A \rightarrow U_l$, h:(g:A→w:X(g)→G),
g:A,w:T(X/t,g/x) >> G

It is noteworthy that X is a new type with parameter over A.

Extraction

The constructive character of the logic requires that with each rule there be explicit instructions for how to extract its computational content. In the formation rule the content is the conclusion, in the introduction and elimination rules the extraction forms are inherited directly from the rules for building nonrecursive types, as illustrated below. But for the induction rule a new computational form is required. The new form must specify how to compute recursively with elements of the recursive type. The key idea for specifying this form is that use of the induction hypothesis of the form h:x:A→y:X(x)→G(y/g) corresponds to a recursive call. We look first at examples and then explain the specific form.

Let us see how elements of rec(t.int|(int#t)) are built. Let T be int|(int#t)

```
>> rec(t.T)  by intro                              [inr(<5,inl(17)>)]
     >> int|(int#rec(t.T))  by intro right         [inr(<5,inl(17)>)]
          >> int#rec(t.T)  by intro (of pairs)     [<5,inl(17)>]
               >> int  by explicit intro 5         [extract 5]
               >> rec(t.T)  by intro               [inl(17)]
                    >> int|(int#rec(t.T))  by intro left   [inl(17)]
                    >> int  by explicit intro 17   [extract 17]
```

The extracted terms are displayed in square brackets and are constructed bottom-up after the proof is complete. Now when we build elements by induction, we are performing a structural analysis of terms such as inr(<5,inl(17)>). Here is an example for T as above.

```
   x:rec(t.T) >> int  by elim x at U1 new X,h
X:U1, h:X→int, x:(int|int#X) >> int  by elim x new x1,x2              [decide(x; x1.x1; x2.h(2of(x2)))]
     X:U1, h:x→int, x:(int|int#X), x1:int >> int  by hyp x1              [x1]
     X:U1, h:X→int, x:(int|int#X), x2:(int#X) >> int  by elim x2 new u,v [h(2of(x2))]
     X:U1, h:X→int, x2:(int#X), u:int, v:X, x2=<u,v> >> int  by elim h   [h(v)]
```

Again the extracted forms are created bottom-up. In the second from last extracted form, decide(x; x1.x1; x2.h(2of(x2))), h represents a recursive call, and 2of(x2) selects the second component of the pair <u,v> (it is defined as spread(z;u,v.v)). A reasonable expression for the final extracted form would be

fix(h,x. decide(x; x1.x1; x2.h(2of(x2)))).

In section III we will present a systematic treatment of such forms.

Equality

Two recursive types, say rec(t. T_1) and rec(t. T_2) are equal when t:U_1 >> T_1=T_2 in U_1. More generally, rec(t,x. T_1;a) = rec(t′,x′. T_2;b) when λx.λt. T_1 = λx′.λt′.T_2 in A→U_1→U_1 and λt. T_1(a/x) = λt′.T_2(b/x) in U_1. For example, if f(0)=int, then rec(t,x. x#t|x;int) = rec(t,y. y#t|y;f(0)). Also rec(t,x. int#t|x;int) = rec(t,x. x#t|x;int). But notice, we do not equate int#int and rec(t. int#int).

Propositions-As-Types

In theories which adopt the propositions-as-types principle, such as Nuprl, AUTOMATH, Martin-Löf's theories, Girard's theories [21,46], etc., recursive definitions of types provide recursive definitions of propositions as well. Thus in such theories we have a version of infinitary logic. We rely on this feature to define the domains of partial recursive functions in section 2.2. The important point is that equalities such as (x=1 in int) can be treated as types in recursive definitions.

Representing Well-Founded Trees

A recursive type such as rec(w. x:A#(B(x)→w)) represents the W-type of well-founded trees used to represent Brouwer ordinals [6,46]. Martin-Löf's rules for the W-type can be derived from rules for recursive types. For example his introduction rule is

$$\frac{a\in A \quad f\in B(a)\rightarrow W}{sup(a,f)\in Wx\in A.B(x)}$$

which corresponds to

```
H >> <a,f> in rec(w. x:A#B(x)→w)
   H >> <a,f> in x:A#B(x)→w
      H >> a in A
      H >> f in B(a)→rec(w. x:A#B(x)→w).
```

The induction rule for rec(w. x:A#B(x)→w) corresponds to Martin-Löf's elimination rule. Essentially this is Martin-Löf's rule in our notation

```
H, x:Wy∈A.B(y) >> G
   H, y:A, f:B(y)→Wy∈A.B(y),
   z:(v:B(y)→G(f(v)/x)) >> G                [ext d(y,f,z)]
```

The extracted term is a tree induction form, let us call it tind(x;y,f,z.d). It satisfies the computation rule tind(sup(a,b);y,f,z.d) = d(a/y,b/f,λv.tind(f(v);y,f,z.d)/z).

This rule can be seen as a special way of using the induction rule as follows.

```
H, x:rec(w.y:A#(B(y)→w)) >> G                                  by induction at U_l, new X, y, h
1. H, X:U_l,h:(x:X→G),x:yA#(B(y)→X) >> G                       by elim x
1.1. H, X:U_l,h:(x:X→G),y:A,f:B(y)→X >> G                      by seq v:B(y)→G(f(v)/x) new 3
1.1.1. H, X:U_l,h:(x:X→G),y:A,f:B(y)→X >> v:B(y→G(f(v)(x)      by explicit intro λv.h(f(v))
1.1.2. H, X:U_l,h:(x:X→G),y:A,f:B(y)→X, z:(v:B(y)→G(f(v)/x)) >> G   [ext d(y,f,z)]
```

Now define g(x,h) = d(1of(x), 2of(x), λv.h(2of(x)(1of(x)))) where 1of(x) = spread(x;u,v.u), 2of(x) = spread(x;u,v.v). Then λx.tind(x; y,f,z.d(y,f,z)) corresponds to fix(h,x.g(x,h)). We see that fix(h,x.g(x,h))(<a,b>) = d(a,b,λv.h(b(v))) = tind(sup(a,b); y,f,z.d(y,f,z)).

III. Recursive Functions

1. Background

For each recursive data type in the theory, there is a computation form associated with its elimination rule. For example, natural number induction provides a form written ind(e;b;u,v.h) in Nuprl, and it satisfies the computation rule.

```
ind(0;b;u,v.h) = b
ind(n;b;u,v.h) = h(n/u,ind(n-1;b;u,v.h)/v).
```

This is recognizable as a form of *primitive recursion* with values in any type. As a special case we have the ordinary primitive recursion scheme for defining functions into the natural numbers, e.g. factorial(n) is

```
ind(n;1;u,v. u*v).
```

Likewise list induction gives rise to a form of primitive recursion on lists. We have also seen that the defined recursive types provide a recursive computation form. We have written them as fix(f,x. F). We have not discussed these forms in detail yet, but it is clear that for any defined recursive type, say rec(t,x. T), the extract form of the induction rule, say fix(f,x. F), is a well defined computable function whose domain is rec(t,x. T).

In order to represent "all algorithms" in the theory, we turn to the insights from Herbrand, Gödel, Church, Kleene and Turing who first tried to formalize the concept. Herbrand's ideas are particularly suitable because they arose in the context of constructive mathematics and logic (see [49]). (They were also the first expression of the concept of algorithm as we now know it.)

Herbrand realized that we could understand a rule and treat it as a precise concept before we understood exactly what the domain of application was. For us this means we can use the rule to define its domain of definition. That domain will depend on what we can prove about the rule, but even without an abstract idea of proof we know how to execute the rule.

One way to develop Herbrand's idea in type theory is to define an internal notion of a rule, for example to define Turing machines or mu-recursive functions as inductive classes of functions. This approach is illustrated in [16]. Another approach is to introduce partial functions into the very formalization of constructive mathematics itself. For example, this is done classically in LCF [22] and by Kleene [26] for number theory. We follow this later path, taking partial functions as basic concepts. We introduce new canonical forms to denote partial functions, written fix(f,x. F) in the style of ML. The computation rule for these forms is fix(f,x. F)[a] = F(a/x,fix(f,x. F)/f). Based on this rule we know how to say that a fix form converges on an input. We could express the domain of convergence of fix(f,x. F) mapping A to B as {y:A | fix(f,x. F)[y] in B}. It would be possible to prove fix(f,x. F)[a] in B for specific a by a series of reduction steps. For example, we can prove fix(f,x. inteq(x;0;1;f(x-1)))[0]=1 in int by one reduction step. We might prove some instances of fix(f,x. F)[y] in B by induction. But a serious disadvantage to this simple approach is that we cannot reason about {y:A | fix(f,x. F)[y] in B} inductively although it posses an inductive structure. We might in fact be able to show that for any element of this domain fix(f,x. F)[y] = b in B if we had access to the inductive structure. We will see a particular example of this below for the "3x+1 function."

In order to provide access to the inductive structure of the domain of partial functions, we introduce a new (noncanonical) form into the theory, dom(f)(g). The type dom(fix(f,x. F))(a) expresses the concept that fix(f,x. F)[a] converges on input a from type A. The rules are arranged so that when dom(fix(f,x. F))(a) is true for a in A and when F(fix(f,x. F)/f,a/x) is functional in B, then fix(f,x. F) is a partial function from A to B which converges on all a for which dom(fix(f,x. F))(a) is true.

It has proven to be useful in programming and in the theory of algorithms to think in terms of the space of all partial functions from A to B. To define this concept in type theory, we introduce the new constructor, x:A~>B, denoting the *partial function space*. The elements of this space are named by expressions which reduce to the fix(f,x. F) canonical forms and which are defined by the introduction and equality rules for the x:A~>B type. The precise rules are given below.

2. Domain Predicates

Syntax for Algorithms

The representation of algorithms that we use is based on the conception that the computation proceeds by successively evaluating a functional and follows closely the style of PPλ of Edinburgh LCF [22]. (In part this decision was made because the ML part of LCF is a component of Nuprl.) We write fix(f_1,x_1. F_1;...;f_n,x_n. F_n; f_i) where F_j is a well-defined expression which may contain occurrences of f_i. We say that occurrences of f_i and x_i in F_j are bound. To minimize the notational complexity, we present in this section the details only for the single function case, fix(f,x. F).

Examples of Domain Predicates

One of the computation forms in Nuprl is inteq(e;e_2;t_1;t_2) which evaluates to t_1 if e_1=e_2 and to t_2 otherwise where e_1 and e_2 are integer expressions. The well-known 3x+ 1 function can be written in terms of inteq and a modulus function mod(x,y), notice mod(x,2)=0 iff x is even. The function is:

fix(f,x. inteq(x;1;0;inteq(mod(x,2);0;f[x/2];f[3*x+ 1])))

Call the function g. The domain on which g converges is the set of natural numbers x such that x=1 or x>1, x is even and x/2 is in the domain or x>1, x is odd and 3*x+ 1 is in the domain. This is defined in the theory as

rec(D,x. (x=1 in int)| x>1 & (mod(x,2)=0 in *int*) & D(x/2)|
x>1 & ¬(mod(x,2)=0 in *int*) & D(3*x+ 1)).

Recall from 1.3 that (x=0 in *int*), (mod(x,2)=0 in *int*) and x>1 can be construed as types. The & operator is just another symbol for # which is used when its operands are thought of as propositions. The idea is that the recursive type is nonempty exactly when the proposition it expresses holds.

Pattern of Definition

To express the relationship between the recursive function g and its domain, we introduce into the theory a new (noncanonical) expression written dom(g)(x); thus dom is a new form in the theory. We must also introduce into the metatheory an interactive procedure for computing the recursive form of dom(g)(x) for any recursive function g. We denote this algorithm by D, the user must supply the type input T at various stages in the evaluation of D.

Definition

We would like the following to hold for *any* terms a and A and hypotheses H.

H >> D[a,A] ⇒ H >> a in A

Thus, the domain predicate for $\varphi \in$ A~>B is λx.D[φ[x],B], where we define D by:

- D[fix(f,x. b)[a],B] = D[a,T]#rec($\hat{f}$,x. D[fix(f,x. b)[x],B]; a)
- D[f[t],B] = D[t,T]#$\hat{f}$(t), if f had been bound by fix(f,x. b).
- D[t[a],B] = D[t,T~>B]#D[a,T]#dom(t)(a)
- D[decide(e; u. t; u′. t′),B] =
  D[e,T]#decide(e; u. D[t,B]; u′. D[t′,B]), and similarly for
  spread, less, inteq and atomeq.
- D[t(a),B] = D[a,T′]#D[t,T→B]
- D[inl(a),A|B] = (A|B in U_i)#D[a,A]
- D[<a,b>,x:A#B] = (x:A#B in U_i)#D[a,A]#D[b,B(a/x)]
- D[λx. b, x:A→B] = (x:A→B in U_i)#x:A→D[b,B]
- D[fix(f,x. b), A~>B] = λx. D[fix(f,x. b)[x],B] in A→U_i
- D[ind(n; u,v. t; b; u′,v′. t′),B] =
  D[n,int]#u:int→v:B→u<0→D[t,B]#
  D[b,B]#u′:int→v′:B→0<u′→D[t′,B], and list and rec induction
  are handled similarly.
- D[v,B] = v in B, if v is a variable.

These rules define dom(f)(x) for any partial function (or algorithm) as a recursive type. Thus we can use the rules for recursive types to prove propositions of the form dom(f)(a) or ∀x:A.dom(f)(x) and so forth. We might have tried to assert that fix(f,x. F) is defined at a by proving the well-formedness assertion fix(f,x. F)[a] in B. We could even use this technique to prove properties of those values for which fix(f,x. F)[y] in B is true. But without dom(fix(f,x. F)) we cannot prove properties of the domain by induction.

3.4 Rules

A partial function f from A into B actually maps {x:A| dom(f)(x)} into B. By this notation we indicate that the domain information is not needed for computing the value of f, only for insuring that the computation is sensible. This is because the set notation {x:A|B} in Nuprl denotes those elements of A such that B(a/x) is true (but unlike in Martin-Löf's theories, the proof information, b∈B(a/x) is not included with the elements). We see these ideas in the elimination rule for partial functions, there the argument to f is simply a, but one of the subgoals requires the proof dom(f)(a).

It is convenient to collect these functions into a single type, such a collection is commonly and easily defined in set theory for instance. This type is essentially the union of the types {x:A| dom(f)(x)}→B for all algorithms f. There are no union types as such in type theory, so this concept is represented by a new constructor written A~>B. The rules for A~>B fall into these categories: formation, introduction, elimination, equality, and computation.

Formation Rule

H >> x:A~>B in U_1
1. H >> A in U_1
2. H,x:A >> B in U_1

Explicit Introduction Rule

H >> fix(f,x. b) in x:A~>B   by intro at U_1
H >> x:A~>B in U_1
H >> λx.D[fix(f,x. b)[x], B] in A→U_1

H >> t[a] in B   by intro using x:A~>B
H >> t in x:A~>B
H >> a in A
H >> dom(t)(a)†

Domain Definition

H >> dom in (x:A~>B)→(A→U_1)
H >> x:A~>B in U_1

H >> dom(t) = λx. D(t[x],B)
H >> t in x:A~>B

Elimination

H,f:(x:A~>B), H′ >> G by elim f on a
1. H,f:(x:A~>B), H′ >> a in A
2′. H,f:(x:A~>B), H′ >> dom(f)(a)
3. H,f:(x:A~>B), H′,y:B(a/x), y=f[a] in B(a/x) >> G

†Noncomputational ⇒ release restrictions on r.h.s. of set types.

Equality

H >> f[a] in B(a/x) by intro using x:A~>B
 1. H >> f in (x:A~>B)
 2. H >> a in A
 3'. H >> dom(f)(a)

H >> fix(f,x. F) = fix(g,y. G) in x:A~>B at U_1
 1. H >> fix(f,x. F) in x:A~>B
 2. H,x:A >> dom(fix(f,x. F))(x) =
 dom(fix(g,x. G))(x) in U_1

H >> fix(f,x. F)[a] = F(a/x, fix(f,x. F)/f) in B(a/x) by computation using x:A~>B
 1. H >> fix(f,x. F) in x:A~>B
 2. H >> a in A
 3. H >> dom(fix(f,x. F))(a)

Among the computation rules, we allow the following reduction.

Computation

fix(f,x. F)[a] → F(a/x, fix(f,x. F))

3.5 Recursive Types Over Partial Function Spaces

The principal difficulty with defining types like rec(t. t→t) is that they allow nonterminating functions as members, even as members of the empty type. This difficulty can be avoided by using the partial function space constructor instead. To this end we allow without restriction the ~> operator in recursive type definitions. Thus in particular rec(t. t~>t) is a legitimate type, and fix(f,x. x[x]) is a member of this type. It is a member because the domain function from R to U_1 is

λy. D[fix(f,x. x[x])[y],R]

where R = rec(t. t~>t), and this computes by the rules for D to

λy. y in R#rec(f̂,x. x in R#x in (R~>R)#dom(x)(x);y)

This function is well-formed, so fix(f,x. x[x]) is an element of R~>R. It is the analogue of λx. x(x) in the lambda calculus. The partial function is defined only on those elements f of R for which dom(f)(f) is true, such as fix(f,x. x).

The total elements of rec(t. t~>t) are defined by {f:rec(t. t~>t) | ∀x:rec(t. t~>t). dom(f)(x)}.

Acknowledgements

We thank Stuart Allen for numerous comments and suggestions at every level from notation to philosophy which helped us present these ideas. We also thank Jim Hook for his thoughtful advice and Donette Isenbarger for preparing the manuscript.

References

[1] Allen, Stuart. The logical foundations of type theory. (To appear as Cornell Ph.D. thesis.)

[2] Aczel, P. An introduction to inductive definitions. *Handbook of Mathematical Logic,* Barwise, J. (ed.), North Holland, NY (1977) 739-782.

[3] Bates, J.L. and Constable, R.L. Proofs as programs. *TOPLAS,* January 1985.

[4] Bishop, E., *Foundations of Constructive Analysis.* McGraw Hill, New York, NY, 1967. 370 pp.

[5] Boyer, R.S. and Moore, J.S. *A Computational Logic.* Academic Press, New York, NY, 1979. 397 pp.

[6] Brouwer, L.E.J. *Collected Works,* Vol. 1, A. Heyting, (Ed.), North-Holland, 1975.

[7] Cartwright, R. User-defined data types as an aid to verifying Lisp programs. *Proc. of the 3rd Int'l. Colloq. on Automata, Languages and Programming,* [Michaelson, S. and Milner, R., eds.], Edinburgh University Press, Edinburgh (1976) 228-256.

[8] Cartwright, R. Toward a logical theory of program data. In *Logics of Programs,* Lecture Notes in Computer Science 131, Springer-Verlag, New York, NY (1982) 37-51.

[9] Church, A. A formulation of the simple theory of types. *J. Symbolic Logic, 5,* (1940), 56-68.

[10] Constable, Robert L. Constructive mathematics and automatic program writers. In *Proc. of IFIP Congress,* Ljubljana, 1971, 229-233.

[11] Constable, Robert L. Constructive mathematics as a programming logic I: some principles of theory. Technical report TR83-554, Dept. of Computer Science, Cornell University, May 1983. (To appear in *Proc. of FCT Conf.,* Springer-Verlag, 1983).

[12] Constable, Robert L. Partial functions in constructive formal theories. In *Proc. of 6th G.I. Conference,* Lecture Notes in Computer Science 45, Springer-Verlag, New York, NY, 1983.

[13] Constable, R.L., and Bates, J.L. The nearly ultimate PRL. Tech. Rep., Dept. of Computer Science, Cornell University, TR 83-551, 1984.

[14] Constable, Robert L. and O'Donnell, M.J. *A Programming Logic.* Winthrop, Cambridge, 1978.

[15] Constable, Robert L. and Zlatin, D.R. The type theory of PL/CV3. *ACM Trans. on Prog. Lang. & Syst., 6*:1 (Jan. 1984) 94-117.

[16] Constable, Robert L. Mathematics as programming. In *Proc. of Workshop on Logics of Programs,* Lecture Notes in Computer Science 164, Springer-Verlag, New York, NY, 1983, 116-128.

[17] Curry, H.B., Hindley, J.R. and Seldin, J.P. *Combinatory Logic, Volume II.* North-Holland Publ. Co., Amsterdam, 1972.

[18] deBruijn, N.G. A survey of the project AUTOMATH. In *To H.B. Curry: Essays on Combinatory Logic, Lambda Calculus and Formalism,* J.P. Seldin and J.R. Hindley (Eds.), Academic Press, New York, NY, 1980, 579-607.

[19] Demers, A.J. and Donahue, J. Revised report on Russell. Tech. Rep., Department of Computer Science, Cornell University, TR 79-389, September 1979.

[20] Feferman, S. Formal theories for transfinite iterations of generalized inductive definitions and some subsystems of analysis, *Intuitionism and Proof Theory,* Kino, A., Myhill, J., and Vesley, R.E. (eds.), North Holland, Amsterdam (1970) 303-326.

[21] Girard, J.-Y. *Interpretation Fonctionelle et Elimination des Coupures de l'arithmeétique d'ordre supérieur.* Ph.D. Thesis, Univ. of Paris VII, 1972.

[22] Gordon, M., Milner, R., and Wadsworth, C. *Edinburgh LCF: A Mechanized Logic of Computation,* Lecture Notes in Computer Science 78, Springer-Verlag, 1979.

[23] Harper, R. Aspects of the implementations of type theory. Ph.D. thesis, Computer Science Department, Cornell University, NY, June 1985.

[24] Hoare, C.A.R. Recursive data structures. *International Journal of Computer and Information Sciences, 4*:2, (June 1975), 105-132.

[25] Kleene, S.C. *Introduction to Metamathematics.* D. Van Nostrand, Princeton, NJ, 1952.

[26] Kleene, S.C. Formalized recursive functionals and formalized realizability. *Memoirs of the American Math. Society,* No. 89, 1969.

[27] Kreisel, G. Generalized inductive definitions, section III. Standard report on the foundations of analysis (mimeographed), 1963.

[28] Knuth, D.E. *The Art of Computer Programming, Vol. I.* Addison-Wesley, Reading, 1968.

[29] MacQueen, D.B., Plotkin, Gordon D. and Sethi, R. An Ideal Model for Recursive Polymorphic Types. *11th ACM Symp. on Principles of Programming Languages,* (1984) 165-174.

[30] MacQueen, D.B., and Sethi, R. A semantic model of types for applicative languages. *ACM Symp. on LISP and Functional Programming,* 1982, 243-252.

[31] Martin-Löf, Per. Constructive mathematics and computer programming. In *6th International Congress for Logic, Methodology and Philosophy of Science,* North-Holland, Amsterdam, 1982.

[32] Martin-Löf, P. Hauptsatz for the intuitionistic theory of iterated inductive definitions. In *Proceedings of the Second Scandinavian Logic Symposium,* J.E. Fenstad (Ed.), North-Holland, Amsterdam, 1971, 179-216.

[33] McCarty, David C. Realizability and recursive mathematics. Computer Science Dept. Tech. Rpt. CMU-CS-84-131, Carnegie-Mellon University (1984).

[34] McGettrick, A.D. *Algol 68, A First and Second Course.* Cambridge University Press, Cambridge, 1978.

[35] Meyer, Albert R. What is a model of the lambda calculus? *Information and Control, 52,* (1982), 87-122.

[36] Moschovakis, Yiannis N. *Elementary Induction on Abstract Structures.* North Holland, London, 1974.

[37] Plotkin, Gordon D. T^{ω} as a universal domain. *J. Computer and System Sciences, 17,* (1978), 209-236.

[38] Plotkin, Gordon D. Private communication.

[39] PRL Staff, The. Constructing proofs: An introduction to the Nuprl proof development system. Computer Science Department, Cornell University, January 1985.

[40] Quine, Willard Van Orman. *Set Theory and Its Logic.* Harvard University Press, Cambridge, 1963.

[41] Reynolds, John C. Types, abstraction, and parametric polymorphism. *Information Processing 83,* IFIP, North Holland Publishers, 1983, 513-523.

[42] Russell, B. Mathematical logic as based on a theory of types. *Am. J. of Math., 30,* (1908), 222-262.

[43] Scott, Dana. Data types as lattices. *SIAM Journal on Computing,* 5:3, (September 1976) 522-587.

[44] Scott, Dana. The lambda calculus, some models, some philosophy. *The Kleene Symposium* [eds., J. Barwise, et al.], North-Holland, 1980, 381-421.

[45] Scott, Dana. Constructive validity. In *Symposium on Automatic Demonstration,* Lecture Notes in Mathematics 125, Springer-Verlag, 1970, 237-275.

[46] Stenlund, S. *Combinators, Lambda-terms, and Proof-Theory.* D. Reidel, Dordrecht, 1972, 183.

[47] Stoy, Joseph E. *Denotational Semantics: The Scott-Strachey Approach to Programming Language Theory.* MIT Press, Cambridge, MA, 1977.

[48] Tait, William W. Intensional interpretation of functionals of finite type. *J. Symbolic Logic, 32*:2, (June 1967), 198-212.

[49] van Heijenoort, Jean. *From Frege to Gödel: A source book in mathematical logic, 1879-1931*, Harvard University Press, Cambridge (1967).

[50] van Wijngaarden, A.B.J. *et al. Revised report on the algorithmic language ALGO 68. Acta Informatica, 5*, (1975), 1-236. (Also a Supplement to *ALGO BULLETIN*, University of Alberta, 1974.)

Errata

(1) The induction rule has an additional hypothesis, asserting X is a subset of rec(t. T):

H,x:rec(t. T) >> G by ind on x at U_l new X,h,y
  H,X:U_l,x:X→(x in rec(t. T)),h:(y:X→G(y/x)),x:T(X/t) >> G

(2) The first line in the definition of D should be:

- D[fix(f,x. b)[a],B] = D[a,T]#rec($\hat{f}$,x. D[b,B];a)

(3) Equality of partial functions is extensional. The proof rule should be:

H >> fix(f,x. F) = fix(g,y. G) in x:A~>B by intro at U_l new z
  H >> {z:A|dom(fix(f,x. F))(z)} = {z:A|dom(fix(g,y. G))(z)} in U_l
  H,z:A,dom(fix(f,x. F))(z) >> fix(f,x. F)[z] = fix(g,y. G)[z] in B(z/x)

AUTOMATA, TABLEAUX, AND TEMPORAL LOGICS
(Extended Abstract)

E. Allen EMERSON[1]

Department of Computer Sciences
University of Texas at Austin
Austin, Texas 78712

1. Introduction

There has recently been a resurgence of interest in the theory of finite automata on infinite trees (cf. [RA69], [RA70]) because of the intimate relationship between such automata and temporal logic (cf. [ST81], [WVS83]). For example, in testing satisfiability of a formula p_o in the branching time logic CTL, a directed graph labelled with appropriate subformulae of p_o, a *tableau*, is constructed (cf. [EH82], [EC82]). This tableau may be viewed as defining a finite automaton on infinite trees which accepts input trees that define models of p_o. The satisfiability problem for CTL is thus reduced to the nonemptiness problem for finite automata on infinite trees. A general framework for applying such automata-theoretic techniques is described in [VW84] where it is shown that for a number of temporal logics, satisfiability can be reduced to testing nonemptiness of Buchi automata on infinite trees resulting in a deterministic exponential time decision procedures. For more expressive logics such as CTL* ([EH83]), more elaborate reductions to tree automata with more complicated acceptance conditions yield superexponential, but still elementary time, decision procedures.

In this paper, we study tree automata in depth, and provide new, more efficient algorithms for testing nonemptiness for various classes of tree automata. Our work should therefore lead to more efficient decision procedures for testing satisfiability of temporal logics. For example, one consequence of our findings is that CTL* can be decided in nondeterministic double exponential time and double exponential space. (The best previous known upper bound was deterministic triple exponential time (cf. [ES84].) and triple exponential space.) Another is that the logic ECTL ([EH83]) is decidable in deterministic exponential time.

We begin by defining the notion of the transition diagram of a tree automaton. It is derived from the "AND/OR graph" formulation of the tableau for CTL as described in [EC82]. (Roughly, the OR-nodes correspond to states of the automaton, while the AND-nodes give the input symbols labelling the transitions between states.) Surprisingly, the transition diagram idea for tree automata has never before appeared in the literature. We believe that it is important because it makes tree automata "easier to think about" and the graph-theoretic

[1]Work supported in part by NSF Grant MCS8302878

nature of the algorithms for testing nonemptiness more apparent. Moreover, in the context of temporal logic, we see that while the tableau can be viewed as an automaton, the converse relationship also holds: we can view a tree automaton as a tableau and apply tableau-theoretic techniques to automata. As we shall see, this can result in improved algorithms for testing nonemptiness of autotmata which, in turn, yield improved decision procedures for temporal logics.

We then define the notion of a tree automaton running on (essentially) an arbitrary directed graph. If the tree automaton accepts a graph, we may think of the graph as a "model" of the (temporal modality) defined by the automaton. We are then able to prove a Linear Size Model Theorem for pairs tree automata: if a pairs tree automata accepts some tree, then in fact it accepts some graph with number of nodes linear in the size of the transition diagram of the tree automaton. The crucial property that makes this possible is that the family of sets of states appearing infinitely often along a path meeting the pairs condition is closed under union. This closure under union was used in [ST81] to get a finite tree-model theorem for complemented pairs automata; we use [HR72] to get a finite tree-model and then use closure under union to collapse down to the linear size model. Our linear size model theorem also applies to automata where acceptance is defined by means of a single complemented pair.

We go on to show that testing nonemptiness for pairs automata is in NP (cf. [RA70], [HR72]) For pairs automata with a single pair, or for complemented pairs automata with a single pair we can do much better: nonemptiness for these automata can be tested in deterministic polynomial time. We believe that this later result will have particularly significant applications in obtaining decision procedures.

Finally, we consider the limits of the "expressive power" of finite automata on infinite trees. We exhibit a natural correctness property, *uniform inevitability*, which is not definable by any type of finite automata on infinite trees. It is, however, definable by a pushdown automaton on infinite tress. This suggests that these automata also merit study (cf. [KP83]).

The remainder of the paper is organized as follows: Section 2 gives preliminary definitions including the important notions of the transition diagram for a tree automaton and runs of a tree automaton on graphs. Section 3 describes how the tree automaton can be viewed as a tableau. The linear size model theorem for pairs and single complemented pairs tree automata are proved in Section 4 while our new algorithms for testing nonemptiness are given in section 5. Section 6 defines the property of uniform inevitability and shows that it not definable by finite state tree automata. Finally, some concluding remarks are presented in Section 7.

2. Preliminaries

2.1. Automata. To simplify the exposition, we only consider automata on infinite binary trees here; the extension to infinite n-ary trees is routine. The set $\{0,1\}^*$ of all infinite strings over alphabet $\{0,1\}$, may be viewed as an *infinite binary tree* where the *root node* is the empty string λ and each *node* $v \in \{0,1\}^*$ has as its *successors* the nodes v0 and v1. A finite (infinite) *path* through the tree is a finite (resp., infinite) sequence $x = v_0, v_1, v_2,$ of nodes such that for all i, v_{i+1} is a successor of v_i. Let Σ be a finite alphabet of infinite symbols. An infinite binary Σ-tree is a labelling T which maps $\{0,1\}^* \dashrightarrow \Sigma$.

A *finite automaton A on infinite binary Σ-trees* consists of a tuple (Σ, S, δ, s_0) plus an *acceptance condition* (which is described subsequently) where

Σ is the *input alphabet* labelling the nodes of the input tree,

S is the set of *states* of the automaton,

$\delta : S \times \Sigma \dashrightarrow$ PowerSet(S $\times$ S is the (nondeterministic) *transition function*, and

$s_0 \in S$ is the *start state* of the automaton.

A *run* of A on the input Σ-tree T is a function $\rho : \{0,1\}^* \dashrightarrow S$ such that for all $v \in \{0,1\}^*$ $(\rho(v0), \rho(v1)) \in \delta(\rho(v), T(v))$ and $\rho(\lambda) = s_0$. We say that A *accepts* input Σ-tree T iff $\exists$ a run ρ of A on T such that $\forall$ path x starting at the root of $\{0,1\}^*$ if $r = \rho|x$, the sequence of states A goes through along path x, then the acceptance condition (as below) holds along r.

For a *Buchi* automaton acceptance is defined in terms of a distinguished set of states, GREEN $\subseteq$ S. A sequence $r = s_1, s_2, s_3, \ldots$ of states meets the Buchi condition specified by GREEN iff there exist infinitely many i such that $s_i \in$ GREEN. If we think of a green light flashing upon entering any state of GREEN then r meets the condition iff $\overset{\infty}{\exists}$ GREEN flashes along r.[2] For a *pairs* automaton we have a finite list $((\mathrm{RED}_1, \mathrm{GREEN}_1), \ldots, (\mathrm{RED}_k, \mathrm{GREEN}_k))$ of pairs of sets of states (think of them as pairs of colored lights where A flashes the red light of the 1st pair upon entering any state of set RED_1, etc.): r meets the pairs condition iff $\exists$ pair i %el [1:k] $(\neg\overset{\infty}{\exists}\mathrm{RED}_i$ flashes and $\overset{\infty}{\exists}\mathrm{GREEN}_i$ flashes). Finally, a complemented pairs automaton is defined by the above pairs condition being false, i.e., $\forall$ pairs $i \in [1:k]$ ($\overset{\infty}{\exists}$ GREEN_i flashes implies $\overset{\infty}{\exists}$ RED_i flashes).

The *transition diagram* of A is an AND/OR-graph where the set S of states of A comprises the the set of OR-nodes while the AND-nodes define the allowable moves of the

---

[2]We use $\overset{\infty}{\exists}$ to mean "there exist infinitely many" or "infinitely often" and $\overset{\infty}{\forall}$ to mean "for all but a finite number of instances" or "almost everywhere".

automaton: Suppose that for $\mathcal{A}$, $\delta(s,a) = \{(t_1,u_1),..., (t_m,u_m)\}$ and $\delta(s,a) = \{(v_1,w_1),...,(v_n,w_n)\}$ then the transition diagram contains the portion shown in figure 1. We merge OR-nodes representing the same of $\mathcal{A}$. See also figure 2. Intuitively, the OR-nodes indicate that a non-deterministic choice of move must be made while the AND-nodes indicate that the automaton must continue down both branches of the input tree.

We now define what it means for a tree automaton to run on a graph. A *Σ-labelled, binary directed graph* $G = (V,A_0,A_1,L)$ consists of

V - a set of underlying *nodes*,

A_0 - a total function mapping V --> V which assigns to each node v
a unique successor node called the *0-successor* of v,

A_1 - defined similarly to A_0,

L - a *labelling* function V --> Σ which assigns to each node
a symbol from Σ

A *run* of $\mathcal{A}$ on G is a mapping ρ:V --> S such that $\forall$ v $\in$ V, $\rho(A_0(v), A_1(v)) \in \delta(\rho(v), L(v))$ and $\rho(v_0) = s_0$. Intuitively, a run is a labelling of G with states of $\mathcal{A}$ consistent with the local structure of $\mathcal{A}$'s transition diagram.

2.2. Temporal Logic. CTL* is the branching time temporal logic with basic modalities of the form, A ("for all paths) or E ("for some path), followed by an arbitrary linear time formula (involving nestings and boolean connectives as desired) over the linear time operators Fp ("sometimes p"), Gp ("always p"), Xp ("nexttime p"), and [p U q] ("q sometime holds and p holds up until then"). In the restricted logic CTL, the basic modalities are of the form: A or E followed by a single F, G, X, or U. We use $\overset{\infty}{F}$p to abbreviate GFp ("infinitely often p") and $\overset{\infty}{G}$p to abbreviate FGp ("almost everywhere p"). ECTL is the logic with basic modalities of the form A or E followed by a single F, G, X, U, $\overset{\infty}{F}$, or $\overset{\infty}{G}$.

3. Automata and Temporal Tableau

In the full paper we will show that tree automata, the tableau as defined in [EC82] or [EH82] or [BMP81], and the maximal model construction of [WVS83], [VW84] are all equivalent formalisms.

4. Linear Size Model Theorem

Note that in testing nonemptiness we can, without loss of generality, restrict our attention to automata over a 1 symbol alphabet (cf. [Hr72]). In the remainder of the paper we restrict our attention to such automata in order to simplify the exposition. Our results generalize in a routine way to automata over multi-symbol alphabets.

4.1. Theorem. Suppose $\mathcal{A}$ is a pairs tree automaton over a single letter alphabet. If $\mathcal{A}$ accepts some tree T then $\mathcal{A}$ accepts some graph G with number of nodes linear in the size of $\mathcal{A}$'s transition diagram.

proof sketch. By [HR72] we know that $\mathcal{A}$ accepts some finitely generated tree with a finite number of nodes. This may be viewed as a finite graph G accepted by $\mathcal{A}$. The accepting run induces a labelling of the nodes of G with the states of $\mathcal{A}$ consistent with $\mathcal{A}$'s transition table. We claim that we can chop out duplicate nodes, i.e., nodes with the same label. Suppose nodes u and v have the same label. If we redirect all the arcs coming into v so that they point instead to u, and then delete all nodes (and incident arcs) that are no longer reachable from the start node v_0, then the resulting graph G' will still be labelled consistently with respect to the transition diagram of $\mathcal{A}$. It will moreover have at least one less pair of duplicate nodes than G since at the very least node u was chopped out. If the run of $\mathcal{A}$ defined on G' is accepting then we have successfully obtained a strictly smaller accepted graph. However, the run of $\mathcal{A}$ defined on G' may not be accepting because we may have introduced a path violating the pairs condition. This path which was not present in G must end in a cycle of the form: w --> u --····--> w where w --> v was an arc in G redirected to be the arc w --> u in G', and u --····--> w is a path from node u to node w that was present in G and is still present in G'. Similarly, we can try to replace u by v. This might yield an accepted smaller graph G" or it might introduce a cycle violating the pairs condition of the form y --> v --····--> y where y --> u was an arc in G changed to y --> v in G" and v --····--> y is a path present both in G and G".

It must be possible to either replace v by u or replace u by v. If both replacements were to lead to a nonaccepting graph, then, as above, we would have present in the original graph G the following arcs and paths: w --> v, u --····--> w, y --> u, v --····--> y. These form the following cycle in the original G: w --> v --····--> y --> u --> ··· --> w which itself violates the pairs condition because it is the union of two violating cycles (those above). This contradiction shows that one of the replacements must be possible.

Hence, given any two duplicate nodes, we can always eliminate one of them. We continue chopping out duplicates until none remain. The final graph contains at most a single node labelled with any given state of $\mathcal{A}$. □

We can similarly establish

4.2. Theorem. Suppose $\mathcal{A}$ is a complemented pairs tree automaton with a single pair over a single letter alphabet. If $\mathcal{A}$ accepts some tree T then $\mathcal{A}$ accepts some graph G with number of nodes linear in the size of $\mathcal{A}$'s transition diagram.

5. Testing Nonemptiness

5.1. Theorem. Testing nonemptiness for pairs type automata $\mathcal{A}$ is in NP.

proof sketch. By the Linear Size Model Theorem we know that there is a graph G accepted by $\mathcal{A}$ of size linear in $\mathcal{A}$. Guess such a G. We must now check that along every path starting in the start node of G, the pairs condition holds, i.e., $\exists$ pair $i \in [1{:}k]$ $(\neg\overset{\infty}{\exists}\mathrm{RED}_i$ and $\overset{\infty}{\exists}\mathrm{GREEN}_i$). But this just amounts to a model checking problem in the logic FCTL of [EL84] which can be solved in polynomial (in fact, linear) time. □

Remark. Note that the proof of the Linear Size Model Theorem really tells us more than the theorem asserts. If the automaton $\mathcal{A}$ accepts some graph then it accepts a graph G contained in the transition diagram of $\mathcal{A}$ in this sense: G is of the form (T, A_0, A_1, L, s_0) where

(1) $T \subseteq S$, the state set of $\mathcal{A}$,
(2) for each $s \in T$, $(A_0(s),A_1(s)) \in \delta(s,\sigma)$
(3) for each $s \in T$, $L(s) = \sigma$, and
(4) $s_0 \in T$.

5.2. Corollary. Testing satisfiability for CTL* is in nondeterministic double exponential time and double exponential space.

Proof sketch. Redo [ES84] using pairs automata instead of complemented pairs automata. The pairs automata constructed will be of size double exponential in the length of the input formula. □

However, we can do much better for pairs automata with a single pair.

5.3. Theorem. There is an algorithm for testing nonemptiness of an input pairs automaton $\mathcal{A}$ with a single pair which runs in deterministic polynomial time.

Proof sketch. By the above remark, if $\mathcal{A}$ accepts any graph then it accepts some graph G contained in (the transition diagram of) $\mathcal{A}$. We must construct G so that each node in G has sufficient successors in G In tableau terms if OR-node s is in G we say that s has sufficient successors in G if there exists an AND-node son d of s in $\mathcal{A}$ which in turn has two OR-node sons t,u in G. We will try to pick sufficient successors for each OR-node s to get a model of the CTL* formula $A[\overset{\infty}{G}P \vee \overset{\infty}{F}Q]$ where $P \equiv \neg\mathrm{RED}$ and $Q \equiv \mathrm{GREEN}$. In other words, we must for each OR-node we include in G, we must strike a link to 2 successor OR-nodes intermediated by an AND-node. (The model we will try to construct is built out of OR-nodes so our approach here is "dual" to that of [EC82] which built the model out of AND-nodes; we could formulate things in the dual approach but the present one seems more direct.)

We will compute the set of states of $\mathcal{A}$ at which $A[\overset{\infty}{G}P \wedge \overset{\infty}{F}Q]$ is satisfiable inductively based on the following fixpoint characterization: $A[\overset{\infty}{G}P \wedge \overset{\infty}{F}Q] = \mu Y.AFAG((P \vee Y) \wedge AF(Q \vee Y))$. (To see that the fixpoint characterization is valid, consider the dual property $E[\overset{\infty}{F}P \vee \overset{\infty}{G}Q]$ which, pretty obviously, has the dual fixpoint characterization $\nu Y.EGEF((P \wedge Y) \vee EG(Q \wedge Y))$.) Let $\tau[Y] = AFAG((P \vee Y) \wedge AF(Q \vee Y))$. Then we compute $Y^1 = \tau[\text{false}]$, $Y^2 = \tau[Y^1]$, etc. As we add add states to Y^i we choose sufficient successors so that if $s \in Y^i$, there really is a model of Y^i at s selected out of the tableau.

Details are provided in the full paper □.

Similarly we can show that

5.4. Theorem. There is an algorithm for testing nonemptiness of an input complemented pairs automaton $\mathcal{A}$ with a single pair which runs in deterministic polynomial time. □

We can reduce the emptiness problem for ECTL to pairs automata with a single pair to establish that

5.5. Corollary. ECTL is decidable in deterministic exponential time. □

6. Limits of Expressive Power of Tree Automata

The correctness property known as *inevitability* of predicate P is expressible in CTL* as, simply, AFQ - meaning that along every future computation path x, there exists a time i along x at which Q is true. The time i in general depends on the particular path x followed. In other words, it has the pattern ∀ path ∃ time P. The property defined by swapping the quantifiers to get the pattern ∃ time ∀ path P - meaning that there exists a time i such that along every future computation path x, P holds at time i - we call *uniform inevitability.* The time i is uniform over all paths x. We have the following

6.1. Theorem. Uniform inevitability is not definable by any finite state tree automaton with any acceptance condition; hence, this property is not expressible in any of the temporal logics shown to be decidable using finite state tree automata.

The proof uses a sort of "pumping lemma" type argument. However, it turns out that a tree automaton with a pushdown store can be used to define this property. (It guesses i by pushing i symbols on its stack initially and decrements the stack as it advances from level to level.)

7. Conclusion

We have studied the problem of testing nonemptiness for tree automata. We have shown that, by viewing the automata as tableaux, it is possible to give better algorithms for testing nonemptiness than were previously known, which, in many cases, also yield improved temporal decision procedures. We have also investigated the limits of the expressive power of tree automata.

Finally, among related work, we mention that some related results regarding the complexity of tree automata and of temporal logics were obtained by Vardi and Stockmeyer ([VS85]).

8. References

[AB80] Abrahamson, K., Decidability and Expressiveness of Logics of Processes, PhD Thesis, Univ. of Washington, 1980.

[BMP81] Ben-Ari, M., Manna, Z., and Pnueli, A., The Temporal Logic of Branching Time. 8th Annual ACM Symp. on Principles of Programming Languages, 1981.

[CE81] Clarke, E. M., and Emerson, E. A., Design and Synthesis of Synchronization Skeletons using Branching Time Temporal Logic, Proceedings of the IBM Workshop on Logics of Programs, Springer-Verlag Lecture Notes in Computer Science #131, 1981.

[CES83] Clarke, E. M., Emerson, E. A., and Sistla, A. P., Automatic Verification of Finite State Concurrent Programs: A Practical Approach, POPL83.

[EC80] Emerson, E. A., and Clarke, E. M., *Characterizing Correctness Properties of Parallel Programs Using Fixpoints*, Proc. ICALP 80, LNCS Vol. 85, Springer Verlag, 1980, pp. 169-181.

[EC82] Emerson, E. A., and Clarke, E. M., Using Branching Time Logic to Synthesize Synchronization Skeletons, Science of Computer Programming, vol. 2, pp. 241-266, 1982.

[EH82] Emerson, E. A., and Halpern, J. Y., Decision Procedures and Expressiveness in the Temporal Logic of Branching Time. 14th Annual ACM Symp. on Theory of Computing, 1982.

[EH83] Emerson, E. A., and Halpern, J. Y., 'Sometimes' and 'Not Never' Revisited: On Branching versus Linear Time. POPL83.

[EL84] Emerson, E. A., and Lei, C. L., *Modalities for Model Checking: Branching Time Strikes Back*, to be presented at the 12th Annual ACM Symposium on Principles of Programming Languages.

[ES84] Emerson, E. A., and Sistla, A. P., *Deciding Branching Time Logic*, 16 Annual ACM Symp. on Theory of Computing, 1984.

[HR72] Hossley, R., and Rackoff, C, The Emptiness Problem For Automata on Infinite Trees, Proc. 13th IEEE Symp. Switching and Automata Theory, pp. 121-124, 1972.

[KP83] Koren, T. and Pnueli, A., There exist decidable context-free propositional dynamic logics, CMU Workshop on Logics of Programs, Springer LNCS #164, pp. 313-325, 1983.

[McN66] McNaughton, R., Testing and Generating Infinite Sequences by a Finite Automaton, Information and Control, vol. 9, 1966.

[MP79] Manna, Z., and Pnueli, A., The modal logic of programs, Proc. 6th Int. Colloquium on Automata, Languages, and Programming, Springer-Verlag Lecture Notes in Computer Science #71, pp. 385-410, 1979.

[ME74] Meyer, A. R., Weak Monadic Second Order Theory of Successor is Not Elementary Recursive, Boston Logic Colloquium, Springer-Verlag Lecture Notes in Mathematics #453, 1974.

[PN77] Pnueli, A., The Temporal Logic of Programs, 19th Annual Symp. on Foundations of Computer Science, 1977.

[RA69] Rabin, M., Decidability of Second order Theories and Automata on Infinite Trees, Trans. Amer. Math. Society, vol. 141, pp. 1-35, 1969.

[RA70] Rabin, M., Automata on Infinite Trees and the Synthesis Problem, Hebrew Univ., Tech. Report no. 37, 1970.

[ST81] Streett, R., Propositional Dynamic Logic of Looping and Converse (PhD Thesis), MIT Lab for Computer Science, TR-263, 1981. (a revised version appears in Information and Control, vol. 54, pp. 121-141, 1982.)

[Wo82] Wolper, P., A Translation from Full Branching Time Temporal Logic to One Letter Propositional Dynamic Logic with Looping, unpublished manuscript, 1982.

[VW83] Vardi, M., and Wolper, P., Yet Another Process Logic, CMU Workshop on Logics of Programs, Springer-Verlag, 1983.

[WVS83] Wolper, P., Vardi, M., and Sistla, A., Reasoning about Infinite Computations, 24th FOCS, 1983.

[VW84] Vardi, M. and Wolper, P., *Automata Theoretic Techniques for Modal Logics of Programs*, pp. 446-455, STOC84.

[VS85] Vardi, M. and Stockmeyer, L., *Improved Upper and Lower Bounds for Modal Logics of Programs*, to be presented at STOC85.

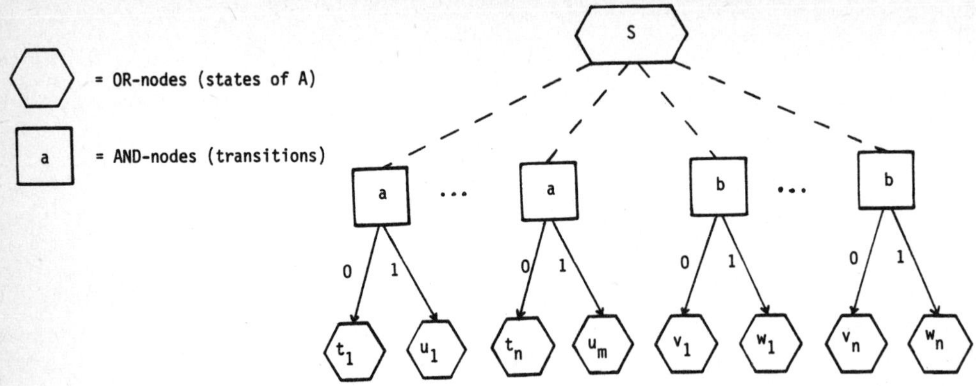

Figure 1.

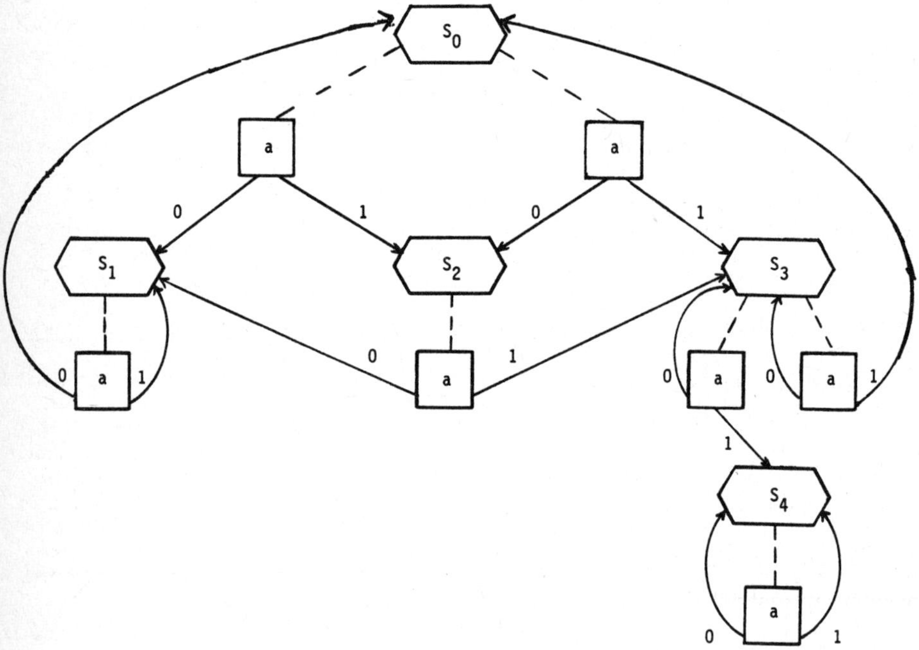

$\delta(s_0,a) = \{(s_1,s_2),\ (s_2,s_3)\}$

$\delta(s_1,a) = \{(s_0,s_1)\}$

$\delta(s_2,a) = \{(s_1,s_3)\}$

$\delta(s_3,a) = \{(s_3,s_4),\ (s_3,s_0)\}$

$\delta(s_4,a) = \{(s_4,s_4)\}$

Transition Diagram for Tree Automaton with
Indicated Transition Function

Figure 2.

PROVING TERMINATION OF PROLOG PROGRAMS

by

Nissim Francez[1], *Orna Grumberg*[1], *Shmuel Katz*[1] *and Amir Pnueli*[2]

1) Computer Science dept., the Technion, Haifa 32000, ISRAEL

2) Dept. of Applied Mathematics, Weizmann institute, Rehovot, ISRAEL

November 1984

Introduction

The results reported in this paper are motivated by two recent trends in computer science:

Prolog:

Since the gain in momentum by the 5th generation computer systems project, much attention is paid to Prolog [NGC]. It is by now the best known programming language based on the *Logic programming* paradigm [KO 77]. Still, most of the foundational issues are treated on the level of logic programming [AvE 82, vEK 76], and very little basic research has been conducted on the basis of Prolog itself (or its derivatives). In contrast, much research has been done on the less theoretical, implementation oriented and application oriented levels. In particular, in the area of program verification, Prolog programs are considered by many researchers as *self specifying*, being non-procedural, and not needing elaborate correctness proofs. Even if this is taken to hold with respect to partial correctness (functional behavior), it certainly is *not* so with respect to *termination*.

Termination proofs:

Since the discovery of the fundamental connection between termination proofs of (deterministic) programs and *well−founded* sets [FL 67], much effort has been devoted to the extensions of this fundamental connection to richer classes of programming language constructs. In particular, the method has been extended to *non−deterministic* programs. The main idea there is that a well-founded quantity, known also as the *variant*, should decrease under *every* non-deterministic choice taken by the program. Recent research, however, in non-determinism and concurrency produced a more refined notion, that of *relativized termination*, where it is required that only a *certain kind* of infinite computations be absent (those that "count" for some semantic reason). A proliferation of proof rules of this kind is exhibited in proving *fair termination* (i.e. termination under the assumption of fair scheduling) [GFMR 81, LPS 81]. As it turns out, a similar phenomenon is present in the case of Prolog. Due to its *leftmost−depthfirst* search mode, certain infinite computation paths will *never* be followed by a terminating program. This is a major difference between Prolog and general logic programming, that considers unrestricted nondeterminism in its proof (goal satisfaction) procedure.

The contribution of this paper is in the formulation of proof rules for proving termination of Prolog programs based on well-foundedness arguments. These rules are an adequate *static* characterization of the differences between the flow of control in Prolog, with its dynamic interaction between recursion and backtracking, and between that of general logic programming, the abstract non-deterministic inference engine. Similar rules may be designed for variants of Prolog, based on different restrictions of the search procedure, and may serve as their abstract definition.

We present two kinds of rules, based on different views of the (operational) semantics. The first is based on a tree oriented semantics. It has a global flavour, viewing the whole program as one unit, having the full context at hand all the time.

The second is a more *compositional* rule, where some properties are proved for each procedure separately, and then used at the point of call. The usual "proof by assumption" paradigm for (mutual) recursion is adopted. This rule is based on *stream* semantics, similar to that of data-flow programs. The assertion language has to be enriched accordingly.

The paper assumes basic familiarity with Prolog, especially with the relationship it induces on the interaction between *backtracking* and *recursion*. This relationship is our primary concern here; we pay less attention to another central issue in Prolog, that of *unification*. To the best of our knowledge, no previous attempt has succeeded in a static, proof-theoretic, characterization of these two dynamic features. For a treatment of these issues on a semantic level, in the context of non-deterministic functional programs, see [FKP 77].

2. The sublanguage considered:

As stated in the introduction, we are interested here in the effect of backtracking+recursion on termination. Thus, we restrict our attention to a sublanguage of Prolog rich enough to serve as a tool for the study.

A *program* P consists of a (finite) collection of *procedures*, denoted by p, q, r, etc. A procedure p consists of a (finite, positive) number of *clauses*. A compound clause has a *head*, the procedure's name and its formal parameters, and a *body*. For simplicity we assume that no two identical procedure names occur with different arities- a common Prolog trick. The body of a compound clause consists of a finite sequence of *subgoals*. A subgoal names a procedure and supplies actual parameters. A simple clause (called also a *fact*) has a head only. As the scope rules of Prolog imply that variable names are local to clauses, we strengthen our assumptions somewhat in assuming that different procedures use different names, avoiding renaming rules or auxiliary indexing, problems orthogonal to the subject under focus here.

We assume here that the data domain is the integers, and avoid the treatment of arbitrary terms of full Prolog, which would require a notational extension only. Thus, *unification* in this context will only match numeric constants and variables. The usual numeric built-in procedures are allowed. Here numeric terms are *always evaluated* (to a constant) before unification.

We use the syntax of [CM 81] in this paper and refer the reader to it for further informal description of the semantics. Following (see figure 1) is an example program, for which a termination proof appears in the sequel.
The order in which clauses are written (and that of subgoals within a goal) is crucial in the semantics of Prolog, while immaterial in the general Logic Programming paradigm.

---

1) $r(x){:-}\,p(x-1,y),q(x-1,y)$.

2) $p(0,0)$.

3) $p(1,1)$.

4) $p(u,v){:-}\,p(u-1,v)$.

5) $p(u,v){:-}\,p(u+1,v)$.

6) $q(0,0)$.

7) $q(a,b){:-}\,a>0,q(a-1,b)$.

Figure 1: a provably B-terminating program

Together with every program P is associated an *initial goal* $g_0=pr_0(f(\sigma_0))$ and the task is to *prove* this goal using the program P. By the semantics of Prolog, at each intermediate stage of a computation (proof), there is a *current goal*, denoted by $g_c = pr_c(\sigma_c)$ consisting of an ordered list of goals to be proved. The head of this list (when the list is not empty) is also referred to as the *immediate goal* (*ig*). In these goals *pr* is a procedure name (within P) and σ a state , assigning values to all the formal parameters and local variables. In a given state, some variables may be *uninstantiated*, having no value at that state. Only a pair (P, g) is capable of termination. Actually, goals should have some *unique labeling* for identification, as multiple occurrences of the same goal may occur. We exclude their consideration to simplify the notation.

Finally, note that the sublanguage used excludes programs that may modify themselves by addition/deletion of rules (clauses), and features like *cut*, altering the flow of control.

3. B-termination

In this section we discuss in more detail the kind of termination properties exhibited by Prolog programs. It is referred to as *B−termination*. We refer to the i'th (in order of appearance) clause as the *i*'th *direction* in the (purely nondeterministic) execution of P. We say that a direction i is *enabled*, denoted by $E(i)$, at a given stage of a computation, if the head of the corresponding clause *unifies* with the head of the *current goal*. We use $U(g_1, g_2)$ for the unification primitive (with its side effect). The set of all directions is denoted by D. We use $G(i)$ to denote the r.h.s of clause number i. We use the operator **d** to denote *definiteness* of variables: a variable is definite if and only if it is bound to a constant by the unification. In case two indefinite variables are equal, each binding to a constant of one of them binds the other as well.

The exposition that follows is inspired by the view of the execution of a program P as the following *iterative* nondeterministic program P^*, in which mutual recursion is hidden by using an explicit stack of goals, the value of the state variable *cg* (current goal). This view mimics the operation of *resolution*, on which the execution of Prolog is actually based.

$$P^*:: *[\ \underset{i\in D}{[]}\ U(head(cg), g_i) \rightarrow cg:=G(i)\ .\ tail(cg)^i]$$

Here the dot denotes list concatenation. Note that $G(i)$ already reflects the side effects caused by the unification in the guard. This side effect is present also in $tail(cg)$, as indicated by the superscript of the unified direction, i. This notation is further elaborated later. The updating of the current goal introduces yet another side effect in causing all variables appearing in $G(i)$ which are not affected by the unification to be indefinite. The program P^* terminates when the *head* of the current goal (i.e. the immediate goal) does not unify with any clause head. This may happen in case the current goal is the empty list, signaling success, or, otherwise, signaling failure. A backtracking execution of P^* (rather uncommon in the usual context of guarded commands) induces a corresponding backtracking execution of P. A standard nondeterministic execution of P induces the Logic Programming interpretation of P.

We define an operational semantics for the language considered by associating with each program P and (initial) state σ_0 an *execution tree* T_{P,σ_0}, representing all possible computations of P on σ_0. The construction is derived from the iterative description of P mentioned above. The nodes of the tree are labeled with states and its edges are labeled with directions.

Rules for constructing T_{P,σ_0}:

(1) The *root* is labeled σ_0.

Suppose some node is labeled σ:

(2) If $\sigma[\![cg]\!]\neq nil$, then the node has a descendant node for each direction i s.t $U(head(\sigma[\![cg]\!]), G(i))$ holds. The edge is labeled i and the descendant node σ', the state obtained after unification, as described

(3) If $\sigma[\![cg]\!] \neq nil$, but for *no* $i \in D$ $U(head(\sigma[\![cg]\!]), G(i))$ holds, then the node is a *failing leaf*.

(4) Otherwise (i.e $\sigma[\![cg]\!]=nil$), the node is a *successful leaf*.

When convenient, we abbreviate the tree to $T_{P,g}$ and depict in the node only the value of cg. Note that for a B-terminating program the tree never degenerates to a single node (being *both* a root and a leaf).

Before passing to discuss termination, we formulate two axioms for the unification operation. This operation is special in serving as a guard with side effects. Both aspects have to be captured by the axioms. In the sequel, we apply these axioms implicitly whenever needed, without further mention. The axioms are shown in figures 2 and 3. They are partial correctness axioms, stating a precondition under which if unification successfully terminates, it yields the post condition.

We start the discussion of termination by considering a very simple example (figure 4). The collection of all possible executions of an initial goal, say $g_0=p(3)$, can be arranged in a tree $T_{(P,p(3))}$ (see figure 5). At each node of this tree reside the current goal, and it has outgoing edges for all the clauses of the procedure specified by this goal that unify with its first subgoal. In case of fact, an extra edge, leading to a *success* leaf, is added. Similarly, in case of failure due to nonunifiability of (the head of) the current goal, a *failure* leaf is added. Clearly, the tree $T_{(P,p(3))}$ contains many infinite paths. However, due to Prolog's *leftmost–depthfirst* traversal of this tree, no infinite path will ever be traversed due to the presence of a successful leaf, a left descendant of $p(0)$, which, when encountered, terminates the computation.

For $1 \leq i \leq n$:

$$\{ (\mathbf{d}(arg_i^1) \vee \mathbf{d}(arg_i^2)) \wedge$$

$$\mathbf{d}(arg_i^1) \rightarrow arg_i^1 = C_i \wedge$$

$$\mathbf{d}(arg_i^2) \rightarrow arg_i^2 = C_i \}$$

$$U(p(arg_1^1, \cdots, arg_n^1), p(arg_1^2, \cdots, arg_n^2))$$

$$\{ (\mathbf{d}(arg_i^1) \wedge \mathbf{d}(arg_i^2)) \wedge arg_i^1 = arg_i^2 = C_i \}$$

Figure 2: definite unification axiom

For $1 \leq i \leq n$:

$$\{ (\neg\mathbf{d}(arg_i^1) \wedge \neg\mathbf{d}(arg_i^2)) \}$$

$$U(p(arg_1^1, \cdots, arg_n^1), p(arg_1^2, \cdots, arg_n^2))$$

$$\{ (\neg\mathbf{d}(arg_i^1) \wedge \neg\mathbf{d}(arg_i^2)) \wedge arg_i^1 = arg_i^2 \}$$

Figure 3: indefinite unification axiom

P:: 1) $p(0)$.

2) $p(x)$:− $p(x-1)$.

3) $p(x)$:− $p(x+1)$.

Figure 4: simple example program P

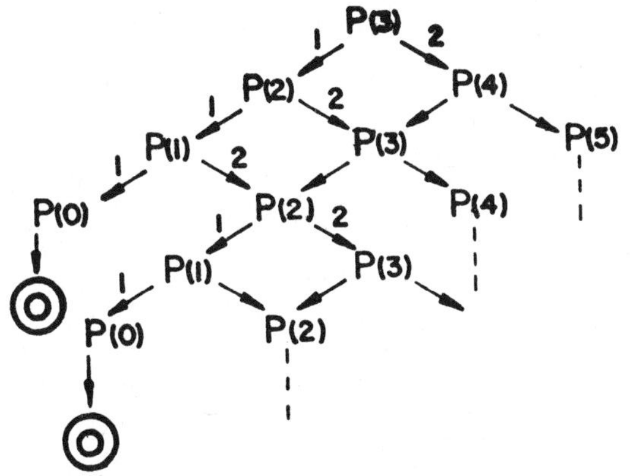

Figure 5: the tree $T_{(P,\,p(3))}$

This example is oversimplified since $(P, p(3))$ terminates without *ever* backtracking. Once backtracking is also considered, one gets the following representation for a terminating program (P, g_0), depicted as a tree $T_{(P,\,g_0)}$ in figure 6. In this tree, the path π is the *leftmost infinite path*. To its left is a *successful* leaf σ_s (in a double circle), and further to its left are $k \geq 0$ *failing* leaves $\sigma_f^j, 1 \leq j \leq k$, where the procedure names in current goals of leaves are omited for brevity.

Thus, $T_{(P,\,g_0)}$ can be divided into two subtrees:

1) The tree $T^f_{(P,\,g_0)}$ to the left (and not including) the leftmost infinite path π, which has to be *finite* and contain a successful (rightmost) leaf, and a finite number of failing leaves.

2) The tree $T^i_{(P,\,g_0)}$ to the right of (and including) π, which may be infinite.

In the sequel, we omit references to the subscripts (P,g_0) when clear from context.

For a nonterminating (P,g_0), we get the dual picture as in figure 7. The tree is again divided as before. However, the leftmost successful leaf (if such is present) is to

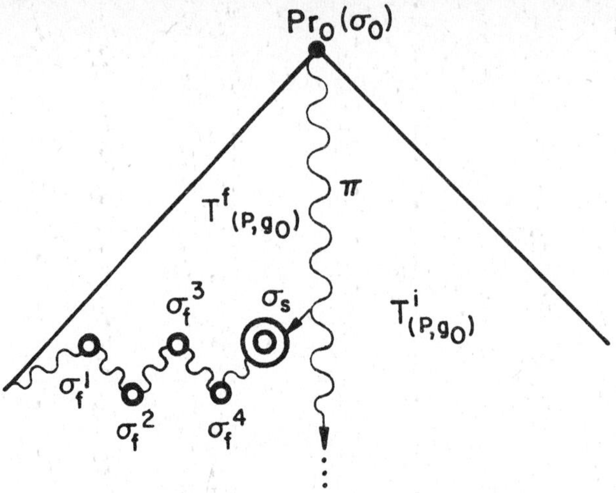

Figure 6: the tree $T_{(P,\, g_0)}$
(terminating program)

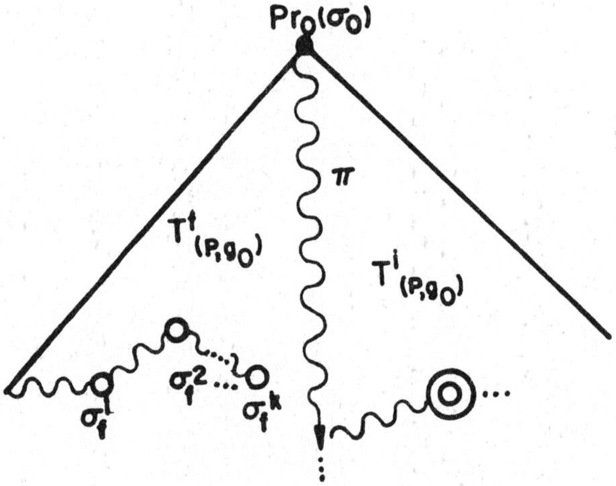

Figure 7: the tree $T_{(P,\, g_0)}$
(nonterminating program)

the right of π, the leftmost infinite path. In this case, Prolog's search mode will not terminate the execution, as it backtracks from all the failing leaves and "bumps into" π, on which it continues indefinitely.

There is yet a third possibility, that of the whole program terminating with a failure of the initial goal. This is an "uninteresting" case, as the tree $T_{(P,g_0)}$ is finite, with all the leaves failing. Thus, our main concern is of statically distinguishing between the first two possibilities., the third being provable using the ordinary rule for non-deterministic termination (decreasing along *every* direction).

We call this kind of termination *B−termination* (for *B*acktracking termination) and denote it by

$$\overset{\mathbf{B}}{[}\, pre\,]\,(\,g_0\,)\,[post\,]$$

where *pre*, *post* are the usual precondition and postcondition, respectively. The proposed proof-rule for *B−termination* is referred to as **BT**, while the usual rule for non-deterministic termination is **NDT**.

The main idea behind the suggested rule **BT** is to identify, by means of decreasing *well−founded variant* the path π^s to the leftmost successful leaf, and showing that all the subtrees to its left are finite and have failing leaves. Thus, for each node on π^s the set of enabled directions is partitioned, depending on its variant value $w \in W$, into three classes:

i. A direction i_w that causes a *decrease* in w,

ii. The set $F_w = \{j \mid 1 \leq j < i_w,\ E(j)\}$, which leads to states to which **NDT** can be applied successfully,

iii. The set of all other directions $i > i_w$, i enabled, on which no restriction whatsoever is imposed.

Also, when a node with variant value $w = 0$ is reached, that state has to imply that the corresponding node is both a leaf (no enabled direction) and a successful one (the initial goal is satisfied and the current goal is empty).

4. the rule BT for B-termination

In this section we present the proof-rule **BT** for proving B-termination of a Prolog goal (g_0) using well-founded sets. (The program P is implicit). For technical reasons we find it more convenient to use a *parametrized invariant* over the state σ and current goal cg, denoted by $pi(\sigma, cg, w)$, whose additional parameter w ranges over a well-founded set W, instead of using variant functions. We use 0 as a generic name for *minimal* elements in W. we use the notation $[[p]]\ U\colon g\ [[q]]$ to assert that if p holds and the current goal is updated by g after unification, then immediately afterwards q holds. The rule is presented in figure 8.

Explanations:

1) The clause INIT takes care that by invoking the initial goal the invariant *pi* is established by some $w \in W$, given the global precondition *pre*.

2) The clause CONT has a double role:
it ensures that, as long as $w > 0$ holds, there is an enabled direction to take; furthermore, this direction is the decreasing direction (for that w), preventing vacuous choices of decreasing directions.

3) The clause TERM ensures the boundary condition: successful termination is reached once $w = 0$ holds. Success is expressed by implying the initial goal.

4) The clause DEC is the central clause, taking care that following a decreasing direction i_w indeed causes decrease in *pi* when the corresponding current goal $G(i_w)$ is taken. Note that σ' denotes the current state *after* the execution of the goal $G(i_w^{BT})$.

5) The clause FIN takes care that for every enabled direction j smaller than i_w the rule **NDT** proves non-deterministic termination with a failing state.

To prove $\overset{B}{[pre]}(g_0)[post]$ (where $g_0 = pr_0(\sigma_0)$):
Find:

1) a well-founded, partially-ordered, set $(W, <)$
2) a *parametrized invariant* $pi(\sigma, cg, w)$
3) for each $w>0$, a *decreasing direction* i_w,

all satisfying:

(INIT)

$$pre(\sigma_0) \wedge cg = g_0 \rightarrow \exists w: pi(\sigma_0, g_0, w)$$

(CONT)

$$pi(\sigma, cg, w) \wedge w>0 \rightarrow E(i_w)$$

(TERM)

$$pi(\sigma, cg, 0) \rightarrow \neg \bigvee_{j \in D} E(j) \wedge g_0 \wedge cg = () \wedge post(\sigma)$$

(DEC)

$$[[pi(\sigma, cg, w) \wedge w>0]]\ U: G(i_w)\ [[\exists w': w' < w \wedge pi(\sigma', cg', w')]]$$

(FIN)

$$\vdash_{\mathbf{NDT}} [pi(\sigma, cg, w) \wedge w>0]\, U: G(j)\, [\neg g_0], \quad j \in F_w.$$

for $j \in F_w$.

Figure 8: the rule BT

As an application of the rules suggested above, we present a proof of

$$\vdash_{\mathbf{BT}} \overset{B}{[C>0]}\, r(C)\, [true]$$

where the program P appeared in figure 1.

As the well-founded set we choose $(N, <)$, the natural numbers with their usual ordering. The parametrized invariant is shown in figure 9.

Clearly, $0 \le w \le 2C + 3$ is implied by pi. Hence, we choose decreasing directions i_w for this range only. Figure 10 presents these values, as well as the sets F_w for the **NDT** rule, as determined from the invariant chosen.

We now present some of the details involved in showing that the clauses of **BT** apply.

INIT

Clearly, $C > 0$ and $cg = r(C)$ imply that pi is satisfied by $w = 2C + 1$.

CONT

For $w = 2C + 1$ we have $i_w = 1$ and $cg = (r(C))$, and indeed $U(r(C), r(x))$ holds.

For $w = 2C$ we have $i_w = 4$ and $cg = p(x-1, y) \cdot q(x-1, y)$.

For $C + 1 < w < 2C$ we have again $i_w = 4$ and $cg = (p(u-1, v) \cdot q(x-1, y))$. In both cases the current goal unifies with $p(u, v)$.

The rest of the cases are checked similarly.

$pi(x, y, u, v, a, b, cg, w) =$

$C > 0 \wedge$

$w = 2C + 1 \rightarrow [\ cg = r(C)\ ] \wedge$

$w = 2C \rightarrow [\ cg = p(x - 1, y).q(x - 1, y) \wedge x = C \wedge \neg \mathbf{d}(y)\ ] \wedge$

$w = C + u \rightarrow [0 < u < x \wedge v = y \wedge x = C \wedge cg = (p(u-1, v) . q(x - 1, y)) \wedge$

$\neg \mathbf{d}(v) \wedge \neg \mathbf{d}(y) \wedge (p(u-1, v) \rightarrow p(x - 1, y))] \wedge$

$w = C \rightarrow [p(x - 1, 0) \wedge cg = q(x - 1, y) \wedge x = C \wedge y = 0\ ] \wedge$

$w = a \rightarrow [0 < a < x \wedge b = y = 0 \wedge p(x - 1, 0) \wedge \wedge x = C \wedge cg = (q(a - 1, 0)) \wedge$

$(q(a - 1, 0) \rightarrow q(x - 1, 0)] \wedge$

$w = 0 \rightarrow [cg = () \wedge p(x - 1, 0) \wedge q(x - 1, 0) \wedge x = C]$

Figure 9: The parametrized invariant

$w = 2C + 1$	$i_w = 1$	ϕ
$C + 1 < w \leq 2C$	$i_w = 4$	if $w > C + 2$ *then* ϕ *else* $\{3\}$
$w = C + 1$	$i_w = 2$	ϕ
$1 < w \leq C$	$i_w = 7$	ϕ
$w = 1$	$i_w = 6$	ϕ

Figure 10: the decreasing directions and NDT sets

TERM

$pi(\sigma, cg, 0)$ implies $cg = ()$ and hence termination. It also implies $x = C \wedge p(x - 1, 0) \wedge q(x - 1, 0)$, which, by clause 1, implies the initial goal $r(C)$ and, hence, success. The post condition *true* is trivially satisfied.

DEC

This is the interesting part of the proof, establishing the correctness of the "guesses" of the decreasing directions. We again do a case analysis according to the value of w.

We first consider

$[[pi(\sigma, cg, 2C + 1)]]\ U{:}\ (p(x - 1, y), q(x - 1, y))\ [[pi(\sigma', cg', w')\ ]]$

After unification, we have that $cg' = (p(C - 1, y) . q(C - 1, y)$ and the invariant is reestablished with $w' = 2C < w$.

The next case is

$[[pi(\sigma, cg, w) \wedge w = 2C]]\ U\colon p(u-1, v)[[pi(\sigma', cg', w')]]$.

As the invariant initially holds, we obtain $cg = p(x-1, y).q(x-1, y)$ *and* $\neg \mathbf{d}(y)$. By the unification we have

$u = x - 1 \wedge v = y \wedge \neg \mathbf{d}(v) \wedge cg' = p(u-1, v).q(x-1, y)$.

By clause 4 (of the program) we also have that $p(u-1, v) \rightarrow p(x-1, y)$. Hence, the invariant is reestablished with $w' = 2C - 1 < w$.

Next, consider the case

$[[pi(\sigma, cg, w) \wedge C + 1 < w < 2C]]\ U\colon p(u-1, v)\ [[pi(\sigma', cg', w')]]$.

As the invariant holds initially, we obtain

$w = C + u$, $0 < u < x$, $cg = (p(u-1, v) . q(x-1, y)), p(u-1, v) \rightarrow p(x-1, y)$.

After the unification we have

$u' = u - 1, v' = v, cg' = (p(u'-1, v') . q(x-1, y))$.

Using clause 4 in the program with the above implication, we get $p(u'-1, v) \rightarrow p(C-1, y)$. Hence, the invariant is reestablished with

$w' = C + u' = C + u - 1 < w$

Note that this holds also for $w = C + 2$, i.e. for the case $cg = p(1, v)$ i.e. $u - 1 = 1$. This is the "real" guess of a successful continuation, leaving direction 3, which is also enabled, to **NDT** in clause *FIN*.

As the last case discussed in detail, consider

$[[pi(\sigma, cg, C + 1)]]\ U\colon()\ [[pi(\sigma', cg', w')]]$

The same precondition as before is obtained. After unification, we get

$u' = v' = 0, cg' = (q(C-1, 0))$

(here an empty r.h.s of this direction is appended to the tail of the previous cg). By Modus Ponens we get $p(x-1, 0)$ and the invariant is reestablished by

$w' = C < w$

We skip the details of the rest of the cases.

Finally,

FIN

As most of the sets F_w are empty, the only fact to be proved using **NDT** amounts to proving termination of $q(C-1, b)$, a simple exercise in termination of recursive procedures (as no backtracking is involved any more). We again skip the details.

This concludes the proof of the example using the rule **BT**. We return to this example in the next section, presenting a more modular proof.

We now state the two basic theorems establishing the soundness and semantic completeness of the rule **BT**. Their proofs rely directly on the observation made before about the form of the tree T_{P, g_0} for a B-terminating program.

Theorem: (soundness of BT)

$$\text{if } \mid\!-_{BT}^{B} [\, pre \,]\, (P, g_0)\, [\, post \,], \text{ then } \models^{B} [\, pre \,]\, (P, g_0)\, [\, post \,].$$

Proof: If all clauses of **BT** are successfully applicable then clearly the tree must have the form shown in figure 6, i.e. the program indeed B-terminates.

[]

Theorem: (semantic completeness of BT)

$$\text{If } \models^{B} [\, pre \,]\, (P, g_0)\, [\, post \,], \text{ then } \mid\!-_{BT}^{B} [\, pre \,]\, (P, g_0)\, [\, post \,].$$

Proof: If the program fairly terminates for an initial state satisfying pre, the tree has the form shown in figure 6. We may choose $W \overset{def.}{=} \{1,...,n\}$ naturally ordered, where $n \overset{def.}{=} length(\pi)$. For the invariant we define $pi(\sigma, cg, w)$ to hold if an occurrence of (σ, cg) occurs on π with distance w. Also, $pi(\sigma, cg, n)$ holds for every (σ, cg) occurring on the tree not on π.

From the fact that the tree is shaped as in figure 6 it clearly follows that all clauses of **BT** apply.

[]

5. Compositional proofs of B-termination

In this section a compositional proof system for B-termination is presented, in which each procedure is treated separately, making use of assumptions about inner calls. This approach is similar to the way mutually recursive procedures are handled in the backtracking-free case.

The main difficulty of adding backtracking to this framework is the absence of *context information* in the isolated treatment of a single procedure. As a consequence, it is impossible to attribute success/failure to the various outcomes of a procedure, as a value that succeeds w.r.t that procedure may be rejected by a subsequent one. Thus, it is impossible to "judge" a procedure call by its first outcome.

This leads naturally to a different view of the semantics of a single procedure (outside of any context of its call). Instead of regarding a procedure as a (single) *state−transformer*, it is now regarded as a *stream−transformer*, in a sense similar to that of *data flow* programs. The idea is to characterize the procedure by the stream of values it produces (under the leftmost depth-first mode of execution) leaving the classification with respect to success to the receiver of the stream.

In the example program discussed above, the procedure p, for a given call with a positive first argument, produces the stream $< 1,0 >$, looping forever after producing its second output value. The procedure q, for a call with a positive first argument, produces an one-element stream $< 0 >$, terminating subsequently with a failure to produce any further results (for the given call). In the procedure r (called with a positive argument) the output stream of p is filtered through q, resulting in an output stream for r consisting of the stream $< 0 >$.

In the more general case, output streams may be infinite also, and some finite prefix will be consumed by the context. Consider for example the following procedure $s(z)$, shown in figure 11. A call $s(k)$ produces the ascending infinite stream

$$< k \,, k + 1 \,, \cdots >$$

Stream-extended assertion language

As a result of the above discussion, we have to extend the assertion language to be able to deal with assertions about streams. We use use Greek letters to refer to assertions from an underlying assertion language, asserting facts about single elements.

1) $s(z)$.

2) $s(z)\text{:-}s(z+1)$.

Figure 11: a program producing an infinite output stream

Finite concatenations of such formulae are interpreted over streams in the natural way: a prefix of the appropriate length is such that its respective elements satisfy the respective assertions from the concatenation. For example, the assertion $\varphi\vartheta$ is satisfied by streams the length of which is at least 2, the first element satisfying φ and the second element satisfying ϑ. A frequently occurring form of stream assertions is that of φ^*. It is satisfied by any stream having a (finite) prefix, each of which elements satisfies φ. The assertion **ff** is the assertion satisfied by the empty stream only. Its main use is in truncating a stream, claiming something about its exact form, without any suffixes. For example, the assertion $\varphi_1\ \varphi_2$ **ff** is satisfied only by streams of length 2. It is *not* satisfied by a diverging computation that fails to produce any output value in a finite time.

The main assertions made about a procedure p is the following:

$[\varphi^*\eta]\ p\ [\psi^*\vartheta]$.

The validity of such an assertion is defined as follows:

If the procedure p is presented with an input stream that has a prefix satisfying the precondition, than it will produce an output stream having a prefix satisfying the postcondition.

We deliberately distinguish between the last state assertion within a stream assertion from its predecessors, as it will represent an assertion about the (intentionally) successful element, all its predecessors being failing elements. This intention is formalized by the proof rules suggested for deriving such *stream correctness assertions* about procedures.

The proof system to follow, for the deduction of assertions of the above form, is called **CBT** (for *C*ompositional **BT**).

The first rule CONJ describe how to compose assertions about conjuncts into assertions about conjunctions. It is the analogue of the more usual rules of sequential compositions. This rule asserts the existence of an appropriate *intermediate stream* between two conjuncts.

CONJ

$[\varphi^*\mu]\ p\ [\eta^*\vartheta]$

$[\eta^*\vartheta]\ q\ [\psi^*\nu]$

$[\varphi^*\mu]\ (p,q)\ [\psi^*\nu]$

Figure 12: the rule CONJ

The next rule COM describes how to combine assertions about "failing" prefixes and assertions about a "successful" element.

The next two rules S and F describe how to obtain assertions about the "successful" and "failing" elements by inspecting the internals of the procedure. Here again the backtracking is considered and similarly to the previous section, decreasing directions are guessed, this time for each procedure independently. In these two rules, and in their recursive analogs, we use the notation φ^i, for a direction i, to denote the assertion obtained from φ after the side effect of unification and updating the current goal. We first ignore the (mutual) recursion and add it at the end by considering proof from assumptions.

The rule F deals with the failing case and is the equivalent of **NDT** in the previous section.

The second rule S deals with success. Here the real guessing occurs.

Finally, to deal with recursion, all the assertions are considered parametrized by a parameter ranging over a well-founded set, as before. The recursion rules S-REC and F-REC state that assumptions about calls with a smaller parameter are permitted to be used when dealing with the directions in the procedure's body. The first uses as an assumption an assertion of the form of the conclusion of S, while the second does the same for F. For both rules, note that the selection of the decreasing direction j_n depends on the rank n. It can be made state dependent instead.

We now present part of the details in showing

COM

$[\varphi]\, p\, [\psi^* \mathbf{ff}]$

$[\eta]\, p\, [\psi^* \vartheta]$

$[\varphi^* \eta]\, p\, [\psi^* \vartheta]$

Figure 13: the rule COM

F

$\forall i{:}\ 1 \le i \le n \wedge E(i){:}\ [\varphi^i]\ G(i)\ [\psi^* \mathbf{ff}]$

$[\varphi]\, p\, [\psi^* \mathbf{ff}]$

Figure 14: the rule F

S for some unifiable direction j and all unifiable directions k, $k < j$:

$[\varphi^j]\, G(j)\, [\psi^*\vartheta]$,

$[\varphi^k]\, G(k)\, [\psi^*\mathbf{ff}]$

$[\varphi]\, p\, [\psi^*\vartheta]$

Figure 15: the rule S

S-REC

For some unifiable direction $j = j(n)$ and all unifiable directions k, $k < j$:

$$[m < n \wedge \varphi(m)]\, p\, [\psi^*\vartheta] \mid\!-_{\mathbf{CBT}} \begin{cases}[\varphi^j(n)]\, G(j)\, [\psi^*\vartheta] \\ [\varphi^k(n)]\, G(k)\, [\psi^*\mathbf{ff}]\end{cases}$$

$[\exists n: \varphi(n)]\, p\, [\psi^*\vartheta]$

Figure 16: the rule S-REC

F-REC

$$[m < n \wedge \psi(m)]\, p\, [\varphi^*\mathbf{ff}] \mid\!-_{\mathbf{CBT}} \forall k: 1 \le k \le n \wedge E(k): [\varphi^k(n)]\, G(k)\, [\psi^*\mathbf{ff}]$$

$[\exists n: \varphi(n)]\, p\, [\psi^*\mathbf{ff}]$

Figure 17: the rule F-REC

$$\mid\!-_{\mathbf{CBT}} [C > 0]\, r(x)\, [\mathit{true}] \qquad 1$$

We want to use the rule S (for the only direction existing in r). To this end, we have to prove

$$[x = C > 0 \wedge \neg\mathbf{d}(y)]\, p(x-1, y).q(x-1, y)\, [\mathit{true}] \qquad 2$$

where $\varphi \equiv C > 0$ and $\varphi^1 \equiv x = C > 0 \wedge \neg\mathbf{d}(y)$(after unification by U: $G(1)$). In order to show 2, we want to use the rule CONJ. Hence, we have to show

$$[u \ge 0 \wedge \neg\mathbf{d}(y) \wedge x > 0]\, p(u, v)\, [(x > 0 \wedge v = 1)^*(x > 0 \wedge v = 0)] \qquad 3$$

and

$$[(a \ge 0 \wedge b = 1)^*(a \ge 0 \wedge b = 0)]\, q(a, b)\, [\mathit{true}]. \qquad 4$$

The parameter substitution used is $x - 1$ for u and a and y for v and b. Note that x

can be substituted for as it is not subject to change in p and q. We omit the proof of 3 and show that of 4. We want to use the rule *COM*. Hence, we have to show

$$[\, a \geq 0 \wedge b = 1\,]\; q(\, a,\, b\,)\,[\, \mathbf{ff}\,] \qquad 5$$

and

$$[\, a \geq 0 \wedge b = 0\,]\; q(\, a,\, b\,)\,[\, \mathit{true}\,] \qquad 6$$

Again the proof of 6 is omitted and we show 5. We want to use the rule F-REC and have, therefore, to chose a parametrized invariant. We take

$$\varphi(\, n\,) \equiv n = a \wedge a \geq 0 \wedge b = 1$$

and use the assumption

$$[\, m < n \wedge \varphi(\, m\,)\,]\; q(\, a,\, b\,)\,[\, \mathbf{ff}\,]. \qquad 7$$

As direction one of q is not unifiable, we show the following for direction 2 in q:

$$[\, \varphi^2(\, n\,)\,]\; a > 0,\, q(\, a - 1,\, b\,)\,[\, \mathbf{ff}\,]. \qquad 8$$

We distinguish between two cases:

a) $a = 0$, and therefore $a > 0$ fails, yielding **ff**.

b) $a > 0$, in which case 8 reduces to

$$[\, \varphi^2(\, n\,) \wedge a > 0\,]\; q(a - 1,\, b\,)\,[\mathbf{ff}\,] \qquad 9$$

which is obtained by the parameter substitution $a - 1$ for a and $n - 1$ for m in the assumption 7.

This finishes the example.

[]

In order to prove the soundness and semantic completeness theorems of the **CBT** system, a formal definition of the stream semantics is needed. This will be provided in a fuller version of the paper. Several attempts at such a stream oriented semantics exist (e.g [JM 83]). however none of them exactly fits the language and proof rules considered here.

Given an appropriate stream semantics, the assertions needed for the completeness proof in order to apply the recursion rules are the following (informally expressed):

For **S–REC**:

Precondition:

$\varphi(\sigma, l, n) \overset{def.}{=}$ The partial σ-computation of length n yields a stream of length l.

Postconditions:

1) $\psi(\sigma, \sigma', n) \overset{def.}{=}$ σ' is the i'th element in the output stream of the σ-computation for some $i<l$.

2) $\vartheta(\sigma, \sigma', l) \overset{def.}{=}$ σ' is the l'th element of the output stream of the σ-computation.

In these assertions l is an auxiliary variable reflecting the context dependency of *failure / success* of the part of the output stream relevant to a given recursive call.

For **F—REC**:

Precondition:

$\varphi(\sigma, n) \overset{def.}{=}$ The full σ-computation is finite and of length n.

Postcondition:

$\psi(\sigma, \sigma') \overset{def}{=} \sigma'$ is an element of the output stream of the full σ-computation.

Recal that the other postcondition is **ff**.

The full details of the completeness proof will appear in the fuller version of the paper.

6. Conclusions

The paper presented two kinds of proof rules to prove B-termination, the kind of termination obtained by the combination of backtracking and recursion as displayed by Prolog. The first kind of rule takes into account the context of the whole program and is based on a tree oriented operational semantics. The second kind is more compositional, dealing with separate procedures in a context independent way. It is based on a stream oriented semantics.

We would like to stress that such proof rules may be successfully used for *defining* other search strategies than the actual one used by prolog. An interesting question is to define in this way a probabilistic backtracking search strategy.

Acknowledgement: The first author was partially supported by the fund for the promotion of research, the Technion.

References:

[AvE 82] K.R.Apt, M.H. Van Emden: "Contributions to the theory of logic programming", JACM 29, 3 (July 1982).

[CM 81] W.F. Clockskin, C.S.Mellish: "*Programming in Prolog*", Springer (1981).

[vEK 76] M.H.Van Emden, R.A.Kowalski: "The semantics of predicate logic as a programming language", JACM 23,4 (1976).

[FL 67] R.M.Floyd: "Assigning meanings to programs", proc AMS symp. in app. math. 19 Providence, R.I (1967)

[FKP 77] N.Francez, B.Klebanski, A.Pnueli: "Backtracking in recursive computations", Acta Informatica 8 (1977).

[GFMR 81] O.Grumberg, N.Francez, J.A.Makovsky, W.P.de Roever: "A proof rule for fair termination of guarded commands", proc. int. symp. on Algorithmic Languages, Amsterdam (1981).

[JM 83] N.D. Jones, A.Mycroft: "Stepwise developement of operational and denotational semantics of Prolog", TR. Univ. of Copenhagen, 1983.

[KO 74] R.A.Kowalski: "Predicate logic as a programming language", in: Info. Proc. 74 (J.Rosenfeld,ed.), North-Holland (1974).

[LPS 81] D.Lehmann, A.Pnueli, J.Stavi: "Impartiality, justice and fairness: the ethics of concurrent termination ", proc. 8th ICALP, ACRE, (1981); LNCS 115 (S.Even, O.Kariv-eds.), Springer 1981.

[NGC] New Generation Computing, Springer; (the existence of a journal devoted to the subject is taken as evidence for interest in that subject).

A HOARE CALCULUS FOR FUNCTIONS DEFINED BY RECURSION ON HIGHER TYPES

Andreas Goerdt
Lehrstuhl für Informatik II
RWTH Aachen
Büchel 29 - 31
D-5100 Aachen (West-Germany)

INTRODUCTION

In [Cl 79] Clarke puts a borderline to the development of Hoare Calculi for increasingly complex programming languages. He shows that for languages with a certain rich procedure concept no Hoare Calculus can exist which is sound and complete relative to the first-order theory of the interpretation, even if we assume it is expressive (cf. [Ur 83, ClGeHa 82]). Programming languages with higher type functions and procedures but without global variables are within the limitations set by Clarke. (Please note the difference between functions and procedures, functions only appear on right hand sides of assignments, whereas procedures define state transformations.)

In recent years quite a few researchers have developed calculi for programming languages with higher type functions or procedures and obtained the following results (completeness as usual only for expressive interpretations):

The calculi in [Ol 84, DaJo 83, La 83] are proved complete relative to an oracle consisting of certain higher-order formulae valid in the underlying interpretation. In [GeClHa 83] a Hoare Calculus for a language with higher type procedures is presented which is complete relative to the first-order theory of the interpretation. In [ErNaOg 82, dBMeKl 82] no completeness proofs are given. Moreover [Si 81] treats similar problems from a different angle and does not obtain completeness results.

In this paper we study the problems arising in the theory of Hoare Logic for higher type concepts in the abstract and general setting of finitely typed λ-terms with fixpoints. We set up a Hoare Calculus for partial correctness properties of λ-terms which is sound and complete relative to the first-order theory of the interpretation, provided the interpretation is expressive (cf. [Ur 83, ClGeHa 82]). That means that the calculus has the same completeness properties as calculi for languages not involving higher type recursion. The results of this paper are interesting in their own right as they show how applicative (functional) concepts like application and abstraction can be explicitly axiomatized using the approach of Hoare Logic. In particular they demonstrate in the environment of λ-terms how to treat higher type recursion with a first order oracle only. Due to the generality of λ-terms our calculus can be readily applied to any incidence of higher type recursion in concrete programming languages. We indicate how to obtain a Hoare Calculus for a programming language with functions defined by recursion on higher types. This solves an open problem stated in [Ol 84, DaJo 83, dBMeKl 82].

Our calculus works as Hoare Calculi normally do: in proving an assertion for a λ-term t, t is split up into its subterms. So even if we are only interested in terms which are functions from individuals to individuals, say, the proof will involve higher type terms. Therefore we need an assertion language for objects of higher type. (Please recall, that in Hoare Logics two formal languages are distinguished , the programming language and the assertion language.) The clue to our results lies in designing the right assertion language which meets two requirements: On the one hand it is *weak* enough to allow for oracle calls, which are normally implications of assertions, to be first-order formulae, but on the other hand it is *strong* enough to express the semantics of terms in expressive interpretations uniquely, which is a prerequisite to completeness proofs of Hoare Logics.

Assertions of type ind → ind, that is of terms denoting a function from individuals to individuals, are rather similar to assertions of imperative programs. They are built up from *pairs of first-order predicates* each of them having a distinguished free variable which is supplied as index, as in $((p)_u, (q)_v)$, where p and q are predicates and u and v indvidual variables. Semantically $((p)_u, (q)_v)$ is interpreted as a pair of pre- and postcondition where u stands for the input and v for the output of the term in question. For example the (simple) term ·5, denoting multiplication with 5, satisfies the assertion $((\text{input} \geq 0)_{\text{inp}}, (\text{output} \geq 0)_{\text{output}})$. As ·5 satisfies the assertion $p = ((\text{input} > u > 0)_{\text{input}}, (\text{output} > u)_{\text{output}})$ for all u , the assertion ∀u.p holds for the term ·5. Accordingly the assertion language is - roughly - defined by: an assertion of type ind (individual) is a predicate which is indexed with an individual variable, an assertion of type $\tau \to \rho$ is a possibly universally quantified pair of assertions (p, q), where p is an assertion of type τ and q of type ρ.

Contrary to the assertion languages in [Ol 84, DaJo 83, La 83, ErNaOg 82] our assertion language contains no higher type variables. This allows on the one hand to give a first-order definition of impl(p, q), meaning assertion p implies assertion q, and thus to restrict oracle calls to first-order formulae. On the other hand the assertion language is strong enough to express the semantics of terms in expressive interpretations uniquely because universal quantification is admissable.

A detailed report of the results of this paper can be found in [Go 85].

1 THE CALCULUS AND ITS SOUNDNESS

We assume familiarity with finitely typed λ-terms with if-then-else and fixpoints. The base types are ind and bv (individuals and Boolean values), we have only functional types, no cartesian ones. All semantic considerations are relative to a fixedly given interpretation consisting of a set of individuals I, a set of Boolean values {tt, ff}, and an interpretation of the operation symbols. We assume the Boolean constants tt, ff among the operation symbols. $D = (D^{\tau} \mid \tau \text{ type})$ is the family of cpo's of continuous functions over $D^{ind} = I_{\perp}$ and $D^{bv} = \{tt, ff\}_{\perp}$. Typed λ-terms are denoted by r, s, t, term variables by y; let μ always be an assignment of term variables in D, then $T[\![t]\!]\mu \in D$ is the semantics of t under μ. Let always be $i, j \in I \cup \{tt, ff\}$ and $c, d \in D$. The assertion language is built up from two-sorted first--order predicates (two-sorted because of the two base types ind and bv of terms). Hence we need a family of individual variables $Indvar = (Indvar^{\tau} \mid \tau \text{ base type})$ ranging over I and {tt, ff} resp. and relation symbols over ind and bv, which are also assumed to be fixedly interpreted. Let Pred be the set of two-sorted first-order predicates over Indvar, the operation and the relation symbols. Let π be an assignment of individual variables and let u, v, inp, outp $\in$ Indvar. Let $\pi \models p$ be the usual notion of validity for a predicate p under the assignment π. $\models p$ means that $\pi \models p$ for all π (p is valid).

1.1 Definition

(a) The family of assertions, $Ass = (Ass^{\tau} \mid \tau \text{ type})$, is given by

if $p \in Pred$, $u \in Indvar^{\tau}$, then $(p)_u \in Ass^{\tau}$, for τ base type
if $p \in Ass^{\tau}$, $q \in Ass^{\rho}$, then (p, q) $Ass^{\tau\to\rho}$
if $p, q \in Ass^{\tau}$, then $p \wedge q$, $\forall u.p \in Ass^{\tau}$, for τ not base type.

Let always $p, q \in Ass$.

(b) The semantics of $p \in Ass^{\tau}$ is the set $A[\![p]\!]\pi \subseteq D^{\tau}$ of cpo elements satisfying p under π and is defined by

$c \in A[\![(p)_u]\!]\pi \iff$ if $c \neq \bot$, then $\pi[c/u] \models p$ ($\pi[c/u]$ is the variant of π, as usual.)

$c \in A[\![(p, q)]\!]\pi \iff$ for all $d \in D$, if $d \in A[\![p]\!]\pi$, then $c(d) \in A[\![q]\!]\pi$

$c \in A[\![p \wedge q]\!]\pi \iff c \in A[\![p]\!]\pi \cap A[\![q]\!]\pi$

$c \in A[\![\forall u.p]\!]\pi \iff$ for all i $c \in A[\![p]\!]\pi[i/u]$.

Please recall, that we only treat partial correctness. Let fr p be the set of free variables of the assertion p (variables are bound by indexing and quantification).

As an example the term $\lambda y.y(5)$ of type (ind → ind) → ind satisfies the assertion $\forall u.(((inp \geq 5)_{inp}, (outp = u)_{outp}), (outp = u)_{outp})$.

The formulae of the calculus consist basically of pairs $t\ p$ meaning semantically that t satisfies p. In the proof process the calculus has to deal with terms containing free variables. In general only trivial assertions can be made of such terms, as free variables can assume any value. It is therefore necessary to "bind" free variables by assumptions restricting their possible values.

1.2 Definition:

(a) The formulae of the calculus consist of all $p \in$ Pred (to make the oracle accessible to the calculus) and of sequents like $y_1\ p_1, y_2\ p_2, \ldots, y_n\ p_n \to t\ p$, where the types of y_k, p_k and t, p resp. are equal. (The $y_k\ p_k$ are assumptions.) We think of the assumptions before the arrow as set and denote assumption sets by A, B, C.

(b) The semantics of formulae is given by a notion of validity $\models$ and is defined by, let $f = y_1\ p_1, \ldots, y_n\ p_n \to t\ p$ then

$\mu, \pi \models f \iff \mu(y_k) \in A[\![p_k]\!]\pi$ for all k implies $T[\![t]\!]\mu \in A[\![p]\!]\pi$.

Meaning, if all assumptions hold then the conclusion holds.

$\models f$ (f is valid) $\iff \mu, \pi \models f$ for all μ, π.

An example of a valid formula is (continuing the example after 1.1)

$y((inp \geq 5)_{inp}, (outp = u)_{outp}) \to y(5)\ (outp = u)_{outp}$.

Now we are ready to give the axioms and rules of the calculus.

1.3 Definition and remark:

The calculus has one rule for each syntactic construct of λ-terms:

(a) Application rule

$$\frac{A \rightarrow t\ (p,\ q) \quad B \rightarrow s\ p}{A \cup B \rightarrow t(s)\ q}$$

(b) Abstraction rule

$$\frac{A,\ y\ p \rightarrow t\ q}{A \rightarrow \lambda y.t\ (p,\ q)} \quad \text{if } y \text{ not in } A$$

(c) Fixpoint rule

$$\frac{A,\ y\ p \rightarrow t(y)\ p}{A \rightarrow fix(t)\ p}$$

if y not in A and not free in t

(d) If-then-else rule

$$\frac{A \rightarrow r\ (p)_u \quad B \rightarrow s\ (q_1)_v \quad C \rightarrow t\ (q_2)_v}{A \cup B \cup C \rightarrow \text{if } r \text{ then } s \text{ else } t \text{ fi } q}$$

with $q = ((p[tt/u] \wedge q_1) \vee (p[ff/u] \wedge q_2))_v$ and v not free in p .

The soundness of the above rules is an easy consequence of the definition of our semantics. As to the fixpoint rule it is imporant that the sets $A[\![p]\!]\pi$ are closed under lubs of ascending ω-chains, that is, they are admissable for Scott's induction. The notation p[tt/u] means substitution of u by tt.

The calculus has the following logical rules:

(e) And-rule

$$\frac{A \rightarrow t\ p \quad B \rightarrow t\ q}{A \cup B \rightarrow t\ p \wedge q}$$

(f) Universal quantification

$$\frac{A \rightarrow t\ p}{A \rightarrow t\ \forall u.p} \quad \text{if } u \text{ not free in } A$$

(g) Implication rule

$$\frac{A \rightarrow t\ p \quad impl(p,\ q)}{A \rightarrow t\ q}$$

The soundness of the rules should be clear, knowing that impl(p, q) stands for a first-order predicate implying $A[\![p]\!]\pi \subseteq A[\![q]\!]\pi$ for all π to be defined in 2.1.

The calculus has the following axioms:
(h) Operation symbol axioms
For simplicity we only regard a two-place operation symbol φ, then the formula

$$\varphi \quad \forall u_1, v_1.(q_1,\ \forall u_2, v_2.(q_2,\ q'))$$

with $q_k = ((v_k = tt \rightarrow inp_k = u_k) \wedge (v_k = ff \rightarrow false))_{inp_k}$

and $q' = ((v_1 = tt \wedge v_2 = tt \rightarrow outp = \varphi(u_1,\ u_2))$

$$\wedge (v_1 = ff \vee v_2 = ff \rightarrow false))_{outp}$$

is axiom. (Operation symbols are interpreted as strict functions.)

(i) Oracle axiom

p ∈ Pred is axiom iff p is a valid predicate.

(j) Assumption introduction

A → y p is axiom iff y p ∈ A .

2 COMPLETENESS AND EXPRESSIVENESS

In this section we show that the calculus is complete for closed terms of first-order type (that is types like $\tau_0 \to \ldots \to \tau_n$ where τ_k is a base type, terms of first order type can of course contain subterms of arbitrary type) provided our fixedly given interpretation is expressive (cf. [Ur 83, ClGeHa 82]). The method normally employed to prove Hoare Logics complete is adapted to our situation. As we have no clear distinction between pre- and postcondition, the notion of strongest assertion of a term with respect to a set of assumptions is defined instead of the usual notion of strongest post- or weakest precondition. We show that for the operation symbols we can derive a strongest assertion and that the rules of the calculus propagate strongest assertions nicely.

Now suppose the above proof method works for our calculus. We then know, if t is a closed term an p a strongest assertion of t , that the formula t p is derivable. This does not yet mean that the calculus is complete. We must proceed to show, if the formula t q for an arbitrary assertion q is valid, it is derivable. For this reason we prove that for p, q as above impl(p, q) ∈ Pred. (cf. def. 1.3 (g)) is valid, because then t q is derivable using the implication rule with t p and impl(p, q) as premises.

We continue now by introducing impl(p, q) for p, q ∈ Ass, which is one of the crucial definitions of this paper, as it gives a *first-order* characterization of a notion of implication for assertions of any type, whose semantics in general is a set of *higher-order* objects. In particular it allows to restrict oracle calls to first-order formulae.

To see which requirements are to be met by impl(p, q) let us once more look at t (of first order type) and its strongest assertion p . How is a strongest assertion of t characterized semantically? As it is the *strongest* assertion such that t p is valid, p is just satisfied by $T[\![t]\!]\mu$ (and all d ∈ D less than $T[\![t]\!]\mu$). Hence it holds, t q is valid iff $A[\![p]\!]\pi \subseteq A[\![q]\!]\pi$ for any π. So our notion of implication impl(p, q) for p, q of the same type has to meet two requirements: If p can occur as a strongest assertion of a term of first-order type and q is an arbitrary assertion of the same type it holds, if for all π $A[\![p]\!]\pi \subseteq A[\![p]\!]\pi$ then $\models$ impl(p, q). This ensures that the above completeness argument holds if t is of first-order type. The second requirement is of course if impl(p, q) is valid, then holds $A[\![p]\!]\pi \subseteq A[\![q]\!]\pi$, this ensures that the implication rule is sound.

2.1 Definition and remark:

(a) The notion of implication impl(p, q) is defined with the help of three mappings

$$\mathrm{impl}^{\tau}: \mathrm{Ass}^{\tau} \times \mathrm{Ass}^{\tau} \to \mathrm{Pred},\ \tau \text{ arbitrary type}$$

$$\mathrm{impl}_r^{\tau}: \mathrm{Ass}^{\tau} \times \mathrm{Ass}^{\tau} \to \mathrm{Pred},\ \tau \text{ not base type}$$

$$\mathrm{impl}_l^{\tau}: \mathrm{Ass}^{\tau} \times \{(q_1, q_2) \mid (q_1, q_2) \in \mathrm{Ass}^{\tau}\} \to \mathrm{Pred},\ \tau \text{ not base type.}$$

(impl_r^{τ} is defined inductively on the right argument, impl_l^{τ} on the left argument.) These mappings are defined by: Let τ be base type, w.l.o.g. $p = (p_1)_u$ $q = (q_1)_u$ then

$$\mathrm{impl}^{\tau}(p, q) = \forall u.p_1 \to q_1.$$

Let $\tau = \rho \to \sigma$ then impl^{τ} is defined using impl_r^{τ}

$$\mathrm{impl}^{\tau}(p, q) = \mathrm{impl}_r^{\tau}(p, q)\ .$$

impl_r^{τ} is now defined inductively on the syntax of q, using impl_l^{τ}

$$\mathrm{impl}_r^{\tau}(p, q_1 \wedge q_2) = \mathrm{impl}_r^{\tau}(p, q_1) \wedge \mathrm{impl}_r^{\tau}(p, q_2)$$

$$\mathrm{impl}_r^{\tau}(p, \forall u.q_1) = \forall u.\mathrm{impl}_r^{\tau}(p, q_1),\ u \text{ not free in } p$$

$$\mathrm{impl}_r^{\tau}(p, (q_1, q_2)) = \begin{cases} \forall v.\mathrm{impl}_l^{\tau}(p, ((q_1' \wedge u = v)_u, q_2)), \\ \text{if } \rho \text{ base type and } q_1 = (q_1')_u,\ v \text{ is a new variable} \\ \mathrm{impl}_l^{\tau}(p, (q_1, q_2)), \text{ otherwise .} \end{cases}$$

(The case distinction in the last clause of the definition is necessary to satisfy the first requirement of impl mentioned above.)

impl_l^{τ} is defined inductively on the first argument, let $q = (q_1, q_2)$

$$\mathrm{impl}_l^{\tau}(p_1 \wedge p_2, q) = \mathrm{impl}_l^{\tau}(p_1, q) \vee \mathrm{impl}_l^{\tau}(p_2, q)$$

$$\mathrm{impl}_l^{\tau}(\forall u.p_1, q) = \exists u.\mathrm{impl}_l^{\tau}(p_1, q),\ u \text{ not free in } q$$

$$\mathrm{impl}_l^{\tau}((p_1, p_2), (q_1, q_2)) = \mathrm{impl}^{\rho}(q_1, p_1) \wedge \mathrm{impl}^{\sigma}(p_2, q_2)\ .$$

For p, q of type τ, the predicate impl(p, q) abbreviates $\mathrm{impl}^{\tau}(p, q)$.

(b) A computation shows $\models$ impl(p, q) implies $A[\![p]\!]\pi \subseteq A[\![q]\!]\pi$, hence the second requirement above is met. The first requirement can be seen to be met only after an exact definition of strongest assertion is given, cf. 2.2.

Our aim now is to show that for a closed term of first order type t and its strongest assertion p, t p is derivable. This statement is not amenable to induction on the syntax of terms, instead a more general statement is proved:

> If $p_1,\ldots,p_n$ are strongest assertions, $A = y_1\ p_1,\ldots,y_n\ p_n$, the free variables of t are among $y_1,\ldots,y_n$, the y_k are pairwise distinct, and p is a strongest assertion of t with respect to A, then $A \rightarrow t\ p$ is derivable.

This can be proved inductively on t by showing that our rules propagate strongest assertions nicely. But to begin with, we have restrict attention to such assumptions for which for any π $\max(p_k, \pi)$, that is the maximum (greatest element) of $A[\![p_k]\!]\pi$, exists. Let the assignment of term variables $\mu(A, \pi)$ be given by $\mu(A, \pi)(y_k) = \max(p_k, \pi)$, that is $\mu(A,\pi)$ is the greatest assignment μ such that A is valid under μ and π. Then the semantics of p, the strongest assertion of t with respect to A, is given by $\max(p, \pi) = T[\![t]\!]\mu(A, \pi)$ for all π. One easily sees that $A \rightarrow t\ p$ is valid and if $A \rightarrow t\ q$ is valid $A[\![p]\!]\pi \subseteq A[\![q]\!]\pi$ holds.

Knowing what strongest assertions are semantically we will now single out additional properties strongest assertions must have to make our inductive argument work. A summing up of these considerations is given in 2.2. The induction proceeds of course by case distinction on the structure of t .

Let t = fix r and let p be a strongest assertion of t with respect to A . From the induction hypothesis we know, A, y p $\rightarrow$ t(y) q is derivable where y is a new variable and q is a strongest assertion of t(y) with respect to A, y p. One easily sees that q is also (semantically) a strongest assertion of t with respect to A, for p and q are semantically equal. Now the question is, does $\models$ impl(q, p) hold? If $\models$ impl(q, p) holds we could derive the desired result A $\rightarrow$ t p using the implication and fixpoint rule. Unfortunately $\models$ impl(p, q) does in general not hold if q, p are semantically equal. Hence we have to require the following property of our strongest assertions: if p, q are strongest assertions and $\max(p, \pi) \sqsubseteq \max(q, \pi)$ for all π then $\models$ impl(p, q) holds. One can say impl restricted to strongest assertions is extensional.

Another instructive case is t = r(s). By induction hypothesis we can derive, with p, q being appropriate strongest assertions, A $\rightarrow$ r p and A $\rightarrow$ s q. As by our definition of strongest assertion p determines the semantics of t uniquely it can in general not look like (q, q') which would be necessary to apply the application rule. Instead p will involve universal quantification. Hence in order to apply the application rule we must be able to extract the information (q, q') with q' a strongest assertion of t with respect to A from p using the implication rule. It must hold $\models \text{impl}(p, (q, q'))$, which allows to derive $A \to r\ (q, q')$ and then with the application rule $A \to t\ q'$.

These observations result in the following definition of strongest assertions:

2.2 Definition and remark:

A family of assertions $Sa = (Sa^{\tau} \mid \tau \text{ type})$ with $Sa^{\tau} \subseteq Ass^{\tau}$ is a family of strongest assertions iff for all $p \in Sa$ whose sets of bound and free variables are disjoint statements (1), (2), (3), (4), (5) hold. In addition statement (6) is to hold.

(1) For all π $\max(p, \pi)$ exists.

If p is of type $\tau \to \rho$, it holds:

(2) If (p_1, p_2) of type $\tau \to \rho$ is a subassertion of p then $p_1 \in Sa^{\tau}$, $p_2 \in Sa^{\rho}$.
(This makes sure that the family Sa is amenable to inductive arguments on the type.)

(3) For all π holds
$\{\max(p_1, \pi') \mid (p_1, p_2) \text{ subbassertion of type } \tau \to \rho \text{ of } p, \pi_{|\text{fr } p} = \pi'_{|\text{fr } p}\}$
$= \{\max(q, \pi') \mid q \in Sa^{\tau}, \pi' \text{ assignment of individual variables}\}$.
(In an assertion of type $\tau \to \rho$ we can find *any* argument assertion which is necessary for the above argument in case $t = r(s)$ to work.)

(4) If (p_1, p_2) of type $\tau \to \rho$ is a subassertion of p and π, π' are assignments with $\pi'_{|\text{fr } p} = \pi_{|\text{fr } p}$ then $\max(p, \pi)(\max(p_1, \pi')) = \max(p_2, \pi')$.
(The subassertions of p, (p_1, p_2), give optimal information about the behaviour of the semantics of p with respect to the argument $\max(p_1, \pi')$. In general only $\sqsubseteq$ holds. This point is also vital for the above case $t = r(s)$.)

(5) For all $q \in Sa^{\tau}$ there exists a $q' \in Sa^{\rho}$, such that *for all* π $\max(p, \pi)(\max(q, \pi)) = \max(q', \pi)$.
(This statement (together with (6)) makes sure that our family contains enough assertions such that for any term and set of assumptions containing only strongest assertions a strongest assertion exists.)

(6) For each closed term there exists $q \in Sa$ with $T[\![t]\!]\mu = \max(q, \pi)$ for all μ, π. (Same reason as (5).)

Additionally (1), (2), (3), (4) together make sure that impl restricted to Sa es extensional. It also holds that the first requirement to be met by impl is satisfied (cf. discussion before 2.1).

The existence of such a family Sa entails the completeness of the calculus. Now the question arises: For which interpretations does such a family exist? From [Ur 83, ClGeHa 82] we know that a Herbrand definable interpretation is expressive for programs involving normal (as opposed to higher type) recursion, if it is finite or strongly arithmetic, that is Peano Arithmetic can be defined in the interpretation using first-order formulae. (Note that the expressiveness of the interpretation is a prerequisite of usual completeness proofs of Hoare Logics.) We show that for finite and strongly arithmetic interpretations a family Sa of strongest assertions exists, so that in case of Herbrand definable interpretations our calculus has the same completeness properties as calculi dealing with normal recursion.

If the interpretation is finite one can readily construct a family of strongest assertions as we have the possibility of finite conjunctions in our assertion language. If the interpretation is strongly arithmetic, we employ the theory of effective domains (similar to [Jo 84]), and restrict attention to computable elements in any type. We then have an indexing of the computable elements of any type with individuals (corresponding to numbers) as our interpretation is strongly arithmetic. For the nature of this indexing see [Ka 79]. The operation apply yields a computable function on the indices. Hence it can be expressed by a first-order predicate. With the help of this predicate we can find universal assertions U^{τ} for any type τ, containing exactly one free variable u^{τ}, such that $\max(U^{\tau}, \pi[i/u^{\tau}])$ is the computable element of type τ having index i.

The family Sa is then defined by

$$p \in Sa \quad \text{iff} \quad \models \exists u^{\tau}.\mathrm{impl}(p, U^{\tau}) \wedge \mathrm{impl}(U^{\tau}, p).$$

Then Sa satisfies 2.2.

3 APPLICATION

We indicate how to apply the calculus to an imperative language involving higher type functions (cf. [dBMeKl 82]) and obtain a relative complete calculus for such languages. To simplify matters we disregard function declarations but assume instead that the right hand sides of assignments are typed λ-terms of base type involving additionally storage variables (which is equivalent to function declarations). The right hand sides are treated by our calculus extended with axioms for storage variables, $x\ (x = outp)_{outp}$, x storage variable. Storage variables are viewed semantically by assertions as normal individual variables. The connection with the imperative Hoare Calculus is made by the following rule which is a substitute for the assignment axiom:

$$\frac{t\ (p)_{outp}}{\{\forall outp.p \rightarrow q[outp/x]\}\ \ x := t\{q\}}$$, where p, q are predicates, outp not free in q .

This rule makes the calculus complete as, if $(p)_{outp}$ is a strongest assertion, it is just satisfied by one element and the above precondition is easily seen to be equivalent to the weakest precondition of x := t with respect to q . In case t is a simple expression (which are special λ-terms) and we have derived the strongest assertion of t in our calculus the above rule has the same effect as the well known assignment axiomof Hoare Logics.

By adding the above rule to our calculus we have solved the open problem stated in [Ol 84, DaJo 83, dBMeKl 82] of finding a satisfactory Hoare Calculus for a language with function prodedures of higher type. Another possibility to apply this calculus is to give proof calculi for programming languages based on their denotational semantics, which consists of λ-terms.

ACKNOWLEDGEMENTS

I should like to thank W. Damm and B. Josko for many helpful discussions and imparting their knowledge of higher type objects to me.

REFERENCES

Cl 79 E.M. Clarke, *Programming language constructs for which it is impossible to obtain good Hoare - like axioms*, JACM 26, 129-147, (1979)

ClGeHa 82 E.M. Clarke, S.M. German, J.Y. Halpern, *On effective axiomatizations of Hoare logics*, Proceedings 9th POPL, 309-321, (1982)

DaJo 83 W. Damm, B. Josko, *A sound and relatively* complete Hoare-Logic for a language with higher type procedures*, Acta Informatica 20, 59-101, (1983)

dBMeKl 82 J.W. deBakker, J.-J.Ch. Meyer, J.W. Klop, *Correctness of programs with function procedures*, Proceedings Logics of programs, LNCS 134, 94-112, (1982)

ErNaOg 82 G.W. Ernst, J.K. Navlakha, W.F. Ogden, *Verification of programs with procedure type parameters*, Acta Informatica 18, 149-169, (1982)

GeClHa 83 S.M. German, E.M. Clarke, J.Y. Halpern, *Reasoning about procedures as parameters*, Proceedings Logics of programs, LNCS 164, 206-220, (1983)

Go 85 A. Goerdt, *Ein Hoare Kalkül für getypte λ-Terme - Korrektheit, Vollständigkeit, Anwendungen*, RWTH Aachen

Jo 84 B. Josko, *On expressive interpretations of a Hoare-logic for Clarke's language* L_4, STACS 1984, LNCS 166, 73-84, (1984)

Ka 79 A. Kanda, *Effektive solutions of recursive domain equations*, Thesis Warwick, (1979)

La 83 H. Langmaack, *Aspects of programs with finite modes*, FCT 83, LNCS 158, 241-254, (1983)

Ol 84 E.-R. Olderog, *Correctness of programs with PASCAL - like procedures without global variables*, TCS 30, 49-90, (1984)

Si 81 M. Sintzoff, *Proof - oriented and applicative valuations in definitions of algorithms*, Proceedings of the 1981 Conference on Functional Programming Languages and Computer Architecture, 155-162, (1981)

Ur 83 P. Urzyczyn, *A necessary and sufficient condition in order that a Herbrand interpretation is expressive relative to recursive programs*, Information and Control 56, 212-219, (1983)

ON THE RELATIVE INCOMPLETENESS OF LOGICS FOR TOTAL CORRECTNESS

/Extended abstract/

Michał Grabowski
Institute of Informatics
University of Warsaw
PKiN p. 850
00-901 Warszawa POLAND

ABSTRACT: It is proved that it does not exist an acceptable /cf.4/ programming language having a sound and relatively complete /in the sense of Cook/ proof system for total correctness. This implies that the result of Clarke, German and Halpern concerning total correctness /cf.[4]/ cannot be essentially strengthened.

On the other hand, a chain $Q_0 \subseteq Q_1 \subseteq \ldots \subseteq Q_k \subseteq \ldots$ of classes of interpretations is defined such that for every $k \in \omega$ and every acceptable programming language with recursion there exists a proof system for total correctness, sound and complete over interpretations in Q_k. For the class $Q_\infty = \bigcup_k Q_k$ /the class of all infinite expressive interpretations/ such system does not exist.

1. INTRODUCTION

Relative completeness is one of the basic notions in the current trend of program verification theory. It has been proposed by Cook, cf.[5], for exhibiting the inherent complexity of proof systems for partial correctness. In order to make the statement of results concise, we investigate this notion in a general setting.

In this paper a <u>logic</u> will denote: The Hoare's logic HL_{PL} or the set TC_{PL} of total correctness formulas /where PL is an acceptable programming language/ or dynamic logic or first-order logic.

Let L be a logic, C be a certain class of interpretations.

The following definition is fundamental for this paper:

<u>def</u>. The logic L is relatively complete in the class C iff there exists a uniform enumeration procedure P with oracle answering questions on validity /in the interpretation involved/ of first-order formulas, such that for every interpretation I in C, P enumerates

/with oracle Th(I)/ all formulas of L valid in I.

It means that for every interpretation I in C, the set of all formulas of L valid in I is uniformly recursively enumerable in the elementary theory of I, Th(I).

Notice, that it is not required that P is sound in all interpretations. It must be sound at least over interpretations in C.

1.1 BACKGROUND

In this section we will review some history of the considered problem and we will quote the known results.

Research by Clarke, cf.[2],[3], has shown that if a programming language PL has certain natural features /e.g. procedures as parameters of procedure calls, recursion, static scope, global variables, internal procedures as parameters of procedure calls/, then its Hoare's Logic, HL_{PL}, is not relatively complete in the class of all expressive interpretations. /An interpretation I is expressive iff the weakest preconditions of programs are first-order definable in I./ This incompleteness result is established by observing that if the Hoare's Logic of a programming language PL is relatively complete in the class of expressive interpretations then the halting problem for PL must be decidable for finite interpretations. Clarke, German and Halpern, cf.[4], proved that for a wide class of programming languages, called acceptable, this last condition is equivalent to the relative completeness of HL_{PL} in the class of expressive and Herbrand-definable interpretations. Moreover, the procedure defined in [4] is a decision procedure. Acceptability of the programming language ensures that every program in PL can be effectively translated into, for example, Friedman's scheme, cf.[6], /PL is not too strong/ and PL is closed under reasonable programming constructs /PL is not too weak/. For instance, almost all Algol-like programming languages are acceptable. We do not quote the long definition and we refer the reader to the paper [4].

Working further on ideas of proof due to Clarke,German and Halpern Grabowski [7] has shown that the requirement of Herbrand-definability of interpretations can be dropped. Moreover, this modification yields a procedure which is sound in all interpretations /not only in expressive ones/. However, Grabowski's version of the theorem does not handle total correctness. So far, the following theorem, cf.[4], stands for the most significant result on total correctness regarded of relative completeness:

Th.1 /Clarke, German, Halpern, 1982/

For every acceptable programming language with recursion the logic TC_{PL} of total correctness for PL is relatively complete in the class of expressive and Herbrand-definable interpretations. Moreover, TC_{PL} is uniformly decidable over this class iff the halting problem for PL is decidable for finite interpretations.

Natural question arises: is it possible /as in the case of partial correctness/ to essentially strengthen the above theorem ? The full answer to this question would provide with better understanding of the nature of program properties proving.

1.2 RESULTS

Let us observe that for an enumeration procedure P with oracle to be a realistic analogue of an axiomatic proof system, it should be uniform, i.e. P should operate in the same way over interpretations with their elementary theories equal to one another. Moreover P should be totally sound, i.e. sound over all interpretations. It is very easy to observe that there does not exist a uniform and totally sound procedure P for total correctness which is complete over expressive interpretations.

Assume that such procedure P exists. Hence, we could prove using P that the program π = "x:=0; while y $\neq$ x do x:=x+1 od" halts in the standard model $\underline{\omega} = \langle \omega; 0, +1, +, \cdot, = \rangle$ /by expressiveness of $\underline{\omega}$ /. Let $\mathfrak{A}$ be a nonstandard model of $Th(\underline{\omega})$. Procedure P is uniform and totally sound, hence π halts in $\mathfrak{A}$ - contrary to the assumption that $\mathfrak{A}$ is nonstandard.

Hence, we could search for a uniform procedure which is complete over expressive interpretations and sound merely over expressive interpretations. Unfortunately, this weaker version has a negative solution also and we are able to prove the following:

Th.2 For every acceptable programming language PL the logic TC_{PL} of total correctness for PL is not relatively complete in the class of expressive interpretations.

Thus, the assumption on Herbrand-definability /in theorem 1/ is essential.

Remark

Let PL be an acceptable programming language, L_1 be the first-order logic. Let for a program P in PL, $A_P(x,y)$ be the input-output relation of the program P. Then, co-$TC_{PL} \overset{df}{=} \{\neg(\forall x)(\varphi(x) \rightarrow (\exists y)(A_P(x,y) \& \& \psi(y))) \mid P \in PL \text{ and } \varphi, \psi \in L_1\}$, i.e. the set of negations of total correctness assertions. It can be proved that co-TC_{PL} is relatively complete in the class of expressive interpretations iff PL has a decidable halting problem for finite interpretations. □

It remains to look for classes of interpretations, different from the class of Herbrand-definable ones, for which total correctness is relatively complete.

def. An interpretation I is weakly arithmetic iff there exist first-order formulas $\mathcal{N}(x)$, $\mathcal{E}(x,y)$, $\mathcal{S}(x,y)$, $\mathcal{Z}(x)$, $\mathcal{Add}(x,y,z)$, $\mathcal{Mult}(x,y,z)$ /with respectively n,2n,2n,n,3n and 3n free variables for some n/ such that $\mathcal{E}$ defines an equivalence relation on I^n and formulas $\mathcal{E}$, $\mathcal{S}$, $\mathcal{Z}$, $\mathcal{Add}$, $\mathcal{Mult}$ define on the set $\{x \mid I \models \mathcal{N}(x)\}$ the model M such that the quotient model $M/\mathcal{E}$ is isomorphic to the standard model $\underline{\omega} = \langle \omega; 0, +1, +, \cdot, = \rangle$.

Let k be a natural number.

def. An interpretation I is in the class Q_k iff I is expressive and there are first-order formulas $\mathcal{N}, \ldots, \mathcal{Mult}$ with at most k quantifiers such that $\mathcal{N}, \ldots, \mathcal{Mult}$ make I weakly arithmetic.

Th.3

For every acceptable programming language PL with recursion and for every $k \in \omega$, the logic TC_{PL} of total correctness for PL is relatively complete in the class Q_k. The logic TC_{PL} is not relatively complete in the class $Q_\infty = \bigcup_k Q_k$.

Proof is deferred to the final paper.

The classes Q_k are less natural than the class of Herbrand-definable and expressive interpretations. However, the theorems 2 and 3 enable to gain insight into the Harel's arithmetical completeness /cf.[9]/. Namely, the set of natural numbers stands for the primitive notion in arithmetical /in sense of Harel/ interpretations. By exploitanation of the theorem 2 proof method it is possible to show that the assumption of Harel's theorem on arithmetical completeness: "the set of natural numbers is primitive" cannot be relaxed to the following one: "the set of natural numbers is first-order definable".

The results related to the arithmetical completeness are not fully presented here and they are deferred to the final papers.

2. RELATIVE INCOMPLETENESS OF TOTAL CORRECTNESS

In this section the proof of theorem 2 is outlined.

In the sequel we will assume that we are working over the fixed type /or signature/ $\Sigma = \{0, S, +, \cdot, =\}$: one constant 0, one unary function symbol S, two binary function symbols +,· and the equality sign =.

Let PL be an acceptable programming language.

<u>def</u>. An interpretation I is said to be algorithmically nontrivial /for PL/ iff there exists a program $\pi \in PL$ such that for every $n \in \omega$, π reaches at least n distinct valuations in a certain computation of π.

Let WP be the programming language of while-programs, $\mathbb{E}$ be the class of expressive /for WP/ interpretations. $\underline{\omega} \stackrel{df}{=} \langle \omega; 0, +1, +, \cdot, = \rangle$.

<u>Lemma 1</u>

If the logic TC_{WP} of total correctness for WP is relatively complete in the class $\mathbb{E}$ then there exist first-order formulas $\varphi, \mathcal{N}, \mathcal{O}, \mathcal{Z}, \mathcal{E}, \mathcal{A}dd, \mathcal{M}ult$ such that $\underline{\omega} \models \varphi$ and for every expressive interpretation I, if $I \models \varphi$ and I is algorithmically nontrivial for WP then the formulas $\mathcal{N}, \ldots, \mathcal{M}ult$ make I weakly arithmetic.

<u>Outline of proof</u>

Assume that TC_{WP} is relatively complete in $\mathbb{E}$. The logic HL_{WP} is relatively complete in $\mathbb{E}$ /Cook's theorem/, hence by Harel's completeness theorem, cf.[9], the dynamic logic for WP, DL_{WP}, is relatively complete in $\mathbb{E}$.

There exists a uniform procedure A with oracle answering questions on validity /in the interpretation involved/ of first-order formulas such that for every expressive and algorithmically nontrivial interpretation I, the procedure A /with oracle Th(I)/ outputs the formulas $\mathcal{N}, \ldots, \mathcal{M}ult$, which make I weakly arithmetic. The procedure A acts as follows:

1. Guess a program π in WP;

2. Treating π as a program which can access an unbounded number of valuations, create /as in the theorem of DeMillo, Lipton, Snyder cf.[10]/ dynamic formulas in DL_{WP} modelling arithmetical notions;

3. Making use of relative completeness of DL_{WP} check that the resulting formulas /from 2/ satisfy axioms of arithmetical successor;

4. Again, making use of relative completeness of DL_{WP} find the first-order formulas $\mathcal{N},\ldots,\mathcal{M}ult$ equivalent to the constructed dynamic formulas.

Hence, with oracle $Th(\underline{\omega})$, procedure A outputs formulas $\mathcal{N},\ldots,\mathcal{M}ult$ which make $\underline{\omega}$ weakly arithmetic. Agregate all queries to the oracle in this computation of A to the single formula φ. Since A is uniform it acts in the same way over all algorithmically nontrivial and expressive interpretations I modelling φ /$I\models\varphi$/. The formulas $\varphi,\mathcal{N},\ldots,\mathcal{M}ult$ satisfy the thesis of lemma 1, since A is sound. □

Th.2

For every acceptable programming language PL, the logic TC_{PL} of total correctness for PL is not relatively complete in the class of all expressive interpretations.

Outline of proof

Proof is elementary. The method of constructing models by Skolemization is used.

Let φ be a formula such that $\underline{\omega}=\langle\omega;0,+1,+,\cdot,=\rangle\models\varphi$. We shall prove that for every formulas $\mathcal{N},\ldots,\mathcal{M}ult$ there exists a model $\mathfrak{A}$ such that:

/1/ $\mathfrak{A}\models\varphi$,

/2/ $\mathfrak{A}$ is expressive and algorithmically nontrivial,

/3/ the formulas $\mathcal{N},\ldots,\mathcal{M}ult$ do not make $\mathfrak{A}$ weakly arithmetic.

Thus, the relative completeness of TC_{WP} would lead to a contradiction, by lemma 1.

Let ArP be the set of Peano axioms for arithmetic.

Let $\mathcal{N}(x)$, $\mathcal{Z}(x)$, $\mathcal{S}(x,y)$, $\mathcal{E}(x,y)$, $\mathcal{A}dd(x,y,z)$, $\mathcal{M}ult(x,y,z)$ be the formulas with respectively $\bar{n},\bar{n},2\bar{n},2\bar{n},3\bar{n}$ and $3\bar{n}$ free variables, for some $\bar{n}$. Let $\mathcal{L}ess(x,y)$ be the formula: $(\exists z)(\mathcal{N}(z)\ \&\ \mathcal{A}dd(x,z,y))$.

If the formulas $\mathcal{N},\ldots,\mathcal{M}ult$ do not make $\underline{\omega}$ weakly arithmetic then the propositions /1/,/2/,/3/ hold, for $\mathfrak{A}=\underline{\omega}$. Hence, suppose the converse: the formulas $\mathcal{N},\ldots,\mathcal{M}ult$ make $\underline{\omega}$ weakly arithmetic.

Let $\mathfrak{z}=(\mathfrak{z}_1,\ldots,\mathfrak{z}_{\bar{n}})$ be a vector of new constants. Let $\alpha_0,\alpha_1,\ldots$ be the formulas defined as follows:

α_0: $(\exists z)(\mathcal{Z}(z)\ \&\ \mathcal{L}ess(z,\mathfrak{z}))$

α_1: $(\exists z,x)(\mathcal{Z}(z)\ \&\ \mathcal{S}(z,x)\ \&\ \mathcal{L}ess(x,\mathfrak{z}))$

.

.

.

.
.
.

$\alpha_n : (\exists z,x)(\exists y_1,\dots,y_{n-1})\ \mathcal{Z}(z) \,\&\, \mathcal{S}(z,y_1) \,\&\, \mathcal{S}(y_1,y_2) \,\&\, \dots \,\&\, \mathcal{S}(y_{n-1},x)$
$\&\ \mathcal{L}ess(x,\mathcal{c}))$

.
.
.

For every $n\in\omega$, the set $ArP\cup\{\varphi\}\cup\{\alpha_0,\dots,\alpha_n\}$ is consistent, since $\mathcal{N},\dots,\mathcal{M}ult$ make $\underline{\omega}$ weakly arithmetic. Hence, the set $Z = ArP \cup \{\varphi\}\cup\{\alpha_0,\alpha_1,\dots\}$ has a model.

Let $\mathfrak{T}$ be a model of Z, i.e. $\mathfrak{T}\models Z$. The formulas $\mathcal{N},\dots,\mathcal{M}ult$ do not make $\mathfrak{T}$ weakly arithmetic, since for every $n\in\omega$, $\mathfrak{T}\models\alpha_n$.

We shall find a submodel $\mathfrak{A}$ of the model $\mathfrak{T}$ such that $\mathfrak{A}$ satisfies the propositions /1/,/2/ and /3/.

Lemma 2

It exists a finite set $X\subseteq ArP$ of formulas such that for every interpretation I, if $I\models X$ then I is algorithmically nontrivial and if $I\models X$ and the set of standard elements of I, i.e. the set $\{0_I, S_I(0_I), S_I^2(0_I), \dots\}$, is first-order definable in I then I is expressive.

Proof of lemma 2 is omitted. The key idea is to gather into X all properties used in the technique of coding finite sequences in arithmetic.

Without loss of generality we may assume that X /that of lemma 2/ is a single formula.

The formulas $\varphi \,\&\, X$ and $\mathcal{L}ess(x,y)$ are equivalent in $\mathfrak{T}$ to the following ones in the quantifier normal forms:

/a/ $X\&\varphi \ .\underset{\mathfrak{T}}{\equiv}.\ (\forall x_1)(\exists y_1)\dots(\forall x_{n_0})(\exists y_{n_0})\alpha(x_1,y_1,\dots,x_{n_0},y_{n_0})$

/b/ $\mathcal{L}ess(x,y) .\underset{\mathfrak{T}}{\equiv}. (\forall x_1)(\exists y_1)\dots(\forall x_{k_0})(\exists y_{k_0})\beta(x,y,x_1,y_1,\dots,x_{k_0},y_{k_0})$

since there is a definable in $\mathfrak{T}$ pairing function. Then

/c/ $\neg(X\&\varphi) \ .\underset{\mathfrak{T}}{\equiv}.\ (\exists x_1)(\forall y_1)\dots(\exists x_{n_0})(\forall y_{n_0})\neg\alpha(x_1,y_1,\dots,x_{n_0},y_{n_0})$

/d/ $\neg\mathcal{L}ess(x,y) .\underset{\mathfrak{T}}{\equiv}. (\exists x_1)(\forall y_1)\dots(\exists x_{k_0})(\forall y_{k_0})\neg\beta(x,y,x_1,y_1,\dots,x_{k_0},y_{k_0})$.

The model $\mathfrak{T}$ is linearly ordered by the relation $x\leqslant y$ which is defined by the following formula: $(\exists z)(x+z=y)$. There are first-order definable in $\mathfrak{T}$ Skolem's functions for /a/,/b/,/c/,/d/. Hence, it exists an increasing function h(x) bounding from above all Skolem's functions involved and h(x) is first-order definable in $\mathfrak{T}$:

$$h(x) = \max\{y \mid y=x+1 \text{ or } (\exists a_1,b_1,\dots,a_{n_0},b_{n_0}\leq x)(\exists a'_1,b'_1,\dots,a'_{k_0},b'_{k_0}, a,b\leq x)(\ y = \text{value of a Skolem's function of } \dots a_i,b_i,\dots,\dots a'_j,b'_j\dots a,b\ )\}\ .$$

Let $\delta_{max} = \max\{\delta_1,\dots,\delta_{\bar{n}}\}$. /Recall that the vector of constants $\delta = (\delta_1,\dots,\delta_{\bar{n}})$ is interpreted in $\mathfrak{T}$ ./

Let $\mathfrak{A} \overset{df}{=} \{a\in\mathfrak{T} \mid a\leq h^i(\delta_{max})$ for some $i\in\omega\}$.

The model $\mathfrak{A}$ is closed under the Skolem's functions involved, hence

/I/ $\mathfrak{T}\models\varphi\&X$ iff $\mathfrak{A}\models\varphi\&X$

/II/ for all $a,b\in\mathfrak{A}$, $\mathfrak{A}\models \mathcal{L}ess(a,b)$ iff $\mathfrak{T}\models\mathcal{L}ess(a,b)$.

By the definition of $\mathfrak{A}$,

/III/ $\delta_i\in\mathfrak{A}$ for $i=1,\dots,\bar{n}$.

Thus we have proved that $\mathfrak{A}\models\varphi$ and $\mathfrak{A}\models X$ and $\mathfrak{A}$ is algorithmically nontrivial /by lemma 2/ and the formulas $\mathcal{N},\dots,\mathcal{M}ult$ do not make $\mathfrak{A}$ weakly arithmetic /by /II/ and /III//. Since $\mathfrak{A}\models X$, it remains to be proved that the set of standard elements of $\mathfrak{A}$, i.e. the set $\{0_{\mathfrak{A}},S_{\mathfrak{A}}(0_{\mathfrak{A}}),\dots\}$, is first-order definable in $\mathfrak{A}$.

The restrictions to $\mathfrak{A}$ of Skolem's functions for /a/,/b/,/c/,/d/ are definable in $\mathfrak{A}$, hence the relation $h(x)=y$ is definable in $\mathfrak{A}$. The ternary relation $h^z(x)=y$ - the z-th iteration of h applied to x is equal to y - is definable in $\mathfrak{T}$, since $\mathfrak{T}$ is a model for ArP. Hence, the relation $h^z(x)=y$ is definable in $\mathfrak{A}$, since $\mathfrak{A}$ is an initial segment of $\mathfrak{T}$ and the relation $h(x)=y$ is definable in $\mathfrak{A}$. Thus, we can define:

/*/ v is a standard element of $\mathfrak{A}$ iff $\mathfrak{A}\models(\forall x)(\exists y)(h^v(x)=y)$.

Intuitively, the condition /*/ holds, since if v is nonstandard then by definition of $\mathfrak{A}$, $h^v(\delta_{max})$ "jumps" out of $\mathfrak{A}$; if v is standard then for every $b\in\mathfrak{A}$, $h^v(b)\in\mathfrak{A}$.

Thus, theorem 2 is proved, since every acceptable programming language incorporates the language WP. □

3. CONCLUSIONS

1. In spite of theorem 2, there exist formal or semiformal proof systems for total correctness. Some of these systems /cf. [1]/ are not of pure-logical character, i.e. they incorporate the standard model for Peano arithmetic or an external well-founded relation.

Another such systems /e.g. dynamic logic/ need the set of natural numbers as a primitive notion. Theorem 2 states that these disadvantages cannot be removed without adding new assumptions like Herbrand-definability or restrictions on the number of quantifiers in the formulas making the interpretation involved weakly arithmetic.

2. From now on, by a logic we mean logic in the sense of abstract model theory, cf. [11].

We could overcome the limitations caused by theorem 2 by strengthening the oracle logic, similarly as in the paper of Halpern [8]. We have shown that if oracle logic is compact then there does not exist a uniform, totally sound and complete over expressive interpretations proof system for total correctness. If oracle logic L is compact and it admits construction of L-elementary submodels by Skolemization then there does not exist a uniform proof system for total correctness, complete and sound over expressive interpretations We conjecture that there does not exist an oracle logic L, strictly weaker than the dynamic logic, and such that L provides a uniform, sound and complete over expressive interpretations, proof system for total correctness.

3. Clarke, German and Halpern have shown /cf. [4]/ that there are programming languages for which total correctness assertions are effectively axiomatizable in the class of expressive and Herbrand-definable interpretations while partial correctness assertions are not. We have given a further information on the relationship between partial and total correctness. Namely, if we pass to the larger class of all expressive interpretations, total correctness assertions become much more complex than partial correctness assertions. Under the assumption that the halting problem is decidable for finite interpretations, partial correctness assertions are effectively axiomatizable in the class of all expressive interpretations, cf. [7], while total correctness assertions are not.

R E F E R E N C E S

[1] Apt, K.R., Ten years of Hoare Logics, TOPLAS 3/4/, 431-483, 1981

[2] Clarke, E.M., Programming language constructs for which it is impossible to obtain good Hoare axiom systems, JACM, 26, 1, January 1979

[3] Clarke, E.M., The characterization problem for Hoare Logics, manuscript

[4] Clarke E.M., German S.M., Halpern J.Y., Effective axiomatizations of Hoare Logics, JACM 30, 612-636, 1983

[5] Cook S.,Soundness and completeness of an axiomatic system for program verification,SIAM J. on Comp.,7,70-90,1978

[6] Friedman H.,Algorithmic procedures, generalized Turing algorithms and elementary recursion theory, Gandy and Yates eds.,Logic Colloquium 69

[7] Grabowski M.,On relative completeness of programming logics, Proc. 11th ACM Symp. POPL,258-261,1984

[8] Halpern J.Y.,A good Hoare axiom system for an Algol-like language, Proc. 11th ACM Symp. on POPL,262-271,1984

[9] Harel D.,Logics of programs: axiomatics and descriptive power, report, MIT/LCS/TR-200, 1978

[10] Lipton R.J.,A necessary and sufficient conditions for the existance of Hoare Logics, 18th IEEE Symp.FOCS,pp.1-6,1977

[11] Makowski J.A., Model theoretical issues in theoretical compute r Science, Logic Colloquium 1982

FROM SYNCHRONIZATION TREE LOGIC TO ACCEPTANCE MODEL LOGIC

S. Graf and J. Sifakis
IMAG - LGI
BP 68
38402 St. Martin d'Hères Cedex
France

1. INTRODUCTION

In the various calculi of communicating systems (CCS, SCCS, TCSP,...) the language used for the description of programs is a term language T with a given congruence relation $\approx$. Operators of the term language correspond to program constructors and the relation $\approx$ defines a concept of equivalence which is supposed to be satisfactory for the comparison of programs.

A requirement for a logic with set of formulas F, to be an adequate tool for the specification and proof of such programs is,

$$\forall t_1, t_2 \in T \ (t_1 \approx t_2 \ \text{ iff } \ \forall f \in F \ (t_1 \models f \ \text{ iff } \ t_2 \models f)),$$

i.e. the congruence $\approx$ and the equivalence relation on programs induced by the logic, agree. Consequences of this requirement are,

- formulas represent unions of congruence classes (congruent terms satisfy the same formulas),
- the logic is sufficiently powerful to distinguish non congruent terms (for each congruence class there exists a formula of the logic representing it).

In a previous paper [GS2] we have defined a logic, called Synchronization Tree Logic (STL) for the specification and proof of programs, described in a simple language. Terms of this language are obtained from a constant **Nil** by using a set **A** of unary operators, a binary operator **+** and **recursion**. This term language is at the base of many calculi for communicating systems, where A represents a set of **action** names, + the **non deterministic choice** and Nil the system performing no action. Its terms can be modelled by trees labelled on A - **synchronization trees** - following the terminology of [Mi].

The logic STL has been defined so as to satisfy the given adequacy requirement for programs described in this language compared by using the strong congruence relation of [Mi]. Its language of formulas contains the term language used for the description of programs (terms are formulas of STL). It can be obtained from the constants **Nil**, **T** by using **logical connectives**, consistent extensions of the operators **a∈A**, **+** and **fixpoint operators**. Its semantics is defined by associating with a formula a set of terms (synchronization trees) representing unions of congruence classes of the strong congruence relation. In this paper we consider a version of STL without recursion and negation.

The aim of this paper is the presentation of a logic called Acceptance Model Logic (AML) whose language of formulas contains a subset of TCSP [BHR], [Ol] and we study its relationship with STL. The subset of TCSP considered is the term language generated from the constants **Chaos** and **Stop** by using unary **action** operators $a \in A$ and the binary **internal** and **external non deterministic choice** operators.

The language of formulas of AML is the same as the language of the formulas of the restricted version of STL. Its semantics is defined by associating with any formula an **acceptance model**. Acceptance models are close variants of the readiness models of Olderog [Ol].

The paper is organized as follows:
In part 2, we present the logic STL. A sound deductive system is given, which is shown to be complete whenever A is finite.
In part 3, we present acceptance models and define semantics for AML.
The relationship between the two logics is studied in part 4 by defining a Galois connection between the classes of the underlying models. By using this connection, it is shown that any theorem of STL is a theorem of AML, and a sound deductive system is obtained for AML which is complete whenever A is finite.

2. THE SYNCHRONIZATION TREE LOGIC STL(A)

2.1 Preliminary results

Consider the term language T(A) built from a constant Nil by using a set A of unary operators and a binary operator +:

- $Nil \in T(A)$
- $at,\ t+t' \in T(A)$ if $a \in A$, $t,t' \in T(A)$.

The terms of T(A) represent finite trees labelled on A, called **synchronization trees**, as in [Mi]. With a synchronization tree can be associated a transition system where A is the set of action names, + represents non deterministic choice and Nil the system performing no action. It is defined as a set of transition relations $\rightarrow^{a} \subseteq T(A) \times T(A)$ for $a \in A$ which are the least relations such that,

- $at \rightarrow^{a} t \quad \forall a \in A\ \forall t \in T(A)$
- $t_1 \rightarrow^{a} t$ implies $t_1+t_2 \rightarrow^{a} t$ and $t_2+t_1 \rightarrow^{a} t \quad \forall a \in A\ \forall t,t_1,t_2 \in T(A)$.

The strong congruence relation $\approx$ defined in [Mi] is the least congruence relation induced by the following axioms [HM]:

T1. $t_1+(t_2+t_3) = (t_1+t_2)+t_3$
T2. $t_1+t_2 = t_2+t_1$
T3. $t+t = t$
T4. $t+Nil = t$.

Denote by CL(A) the set of the subsets of T(A) representing unions of congruence classes of $\approx$, i.e.

$$CL(A) = \{w \subseteq T(A) \mid t \in w \text{ and } t' \approx t \text{ implies } t' \in w\}$$

Denote by P(X) the set of <u>finite</u> subsets of a set X and extend the operators $a \in A$ and $+$ in the following manner:

$$aw \quad = \bigcup_{X \in P(w)} \{t \in T(A) \mid t \approx \textstyle\sum_{t_i \in X} at_i\},$$
$$w_1+w_2 \quad = \{t \in T(A) \mid t \approx t_1+t_2 \text{ where } t_1 \in w_1 \text{ and } t_2 \in w_2\}.$$

Consider the set **STM(A)**$\subseteq$CL(A) generated from $\emptyset$, T(A) and $\{t \mid t \approx Nil\}$ by using operators $a \in A$, $+$ and $\bigcup$, where all infinite unions are of the form $\bigcup \sum a_i w_i$ in which only a finite number of different w_i's occur.

The following properties of monotonicity are easy to prove.

<u>Properties 1</u> (monotonicity of a and +)
- $w_1 \subseteq w_2$ implies $aw_1 \subseteq aw_2$,
- $w_i \subseteq w_i'$, $i=1,2$ implies $w_1+w_2 \subseteq w_1'+w_2'$. □

2.2 <u>Syntax and semantics of STL</u>

For a given set A, represent by F(A) the language of formulas defined by,
- Nil, T, $\perp \in F(A)$,
- $bf \in F(A)$ if $b \subseteq A$ and $f \in F(A)$,
- $f+f'$, $f \vee f'$, $f \wedge f' \in F(A)$ if $f, f' \in F(A)$.

Notice, that $T(A) \subseteq F(A)$.

The semantics of F(A) is defined by giving a function $[\![\ ]\!]_1$: F(A) $\rightarrow$ STM(A) associating with any formula f a set of synchronization trees $[\![f]\!]_1$ representing a union of congruence classes of $\approx$.

<u>Definition of $[\![\ ]\!]_1$</u>: For $f, f' \in F(A)$, $b \subseteq A$,
- $[\![T]\!]_1 = T(A)$
- $[\![\perp]\!]_1 = \emptyset$
- $[\![Nil]\!]_1 = \{t \in T(A) \mid t \approx Nil\}$

- $[\![bf]\!]_1 = \bigcup_{b'\in P(b)-\emptyset} \sum_{a\in b} a[\![f]\!]_1$
- $[\![f+f']\!]_1 = [\![f]\!]_1 + [\![f']\!]_1$
- $[\![f \vee f']\!]_1 = [\![f]\!]_1 \cup [\![f']\!]_1$
- $[\![f \wedge f']\!]_1 = [\![f]\!]_1 \cap [\![f']\!]_1$

Notations:

- We write $\models_{STL} f$ for $[\![f]\!]_1 = T(A)$,
- We write $\models_{STL} f \supset f'$ for $[\![f]\!]_1 \subseteq [\![f']\!]_1$ and $\models_{STL} f \equiv f'$ for $[\![f]\!]_1 = [\![f']\!]_1$,
- If no confusion is possible, we write simply $\models$ instead of $\models_{STL}$.
- The following operators have progressively increasing priority: $\vee$, $\wedge$, $+$, $b \subseteq A$.
- For $a \subseteq A$ we write af instead of $\{a\}f$.

Property 2

For $t, t' \in F(A)$, $t \approx t'$ iff $[\![t]\!]_1 = [\![t']\!]_1$. □

The table of next page gives an equational deductive system AX_{STL} for STL(A). Its soundness has been proved in [GS2].

The axioms D1 to D5 are distributivity axioms. The axioms ST1 to ST3 express strictness properties and the axiom DE is a decomposition property. The following theorems can be proved for AX_{STL}.

A more complete version of STL(A) with fixpoint operators and classes of finite and infinite synchronization trees as models has been studied in [GS2].

Proposition 1

Th1. $AT+T \equiv T$

Th2. $f+f'+T \equiv (f+T) \wedge (f'+T)$

Th3. $(b_1 \cup b_2)f+T \equiv b_1 f+T \vee b_2 f+T$

Th4. $b(f \vee f')+T \equiv bf+T \vee bf'+T$

Th5. $b_1 f \supset b_2 f$ if $b_1 \subseteq b_2$. □

Remarks :

1. Notice that the elements of 2^A represent some kind of "weakest precondition" operators, as $b\bot \equiv \bot$ and $b(f_1 \wedge f_2) \equiv bf_1 \wedge bf_2$ for $b \subseteq A$. These operators do not distribute over $\vee$. However, due to D3 $b(f_1 \vee f_2)$ has an interesting decomposition in terms of bf_1 and bf_2 where the non deterministic construct + plays an important role.
2. By using the axioms for distributive lattice, axioms of distributivity and NC, a formula can be transformed into an equivalent one without occurrences of conjunction. In fact, conjunction can be expressed in terms of + and disjunction, as shows the following example. For $a,b,c \in A$ we have,

   $(\{a,b\}T + cNil) \wedge (\{a,c\}Nil + \{a,d\}T) \equiv$

Table 1 : AX_{STL}, a deductive system for STL(A)

Axioms

DL. axioms for distributive lattice

T1. $f_1+(f_2+f_3) \equiv (f_1+f_2)+f_3$

T2. $f_1+f_2 \equiv f_2+f_1$

T3. $f+f \equiv f$ where $f=\sum f_i$ with f_i of the form bf_i', T or Nil

T4. $f+Nil \equiv f$

D1. $f_1+(f_2 \vee f_3) \equiv (f_1+f_2)\vee(f_1+f_3)$

D2. $(b_1 \cup b_2)f \equiv b_1 f \vee b_2 f \vee b_1 f+b_2 f$

D3. $b(f_1 \vee f_2) \equiv bf_1 \vee bf_2 \vee bf_1+bf_2$

D4. $b_1 f_1 \wedge b_2 f_2 \equiv (b_1 \cap b_2)(f_1 \wedge f_2)$

D5. $(\sum_I f_i)\wedge(\sum_K g_k) \equiv [\sum_I (f_i \wedge \bigvee_K g_k)]+[\sum_K (g_k \wedge \bigvee_I f_i)]$ where the f_i's and g_k's are of the form bf, T or Nil

NC. $Nil \wedge bf \equiv \bot$

ST1. $\emptyset f \equiv \bot$

ST2. $b\bot \equiv \bot$

ST3. $f+\bot \equiv \bot$

DE. $Nil \vee AT \equiv T$

Rules

R1. $\dfrac{\vdash f,\ \vdash f \supset g}{\vdash g}$

R2. $\dfrac{\vdash f \supset g}{\vdash bf \supset bg}$

R3. $\dfrac{\vdash f \supset g,\ \vdash f' \supset g'}{\vdash f+f' \supset g+g'}$

$[\{a,b\}T \wedge (\{a,c\}Nil \vee \{a,d\}T)] + [cNil \wedge (\{a,c\}Nil \vee \{a,d\}T)] +$
$[\{a,c\}Nil \wedge (\{a,b\}T \vee cNil)] + [\{a,d\}T \wedge (\{a,b\}T \vee cNil)] \equiv$
$(aNil \vee aT) + cNil + (aNil \vee cNil) + aT \equiv$
$aT + cNil + (aNil \vee cNil) \equiv aT + cNil.$

3. Notice, that due to DE, the equivalence of formulas depends on the set A. The following are theorems when $A=\{a\}$.
$Nil \vee aT \equiv T$ which implies by R2
$a(Nil \vee aT) \equiv aT$ which by D3 is equivalent to
$aNil \vee aaT \vee aNil+aaT \equiv aT$. This implies,
$(aNil \vee aaT \vee aNil+aaT) + (aNil+aaNil) \equiv aT + (aNil+aaNil)$, equivalent to
$aaT + aNil + aaNil \equiv aT + aNil + aaNil.$

Proposition 2
For any formula $f \in F(A)$ there exists $f' \in F(A)$ without occurrences of conjunction such that $\vdash f \equiv f'$.
Proof:
Using axioms D1 and DL, one can transform any formula of F(A) into a disjunction of conjunctions of formulas of the form $\sum f_i$, where f_i of the form bf_i' ,T or Nil. By D5, D2 and D4 conjuntions can be pushed into a lower level as shown in the example of the remark 2. By repeating this transformation and application of NC, conjunction can finally be eliminated. □

Proposition 3
If A is finite, for any formula $f \in F(A)$ there exists f', $\vdash f \equiv f'$ such that either $\vdash f' = \bot$ or f' is a disjunction of formulas where neither $\bot$ nor logical connectives occur.
Proof :
Let f be a formula without occurrences of conjunction. By using ST1 to ST3, $\bot \wedge f = \bot$ and $\bot \vee f = f$ we get a formula f' such that $f' = \bot$ or f' has no occurrence of the constant $\bot$. By using D1 to D3, we can transform f' into a disjunction of formulas without occurrences of logical connectives. □

Proposition 4
If A is finite, then the deductive system AX_{STL} is sound and complete for STL(A).
Sketchy proof of completeness :
In [GS2] a normal form has been defined for formulas of F(A). By application of proposition 3 and axiom DE, a formula f is put into normal form $f' = \vee f_i$ where in the f_i's neither the constant $\bot$ not logical connectives occur.
To prove completeness, it is sufficient to prove that for any f_1, f_2 $\models f_1 \equiv f_2$ implies $\vdash f_1 \equiv f_2$.
By putting f_1, f_2 into normal form $f_i' = \vee_{k \in I_i} f_{ik}$ for i=1, 2 we have $\vdash f_i \equiv f_i'$.
The result is obtained by proving that for those formulas, $\models f_{1i} \equiv f_{2k}$ implies,
$\forall i \in I_1\ \exists k \in I_2\ \vdash f_{1i} \equiv f_{2k}$ by the axioms T1 to T4 and
$\forall k \in I_2\ \exists i \in I_1\ \vdash f_{1i} \equiv f_{2k}$ by the axioms T1 to T4. □

3. THE ACCEPTANCE MODEL LOGIC AML(A)

3.1 Preliminary results

An **acceptance model** on a set of action names A is a subset m of $A^*\times P(A)$ such that

$\forall s\in A^*\ \forall a\in A\ (\ \exists X\in P(A)\ (sa,X)\in m$ iff $\exists Y\in P(A)\ a\in Y$ and $(s,Y)\in m\ )$.

Notation : For $s\in A^*$ denote by m[s] the set $m[s] = \{X \mid (s,X)\in m\}$.
For m, m_1, m_2 acceptance models, ϵ the empty string of A^*, we define operators $a\in A$ and +:

$$am = \begin{cases} \emptyset & \text{if } m=\emptyset \\ \{(\epsilon,\{a\})\} \cup \{(as,X) \mid (s,X)\in m\} & \text{otherwise} \end{cases}$$

$$m_1+m_2 = \begin{cases} \emptyset & \text{if } m_1=\emptyset \text{ or } m_2=\emptyset \\ \{(\epsilon,X_1\cup X_2) \mid X_i\in m_i[\epsilon] \text{ for } i=1,2\} \cup \{(s,X) \mid (s,X)\in m_1\cup m_2,\ s\neq\epsilon\} & \text{otherwise.} \end{cases}$$

Notice that the union of acceptance models is an acceptance model, too. The following properties of monotonicity of the operators a and + are easy to prove.

Properties 3

- $m_1\subseteq m_2$ implies $am_1\subseteq am_2$,
- $m_i\subseteq m_i'$, i=1,2 implies $m_1+m_2\subseteq m_1'+m_2'$. □

Acceptance models are a very close variant of readiness models defined in [O1]. We consider them as systems where A is a set of action names, + and $\cup$ represent external and internal non deterministic choice, $\{(\epsilon,\emptyset)\}$ the system performing no action and $A^*\times P(A)$ the completely undefined system. To this purpose, we define transition relations $\rightarrow^a$ for $a\in A$ by

$m \rightarrow^a m_a$ where $m_a = \{(s,X) \mid (as,X)\in m\}$.

The following properties are easy to verify.

Properties 4

For acceptance models m, m_i and m_i' and $a\in A$, we have the following properties:

- $(\{(\epsilon,\emptyset)\})_a = \emptyset_a = \emptyset$ and $(A^*\times P(A))_a = A^*\times P(A)$,
- $am \rightarrow^a m$, i.e. $(am)_a = m$ and $(am)_b = \emptyset\ \forall b\neq a$,
- $(m_1+m_2)_a = (m_1\cup m_2)_a = (m_1)_a\cup(m_2)_a$
- $m_1 \rightarrow^a m_1'$ and $m_2 \rightarrow^a m_2'$ implies $m_1+m_2 \rightarrow^a m_1'\cup m_2'$ and $m_2+m_1 \rightarrow^a m_1'\cup m_2'$,
- $$m = \begin{cases} m' = \bigcup_{X\in m[\epsilon]} \Sigma_{a\in X}\, am_a & \text{if } \emptyset\notin m[\epsilon] \\ m' \cup \{(\epsilon,\emptyset)\} & \text{otherwise.} \end{cases}$$

Now, we define the subset AM(A) of acceptance models which will be considered in the sequel. AM(A) is defined as the least subset of $2^{A^*\times P(A)}$ such that,

- $\emptyset \in AM(A)$
- $Stop = \{(\epsilon,\emptyset)\} \in AM(A)$,
- $Chaos = A^*\times P(A) \in AM(A)$,
- $am \in AM(A)$ if $m \in AM(A)$
- $m_1+m_2 \in AM(A)$ if $m_1,m_2 \in AM(A)$,
- $\bigcup m_i \in AM(A)$ if $m_i \in AM(A)$ and only a finite number of the $(\bigcup m_i)_a$'s are different.

We order AM(A) by set inclusion ($\subseteq$). The lub operation is $\cup$; we denote by $\sqcap$ the glb operation, i.e.

$$m_1 \sqcap m_2 = \bigcup\{m \in AM(A) \mid m \subseteq m_i \text{ for } i=1,2\}.$$

Notice that in general $m_1 \sqcap m_2 \neq m_1 \cap m_2$.

<u>Proposition 5</u>

$\forall m \in AM(A)\ \forall a \in A\ \ m_a \in AM(A)$.

<u>Proof</u> :

The proposition is a direct consequence of properties 4. □

<u>Proposition 6</u>

$\forall m_1,m_2 \in AM(A)\ \ m_1 \sqcap m_2 \in AM(A)$.

<u>Proof</u> :

By induction on the structure of $m_1 \in AM(A)$.

- It is obvious that for $m_1=\emptyset$, $m_1=Stop$ or $m_1=Chaos$, $m_1 \sqcap m_2 \in AM(A)$.
  From the fact that $\{(\epsilon,\emptyset)\} \in AM(A)$ we have:
  $m_1 \sqcap m_2 \in AM(A)$ iff $(m_1-\{(\epsilon,\emptyset)\}) \sqcap (m_2-\{(\epsilon,\emptyset)\}) \in AM(A)$.
- Thus, it is sufficient to consider only m_i (for i=1,2) of the form
  (1) $m_i = \bigcup_{X \in m_i[\epsilon]} \Sigma_{a \in X}\, a(m_i)_a$, where only a finite number of $(m_i)_a$'s are different
  Suppose that $\forall a \in A\ \forall m'\ (m_1)_a \sqcap m' \in AM(A)$.

  For models of the form am it is easy to prove that,

$$\forall m,m' \quad a_1 m \sqcap a_2 m' = \begin{cases} a_1(m \sqcap m') & \text{if } a_1=a_2 \\ \emptyset & \text{otherwise.} \end{cases}$$

  From this we deduce for m_1,m_2 of form (1)

$$m_1 \sqcap m_2 = \bigcup_{X \in m_1[\epsilon] \cap m_2[\epsilon]} \Sigma_{a \in X}\, a(\,(m_1)_a \sqcap (m_2)_a\,).$$

  By induction hypothesis $\forall a \in A\ \ (m_1)_a \sqcap (m_2)_a \in AM(A)$ and obviously only a finite number of the $(m_1)_a \sqcap (m_2)_a$'s are different. □

3.2 Syntax and semantics of AML(A)

The language of formulas of AML(A) is F(A). Its semantics is defined by a function $[\![\ ]\!]_2: F(A) \to AM(A)$, associating with a formula f an acceptance model $[\![f]\!]_2 \in AM(A)$.

Definition of $[\![\ ]\!]_2$: For $f,f' \in F(A)$, $b \subseteq A$,

- $[\![T]\!]_2$ = Chaos,
- $[\![\bot]\!]_2 = \emptyset$,
- $[\![Nil]\!]_2$ = Stop,
- $[\![bf]\!]_2 = \bigcup_{b' \in P(b)-\emptyset} \sum_{a \in b'} a[\![f]\!]_2$,
- $[\![f+f']\!]_2 = [\![f]\!]_2 + [\![f']\!]_2$,
- $[\![f \vee f']\!]_2 = [\![f]\!]_2 \cup [\![f']\!]_2$,
- $[\![f \wedge f']\!]_2 = [\![f]\!]_2 \cap [\![f']\!]_2$.

We adopt analogous notations and conventions as in 2.2.

Notice that the subset of F(A) generated from T and Nil by using operators $a \in A$, $\vee$ and $+$, can be considered as the subset of TCSP interpreted in terms of readiness models [OI] which is generated from Chaos and Stop by using the operators $a\to$, or and $\square$. In fact, the differences between acceptance models and readiness models have, in the case of finitary formulas, no influence on the results obtained.

4. CONNECTION BETWEEN STM(A) AND AM(A) - THE INDUCED RELATIONSHIP ON THE LOGICS

In this section we present the main results of the paper. We introduce two functions φ:STM(A)→AM(A) and ψ:AM(A)→STM(A) which define a Galois connection between these two classes of models. By using this connection , we obtain from AX_{STL} a deductive system for AML(A) which is complete in the case where A is finite.

Definition of φ : STM(A) → AM(A) :

$\varphi(w) = \{\varphi'(t) \mid t \in w\}$ where φ' is defined by,

- $\varphi'(Nil)$ = Stop,
- $\varphi'(at) = a\varphi'(t)$ for $t \in T(A)$,
- $\varphi'(t+t') = \varphi'(t)+\varphi'(t')$ for $t,t' \in T(A)$.

Properties 5

a) $\varphi(w) = \varphi'(t)$ for $w=\{t' \mid t' \approx t\}$,

b) $\varphi(w \cup w') = \varphi(w) \cup \varphi(w')$ for $w,w' \in STM(A)$,

c) $\varphi(aw) = a\varphi(w)$ for $a \in A$ and $w \in STM(A)$,

d) $\varphi(w+w') = \varphi(w) + \varphi(w')$ for $w,w' \in STM(A)$,

e) $w \leq w'$ implies $\varphi(w) \leq \varphi(w')$ for $w,w' \in STM(A)$,

f) $\varphi(\emptyset) = \emptyset$ and $\varphi(T(A)) = Chaos$,

g) $\varphi(w) \in AM(A)$ for $w \in STM(A)$.

Proof :

a) is a consequence of the fact that T1 to T4 are valid for AM(A).

b) is a direct consequence of the definition of φ.

c) and d) are consequences of the definition of φ' and b).

e) is a consequence of b).

f) is a consequence of the definition of φ, the fact that $\forall s \in A^* \ \forall X \in P(A)$
(1) $\exists t,t' \in STM(A)\ t \to^s t'$ and $t' = \sum_{a \in X} aT$ and the fact that (1) implies $(s,X) \in \varphi'(t) \leq \varphi(T(A))$.

Thus, it remains to prove g) in the case where w is an infinite union. In this case w is of the form $w = \bigcup_{i \in I} \sum_{k \in K_i} a_{ik} f_{ik}$ where only a finite number of the f_{ik}'s are different.
From the properties b) to d) we obtain $\varphi(w) = \bigcup_{i \in I} \sum_{k \in K_i} a_{ik} \varphi(f_{ik})$ where only a finite number of the $\varphi(f_{ik})$'s are different because φ is a function. □

Definition of ψ : AM(A) → STM(A) :

- $\psi(\emptyset) = \emptyset$,
- $\psi(Stop) = \{t \mid t \approx Nil\}$,
- $\psi(Chaos) = T(A)$,
- For $m \neq \emptyset$, $m \neq Stop$ and $m \neq Chaos$,

$$\psi(m) = \begin{cases} w = \bigcup_{X \in m[\epsilon]} \sum_{a \in X} a\psi(m_a) & \text{if } \emptyset \notin m[\epsilon], \\ w \cup \{t \mid t \approx Nil\} & \text{otherwise.} \end{cases}$$

Properties 6 :

a) $\psi(am) = a\psi(m)$ for $a \in A$ and $m \in AM(A)$.

b) $m \leq m'$ implies $\psi(m) \leq \psi(m')$ for $m,m' \in AM(A)$.

c) $\psi(m) \in STM(A)$ for $m \in AM(A)$.

Proof :

a) and c) are obvious from the definition of ψ.

The proof of b) is done by structural induction.

- For m=Chaos or $m=\emptyset$ property b) is trivially true.
  For m=Stop we have $m \leq m'$ implies $\{t \mid t \approx Nil\} \leq \psi(m')$ by the definition of ψ.
  We also have $\{t \mid t \approx Nil\} \in \psi(m)$ iff $Stop \in m$, so it is enough to consider models m such that $Stop \notin m$.
- Let $m = \bigcup_{X \in m[\epsilon]} \sum_{a \in X} am_a$ such that $\forall m'\ m_a \leq m'$ implies $\psi(m_a) \leq \psi(m')$.
  From $m \leq m'$ we deduce $m[\epsilon] \leq m'[\epsilon]$ and $\forall a \in A\ m_a \leq m'_a$. Thus, we obtain

$$\begin{aligned} \psi(m) &= \bigcup_{X \in m[\epsilon]} \sum_{a \in X} a\psi(m_a) \\ &\leq \bigcup_{X \in m[\epsilon]} \sum_{a \in X} a\psi(m'_a) && \text{by the induction hypothesis and properties 3} \\ &\leq \bigcup_{X \in m'[\epsilon]} \sum_{a \in X} a\psi(m'_a) && \text{because } m[\epsilon] \leq m'[\epsilon] \\ &= \psi(m'). \end{aligned}$$
□

Proposition 7

$\forall m \in AM(A)\ \varphi\psi(m) = m$ and $\forall w \in STM(A)\ w \le \psi\varphi(w)$, i.e. (φ,ψ) is a Galois connection as φ and ψ are order preserving.

Proof :

a) First we prove $\forall m \in AM(A)\ \varphi\psi(m) = m$ by induction on the structure of m.

- For $m=\emptyset$ or m=Stop or m=Chaos this is obvious.
- Let $m = \bigcup_{X \in m[\epsilon]} \sum_{a \in X} am_a$ such that $\forall a \in A\ \varphi\psi(m_a) = m_a$. We obtain,

$$\begin{aligned}\varphi\psi(m) &= \varphi(\textstyle\bigcup_{X \in m[\epsilon]} \sum_{a \in X} a\psi(m_a)) && \text{by the definition of } \psi \\ &= \textstyle\bigcup_{X \in m[\epsilon]} \sum_{a \in X} a\ \varphi\psi(m_a) && \text{by properties 5} \\ &= m && \text{by induction hypothesis.}\end{aligned}$$

In the case where $m = \bigcup_{X \in m[\epsilon]} \sum_{a \in X} am_a \cup \{(\epsilon,\emptyset)\}$ a similar proof can be done.

b) We prove $\forall w \in STL(A)\ w \le \psi\varphi(w)$ by induction on the structure of w.

- For $w=\emptyset$, $w=\{t \mid t \approx Nil\}$ and $w=T(A)$ this is obvious.

  Furthermore, we have $\{t \mid t \approx Nil\} \in \psi\varphi(w)$ iff $\{t \mid t \approx Nil\} \in w$. Thus, it is sufficient to consider w such that $\{t \mid t \approx Nil\} \notin w$. Any such w can be put into the form

  (1) $w = \bigcup \sum a_i w_i$.

- Let $w \in STM(A)$ of the form (1) such that $\forall w_i\ \ w_i \le \psi\varphi(w_i)$.

  We prove first that $\sum_{i \in I} a_i w_i \le \psi\varphi(\sum_{i \in I} a_i w_i)$. We obtain,

$$\begin{aligned}\psi\varphi(\textstyle\sum_{i \in I} a_i w_i) &= \psi(\textstyle\sum_{i \in I} a_i \varphi(w_i)) && \text{by properties 5} \\ &= \textstyle\sum_{i \in I} a_i \psi\varphi(w_i) && \text{by the definition of } \psi \\ &\ge \textstyle\sum a_i w_i && \text{by induction hypothesis and properties 3.}\end{aligned}$$

To complete the proof, it is sufficient to show that for any w of the form $w=\bigcup w_i$ $w \le \psi\varphi(w)$. From the monotonicity of φ and ψ, we deduce,

$$\bigcup w_i \le \bigcup \psi\varphi(w_i) \le \psi\varphi(\bigcup w_i). \quad \Box$$

The following properties are well-known facts about Galois connections.

Properties 7

- φ is surjective and ψ is one-to-one,
- $\psi(m \sqcap m') = \psi(m) \cap \psi(m')$,
- $m \sqcap m' = \varphi(\psi(m) \cap \psi(m')$. $\Box$

The following propositions concern the relationship of STL and AML induced by this connection.

Proposition 8

$$\varphi [\![f]\!]_1 \le [\![f]\!]_2.$$

Proof :

The proof is done by induction on the structure of the formulas.

- For $f=\bot$ or $f=T$ or $f=Nil$ this is obvious.
- Let f,f' such that $\varphi [\![f]\!]_1 \subseteq [\![f]\!]_2$ and $\varphi [\![f']\!]_1 \subseteq [\![f']\!]_2$. We obtain,

$$\varphi [\![af]\!]_1 = a\varphi [\![f]\!]_1 \subseteq a[\![f]\!]_2 = [\![af]\!]_2,$$
$$\varphi [\![f+f']\!]_1 = \varphi ([\![f]\!]_1+[\![f']\!]_1) = \varphi ([\![f]\!]_1)+ \varphi ([\![f']\!]_1) \subseteq [\![f]\!]_2+[\![f']\!]_2 = [\![f+f']\!]_2,$$
$$\varphi [\![f\vee f']\!]_1 = \varphi ([\![f]\!]_1\cup[\![f']\!]_1) = \varphi ([\![f]\!]_1)\cup \varphi ([\![f']\!]_1) \subseteq [\![f]\!]_2\cup[\![f']\!]_2 = [\![f\vee f']\!]_2,$$
$$\varphi [\![f\wedge f']\!]_1 = \varphi ([\![f]\!]_1\cap[\![f']\!]_1) = \varphi ([\![f]\!]_1)\cap \varphi ([\![f']\!]_1) \subseteq [\![f]\!]_2\cap[\![f']\!]_2 = [\![f\wedge f']\!]_2. \quad \square$$

<u>Proposition 9</u>
Any valid formula of STL(A) is a valid formula of AML(A).
<u>Proof</u> :
Let f be a valid formula of STL(A), i.e. $[\![f]\!]_1= T(A)$. Thus, $\varphi [\![f]\!]_1$=Chaos. By proposition 8 we get $[\![f]\!]_2$=Chaos, i.e. f is a valid formula of AML(A). □

A consequence of this proposition is, that any sound deductive system for STL(A) (and in particular AX_{STL}) is sound for AML(A).

<u>Proposition 10</u>
The deductive system AX_{AML} obtained by adding to AX_{STL} the following axioms, is sound for AML(A).

AM1. $bf+bf' \equiv b(f\vee f')$,
AM2. $bf+g \vee bf'+g' \equiv b(f\vee f')+g \vee b(f\vee f')+g'$,
AM3. $bf+T \equiv bT+T$,
AM4. $f+T \vee \sum_{i\in I}b_if_i \equiv f+T \vee \sum_{i\in I}b_iT$.

<u>Proof</u> :
AM1. If $b=\emptyset$ this is trivially true. Otherwise,

$$\begin{aligned}[\![bf+bf']\!]_2 &= [\{(\epsilon,b')|b'\subseteq b, b'\neq\emptyset\} \cup \{(as,X)|(s,X)\in f \text{ and } a\in b\}] + \\ &\quad [\{(\epsilon,b')|b'\subseteq b, b'\neq\emptyset\} \cup \{(as,X)|(s,X)\in f' \text{ and } a\in b\}] \\ &= \{(\epsilon,b')|b'\subseteq b, b'\neq\emptyset\} \cup \{(as,X)|(s,X)\in f\cup f' \text{ and } a\in b\} \\ &= [\![b(f\cup f')]\!]_2.\end{aligned}$$

The proof of AM2 can be done in a similar manner.
AM3. If $b=\emptyset$ this is trivially true. Otherwise,

$$\begin{aligned}[\![bf+T]\!]_2 &= [\{(\epsilon,b')|b'\subseteq b, b'\neq\emptyset\} \cup \{(as,X)|(s,X)\in f \text{ and } a\in b\}] + A^*\times P(A) \\ &= \{(\epsilon,b'\cup b'')|b'\subseteq b, b'\neq\emptyset, b''\subseteq A\} \cup \{(as,X)|(s,X)\in A^*\times P(A), a\in A\} \\ &= [\![bT+T]\!]_2.\end{aligned}$$

The proof of AM4 can be done in a similar manner. □

The following theorems can be deduced from AX_{AML}.

<u>Proposition 11</u>

Th1. $bf \vee bf' \equiv b(f \vee f')$,
Th2. $\sum_{i\in I}b_if_i \vee \sum_{i\in J}b_if_i' \equiv \sum_{i\in I\cap J}b_i(f_i\cup f_i') + (\sum_{i\in I-J}b_if_i \vee \sum_{i\in J-I}b_if_i')$,

Th3. $\sum_{i\in I} b_i f_i + \sum_{i\in J} b_i f_i' \equiv \sum_{i\in I\cap J} b_i(f_i \cup f_i') + \sum_{i\in I-J} b_i f_i + \sum_{i\in J-I} b_i f_i'$. □

We give hereafter a transformation which has been used to prove the completeness of AX_{AML} for AML(A) in the case where A is finite.

Proposition 12

In the case where A is finite, any formula f of AML(A) can be transformed into an equivalent formula of the form

(1) $\perp$ or T or Nil

or (2) $\bigcup \sum a_{ik} f_{ik}$ where $a_{ik}=a_{jn}$ implies $f_{ik}=f_{jn}$ and all f_{ik} are in one of the forms (1) to (3)

or (3) $\bigcup \sum a_{ik} T$ [+T] where [+T] means that the term +T is optional.

Proof :

The proof is done by induction on the structure of formulas.

- The constants $\perp$, T and Nil are of form (1).
- By the proposition 9 we can, as in STL(A), transform any formula f into an equivalent formula f' such that $f'=\perp$ or f' is of the form $f'=\bigvee\sum f_{ik}$ where the f_{ik}'s are of the form af, T or Nil and without occurences of conjunction and of the constant $\perp$.
- If one of the sums of this disjunction is of the form f'+T, then we get by exhaustive application of AM3 and AM4 a formula of the form (3).

  Otherwise, we can suppose that f' is of the form $f'=\bigcup \sum b_{ik} f_{ik}$ where all the f_{ik}'s are in one of the forms (1) to (3). By application of D2, we obtain a formula of the same form where all the b_{ik}'s are singletons. Finally, by exhaustive application of AM1, AM2 and Th1 (of proposition 11) a formula of the form (2) can be obtained. □

Proposition 13

Let f be a formula in one of the forms (1) to (3) given in proposition 12, and let A be finite. Then,

$$\psi([\![f]\!]_2) \subseteq [\![f]\!]_1.$$

Proof :

- For f of the form (1), this is certainly true.
- Let f be of the form (2), i.e. $f=\bigcup \sum a_{ik} f_{ik}$, such that $\forall i,k\ \psi([\![f_{ik}]\!]_2) \subseteq [\![f_{ik}]\!]_1$.

  From the fact that for all i,k such that $a_{ik}=a$ the f_{ik}'s are identical, we have $([\![f]\!]_2)_a=([\![f_{ik}]\!]_2)_a$ for all those i,k. Put $f_a= f_{ik}$. We get,

  (*) $\vdash \bigcup \sum a_{ik} f_{ik} \equiv \bigcup_{X\in[\![f]\!]_2[\epsilon]} \sum_{a\in X} af_a$ by the axioms T1 to T4. We deduce,

  $\psi([\![f]\!]_2) = \psi(\bigcup_{X\in[\![f]\!]_2[\epsilon]} \sum_{a\in X} af_a)$

  $= \bigcup_{X\in[\![f]\!]_2[\epsilon]} \sum_{a\in X} a\psi(f_a)$ by the definition of ψ

  $\subseteq \bigcup_{X\in[\![f]\!]_2[\epsilon]} \sum_{a\in X} a[\![f_a]\!]_1$ by induction hypothesis

  $= [\![\bigcup_{X\in[\![f]\!]_2[\epsilon]} \sum_{a\in X} af_a]\!]_1$

  $= [\![f]\!]_1$ by (*). □

Theorem 1

If A is finite, then AX_{AML} is sound and complete for AML(A).

Proof :

Soundness has been proved in proposition 10.

The proof of the completeness can be done as follows:

$\vDash_{AML} f$ iff $[\![f]\!]_2$ = Chaos. By proposition 12 we obtain,

$\exists f^*$ in one of the forms (1) to (3) such that $\vdash_{AML} f \equiv f^*$ and $[\![f^*]\!]_2$=Chaos.

This implies $\psi([\![f^*]\!]_2)$ = T(A). By proposition 13 we get $[\![f^*]\!]_1$ = T(A), which implies by the completeness of AX_{STL}, $\vdash_{STL} f^*$. From the fact that $AX_{STL} \subseteq AX_{AML}$, we get finally $\vdash_{AML} f$. □

5. DISCUSSION

This paper is a contribution to the solution of the following general problem, discussed also in [GS1], [GS2]: For a given term language with a congruence relation, used for the description of programs, find a logic whose formulas express program properties. This problem arises in particular when a logic is to be used for the specification and proof of programs in calculi for communicating systems.

The logics proposed provide a uniform frame to deal with both, programs and their properties. Programs are formulas of the logic, and the proof of the validity of an assertion $t \vDash f$ (t is a programm and f is a formula) is reduced to the proof of the validity of the formula $t \supset f$. Another interesting feature of these logics is, that they lend themselves to the definition of syntax directed proof methods, as their non logical operators are consistent extensions of the term languages integrated in them.

Finally, the comparison between STL and AML has shown that the semantics of the subset of TCSP considered, can be defined in terms of synchronization tree models. The extension of this comparison to the case where both logics have fixpoint operators is under study.

REFERENCES

[BHR] Brookes S.D., Hoare C.A.R., Roscoe A.W. "*A Theory of Communicating Sequential Processes*", JACM, Vol.31, N°3, 84

[GS1] Graf S., Sifakis J. "*A logic for the specification and proof of controllable processes of CCS*", Advanced Seminar "Logics and Models for Verification and

Specification of concurrent Systems", La Colle sur Loup, Octobre 84, (to appear in LNCS).

[GS2] Graf S., Sifakis J. "*A logic for the description of non deterministic programs and their properties*", RR511, IMAG-LGI, Grenoble, February 85.

[HM] Hennessy M., Milner R. "*On observing non determinism and concurrency*", Proc. of 7th ICALP, 80, LNCS 85.

[Mi] Milner R. "*A calculus for communicating systems*" LNCS 92.

[Ol] Olderog E.R. "*Specification oriented programming in TCSP*", Advanced Seminar 'logic and models for verification and specification of concurrent systems', La Colle sur Loup,84, To appear in LNCS.

A FASE Specification of FP[1]

Sam Kamin
Computer Science Dept.
Univ. of Illinois at Urbana-Champaign
Urbana, IL 61801
1304 W. Springfield

Abstract

The purpose of this paper is to describe the FASE system of executable specifications of data types via a specification of Backus's FP language. We illustrate the ability to execute specifications as well as our more recent efforts to incorporate formal proofs into the system.

1. Introduction

The purpose of this paper is to describe the FASE system of executable specifications of data types [1] via a specification of Backus's FP language [2]. We illustrate the ability to execute specifications as well as our more recent efforts to incorporate formal proofs into the system.

FASE stands for Final Algebra Specification and Execution. It is a data type specification system, based upon the notion of final algebras [3], which emphasizes the direct execution of specifications. As such, it is comparable to OBJ2 [4]. Our more recent development of the system is toward including formal proofs. As such, it is comparable to AFFIRM [5]. In contrast to these systems, we do not use algebraic (i.e. equational) specifications. However, in [3] we emphasized the inherent abstract-ness of the method of final algebras; we will see that the FP specification illustrates this point particularly well. In particular, the theory of FP as specified in FASE is exactly the theory of FP given by Backus, and this can be stated unequivocally on general grounds: no special pains have been taken in writing this specification aside from making certain that the *externally-observable* behavior of the operations is correct.

2. FP

FP, or "functional programming," is a programming language devised by John Backus to help solve some of our critical problems in software engineering. He first presented it in his famous Turing Award lecture [2]. An interesting property from the point of view of the current study is that FP does away with *variables*, developing instead an algebra in which functions are formed by applying one of a fixed set of operators ("functional forms") to built-in or user-defined functions. In other words, this is an algebra whose elements are functions, and whose operators are functionals.

Thus, FP divides the world into Objects, Functions, and functional forms. (It must be emphasized that we are treating FP, not FFP; the former is distinguished by its having no user-defined functional forms.) Here is a brief synopsis of the three categories:

---

[1] This work was supported in part by NSF under grant MCS-81-10087.

Objects — Primitive values, or lists of Objects.

Functions — Functions take Objects to Objects. Each function has exactly one argument (which of course may be a sequence). There are some primitive functions, such as arithmetic operations (e.g. + takes a sequence of length 2 and returns a number), and list operations. Other functions can be defined by applying functional forms to primitive or previously-defined functions.

Functional forms — These take Functions or sequences of Functions (or, in one case, Objects) to Functions. The most commonly-used is composition, denoted $\circ$, which takes two Functions as arguments. The "constant" functional form takes an Object x, and returns a function, denoted $\bar{x}$, such that $\bar{x} : y = x$ for any y (: denoting function application). Another important functional form, called "construction," takes a sequence of functions f, ..., g, and returns the function denoted [f,...,g], such that $[f,...,g] : x = \langle f : x, \ldots, g : x \rangle$.

As a simple example, the function to subtract one from its argument is:

$$\text{def } \mathbf{sub1} = - \circ [\mathbf{id}, \bar{1}].$$

The computation of sub1 applied to 4 proceeds as follows:

$$\mathbf{sub1} : 4 \rightarrow - \circ [\mathbf{id}, \bar{1}] : 4 \rightarrow - : ([\mathbf{id}, \bar{1}] : 4) \rightarrow - : \langle \mathbf{id} : 4, \bar{1} : 4 \rangle \rightarrow - : \langle 4,1 \rangle \rightarrow 3.$$

Many more examples appear in [2], as well as [6, 7, 8].

3. Final Algebra Specifications

FASE is a system in which data type specifications are given using the method of *final data type specification*[3], and are presented for immediate execution.

The principal idea underlying this method is that a data type is best characterized not by the operators which construct elements of the type, but by the operators which *distinguish between* elements of the type. For instance, the "set-ness" of sets is not due so much to the fact that they are constructed using operations like **addelt**: Elt × Set → Set, but to the fact that sets are distinguished from one another using the operator **iselt**: Elt × Set → Bool. In the terminology of final algebra specifications, **iselt** is called a "distinguishing function." The specifier always starts by asking the question: what are the distinguishing functions of this type?

The answer to this question leads to an immediate choice of a carrier for the algebra being specified. For example, if **iselt** is the only distinguishing function for Set, it follows that sets may be represented by functions from Elt to Bool. This choice is in some sense "most abstract" in that any other method of representing sets concretely (for example, by a list, a bit string, or a search tree) can be regarded as a representation of such functions.

For FP, the proper answer to the question "how are FP programs distinguished from one another" is: *application*. That is, FP program f is distinct from FP program g if there is some object o such that $f : o \neq g : o$[2]. From this observation, essentially all of what follows is inevitable. In particular, we see that the carrier of the abstract algebra of FP programs is the space of functions from Object to Object[3]. It follows that the specified algebra is exactly the algebra intended by Backus, as long as we make sure in our specification that all functions have the externally-observable behavior ascribed to them by Backus.

---

[2] Actually, the environment of user-defined functions is an implicit argument to both f and g, so we should say f is distinct from g if there is some set of definitions d and object o such that ... .

[3] Following up on the previous footnote, it is actually functions from Defs × Object to Object.

4. FASE Specification of FP

The specification appears as appendix 1. (Due to space limitations, we have included only the specifications of functions that are used in the examples in this paper.) Although the only important data types are Object and Function, the specification consists of five data types: Object, Sequence, Function, FunctionSeq, and Defs. The explanations for each data type follow.

4.1. Object and Sequence

Object and Sequence together recursively define Object. That is, in effect,

$$\begin{aligned} \text{Object} &= \text{Int} + \text{Symbol} + \text{Sequence} \\ \text{Sequence} &= \text{list of Object} \end{aligned}$$

An Object is characterized by its value as an Int or Symbol (the two types of atoms we have included) or Sequence. It is necessary to include explicitly operations to coerce Int's, Symbol's, and Sequence's into Object's, and vice-versa; coercions into Object are called intobj, etc., and those out of Object are called objint, etc. (It is not, however, the case that the ultimate user of FASE will have to be aware of these coercions; rather, they will be added by the program that parses user inputs, as is discussed below.) A Sequence is characterized by the values of its head, of the head of its tail, and so on, each taken as an Object. Aside from that, all definitions in Object are primitive operations as defined in [2]. Also, there are two equality predicates — eqObject and equalObject; this is because eqObject is automatically added by the system, and is a function from pairs of objects to the built-in type Bool; equalObject is an FP function, and is therefore a function from Object to Object.

4.2. Function and FunctionSeq

The data type Function has as elements all functions, and as operators all functional forms. In our formulation, the primitive operations have been included as nullary functions; the "functional forms" of [2] correspond to the non-nullary functions. As mentioned in an earlier footnote, the environment of user-defined functions must be included as an explicit argument to every function. Then, the use of a user-defined function must be explicitly indicated by writing "userfun(functionname)."

The rationale behind the type Function, as has already been explained, is that a function is characterized by its values on all objects, in all possible environments. That is why the distinguishing function in Function is **funapply**, which in turn implies that the carrier of Function is the set of functions from Defs × Object to Object. For example, **compose** takes two such functions, say f and g, and returns the function that applies g to its argument, then applies f to the result, using the same environment in both applications.

FunctionSeq is defined in order that the **construct** functional can take an indefinite number of arguments (all functions in FASE must take a fixed number of arguments).

4.3. Defs

The type Defs simply contains tables of user-defined functions; in practice, there will be one global element of type Defs which will be passed around to all functions. In the current system, there is no way to hide this totally from the user.

5. Using FASE

5.1. Signature files

The interaction of the user with these definitions is mediated by "signature files." In these, the user gives a syntax-directed translation scheme from some syntax for FP expressions (and objects, etc.), into the internal, function-application form. The signature files appear in appendix 2. We have followed the syntax of Berkeley FP [9], including precedences where appropriate. (The syntax for the built-in types Integer and Symbol are not shown.)

5.2. Interacting with FASE

Here is a brief session with FASE. Expressions in the user's syntax must be enclosed in exclamation marks. This decision was made to avoid having to introduce a new top-level for FASE, the integration of specifications into the existing programming environment having been one of our principal design goals.

```
-> (load '/mnta/1/kamin/fase2/franz/sys/fase2)
-> (entertype Defs.sig Defs.spec Function.sig Function.spec ... )
-> !Object: + : <2,3>!          ; the internal representation of this object is printed
(addobj NOBIND NOBIND NOBIND NOBIND (seqobj nil NOBIND NOBIND NOBIND ... ))
-> (load 'printobj.l)                    ; this will print Objects readably
[load printobj.l]
-> (pp printobj)                         ; note use of specified operations within LISP program
(def printobj
  (lambda (object)
    (cond ((iserrObject object) (print 'errObject) (terpri))
          ((isinteger object) (print (getint object)) (terpri))
          ((issymbol object) (print (getsym object)) (terpri))
          (t (print (getlist object)) (terpri)))))          ; calls getlist, not shown
-> (printobj !+ : <2,3>!)
5
-> (putq Env !Defs: emptydefs!)          ; putq is setq without printing the entire value
(adddef --)
; Need to define sub1 and eq0 before defining fac.
-> (putq Env !define sub1 = - @ [id,%1] in Env!)          ; @ = o , %1 = 1̄, as in Berkeley FP
(adddef --)
-> (printobj !sub1 : 4 { Env }!)
3
-> (putq Env !Defs: define eq0 = eq @ [id,%0] in Env!)
(adddef --)
-> (putq Env !Defs: define fac = eq0 -> %1; * @ [id,fac @ sub1] in Env!)
(adddef --)
-> (printobj !fac : 7 {Env}!)
5040
-> (putq Env ! define ninetyone = > @ [id,%100] -> - @ [id,%10] ;
                         ninetyone @ ninetyone @ + @ [id,%11] in Env!)
(adddef --)
-> (printobj !ninetyone : 60 {Env}!)
91
-> (exit)
Exited
```

6. Doing Proofs in FASE

We have recently begun to incorporate theorem-proving into our system. The types of things one wants to prove are properties of the specified data types (in this case, the "algebra of functional programs"[2]), and correctness of implementations of data types and of programs that use the data types. A related activity is program transformation, which might be regarded as the "dual" of program equivalence proofs.

6.1. TED

Our theorem-proving effort has centered around the tree-editor TED. With a resolution-based theorem prover[4] as the underlying inference mechanism, doing realistic-sized formal proofs such as arise in program verification becomes a problem of developing a large proof tree [5]. The TED philosophy is to give the user complete control over the construction of the tree, but to provide various methods by which a given node in the tree can be "certified." An assertion is considered proven when it is the top node of a tree all of whose nodes have been certified.

Some of the methods of certification currently available are:

Assertion: A leaf node in a proof tree may be certified by labelling it an AXIOM, SIMPlification, or DEFinition node. In each case, the node is assumed to contain a list of true formulas. The only difference among these three labels is in how the nodes are used by other certification methods, especially theorem-proving.

Theorem-proving:

A node containing formula P, whose children contain formulas $Q_1, \ldots, Q_n$, is certified if a theorem-prover can prove $Q_1 \& \cdots \& Q_n \supset P$. The list $Q_1, \cdots, Q_n$ generally omits formulas contained in DEF nodes, and may treat in a special way those contained in SIMP nodes, but includes all formulas in AXIOM or other ("lemma") nodes.

Definition expansion:

Suppose a formula "...f(a)..." is to be proved; its children in the tree include a DEF node containing the formula "$\forall$x. f(x)=e", and non-DEF nodes containing formulas $Q_1, \ldots, Q_n$. When the user indicates that the definition of f is to be expanded, the system sends the formula "$Q_1 \& \cdots \& Q_n \supset$ ...e[a/x]..." to the theorem-prover; if it is proved, the node containing "...f(a)..." is certified.

Other methods include a data type induction facility; given an induction hypothesis, it forms the base and induction cases, and attempts to prove each of them from the children of this node, certifying the node if successful.

6.2. The Algebra of FP

We now present a TED session in which two facts about FP are proven. The first is the fact that Backus writes as $[f,g] \circ h = [f \circ h, g \circ h]$, and the second is $[[f,g],h] \circ i = [[f \circ i, g \circ i], h \circ i]$. The user-defined syntax is not yet incorporated into TED, so all assertions are written out using the operators of the type. For simplicity, we have departed from the specification by using a binary "construct" instead of the construct that takes a function sequence argument.

```
ted version 0.1
```

---

[4] We have used primarily the theorem-provers developed here by Dave Plaisted's research group.

```
⊢ r fp.pf1
⊢ p*                         ; Tree has been previously created
/ : unproven
  (A (f g h)
    (== (compose (construct f g) h) (construct (compose f h) (compose g h))))

    /1 : DEF                     ; == is function equality
      (A (f g) (= (== f g) (A (d o) (= (funapply f d o) (funapply g d o)))))

    /2 : SIMP                    ; Only the first item in the nodes is printed here
      (A (d o) (= (funapply idfun d o) o))
⊢ 2p                             ; Here are all the simplifications
/2 : SIMP
  (A (d o) (= (funapply idfun d o) o))
  (A (f g d o)
    (= (funapply (compose f g) d o) (funapply f d (funapply g d o))))
  (A (f g d o)
    (= (funapply (construct f g) d o)
      (seq (funapply f d o) (funapply g d o))))
⊢ /c defn == : pv4               ; Use definition expansion for ==, then prover pv4
PROOF:
 49 CONTRADICTION    <- (186 160)
Time (sec):    CPU: 29.616      GC: 0.0      Total: 29.616

⊢ w                              ; save this tree
⊢ f fp.pf2                       ; and us it as the basis for the next one
File now : fp.pf2
⊢ w
⊢ e                              ; enter session (not shown) to edit node for second proof
⊢ p*
/ : unproven
  (A (f g h)
    (== (compose (construct (construct f g) h) i)
        (construct (construct (compose f i) (compose g i)) (compose h i))))

    /1 : DEF
      (A (f g) (= (== f g) (A (d o) (= (funapply f d o) (funapply g d o)))))

    /2 : SIMP
      (A (d o) (= (funapply idfun d o) o))

⊢ w
⊢ c defn == : pv4
Aborting defn                    ; proof taking too long, aborted by user
⊢ 3r fp.pf1                      ; create third child, with previous theorem as lemma
⊢ p
/3 : (c defn == : pv4 1 3)
  (A (f g h)
    (== (compose (construct f g) h) (construct (compose f h) (compose g h))))
        & &
; The best use we can make of this lemma is as a simplification.
⊢ s SIMP
⊢ e                              ; The == must be changed to = to be a simplification.
⊢ p
/3 : SIMP
```

```
    (A (f g h)
       (= (compose (construct f g) h) (construct (compose f h) (compose g h))))
         & &
|- /c defn == : pv4
PROOF:
 55 CONTRADICTION   <- (16 2 216 12)
Time (sec):    CPU: 39.4     GC: 0.0     Total: 39.4

|- w
|- q
Exited
```

Space limitations prevent us from discussing proofs of FP implementations, or the incorporation of program transformations into TED. Concerning the latter, we might just mention that a program transformation in the traditional sense we regard as simultaneously the construction of a new node containing a transformed program, and the certification of that node. Thus, in TED it is essentially just a process of adding a new certification method.

7. Conclusions

We have illustrated the two parts of our system — the direct execution of specifications, and the proof-editing tool TED. Some further comments on each are now in order.

An aspect of direct execution which is not illustrated by the FP specification is quantification, which is sometimes necessary in specifications. For example, the maximum of a set is most easily defined by

max (S) => (some x: Integer) isin(x,S) & ((forall y: Integer) isin(y,S) => y ≤ x)

FASE is capable of evaluating expressions containing max. Some details are in [10], and more will be contained in Stan Jefferson's PhD. thesis.

A serious shortcoming of FASE is the simplicity of the type system. In particular, we have no generic types or type expressions, whereby we could say "Object = Int + Symbol + list(Object)", without having to define it explicitly (since all definitions of union types in FASE look essentially the same).

The ability to do proofs in TED is limited by the weakness of the theorem-provers available to us (even though, as resolution-based refutation procedures go, they are excellent). On the other hand, TED itself is a major win. Theorems whose proof trees contain on the order of a hundred nodes — of which we have several — would be totally impractical to prove without TED.

The main work we want to do to improve our theorem-proving capability is to integrate the two parts of the system. For one example, theorems to be proved by TED should be expressed in the user's syntax. In the long run, we want to create a visual version of TED, which can run on workstations. It should also be programmable, so that users can program proof strategies, somewhat after the "tactics" of LCF, as well as program transformations.

8. Acknowledgements

It is a pleasure to acknowledge the help of several students who have worked on this project, and have contributed to this paper. Stan Jefferson wrote the evaluator of FASE. Myla Archer actually entered the FP specification, uncovering some bugs in the process, and wrote the signature file. TED is the work of Dave Hammerslag, and Dave Carr has contributed to the project in a variety of ways.

9. References

1. S. Kamin, S. Jefferson, and M. Archer, "The Role of Executable Specifications: The FASE System," *Proc. IEEE Symp. on Application and Assessment of Automated Tools for Software Development*, San Francisco (Nov. 1983).

2. John Backus, "Can Programming Be Liberated from the von Neumann Style? A Functional Style and Its Algebra of Programs," *CACM* **21**(8), pp. 613-641 (August, 1978).

3. S. Kamin, "Final Data Types and Their Specification," *ACM TOPLAS* **5**(1), pp. 97-123 (Jan. 1983).

4. K. Futatsugi, J. A. Goguen, Jean- Pierre Jouannaud, and J. Meseguer, *Principles of OBJ2*, Centre de Recherche en Informatique, University de Nancy, Nancy, France (1984).

5. S. L. Gerhart, D. R. Musser, D. H. Thompson, D. A. Baker, R. L. Bates, R. W. Erickson, R. L. London, D. G. Taylor, and D. S. Wile, *An Overview of AFFIRM: A Specification and Verification System*, USC Information Sciences Institute (Nov. 1979).

6. John Williams, "On the Development of the Algebra of Functional Programs," *TOPLAS* **4**(4), pp. 733-757 (October, 1982).

7. J. W. Backus, "The algebra of functional programs: Function-level reasoning, linear equations, and extended definitions," *LNCS 107: Formalization of Programming Concepts*, Springer-Verlag, New York, pp. 1-43 (1981).

8. R. B. Kieburtz and J. Shultis, "Transformation of FP Program Schemas," *Proc. Conf. on Functioanl Programming Languages and Computer Architecture*, Portsmouth, MA, pp. 41-48 (1981).

9. Scott Baden, "Berkeley FP User's Manual, Rev. 4.1," in *UNIX Programmer's Manual, 4.2bsd*, (July, 1983).

10. S. Kamin and S. Jefferson, *On λ-expressions That Define Finite Functions*, Univ. of Illinois (1984).

Appendix 1 - FP Specification Files

Function

```
funapply: Function Defs Object -> Object
idfun: -> Function
eqfun: -> Function
gtfun: -> Function
addfun: -> Function
subfun: -> Function
multfun: -> Function
nthfun: Int -> Function
constantfun: Object -> Function
compose: Function Function -> Function
funcond: Function Function Function -> Function
construct: FunctionSeq -> Function
userfun: Symbol -> Function

DISTINGUISHING SET funapply;

userfun(s) => [ <d,o> |-> funapply(getfunc(s,d),d,o) ];
idfun => [ <d,o> |-> o ];
eqfun => [ <d,o> |-> equalObject(o) ];
gtfun => [ <d,o> |-> gtobj(o) ];
addfun => [ <d,o> |-> addobj(o) ];
subfun => [ <d,o> |-> subobj(o) ];
multfun => [ <d,o> |-> multobj(o) ];
nthfun(n) => [ <d,o> |-> nthobj(n,o) ];
constantfun(o) => [ <d,oo> |-> o ];
compose (f, g) => [ <d,o> |-> funapply(f,d,funapply(g,d,o)) ];
funcond (p, f, g) =>
            [ <d,o> |-> if getsym(funapply(p,d,o)) = T
                then funapply(f,d,o) else funapply(g,d,o) ];
construct ( fs ) => [ <d,o> |-> applyseq(fs,d,o) ];
```

FunctionSeq

```
applyseq: FunctionSeq Defs Object -> Object
nullfuncseq: -> FunctionSeq
apndlfunc: Function FunctionSeq -> FunctionSeq

DISTINGUISHING SET applyseq;

nullfuncseq => [ <d,o> |-> phi ];
apndlfunc ( f, fs ) => [ <d,o> |->
            seqobj(apndlSeq( funapply(f,d,o),
                getseq(applyseq(fs,d,o)) )) ];
```

Object

```
intobj : Int -> Object
symobj : Symbol -> Object
seqobj : Sequence -> Object
getint : Object -> Int
getsym : Object -> Symbol
getseq : Object -> Sequence
eqObject : Object Object -> Bool
equalObject: Object -> Object
gtobj: Object -> Object
addobj: Object -> Object
subobj: Object -> Object
multobj: Object -> Object
hd: Object -> Object
tl: Object -> Object
phi: -> Object
nthobj: Int Object -> Object

DISTINGUISHING SET getint getsym getseq;

intobj (n) => [n, errSymbol, errSequence];
symobj (s) => if s = NIL then phi else [errInt, s, errSequence];
seqobj (s) => if s = nullSeq then phi else [errInt, errSymbol, s];
eqObject (v1,v2) => ( getint (v1) = getint (v2)
            & getsym (v1) = getsym (v2)
                & getseq (v1) = getseq (v2) );
equalObject (v) => if eqObject(hd(v),hd(tl(v)))
                then symobj(T) else symobj(F);
gtobj (v) => if getint(hd(v)) > getint(hd(tl(v)))
                then symobj(T) else symobj(F);
addobj(v) => intobj(getint(hd(v))+getint(hd(tl(v))));
subobj(v) => intobj(getint(hd(v))-getint(hd(tl(v))));
multobj(v) => intobj(getint(hd(v))*getint(hd(tl(v))));
nthobj(i,v) => if i=1 then hd(v) else nthobj(i-1,tl(v));
hd(v) => hdSeq(getseq(v));
tl(v) => tlSeq(getseq(v));
phi => [errInt, NIL, nullSeq];
```

```
Sequence

hdSeq: Sequence -> Object
tlSeq: Sequence -> Sequence
lengthSeq: Sequence -> Int
nullSeq: -> Sequence
apndlSeq: Object Sequence -> Sequence
eqSequence: Sequence Sequence -> Bool

DISTINGUISHING SET hdSeq tlSeq lengthSeq;

nullSeq => [errObject, nullSeq, 0];
apndlSeq(o,s) => [o,s,lengthSeq(s)+1];
```

```
Defs

getfunc: Symbol Defs -> Function
emptydefs: -> Defs
adddef: Symbol Function Defs -> Defs

DISTINGUISHING SET getfunc;

adddef (s,f,d) => [ <ss> ⊢> if s==ss then f else getfunc(ss,d) ];

emptydefs => [ <s> ⊢> errFunction ];
```

Appendix 2 - FP Signature File for Function

```
Function

AUXILIARY NONTERMINALS Function1 Function2 Function3 Function4

Function ::= Function1 ⊢> Function1
        | while Function Function ⊢> funwhile ( Function 1 , Function 2 )
        | bu Function Object ⊢> bufun ( Function , Object )

Function1 ::= Function2 ⊢> Function2
          | Function2 - > Function1 ; Function1
                ⊢> funcond ( Function2 , Function1 1 , Function1 2 )

Function2 ::= Function3 ⊢> Function3
        | Function2 @ Function3 ⊢> compose ( Function2 , Function3 )

Function3 ::= Function4 ⊢> Function4
          | & Function4 ⊢> applytoall ( Function4 )
          | / Function4 ⊢> insertright( Function4 )
          | % Object ⊢> constantfun ( Object )

Function4 ::= ( Function ) ⊢> Function
          | [ FunctionSeq ] ⊢> construct ( FunctionSeq )
          | id ⊢> idfun ()
          | eq ⊢> eqfun ()
          | > ⊢> gtfun ()
          | + ⊢> addfun ()
          | - ⊢> subfun ()
          | * ⊢> multfun ()
          | Int ⊢> nthfun ( Int )
          | Symbol ⊢> userfun ( Symbol )

Object ::= Function : Object ⊢> funapply( Function , emptydefs() , Object )
        | Function : Object { Defs } ⊢> funapply( Function , Defs , Object )
```

ON ASYMPTOTIC PROBABILITIES OF INDUCTIVE QUERIES AND THEIR DECISION PROBLEM

Phokion G. Kolaitis

Department of Mathematics, Occidental College, Los Angeles, California 90041
and
Department of Mathematics*, University of California, Los Angeles, California 90024

§1. Introduction and Summary of Results

In recent years several research articles have been devoted to the study of inductive queries on finite relational structures, including the papers by Aho and Ullman [1979], Chandra and Harel [1982], Harel and Kozen [1984]. The inductive queries are the ones expressible in the language obtained from first-order logic by adding the least fixed point operator for positive formulas. These queries are always computable in PTIME and can capture interesting properties, such as connectivity and acyclicity, which in general are not expressible in first-order logic.

At about the same time a different direction of research focused on the asymptotic probabilities of first-order properties on finite relational structures. Fagin [1976] established both a labeled and an unlabeled 0-1 law for first-order sentences on the class of all finite graphs. Compton [1980, 1984a] investigated asymptotic probabilities of first-order sentences on restricted classes of finite structures which arise naturally in combinatorics, such as equivalence relations, permutations, various classes of forests, and others. After this, in Compton [1984b], he showed that in many of these classes a 0-1 law holds for first-order queries if and only if a 0-1 law holds for queries expressible in monadic second order logic.

The recent paper by Blass, Gurevich and Kozen [1984] brings together the two areas of research mentioned above. It is shown there that both labeled and unlabeled 0-1 laws hold for the inductive queries on the class of all finite graphs. Moreover, the problem of deciding the asymptotic probability of an inductive query on the class of all finite graphs is EXPTIME complete. The proofs of these results depend on the fact that the first-order almost sure theory of finite graphs is ω-categorical, that is to say it has only one countable model up to isomorphism.

Our aim in this paper is to investigate inductive queries and their probabilities on certain classes of finite relational structures for which the first-order almost sure theory is not ω-categorical. More specifically, in §3 we show:

---

*Author's address for 1984-85.

<u>Theorem.</u> Let $\mathcal{FE}$ be the class of all finite equivalence relations.

<u>(i)</u> The inductive queries coincide with the first-order ones on $\mathcal{FE}$, that is to say if φ is an inductive query on $\mathcal{FE}$, then there is a first-order query ψ which is equivalent to φ on every finite equivalence relation. Consequently, the inductive queries on $\mathcal{FE}$ have both a labeled and an unlabeled 0-1 law.

<u>(ii)</u> The problem of deciding the asymptotic probability of an inductive query on $\mathcal{FE}$ is EXPTIME complete.

In addition, the same conclusions are true for the class $\mathcal{F}$ of finite oriented forests of height 1.

The main tool developed and used here is a theorem about the languages $L^k_{\infty\omega}$, $1 \leq k < \omega$, which allow for arbitrary disjunctions and conjunctions, but only for a fixed finite number of variables. This result is proved in §2 using an "infinitary" pebble game. The languages $L^k_{\infty\omega}$ are relevant to the study of inductive queries, because the stages of an inductive definition can be expressed by formulas having a fixed finite number of variables.

We also show in §4:

<u>Theorem.</u> Let $\mathcal{K}$ be the class of all finite graphs which are unions of cycles.

<u>(i)</u> The queries expressible in monadic second-order logic on $\mathcal{K}$ (and hence the first-order ones) have an unlabeled 0-1 law. However, the first-order queries on $\mathcal{K}$ do not have a labeled 0-1 law.

<u>(ii)</u> The query Q which says that "the largest cycle has an even number of elements" is inductive on $\mathcal{K}$ and has unlabeled probability equal to 1/2. Thus, the inductive queries on $\mathcal{K}$ do not have an unlabeled 0-1 law and moreover Q is not equivalent to any monadic second-order query on almost all members of $\mathcal{K}$.

Similar conclusions are true for the class $\mathcal{P}$ of permutations (viewed as binary relational structures) and the class $\mathcal{LF}$ of finite linear forests.

The different behavior of inductive queries between equivalence relations and unions of cycles is due mainly to the existence of "long" inductive definitions on cycles.

§2. <u>Inductive Queries and Languages with a Fixed Number of Variables</u>

<u>2.1.</u> Let $\sigma = (R_1, R_2, \ldots, R_\ell)$ be a vocabulary consisting of predicate symbols and let C be a class of relational structures on this vocabulary. The <u>inductive queries over C</u> are the ones expressible in the logic FO + LFP which is first-order logic augmented with the least fixed point operator. This operator allows for the formation of the least fixed point $\varphi^\infty(x_1, x_2, \ldots, x_n)$ of a first-order formula $\varphi(x_1, x_2, \ldots, x_n, S)$, in which S is a new n-ary predicate symbol having <u>only</u> positive occurrences. The least fixed point φ^∞ can be constructed "from

below" by defining first the stages φ^ξ, ξ an ordinal, of the formula φ, where

$$\varphi^\xi(x_1,\ldots,x_n) \Leftrightarrow \varphi(x_1,\ldots,x_n, \bigcup_{\lambda<\xi} \varphi^\lambda)$$

and verifying then that

$$\varphi^\infty = \bigcup_\xi \varphi^\xi$$

Of course over finite structures we have that $\varphi^\infty = \bigcup_{m<\omega} \varphi^m$, and actually if the universe of the structure has s elements, then $\varphi^\infty = \varphi^m$ for some $m \le s^n$.

If $\mathcal{G} = \langle A,R\rangle$ is an undirected graph, then $\mathcal{G}$ is connected if and only if $\mathcal{G} \models (\forall x)(\forall y)\varphi^\infty(x,y)$, where $\varphi(x,y,S)$ is the formula $R(x,y) \vee (\exists z)(R(x,z) \wedge S(z,y))$.

It is well known that if $\varphi(x_1,\ldots,x_n,S)$ is a positive formula in S having ℓ variables, then the stages φ^ξ of φ can be expressed by infinitary formulas having $k = n + \ell$ distinct free and bound variables. In particular, the finite stages φ^m, $m < \omega$, are equivalent to first-order formulas with k distinct variables. In the example above, where the least fixed point φ^∞ gives the transitive closure query, we have that each stage is expressible by formulas with 5 distinct variables, since if $\varphi^m(x,y)$ is equivalent to such a formula, then $\varphi^{m+1}(x,y)$ is equivalent to

$$(R(x,y) \vee (\exists z)R(x,z) \wedge [(\exists w_1)(\exists w_2)((w_1 = z) \wedge (w_2 = y) \wedge (\exists x)(\exists y)(w_1 = x \wedge w_2 = y \wedge \varphi^m(x,y)]).$$

2.2. For each $k < \omega$ we consider the infinitary language $L^k_{\infty\omega}$ over the vocabulary σ which allows for arbitrary disjunctions and conjunctions, but whose formulas have at most k distinct free and bound variables. The sentences of $L^k_{\infty\omega}$ are exactly the sentences of $L_{\infty\omega}$ with at most k bound variables.

Let $\mathfrak{A}$ and $\mathfrak{B}$ be relational structures over the vocabulary σ. We say that $\mathfrak{A}$ is $L^k_{\infty\omega}$-equivalent to $\mathfrak{B}$, and we write $\mathfrak{A} \equiv^k_{\infty\omega} \mathfrak{B}$, in case $\mathfrak{A}$ and $\mathfrak{B}$ satisfy the same sentences of $L^k_{\infty\omega}$.

The languages $L^k_{\infty\omega}$ and the relations $\equiv^k_{\infty\omega}$ were introduced by Barwise [1977] and used in characterizing closure ordinals of inductive definitions on infinite structures. Immerman [1982b] studied these languages on finite relational structures and obtained lower bounds for the definability of certain combinatorial queries.

There is an infinitary k-pebble game which is related to $\equiv^k_{\infty\omega}$. The game is played between Players I and II on a pair of structures $\mathfrak{A}$ and $\mathfrak{B}$. Player I picks up a pebble and places it on an element of $\mathfrak{A}$ (or $\mathfrak{B}$) and Player II responds by placing a pebble on an element of $\mathfrak{B}$ (or $\mathfrak{A}$). If, after k pebbles have been placed on each structure, the corresponding substructures are not isomorphic, then I wins the game. Otherwise, Player I removes some corresponding pairs of pebbles from $\mathfrak{A}$ and $\mathfrak{B}$ and the game is resumed until again k pebbles are placed on each structure. Player II wins if he can continue this game "forever".

It is not hard to see that Player II has a winning strategy for the infinitary k-pebble game if and only if there is a non-empty family J of partial isomorphisms from $\mathfrak{A}$ to $\mathfrak{B}$ with the following properties:

(i) J is closed under subfunctions, that is to say if $f \subseteq g$ and $g \in J$, then $f \in J$.

(ii) J has the back and forth property up to k, namely if $f \in J$ and $\text{card}(f) < k$, then for all $a \in A$ (respectively $b \in B$) there is a $g \in J$ such that $f \subseteq g$ and $a \in \text{dom}(g)$ (respectively $b \in \text{rng}(g)$).

We should point out that the infinitary k-pebble game is quite different from the usual Ehrenfeucht-Fraisse game with k moves. For example, if C_n denotes the undirected cycle on n elements, then it is well known that for any k there is an integer N such that for all $m,n \geq N$ Player II wins the Ehrenfeucht-Fraisse game with k moves on the structures C_m and C_n. In contrast, it is easy to show that for any $k \geq 4$ and any m, n Player II wins the infinitary k pebble game on C_m and C_n if and only if $m = n$.

The next theorem, due to Barwise [1977] (see also Immerman [1982b]), provides the connection between $\equiv^k_{\infty\omega}$ and the infinitary k-pebble game.

Theorem 2.3. Let $\mathfrak{A}$ and $\mathfrak{B}$ be relational structures. Then

$\mathfrak{A} \equiv^k_{\infty\omega} \mathfrak{B}$ if and only if Player II has a winning strategy for the infinitary k-pebble game on $\mathfrak{A}$ and $\mathfrak{B}$. ⊣

2.4. The main result in this section is a criterion for $L^k_{\infty\omega}$-equivalence between structures which are members of a class C closed under disjoint unions and components. Classes having these closure properties arise naturally in combinatorics and the study of asymptotic probabilities on such classes has been pursued by Compton [1980, 1984a,b]. Intuitively, a component of a structure $\mathfrak{A}$ is a "connected piece" of $\mathfrak{A}$. More precisely, let $\mathfrak{A}$ be a structure of vocabulary $\sigma = (R_1,\ldots,R_\ell)$ and define the binary relation $\sim$ on A by:

$$a_1 \sim a_2 \text{ if for some predicate symbol } R_i \ (1 \leq i \leq \ell)$$

$\mathfrak{A} \models \exists\bar{x}\exists\bar{y}\exists\bar{z}\, R_i(\bar{x},a_1,\bar{y},a_2,\bar{z})$. The components of $\mathfrak{A}$ are the substructures of $\mathfrak{A}$ with universe an equivalence class of the smallest equivalence relation extending $\sim$. A structure $\mathfrak{A}$ is connected if it has only one component.

Notice that a component of a graph $\mathfrak{A}$ is a connected subgraph, while if $\mathfrak{A}$ is a permutation (viewed as a binary relational structure), then the components are exactly the cycles. Similarly, the components of an equivalence relation

$\mathfrak{A} = \langle A,R\rangle$ coincide with the equivalence classes of R.

Let C be a class of relational structures over the vocabulary σ. We say that C is closed under disjoint unions and components if (i) whenever $\mathfrak{A}$ and $\mathfrak{B}$ are in C, then the disjoint union $\mathfrak{A} \cup \mathfrak{B}$ is also in C, and (ii) if $\mathfrak{A} \in C$ and $\mathfrak{B}$ is a component of $\mathfrak{A}$, then $\mathfrak{B}$ is in C. If every member of such a class C has finitely many components, then C is completely determined by its connected structures.

Assume that $C_1, C_2, \ldots, C_n, \ldots$ is a finite or countably infinite sequence of distinct $\equiv^k_{\infty\omega}$-equivalence classes of the connected structures in a class C closed under disjoint unions and components. We write $\mathfrak{A} = \ell_1 C_1 \cup \ell_2 C_2 \cup \cdots \cup \ell_n C_n \cup \cdots$ for a structure in C which has exactly ℓ_i components in the equivalence class C_i, for each i. We now can state and prove the following:

Theorem 2.5. Let k be a positive integer and C a class of relational structures which is closed under disjoint unions and components. Let $\mathfrak{A} = \ell_1 C_1 \cup \ell_2 C_2 \cup \cdots \cup \ell_n C_n \cup \cdots$ and $\mathfrak{B} = m_1 C_1 \cup m_2 C_2 \cup \cdots \cup m_n C_n \cup \cdots$ be two structures in C, where $C_1, C_2, \ldots, C_n, \ldots$ is a sequence of distinct $\equiv^k_{\infty\omega}$-equivalence classes of the connected structures in C.

If $(\ell_i = m_i < k)$ or $(\ell_i \geq k$ and $m_i \geq k)$ for each i, then $\mathfrak{A} \equiv^k_{\infty\omega} \mathfrak{B}$.

Proof. For each $\equiv^k_{\infty\omega}$-equivalence class C_i and each pair $\mathfrak{D}$ and $\mathfrak{H}$ of connected structures in C_i which are components of $\mathfrak{A}$ and $\mathfrak{B}$ respectively, pick a family $J(\mathfrak{D},\mathfrak{H})$ of partial isomorphisms from $\mathfrak{D}$ to $\mathfrak{H}$, such that $J(\mathfrak{D},\mathfrak{H})$ gives a winning strategy for Player II in the infinitary k-pebble game on $\mathfrak{D}$ and $\mathfrak{H}$.

Let J be the family of all partial isomorphisms from $\mathfrak{A}$ to $\mathfrak{B}$ with the following properties:

(i) if $f \in J$, then $\mathrm{card}(f) \leq k$.

(ii) if $f \in J$ and $\mathfrak{D}$ is a component of $\mathfrak{A}$ in some C_i such that $(f \upharpoonright \mathfrak{D}) \neq \emptyset$, then $f[\mathfrak{D}] \subseteq \mathfrak{H}$ with $\mathfrak{H}$ a component of $\mathfrak{B}$ in C_i and $(f \upharpoonright \mathfrak{D}) \in J(\mathfrak{D},\mathfrak{H})$, where $(f \upharpoonright \mathfrak{D})$ denotes the restriction of the function f on $\mathfrak{D}$.

(iii) if $f \in J$ and $\mathfrak{H}$ is a component of $\mathfrak{B}$ in some C_i such that $(f^{-1} \upharpoonright \mathfrak{H}) \neq \emptyset$, then $f^{-1}[\mathfrak{H}] \subseteq \mathfrak{D}$ with $\mathfrak{D}$ a component of $\mathfrak{A}$ in C_i and $(f \upharpoonright \mathfrak{D}) \in J(\mathfrak{D},\mathfrak{H})$.

We have to show that the family J gives a winning strategy for Player II in the infinitary k-pebble game on $\mathfrak{A}$ and $\mathfrak{B}$. It is obvious that J is non-empty and closed under subfunctions. Moreover, because of the symmetry in the definition of J, it is enough to verify only one of the two directions in the back and forth property up to k. Let $f \in J$ be such that $\mathrm{card}(f) < k$ and let $a \in (A - \mathrm{dom}(f))$. We must find some $g \in J$ such that $f \subseteq g$ and $a \in \mathrm{dom}(g)$. Assume that the component of a is the connected structure $\mathfrak{D}$ and that $\mathfrak{D}$ is in the $\equiv^k_{\infty\omega}$-equivalence class C_i. We consider the following cases:

Case 1: $(f \upharpoonright \mathfrak{D}) \neq \emptyset$.

The definition of the family J implies that there is a component $\mathfrak{H}$ of $\mathfrak{B}$ such that $f[\mathfrak{D}] \subseteq \mathfrak{H}$, $\mathfrak{D} \equiv^k_{\infty\omega} \mathfrak{H}$ and $(f \upharpoonright \mathfrak{D}) \in J(\mathfrak{D},\mathfrak{H})$. Since $\text{card}(f \upharpoonright \mathfrak{D}) < k$ and $J(\mathfrak{D},\mathfrak{H})$ has the back and forth property up to k, there is some $h \in J(\mathfrak{D},\mathfrak{H})$ such that $(f \upharpoonright \mathfrak{D}) \subseteq h$ and $a \in \text{dom}(h)$. Take $g = f \cup h$ and observe that g is a partial isomorphism from $\mathfrak{A}$ to $\mathfrak{B}$ which is in J.

Case 2: $(f \upharpoonright \mathfrak{D}) = \emptyset$.

Let ℓ_i and m_i be the number of components of $\mathfrak{A}$ and $\mathfrak{B}$ respectively which are in C_i.

Subcase 2.1: $\ell_i = m_i < k$.

Since f induces a 1-1 correspondence from the components of $\mathfrak{A}$ to the components of $\mathfrak{B}$ and $(f \upharpoonright \mathfrak{D}) = \emptyset$, there exists a component $\mathfrak{H}$ of $\mathfrak{B}$ such that $\mathfrak{H} \in C_i$ and $(f^{-1} \upharpoonright \mathfrak{H}) = \emptyset$. Using the back and forth property up to k of the family $J(\mathfrak{D},\mathfrak{H})$, we can find a partial isomorphism $h \in J(\mathfrak{D},\mathfrak{H})$ such that $a \in \text{dom}(h)$. The function $g = f \cup h$ gives a partial isomorphism from $\mathfrak{A}$ to $\mathfrak{B}$ which is in J and is defined on a.

Subcase 2.2: $\ell_i \geq k$ and $m_i \geq k$.

Since $\text{card}(f) < k$, there are at most $(k - 1)$ components $\mathfrak{A}$ in C_i on which f is defined. Therefore condition (ii) in the definition of J and the fact that $m_i \geq k$ imply that there is a component $\mathfrak{H}$ of $\mathfrak{B}$ in C_i such that $(f^{-1} \upharpoonright \mathfrak{H}) = \emptyset$. Apply now the back and forth property of $J(\mathfrak{D},\mathfrak{H})$ to get a partial isomorphism $h \in J(\mathfrak{D},\mathfrak{H})$ such that $a \in \text{dom}(h)$, and verify that $g = f \cup h$ is a member of J. $\dashv$

In the next two sections of this paper we will apply Theorem 2.5 to concrete combinatorial classes in order to analyze definability in the languages $L^k_{\infty\omega}$, $1 \leq k < \omega$. In all the classes we consider here the components are fairly "homogeneous" and, as a result, the sufficient condition for $L^k_{\infty\omega}$-equivalence given by Theorem 2.5 will turn out to be a necessary one as well.

§3. Equivalence Relations

3.1. Let $\mathcal{E}$ be the class of all equivalence relations, that is to say structures of the form $\mathfrak{A} = \langle A,R \rangle$, where R is a reflexive, symmetric, transitive binary relation. Of course $\mathcal{E}$ can be also identified with the class of graphs which are disjoint unions of reflexive, complete graphs. The connected structures in $\mathcal{E}$ are the equivalence relations with only one equivalence class. For each cardinal λ let $\mathfrak{D}_\lambda$ be a fixed connected equivalence relation on a set of cardinality λ. It is quite obvious that for any positive integer k there are exactly k distinct $\equiv^k_{\infty\omega}$-equivalence classes of connected structures in $\mathcal{E}$, namely the classes $C_i = \{\mathfrak{A} \in \mathcal{E} : \mathfrak{A} \cong \mathfrak{D}_i\}$ for $1 \leq i < k$, and the class

$C_k = \{\mathfrak{A} \in \mathcal{E} : \mathfrak{A} \cong \mathfrak{D}_\lambda$ for some $\lambda \geq k\}$.

3.2. Theorem. Let $\mathfrak{A}$, $\mathfrak{B}$ be two equivalence relations and let $c(\mathfrak{A},\lambda)$, $c(\mathfrak{B},\lambda)$ denote the number of equivalence classes of cardinality λ in $\mathfrak{A}$ and $\mathfrak{B}$ respectively.

(i) $\mathfrak{A} \equiv^k_{\infty\omega} \mathfrak{B}$ if and only if the following conditions hold:

1. $c(\mathfrak{A},i) = c(\mathfrak{B},i) < k$ or both $c(\mathfrak{A},i) \geq k$ and $c(\mathfrak{B},i) \geq k$, for each $i < k$
2. $\sum_{\lambda \geq k} c(\mathfrak{A},\lambda) = \sum_{\lambda \geq k} c(\mathfrak{B},\lambda) < k$ or both $\sum_{\lambda \geq k} c(\mathfrak{A},\lambda) \geq k$ and $\sum_{\lambda \geq k} c(\mathfrak{B},\lambda) \geq k$

(ii) There are exactly $(k + 1)^k$ distinct $\equiv^k_{\infty\omega}$-equivalence classes on $\mathcal{E}$ with representatives the finite structures $m_1\mathfrak{D}_1 \cup m_2\mathfrak{D}_2 \cup \cdots \cup m_k\mathfrak{D}_k$, where $0 \leq m_i \leq k$ for each $i = 1,2,\ldots,k$. Moreover, each equivalence class is definable by a sentence of first-order logic with at most k distinct variables.

Proof. (i) Theorem 2.4 and the remarks about the connected equivalence relations show immediately that if the conditions 1. and 2. hold, then $\mathfrak{A} \equiv^k_{\infty\omega} \mathfrak{B}$. For the other direction assume that $\mathfrak{A} = \ell_1 C_1 \cup \cdots \cup \ell_k C_k$ and $\mathfrak{B} = m_1 C_1 \cup \cdots \cup m_k C_k$ are two equivalence relations such that $\ell_i < k$ and $m_i \geq k$ for some $i \leq k$. We will show that $\mathfrak{A} \not\equiv^k_{\infty\omega} \mathfrak{B}$ by exhibiting a winning strategy for Player I in the infinitary k pebble game on $\mathfrak{A}$ and $\mathfrak{B}$. Player I places successively ℓ_i pebbles on elements $a_1,\ldots,a_{\ell_i}$ of different components of $\mathfrak{A}$ in C_i. If in one of these moves Player II responds with an element b_j in $\mathfrak{B}$ whose component is not in C_i, then Player I keeps the pebbles on a_j and b_j, removes all the other pebbles and proceeds to win the game on the $\equiv^k_{\infty\omega}$-inequivalent components of a_j and b_j. Thus, in order to keep the game going, Player II is forced to put pebbles on elements $b_1,\ldots,b_{\ell_i}$ of different components of $\mathfrak{B}$ in C_i. Player I places next a new pebble on an element of a component of $\mathfrak{B}$ in C_i which carries no pebbles. At this point, Player II is forced to either place a pebble on an element of a component of $\mathfrak{A}$ in C_i, in which case he looses immediately, or places it on an element of some component in C_j, with $C_j \not\equiv^k_{\infty\omega} C_i$, and so Player I can win the game in at most $k - 1$ more moves.

(ii) The existence of $(k + 1)^k$ distinct $\equiv^k_{\infty\omega}$-equivalence classes on $\mathcal{E}$ with the indicated representatives is a direct consequence of part (i). It is also quite straightforward to verify that each equivalence class is definable by first-order formulas with at most k distinct variables. For example, the $\equiv^k_{\infty\omega}$-equivalence class of the structure $k\mathfrak{D}_{k-1} \cup (k - 1)\mathfrak{D}_k$ is given by the formula $\varphi_1 \wedge \varphi_2 \wedge \varphi_3$, where φ_1 says "there are at least k unrelated elements each of which is related to exactly $k - 2$ different elements," φ_2 says "there are exactly $k - 1$ unrelated elements each related to at least $k - 1$ different elements," and φ_3 states that "every element is related to either exactly $k - 2$ or to at least $k - 1$ elements." ⊣

3.3. Remarks. We can give a different proof of the fact that if $\mathfrak{A} \equiv^k_{\infty\omega} \mathfrak{B}$, then conditions 1. and 2. hold by using the argument in part (ii) to exhibit directly a sentence ψ of $L^k_{\infty\omega}$ such that $\mathfrak{A} \models \psi$ and $\mathfrak{B} \models \neg \psi$ whenever $\ell_i < k$ and $m_i \geq k$ for some i with $1 \leq i \leq k$.

The conditions 1. and 2. in the above Theorem 3.2 were studied first by Tenney [1975] who showed that they imply the existence of a winning strategy for Player II in the usual Ehrenfeucht-Fraisse game with k moves. As a corollary of Theorem 3.2 we prove now that on any collection of equivalence relations the infinitary language $L^k_{\infty\omega}$ is no more expressive than $L^k_{\omega\omega}$, the first-order language with at most k distinct variables.

3.4. Corollary. Let $\mathcal{C}$ be a collection of equivalence relations and let $\mathfrak{D}$ be a non-empty subclass of $\mathcal{C}$. The following are equivalent:

(i) There is a sentence φ of $L^k_{\infty\omega}$ such that

$$\mathfrak{D} = \{\mathfrak{A} \in \mathcal{C} : \mathfrak{A} \models \varphi\}.$$

(ii) If $\mathfrak{A} \in \mathfrak{D}$, $\mathfrak{B} \in \mathcal{C}$ and $\mathfrak{A} \equiv^k_{\infty\omega} \mathfrak{B}$, then $\mathfrak{B} \in \mathfrak{D}$.

(iii) There is a sentence ψ of $L^k_{\omega\omega}$ such that

$$\mathfrak{D} = \{\mathfrak{A} \in \mathcal{C} : \mathfrak{A} \models \psi\}.$$

Proof. (ii) $\Rightarrow$ (iii): Let $\varphi_1, \ldots, \varphi_m$ be the sentences of $L^k_{\omega\omega}$ which define the $\equiv^k_{\infty\omega}$-equivalence classes of members of $\mathfrak{D}$. Then

$$\mathfrak{D} = \{\mathfrak{A} \in \mathcal{C} : \mathfrak{A} \models \varphi_1 \vee \cdots \vee \varphi_m\}. \qquad \dashv$$

3.5. Let $\mathcal{C}$ be a class of finite structures such that the universe of a member of $\mathcal{C}$ is $\{1,2,\ldots,n\}$ for some integer n. If P is a statement about structures in $\mathcal{C}$, then $\mu_n(P)$ is the fraction of structures in $\mathcal{C}$ with universe $\{1,2,\ldots,n\}$ satisfying P. The labeled asymptotic probability $\mu(P)$ on the class $\mathcal{C}$ is defined by the equation $\mu(P) = \lim_{n\to\infty} \mu_n(P)$ provided this limit exists. The unlabeled asymptotic probability $\nu(P)$ on the class $\mathcal{C}$ is $\nu(P) = \lim_{n\to\infty} \nu_n(P)$ (if the limit exists), where $\nu_n(P)$ is the fraction of isomorphism types of structures in $\mathcal{C}$ with universe $\{1,2,\ldots,n\}$ satisfying P. If $\mathcal{P}$ is a collection of statements about structures in $\mathcal{C}$, then a labeled 0-1 law holds for $\mathcal{P}$ in case $\mu(P) = 0$ or $\mu(P) = 1$ for every $P \in \mathcal{P}$. We define the unlabeled 0-1 law in an analogous way. As mentioned in the introduction, Fagin [1976] showed that both labeled and unlabeled 0-1 laws hold for first-order sentences on the class $\mathcal{G}$ of all finite graphs, while Blass-Gurevich-Kozen [1984] extended this result to the collection of inductive queries on $\mathcal{G}$ by proving that every inductive query is equivalent to a first-order one on almost all graphs. The problem of deciding the asymptotic probability of first-order sentences on finite graphs is PSPACE complete (Grandjean [1983]) and of inductive queries is EXPTIME complete (Blass-Gurevich-Kozen [1984]).

Let $\mathcal{FE}$ be the class of all finite equivalence relations. Compton [1980, 1984a] proved that both labeled and unlabeled 0-1 laws hold for first-order sentences on $\mathcal{FE}$, and moreover $\mu(\varphi) = \nu(\varphi)$ for every first-order sentence φ. The <u>first-order almost sure theory of $\mathcal{FE}$</u> is the set

$$T = \{\varphi : \varphi \text{ is a first-order sentence and } \mu(\varphi) = 1 \text{ on } \mathcal{FE}\}.$$

Compton [1980, 1984a] shows that a countable model of T is the equivalence relation $\mathfrak{A}_0 = \langle A,R\rangle$ which has infinitely many equivalence classes of each finite cardinality. Using this fact one can prove that deciding the asymptotic probability of first-order sentences on $\mathcal{FE}$ is a PSPACE-complete problem. The equivalence relation $\mathfrak{A}_0$ is not an ω-saturated structure and therefore the first-order almost sure theory T is not ω-categorical. As a result of this, the methods of Blass-Gurevich-Kozen [1984] do not seem to apply here in studying inductive queries. We use instead the definability analysis of $L^k_{\infty\omega}$ on $\mathcal{E}$ in order to establish the following:

<u>3.6. Theorem.</u> Let $\mathcal{FE}$ be the class of all finite equivalence relations.

<u>(i)</u> The inductive queries coincide with the first-order ones on $\mathcal{FE}$, that is to say if φ is an inductive query on $\mathcal{FE}$, then there is a first-order query ψ which is equivalent to φ on every finite equivalence relation. Consequently the inductive queries on $\mathcal{FE}$ have both a labeled and an unlabeled 0-1 law.

<u>(ii)</u> The problem of deciding the asymptotic probability of any inductive query on $\mathcal{FE}$ is EXPTIME complete.

<u>Proof.</u>

<u>(i)</u> Let $\varphi(x_1,\ldots,x_n,S)$ be a positive formula and let $k = n + \ell$, where ℓ is the total number of variables in φ. There are $(k+1)^k$ finite equivalence relations of the form $\mathfrak{B} = m_1\mathfrak{D}_1 \cup \cdots \cup m_k\mathfrak{D}_k$ with $0 \le m_i \le k$ for $i = 1,\ldots,k$. Therefore there is a finite number $s \le \left(\frac{k^3+k^2}{2}\right)^n$ such that φ closes off in at most s steps on each such structure $\mathfrak{B}$. It follows then that the $L^k_{\omega\omega}$ sentence $(\forall\bar{x})(\varphi^{s+1}(\bar{x}) \rightarrow \varphi^s(\bar{x}))$ is true on all such structures. But, by Theorem 3.2, any equivalence relation $\mathfrak{A} = \langle A,R\rangle$ satisfies exactly the same $L^k_{\omega\omega}$ sentences as one of these structures $\mathfrak{B}$, and hence $\mathfrak{A} \models (\forall\bar{x})(\varphi^{\infty}(\bar{x}) \leftrightarrow \varphi^s(\bar{x}))$. Thus every inductive query on $\mathcal{FE}$ is first-order and so the 0-1 laws for such queries follow from the results of Compton [1980, 1984a].

<u>(ii)</u> Consider the countable model $\mathfrak{A}_0$ of the first-order almost sure theory of $\mathcal{FE}$ which has infinitely many equivalence classes of each finite cardinality.

In view of (i), we have to show that the problem of deciding the truth value of an inductive query on $\mathfrak{A}_0$ is EXPTIME complete. Blass-Gurevich-Kozen [1984] proved that the decision problem for inductive queries is EXPTIME hard on any non-trivial structure. Thus to establish (ii) it is enough to find an algorithm which determines the truth value of any inductive query on $\mathfrak{A}_0$ in EXPTIME. By Theorem 3.2 we have that if ψ is any inductive query of length k (as a sentence of the logic FO + LFP), then $\mathfrak{A}_0 \models \psi$ if and only if $\mathfrak{B}_k \models \psi$, where $\mathfrak{B}_k = k\mathfrak{D}_1 \cup \cdots \cup k\mathfrak{D}_k$. However, inductive queries of length k are computable on any finite structure $\mathfrak{A}$ in time $p(|\mathfrak{A}|)$, where $|\mathfrak{A}|$ is the size of the structure, for some polynomial p of degree $\leq 3k$ (see Immerman [1982a]). Since $\mathfrak{B}_k$ has cardinality $\frac{k^3 + k^2}{2}$, we conclude that the problem of deciding the asymptotic probabilities of inductive queries on $\mathfrak{FE}$ is solvable in time $2^{q(k)}$ for some polynomial $q(k)$. ⊣

3.7. Remarks. We have shown that inductive and first-order queries possess identical expressive power on $\mathfrak{FE}$, but there is a complexity difference in the computation of their asymptotic probabilities (EXPTIME vs. PSPACE). Intuitively, the reason for this fact is that a query can be expressed by a formula of FO + LFP having shorter length than an equivalent first-order formula.

Similar results can be derived for other combinatorial classes of finite structures which have only a finite number of $\equiv^k_{\infty\omega}$-inequivalent components. One such example is the class $\mathfrak{F}$ of oriented forests of height 1.

§4. Unions of Cycles

We consider now the class $\mathcal{K}$ of finite undirected graphs $\mathfrak{A} = \langle A,R\rangle$ which are disjoint unions of cycles and we obtain:

4.1. Theorem. (i) An unlabeled 0-1 law holds for the queries expressible in monadic second order logic on $\mathcal{K}$, and hence for the first-order queries as well. However, the first-order queries on $\mathcal{K}$ do not have a labeled 0-1 law.

(ii) The query Q which says that "the largest cycle has an even number of elements" is inductive on $\mathcal{K}$ and has unlabeled probability equal to 1/2. Thus, the inductive queries on $\mathcal{K}$ do not have an unlabeled 0-1 law and moreover Q is not equivalent to any monadic second order query on almost all members of $\mathcal{K}$.

Proof.

(i) The ordinary generating series for the unlabeled structures in $\mathcal{K}$ is $b(x) = \prod_{n\geq 1} (1 - x^n)^{-1}$, since there is exactly one unlabeled component of cardinality n for each $n \geq 1$. Theorem 6.4 of Compton [1984b] implies immediately that an unlabeled 0-1 law holds for monadic second order logic on $\mathcal{K}$. A straightforward computation shows that the exponential generating series for the labeled structures in $\mathcal{K}$ is $a(x) = (1 - x)^{-1/2}$. From Theorem 5.9 of Compton [1984a] it follows that the first-order queries on $\mathcal{K}$ do not have a labeled 0-1 law, since the radius of convergence of $a(x)$ is a positive finite number.

(ii) Before proving that the query "the largest cycle has an even number of elements" is inductive on $\mathcal{K}$, we state the Stage Comparison Theorem 2A.2 of Moschovakis [1974] which we will use twice in the proof. Informally, this result says that we can compare the stages of an inductive definition in an inductive way. More precisely, if $\varphi(x_1,\ldots,x_n,S)$ is a positive formula in S and $\bar{x} = (x_1,\ldots,x_n)$ is a member of the least fixed point φ^∞, then the rank $|\bar{x}|_\varphi$ is the smallest ordinal ξ such that $\bar{x} \in \varphi^\xi$. The Stage Comparison Theorem asserts that given a positive formula $\varphi(x_1,\ldots,x_n,S)$ the relations $\leq^*_\varphi$ and $<^*_\varphi$ are inductive (actually they are least fixed points of positive formulas), where

$$\bar{x} \leq^*_\varphi \bar{y} \Leftrightarrow (\bar{x} \in \varphi^\infty) \wedge (\bar{y} \notin \varphi^\infty \vee |\bar{x}|_\varphi \leq |\bar{y}|_\varphi)$$

and

$$\bar{x} <^*_\varphi \bar{y} \Leftrightarrow (\bar{x} \in \varphi^\infty) \wedge (\bar{y} \notin \varphi^\infty \vee |\bar{x}|_\varphi < |\bar{y}|_\varphi).$$

Let $\varphi(x,y,z,S)$ be the first-order positive in S formula

$$(R(x,y) \wedge R(y,z) \wedge (x \neq z)) \vee (\exists w)(S(x,w,y) \wedge S(w,y,z) \wedge R(y,z)),$$

where R is the edge relation on the graph and S a ternary relation variable. The effect of this formula is that it determines a direction on any cycle. It is easy to verify that if x is in a cycle of cardinality $n \geq 3$, then $|(x,y,x)|_\varphi = n - 1$ for any y such that $(x,y,x) \in \varphi^\infty$. Let σ be a first-order sentence saying "the largest cycle has cardinality 2." Using the Stage Comparison Theorem, we can now show that the query

$$Q_1(x) \Leftrightarrow \text{"the component of } x \text{ is of biggest cardinality"}$$

is inductive on $\mathcal{K}$, since

$$Q_1(x) \Leftrightarrow (\sigma \wedge (\exists y)R(x,y)) \vee (\exists y)(\forall x')(\forall y')(\forall z')[\varphi^\infty(x,y,x) \wedge$$
$$\wedge (\varphi^\infty(x',y',z') \rightarrow (x',y',z') \leq^*_\varphi (x,y,x))].$$

Let $\psi(x,y,T)$ be the formula $(x \neq y) \wedge (R(x,y) \vee (\exists w)(T(w) \wedge R(w,y)))$, where T is a unary relation variable. By treating x as a parameter, we obtain a positive operator $\psi_x(y,T) \equiv \psi(x,y,T)$ for each x, which we can then iterate and get the least fixed point ψ_x^∞, such that $y \in \psi_x^\infty \Leftrightarrow y$ is connected to x. Notice that exactly two new elements enter into every stage ψ_x^n of ψ_x^∞, with the possible exception of the last stage. If x belongs to a cycle of even cardinality, then only one new element gets into the last stage, otherwise two new elements enter.

Using a relativized version of the Stage Comparison Theorem for positive formulas with parameters, we can show that the query

$$Q_2(x,y) \Leftrightarrow \text{"}y \text{ enters } \psi_x^\infty \text{ in the last stage"}$$

is inductive on $\mathcal{K}$, since

$$Q_2(x,y) \Leftrightarrow \psi_x^\infty(y) \wedge (\forall z)(\psi_x^\infty(z) \rightarrow z \leq_{\psi_x}^* y).$$

It follows now that the query Q which says that "the largest cycle has an even number of elements" is inductive on $\mathcal{K}$, because

$$Q \Leftrightarrow \sigma \vee (\exists x)(Q_1(x) \wedge (\exists! y) Q_2(x,y)),$$

where $\exists! y$ abbreviates "there is exactly one y."

Finally, we can easily see that $\nu(Q) = 1/2$ using the well known fact from the theory of partitions that $\lim_{n\to\infty}\left(\frac{p(n)}{p(n+1)}\right) = 1$ and the obvious inequalities $p_e(n) \leq p_o(n+1) \leq p_e(n+2)$, where $p(n) = \#$ of partitions of n (= # of ways n can be written as the sum of smaller integers), $p_e(n) = \#$ of partitions of n such that the largest part is even, and $p_o(n) = \#$ of partitions of n such that the largest part is odd. ⊣

4.2. Remarks. For each $n \geq 1$ let C_n be a cycle of cardinality n. Every member of $\mathcal{K}$ is isomorphic to a structure of the form $m_1C_1 \cup m_2C_2 \cup \cdots \cup m_nC_n$ for some $n \geq 1$ and nonnegative integers $m_1, m_2, \ldots, m_n$ (here the notation m_iC_i denotes the disjoint union of m_i copies of C_i). Thus every unlabeled structure $\mathfrak{A}$ in $\mathcal{K}$ can be identified with a partition of $|\mathfrak{A}|$. Using the method of proof in the above Theorem 4.1(ii), we can show that many queries expressing interesting partition properties, such as "all parts are distinct" or "all parts are odd," are inductive on $\mathcal{K}$. In contrast we will see that the query "the graph is of even cardinality" is not inductive on $\mathcal{K}$ and, as a matter of fact, is not expressible by any infinitary formula in $\bigcup_{k\geq 1} L_{\infty\omega}^k$. This will be an easy consequence of the following:

4.3. Theorem. Let k be a positive integer ≥ 4 and let $\mathfrak{A} = \ell_1C_1 \cup \cdots \cup \ell_iC_i \cup \cdots$ and $\mathfrak{B} = m_1C_1 \cup \cdots \cup m_iC_i \cup \cdots$ be two finite graphs which are disjoint unions of cycles.

(i) $\mathfrak{A} \equiv_{\infty\omega}^k \mathfrak{B}$ if and only if $\ell_i = m_i < k$ or both $\ell_i \geq k$ and $m_i \geq k$, for each i.

(ii) There are countably many distinct $\equiv_{\infty\omega}^k$-equivalence classes on $\mathcal{K}$ with representatives the structures $m_1C_1 \cup \cdots \cup m_nC_n$, where $n \geq 1$ and $0 \leq m_i \leq k$ for each $i = 1,2,\ldots,n$. Moreover, if $k \geq 8$, then the equivalence classes are definable by formulas of $L_{\omega\omega}^k$.

(iii) If $k \geq 8$, then every formula of $L^k_{\infty\omega}$ is equivalent on $\mathcal{K}$ to a countable disjunction of $L^k_{\omega\omega}$ formulas.

Hint of Proof. For part (i) we use Theorem 2.5, the fact that for any $k \geq 4$ we have $C_m \equiv^k_{\infty\omega} C_n$ if and only if $m = n$, and an argument similar to the one in Theorem 3.2. The $\equiv^k_{\infty\omega}$-equivalence classes can be defined in $L^k_{\omega\omega}$ (for $k \geq 8$) using the stages of the formula $\varphi(x,y,z,S)$ in the proof of Theorem 4.1(ii). ⊣

4.4. Corollary. The query "there is an even number of vertices" is not expressible on $\mathcal{K}$ by any infinitary formula with a fixed finite number of variables. ⊣

4.5. Remarks. It follows from Corollary 4.4 that the inductive queries on $\mathcal{K}$ are propertly contained in the class of queries computable in PTIME. The query "there is an even number of vertices" is inductive on each $\mathcal{K}^n$ $(n \geq 1)$, where $\mathcal{K}^n$ is the subclass of $\mathcal{K}$ consisting of graphs with at most n components. Moschovakis (unpublished) has actually proved that inductive = PTIME on each $\mathcal{K}_n$ $(n \geq 1)$.

Compton [1984a,b] isolated and studied a certain growth condition on the coefficients of the ordinary generating series $b(x)$ of a class $\mathcal{C}$ closed under disjoint unions and components. He showed that, whenever $b(x)$ has a positive radius of convergence, this growth condition is equivalent to the existence of unlabeled 0-1 laws for first-order and monadic second order properties. If the ordinary generating series is $b(x) = \prod_{n\geq 1} (1 - x^n)^{-1}$, then the growth condition is automatically satisfied. This is for example the case for the class $\mathcal{FE}$ of the finite equivalence relations and the class $\mathcal{K}$ of disjoint unions of cycles. Thus our results here show that unlabeled 0-1 laws for first-order or monadic second order queries do not imply in general an unlabeled 0-1 law for inductive queries. The asymptotic probabilities of inductive queries on a class $\mathcal{C}$ seem to depend on uniform definability properties of the structures in $\mathcal{C}$ rather than combinatorial properties of their isomorphism types. In particular, as the proof of Theorem 4.1 reveals, the different behavior of inductive queries between $\mathcal{FE}$ and $\mathcal{K}$ is due mainly to the existence of "long" uniform inductive definitions on cycles.

We conclude by pointing out that we can obtain results analogous to Theorems 4.1 and 4.3 for other combinatorial collections of finite structures, including the class $\mathcal{P}$ of permutations and the class $\mathcal{LF}$ of linear forests.

Acknowledgement. This research was partially supported by a John D. MacArthur Research Professorship from Occidental College during the Fall of 1984.

References

A. Aho and J. Ullman [1979]: Universality of data retrieval languages, Proc. 6th ACM Symposium of Programming Languages, 1979, 110-120.

J. Barwise [1977]: On Moschovakis closure ordinals, J. Symbolic Logic 42 (1977), 292-296.

A. Blass, Y. Gurevich, D. Kozen [1984]: A zero-one law for logic with a fixed-point operator, Technical Report CRL-TR-38-84, University of Michigan, 1984.

A. Chandra and D. Harel [1982]: Structure and complexity of relational queries, J. Comp. System Sci. 25 (1982), 99-128.

K. Compton [1980]: Applications of logic to finite combinatorics, Ph.D. Thesis, University of Wisconsin, Madison, 1980.

K. Compton [1984a]: A logical approach to asymptotic combinatorics I: First order properties, to appear in: Advances in Mathematics.

K. Compton [1984b]: A logical approach to asymptotic combinatorics II: Monadic second order properties, to appear in: Advances in Mathematics.

R. Fagin [1976]: Probabilities on finite models, J. Symbolic Logic 41 (1976), 50-58.

E. Grandjean [1983]: Complexity of the first-order theory of almost all structures, Information and Control 57 (1983), 180-204.

D. Harel and D. Kozen [1984]: A programming language for the inductive sets and applications, to appear in: Information and Control.

N. Immerman [1982a]: Relational queries computable in polynomial time, Proc. 14th ACM Symposium on Theory of Computing, 1982, 147-152.

N. Immerman [1982b]: Upper and lower bounds for first-order expressibility, J. Comp. System Sci. 25 (1982), 76-98.

Y. N. Moschovakis [1974]: Elementary Induction on Abstract Structures, North-Holland, 1974.

R. L. Tenney [1975]: Second-order Ehrenfeuct games and the decidability of the second-order theory of an equivalence relation, J. Austral. Math. Soc. 20 (Series A) 1975, 323-331.

COMPOSITIONAL SEMANTICS
FOR
REAL-TIME DISTRIBUTED COMPUTING

R. Koymans[1,4]
R.K. Shyamasundar[3,5]
W.P. de Roever[1,2]
R. Gerth[2,4]
S. Arun–Kumar[3]

March 1985

ABSTRACT

We give a compositional denotational semantics for a real-time distributed language, based on the linear history semantics for CSP of Francez et al. Concurrent execution is *not* modelled by interleaving but by an extension of the maximal parallelism model of Salwicki, that allows the modelling of transmission time for communications. The importance of constructing a semantics (and in general a proof theory) for real-time is stressed by such different sources as the problem of formalizing the real-time aspects of Ada and the elimination of errors in real-time flight control software ([Sunday Times 7-22-84]).

1. INTRODUCTION

Although concurrency in programming has been seriously investigated for more than 25 years ([Dij 59]), the specific problems of real-time have been the object of little theoretical reflection. Currently used real-time languages represent almost no evolution with respect to assembly language ([Cam 82]). Consequently no serious analysis of complexity, no design methodology, no standard for implementation and no concept of portability exist for real-time languages. This state of affairs is astonishing, for the confrontation with real-time lends a nervous twitch of actuality to arguments in favour of formalization; don't the dangers of malfunctioning real-time systems affect all of us?

Errors occurring in Boeing 747's real-time flight control are a closely guarded secret ([ST 84]), yet most of us fly in such planes. Software for space vehicles and nuclear power stations belong to the world's most prestiguous projects, yet *remain* notoriously unreliable ([CACM 84], The Three-Miles Island Disaster), with no prospect of improvement in the immediate future. Every industrialized country has computer controlled chemical plants in densely populated areas.

But even commercial interest points to a need for real-time systems developed as a hierarchy of modules. For example, the development of digitized telephone-switching networks suitable for adaptation to local circumstances as occurring in, e.g., Asia, is often problematic because designs lack the required transparancy. And what to think of the advent of industrial robots?

The response to this need, has been the development of new real-time languages such as (1) Ada - developed for the military, (2) CHILL - within the context of telecommunication industries and (3) Occam - which is even chip-implemented, for those interested in experimenting with structure. All of these are claimed to have been rigorously defined ([Ada 83], [BO 80], [BLW 82], [Occ 84]). Yet their official standards lack any acceptable

---

[1] Department of Computer Science, University of Nijmegen, Toernooiveld, 6525 ED Nijmegen, the Netherlands.

[2] Department of Computer Science, University of Utrecht, P.O. Box 80.012, 3508 TA Utrecht, the Netherlands.

[3] NCSDCT, Tata Institute for Fundamental Research, Homi Bhaba Road, Bombay - 400 005, India.

[4] supported by the Foundation for Computer Science Research in the Netherlands (SION) with financial aid from the Netherlands Organization for the Advancement of Pure Research (ZWO).

[5] supported by a visitors grant from the Netherlands Organization for the Advancement of Pure Research (ZWO).

characterization of concurrency (with the exception of Occam), let alone of real-time (, which is lacking for Occam, too).
All these arguments emphasize the need to develop formal models for real-time concurrency, and, more importantly, to discover structuring methods which lead to hierarchical and modular development of real-time concurrent systems. Obviously, models based on interleaving, such as [BH 81] can be immediately discarded as being unrealistic.
Models allowing truly concurrent activity such as SCCS ([Mil 83]) or MIJE ([BC 84]), although an improvement, remain unsatisfactory because they either enforce complete synchronicity in executions (so that any communication must be performed immediately to circumvent deadlock) or do not exclude interleaving. Petri-net theory remains a viable direction for discovering structuring methods, yet is still unsatisfactory because it does not incorporate (1) satisfactory verification methods for liveness properties, such as temporal logic has, or (2) (machine checkable) formalisms for representing (concurrently implemented) data structures. And certainly none of these models apply to real-time features of realistic programming languages such as Ada.

The present paper aims at providing a model of real-time concurrency

- which is *realistic* in the sense that concurrent actions can and will overlap in time unless prohibited by synchronization constraints, no unrealistic waiting of processors is modelled, and yet the many parameters involved in real-time behaviour are reflected by a corresponding parametrization of our models; it is based on Salwicki's notion of maximal concurrency ([SM 81]),

- which applies to programming languages for distributed computing such as Ada and Occam which are based on *synchronized communication* (, for asynchronized communication as in CHILL, see [KVR 83]),

- which implies a sound and relatively complete method for verification since it is *compositional*; we base ourselves in this respect on the method developed by Soundararajan ([Sou 83],[Sou 84]), and joint research together with Pnueli leading to the incorporation of maximal parallelism within the temporal framework of [BKP 84],

- which meets the standard of rigour as provided by the denotational semantics of concurrency.

Some of these aspects are also covered by work of Zijlstra ([Zij 84]) and G. Jones ([Jon 82]).

We have developed a real-time variant of CSP, called CSP-R, which allows the modelling of the essential Ada ([Ada 83]) real-time features (see Appendix A). Our study of real-time distributed computing is carried by a subset of this language, Mini CSP-R. Extending our techniques to CSP-R introduces some notational complications, but is straightforward and is briefly discussed in Appendix A. In the paper we develop a denotational semantics for Mini CSP-R, stressing compositionality, based on the linear history semantics for CSP of [FLP 84]:

- the basic domain consists of non-empty *prefix-closed sets* of pairs of states and (finite) histories of communication assumptions leading to that state,

- the ordering on this domain is simply set-inclusion,

- the denotation for the parallel execution of two processes yields a denotation *in the same domain* for a new combined process replacing the original two (this makes the approach applicable to nested parallelism),

- the histories contain enough information to detect deadlock, eliminating the expectation states of [FLP 84].

Histories are modelled as sequences of *bags* of communication assumption records as we allow truly concurrent actions:
There is a clear operational difference between one process offering a particular communication capability and two (or more) processes, executing in parallel, each offering the same capability. It is to model this distinction that we have to use bags instead of sets (see also example 3 in section 8).

Real-time is modelled in the histories by relating the i-th element of a history with the i-th tick of a **conceptual** *global clock* (see section 4).

There are two kinds of records for expressing communication assumptions in the histories:

- communication claims <i,j,v>, modelling the execution of an I/O command: <i,j,v> claims that the value v is passed from process i (the sender) to process j (the receiver),

- no-match claims <i,j>, modelling the absence of a possibility for the execution of an I/O command α (this means that there is no matching I/O command $\bar{\alpha}$ such that α and $\bar{\alpha}$ can be executed simultaneously): <i,j> claims that no value could be passed from process i (the sender) to process j (the receiver).

The combination of the records <i,j,v> and <i,j> can be used to describe all possible behaviours when executing an I/O command concerning communication from i to j:
<i,j,v> claims that communication from i to j (transferring value v) is *possible* and <i,j> claims that a communication from i to j is *impossible*. Note that a no-match claim <i,j> implies the *waiting* for a possibility to communicate from i to j. The constraint of no unrealistic waiting that the maximal parallelism model imposes on parallel execution, can now be formulated as: two processes may not make the same no-match claim, i.e., waiting at both sides for the same communication between each other is prohibited.

The communication claim record is the same as the communication record of [FLP 84]. Internal moves within a process (the δ-record of [FLP 84]) are modelled by empty bags.
The no-match claim record is new and allows

- the checking of the maximal parallelism constraints, i.e., no unnecessary waiting (see above),

- the detection of (established) deadlock (i.e., waiting for a communication that will never come), rendering expectation states as in [FLP 84] unnecessary.

2. MINI CSP-R

In this section we describe our language Mini CSP-R. Mini CSP-R consists of the programming constructs of our interest in their basic form without syntactic sugar. In appendix A we show how Mini CSP-R can easily be extended to a language CSP-R that can simulate the basic Ada real-time and communication primitives.
Mini CSP-R essentially is CSP (see [Hoa 78]) with the addition of the real-time construct **wait** d. This construct can be used both as instruction and as guard in a selection or loop. As guard it functions as a time-out, revoking a process' willingness to communicate (through one of the I/O guards).
In the syntax we use the following conventions:

- a *process identification* is an element of $\{P_1, P_2, \ldots\}$,
- a *duration* is an integer-valued expression.

We assume that expressions e and boolean expressions b have some unspecified syntax.

The primitive language elements are the *instructions:*
1. x := e - assignment
2. **wait** d - wait instruction (d is a duration)
3.1 $P_i!e$ - output (send) to process i the value of the expression e
3.2 $P_i?x$ - input (receive) from process i a value and assign this value to the variable x.

Instructions of form 3 are called I/O commands: $P_i!e$ is an output command and $P_i?x$ an input command.
The important notion of *syntactic matching* of two I/O commands in two processes is defined as follows: two pairs $\langle P_i,\alpha\rangle$ and $\langle P_j,\beta\rangle$ (α,β I/O commands) match syntactically iff:
($\alpha \equiv P_j!e$ and $\beta \equiv P_i?x$) or ($\alpha \equiv P_j?x$ and $\beta \equiv P_i!e$).

Communication between processes i and j takes place when $\langle i,\alpha\rangle$ *semantically matches* $\langle j,\beta\rangle$:
- $\langle P_i,\alpha\rangle$ and $\langle P_j,\beta\rangle$ match syntactically,
- control in P_i and P_j is in front of α, respectively β.

The result of a semantic match is the simultaneous execution of the I/O commands as indicated by 3.1 and 3.2. Its effect is the assignment of the value of the expression of the sending process to the variable of the receiving process.

A *guard* is of one of the following forms:
1. b - pure boolean guard
2.1 α - pure I/O guard
2.2 b; α - boolean I/O guard
3.1 **wait** d - pure wait guard
3.2 b; **wait** d - boolean wait guard.

Here, b is a boolean expression, e.g. x>0, α is an I/O command and d a duration. For a guard g, its *boolean part* $\bar{g}$ is defined as: $\bar{b} = b$, $\bar{\alpha} = \textbf{true}$, $\overline{b;\alpha} = b$, $\overline{\textbf{wait}\ d} = \textbf{true}$, $\overline{b;\textbf{wait}\ d} = b$.
A guard g is called *open* if $\bar{g}$ evaluates to true.

To complete the definition of Mini CSP-R, we define *commands,* notation Comm, together with *parallel commands,* notation ParComm, and the set of *visible subprocesses,* notation vsp, of a command inductively as follows:

1. every instruction is a command; its set of visible subprocesses is empty
2. if T_1 and T_2 are commands, then T_1; T_2 is a (sequential composition) command with $vsp(T_1;T_2) = vsp(T_1) \cup vsp(T_2)$
3. if $T_1,\ldots,T_n$ are commands and $g_1,\ldots, g_n$ guards ($n \geq 1$), then $[\mathop{\square}_{j=1}^{n} g_j \rightarrow T_j]$ is an (alternative) command and $*[\mathop{\square}_{j=1}^{n} g_j \rightarrow T_j]$ is a (repetitive) command with
$vsp([\mathop{\square}_{j=1}^{n} g_j \rightarrow T_j]) = vsp(*[\mathop{\square}_{j=1}^{n} g_j \rightarrow T_j]) = \bigcup_{j=1}^{n} vsp(T_j)$

4.1 if T is a command then P_i::T is a (named) parallel command
4.2 if T_1 and T_2 are parallel commands and the following two restrictions are satisfied:
(r1) the variables occurring in T_1 are different from those occurring in T_2,
(r2) the visible subprocesses of T_1 are different from those of T_2
then $(T_1 \parallel T_2)$ is a (composite) parallel command
5. if T is a parallel command, then it is also a command with
$vsp(P_i::T) = \{i\}$ and $vsp((T_1 \parallel T_2)) = vsp(T_1) \cup vsp(T_2)$.

We further adopt the naming conventions of [Hoa 78, FLP84]: any I/O command may only address either one of its sibling processes or one of its ancestor's sibling processes. Note that such a naming convention may result in a match with a subprocess of the named sibling (see example 5 in section 8).

We can interpret Mini CSP-R informally as follows (this interpretation applies also to CSP-R).
An assignment has its usual interpretation: the value of the expression e is assigned to the variable x.
The wait instruction suspends execution of the process in which it occurs for the value of d (but at least one) time units.
The interpretation of I/O commands was already indicated above: an I/O command α in process i waits for a semantic match with an I/O command β in a process j.
The interpretation of sequential composition is as usual: the execution of T_1 is followed by the execution of T_2.
The interpretation of an alternative command is as follows: First check if none of the guards is open. If this is the case, execution aborts. Otherwise, check whether there is at least one open pure boolean guard. If this is the case select non-deterministically one of these guards. In the case that at least one of the guards is open but there are no open pure boolean guards, execution of an alternative command proceeds as follows. Compute the minimum of the values of the durations of the open wait guards and 1. The waitvalue is defined to be infinite if there are no open wait guards and otherwise the just computed minimum. For waitvalue time units wait for a semantic match with one of the open I/O guards. If at least one semantic match occurs within this time period, non-deterministically take one of them. Otherwise, after waitvalue time units one of the open wait guards with a minimal duration is selected. A selection of a guard g_j in all these cases is followed by the execution of the corresponding command T_j.

The interpretation of a repetitive command is the repeated execution of the alternative command contained in it. Now, however, execution terminates normally whenever in this repetition none of the guards is open.
The interpretation of a named parallel command is as follows:
P_i::T executes its body T. Furthermore, for a semantic match of *any* I/O command α in T with an I/O command outside T, α is considered to be part of process i and process i only. Hence if α occurs in the body of some visible subprocess of T, α is not addressable by the name of that visible subprocess from outside T anymore. Even more, the visible subprocesses of T are no longer visible outside P_i::T.
The interpretation of a composite parallel command involves the parallel execution of the parts T_1 and T_2. The underlying parallel execution semantics is *not* interleaving semantics, but a semantics based on the maximal parallelism model (see sections 3 and 9). For Mini CSP-R this means that whenever there is a choice between different semantic matches for some I/O command in a process, always one of the semantic matches that occurred earliest in time is non-deterministically chosen.

3. THE MAXIMAL PARALLELISM MODEL

Under maximal parallelism, the number of instructions in concurrently executing processes that can be executed simultaneously without violating synchronization requirements, is maximalized (see [SM 81] for a formal definition). So, in the program [P_1:: x := 1 ‖ P_2:: x := 3 ‖ P_3:: y := 2] *either* P_1 and P_3 *or* P_2 and P_3 will execute their first move simultaneously, but *not* P_1 and P_2; all this, under the assumption that multiple accesses to a single (shared) variable are mutually exclusive.
Implementing maximal parallelism requires separate processors for the various processes. The connection with real-time behaviour is, that when execution speed is a critical factor, separate processors should be available to all processes.
For distributed computing, we take maximal parallelism to mean "first-come first-served" (fcfs) in some global time scale (see section 4). Consider the Mini CSP-R program (P_1::(P_{11}::P_2!0 ‖ (P_{12}::P_{13}!1 ‖ P_{13}::P_{12}?x; P_2!x)) ‖ P_2::P_1?y; P_1?y).
According to *interleaving* semantics two scenarios are possible:
(1) P_{11} communicates with P_2 while P_{12} communicates with P_{13}; after that P_{13} communicates with P_2
(2) P_{12} first communicates with P_{13}; after that P_{13} communicates with P_2; finally, P_{11} communicates with P_2.
According to *maximal parallelism* semantics, only (1) is possible since P_{11} and P_2 can *immediately* become engaged in a rendezvous and hence do not wait for P_{12} and P_{13} to communicate earlier.
As we will reason in section 9, the maximal parallelism model is unrealistic for distributed systems in general. We will develop a whole family of real-time models ranging from interleaving to maximal parallelism semantics and incorporating the transmission time for messages in a system.

4. OUR VIEW OF TIME

To express real-time properties such as "the system responds to a certain request within a fixed number of seconds" there must be some measure of time to relate these properties to. When we talk about abstract, i.e., implementation independent, properties of a system *as a whole,* this measure must be relative to some *global* time scale. For distributed systems this means that all events in the various processes are related to each other by means of one *conceptual* global clock, introduced at a metalevel of reasoning.
Clearly, no physical realization of such a global clock is possible; processors always drift from one time mutual synchronization as exemplified by the existence of clock synchronization algorithms. In our model, drifting can always be modelled by allowing (small) unpredictable variations in the execution time of basic actions.

5. NOTATIONS AND TECHNICAL PRELIMINARIES

5.1 *Numbers, sets, cartesian product and finite sequences*

$\mathcal{N} = \{ 0,1,2,... \}$ is the set of natural numbers ordered by $0 < 1 < 2 < ...$
$\mathcal{N}^\infty = \mathcal{N} \cup \{\infty\}$, inherits the ordering on $\mathcal{N}$ and is additionally ordered by $n<\infty$ for all $n \in \mathcal{N}$.
The empty set is denoted by $\emptyset$.
The powerset of a base set E, i.e., the set of all subsets of E, is denoted by $\mathcal{P}(E)$.
If $E_1,...,E_n$ are sets, then $\overset{n}{\underset{i=1}{X}} E_i$ denotes their cartesian product.
If all E_i's are equal (to E), we write E^n for $\overset{n}{\underset{i=1}{X}} E_i$.
π_i, for $1 \leq i \leq n$, denote the associated projection functions for elements of $\overset{n}{\underset{i=1}{X}} E_i$: $\pi_i (< e_1,...,e_n >) = e_i$.
A finite sequence over a base set E is an element of $\mathcal{S}(E) \overset{def.}{=} \bigcup_{n \in \mathcal{N}} E^n$, denoted by $<e_1,...,e_n>$ or $<e_i>_{i=1}^n$ where $e_i \in E$, $1 \leq i \leq n$.
If all e_i's are equal (to e), we write $<e>^n$ for $<e_i>_{i=1}^n$.
A special case is n=0: it is called the empty sequence, notation λ.
The length of a sequence $s = <e_1,...,e_n>$, notation $|s|$, is n.
For a sequence $s = <e_1,...,e_n>$ and $1 \leq k \leq n$ we define the k-th element of s, notation s(k), as e_k.
For $e \in E$ and $s \in \mathcal{S}(E)$, we say that e is an element of s, notation $e \lessdot s$, if there exists a k, $1 \leq k \leq |s|$, such that $s(k) = e$.
Given $s_1, s_2 \in \mathcal{S}(E)$, we can concatenate them, notation $s_1\hat{}s_2$: if $s_1 = <e_1, ...,e_n>$ and $s_2 = <e_1',...,e_m'>$, then $s_1\hat{}s_2 = <e_1,...,e_n, e_1',..., e_m'>$. ^ is closed, associative and has identity element λ:
$s_1, s_2 \in \mathcal{S}(E) \Rightarrow s_1\hat{}s_2 \in \mathcal{S}(E)$, $(s_1\hat{}s_2)\hat{}s_3 = s_1\hat{}(s_2\hat{}s_3)$ and $s\hat{}\lambda = \lambda\hat{}s = s$.
For $s,s' \in \mathcal{S}(E)$ we say that s' is a prefix of s, notation $s' \leq s$, if there exists a $s'' \in \mathcal{S}(E)$ such that $s = s'\hat{}s''$.

5.2 *Functions and partial functions*

The set of all functions from X (the domain) to Y (the range) is denoted by Y^X. The domain and range of a function f are denoted by dom(f), respectively ran(f). A partial function from X to Y is an element of $Y^{X'}$ where $X' \in \mathcal{P}(X)$, i.e., a function from a subset of X to Y.
For f a partial function from X to Y, $x \in X$ and $y \in Y$, f[y/x] is the partial function with $dom(f[y/x]) = dom(f) \cup \{x\}$ and $ran(f[y/x]) = Y$ defined by

$$(f[y/x])(x') = \begin{cases} y \text{ if } x' = x \\ f(x') \text{ if } x' \in dom(f)\backslash\{x\}. \end{cases}$$

For f_1,f_2 partial functions from X to Y, such that $f_1(x) = f_2(x)$ for all $x \in dom(f_1) \cap dom(f_2)$,
we can define $f_1 \cup f_2$, the union of f_1 and f_2: $dom(f_1 \cup f_2) = dom(f_1) \cup dom(f_2)$, $ran(f_1 \cup f_2) = Y$ and

$$(f_1 \cup f_2)(x) = \begin{cases} f_1(x) \text{ if } x \in dom(f_1) \\ f_2(x) \text{ if } x \in dom(f_2). \end{cases}$$

5.3 *Bags*

A bag (or multiset) over a base set E is an element of $\mathcal{B}(E) \overset{def.}{=} \mathcal{N}^E$, i.e., a function from E to $\mathcal{N}$.
For $e \in E$ and $B \in \mathcal{B}(E)$ we say that e is an element of B, notation eEB, if $B(e) > 0$.
For finite bags we often use the notation $[e_1^{i_1}, \ldots , e_n^{i_n}]$ where $n \in \mathcal{N}$, $i_k \geq 1$, $e_k \in E$, all e_k different $(1 \leq k \leq n)$ which corresponds to the bag $B \in \mathcal{B}(E)$ defined by

$$B(e) = \begin{cases} i_k & \text{if } e = e_k,\ 1 \leq k \leq n \\ 0 & \text{otherwise.} \end{cases}$$

If $i_k = 1$, we just write e_k instead of e_k^1.
A special case is n=0, the empty bag, notation [].

6. THE SEMANTIC DOMAIN AND ITS INTERPRETATION

6.1 The semantic domain

Because our basic domain consists of state-history pairs, we first explain what states and histories are.
Let Id be a (fixed) set of identifiers (i.e., a set of strings over some alphabet). Since we gave no syntax for expressions in Mini CSP-R, we assume furthermore the existence of a set V of expression values.
S, the set of *proper* states, is defined to be the set of partial functions from Id to V. So a proper state $s \in S$ maps *certain* identifiers to their value.
Σ, the total set of states, can now be defined as $S \cup \{\perp, \bullet\}$ where $\perp$ denotes an incomplete computation and $\bullet$ denotes failure (both explained later).
Let CAR = $(\mathcal{N} \times \mathcal{N}) \cup (\mathcal{N} \times \mathcal{N} \times V)$ be the set of communication assumption records.
H, the set of histories, is, as was motivated in the introduction, $\mathcal{S}(\mathcal{B}(CAR))$. It would in fact suffice to take H = $\mathcal{S}(\mathcal{P}(\mathcal{N} \times \mathcal{N}) \times \mathcal{B}(\mathcal{N} \times \mathcal{N} \times V))$, as bags are only needed to collect communication claims. Obviously, for claiming the *absence* of a communication possibility between process i and j, it suffices to do this only once. However, we prefer the first denotationally simpler definition.
The technical reason for using bags instead of sets is illustrated in example 3 of section 8.
Our central domain is that of non-empty prefix-closed sets of state-history pairs, notation ΣH.

Definition: A set $X \in \mathcal{P}(\Sigma \times H)$ is *prefix-closed* iff for all $\langle \sigma, h \rangle \in X$, if $h' \leq h$, then $\langle \perp, h' \rangle \in X$.

The *prefix-closure* of X, PFC(X), is defined as $X \cup \{\langle \perp, \lambda \rangle\} \cup \{\langle \perp, h' \rangle \mid \exists \sigma \exists h (\langle \sigma, h \rangle \in X \wedge h' \leq h)\}$.

Note that $PFC(X) \in \Sigma H$, for all $X \in \mathcal{P}(\Sigma \times H)$.

ΣH can be turned into a complete lattice:
- the partial ordering is $\subseteq$, set-inclusion
- the least upper bound is obtained by $\cup$, set-union.

Its least element is $\{\langle \perp, \lambda \rangle\}$.

The technical motivation for the introduction of $\perp$ lies in the simplicity of the ordering of ΣH: several proofs, in particular those for continuity of operators, become very simple.
The introduction of a separate failure state $\bullet$ is needed for the detection of non-deterministic failure (see below, in section 6.2).
We want elements of ΣH to be non-empty, because otherwise the least element of ΣH would be $\emptyset$. Since $\emptyset$ contains no history at all, and sequential composition is essentially modelled by concatenation of histories, this choice of least element would imply that the denotation of *[**true** $\rightarrow$ P_2!5] would be empty. Although consistent with the view that a command is a transformation of initial states to final states when characterizing sequential constructs relationally, this does not capture our intuition that an unbounded set of communication possibilities may have been offered by *[**true** $\rightarrow$ P_2!5] (cf. example 1 in section 8).

Remark: As E.-R. Olderog observed in the context of the linear history semantics for CSP (see [FLP 84]), here too, we do not need to order our domain. This is a consequence of the fact that our recursions are always guarded (see loops) and that histories, once they have been generated, can not 'shrink', i.e., they remain the same or are extended to a longer history. For details, see the Appendix of [FLP 84].

6.2 Interpretation of ΣH

We can interpret $X \in \Sigma H$ as the set of all possible computations of a program P(cf. [FLP84]):

- $<s,h> \in X$ with $s \in S$, models a computation of P with history h that terminates in s,
- $<\bullet,h> \in X$ models a failure of P after history h,
- $<\perp,h> \in X$ models an incomplete computation of P which is *either* an approximation of a computation $<\sigma,h'>$ with $\sigma \neq \perp$ and $h \leqslant h'$ *or* an element in a chain of approximations $<\perp,h_o>,<\perp,h_o\hat{\ }h_1>,\ldots$ (all $h_i \neq \lambda$) which models an *infinite* computation of P with history $h_0\hat{\ }h_1\hat{\ }\ldots$ (this interpretation is justified by an appeal to König's Lemma, based on an intuitive operational semantics).

If only deterministic failure can occur, there is no need for a separate failure state $\bullet$ because $\perp$ can be used for that purpose: deterministic failure of P after history h is then modelled by $<\perp,h> \in X$ such that there exists no $<s,h'> \in X$ with $s \in S$, $h \leqslant h'$ nor $<\perp,h'> \in X$ with $h \leqslant h'$, $h \neq h'$. However, we have to include the possibility of a non-deterministic failure as is demonstrated by the following CSP-R program fragment:
[**true** → [**false** → x := 0] □ **true** → x := 1].

Using the above interpretation of ΣH, we can informally define a notion of observable behaviour.
The observable entities are: a communication history, termination, failure and infinite computation.
The observable behaviour of a communication history has already been given in the introduction. The other observable entities are given in the above interpretation of ΣH:

- termination: indicated by a proper state $s \in S$,
- failure: indicated by $\bullet$,
- infinite computation: indicated by an infinite chain of approximations.

Both divergence and established deadlock are viewed as infinite computations: divergence is making internal steps while time passes, established deadlock is waiting for a communication that will not come, while time passes. This means that divergence and established deadlock are observed in the same way, and hence that they can not be distinguished! In our view this is a perfectly reasonable standpoint: the only observation that can be made from the outside is the ticking of the global clock while no communication with the environment can occur. In other words: there is no context that can distinguish a diverging process from such a deadlocked one.

6.3 Extending the meaning function

The meaning of a construct T, notation $\mathcal{M}[T]$, only depends on a proper state $s \in S$: $\mathcal{M}[T]s \in \Sigma H$ represents all possible state changes and computational histories produced by T starting from s. It therefore seems sufficient to let $\mathcal{M}[T]$ be a function from S to ΣH. However, to define sequential composition we have to extend the meaning function to a function from ΣH to ΣH (this situation is analogous to that for a purely sequential non-deterministic language where the meaning function is generalized to sets of states). To that end we first extend a function ϕ from S to ΣH to a function ϕ^* from Σ to ΣH and next to a function $\boldsymbol{\phi}$ from ΣH to ΣH.

Definition: Let ϕ be a function from S to ΣH. Then ϕ^* is the function from Σ to ΣH defined by

$$\phi^*(\sigma) = \begin{cases} \phi(\sigma) \text{ if } \sigma \in S \\ PFC(\{<\sigma,\lambda>\}) \text{ otherwise.} \end{cases}$$

Furthermore, $\boldsymbol{\phi}$ is the function from ΣH to ΣH defined by

$$\boldsymbol{\phi}(X) = \{<\sigma',h\hat{\ }h'> \mid <\sigma,h> \in X \wedge <\sigma',h'> \in \phi^*(\sigma)\}.$$

$\boldsymbol{\phi}$ extends ϕ in a canonical way: for $X \in \Sigma H$ it takes $<\sigma,h> \in X$ and extends h with an additional history h' formed by applying ϕ^* to σ; ϕ^* behaves like ϕ on S but does not extend the histories of pairs $<\sigma,h> \in X$ with $\sigma \notin S$; the new state σ' is the state after applying ϕ^* to σ.
The histories h represent communication assumptions that have been made and can only be supplemented with additional communication assumptions. In other words: the extension of histories is independent of their contents. The meaning function should certainly have this property. A further property of $\boldsymbol{\phi}$ is that it is always strict and continuous. This means that we do not have to worry about the continuity of operators in our semantics!

Proposition: For all ϕ from S to ΣH, $\hat{\phi}$ is a strict and continuous function from ΣH to ΣH.

Proof: $\hat{\phi}(\{<\perp,\lambda>\}) = \{<\sigma',\lambda\hat{\ }h'> \mid <\sigma',h'> \in \phi^*(\perp)\} = \phi^*(\perp) = \{<\perp,\lambda>\}$ and

$$\hat{\phi}(\bigcup_{i\in I} X_i) = \{<\sigma',h\hat{\ }h'> \mid <\sigma,h> \in \bigcup_{i\in I} X_i \wedge <\sigma',h'> \in \phi^*(\sigma)\}$$
$$= \bigcup_{i\in I}\{<\sigma',h\hat{\ }h'> \mid <\sigma,h> \in X_i \wedge <\sigma',h'> \in \phi^*(\sigma)\}$$
$$= \bigcup_{i\in I} \hat{\phi}(X_i). \qquad \blacksquare$$

7. MAXIMAL PARALLELISM SEMANTICS FOR MINI CSP-R

7.1 *Introduction*

The meaning of Mini CSP-R commands is defined *denotationally* by giving for all commands T, an equation for $\mathcal{M}[T]$ which relates the meaning of T to the meaning of T's constituents in a compositional way. As demonstrated at the end of the previous section it suffices to define $\mathcal{M}[T]$ as a function from S to ΣH.

To define the alternative command $[\mathop{\square}_{j=1}^{n} g_j \rightarrow T_j]$ compositionally, we use an auxiliary semantic function $\mathcal{G}[g,A]$ from S to ΣH which gives the meaning of guard g in the context of a set A of alternative guards (the other guards in the alternative command). We use the context A in a compositional way, i.e., A depends only on the construct in which g occurs. In the definition of $\mathcal{M}$ we use $\mathcal{G}$ too, in defining the meaning of guards g that occur as instructions (these are the pure waitguards and pure I/O guards). Its meaning is simply the meaning of g as a guard in an empty context.

Since we gave no syntax for (boolean) expressions in Mini CSP-R, we assume the existence of semantic functions $\mathcal{V}$ and $\mathcal{B}$, such that $\mathcal{V}[e]$ for e an expression is a function from S to V and $\mathcal{B}[b]$ for b a boolean expression is a predicate on S, i.e., for $s \in S$ $\mathcal{B}[b]s$ is either true or false.

To define the meaning of constructs like $P_1::P_2!5$ compositionally, we have to give a meaning for $P_2!5$ separately, i.e., in a context where it is not known that this construct belongs to the process with identification 1. In order to do so, we introduce as semantic entity the 'unknown process', with process identification 0, and use this e.g. to generate records $<0,2,5>$ in the meaning for $P_2!5$ and later, in the meaning for $P_1::P_2!5$, replace 0 by 1. Therefore, we identify process identifications with natural numbers.

Just as for the syntax we need a notion of visible subprocesses of a command T, vsp(T). The difference with the definition in section 2 is the use of $\{0\}$ instead of $\varnothing$:

$vsp(T) = \{0\}$ for T an instruction
$vsp(T_1;T_2) = vsp((T_1 \parallel T_2)) = vsp(T_1) \cup vsp(T_2)$
$vsp([\mathop{\square}_{j=1}^{n} g_j \rightarrow T_j]) = vsp(*[\mathop{\square}_{j=1}^{n} g_j \rightarrow T_j]) = \bigcup_{j=1}^{n} vsp(T_j)$
$vsp(P_i::T) = \{i\}$.

To keep the semantics simple, we assume that the evaluation of expressions takes no time. However, this restriction can easily be relaxed by introducing time-parameters that represent evaluation times of expressions. Furthermore, we make the realistic assumption that the execution of commands takes at least one unit of time unless failure occurs (this can only occur if an alternative command is executed which has no open guard).

7.2 *Definition of* $\mathcal{G}$

In the definition of $\mathcal{G}$ we use the following two auxiliary notions for guards:

Definition 1:

For a set of guards G and $s \in S$, define $RTA(G,s) \in \mathcal{B}(CAR)$, the bag of real-time assumptions concerning the open I/O guards of G in state s, as follows:

$$RTA(G,s)(r) = \begin{cases} 1 \text{ if } r \in \{<0,i> \mid \exists g \in G(g \equiv P_i!e \vee (g \equiv b;P_i!e \wedge \mathcal{B}[b]s))\} \\ \qquad \cup \{<i,0> \mid \exists g \in G(g \equiv P_i?x \vee (g \equiv b;P_i?x \wedge \mathcal{B}[b]s))\} \\ 0 \text{ otherwise.} \end{cases}$$

Remark:

If e.g. $P_2!4$ and $P_2!6$ occur in G one might expect a multiplicity 2 (instead of 1) for the record <0,2> in the above definition. This is unnecessary (see the discussion of bags versus sets in section 6.1).

Definition 2:

For a guard g and $s \in S$, define waitvalue(g,s)$\in \mathcal{N}^\infty$ as follows:

$$\text{waitvalue}(g,s) = \begin{cases} 0 \text{ if } g \equiv b \wedge \mathcal{B}[b]s \\ \max\{\mathcal{V}[d]s,1\} \text{ if } g \equiv \textbf{wait } d \vee (g \equiv b; \textbf{wait } d \wedge \mathcal{B}[b]s) \\ \infty \text{ otherwise.} \end{cases}$$

Furthermore, for a set of guards G and $s \in S$, define minwait(G,s)$\in \mathcal{N}^\infty$ as min {waitvalue(g,s)|$g \in G$} (where by convention min $\emptyset = \infty$).

Note that the guard **true** has waitvalue 0 while the guards **wait** 0 and **wait** 1 have waitvalue 1. The reason for this anomaly with **wait** 0 is that **wait** d can also be used as an instruction, hence as a command, and the execution of commands should take at least one time unit. This leads however not to a loss of expressive power because **true** can be used if one wants a guard with waitvalue 0.

The equations for $\mathcal{G}$ are:

$$\mathcal{G}[b,A]s = \begin{cases} PFC(\{<s,\lambda>\}) \text{ if } \mathcal{B}[b]s \\ \{<\bot,\lambda>\} \text{ otherwise.} \end{cases}$$

A boolean acts as a filter: s is maintained only if b evaluates to true in s.

$$\mathcal{G}[\textbf{wait } d,A]s = PFC(\{<s,<RTA(A,s)>^T> \mid \max\{\mathcal{V}[d]s,1\} = \text{minwait}(A \cup \{\textbf{wait } d\},s) \overset{\text{def.}}{=} T\}).$$

A pure wait guard in the context A can be selected after its waitvalue time units elapsed provided this value equals the minimal waitvalue T (note that $T \in \mathcal{N}$) *and* no communication with an open I/O guard in A was possible during this period. If there is at least one open boolean guard in A, then T=0 and no wait guard can be selected.

$$\mathcal{G}[P_j!e,A]s = PFC(\{<s,<RTA(GRDS,s)>^t \hat{} < [<0,j,\mathcal{V}[e]s>]>> \mid 0 \leq t < \text{minwait}(GRDS,s)\})$$
where $GRDS = A \cup \{P_j!e\}$.

A pure I/O guard in the context A can be selected (indicated by the last triple of the history above) within the minimum waitvalue of GRDS (the bound on t above) under the condition that no match for any open I/O guard in GRDS was possible earlier (indicated by the first t elements of the history above). If there is at least one open boolean guard in A, then minwait(GRDS,s) = 0 and no output guard (in fact, no I/O guard) can be selected. The possibility that no guard at all is selected can only occur if there are no open boolean guards and no open wait guards (hence minwait(GRDS,s) = ∞) and furthermore no communication with an open I/O guard ever occurs. This case is represented by the subset $\{<\bot, <RTA(GRDS,s)>^t> \mid t \in \mathcal{N}\}$ of $\mathcal{G}[P_j!e,A]s$.

$\mathcal{G}[P_j?x,A]s = PFC(\{<s[v/x],<RTA(GRDS,s)>^t \hat{} <[<j,0,v>]>> \mid v \in V, 0 \leq t < minwait(GRDS,s)\})$
where $GRDS = A \cup \{P_j?x\}$.

The same remarks as for $\mathcal{G}[P_j!e,A]s$ apply here. In comparison with $\mathcal{G}[P_j!e,A]s$ we see that in the last triple of the history sender and receiver are reversed. Furthermore, for an input command $P_j?x$ we have to 'guess' the value v that will be assigned to x. When binding the inputting process with the outputting process we check that the values correspond (see the last three examples in section 8). This 'guessing' models Bekiç's and Milner's concept of renewal (see [Mil 73]).

$\mathcal{G}[b;g,A]s = \mathcal{G}\hat{[g,A]}(\mathcal{G}[b,A]s)$ where $g \equiv P_j!e$ or $g \equiv P_j?x$ or $g \equiv$ **wait** d.

The meaning of a sequential composition of guards is the functional composition (using the extension operator ^) of the meanings of the separate guards.

7.3 Definition of $\mathcal{M}$

7.3.1 $\mathcal{M}[T]$ for $T \in$ Comm \ ParComm

In this subsection we give the meaning of the 'standard' commands of Mini CSP-R, the non-parallel commands.

$\mathcal{M}[x := e]s = PFC(\{<s[\mathcal{V}[e]s/x],<[\,]>>\})$

To keep the semantics simple, an assignment takes exactly one time unit (indicated by the empty bag).

$\mathcal{M}[g]s = \mathcal{G}[g,\varnothing]s$ for $g \equiv$ **wait** d or $g \equiv P_j!e$ or $g \equiv P_j?x$.

This was already discussed when introducing the auxiliary function $\mathcal{G}[g,A]$.

$\mathcal{M}[T_1;T_2]s = \hat{\mathcal{M}}[T_2](\mathcal{M}[T_1]s)$.

$$\mathcal{M}[[\mathop{\Box}_{j=1}^{n} g_j \rightarrow T_j]]s = \begin{cases} \bigcup_{j=1}^{n} \hat{\mathcal{M}}[T_j](\mathcal{G}[g_j,\{g_k \mid 1 \leq k \leq n, k \neq j\}]s) & \text{if } \bigvee_{j=1}^{n} \mathcal{B}[\bar{g}_j]s \\ PFC(\{<\bullet,\lambda>\}) & \text{otherwise.} \end{cases}$$

The meaning of the alternative command depends on the presence of an open guard: if no such guard is present this means failure, otherwise one guard is selected where each guard is considered in the context of the remaining guards ($\bar{g}_j$ is the boolean part of g_j, see section 2).

Let C abbreviate $[\mathop{\Box}_{j=1}^{n} g_j \rightarrow T_j]$.
$\mathcal{M}[*C]s = \bigcup_{i \in \mathcal{N}} \phi_i(s)$

where the ϕ_i ($i \in \mathcal{N}$) are functions from S to ΣH defined inductively by

$\phi_0(s) = \{<\perp,\lambda>\}$ for all $s \in S$,

$$\phi_{i+1}(s) = \begin{cases} \hat{\phi}_i(\mathcal{M}[C]s) & \text{if } \bigvee_{j=1}^{n} \mathcal{B}[\bar{g}_j]s \\ PFC(\{<s,<[\,]>>\}) & \text{otherwise.} \end{cases}$$

The ϕ_i's represent as usual the i-th iteration step of the loopbody. If at some point of iteration there are no open guards anymore, the loop terminates (this last iteration is indicated by the empty bag because the execution of commands takes at least one time unit).
For an illustration of the loop equation see the first two examples in section 8 (these give also a demonstration why $\{<\perp,\lambda>\}$ and not $\varnothing$ should be the least element of ΣH).
The loop equation can alternatively be written as a fixed-point equation over the complete partial order of functions from S to ΣH with the usual ordering on function domains:

$$\mathcal{M}[*C] = \mu(\lambda\phi.\lambda s.\textbf{if} \bigvee_{j=1}^{n} \mathcal{B}[\bar{g}_j]s \textbf{ then } \phi(\mathcal{M}[C]s) \textbf{ else } PFC(\{<s,<[\ ]>>\}) \textbf{ fi})$$

where μ is the least fixed-point operator.

7.3.2 *The meaning of* P_i::T

The effect caused by P_i::T is the renaming of the visible subprocesses of T by i. To this end, we need a definition for substitution of a certain process, c.q. i, in place of a collection of processes I, c.q. the visible subprocesses of T, both for bags over CAR as for elements of ΣH. Although the substitution for bags over CAR is intuitively clear, the technical definition is rather awkward and is therefore given in Appendix B. So, assuming we have for $B \in \mathcal{B}(CAR)$, $I \in \mathcal{P}(\mathcal{N})$ and $i \in \mathcal{N}$ defined $B[I \rightarrow i] \in \mathcal{B}(CAR)$ we can extend this componentwise for elements of ΣH:

$$X[I \rightarrow i] = \{<s,<h(k)[I \rightarrow i]>_{k=1}^{|h|}> \mid <s,h> \in X\}.$$

Note that $X[I \rightarrow i] \in \Sigma H$ for $X \in \Sigma H$, $I \in \mathcal{P}(\mathcal{N})$ and $i \in \mathcal{N}$.

Now we can define
$\mathcal{M}[P_i::T]s = (\mathcal{M}[T]s)[vsp(T) \rightarrow i]$.

7.3.3 *The meaning of* $(T_1 \parallel T_2)$

7.3.3.1 Intuition for parallel composition

It remains to define the meaning of the most important construct, the parallel composition. Intuitively, when binding two processes, the information of the states is combined, the histories are checked for consistency and then are merged. This consistency check can actually be split into two independent parts to be applied at each instant of time:

(c1) the histories must have matching communication claims, i.e., the histories agree on the communications that occur between the two processes (the internal communications)

(c2) there is no unnecessary waiting, i.e., the histories do not indicate a situation where both processes are waiting for a communication that the other process can provide (in other words: two processes do not wait if there is a semantic match between them).

7.3.3.2 Using the syntactic restrictions

The syntactic restrictions for $(T_1 \parallel T_2)$ are:

(1) the variables of T_1 and T_2 are disjoint

(2) the visible subprocesses of T_1 and T_2 are disjoint.

Translated to the semantics we may assume:

(a1) if s_i is a proper state in the meaning of T_i (i=1,2), then $dom(s_1) \cap dom(s_2) = \emptyset$

(a2) $vsp(T_1) \cap vsp(T_2) = \emptyset$ (in this case the visible subprocesses for syntax and semantics coincide).

7.3.3.3 Combining states

We denote the combination of states by union $\cup$. This is because the condition (a1) is strong enough to use the union $\cup$ of partial functions (see section 5.2) when $s_1,s_2 \in S$.

It remains to extend $\cup$ for $s_1,s_2 \in \Sigma$. The idea is that whenever one of the states represents an incomplete computation the combination represents the same; otherwise, when one of the states represents failure, the combination represents failure:

$\bot \cup \sigma = \sigma \cup \bot = \bot$ for all $\sigma \in \Sigma$ and

$\bullet \cup \sigma = \sigma \cup \bullet = \bullet$ for all $\sigma \in \Sigma \setminus \{\bot\}$.

7.3.3.4 The consistency check

There is a direct correspondence between the two parts of the consistency check and the two types of communication assumption records:

(c1) concerns triples <i,j,v> such that i and j are internal processes, i.e., processes that belong to the collection of processes represented by the two histories whose consistency is checked; check (c1) corresponds to: each such triple in one history should also occur in the other history at the same time and vice versa

(c2) concerns pairs <i,j>; it corresponds to: no pair <i,j> in one history may occur at the same time in the other history.

Note that for (c1) we need to know the set of internal processes while this is not necessary for (c2). The reason for this is that in an element of CAR one of the processes i and j refers to the process that generated this record. Because (c2) checks that two histories representing different processes do not contain at the same time a common record <i,j>, this means that i and j must be internal processes anyway.
We call (c2) the real-time consistency check; it is formulated by

$$h_1 ¢^{RT} h_2 \stackrel{\text{def.}}{=} \neg\exists\, i,j,k\in\mathcal{N}\ (1\leq k\leq \min\{|h_1|, |h_2|\} \wedge <i,j>E\ h_1(k) \wedge <i,j>E\ h_2(k)).$$

Of course, the consistency check as a whole (and similarly for its part (c1)) could be applied pairwise to histories with the set of internal processes, say I, as parameter: $h_1\ ¢_I\ h_2$. However, we prefer to pair histories without such a parameter. Ideally, we would like to combine state-history pairs (states are united, histories merged) for which the histories are real-time consistent and *after that* apply the check (c1). This approach is unfeasible, as is shown by the programs (P_1::P_2!0 ∥ P_2::P_1?x) and (P_1::(P_{11}::P_2!0 ∥ P_{12}::P_2!0) ∥ P_2:: x:=0). If we would follow the strategy above, the meanings of these programs would both contain the history $<[<1,2,0>^2]>$. The problem is that now, we somehow must remove this history from the meaning of the second program (it deadlocks), but reduce the same history to <[ ]> in the meaning of the first one (showing a successful internal communication); this is clearly an impossibility.

There is, however, an easy trick to circumvent this problem. The above example suggests that we should *subtract equal communication claim records from each other* while merging: for the first program this would result in no <1,2,0>-records at all while for the second program the two <1,2,0>-records would still be maintained. Check (c1) can then be completed by testing whether after this special merging there are any 'internal communications' left, i.e., communication claims <i,j,v> with i and j internal.
Formally:

$$¢_I^{IC}(X) = X\text{-}\{<\sigma,h>|\exists B\lessdot h\ \exists i,j\in I\ \exists v\in V\ <i,j,v>EB\}.$$

$¢_I^{IC}$ maps $X\in\Sigma H$ to $¢_I^{IC}(X)\in\Sigma H$.

The above mentioned special merge is denoted by # and does the following.
Up to the length of the shortest history, # subtracts equal records (of course taking the absolute value). It is unnecessary to check especially for communication claim records because histories with equal <i,j>-pairs were previously removed in the real-time consistency check. After the length of the shortest history, the longer history is just copied.

Formally:
Let $h_1,h_2\in H$.
Then $h_1 \# h_2 = <B_k^{h_1,h_2}>_{k=1}^{\max\{|h_1|,|h_2|\}}$,
where $B_k^{h_1,h_2}\in\mathcal{B}(CAR)$ are defined as follows:

for $1\leq k\leq\min\{|h_1|, |h_2|\}$, $B_k^{h_1,h_2}(r) = |h_1(k)(r) - h_2(k)(r)|$,

for $\min\{|h_1|, |h_2|\}<k\leq\max\{|h_1|, |h_2|\}$, $B_k^{h_1,h_2}(r) = \begin{cases} h_1(k)(r) & \text{if } |h_1|>|h_2| \\ h_2(k)(r) & \text{if } |h_2|>|h_1|. \end{cases}$

Had it not been for the restriction on the visible subprocesses (a2), see subsection 7.3.3.2, # would not have been associative and as a consequence of that $\mathcal{M}[((T_1 \parallel T_2) \parallel T_3)]$ would not equal $\mathcal{M}[(T_1 \parallel (T_2 \parallel T_3))]$. However, in the context of $((T_1 \parallel T_2) \parallel T_3)$ and $(T_1 \parallel (T_2 \parallel T_3))$ we may assume: $vsp(T_i) \cap vsp(T_j) = \varnothing$ for $1\leq i<j\leq 3$.

Associativity of # is now implied by this restriction on account of the fact that, when subtracting equal records, $||a-b|-c| = |a-|b-c||$ holds in case one of a,b and c equals zero. This is elaborated in the full paper [KSRGA85].

7.3.3.5 An additional condition for combining state-history pairs

When combining state-history pairs $<\sigma_i, h_i>$, $1 \leqslant i \leqslant 2$, in the parallel composition of two processes, we should only do that under the condition that $\sigma_i = \bot \Rightarrow |h_i| \geqslant |h_{3-i}|$, $1 \leqslant i \leqslant 2$, i.e., that neither history that can be extended ($\sigma_i = \bot$) is shorter than the other one. Here is why:
Consider the program fragment $(P_1::P_3!5 \parallel P_2:: x:=0)$.
For $s \in S$, $<\bot,\lambda> \in \mathcal{M}[P_1::P_3!5]s$ and $<s[0/x], <[\ ]>> \in \mathcal{M}[P_2:: x:=0]s$.
If we would combine these two state-history pairs without the extra condition above, we get the combined pair $<\bot,<[\ ]>>$. However, this pair should *not* belong to the parallel composition of processes 1 and 2, because only the internal step (the assignment) of P_2 is represented and *not* the attempt of P_1 to communicate with P_3 that occurs *at the same time*.

7.3.3.6 The removal of real-time assumptions

When giving the meaning of $(T_1 \parallel T_2)$ the real-time assumptions concerning the visible subprocesses of T_1 and T_2 should be checked. It is our policy to do this as soon as possible, c.q. in the first context in which the processes i and j of a real-time assumption $<i,j>$ can be identified. The following program fragment illustrates this: $(P_1::P_2!5 \parallel P_2::P_1!5)$.
In this case some histories of process 1 contain the real-time assumption $<1,2>$ and some of process 2 $<2,1>$. After binding process 1 and 2, the real-time assumptions concerning the collection of processes {1,2} should be checked; in this case, exactly $<1,2>$ and $<2,1>$. After this check they are not needed anymore and will be removed.

In general, for $B \in \mathcal{B}(CAR)$ and a collection of processes $I \in \mathcal{P}(\mathcal{N})$, we can define $RTA_I(B) \in \mathcal{B}(CAR)$ which removes from B the real-time assumptions concerning I:

$$RTA_I(B)(r) = \begin{cases} 0 & \text{if } r = <i,j> \text{ with } i,j \in I \\ B(r) & \text{otherwise.} \end{cases}$$

We have to extend this operator to elements of ΣH in the same way as we extended $B[I \rightarrow i]$ to $X[I \rightarrow i]$ (see section 7.3.2):

$$RTA_I(X) = \{<s,<RTA_I(h(k)) >_{k=1}^{|h|} >|\ <s,h> \in X\}.$$

Note that $RTA_I(X) \in \Sigma H$ for $X \in \Sigma H$ and $I \in \mathcal{P}(\mathcal{N})$.

7.3.3.7 Putting it altogether: the meaning of $(T_1 \parallel T_2)$

$$\mathcal{M}[(T_1 \parallel T_2)]s =$$
$$RTA_{tvsp}(¢_{tvsp}^{IC}(\{<\sigma_1 \cup \sigma_2, h_1 \# h_2>|<\sigma_i, h_i> \in \mathcal{M}[T_i]s \wedge h_1 ¢^{RT} h_2 \wedge \sigma_i = \bot \Rightarrow |h_i| \geqslant |h_{3-i}|, 1 \leqslant i \leqslant 2\}))$$

where $tvsp = vsp((T_1 \parallel T_2)) = vsp(T_1) \cup vsp(T_2)$, the total visible subprocesses.

Lemma: $\{<\sigma_1 \cup \sigma_2, h_1 \# h_2>|\ <\sigma_i, h_i> \in \mathcal{M}[T_i]s \wedge h_1 ¢^{RT} h_2 \wedge \sigma_i = \bot \Rightarrow |h_i| \geqslant |h_{3-i}|, 1 \leqslant i \leqslant 2\} \in \Sigma H$.

Proof: see the full paper [KSRGA85]. ■

Proposition: For all $s \in S$, $\mathcal{M}[(T_1 \parallel T_2)]s \in \Sigma H$.

Proof: Immediate by the lemma and the fact that $¢_I^{IC}$, respectively RTA_I, maps elements of ΣH to elements of ΣH (see the sections 7.3.3.4, respectively 7.3.3.6). ■

We want pairwise binding of processes to be independent of the order in which the processes are bound. E.g. for three processes $\mathcal{M}[((T_1 \parallel T_2) \parallel T_3)]$ should equal $\mathcal{M}[(T_1 \parallel (T_2 \parallel T_3))]$. This associativity property together with commutativity $\mathcal{M}[(T_1 \parallel T_2)] = \mathcal{M}[(T_2 \parallel T_1)]$ justifies the writing of $\mathcal{M}[(T_1 \parallel T_2 \parallel T_3)]$ for any order of binding T_1,T_2 and T_3. This immediately generalizes to $\mathcal{M}[(T_1 \parallel \ldots \parallel T_n)]$ for any order of binding $T_1, \ldots ,T_n$ $(n \geqslant 2)$. The commutativity and associativity of binding are stated in the following theorem.

Theorem: $\mathcal{M}[(T_1 \| T_2)] = \mathcal{M}[(T_2 \| T_1)]$ and
$\mathcal{M}[((T_1 \| T_2) \| T_3)] = \mathcal{M}[(T_1 \| (T_2 \| T_3))]$.
Proof: see the full paper [KSRGA 85]. ■

7.4 Concluding remarks

The remark at the end of section 6 shows that we do not have to worry about continuity of the meaning function.
After all these technicalities the next section gives some examples which illustrate the basic ideas, and illustrate what is observable.

8. EXAMPLES

In the examples below E_n abbreviates the program (fragment) of example n and s is an arbitrary element of S.

Example 1: $E_1 \equiv P_1::*[\ \mathbf{true} \rightarrow P_2!5]$.
First we compute

$$\mathcal{M}[\ [\mathbf{true} \rightarrow P_2!5]]s = \bigcup_{j=1}^{1} \mathcal{M}[\hat{P}_2!5](\mathcal{G}[\mathbf{true},\varnothing]s) = \mathcal{M}[\hat{P}_2!5]\ (PFC(\{<s,\lambda>\})) = \mathcal{M}[P_2!5]s =$$
$$\mathcal{G}[P_2!5,\varnothing]s = PFC\ (\{<s,<[<0,2>]>^t \,\hat{}\, <[<0,2,5>]>>|t\in\mathcal{N}\}).$$

Then $\mathcal{M}[*[\mathbf{true} \rightarrow P_2!5]]s = \bigcup_{i\in\mathcal{N}} \phi_i(s)$ where

$$\phi_o(s) = \{<\perp,\lambda>\},\ \phi_{i+1}(s) = \hat{\phi}_i\ (\mathcal{M}[[\mathbf{true} \rightarrow P_2!5]]s).$$

By induction we can prove for all $n\in\mathcal{N}$

$$\phi_n(s) = PFC\ (\{<\perp,<[<0,2>]>^{t_1} \,\hat{}\, <[<0,2,5>]> \,\hat{}\, \ldots \,\hat{}\, <[<0,2>]>^{t_n} \,\hat{}\, <[<0,2,5>]>>|\ t_1,\ldots,t_n \in\mathcal{N}\}).$$

Hence

$$\mathcal{M}[E_1]s = PFC\ (\{<\perp,<[<1,2>]>^{t_1} \,\hat{}\, <[<1,2,5>]> \,\hat{}\, \ldots \,\hat{}\, <[<1,2>]>^{t_n} \,\hat{}\, <[<1,2,5>]>>\ |\ n\in\mathcal{N},t_1,\ldots,t_n\in\mathcal{N}\}).$$

Remark: This example shows why elements of ΣH should be non-empty. Otherwise $\varnothing$ would be the least element of ΣH and for the ϕ_i above we would then get $\phi_n(s) = \varnothing$ for all $n\in\mathcal{N}$ and hence $\mathcal{M}[E_1]s = \varnothing$. This is caused by the fact that we should have a starting point for the histories and $\varnothing$ contains no histories at all.

Example 2: $E_2 \equiv P_1::(P_{11}::*[P_2!5 \rightarrow \mathbf{wait}\ 1 \ \square\ \mathbf{wait}\ 1 \rightarrow \mathbf{wait}\ 1] \ \|$
$P_{12}::\mathbf{wait}\ 1;\ *[P_2!5 \rightarrow \mathbf{wait}\ 1 \ \square\ \mathbf{wait}\ 1 \rightarrow \mathbf{wait}\ 1])$.
We should have $\mathcal{M}[E_1] = \mathcal{M}[E_2]$!
E_1 and E_2 have indeed the same observable behaviour: they both continuously try to output value 5 to process 2.
Let C abbreviate $[P_2!5 \rightarrow \mathbf{wait}\ 1 \ \square\ \mathbf{wait}\ 1 \rightarrow \mathbf{wait}\ 1]$
(then $E_2 \equiv P_1::(P_{11}::*C \ \|\ P_{12}::\mathbf{wait}\ 1;\ *C)$).
We first compute

$$\mathcal{M}[C]s = \mathcal{M}[\hat{\mathbf{wait}}\ 1]\ (\mathcal{G}[P_2!5,\{\mathbf{wait}\ 1\}]s) \cup \mathcal{M}[\hat{\mathbf{wait}}\ 1]\ (\mathcal{G}[\mathbf{wait}\ 1,\{P_2!5\}]s)$$
$$= \mathcal{M}[\hat{\mathbf{wait}}\ 1]\ (PFC(\{<s,<[<0,2>]>^t \,\hat{}\, <[<0,2,5>]>>|0\leq t<1\}))$$
$$\cup\ \mathcal{M}[\hat{\mathbf{wait}}\ 1]\ (PFC(\{<s,<[0,2>]>^1>\}))$$
$$= PFC\ (\{<s,<[<0,2,5>],[\ ]>>\}) \cup PFC\ (\{<s,<[<0,2>],[\ ]>>\}).$$

Then

$$\mathcal{M}[*C]s = \bigcup_{i\in\mathcal{N}} \phi_i(s) \text{ where}$$

$\phi_0(s) = \{<\perp,\lambda>\}, \phi_{i+1}(s) = \hat{\phi}_i\,(\mathcal{M}[C]s)$.

By induction we can prove for all $n \in \mathcal{N}$

$\phi_n(s) = PFC(\{<\perp,<[r_1],[\ ]>\hat{}\ldots\hat{}<[r_n],[\ ]>> \mid \forall i,\ 1 \le i \le n,\ r_i = <0,2,5> \vee r_i = <0,2>\})$.

Hence

$\mathcal{M}[P_{11}::{}^*C]s = PFC(\{<\perp,<[r_1],[\ ]>\hat{}\ldots\hat{}<[r_n],[\ ]>> \mid$
$\quad n \in \mathcal{N},\ \forall i,\ 1 \le i \le n,\ r_i = <11,2,5> \vee r_i = <11,2>\})$ and

$\mathcal{M}[P_{12}::\mathbf{wait}\ 1;{}^*C]s = (\mathcal{M}[{}^*C]\ (\mathcal{M}[\mathbf{wait}\ 1]s))[\{0\}\to 12]$
$\quad = PFC(\{<\perp,<[\ ]>\hat{}<[r_1],[\ ]\hat{}\ldots\hat{}<[r_n],[\ ]>> \mid$
$\quad n \in \mathcal{N},\ \forall i,\ 1 \le i \le n,\ r_i = <12,2,5> \vee r_i = <12,2>\})$.

Next we compute the parallel composition of $P_{11}::{}^*C$ and $P_{12}::\mathbf{wait}\ 1;\ {}^*C$:

$\mathcal{M}[(P_{11}::{}^*C \parallel P_{12}::\mathbf{wait}\ 1;\ {}^*C)]s =$

$RTA_{\{11,12\}}\ (\not{c}^{IC}_{\{11,12\}}\ (\{<\sigma_1 \cup \sigma_2,\ h_1 \# h_2> \mid$
$\quad <\sigma_1,h_1> \in \mathcal{M}[P_{11}::{}^*C]s \wedge <\sigma_2,h_2> \in \mathcal{M}[P_{12}::\mathbf{wait}\ 1;{}^*C]s \wedge h_1 \not{c}^{RT} h_2 \wedge$
$\quad \sigma_{i=\perp} \Rightarrow |h_i| \ge |h_{3-i}|,\ 1 \le i \le 2\}))$

$= \{<\perp,<[r_i]>^n_{i=1}> \mid n \in \mathcal{N},\ \forall i,\ 1 \le i \le n,\ odd(i) \Rightarrow r_i{=}<11,2,5> \vee r_i{=}<11,2>$
$\qquad \wedge\ even(i) \Rightarrow r_i{=}<12,2,5> \vee r_i{=}<12,2>\}$.

Hence

$\mathcal{M}[E_2]s = \{<\perp,\ <[r_i]>^n_{i=1} \mid n \in \mathcal{N},\ \forall i,\ 1 \le i \le n,\ r_i = <1,2,5> \vee r_i = <1,2>\}$.

That $\mathcal{M}[E_1] = \mathcal{M}[E_2]$ holds, can be easily seen by an analogy with formal language theory: $Prefixes((b^*a)^*) = (a \cup b)^*$.

Remark: These two examples illustrate that established deadlock is just a special case of an infinite computation (and is not distinguishable from other infinite computations such as divergence: see the end of section 6.2): E_1 deadlocks when process 2 from some point on does not ask for a value to be input from process 1; in the same context E_2 behaves more or less as 'busy waiting' which is another form of infinite computation.

Example 3: $E_3 \equiv (P_1::(P_{11}::P_2!3 \parallel P_{12}::P_2!7) \parallel P_2::P_1?x)$.

We should get an infinite computation, c.q. an established deadlock of either P_{11} or P_{12} after the succesful communication of the other wtih P_2.

First compute

$\mathcal{M}[P_{11}::P_2!3]s = PFC\ (\{<s,<[<11,2>]>^t\ \hat{}\ <[<11,2,3>]>> \mid t \in \mathcal{N}\})$,

$\mathcal{M}[P_{12}::P_2!7]s = PFC\ (\{<s,<[<12,2>]>^t\ \hat{}\ <[<12,2,7>]>> \mid t \in \mathcal{N}\})$ and

$\mathcal{M}[P_2::P_1?x]s = PFC\ (\{<s[v/x],<[<1,2>]>^t\ \hat{}\ <[<1,2,v>]>> \mid v \in V,\ t \in \mathcal{N}\})$.

Next

$\mathcal{M}[P_{11}::P_2!3 \parallel P_{12}::P_2!7)]s =$

$RTA_{\{11,12\}}\ (\not{c}^{IC}_{\{11,12\}}\ (\{<\sigma_1 \cup \sigma_2,\ h_1 \# h_2> \mid$
$\quad <\sigma_1,h_1> \in \mathcal{M}[P_{11}::P_2!3]s \wedge <\sigma_2,h_2> \in \mathcal{M}[P_{12}::P_2!7]s \wedge h_1 \not{c}^{RT} h_2$
$\qquad \wedge\ \sigma_i = \perp \Rightarrow |h_i| \ge |h_{3-i}|, 1 \le i \le 2\}))$

$= PFC\ (\{<s,<[<11,2>,<12,2>]>^{t_1}\ \hat{}\ <[<11,2,3>,<12,2>]>\ \hat{}$
$<[<12,2>]>^{t_2}\ \hat{}\ <[<12,2,7>]>> \mid t_1,t_2 \in \mathcal{N}\}$
$\quad \cup\ \{<s,<[<11,2>,<12,2>]>^t\ \hat{}\ <[<11,2,3>,<12,2,7>]>> \mid t \in \mathcal{N}\}$
$\quad \cup\ \{<s,<[<11,2>,<12,2>]>^{t_1}\ \hat{}\ <[<11,2>,<12,2,7>]>\ \hat{}\ <[<11,2>]>^{t_2}\ \hat{}\ <[<11,2,3>]>> \mid$
$\quad t_1,t_2 \in \mathcal{N}\})$.

Hence

$\mathcal{M}[P_1::(P_{11}::P_2!3 \parallel P_{12}::P_2!7)]s =$

$PFC\ (\{<s,<[<1,2>^2]>^{t_1}\ \hat{}\ <[<1,2,3>,<1,2>]>\ \hat{}\ <[<1,2>]>^{t_2}\ \hat{}\ <[<1,2,7>]>> \mid t_1,t_2 \in \mathcal{N}\}$
$\quad \cup\ \{<s,<[<1,2>^2]>^t\ \hat{}\ <[<1,2,3>,<1,2,7>]>> \mid t \in \mathcal{N}\}$
$\quad \cup\ \{<s,\ <[<1,2>^2]>^{t_1}\ \hat{}\ <[<1,2>,<1,2,7>]>\ \hat{}\ <[<1,2>]>^{t_2}\ \hat{}\ <[<1,2,3>]>> \mid t_1,t_2 \in \mathcal{N}\})$.

Note that here the use of bags instead of sets is essential, especially if we replace 3 and 7 both by 5 !

Then

$\mathcal{M}[E_3]s =$
$\quad RTA_{\{1,2\}}\ (\not{c}^{IC}_{\{1,2\}}\ (\{<\sigma_1 \cup \sigma_2,\ h_1 \# h_2> \mid$
$\quad <\sigma_1,h_1> \in \mathcal{M}[P_1::(P_{11}::P_2!3 \parallel P_{12}::P_2!7)]s \wedge <\sigma_2,h_2> \in \mathcal{M}[P_2::P_1?x]s \wedge h_1 \not{c}^{RT} h_2 \wedge$

$\sigma_{i=\perp} \Rightarrow |h_i| \geq |h_{3-i}|, 1 \leq i \leq 2\}))$
$= RTA_{\{1,2\}}\ (PFC\ (\{<\perp,<[<1,2>]>\ \hat{}\ <[<1,2>]>^{t_2}>|t_2 \in \mathcal{N}\}))$
$= \{<\perp,<[\ ]>^{t}>|t \in \mathcal{N}\}$.

Example 4: $E_4 \equiv (P_1::(P_{11}::P_2!3 \parallel P_{12}::P_2!7) \parallel P_2::P_1?x;\ P_1?x)$.
In this example one of the processes 11 and 12 first communicates with P_2 and then the other. The total program terminates in two time units. For $\mathcal{M}[P_1::(P_{11}::P_2!3 \parallel P_{12}::P_2!7)]s$ see example 3.
Furthermore
$\mathcal{M}[P_2::P_1?x;\ P_1?x]s =$
$PFC\ (\{<s[v_2/x],<[<1,2>]>^{t_1}\ \hat{}\ <[<1,2,v_1>]>\ \hat{}\ <[<1,2>]>^{t_2}\ \hat{}\ <[<1,2,v_2>]>>|v_1,v_2 \in V, t_1,t_2 \in \mathcal{N}\})$.
Then
$\mathcal{M}[E_4]s =$
$RTA_{\{1,2\}}\ (PFC\ (\{<s[7/x],<[<1,2>],[\ ]>>\} \cup \{<s[3/x],<[<1,2>],[\ ]>>\}))$
$= PFC\ (\{<s[v/x],<[\ ]>^2>|v \in \{3,7\}\})$.

Example 5: $E_5 \equiv (P_1::(P_{11}::P_2!3 \parallel P_{12}::P_2!7) \parallel P_2::(P_{21}::P_1?x \parallel P_{22}::P_1?y))$.
In this example processes 11 and 12 communicate *simultaneously* with processes 21 and 22. The total program terminates in one time unit.
For $\mathcal{M}[P_1::(P_{11}::P_2!3 \parallel P_{12}::P_2!7)]s$ see example 3.
Similarly we can compute
$\mathcal{M}[P_2::(P_{21}::P_1?x \parallel P_{22}::P_1?y)]s =$
$PFC\ (\{<s[v_1/x][v_2/y],<[<1,2>^2]>^{t_1}\ \hat{}\ <[<1,2,v_1>,<1,2>]>\ \hat{}\ <[<1,2>]>^{t_2}\ \hat{}\ <[<1,2,v_2>]>>\ |$
$v_1,v_2 \in V, t_1,t_2 \in \mathcal{N}\} \cup \{<s[v_1/x][v_2/y],<[<1,2>^2]>^{t}\ \hat{}\ <[<1,2,v_1>,<1,2,v_2>]>>|$
$v_1,v_2 \in V, t_1,t_2 \in \mathcal{N}\} \cup \{<s[v_1/x][v_2/y],<[<1,2>^2]>^{t_1}\ \hat{}\ <[<1,2>,<1,2,v_2>]>\ \hat{}\ <[<1,2>]>^{t_2}\ \hat{}$
$<[<1,2,v_1>]>>\ |\ v_1,v_2 \in V, t_1,t_2 \in \mathcal{N}\})$.
Then
$\mathcal{M}[E_5]s = RTA_{\{1,2\}}\ (PFC\ (\{<s[v_1/x][v_2/y],<[\ ]>>|(v_1 = 3 \wedge v_2 = 7) \vee (v_1 = 7 \wedge v_2 = 3)\}))$
$= PFC\ (\{<s[v_1/x][v_2/y],<[\ ]>>|(v_1 = 3 \wedge v_2 = 7) \vee (v_1 = 7 \wedge v_2 = 3)\})$.

9. REAL-TIME MODELS

9.1 Introduction

The following example illustrates the conceptual problems associated with applying (pure) maximal parallelism to communication based systems, motivating the introduction of a whole family of real-time models in which the maximal parallelism model is incorporated.

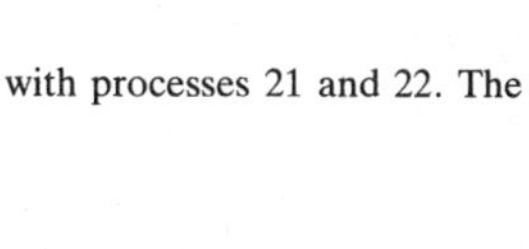

Consider a network with distributed control, and two processes A and B in different nodes that want to communicate with a process C in a third node. If A wants to communicate at an earlier time than B, relative to some global time scale, then according to the fcfs-principle, indeed, A schould communicate first. Whether A's message *arrives* in C before B's message or not, depends on the topology of the network. So, it makes no sense to impose fcfs unless many more details are known about the network. Similar problems occur if processors communicate, e.g., via a common bus where assumptions about bus-arbitration have to be taken into account.
This analysis shows that the fcfs-principle is applied to the order of initiation of communication requests while the above example shows that the time at which communication requests are noticed is relevant. This time gap between initiation and receipt is the essential feature of the $MAX_\gamma(\delta,\varepsilon)$ model of distributed concurrency. As we want to abstract from the properties of communication media, we introduce an uncertainty, bounded by δ an ε, in the length of such time gaps. As a consequence, communications that are initiated too close in time (relative to a global clock) cannot be temporally ordered anymore.

9.2 $MAX_\gamma(\delta,\varepsilon)$ model of concurrency

The model is based on the Salwicki/Müldner maximal parallelism model: there is no unnecessary waiting between the execution of actions. Communication between processes is served on a first-come first-served basis.
Additionally, the following model pertains to process-communication:

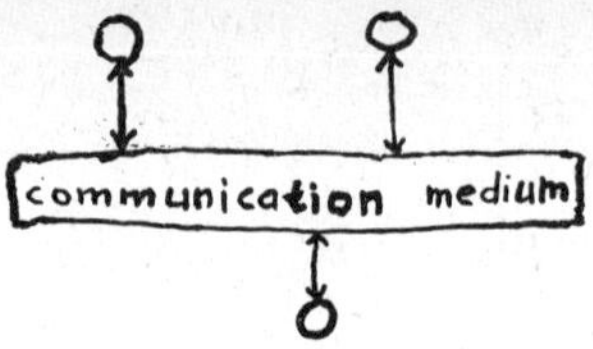

- processes communicate via a medium,
- it takes between δ and ε time units (ε *not* included) for the medium to become aware of a process expressing its willingness to communicate or withdrawing its willingness (time-out),
- communication between two processes only occurs after the medium has become aware of both processes willingness,
- a communication takes an additional γ time units during which period the processes remain synchronized,
- a communication that is in progress at a time when the medium receives a time-out from one of the participating processes, will be completed; a communication that might be started at such a time, will not be executed.

Remarks:

- Communication always takes at least $\delta+\gamma$ time units.
- Let CP(t) denote the set of processes whose willingness to communicate the medium is aware of at time t and let $P \in CP(t)$. A communication-partner for P may be found in the set CP(t') only if no set $CP(\bar{t})$ with $t \leq \bar{t} \leq t'$ contains a partner for P.
- $Max_\gamma(0,2) \not\models \{true\}\ (P_1::P_2?x;P_2?y \parallel P_2::(P_{21}::P_1!1 \parallel P_{22}::\mathbf{wait}\ 1;P_1!2))\ \{x=1\}$, and
  $Max_\gamma(0,1) \models \{true\}\ (P_1::P_2?x;P_2?y \parallel P_2::(P_{21}::P_1!1 \parallel P_{22}::\mathbf{wait}\ 1;P_1!2))\ \{x=1\}$.
  In other words, there is an uncertainty interval of ε-δ: if requests for communication are initiated ε-δ or more time units apart, the first request will indeed be served first; if, on the other hand, these requests are initiated within this interval, the order in which these requests are served is undefined.
- $Max_0(0,1)$ gives vise to pure maximal parallelism;
  $Max_0(0,\infty)$ to pure interleaving semantics (with respect to the communication actions).

10. REAL-TIME SEMANTICS FOR MINI CSP-R

The $Max_\gamma(\delta,\varepsilon)$ model only influences the semantics of communication actions. So, we may expect no changes in the definition of $\mathcal{M}$. The definition of the auxiliary function $\mathcal{G}$ will undoubtedly have to change. The intention of these changes is to have $\mathcal{G}$ "generate" any history that is consistent with the parameters of the model. As these (additional) consistency-requirements are a purely local affair, the parallel composition of processes requires no additional effort.
Consider an I/O command. The changes in the sets of generated histories that $Max_\gamma(\delta,\varepsilon)$ induces, are threefold:

1. histories must be generated in which the first waiting-action (i.e., the first no-match claim record) occcurs τ time units later than the time at which communication was requested; and this for any τ such that $\delta \leq \tau < \varepsilon$,
2. in no history can communication or waiting start within δ time units of the request,
3. communication takes γ time units; this is modelled by having the associated communication claim record mark the time, in a history, at which communication starts and by appending empty bags to trace out γ time units.

The changes to $\mathcal{G}$ are complicated by the necessity of applying the above considerations to every I/O command in the environment (i.e., in the selection or repetition).

First, two auxiliary functions:

Definition: For two equipotent sets of guards G and times (i.e., natural numbers) T, time t and state s, define

- $A(G,T,t) = \{g_i \in G \mid t_i < t,\ 1 \leq i \leq n\}$, where
  $\{g_i,\ldots,g_n\} \subseteq G$ are the I/O guards in G and $T = \{t_1,\ldots,t_n\}$,
- $Ext(G,T,t,s) = <RTA(A(G,T,k),s)>_{k=1}^{t}$.

$Ext(\{\alpha_1,\ldots,\alpha_n\},\{t_1,\ldots,t_n\},t,s)$ yields a sequence of bags of no-match claim records for the I/O commands $\alpha_1,\ldots,\alpha_n$. The time t_i represents the delay of the first waiting action (i.e., no-match claim record) for α_i; t is the time at which a communication or a time-out occurs. The state s would be needed if mixed guards were present. The function A is an auxiliary to define Ext.

Now, we are ready to define $\mathcal{G}$ (terminology as in section 7):

$$\mathcal{G}[b,A]s = \begin{cases} PFC(\{\langle s,\lambda\rangle\}) & \text{if } B[b]s \\ \{\langle\perp,\lambda\rangle\} & \text{otherwise.}\end{cases}$$

$$\mathcal{G}[\mathbf{wait}\ d,A]s = PFC(\{\langle s,Ext(A,T,t+\tau,s)\rangle \mid \max\{\mathcal{V}[d]s,1\} = minwait(A \cup \{\text{ wait } d\},s) \overset{def.}{=} t,$$
$$T \overset{def.}{=} \{t_1,\ldots,t_n\},\ \delta \leqslant t_i < \varepsilon\ (1\leqslant i\leqslant n),\ \delta\leqslant\tau<\varepsilon\}),$$
where n is the number of I/O guards in A.

$$\mathcal{G}[P_j!e,A]s = PFC(\{\langle s,Ext(GRDS,T,t,s) \mathbin{\hat{}} \langle[\langle 0,j,\mathcal{V}[e]s\rangle]\rangle \mathbin{\hat{}} \langle[\,]\rangle^{\gamma}\rangle \mid$$
$$\delta\leqslant t<minwait(GRDS,s)+\varepsilon\text{-}1,\ T \overset{def.}{=} \{t_1,\ldots,t_n\},\ \delta\leqslant t_i<\varepsilon\ (1\leqslant i\leqslant n)\}),$$
where $GRDS = A \cup \{P_j!e\}$ and n is the number of I/O guards in GRDS.

The upperbound on t takes the delay of the arrival of the time-out message in the medium into account.

$$\mathcal{G}[P_j?x,A]s = PFC(\{\langle s[v/x],Ext(GRDS,T,t,s) \mathbin{\hat{}} \langle[\langle j,0,v\rangle]\rangle \mathbin{\hat{}} \langle[\,]\rangle^{\gamma}\rangle \mid$$
$$v\in V,\ \delta\leqslant t<minwait(GRDS,s)+\varepsilon\text{-}1,\ T \overset{def.}{=} \{t_1,\ldots,t_n\},\ \delta\leqslant t_i<\varepsilon\ (1\leqslant i\leqslant n)\}),$$
where $GRDS = A \cup \{P_j?x\}$ and n is the number of I/O guards in GRDS.

$\mathcal{G}[b;g,A]s = \hat{\mathcal{G}[g,A]}\ (\mathcal{G}[b,A]s)$, where g is either a pure I/O guard or a pure wait guard.

We illustrate these equations by the example in the remarks of section 9.2.
Let $P \equiv (P_1::P_2?x;P_2?y \parallel P_2::(P_{21}::P_1!1 \parallel P_{22}::\mathbf{wait}\ 1;P_1!2))$.
We claim that $Max_0(0,2) \not\models \{true\}P\ \{x=1\}$ but
$Max_0(0,1) \models \{true\}\ P\ \{x=1\}$. In other words, we claim that
$Max_0(0,2)$ allows computations in which P_{22} communicates first, that are disallowed by $Max_0(0,1)$.
So, assume $\gamma = 0,\ \delta = 0,\ \varepsilon = 2$:

$\mathcal{M}[P_1!2]s = \mathcal{G}[P_1!2,\varnothing]s = PFC(\{\langle s,Ext(\{P_1!2\},\{t_1\},t,s) \mathbin{\hat{}} \langle[\langle 0,1,2\rangle]\rangle\rangle \mid t\in\mathcal{N},\ 0\leqslant t_1\leqslant 1\})$.
Now, $Ext(\{P_1!2\},\{0\},t,s) = \langle RTA(\{P_1!2\},s)\rangle^t = \langle[\langle 0,1\rangle]\rangle^t,\ t\in\mathcal{N},\ Ext(\{P_1!2\},\{1\},0,s) = \lambda$, and
$Ext(\{P_1!2\},\{1\},t,s) = \langle RTA(\varnothing,s)\rangle \mathbin{\hat{}} \langle RTA(\{P_1!2\},s)\rangle^{t-1} = \langle[\,]\rangle \mathbin{\hat{}} \langle[\langle 0,1\rangle]\rangle^{t-1},\ t>0$.
Hence
$\mathcal{M}[P_1!2]s = PFC((\{\langle s,\langle[\,]\rangle^{\tau} \mathbin{\hat{}} \langle[\langle 0,1\rangle]\rangle^{t} \mathbin{\hat{}} \langle[\langle 0,1,2\rangle]\rangle\rangle \mid 0\leqslant\tau\leqslant 1,\ t\in\mathcal{N}\})$.
Analogously, we obtain the semantics of $P_1!1$ and of the input commands of P_1.
Moreover, $\mathcal{M}[\mathbf{wait}\ 1]s = PFC(\{\langle s,\langle[\,]\rangle^{\tau}\rangle \mid 1\leqslant\tau\leqslant 2\})$, hence
$\mathcal{M}[P_{21}::P_1!1]s = PFC(\{\langle s,\langle[\,]\rangle^{\tau_{21}} \mathbin{\hat{}} \langle[\langle 21,1\rangle]\rangle^{t_{21}} \mathbin{\hat{}} \langle[\langle 21,1,1\rangle]\rangle\rangle \mid 0\leqslant\tau_{21}\leqslant 1,t_{21}\in\mathcal{N}\})$
$\mathcal{M}[P_{22}::\mathbf{wait}\ 1;P_1!2]s = PFC(\{\langle s,\langle[\,]\rangle^{\tau_{22}} \mathbin{\hat{}} \langle[\langle 22,1\rangle]\rangle^{t_{22}} \mathbin{\hat{}} \langle[\langle 22,1,2\rangle]\rangle\rangle \mid 1\leqslant\tau_{22}\leqslant 3,t_{22}\in\mathcal{N}\})$
$\mathcal{M}[P_1::P_2?x;P_2?y]s = PFC(\{\langle s[v_1/x][v_2/y],\langle[\,]\rangle^{\tau_{11}} \mathbin{\hat{}} \langle[\langle 2,1\rangle]\rangle^{t_{11}} \mathbin{\hat{}} \langle[\langle 2,1,v_1\rangle]\rangle$
$\quad \mathbin{\hat{}} \langle[\,]\rangle^{\tau_{12}} \mathbin{\hat{}} \langle[\langle 2,1\rangle]\rangle^{t_{12}} \mathbin{\hat{}} \langle[\langle 2,1,v_2\rangle]\rangle\rangle \mid 0\leqslant\tau_{11},\tau_{12}\leqslant 1,t_{11},t_{12}\in\mathcal{N},v_1,v_2\in V\})$.

Consider the histories for P_{21} and P_{22} in which $\tau_{21} = \tau_{22} = t_{21} = 1,\ t_{22} = 0$.
In particular consider P_{21}'s history $\langle[\,],[\langle 21,1\rangle],[\langle 21,1,1\rangle]\rangle$ and P_{22}'s history $\langle[\,],[\langle 22,1,2\rangle]\rangle$. These compatible histories yield the following history for P_2: $\langle[\,],[\langle 2,1\rangle,\langle 2,1,2\rangle],[\langle 2,1,1\rangle]\rangle$.
This is compatible with P_1's history $\langle[\,],[\langle 2,1,2\rangle],[\langle 2,1,1\rangle]\rangle$, obtained by taking
$\tau_{11} = 1,\ \tau_{12} = t_{11} = t_{12} = 0,\ v_1 = 2,\ v_2 = 1$.
From these two histories we can compute the following element in the denotation for P: $\langle s[2/x][1/y],\langle[\,]\rangle^3\rangle$.
To show that this computation cannot be generated by the $Max_0(0,1)$-model (i.e., the maximal parallelism model, as used in section 7) is straightforward: now, choosing $\tau_{11} = \tau_{21} = 1$ is illegal (cf. example 4 in section 8).

Conclusions

We have given a denotational semantics for real-time distributed computing stressing:

(1) compositionality, thus supplying a basis for compositional specification and verification techniques,
(2) a model of concurrency that is realistic, in contrast with interleaving, in the context of real-time: the maximal parallelism model,
(3) simplicity by basing our techniques upon the linear history semantics for CSP of Francez et al.

We feel that our way of dealing with real-time is particularly simple. Timing aspects of programs relate to the length of the histories. Maximal parallelism constraints are made explicit by recording not only the occurrence of communications but also the act of waiting for one. When binding two processes, these constraints imply that at

no instant of time both processes are waiting for a mutual communication.
Exact clocking of instructions is unrealistic because then all actions can be exactly determined in time. In a shared variables context, this would imply that mutual exclusion, for example, could be programmed without any additional means such as semaphores. This is resolved in Milner's SCCS by introducing the nondeterministic but bounded wait synchronization primitive δ *which may violate* the maximal parallelism constraints. In our set-up, however, shared variables are excluded, so the mutual exclusion anomaly above does not occur. Additionally, by extending the maximal parallelism model by introducing non-deterministic intervals modelling synchronization delays, again this anomaly disappears. Joe Halpern arrived independently at the same extended model, in his case to achieve coordinated actions in a real-time distributed system [HMM85]. This extension furthermore shows that our techniques can easily accomodate more detailed real-time features. Another example of this is modelling the drifting of local clocks. Since only initial and final states and histories are observable, we hope that exact clocking of instructions together with the extension of the maximal parallelism model result in a realistic simplification of the phenomena inherent in the description of real-time *distributed* computing.
We based our research on CSP-R, a language that captures the essential real-time features of Ada, as supported by the simulation of Ada by CSP-R in Appendix A2. In fact, we had to solve two problems: Firstly, how to model maximal concurrency in a compositional way and secondly, how to deal with CSP-R's and Ada's particular form of communication, involving the naming of communication partners and hence inducing process-naming. This is a non-trivial problem and its solution definitly complicates our semantics: the use of bags instead of sets in our histories and many of the complications in parallel composition are a direct consequence of it. Our ideas about modelling maximal paralellism are independent of this and, we maintain, are of general applicability. This is illustrated by [Ger 85] in which a formal semantics for (recursive) Occam is given, that is surprisingly simple because of the much cleaner communication mechanism of Occam, using communication channels between pairs of processes.

Ongoing research

There is a clear correspondence between the readiness semantics of CSP (see [HH 83] and ours: Our sets of no match records - like the ready sets - indicate the set of next possible communications. Certain aspects which cause the readiness model to be not fully abstract, thus leading to the failure set model (see [BHR 84]), are also present in our model:
Our semantics differentiates the two program fragments
[**true** → P_1!0; **wait** 1 □ **true** → P_2!0; **wait** 1] and
[**true** → P_1!0; **wait** 1 □ **true** → P_2!0; **wait** 1 □ **true** → [P_1!0 → **wait** 1 □ P_2!0 → **wait** 1]],
although their observable behaviour is the same. Interestingly, we cannot turn to failure set like semantics, because knowing the maximal set of possible communications at a time, is crucial for checking maximal parallelism.
The precise relation of our model to the readiness and failure set models and the question of how to make our model fully abstract are currently being investigated.
Having discovered on a semantic level how to reason compositionally about maximal parallelism we now have a firm basis for developing compositional specification and verification methods. These are presently under development. A first attempt to use our compositional semantics to get, along the line of the work of Soundararajan, a compositional proof system was made in [Shy 84].

Acknowledgements

We are indebted to the second author, who, during a four-month visit to Utrecht at the end of 1983, started this research by writing [SR 83].
Our thanks goes to Amir Pnueli, who assisted at several occasions in correcting and improving previous versions of this paper.
We especially want to thank JH for his suggestion that a juicy introduction would do the job.

References

[Ada 83] *The programming language Ada. Reference manual.* LNCS 155, Springer, 1983.

[BC 84] G. Berry, L. Cosserat. *The ESTEREL Synchronous Programming Language and its Mathematical Semantics.* R de R No 327, INRIA, Centre Sophia Antipolis, 1984.

[BH 81] A. Bernstein, P.K. Harter jr. *Proving Real-time Properties of Programs with Termporal Logic.* 8th ACM SOSP, pp. 1-11, 1981.

[BHR 84] S.D. Brookes, C.A.R. Hoare, A.W. Roscoe. *A theory of Communicating Sequential Processes.* JACM 31-3, pp. 560-599, July 1984.

[BKP 84] H. Barringer, R. Kuiper, A. Pnueli. *Now You May Compose Temporal Logic Specifications.* 16th ACM STOC, pp. 51-63, 1984.

[BLW 82] P.Branquart, G. Louis, P. Wodon. *An Analytical Description of CHILL, the CCITT High Level Language VI* , LNCS 128, Sspringer, 1982.

[BO 80] D. Bjørner, O.N. Oest (eds). *Towards a Formal Description of Ada.* LNCS 98, Springer, 1980.

[CACM 84] *A Case Study: The Space Shuttle Software System.* CACM 27-9, 1984.

[Cam 82] J. Camerini. *Semantique Mathematique de Primitives Temps Reel.* These de 3 eme cycle, IMA, Université de Nice, 1982.

[Dij 59] E.W. Dijkstra. *Communication with an automatic computer.* Ph.D. thesis, Mathematical Centre, Amsterdam, 1959.

[FLP 84] N. Francez, D. Lehmann, A. Pnueli. *A linear-history semantics for languages for distributed programming.* TCS 32, pp. 25-46, 1984.

[Ger 85] R. Gerth. *A Maximal Parallelism Semantics for Occam.* Notes, 1985.

[HH 83] E.C.R. Hehner, C.A.R. Hoare. *A more complete model of communicating processes.* TCS 26, pp. 105-120, 1983.

[HMM85] J. Y. Halpern, N. Megiddo, A. A. Munshi. *Optimal Precision in the Presence of Uncertainty.* IBM Research Lab., San Jose, 1985.

[Hoa 78] C.A.R. Hoare. *Communicating Sequential Processes.* CACM 21-8, 1978.

[Jon 82] G. Jones.D. Phil.thesis, Oxford, unpublished, 1982.

[Koy 84] R. Koymans. *Denotational semantics for real-time programming constructs in concurrent languages.* Notes, 1984.

[KSRGA85] R. Koymans, R.K. Shyamasundar, W.P. de Roever, R. Gerth, S. Arun-Kumar. *Compositional Semantics for Real-time Distributed Computing.* KUN Report, Informatics Department, Nijmegen University, 1985.

[KVR 83] R. Koymans, J. Vytopil, W.P. de Roever. *Real-time Programming and Asynchronous Message Passing.* 2nd ACM PODC, pp. 187-197, 1983.

[Mil 73] R. Milner. *An approach to the semantics of parallel programs.* Proc. of the Convegno di Informatica Teorica, Pisa, 1973.

[Mil 83] R. Milner. *Calculi for Synchrony and Asynchrony.* TCS 25, pp. 267-310, 1983.

[Occ 84] *The Occam language reference manual.* Prentice Hall, 1984.

[Shy 84] R.K. Shyamasundar. *A total correctness proof system for a real-time distributed language* . Notes, 1984.

[SM 81] A. Salwicki, T. Müldner. *On the algorithmic properties of concurrent programs.* LNCS 125, Springer, 1981.

[Sou 83] N. Soundararajan. *Correctness Proofs for CSP Programs.* TCS 23-4, 1983.

[Sou 84] N. Soundararajan. *Axiomatic Semantics of Communicating Sequential Processes.* TOPLAS 6-4, pp. 647-662, 1984.

[SR 83] R.K. Shyamasundar, W. P. de Roever. *Semantics of real-time Ada.* Notes, 1983.

[ST 84] Sunday Times July 22, 1984.

[Zij 84] E. Zijlstra. *Real-time semantics.* submitted, 1984.

Appendix A: CSP-R and the simulation of Ada

A1. CSP-R

The only difference between Mini CSP-R (see section 2) and CSP-R lies in the definition of I/O commands. CSP-R extends Mini CSP-R in the following ways:

- communication takes place via (a form of) channels,
- the expressions in output commands and the variables in input commands are vectors,
- process identifiers can be communicated and can be used in subsequent communications to determine the target process,

- communication with an arbitrary process can be requested instead of only addressing a particular process.

The syntax of Mini CSP-R is changed in the following way:
Replace forms 3.1 and 3.2 of instructions by

3.1.1 $P_i.c!\vec{e}$	- output to process i via channel c the values of the expressions in the list $\vec{e}$, together with the identification of the sending process
3.1.2 $id.c!\vec{e}$	- as 3.1.1, but now the target process is determined by the value of the identification variable id
3.1.3 $.c!\vec{e}[\#id]$	- output via channel c to *any* process the values of the expressions in the list $\vec{e}$, together with the identification of the sender; record the identity of the receiving process in the identification variable id (the brackets [and] indicate that the identification variable is optional, i.e., $.c!\vec{e}$ is allowed, too)
3.2.1 $P_1.c?\vec{x}$	- the analogon of 3.1.1, but now values are received and are assigned to the variables in the list $\vec{x}$
3.2.2 $id.c?\vec{x}$	- the analogon of 3.1.2
3.2.3 $.c?\vec{x}[\#id]$	- the analogon of 3.1.3.

An identification variable is a variable ranging over $\{P_1,P_2,...\}$. It can only be assigned to using an instruction of the form 3.1.3 or 3.2.3.
The notions of syntactic and semantic matching of I/O commands have to be reformulated.
$\langle P_i,\alpha\rangle$ and $\langle P_j,\beta\rangle$ match syntactically iff:
1. α and β specify the same channel,
2. the vectors have equal length,
3. if α is an input command, then β is an output command and vice versa, and
4. if $\alpha(\beta)$ is of the form 3.1.1 or 3.2.1 then the specified target process should be $P_j(P_i)$.

$\langle i,\alpha\rangle$ and $\langle j,\beta\rangle$ match semantically iff:
1. $\langle P_i,\alpha\rangle$ and $\langle P_j,\beta\rangle$ match syntactically,
2. control in P_i and P_j is in front of both α and β, and
3. if $\alpha(\beta)$ is of the form 3.1.2 or 3.2.2, then the identification variable must have the value $P_j(P_i)$.

The result of two semantically matching I/O commands is the simultaneous execution of those commands as indicated by 3.1.1 - 3.2.3 above. Its effect is the assignment of the expression values to the variables and, possibly, the assignment to identification variables.

The remaining syntax and interpretation of CSP-R is the same as for Mini CSP-R.
As for the extension of our denotational semantics to CSP-R, like the assumptions we have to record about values in the denotations for input commands, we now additionally record assumptions about the communication target in the denotations for I/O commands of the form 3.1.3 and 3.2.3.
Of course, the communication assumption records have to change. The communication claim records now have to record the communication channel and the communicated *vector* of values (instead of a single value). The no-match claim records now record the communication channel and the *length* of the communicated vector of values. Additionally, because of the I/O commands of the form 3.1.3 and 3.2.3, no-match claim records have to indicate with which *set* of processes a match is impossible (a single process for the forms 3.1.1, 3.1.2, 3.2.1 and 3.2.2, and all processes for the forms 3.1.3 and 3.2.3).
The denotations and techniques such as the consistency check have to be adapted corresponding to the above changes. These adaptations are straightforward except for a slight complication in the meaning of P_i::T: Because any communication target is assumed in the denotations for I/O commands of the form 3.1.3 and 3.2.3, now constructs like $P_i::.c!\vec{e}$ generate communication claim records in which process i communicates with itself. This is clearly impossible and such records should be removed by an additional operator. (Notice that this problem did not occur for Mini CSP-R, because constructs like $P_i::P_i!e$ were prohibited syntactically by the naming conventions, see section 2).
The resulting semantics can be found in [Koy 84].

A2. Simulating Ada

To illustrate the power of CSP-R we translate the basic Ada communication primitives into CSP-R. This translation is denoted by τ. The Ada rendezvous is assumed to be understood.

1. the timed entry call ([Ada 83, § 9.7.3]).
   select call $T_i.a(\vec{e},\vec{x});S_1$ $\vee$ **delay** $t;S_2$ **endselect**.

   The semantics of this statement prescribes that if a rendezvous can be started within the specified duration t (or immediately), then it is performed and S_1 is executed afterwards. Otherwise, when the duration has expired, S_2 is executed.
   We offer as translation:
   $[T_i.a(\vec{e},\vec{x}) \rightarrow T_i.a?\vec{x};\ \tau(S_1)\ \Box\ \mathbf{wait}(t+1) \rightarrow \tau(S_2)]$.

2. the selective wait (without terminate alternative)([Ada 83, § 9.7.1]).
   select $\vee(i=1..n)$**when** $b_i \Rightarrow S_i$ $\vee(j=1..m)$**when** $b^j \Rightarrow$ **delay** $E^j;S^j$ **endselect**,
   where $S_i \equiv$ **accept** $a_i(\vec{u}_i \# \vec{v}_i)$**do** S_{i_1} **endaccept**; S_{i_2} $(i=1..n)$.

   The semantics is, that first the minimum value MIN, of those E^j whose guard, b^j, is open is evaluated. If a rendezvous with one of the a_i's whose guard, b_i, is open, can be started either immediately or within duration MIN, then it is performed and S_{i_2} is executed afterwards. Otherwise, when MIN time units elapsed, one of the delay alternatives S^j for which E^j = MIN (and whose associated guard is open) is executed.
   Our translation:
   $$[\mathop{\Box}_{i=1}^{n} b_i;.a_i?(\vec{u}_i,\vec{v}_i)\#\ id \rightarrow \tau(S_{i_1});\ id.a_i!\vec{v}_i;\ \tau(S_{i_2})$$
   $$\Box$$
   $$\mathop{\Box}_{j=1}^{m} b^j;\ \mathbf{wait}(E^j+1) \rightarrow \tau(S^j)].$$

Appendix B: definition of B[I→i]

Definition 1: For $I,J\in\mathcal{P}(\mathcal{N})$ define $R(I,J)\in\mathcal{P}(CAR)$ as $R(I,J) = \{r'\in CAR|\pi_1(r')\in I \wedge \pi_2(r')\in J\}$. R(I,J) restricts the first and second component of pairs and triples in CAR.

Definition 2: For $r\in CAR$ define $ETC(r)\in \mathcal{P}(CAR)$ as $ETC(r) = \{r'\in CAR|\ |r'| = |r| \wedge |r| = 3 \Rightarrow \pi_3(r') = \pi_3(r)\}$. Equal Third Component of r selects pairs r' if r is a pair (and hence contains no third component) and otherwise triples r' with the same third component as r.

Definition 3: For $B\in\mathcal{B}(CAR)$, $I\in\mathcal{P}(\mathcal{N})$ and $i\in\mathcal{N}$ we define $B[I\rightarrow i]\in\mathcal{B}(CAR)$ as follows:

$$B[I\rightarrow i](r) = \begin{cases} 0 & \text{if } \pi_1(r)\in I\setminus\{i\} \vee \pi_2(r)\in I\setminus\{i\} \\ B(r) + \displaystyle\sum_{r'\in ETC(r)\cap R(I\setminus\{i\},\{\pi_2(r)\})} B(r') & \text{if } \pi_1(r)=i \wedge \pi_2(r)\notin I\cup\{i\} \\ B(r) + \displaystyle\sum_{r'\in ETC(r)\cap R(\{\pi_1(r)\},I\setminus\{i\})} B(r') & \text{if } \pi_1(r)\notin I\cup\{i\} \wedge \pi_2(r)=i \\ B(r) + \displaystyle\sum_{r'\in ETC(r)\cap(R(\{i\},I\setminus\{i\})\cup R(I\setminus\{i\},\{i\})\cup R(I\setminus\{i\},I\setminus\{i\}))} B(r') & \text{if } \pi_1(r)=\pi_2(r)=i \\ B(r) & \text{otherwise.} \end{cases}$$

Partial-correctness theories as first-order theories*

Daniel Leivant
Department of Computer Science
Carnegie-Mellon University

Abstract.

We show that any predicate transformer is rendered (semantically) by a first-order theory, provided it is *propositionally closed*, i.e. closed under the rules of Consequence, Conjunction and Disjunction.

It follows that fundamental results in the metamathematics of first-order theories can be applied to propositionally closed predicate transformers, and therefore also to partial-correctness theories of programs. In particular, any such theory is complete for the Hoare semantics it induces, by Godel's Strong Completeness Theorem. From this it also follows that a predicate transformer is a partial-correctness theory of some I/O relation iff it is propositionally closed [Par83].

Introduction.

Hoare-style formalisms for partial-correctness of programs have had a dual nature. They were invented by Hoare as defining the *axiomatic semantics* of **while** programs, and used by others to define the axiomatic semantics of richer programming languages. At the same time, Hoare-style formalisms have been used as vehicles for reasoning about programs, and for guiding program development.

We address two issues related to both goals of Hoare-style formalisms. First, the inference rules cannot be confined to operate on partial-correctness assertions (pca's) alone: such assertions must sometimes refer to formulas in the assertion language, as in the Rule of Consequence. It is natural then to ask whether a particular set of closure conditions on a Hoare formalism (such as the Rule of Consequence) is sufficiently inclusive.

A second issue is to relate a Hoare-style formalism for a given programming language to the I/O semantics, or other semantics, of programs in the language in hand. Obviously, no reasonable formalism can deduce all pca's that are valid in all structures, with respect to the standard I/O semantics of programs, because these pca's do not form an effectively-enumerable set. Bergtra and Tucker [BT83] have therefore proposed to relate a Hoare-style formalism not to the standard (intended) I/O semantics of programs, but rather to the I/O semantics induced, in a natural sense, by the Hoare formalism itself.

The purpose of this note is to show that both questions can be suitably addressed in the context of comparing Hoare-style reasoning about programs to reasoning about programs (as I/O relations) within first-order logic. The first question may be precisely formulated by asking whether a Hoare style formalism H proves all pca's which can be proved, via their first-order rendition, from pca's in H by *any* first-order deduction about properties of I/O relations. Such deductions do not have, of course, to be confined to addressing I/O relation via pca's only. We show that a formalism H is indeed complete for first-order reasoning about I/O relations provided H is propositionally closed, i.e. closed under the Rules of Consequence, Conjunction and Disjunction, and a Rule of Persistence (see §1).

(*) Research partially supported by ONR grant N00014-84-K-0415 and by DARPA grant F33615-81-K-1539.

It then follows that a formalism H as above can in fact be treated as a first-order theory. The metamathematical properties of first-order logic can then be used. In particular, the I/O semantics induced by H, in the sense proposed in [BT83], turns out to be simply the standard semantics of the rendition of H as a first-order theory. That H is complete for validity in its own models falls out then as a case of Godel's Strong Completeness Theorem. Thus, the completeness of H for the I/O semantics it induces depends only on H being closed under trivial conditions. This suggests that axiomatic semantics, understood as an I/O semantics, is of limited interest.

The rest of the paper is organized as follows. In §1 we introduce concepts that encapsulate the essentials of the subject (our definitions resemble those of [Par83]). We define a simple notion of predicate transformer, which we relate to arbitrary I/O relations over structures. In §2 we make the simple observation that the I/O semantics induced by a predicate transformer has a simple and direct first-order rendition. §3 contains our principal and only non-trivial technical proof: we show that every propositionally closed predicate transformer is complete under first-order reasoning about its first-order rendition. In §4 we use this to show that every propositionally closed predicate transformer is complete for the I/O semantics it induces. We also point out that our main result implies a theorem of Parikh, stating that a predicate transformer is determined by some I/O relation iff it is propositionally closed.

1. Predicate transformers and axiomatics semantics.

1.1. Predicate transformers.

Let L be a first-order language over some similarity type. A *predicate transformer* (*over* L) is a binary relation over L.

Let S be an L-structure. An S-*state* is a mapping ξ from variables of L to values in S (of the appropriate sorts, when sorts are present). An *I/O relation over* S is a relation ρ over the space of S-states. We write $\xi \to_\rho \eta$ for $(\xi,\eta) \in \rho$.

A pair (φ,ψ) of L-formulas is *(partially) correct in* S *with respect to the* S-*states* ξ *and* η,

$$S \models (\varphi,\psi)\,[\xi \to \eta],$$

if

$$S \models \varphi\,[\xi] \quad \text{implies} \quad S \models \psi\,[\eta].$$

A pair (φ,ψ) is *valid in* (S,ρ),

$$(S,\rho) \models (\varphi,\psi),$$

if $S \models (\varphi,\psi)\,[\xi \to \eta]$ whenever $\xi \to_\rho \eta$. A predicate transformer P is *valid in* (S,ρ) if every $\pi \in P$ is.

If ρ is an I/O relation over S, then the *predicate transformer determined by* ρ, $P \equiv P(S,\rho)$, is the set of pairs (φ,ψ) that are valid in (S,ρ). That is, $P(S,\rho)$ is the largest predicate transformer valid in (S,ρ). Dually, each predicate transformer P generates an I/O relation $\rho \equiv \rho(S,P)$ over S, defined by

$$\xi \to_\rho \eta \quad \text{iff} \quad S \models (\varphi,\psi)[\xi \to \eta] \ \text{for all} \ (\varphi,\psi) \in P.$$

That is, $\rho(S,P)$ is the largest I/O relation ρ on S such that P is valid in (S,ρ).

π is *valid in* S *with respect to the axiomatic semantics of* P,

$$S \models_P \pi,$$

if it is valid in (S,ρ) for $\rho \equiv \rho(S,P)$. π is *valid with respect to the axiomatic semantics of* P

$$\models_P \pi,$$

if $S \models_P \pi$ for every structure S for L.

1.2. Closure conditions.

Let Th be a theory in L. A predicate transformer P is *propositionally closed with respect to* Th if it satisfies the following closure conditions:

Persistence: if φ is a closed sentence of L, then $(\varphi,\varphi) \in P$.

Consequence: if $(\varphi,\psi) \in P$, $Th \vdash \varphi_0 \to \varphi$ and $Th \vdash \psi \to \psi_1$, then $(\varphi_0,\psi_1) \in P$, where $\vdash$ denotes provability in first-order logic.

Conjunction: if $(\varphi,\psi_i) \in P$, $(i=0,1)$, then $(\varphi,\psi_0 \wedge \psi_1) \in P$.

Disjunction: if $(\varphi_i,\psi) \in P$, $(i=0,1)$, then $(\varphi_0 \vee \varphi_1,\psi) \in P$.

From the Rules of Consequence and Conjunction it immediately follows that,

if $(\varphi_i,\psi_i) \in P$, $(i=0,1)$, then $(\varphi_0 \wedge \varphi_1,\psi_0 \wedge \psi_1) \in P$.

Similarly, from the Rules of Consequence and Disjunction,

if $(\varphi_i,\psi_i) \in P$, $(i=0,1)$, then $(\varphi_0 \vee \varphi_1,\psi_0 \vee \psi_1) \in P$.

When $Th = \emptyset$ we simply say that P is *propositionally closed.*

1.3. Axiomatic semantics for partial-correctness theories.

A *partial-correctness theory* is a set of partial-correctness assertions. Given a partial-correctness theory H and a program α, define a predicate transformer $H(\alpha) \equiv \{ (\varphi,\psi) \mid \varphi[\alpha]\psi \text{ is in } H\}$. Bergstra and Tucker [BT83] define the *axiomatic semantics induced by* H as the I/O semantics which interprets a program α in a structure S as the axiomatic semantics of $H(\alpha)$ in S (as defined above), i.e. as $\rho(S,H(\alpha))$. Note that

1. only the input-output relations generated by the program α matter here, not the program's operational behavior;
2. only the set $H(\alpha)$ matters, not the inference rules used in generating it;
3. the program α is considered in isolation, and its relation to other programs, be they even its subprograms, is irrelevant.

The notion of axiomatic semantics was introduced in Hoare's seminal paper [Hoa69], and was developed subsequently by Hoare, Lauer, Wirth, Dijkstra, Meyer and others [HL74, Lau72, Man69, Dij76, HW73, MH82, Par83]. Hoare's original intention was to view $H(\alpha)$ itself as the semantics of α. The contribution of [BT83] was to reinterpret $H(\alpha)$ by I/O relations $\rho(S,H(\alpha))$.

2. First-order rendering of predicate transformers.

Let $x_1,\ldots$ be a listing of all variables of L. Consider an extension L^+ of L, with new constants $\mathbf{a}_i$ and $\mathbf{z}_i$ $(i \geq 1)$. Our intention is that $\mathbf{a}_i$ and $\mathbf{z}_i$ denote the initial and final values of the variable x_i for some I/O relation. For each pair $\pi \equiv (\varphi,\psi)$ in P, let $\hat{\pi}$ be the first-order formula

$$\hat{\pi} \equiv \varphi[\bar{a}] \rightarrow \psi[\bar{z}],$$

where $\varphi[\bar{a}] \equiv \varphi[\bar{a}/\bar{x}]$, $\psi[\bar{z}] \equiv \psi[\bar{z}/\bar{x}]$ (i.e., a_i and z_i are substituted for the free occurrences of x_i). We denote by $\Gamma(P)$ the first-order theory whose axioms are all formulas $\hat{\pi}$ where $\pi \in P$. For example, if P is the partial correctness theory of the single-line program $x_1 \leftarrow x_1+1$, then all formulas of the form $\varphi[a_1+1] \rightarrow \varphi[z_1]$ are axioms of $\Gamma(P)$. Write $S,\Gamma(P) \models \varphi$ if

$$S^+ \models \Gamma(P) \quad \text{implies} \quad S^+ \models \varphi$$

for *all* expansions S^+ of S in which the new constants a_i, z_i are interpreted.

Given a structure S for L, and S-states ξ and η, let $S(\xi,\eta)$ be the structure for L^+ which is like S, with the additional proviso that each a_i is interpreted as $\xi[x_i]$, and each z_i as $\eta[x_i]$. Of course, every structure S^+ for L^+ is $S(\xi,\eta)$ for some S-states ξ, η.

Lemma 2.1. Let $\pi \equiv (\varphi,\psi)$, let S be a structure for L, and let ξ and η be S-states.

$S \models \pi[\xi \rightarrow \eta]$ iff $S(\xi,\eta) \models \hat{\pi}$.

Proof. Immediate from the definitions. ■

Representation Lemma 2.2. Let $\pi \equiv (\varphi,\psi)$, and let P be a predicate transformer.

(1) $\qquad S \models_P \pi$ iff $S,\Gamma(P) \models \hat{\pi}$.

(2) $\qquad \models_P \pi$ iff $\Gamma(P) \models \hat{\pi}$.

Proof. We prove (1), of which (2) is an immediate consequence.

$S \models_P \pi$ iff
$S \models \pi[\xi \rightarrow \eta]$ whenever $\xi \rightarrow_\rho \eta$, for $\rho \equiv \rho(S,P)$, iff
$S \models \pi[\xi \rightarrow \eta]$ whenever $S \models \pi'[\xi \rightarrow \eta]$ for all $\pi' \in P$, iff
$S(\xi,\eta) \models \hat{\pi}$ whenever $S(\xi,\eta) \models \hat{\pi}'$ for all $\pi' \in P$, by lemma 2.1, iff
$S^+ \models \hat{\pi}$ whenever $S^+ \models \Gamma(P)$ for all extension S^+ of S to L^+, iff
$S,\Gamma(P) \models \hat{\pi}$. ■

3. Completeness of propositionally closed predicate transformers for first-order reasoning.

Reasoning about pca's in first-order logic is not restricted to the particular format of pca's. However, we show that this freedom of style does not increase the set of provable pca's: if a pca π is first-order derivable from the partial-correctness theory of α, i.e. if $\hat{\pi}$ is first-order derivable from $\Gamma(H(\alpha))$, then π itself is in $H(\alpha)$.

Theorem 1. Let *Th* be a first-order theory over L (all axioms of whose are closed L-sentences). Let P be a predicate transformer propositionally closed with respect to *Th*. Let $\pi \equiv (\varphi,\psi)$. If $Th, \Gamma(P) \vdash \hat{\pi}$ then $\pi \in P$.

Proof. Suppose

$$Th, \{\hat{\pi}_i\}_{i<k} \vdash \hat{\pi},$$

where $\pi_i \equiv (\varphi_i,\psi_i)$ are all in P. I.e.,

(1) $\qquad Th, \{\varphi_i[\bar{a}] \rightarrow \psi_i[\bar{z}]\}_{i<k} \vdash \varphi[\bar{a}] \rightarrow \psi[\bar{z}].$

Let $[k] \equiv \{0, \cdots, k-1\}$. For $I \subset [k]$ let

$$\bar{I} \equiv [k]-I,$$
$$\Phi_I^+ \equiv \wedge_{i \in I}\varphi_i \; ; \quad \Phi_I^- \equiv \wedge_{i \in \bar{I}} \neg \varphi_i$$
$$\Psi_I^+ \equiv \wedge_{i \in I}\psi_i$$

From (1) we get by propositional logic, for each $I \subset [k]$,

$$Th, \Phi_I^-[\bar{a}] \wedge \varphi[\bar{a}] \vdash \Psi_I^+[\bar{z}] \rightarrow \psi[\bar{z}].$$

Since Th is a theory in L, no $\mathbf{a}_j$ or $\mathbf{z}_j$ occurs free in Th. By the Interpolation Theorem for First-Order Logic (see e.g. [Sch77]) it therefore follows that there exist closed first-order sentences ξ_I $(I \subset [k])$, with no occurrence of any $\mathbf{a}_j$ or $\mathbf{z}_j$, such that

(2) $$Th, \Phi_I^-[\bar{a}] \wedge \varphi[\bar{a}] \vdash \xi_I,$$

and

(3) $$\xi_I \vdash \Psi_I^+[\bar{z}] \rightarrow \psi[\bar{z}].$$

In propositional logic we can prove

(4) $$\vee_{I \subset [k]}(\Phi_I^+ \wedge \Phi_I^-).$$

Therefore

$$\varphi \vdash \vee_{I \subset [k]}(\Phi_I^+ \wedge \Phi_I^- \wedge \varphi),$$

and so we get from (2)

(5) $$Th, \varphi \vdash \vee_{I \subset [k]}(\Phi_I^+ \wedge \xi_I).$$

Also, by (3),

(6) $$\vee_{I \subset [k]}(\xi_I \wedge \Psi_I^+) \vdash \psi.$$

We now show that π is in P. Since all π_i's are in P it follows, by the closure of P under Conjunction, that

$$(\Phi_I^+, \Psi_I^+)$$

is in P for each $I \subset [k]$. Also, by the Persistence property of P,

$$(\xi_I, \xi_I) \in P.$$

So, by closure under Conjunction,

$$(\Phi_I^+ \wedge \xi_I, \Psi_I^+ \wedge \xi_I)$$

is in P, and by closure under Disjunction so must be

$$(\vee_{I \subset [k]}(\Phi_I^+ \wedge \xi_I), \vee_{I \subset [k]}(\Psi_I^+ \wedge \xi_I)).$$

By (5), (6) and closure under Consequence it follows that $(\varphi, \psi) \equiv \pi$ is in P. ■

4. Partial correctness theories as first-order theories.

Theorem 1 shows that the notion of validity of a pca $\pi \equiv \varphi[\alpha]\psi$ with respect to the axiomatic semantics induced by a Hoare Logic H can be treated as validity of $\hat{\pi}$ with respect to usual (Tarskian) semantics of the first-order theory $\Gamma(H(\alpha))$. It follows that the metamathematics of first-order theories can be applied to partial-correctness theories. The following theorem shows that each propositionally closed Hoare logic H is complete for pca's that are valid with respect to the axiomatic semantics induced by H. This is analogous to a first-order theory, such as Peano Arithmetic or ZF Set Theory, being complete for formulas valid in all its models. This completeness property was proved, for Hoare's Logic for **while** programs, in [BT83], by essentially reproving the Completeness Theorem for First-Order Logic for the case in hand.

Theorem 2. Let P be a propositionally closed predicate transformer. A pair $\pi \equiv (\varphi,\psi)$ is valid with respect to the axiomatic semantics induced by P iff π is in P.

Proof.

π is valid with respect to the axiomatic semantics induced by P iff
$\hat{\pi}$ is valid in all models of $\Gamma(P)$, by the Representation Lemma 2.2, iff
$\Gamma(P)\vdash\hat{\pi}$, by the Strong Completeness Theorem for First-Order Logic, iff
π is in P, by Theorem 1. ■

Theorem 3 [Par83]. Let S be a structure for L. A predicate transformer P is the predicate transformer determined by some I/O relation ρ, i.e. $P \equiv P(S,\rho)$, iff P is propositionally closed.

Proof. If P is propositionally closed then $P = P(S,\rho)$, where $\rho \equiv \rho(S,P)$, by theorem 2. Conversely, if P is determined by some ρ, then it trivially satisfies the Rules of Persistence, Consequence, Conjunction and Disjunction. ■

References.

[BT83] Jan A. Bergstra and John V. Tucker, *The axiomatic semantics of programs based on Hoare's Logic*; Preprint, Technical Report IW 236/83, September 1983, Mathematisch Centrum, Amsterdam.

[Dij76] Edsger W. Dijkstra, **A Discipline of Programming**; Prentice-Hall, Englewood Cliffs (1976) xvii+217pp.

[End70] Herbert B. Enderton, **A Mathematical Introduction to logic**; Academic Press, New York (1970) xiii+295pp.

[HL74] C.A.R. Hoare and P. Lauer, *Consistent and complementary formal theories of the semantics of programming languages;* **Acta Informatica** 3 (1974) 135-155.

[Hoa69] C.A.R. Hoare, *An axiomatic basis for computer programming;* **Communications of the ACM** 12 (1969) 576-580.

[MH82] Albert Meyer and Joseph Halpern, *Axiomatic definition of programming languages: a theoretical assessment,* **Journal of the ACM** 29 (1982) 555-576.

[HW73] C.A.R. Hoare and Nicolas Wirth, *An axiomatic definition of the programming language PASCAL;* **Acta Informatica** 2 (1973) 335-355.

[Lau72] P. Lauer, **Consistent and complementary formal theories of the semantics of programming languages**; PhD Thesis, Queens University, Belfast (1972).

[Man69] Zohar Manna, *The correctness of programs;* **Journal of Computer and Systems Science** 3 (1969) 119-127.

[Par83] Rohit Parikh, *Some applications of topology to program semantics;* **Math. Systems Theory** 16 (1983) 111-131.

[Sch77] Kurt Schutte, **Proof Theory**; Springer-Verlag, Berlin (1977) xii+299pp.

The Glory of The Past

Orna Lichtenstein
Dept. of Computer Science
Tel Aviv University
Ramat Aviv, Israel

Amir Pnueli
and
Lenore Zuck*
Dept. of Applied Mathematics
The Weizmann Institute of Science
Rehovot, 76100 Israel

Abstract

An extension of propositional temporal logic that includes operators referring to a bounded past is considered. An exponential time decision procedure and a complete axiomatic system are presented. A suggested normal form leads to a syntactic classification of safety and liveness formulae. The adequacy of temporal logic to modular verification is examined. Finally we present the notion of *α-fairness* which is proved to fully capture the behavior of probabilistic finite state programs.

Introduction

The classical temporal logic systems (see [Pr],[K],[RU], [Bur]) are usually symmetric, including operators for describing both future and past events. The application of temporal logic in computer science for the specification and verification of reactive systems, usually included only the future fragment. Resistance to the inclusion of the past operators was based on the strive for minimality and on the observation implied in [GPSS] that if we restrict the domain to executions of systems that have a definite start point in time, then the past operators do not add any expressive power.

Several recent developments provide convincing indications that enriching temporal logic with the past operators, or an equivalent construct, can prove most advantageous.

A first observation is that many statements that arise naturally in specifications, are easier to express using the past operators. For example, the fact that every q is preceded by a p is easily expressed by the past-augmented formula $\Box(q \rightarrow \diamondminus p)$. In this formula, $\diamondminus$ is the past version of the future $\Diamond$. See [KVR] for example of such statements.

* The work of this author was supported by the Eshkol Fund.

A more important motivation is the use of past in compositional proof systems. The pioneering work in [OG] indicated that completeness of verification systems for concurrent programs cannot be achieved unless the program is augmented by auxiliary variables that the proof may refer to. In the same work, it is suggested that the most general auxiliary variables are ***history variables*** that record a sequence of selected values that some variables assumed in the past. The idea of maintaining history variables and using them in the proof has been extended to other models of computations, such as messages based systems, where they are usually refered to as ***traces*** ([HO],[MC],[CH],[H],[NGO]). In contrast, advocates of the global approach to temporal verification, such as ([OL],[L],[MP3]) suggested that it is sufficient to allow references to ***locations*** in the program instead of the structurally complex history variables. Indeed, [MP2] shows relative completeness of the location based approach for the first order case, and [LP] shows absolute completeness for the finite state case.

Unfortunately (Fortunately?), when we consider modular verification, it is forbidden when specifying a module to refer to any but its externally observable variables. Mentioning locations within a module is definitely abhorred. The usefulness of locations in program verification can be explained by saying that each location provides a succinct but indirect representation of the history that leads to this location. Hence, the alternative approach which will satisfy the rules required by modularity is to have tools for the efficient ***direct*** characterization of the history.

One such tool is, of course, the ***history variables.*** The alternative tool, which we explore in this paper, is the extension of the temporal logic system to include past operators. One of the conclusions offered by the paper is that these tools are indeed equivalent, and preferring one to the other is merely a matter of personal taste. The works in [BK] and [Pn2] illustrate the utility of the past extension of temporal logic for modular verification.

Once we added the past operators into temporal logic we found out that they help to clarify several issues. In particular they contribute to a natural definition of the basic and important notions of safety and liveness properties. They help to clarify the additional specification power that temporal logic has over regular expressions which may be described as adequate only for expressing safety properties. (Of course, the same specification power, i.e., ability to also express liveness properties, is shared by ω-regular expressions, and we must take extended temporal logic [W] in order to make the above statement precise).

Investigation of these issues also lead us to refine the notion of extreme fairness which was first introduced in [Pn3] in order to deal with finite state probabilistic programs. We present a revised version of this fairness and show that it precisely captures all the properties of such programs which hold with probability 1.

We should emphasize again that augmentation by the past operators does not increase the expressive power of temporal logic. On the other hand it provides in many cases a more natural and succinct presentation and verification of specifications. Fortunately, neither does this augmentation increase the complexity of the decision procedures for the logic. The version of the past operators we introduce appeared already in [Pr] and is attributed there to Dana Scott. An identical version appears in [SC] where it is proved that the validity problem for the full logic is P-space complete.

A Temporal Logic that Includes the Past

Let S be a set of states, Π be a set of ***propositional variables*** and I an ***evaluation*** $I: S \to 2^{\Pi}$ mapping each state $s \in S$ to the set of propositions $I(s) \subseteq \Pi$ that are true in s.

A ***computation*** is a (possibly infinite) sequence of states:

$$\sigma : s_0, s_1, \ldots \qquad s_i \in S$$

Usually a computation is generated by an underlying program, however, in most of our discussions we shall not directly use this fact.

If the computation is finite:

$$\sigma : s_0, s_1, \ldots s_k$$

We define the ***length*** of σ to be $|\sigma| = k+1$. Otherwise we write $|\sigma| = \omega$.

We introduce a temporal language over the propositions in $\Pi \cup \{true, false\}$ using the boolean connectives $\neg$ and $\vee$, and the temporal operators $\odot$ (strong ***next***), $\mathcal{U}$ (***until***), $\ominus$ (strong ***previous***) and $\mathcal{S}$ (***since***).

We define a satisfiability relation $\models$ between a temporal formula, a finite or infinite computation σ, and a position j, $0 \leq j < |\sigma|$, within the computation. The satisfiability relation is defined as follows:

$$(\sigma, j) \models true, \qquad (\sigma, j) \not\models false \quad \text{for every } \sigma \text{ and } j < |\sigma|$$

For a proposition $Q \in \Pi$,

$(\sigma, j) \models Q$ *iff* $Q \in I(s_j)$.

$(\sigma, j) \models \neg\varphi$ *iff* $(\sigma, j) \not\models \varphi$.

$(\sigma, j) \models (\varphi_1 \vee \varphi_2)$ *iff* $(\sigma, j) \models \varphi_1$ or $(\sigma, j) \models \varphi_2$.

$(\sigma, j) \models \odot\varphi$ *iff* $j+1 < |\sigma|$ and $(\sigma, j+1) \models \varphi$.

$(\sigma, j) \models (\varphi \mathcal{U} \psi)$ *iff* For some k, $j \leq k < |\sigma|$, $(\sigma, k) \models \psi$ and for every i, $j \leq i < k$, $(\sigma, i) \models \varphi$.

$(\sigma, j) \models \ominus\varphi$ *iff* $j > 0$ and $(\sigma, j-1) \models \varphi$.

$(\sigma, j) \models (\varphi \mathcal{S} \psi)$ *iff* For some k, $0 \leq k \leq j$, $(\sigma, k) \models \psi$ and for every i, $k < i \leq j$, $(\sigma, i) \models \varphi$.

Additional boolean connectives (such as $\wedge$, $\to$, $\equiv$) can be defined in the usual way. Additional temporal operators can be defined by:

$\bigcirc p \equiv \neg\odot\neg p$ (weak ***next***).

$\Diamond p \equiv true\,\mathcal{U} p$ (***eventually p***).

$\Box p \equiv \neg\Diamond\neg p$ (always in the future).

$\circleddash p \equiv \neg\ominus\neg p$ (weak ***previous***).

$\diamondminus p \equiv true\,\mathcal{S} p$ (sometime in the past).

$\boxminus p \equiv \neg\diamondminus\neg p$ (always in the past).

If $(\sigma, j) \models \varphi$, for some j, $0 \leq j < |\sigma|$, we say that φ is satisfiable in σ. If there is a computation σ such that φ is satisfiable in σ, we say that φ is satisfiable.

A formula φ such that all computations σ and all positions j, $0 \leq j < |\sigma|$ satisfy $(\sigma, j) \models \varphi$ is called *valid*.

For example, $\diamondminus \circleddash$ *false* is a valid formula. It states that all computations have a starting point (position 0).

In the following we refer to general formulae in the described language as TL-formulae. Formulae that have no past operators are called TLF-formulae, and those that have no future operators are called TLP-formulae.

Decidability

As we already mentioned above, the validity problem for the full TL has been solved in [SC]. Sistla and Clarke present in that paper a P-space decision procedure for satisfiability and also show that the problem is P-space complete. We, however, prefer to outline a different decision procedure that is connected to the completeness proof and has a better time complexity than the naive implementation of the procedure in [SC]. The decision procedure is very similar to the one presented in [LP] for model checking of TL formulae, which is simplified here by removing the constraints imposed by the underlying program.

A Procedure for Checking Satisfiability

Let φ be a temporal formula. The *closure* of φ, $CL(\varphi)$, is the smallest set of formulae containing φ and satisfying:

$$\begin{array}{lcl}
\textit{true}, \textit{false} \in CL(\varphi) & & \\
\neg\psi \in CL(\varphi) & \Leftrightarrow & \psi \in CL(\varphi) \text{ (We identify } \neg\neg\psi \text{ with } \psi \text{ and } \neg \textit{true} \text{ with } \textit{false}) \\
\psi_1 \vee \psi_2 \in CL(\varphi) & \Rightarrow & \psi_1, \psi_2 \in CL(\varphi) \\
\bigcirc\psi \in CL(\varphi) & \Rightarrow & \psi \in CL(\varphi) \\
\psi_1 \, \mathcal{U} \, \psi_2 \in CL(\varphi) & \Rightarrow & \psi_1, \psi_2, \bigcirc(\psi_1 \, \mathcal{U} \, \psi_2) \in CL(\varphi) \\
\ominus\psi \in CL(\varphi) & \Rightarrow & \psi \in CL(\varphi) \\
\psi_1 \, \mathcal{S} \psi_2 \in CL(\varphi) & \Rightarrow & \psi_1, \psi_2, \ominus(\psi_1 \, \mathcal{S} \psi_2) \in CL(\varphi).
\end{array}$$

It can be shown by induction on the structure of φ that $|CL(\varphi)| \leq 4|\varphi|$.

An *atom* is a set of formulae $A \subseteq CL(\varphi)$ such that

$$\begin{array}{lcl}
\textit{true} \in A, & & \\
\text{For every } \psi \in CL(\varphi), \quad \psi \in A & \Leftrightarrow & \neg\psi \notin A \\
\text{For every } \psi_1 \vee \psi_2 \in CL(\varphi), \psi_1 \vee \psi_2 \in A & \Leftrightarrow & \psi_1 \in A \text{ or } \psi_2 \in A \\
\text{For every } \psi_1 \, \mathcal{U} \, \psi_2 \in CL(\varphi), \psi_1 \, \mathcal{U} \, \psi_2 \in A & \Leftrightarrow & \psi_2 \in A \text{ or } \psi_1, \bigcirc(\psi_1 \, \mathcal{U} \, \psi_2) \in A \\
\text{For every } \psi_1 \, \mathcal{S} \psi_2 \in CL(\varphi), \psi_1 \, \mathcal{S} \psi_2 \in A & \Leftrightarrow & \psi_2 \in A \text{ or } \psi_1, \ominus(\psi_1 \, \mathcal{S} \psi_2) \in A
\end{array}$$

The set of all atoms is denoted by At. Clearly $|At| \leq 2^{4|\varphi|}$.

An atom A that does not contain any formula of the form $\ominus\psi$ is called ***initial***. An atom A that does not contain any formula of the form $\odot\psi$ is called ***terminal***.

The procedure for checking satisfiability attempts to construct a structure of atoms, interpreted as states, which contains a path satisfying φ. When interpreting atoms as states we take the natural evaluation I defined by $I(A) = A \cap \Pi$, i.e., the propositions taken to be true in A are all the propositions contained in A.

Initially we construct a structure $\mathcal{A} = (At, R)$ which is a graph whose nodes are all the atoms and whose edges are defined by the relation R:

$$(A, B) \in R \Leftrightarrow \begin{cases} \text{for every } \odot\psi \in CL(\varphi), \\ \qquad\qquad \odot\psi \in A \Leftrightarrow \psi \in B, \text{ and} \\ \text{for every } \ominus\psi \in CL(\varphi), \\ \qquad\qquad \psi \in A \Leftrightarrow \ominus\psi \in B \end{cases}$$

We denote by R^* the reflexive transitive closure of R.

A path $\pi = A_0, A_1, \ldots$ in $\mathcal{A}$ is said to ***fulfill*** φ if:

a) Every A_i, $A_{i+1} \in \pi$ are R-connected $((A_i, A_{i+1}) \in R)$. This repeats the requirement that π be a path in $\mathcal{A}$.

b) A_0 is initial.

c) If π is finite then its last atom is terminal.

d) For every $j \geq 0$ and every $\psi_1 \mathcal{U} \psi_2 \in A_j$ there exists some ℓ, $j \leq \ell < |\pi|$ such that $\psi_2 \in A_\ell$.

e) For some j, $0 \leq j < |\pi|$, $\varphi \in A_j$.

Proposition 1

The formula φ is satisfiable ***iff*** there exists a path π in $\mathcal{A}$ which fulfills φ.

Proof: Let π be a path in $\mathcal{A}$ which fulfills φ. It is easy to show by induction that for every $A_k \in \pi$ and $\psi \in A_k$, $(\pi, k) \models \psi$. This is true in particular for the $A_j \in \pi$ such that $\varphi \in A_j$ guaranteed by e).

Given any computation $\sigma = s_0, s_1, \ldots$ over an arbitrary set of states, it is easy to associate with it a path $\pi = A_0, A_1, \ldots$ in $\mathcal{A}$ by defining
$A_i = \{\psi \in CL(\varphi) \mid (\sigma, s_i) \models \psi\}$. ∎

Our construction proceeds by successively removing from $\mathcal{A}$ atoms that could never participate in a path fulfilling φ. For efficiency sake we remove complete strongly connected subgraphs at a time. The removal process can be described by the sequence of successively smaller structures $\mathcal{A}_i = (W_i, R_i)$, $i = 0, 1, \ldots$ defined by taking:

$$\mathcal{A}_0 = \mathcal{A}, \qquad \text{i.e.,} \quad W_0 = At, \quad R_0 = R.$$

the transition from $\mathcal{A}_i$ to $\mathcal{A}_{i+1}$ can be described as follows:

Let C be a maximal strongly connected subgraph (MSCS) of W_i. C is defined to be ***initial*** in W_i if it has no incoming R_i edges.

C is defined to be ***terminal*** in W_i if it has no outgoing R_i edges.

C is defined to be ***self-fulfilling*** if for every formula $\psi_1 \mathcal{U} \psi_2 \in A \in C$, there exists an atom $B \in C$ such that $\psi_2 \in B$.

An MSCS C is defined to be ***useless*** in W_i if it falls into one of the following cases:

a) C is initial but contains no initial atom.

b) C is terminal but is not self-fulfilling.

c) C consists of a non-terminal atom that has no R_i-successors.

We observe that a fulfilling path in $\mathcal{A}_i$ must start at an initial atom and eventually remain contained in a self-fulfilling MSCS. Hence we obtain the following construction:

Let C be a useless MSCS in $\mathcal{A}_i$. Define $\mathcal{A}_{i+1} = (W_{i+1}, R_{i+1})$ by $W_{i+1} = W_i - C$, $R_{i+1} = R_i \cap (W_{i+1} \times W_{i+1})$, i.e., R_{i+1} is R_i restricted to the atoms remaining in W_{i+1}.

<u>Proposition 2</u>

The formula φ is satisfiable in $\mathcal{A}_i$ ***iff*** it is satisfiable in $\mathcal{A}_{i+1}$.

This is justified by the previous observation that by removing C we do not damage any fulfilling path in $\mathcal{A}_i$.

When $\mathcal{A}_i$ is empty or contains no useless MSCS's the removal process terminates. Let this terminal structure be $\mathcal{A}_k$.

<u>Proposition 3</u>

The formula φ is satisfiable ***iff*** there exists an atom $A \in W_k$ such that $\varphi \in A$.

<u>Proof</u>: If φ is satisfiable we had a fulfilling path already in $\mathcal{A}_0$. None of the removals damaged it and consequently it still exists in $\mathcal{A}_k$ including the particular atom A_j which by clause e) of the definition of fulfilling paths contains φ.

Assume, for the converse direction, that $\varphi \in A \in W_k$. By the absence of useless MSCS's in the $\mathcal{A}_k$ we can construct a path π that starts at an initial atom, goes through A and proceeds to a terminal self-fulfilling MSCS C. If C consists of a single terminal atom B, the path π stops there. Otherwise it continues in a periodic loop that traverses each of the atoms of C infinitely many times. It can be shown that in both cases π is fulfilling for φ. ∎

The satisfiability checking procedure outlined above can be executed in time linear in $|At| \cdot |\varphi|$, hence in $O(|\varphi| \cdot 2^{4|\varphi|})$.

Completeness

We propose the following deductive system for establishing the validity of full TL formulae. Due to the symmetry between the past and future parts, we organized the axioms by having a past and a future clause for each axiom.

Axioms

	Past Clause	Future Clause
A1.	$\neg \circledequal p \equiv \ominus \neg p$	$\neg \odot p \equiv \bigcirc \neg p$
A2.	$\circledequal p \rightarrow \ominus p$	$\odot p \rightarrow \bigcirc p$
A3.	$p \rightarrow \ominus \odot p$	$p \rightarrow \bigcirc \circledequal p$
A4.	$\ominus(p \rightarrow q) \rightarrow (\ominus p \rightarrow \ominus q)$	$\bigcirc(p \rightarrow q) \rightarrow (\bigcirc p \rightarrow \bigcirc q)$
A5.	$\neg \diamondminus p \equiv \boxminus \neg p$	$\neg \Diamond p \equiv \Box \neg p$
A6.	$\boxminus(p \rightarrow q) \rightarrow (\boxminus p \rightarrow \boxminus q)$	$\Box(p \rightarrow q) \rightarrow (\Box p \rightarrow \Box q)$
A7.	$\boxminus p \rightarrow \ominus p$	$\Box p \rightarrow \bigcirc p$
A8.	$\boxminus(p \rightarrow \ominus p) \rightarrow (p \rightarrow \boxminus p)$	$\Box(p \rightarrow \bigcirc p) \rightarrow (p \rightarrow \Box p)$
A9.	$p \mathcal{S} q \equiv q \vee [p \wedge \circledequal(p \mathcal{S} q)]$	$p \mathcal{U} q \equiv q \vee [p \wedge \odot(p \mathcal{U} q)]$
A10.	$\diamondminus \ominus \mathit{false}$	$p \mathcal{U} q \rightarrow \Diamond q$

Inference Rules

R1. For each substitution instance of a propositional tautology p, $\vdash p$.

R2. If $\vdash p \rightarrow q$ and $\vdash p$ then $\vdash q$.

R3. If $\vdash p$ then both $\vdash \boxminus p$ and $\vdash \Box p$.

<u>Theorem</u>

The deductive system presented above is sound and complete for propositional TL.

Because of space limitations we outline below only the major steps in the proof of the completeness part.

Assume that the formula φ is valid. Then $\neg\varphi$ is unsatisfiable. Apply the above satisfiability checking procedure to $\neg\varphi$. In the application we construct a sequence of structures $\mathcal{A}_0, \ldots \mathcal{A}_k$ which eventually converges. Since $\neg\varphi$ is unsatisfiable, either $W_k = \emptyset$ or for all atoms $A \in W_k$, $\neg\varphi \notin A$.

For an atom A we denote $\hat{A} = \bigwedge_{\psi \in A} \psi$

We prove the following list of lemmas:

L1:

$$\vdash \bigvee_{B \in W_0} \hat{B}$$

Recall that $W_0 = At$.

L2: For every $B \in W_0$,

$$\vdash \hat{B} \rightarrow \left[\ominus \Big(\bigvee_{(A,B)\in R_0} \hat{A} \Big) \wedge \bigcirc \Big(\bigvee_{(B,C)\in R_0} \hat{C} \Big) \right]$$

The empty disjunction, arising in the case that B has no R_0-predecessors or no R_0-successors, is interpreted as *false*.

Denote by R_0^* the reflexive transitive closure of R_0. Then from L2 and the axiom A8 we can obtain:

L3:

$$\vdash \hat{B} \rightarrow \left[\boxminus \Big(\bigvee_{(A,B)\in R_0^*} \hat{A} \Big) \wedge \Box \Big(\bigvee_{(B,C)\in R_0^*} \hat{C} \Big) \right]$$

We now wish to generalize L2 and L3 to R_i, $i = 1, \ldots, k$. We will prove by induction on $i = 0, 1, \ldots, k$ the following three statements:

L4: For every atom $B \notin W_i$, $\vdash \neg \hat{B}$
i.e., a removed atom is useless.

L5: For every $B \in W_i$

$$\vdash \hat{B} \rightarrow \left[\ominus \Big(\bigvee_{(A,B)\in R_i} \hat{A} \Big) \wedge \bigcirc \Big(\bigvee_{(B,C)\in R_i} \hat{C} \Big) \right]$$

L6: For every $B \in W_i$,

$$\vdash \hat{B} \rightarrow \left[\boxminus \Big(\bigvee_{(A,B)\in R_i^*} \hat{A} \Big) \wedge \Box \Big(\bigvee_{(B,C)\in R_i^*} \hat{C} \Big) \right]$$

For $i = 0$, L4 is vacuously true and L5 and L6 follow from L2 and L3 respectively. Consider the passage from i to $i+1$. It is effected by removing a strongly connected component $\mathcal{C}$ from $\mathcal{A}_i$. Consider the three different reasons for $\mathcal{C}$ being declared useless in $\mathcal{A}_i$.

a) $\mathcal{C}$ is initial but contains no initial atom.

Since every atom $A \in \mathcal{C}$ is non initial it contain some formula of the form $\ominus\psi$. Hence we can prove

L7: $\vdash \hat{A} \rightarrow \ominus true.$

For each $B \in \mathcal{C}$ we may apply the past part of L6 and observe that since $\mathcal{C}$ is initial in $\mathcal{A}_i$ any A such that $(A, B) \in R_i^*$ is necessarily contained in $\mathcal{C}$ and satisfies L7. Hence we obtain:

$$\vdash \hat{B} \rightarrow \boxminus \ominus true$$

Since the right hand side of this implication contradicts $\Diamond\!\!\!\!\ominus false$ of A10 we conclude that for each $B \in \mathcal{C}$

$$\vdash \neg\hat{B}.$$

b) $\mathcal{C}$ is terminal but is not self-fulfilling.

In this case for each $B \in \mathcal{C}$ there exists a formula $\psi_1 \mathcal{U} \psi_2 \in B$ such that no $C \in \mathcal{C}$ contains ψ_2. We may then use the future part of L6 to derive

$$\vdash \hat{B} \rightarrow [\psi_1 \mathcal{U} \psi_2 \wedge \Box(\neg\psi_2)]$$

which is equivalent to

$$\vdash \neg\hat{B}.$$

c) $\mathcal{C}$ consists of a non-terminal atom that has no R_i-successors.

Let $\mathcal{C} = \{B\}$. Since B is a non-terminal atom it contains some $\odot\psi \in B$. Hence we may derive from the future part of L5:

$$\vdash \hat{B} \rightarrow [\odot\psi \wedge \bigcirc false]$$

which again leads to

$$\vdash \neg\hat{B}.$$

This case splitting established L4 for W_{i+1}, and it is easy to utilize this additional information (i.e., that all removed atoms B satisfy $\vdash \neg\hat{B}$) to update L5 and L6 to their R_{i+1} version.

Consider now the final structure W_k. Combining L4 for $i = k$ with L1 we obtain:

$$\vdash \bigvee_{B \in W_k} \hat{B}.$$

Since the satisfiability check for $\neg\varphi$ failed we know that for each $B \in W_k$, $\neg\varphi \notin B$, hence $\varphi \in B$ and trivially $\vdash \hat{B} \rightarrow \varphi$. It follows that $\vdash \varphi$. ∎

Extending TL by Quantification

In [W] Wolper complained that temporal logic is not expressive enough, and suggested an extended language, ETL. He also showed that an equivalent extension can be obtained by allowing quantifiers over propositions.

Since most of the subsequent results hold for both TL and ETL, we consider the same extension and introduce a quantified version of our richer language, where quantification over propositions is allowed. We refer to this language as QTL (QTLF and QTLP denoting the future and past fragments respectively).

The syntax of TL is extended by adding formulae of the form $\exists p\ \varphi$ where $p \in \Pi$. We introduce $\forall p\ \varphi$ as abbreviation for $\neg\exists p(\neg\varphi)$.

Given two evaluations $I, I': S \to 2^{\Pi}$, we say that I and I' differ (at most) in p if for every $s \in S$, $I(s) - \{p\} = I'(s) - \{p\}$. Then the semantics of $\exists p\, \varphi$ is given by:

$$(I, \sigma, j) \models \exists p\, \varphi \Leftrightarrow (I', \sigma, j) \models \varphi \quad \text{for some } I' \text{ such that } I \text{ and } I' \text{ differ in } p.$$

For this definition we had to make the dependence of $\models$ on the evaluation I explicit.

Regular and Star-Free Expressions over Computations

Let Σ denote the set of all propositional formulae over Π. We define a language of regular expressions over Σ using the operators $\neg$ (negation), $+$ (union), ; (concatenation) and $*$ (Kleene closure).

Let $\sigma = \sigma_0, \ldots, \sigma_k$, $\sigma' = \sigma'_0, \ldots, \sigma'_m$. The concatenation of the two sequences is $\sigma;\sigma' = \sigma_0, \ldots, \sigma_k, \sigma'_0, \ldots, \sigma'_m$. In the case that σ (σ') is empty, we define $\sigma;\sigma'$ to be σ' (σ).

We define a satisfiability relation between a *finite* (possibly empty) sequence σ and a regular expression as follows:

For $a \in \Sigma$, a propositional formula over Π, $\sigma \models a$ *iff* σ is a singleton computation $\sigma = (s)$, and $s \models a$. In evaluating a over s, we use $I(s)$ for evaluating the propositions that appear in a.

$\sigma \models (\neg\alpha)$	*iff*	$\sigma \not\models \alpha$.
$\sigma \models (\alpha + \beta)$	*iff*	$\sigma \models \alpha$ or $\sigma \models \beta$.
$\sigma \models (\alpha;\beta)$	*iff*	$\sigma = \sigma_1;\sigma_2$ with $\sigma_1 \models \alpha$ and $\sigma_2 \models \beta$.
$\sigma \models (\alpha^*)$	*iff*	either σ is empty, or $\sigma = \sigma_1;\ldots;\sigma_k$ such that $\sigma_i \models \alpha$ for $i = 1, \ldots, k$.

Thus every finite computation satisfies $(true)^*$.

A regular expression is called ***star-free*** if it does not contain the $*$ operator, except perhaps in the form $true^*$.

History Variables and Predicates

In the current propositional version it is natural to define a ***history variable*** as the variable h, such that in position j of a computation σ its value is given by $h|_{\sigma}^{j} = [s_0, \ldots, s_j]$. That is, h is a ***sequence*** variable that accumulates the ***complete*** history of the computation, up to the current state. The expressive power of a language that uses history variables depends on the type of ***predicates*** we may apply to the history variables. In the current framework, we suggest to use star-free (regular) expressions as the history variables. Consequently, we extend the temporal language by allowing formulae of the type $[\alpha]_H$, where α is a star-free (regular) expression over Π, as defined above.

The semantics of these formulae is given by:

$$(\sigma, j) \models [\alpha]_H \quad \textit{iff} \quad (s_0, \ldots, s_j) \models \alpha$$

We denote by TL_H (QTL_H) the extension of temporal logic by the inclusion of the history predicates.

Finite State Automata on Finite and Infinite Sequences

There is of course a strong connection between regular expressions and finite state automata. A *semi-automaton* is a system consisting of

Q – A finite set of states.
Σ' – An alphabet.
δ – A non deterministic transition function $\delta: Q \times \Sigma' \rightarrow 2^Q$.

We can easily extend δ to map $\delta: Q \times \Sigma'^* \rightarrow 2^Q$. A semi-automaton $B = (Q, \Sigma', \delta)$ is defined to be *counter-free* if there does not exist a sequence of states $q_1, q_2, \ldots q_n \in Q$ for $n > 1$ and a word $w \in \Sigma'^*$, such that $q_{i+1} \in \delta(q_i, w)$ for $i = 1, \ldots, n-1$ and $q_1 \in \delta(q_n, w)$.

Semi-automata can be completed to automata by adding an initial state and acceptance criteria. A *regular* automaton $A = (Q, \Sigma', \delta, q_0, F)$ is a system consisting of a semi-automaton (Q, Σ', δ) plus:

$q_0 \in Q$ an initial state.
$F \subseteq Q$ an accepting set.

The finite string language accepted by the automaton A is defined by:

$$L(A) = \{w \in \Sigma'^* \mid \delta(s_0, w) \cap F \neq \emptyset\}$$

A regular automaton is defined to be a *counter free* automaton if its semi-automaton (Q, Σ', δ) is counter-free.

Finite state automata can also be used to define languages of infinite strings.

An ω-*regular* automaton $A = (Q, \Sigma', \delta, q_0, \Omega)$ is a system consisting of a semi-automaton (Q, Σ', δ) plus:

$q_0 \in Q$ an initial state.
$\Omega \subseteq 2^Q$ a family of accepting sets.

Given an infinite word $\sigma = a_0, a_1, \ldots \in (\Sigma')^\omega$, a ***run*** of A on σ, $r_A(\sigma)$ is defined to be an infinite sequence of states $r_A(\sigma) = q_0, q_1, \ldots \in Q^\omega$ such that the first state is the initial state q_0, and for each $i = 0, 1, \ldots$ $q_{i+1} \in \delta(q_i, a_i)$. For a run $r_A(\sigma)$, $\inf(r_A(\sigma)) \subseteq Q$ is the set of states that appear infinitely many times in the sequence $r_A(\sigma)$.

The language of infinite strings that is accepted by A is defined by

$$L(A) = \{\sigma \in (\Sigma')^\omega \mid \text{There exists a run } r_A(\sigma) \text{ such that } \inf r_A(\sigma)) \in \Omega\}$$

An ω-*regular* automaton is defined to be an ω-*counter-free* automaton if its semi-automaton (Q, Σ', δ) is counter-free.

Equivalence of Star-Free Expressions and Temporal Logic

The following two theorems form the main support for most of the results that follow.

Theorem 1

Let L be a language of *finite* computations (i.e., a subset of S^*). The following conditions are equivalent:

a. L is definable by a star-free (regular) expression.

b. L is definable by a TLF (QTLF) formula.

c. L is accepted by a counter-free (regular) automaton.

In order to consider the case of infinite computations, we introduce the notion of a *limit* of star-free (regular) expressions. For a star-free (regular) expression α, we define $lim(\alpha)$ to be the language of all infinite S sequences, such that $\sigma \in lim(\alpha)$ *iff* infinitely many finite prefices of σ, $\sigma'' < \sigma$, satisfy $\sigma'' \models \alpha$.

Theorem 2

Let L be a language of *infinite* computations (i.e., a subset of S^ω). Then the following conditions are equivalent:

d. L is representable as $\bigcup_{i=1}^{n} lim(\alpha_i) \cap \overline{lim(\beta_i)}$, where α_i, β_i, $i = 1, \ldots, n$, are star-free (regular) expressions.

The operator of complementation is defined by $\overline{L} = S^\omega - L$.

e. L is definable by a TLF (QTLF) formula.

f. L is accepted by an ω-counter-free (ω-regular) automaton.

The proof of these two theorems is based on many previous results, including [Buc], [MNP], [C], [T] and [GPSS], which, when combined, yield the theorems almost immediately. An independent proof of theorem 2 appears in [Pe]. The regular-QTLF part of theorem 2 has already been observed in [VW].

Past, Future and History Predicates over Finite Sequences

- For every TLF (QTLF) formula φ, there exists a TLP (QTLP) formula φ', such that for every *finite* sequence of length $j+1$, $(\sigma, 0) \models \varphi$ *iff* $(\sigma, j) \models \varphi'$. That is, φ stated from the beginning of σ is equivalent to φ' stated from the end of σ.

This translation is based on translating φ into a star-free (regular) expression α, taking α^R (reverse of α) and then retranslating into TL according to Theorem 1 with the substitution of $\ominus$ for $\odot$ and $\mathcal{S}$ for $\mathcal{U}$.

To illustrate this translation, consider $\varphi : p\mathcal{U}q$. Its corresponding star free expression is $\alpha : p^*; q; true^*$. The appearance of p^* does not violate the star-freedom requirement since it is an abbreviation to $\neg(true^*; \neg p; true^*)$. The reversed expression α^R is of course $true^*; q; p^*$. Its obvious TLF translation is $\Diamond(q \wedge \bigcirc \Box p)$. Replacing once more future by past we obtain the TLP formula $\varphi' : \Diamond\!\!\!\!-(q \wedge \ominus \boxminus p)$. Thus for any finite sequence σ, $|\sigma| = k+1$,

$$(\sigma, 0) \models p\mathcal{U}q \Leftrightarrow (\sigma, k) \models \Diamond\!\!\!\!-(q \wedge \ominus \boxminus p)$$

- The converse translation from φ' to φ also exists.
- This yields immediately the translatability of TLF_H to TL. Since any star-free (regular) history predicate $[\alpha]_H$ appearing in a TLF_H formula can be replaced by a TLP (QTLP) formula φ_α, which expresses the same property of the prefix of the sequence up to this point.

Past and Future over infinite Sequences

The past operators do not add expressive power to temporal logic. In order to compare formulae involving past and future operators we introduce the notion of ***initial equivalence***. Two formulae φ and φ' are defined to be initially equivalent if for every infinite computation σ:

$$(\sigma, 0) \models \varphi \Leftrightarrow (\sigma, 0) \models \varphi'$$

This is the same as requiring that $\ominus false \rightarrow [\varphi \equiv \varphi']$ be valid over all infinite computations. The following lemmas compare the past and future fragments.

- For every TL (QTL) formula φ that may contain past operators, there exists a TLF (QTLF) formula φ', which is initially equivalent to φ.

A possible proof to this claim (for the TL case) is to first translate φ into the first order theory of linear order, a translation which is readily available from the definition of $\models$. Then we may invoke the translation from this language into TLF as is outlined in [GPSS] . For the QTL case we may use a similar translation into the weak second order theory of the successor (see [Buc], [W] and [T] for details).

We cannot hope to translate TLF formulae completely into TLP formulae, but, we can restrict the number of future operators. This is expressed in the following normal form theorems:

- Every TL (QTL) formula φ (over infinite sequences) is initially equivalent to a formula of the form:

$$\bigvee_{i=1}^{n} (\Box\Diamond[\alpha_i]_H \wedge \Diamond \Box[\beta_i]_H)$$

where α_i, β_i $(i = 1, \ldots, n)$, are star-free (regular) expressions.

To effect this translation we use first Theorem 2 in order to obtain the normal form:

$$\bigcup_{i=1}^{n} [\lim(\alpha_i) \cap \overline{\lim(\beta_i)}]$$

which is obviously equivalent to the formula above.

- In view of the equivalence between past formulae and star-free (regular) history predicates, every TL (QTL) formula is also initially equivalent to a formula of the form:

$$\bigvee_{i=1}^{n}(\Box\Diamond(\varphi_i)\wedge\Diamond\Box(\psi_i))$$

where φ_i,ψ_i $(i=1,\ldots,n)$, are TLP (QTLP) formulae.

As an example to this translation, let p,q be two state formulae which, for simplicity, we assume to be exclusive. The formula $\Box(p\rightarrow p\mathcal{U}q)$ is then equivalent to the normal form formula:

$$\Box((\neg p)\rightarrow(\neg p)\mathcal{S}q)\wedge\Box\Diamond((\neg p)\mathcal{S}q)$$

In this representation we used the *weak since* operator, defined by $p\mathcal{S}q=\boxminus p\vee p\mathcal{S}q$. While the normal form did not allow formulae of the form $\Box\varphi$ where φ is a past-formula, such a formula is initially equivalent to $\Box\Diamond(\boxminus\varphi)$, which is allowed in the normal form.

Classification of Safety and Liveness Properties

Observing as before, that for past formulae φ and ψ, $\Box\varphi$ and $\Diamond\psi$ are initially equivalent to $\Box\Diamond(\boxminus\varphi)$ and $\Box\Diamond(\diamondminus\psi)$ respectively, we may extend the normal form theorem in the following way:

- Every TL (QTL) formula is initially equivalent to a *positive* boolean combination of formulae of the following forms:
  $\Box\varphi$, $\Diamond\psi$, $\Box\Diamond\theta$, $\Diamond\Box\pi$ for TLP (QTLP) formulae φ,ψ,θ and π.

In view of several recent attempts ([AS],[S]) to give characterization of safety and liveness properties, we suggest the following classification:

A formula represents a safety property *iff* it is initially equivalent to a formula of the form $\Box\varphi$ for some past formula φ.

A formula is a *simple* liveness property *iff* it is *not* a safety property and it is representable in one of the forms $\Diamond\psi$, $\Box\Diamond\psi$, $\Diamond\Box\psi$ for some past formula ψ.

A liveness property is any positive boolean combination of simple liveness properties, which is not a safety property.

For example, the formula $\Box(p\rightarrow p\mathcal{U}q)$ (for exclusive p and q) is representable as the conjunction of a safety formula $\Box((\neg p)\rightarrow(\neg p)\mathcal{S}q)$ and a simple liveness property $\Box\Diamond((\neg p)\mathcal{S}q)$. On the other hand, it is also representable as a single simple liveness formula $\Box\Diamond[(\neg p)\mathcal{S}q\wedge\boxminus((\neg p)\rightarrow(\neg p)\mathcal{S}q)]$.

Comparing our characterization of safety and liveness to the ones given in [AP] we observe the following:

1. The notions of safety presented here and the one defined in [AP] coincide.
2. The class of liveness properties according to [AP] is strictly contained in our class of liveness properties.

Thus, for example, we classify the property $p\mathcal{U}q$ as a simple liveness property since it is representable as $\Diamond(q \wedge \ominus\boxminus p)$. According to [AP] $p\mathcal{U}q$ is neither a safety nor a liveness property.

Our classification is mainly motivated by the two proof principles that have been advocated in [MP1] and [MP3] for establishing safety and liveness properties respectively. In the presence of the past operators, these proof principles can be considerably strengthened and their adequacy for establishing safety and liveness properties made more apparent.

Consider an underlying program P which produces the computations we wish to specify. Let φ and ψ be two TLP (QTLP) formulae. We say that P ***leads from*** φ ***to*** ψ (denoted by $\varphi \hookrightarrow \psi$) if for every σ, a computation of P, and every position $0 \leq j < |\sigma| - 1$:

$$(\sigma, j) \models \varphi \Longrightarrow (\sigma, j+1) \models \psi.$$

Then we have the following two rules:

(Safety)
Let φ be a past formula (TLP, QTLP)

$$\frac{\varphi \hookrightarrow \varphi}{\varphi \rightarrow \Box\varphi}$$

(Liveness)
Let φ and ψ be past formulae (TLP, QTLP)

$$\frac{\begin{array}{l}\varphi \hookrightarrow (\varphi \vee \psi) \\ \text{Eventually } \varphi \hookrightarrow \psi\end{array}}{\varphi \rightarrow \Diamond\psi}$$

The "Eventually $\varphi \hookrightarrow \psi$" premise usually corresponds to some fairness requirement that guarantees an eventual execution of a step that leads from φ to ψ. The basic liveness rule is developed into the general liveness rule by the addition of explicit well founded induction.

Note that the safety rule with a TLP formula φ now covers all the different cases of ***unless*** formulae that previously required separate rules. Similarly the liveness rule covers the ***until*** case and many others.

Adequacy of TL for Compositional Verification

In the earlier works on the use of TL for verification, we find a style of proof that can be described as ***global***.

The proof reasons about the complete program and formulates assertions that unrestrictedly refer to all variables and parts of the program. In particular, a heavy use is made of location pointers that represent the control site in each module and process. It has been shown in [LP] that for the finite state case the proof system for TL presented in [MP1] is complete for global verification.

However, a very important recent trend represented in [BKP] and [NGO], insists on ***compositional*** or ***modular*** proof style. In this style when proving a property of $S_1 \| S_2$, we must derive first the formulae φ_1 and φ_2 that give a partial specification of S_1 and S_2 respectively, and then infer φ from the conjunction of φ_1 and φ_2. The principle of modularity forbids φ_1 to mention any but the variables which are externally observable. In particular φ_1 should not mention the location pointers, since they are obviously unobservable outside of S_1.

An important question is therefore whether the proof system and the language are equal to the task.

Consider the following CSP-like example:

$$S_1 :: *[[\ell_0 : a! \rightarrow \ell_c : \text{ Critical Section}]; [\ell_1 : b! \rightarrow \textit{skip} \;]]$$

$$\|$$

$$S_2 :: *[[m_0 : a? \rightarrow \; \textit{skip}]; [m_1 : b? \rightarrow m_c : \text{ Critical Section}] \;]$$

The property that we wish to establish is

$$\varphi : \; \Box\neg(\textit{at } \ell_c \wedge \; \textit{at } m_c)$$

Were we allowed to use global proof style it would have been easy to establish the global invariant:

$$\Box([\textit{at } \ell_0 \equiv (\textit{at } m_0 \vee \; \textit{at } m_c)] \wedge [(\textit{at } \ell_1 \vee \; \textit{at } \ell_c) \equiv \textit{at } m_1])$$

from which φ immediately follows.

In the modular style we can establish first

$$\varphi_1 : \; \Box\{\textit{at } \ell_c \rightarrow (\neg b S(a \wedge \neg b))\} \quad \text{for } S_1, \text{ and}$$
$$\varphi_2 : \; \Box\{\textit{at } m_c \rightarrow (\neg a S(b \wedge \neg a))\} \quad \text{for } S_2$$

Here a and b are propositions that hold exactly when the a and b communications take place.

From these we again obtain φ immediately. Note that we replaced the forbidden location pointers by a behavioral description of the histories leading to ℓ_c and m_c respectively.

Consider the slightly modified program:

$$S_3 :: *[[c![\textit{true} \rightarrow \ell_c : \text{ Critical Section } \;\Box\; \textit{true} \rightarrow \; \textit{skip}]];$$
$$[c! \rightarrow \; \textit{skip}]] \qquad \|$$
$$S_4 :: *[[c? \rightarrow \; \textit{skip}];$$
$$[c? \rightarrow \quad [\textit{true} \rightarrow m_c : \text{ Critical Section } \;\Box\; \textit{true} \rightarrow \; \textit{skip}]]]$$

The differences between $S_3 \parallel S_4$ and $S_1 \parallel S_2$ are that the two communication a and b have been identified into a single c, and the entry into the critical section has been made non-deterministic.

Using $\mathrm{QTLF_H}$ it is easy to handle this case with similar ease. We take

$$\varphi_1 : \Box\{at\ \ell_c \rightarrow [(true^*; c; true^*; c)^*; true^*; c; true^*]_{\mathrm{H}}\}$$

i.e., $at\ell_c$ may hold only after an *odd* number of c's.

$$\varphi_2 : \Box\{atm_c \rightarrow [(true^*; c; true^*; c)^*; true^*]_{\mathrm{H}}\}$$

In comparison $at\ m_c$ may hold only after an *even* number of c's.

Obviously φ follows.

By the previous equivalence results, these formulae can be expressed also in QTL.

Can we do equally well in TL? If we could, then we could count modulo 2 in TL. As already shown in [W] this is impossible. We must conclude:

Proposition 3

Unextended TL is inadequate for modular verification.

In comparison we have:

Proposition 4

QTL is adequate for modular verification.

Consider a generic program $S_1 \parallel S_2$. Let $\bar{y}_1$ be all the externally observable variables of S_1 and $\bar{x}_1$ the externally unobservables in S_1, including the location pointers. It is a standard exercise to define $\psi_1(\bar{x}_1; \bar{y}_1)$ a TL formula that fully specifies all the computations admitted by S_1. Similarly construct $\psi_2(\bar{x}_2; \bar{y}_2)$. We now take $\varphi_1 : \exists\bar{x}_1\psi_1(\bar{x}_1; \bar{y}_1)$ and $\varphi_2 : \exists\bar{x}_2\psi_2(\bar{x}_2; \bar{y}_2)$. Note that φ_1 and φ_2 obey the modularity principle: they do not have any unobservables as free variables. The proof of $\varphi_1 \wedge \varphi_2 \rightarrow \varphi$ is easy to establish. Since we know that TL is complete for global proofs we may use the complete TL proof system to prove $\psi_1 \wedge \psi_2 \rightarrow \varphi$. We only need the simple $\exists$-introduction rules in order to infer $\varphi_1 \wedge \varphi_2 \rightarrow \varphi$ as required.

P-Validity and α-Fairness

In [Pn3] the problem of verification of concurrent probabilistic programs was studied. It was suggested that the probabilistic behaviour of *finite state* programs can be captured by a special type of fairness, called extreme fairness. It was shown that every temporal property that is proved under the assumption of extreme fairness, is also P-valid, i.e., satisfied with probability 1 over all probabilistic computations of the program. However, we also showed a particular property and program, such that the property was P-valid but could not be proven using extreme fairness.

In this paper we suggest another notion of fairness, called α-fairness, that captures precisely the extent of P-validity. That is, every property is P-valid *iff* it holds over all α-fair computations.

For our computational model we consider finite state concurrent probabilistic programs that are represented by a finite graph with labelled complex transitions. Each node in the graph corresponds to a global state of the program (i.e., in case the program was originally represented as several separate processes, the graph we consider here is their cartesian product). A transition

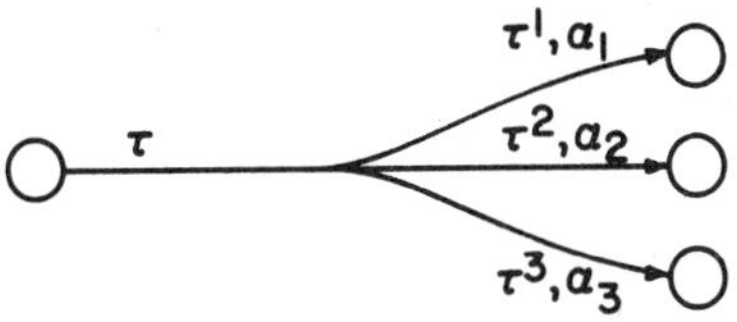

in the graph is a complex edge which has a single source and several destinations. The branching structure represents the probabilistic multiplicity of outcomes in which the execution of τ may result. The different branches $\tau', \ldots \tau^m$ are called the *modes* of τ and they are each associated with a positive probabilities $\alpha_i > 0$, $i = 1, \ldots m$. The transitions τ are partitioned into processes $P_1, \ldots, P_k$ such that the set of transitions associated with P_j are all the transitions that P_j may effect. We require that for each node n and each process P_j, $j = 1, \ldots k$ there is a transition belonging to P_j that departs from n. One node in the graph is distinguished at the *initial node.* It corresponds to the initial global state.

A *computation tree* for a program G is a infinite unwinding tree of G that satisfies the following:

a. The root of the computation tree is the initial node.

b. For each instance of a node n appearing in the tree we choose one transition τ that departs from n in G, and include in the tree all of its modes and instances of all the nodes that are its destinations in G.

c. (Justice) Each (infinite) path in the tree must contain infinitely many P_j-transitions for each P_j, $j = 1, \ldots k$.

For example, the tree of Figure 2 is a computation tree for the program in Fig. 1.

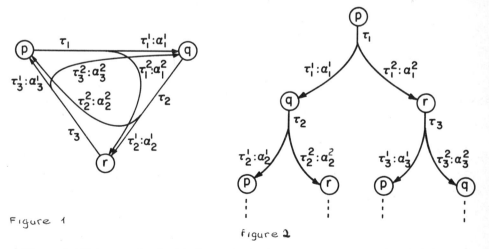

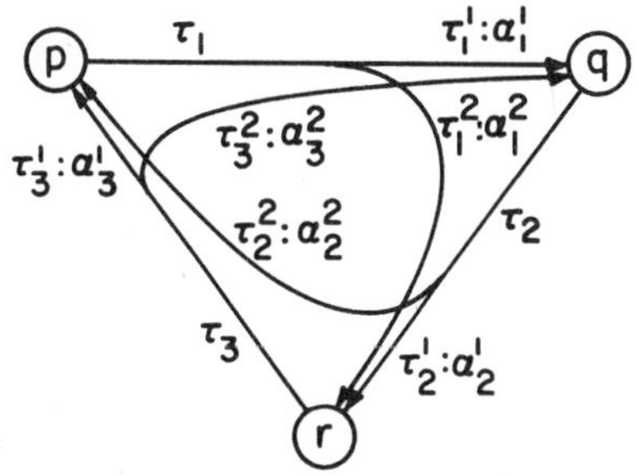

Figure 1

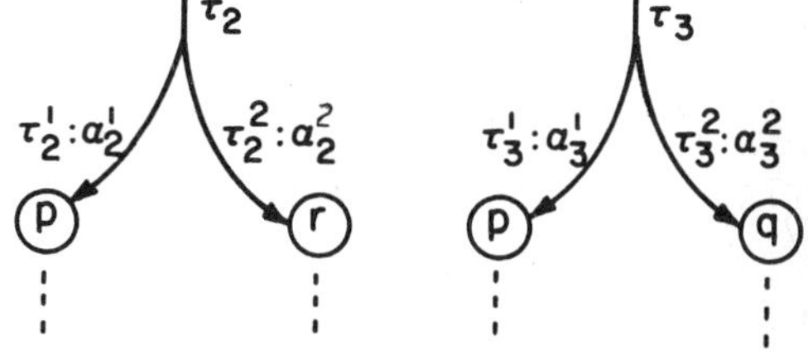

figure 2

The probabilities associated with the modes in the tree induce a natural probability measure on the paths in T.

Thus, for example the measure of the set of all paths that share a common prefix of the form:

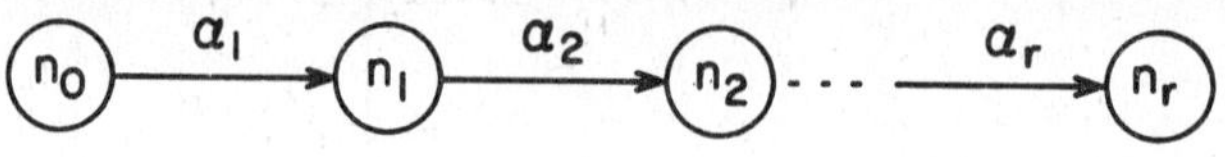

is $\alpha_1 \cdot \alpha_2 \cdot \ldots \cdot \alpha_n$.

Actually, we may relax requirement c. above by requiring that the set of just paths in T is of measure 1.

A path property ψ is said to hold with probability 1 over a computation tree T, if the set of paths in T that satisfy ψ has a measure 1. A path property ψ is said to be ***P-valid*** (probabilistic valid) for a program G, if it holds with probability 1 over all computation trees of G.

A ***computation*** for a program G is an infinite path in some computation tree. Note that a computation singles out a particular mode τ^j for each transition τ.

Let τ be a probabilistic transition that can result in m ***modes***, $\tau^1, \ldots \tau^m$. Let β be a star-free (regular) expression and σ an infinite computation. A finite prefix $\sigma' < \sigma$ is said to be a ***β-prefix*** if $\sigma' \models \beta$. The computation σ is said to be ***γ-fair*** (***α-fair***) with respect to the transition τ and the star-free (regular) expression β, if ***either*** the τ transition is taken only finitely many times from β-prefices, ***or*** each of the $\tau^1, \ldots, \tau^m$ modes is taken infinitely many times from β-prefices in σ.

The computation σ is defined to be ***γ-fair*** (***α-fair***) if it is γ-fair (α-fair) with respect to all the probabilistic transitions in the program, and all the star-free (regular) expressions β.

A TL (QTL) formula ψ is said to be ***γ-valid*** (***α-valid***) over a program G, if it is valid over all the γ-fair (α-fair) computations of G.

Lemma 1 (Completeness)

Let ψ be a TL (QTL) formula.

$$\psi \text{ is not } \gamma\text{-valid } (\alpha\text{-valid}) \Longrightarrow \psi \text{ is not P-valid.}$$

Outline of Proof

To establish the lemma, we assume a computation w that is γ-fair (α-fair) and does not satisfy ψ. As $\neg\psi$ is a TL (QTL) formula, there exists an ω-counter-free (ω-regular) automaton that defines $\neg\psi$. We consider one of its accepting runs on w. This run can be viewed as a sequence of pairs, where each pair consists of a program state and an automaton state. Let $\hat{w}$ denote the suffix of the sequence that satisfies:

a. Each pair appearing at least once in $\hat{w}$ appears there infinitely many times.

b. Each combination of consecutive pairs that appears in $\hat{w}$ at least once, appears there infinitely many times.

The number of distinct pairs in $\hat{w}$ is finite. Assume there are m such pairs, $\Pi_1, \ldots, \Pi_m$. For each such pair Π_i $(1 \leq i \leq m)$, we assign a set of processes

$$h_i = \{P_1^i, \ldots, P_{n_i}^i\}$$

which is the set of processes activated from Π_i in $\hat{w}$. As w is γ-fair (α-fair), it is also just, and

$$\bigcup_{i=1}^{m} h_i = \mathcal{P} \qquad \text{where } \mathcal{P} = \{P_1, \ldots, P_k\} \text{ is the set of all processes.}$$

The sequence $\hat{w}$ can be represented by

$$\hat{w} = \Pi^0, \Pi^1, \ldots \qquad (\Pi^j \in \{\Pi_1, \ldots, \Pi_m\})$$

From $\hat{w}$ we construct a computation tree T as follows:
Each vertex in the tree is labelled by some

$$\Pi_i \times |h_1| \times \ldots \times |h_m| \qquad i \in \{1 \ldots m\}$$

The root of the tree is labelled by

$$(\Pi^0, 1, \ldots, 1)$$

The tree is inductively constructed as follows:

From a leaf v labelled by $(\Pi_j, i_1, \ldots, i_m)$, the process $P_k = P^j_{i_j}$ is activated. For each Π_l such that $\Pi_j \xrightarrow{P_k} \Pi_l$, a vertex labelled by

$$(\Pi_l, i_1, \ldots, (i_j \bmod n_j) + 1, \ldots, i_m)$$

is constructed, and connected as a son of v.

We claim that the computation tree is fair with probability 1, and satisfies $\neg\psi$ with probability 1. This is proved by showing the existence of a finite path of bounded length, from each vertex $(\Pi_j, \ldots)$ to each vertex $(\Pi_k, \ldots)$, for each $1 \leq j, k \leq m$. From that, we can derive that an infinite path in T reaches each vertex of the type $(\Pi_k, \ldots)$ $(1 \leq k \leq m)$ infinitely many times, with probability 1. Each such path has an infinity set of states that is identical to the infinity set of states of the ω-counter-free (ω-regular) automaton that defines ψ, when running on w, and thus satisfies $\neg\psi$. Hence, the tree satisfies $\neg\psi$ with probability 1.

In a path that reaches every vertex of the type $(\Pi_j, \ldots)$ $(1 \leq j \leq m)$ infinitely many times, each process of h_j is taken infinitely many times. As $\bigcup_{i=1}^{m} h_i = \mathcal{P}$, it follows that the tree is just with probability 1.

Given a TL (QTL) formula ψ, we constructed a fair computation tree in which $\neg\psi$ is satisfied with probability 1. It follows that ψ is not P-valid. ∎

Lemma 2 (Soundness)

Let ψ be a TL (QTL) formula.

$$\psi \text{ is } \gamma\text{-valid } (\alpha\text{-valid}) \Longrightarrow \psi \text{ is P-valid.}$$

<u>Outline of Proof</u>

The statement that ψ is γ-valid (α-valid) means that all γ-fair (α-fair) computations satisfy ψ. We proceed to show that the measure of computations which are not γ-fair (α-fair) is 0, leaving a measure 1 set of computations that satisfy ψ.

Let G be a program with a bounded probability distribution, and T one of its computation trees. Define COM_β to be the set of all computations of T, which are not γ-fair (α-fair) with respect to a star-free (regular) expression β. Thus, $\sigma \in COM_\beta$ if in σ some probabilistic transition τ is taken infinitely often after β-prefices, and some mode τ^j of τ is taken only finitely often after β-prefices.

The set COM_β can be partitioned to $COM_\beta^{\tau^j}$, according to the neglected mode τ^j. (The $COM_\beta^{\tau^j}$-s may not be disjoint).

We claim that for each τ^j, $\mu(COM_\beta^{\tau^j}) = 0$.

Taking the union of $COM_\beta^{\tau^j}$ over the finitely many different τ^j-s in the program G and the countable star-free (regular) expressions on the alphabet $\Sigma = \{\text{The set of states in } G\}$, we obtain a set of measure 0. We conclude that the set of computations in T which are not γ-fair (α-fair) is of measure 0. ∎

Discussions

A version of TL which does not assume bounded past is also possible. The approach we have taken here can be easily extended to cover this version. We have to consider sequences that may be infinite at both directions (i.e., indexed by positive and negative integers). In the decision procedure we have to define a criterion of self fulfillment of initial MSCS's that requires the presence of the formula ψ_2 in the component for each formula $\psi_1 \mathcal{S} \psi_2$ that appears in the component. In the axiomatic system we have to replace the clause $\diamondminus\ominus \mathit{false}$ in A by $p\mathcal{S}q \rightarrow \diamondminus q$.

Another extension which is easy to obtain is to consider formulae over a given finite state program. This is usually referred to as model checking. The decision procedure is very similar to the one presented in [LP]. For a corresponding deductive system it is sufficient to add the program dependent axioms of [LP] in order to ensure a complete system.

Acknowledgement

We wish to thank Joe Halpern for helpful suggestions, Carol Weintraub for her excellent typing and Y. Barbut for the drawings.

References

[AS] Alpern, B., Schneider, F.B., - Defining Liveness, Cornell University, (Oct. 1984).

[BK] Barringer, H., Kuiper R., - A Temporal Logic Specification Method Supporting Hierarchical Development, University of Manchester, (Nov. 1983).

[BKP] Barringer, H., Kuiper, R., Pnueli, A. - Now You May Compose Temporal Logic Specifications, *16th Symposium on Theory of Computing* (April 84), 51-63.

[Buc] Büchi, J.R., - On a Decision Method in Restricted Second Order Arithmetic, *Proc. Intern. Congr. Logic, and Philos. Sci. 1960*, 1960, Stanford University Press (1962) 1-11.

[Buc] Büchi, J.R., - Weak Second Order Arithmetics and Finite Automata, Z. Math. Logik Grundlagen Math 6 (1960) 66-92.

[Bur] Burgess, J., - Basic Tense Logic, in Handbook of Philosophical Logic, Vol. 2 (D. Gabbay and F. Guenthner eds.) D. Reidel Pub. Co., (1984).

[C] Choueka, Y., - Theories of Automata on ω-Tapes: A Simplified Approach, *Journal of Computers and Systems Sciences* 8 (1974) 117-141.

[CH] Chen, Z.C., Hoare, C.A.R., - Partial Correctness of Communicating Processes and Protocols, Technical Monograph, PRG-20 Oxford University Computing Laboratory (May 1981).

[GPSS] Gabbay, D., Pnueli, A., Shelah, S., Stavi, J., - On the Temporal Analysis of Fairness, *Proc of the 7th ACM Symp. on Principles of Programming Languages* (1980) 163-173.

[H] Hoare, C.A.R., - A Calculus of Total Correctness for Communicating Precesses, Technical Monograph, RPG-23 Oxford University Computing Laboratory (May 1981).

[HO] Hailpern, B., Owicki, S., - Modular Verification of Computer Communication Protocols, *IEEE Trans. on Communications*, COM-31, 1 (Jan. 1983) 56-68.

[K] Kamp, H.W., - Tense Logic and the Theory of Linear Order, Ph.D. Thesis, University of California Los Angeles (1968).

[KVR] Koymans, R., Vytopil, J., DeRoever, W.P., - Real Time Programming and Asynchronous Message Passing, *2nd ACM Symp. of Distributed Computing*, Montreal (1983) 187-197.

[L] Lamport, L., - What is Good in Temporal Logic?, Proceeding IFIP (1983) 657-668.

[Li] Lichtenstein, O., - Decidablity and Completeness of a Temporal Proof System for Finite State Programs, M.Sc. Thesis, Tel Aviv University (1984).

[LP] Lichtenstein, O., Pnueli, A., - Checking That Finite State Concurrent Programs Satisfy Their Linear Specification, *ACM Symp. on Principles of Programming Languages* (1985).

[MC] Misra, J., Chandy, K.M., - Proofs of Networks of Processes, *IEEE Trans. on Software Engineering* 5E-7, 4 (July 1981).

[MNP] McNaughton, R., Papert, S., - Counter Free Automata, MIT press, Cambridge, Mass (1971).

[MP1] Manna, Z., Pnueli, A., - Verification of Concurrent Programs: A Temporal Proof System, *Proc. 4th School on Advanced Programming*, Amsterdam (June 1982) 163-255.

[MP2] Manna, Z., Pnueli, A., - How to Cook a Temporal Proof System for your Pet Programming Language *Proc of the 10th ACM Symp. on Principles of Programming Languages* (1983).

[MP3] Manna, Z., Pnueli, A., - Adequate Proof Principles for Invariance and Liveness Properties of Concurrent Programs, Science and Computer Programming, Forthcoming.

[NGO] Nguyen, V., Gries, D., Owicki, S., - A Model and Temporal Proof System for Networks of Processes, *Proc of the 12th ACM Symp. on Principles of Programming Languages*

(1985).

[OG] Owicki, S., Gries, D., - An axiomatic Proof Technique for Parallel Programs, *Acta Informatica 6* (1976) 319-340.

[OL] Owicki, S., Lamport, L., - Proving Liveness Properties of Concurrent Programs, *ACM TOPLAS 4,3* (July 1982) 455-495.

[Pe] Peikert, R., - Propositional Temporal Logic and ω-regular Languages, Manuscript, ETH-Zürich.

[Pn1] Pnueli, A., - The Temporal Logic of Programs, *18th Annual Symp. on Foundation of Computer Science* (1977) 46-57.

[Pn2] Pnueli, A., - In Transition from Global to Modular Temporal Reasoning about Programs, *Proc. Advanced NATO Institute on Logic and Models for Verification and Specification of Concurrent Systems*, La Colle-Sur-Loupe (Oct. 1984).

[Pn3] Pnueli, A., - On the Extremely Fair Treatment of Probabilistic Algorithms, *Proc. of the 15th Annual ACM Symp. on Theory of Computing* (1983).

[Pr] Prior, - Past Present and Future, Oxford Press.

[RU] Rescher, N., Urquhart, A., - Temporal Logic, Springer Verlag (1971).

[S] Sistla, A.P., - Characterization of Safety and Liveness Properties in Temporal Logic, University of Massachusetts, Amherst (Nov. 1984).

[SC] A.P. Sistla, E.M. Carke, The Complexity of Propositional Temporal Logic, *14th ACM Symposium on Thoery of Computing*, (May 1982) 159–167.

[T] Thomas, W., - A Combinatorial Approach to the Theory of ω-Automata, *Information and Control 48,3* (March 1981) 261-283.

[VW] Vardi, M.Y., Wolper, P., - Expressiveness and Complexity of Languages for Describing Sequences, Stanford University.

[W] Wolper, P., - Temporal Logic can be More Expressive, *Proc. of the 22nd Annual Symp. on Foundation of Computer Science* (1981) 340-348.

Continuation Semantics in Typed Lambda-Calculi

(summary)

Albert R. Meyer
Massachusetts Institute of Technology
Laboratory for Computer Science
545 Technology Square
Cambridge, MA 02139

Mitchell Wand
Computer Science Department
Brandeis University
Waltham, MA 02254

1. Abstract. This paper reports preliminary work on the semantics of the continuation transform. Previous work on the semantics of continuations has concentrated on untyped lambda-calculi and has used primarily the mechanism of inclusive predicates. Such predicates are easy to understand on atomic values, but they become obscure on functional values. In the case of the typed lambda-calculus, we show that such predicates can be replaced by retractions. The main theorem states that the meaning of a closed term is a retraction of the meaning of the corresponding continuationized term.

2. Introduction. The method of continuations was introduced in [Strachey & Wadsworth 74] as a device for formalizing the notion of control flow in programming languages. In this method, a term is evaluated in a context which represents "the rest of the computation". If the term involves the evaluation of a subterm, then the subterm is evaluated in a new context which evaluates the rest of the term and then proceeds to the old context. If the term can be evaluated immediately, then the value is passed to the context. Such a context is called a *continuation*.

In many cases, one may write either a direct or a continuation semantics for a language. Then one is faced with the problem of formulating the relationship between the two semantics. This relationship has been studied by [Reynolds 74], [Stoy 81], and [Sethi & Tang 80]. All of these papers discussed essentially an untyped lambda calculus with atoms, interpreted in Scott's D_∞ model or something like it. The result in each case was that the two semantics for a given term were connected by a relation which was the identity relation on atoms. The key was the construction of a suitable relation. This was done by the method of *inclusive predicates,* which depended on the details of the models. As a result, the significance of these predicates on values other than atoms was obscure.

In this paper, we show that for the case of the *typed* lambda-calculus, one may replace these inclusive predicates by retractions, which are far easier to understand. Rather than have the direct and continuation meanings of a term connected by a relation, we show that the direct meaning may be recovered from the continuation meaning by a retraction. In this way, the continuation semantics appears as a representation of the direct semantics in the sense of [Hoare 72], with the retraction as Hoare's "abstraction mapping". Hoare's notion of a "concrete invariant" appears as a crucial part of the proof.

Furthermore, the reasoning in the proof lies entirely in the λ-calculus, and hence the theorem holds in *any* model. Thus we avoid the detailed model-theoretic manipulation characteristic of the inclusive predicate approach.

3. Language. We consider the simply-typed lambda-calculus. The types are either ground types $\sigma_1, \sigma_2, \ldots$ or functional types $\alpha \to \beta$. Among the types is a distinguished type o (not necessarily a ground type) of *answers*. These are the only types. Terms are either variables, combinations, or abstractions $\lambda v{:}\,\alpha.\, M$, where v is a variable, α is a type, and M is a term. We assume that the semantics is given using a many-sorted environment model [Meyer 82, Wand 84].

4. Interpretation of Types. The continuation semantics will manipulate representations of the objects that appear in the direct semantics. We assign to each type α a type α' of representations of objects of type α. Ground types are represented as themselves. Corresponding to a function of type $\alpha \to \beta$, we will have in the continuation semantics a function that takes two arguments: a representation of an α and a continuation that expects a representation of a β. With this information, the function computes an answer. Thus we have:

$$\sigma' = \sigma$$

$$(\alpha \to \beta)' = \alpha' \to (\beta' \to o) \to o$$

5. The Transformation. For each term M of type α, we construct a term $\overline{M}$ of type $(\alpha' \to o) \to o$ as follows:

$$\overline{x} = \lambda\kappa.\, \kappa x$$

$$\overline{\lambda x.\, M} = \lambda\kappa.\, \kappa(\lambda x.\, \overline{M})$$

$$\overline{MN} = \lambda\kappa.\, \overline{M}(\lambda m.\, \overline{N}(\lambda n.\, mn\kappa))$$

Here we have deleted the type annotations for clarity. If we have a variable, we send the result to the continuation κ. If we have an abstraction, we return an appropriate function to the continuation. If we have a combination, we evaluate the operator in a continuation which in turn evaluates the operand in a continuation which applies the value of the operator to the value of the operand and the current continuation. This fits nicely with the definition of $(-)'$: if M is of type $\alpha \to \beta$, then m must be of type $(\alpha \to \beta)' = \alpha' \to (\beta' \to o) \to o$, n of type α', and κ of type $\beta' \to o$.

Operationally, the pleasant fact about $\overline{M}$ is that it is *tail-recursive*: no operand is a combination. (This property, furthermore, is preserved under beta-reduction). Thus there is at most one redex which is not inside the scope of a lambda, and thus call-by-value reduction coincides with outermost or call-by-name reduction [Plotkin 75]. This also allows simpler implementation on standard machines [Abelson & Sussman 85].

6. Retractions. We say α is a *retract* of β (we write $\alpha \lhd \beta$) iff there exist lambda-definable maps $i: \alpha \to \beta$ and $j: \beta \to \alpha$ such that $j \circ i$ is the identity function on α. We can formulate retractions between the various domains used in the semantics, as follows:

7. Theorem. (Statman) If $i \lhd o$ for every ground type ι, then $\alpha \lhd (\alpha \to o) \to o$.

Proof: Define $I: \alpha \to (\alpha \to o) \to o$ by $I = \lambda x \kappa . \kappa x$. To define the inverse mapping, observe that α must be of the form $\alpha_1 \to \alpha_2 \to \ldots \to \gamma$, where γ is a ground type. Let $r: \gamma \to o$ be the injection of the retraction from γ to o, with left inverse l. Then we define $J = \lambda u: (\alpha \to o) \to o . \lambda x_1: \alpha_1 \ldots \lambda x_n: \alpha_n . l(u(\lambda a: \alpha . r(a x_1 \ldots x_n)))$.

We will use I_α and J_α to denote these retractions. Note that I_α does *not* denote the usual combinator $\lambda x: \alpha . x$.

We can "apply" an element m of type $(\alpha \to \beta)'$ to an element n of type α' and get an element of type β' by writing $J(mn)$. We use $m \bullet n$ to denote this combination, which we call *pseudo-application.*

8. Theorem. For any type α, $\alpha \lhd \alpha'$.

Proof: For basic types, the retraction is the identity. At functional types, define

$$i_{\alpha \to \beta} = \lambda f: (\alpha \to \beta) . I_{\beta'} \circ i_\beta \circ f \circ j_\alpha$$

$$j_{\alpha \to \beta} = \lambda f': (\alpha \to \beta)' . j_\beta \circ J_{\beta'} \circ f' \circ i_\alpha$$

We may now state the main theorem:

9. Main Theorem. Let M be any closed term of type α. Then $M = j_\alpha(J_{\alpha'} \overline{M})$.

10. Concrete Invariants. To prove the theorem, we need to consider terms with free variables as well. To do this, we must consider which elements of α' are legal representations of elements of α, that is, what constitutes an appropriate concrete invariant for this representation scheme. For each type α, we need a predicate P_α on the elements of type α' in any environment model.

Define a set of such predicates P_α to be *acceptable* iff it has the following properties:

(1) For all types α, β, and γ, and all values x of type α, the following hold:

$$P_\alpha(i_\alpha x)$$

$$P_{\alpha\to(\beta\to\alpha)}(J\overline{K})$$

$$P_{(\alpha\to\beta\to\gamma)\to(\beta\to\gamma)\to(\alpha\to\gamma)}(J\overline{S})$$

(2) If $P_{\alpha\to\beta}(m)$ and $P_\alpha(n)$, then

$$P(m\bullet n)$$

$$(j_{\alpha\to\beta}m)(j_\alpha n) = j_\beta(m\bullet n)$$

$$mn = I_{\beta'}(m\bullet n)$$

Property (1) says that the canonical representations and the images of the standard combinators S and K are legal. Property (2) says that (a) the legal representations are closed under pseudo-application, (b) conventional application is a homomorphic image of pseudo-application, and (c) that real application of representations is well-behaved: that is, it sends a value to its continuation.

With this definition we can state the key result:

11. Theorem. Let P be any acceptable predicate. For any term M and any environment ρ' such that for all x, $P(\rho'[x])$ holds, we have $[M](j\circ\rho') = j(J([\![\overline{M}]\!]\rho'))$.

Proof (Sketch): We first show that $\overline{\lambda x.M} = \overline{[x]M}$, where $[x]M$ denotes the usual bracket-abstraction (lambda-elimination) algorithm. This allows us to concentrate on combination. The theorem then follows by algebraic manipulation, using the additional induction hypotheses that $[\![\overline{M}]\!]\rho' = I(J([\![\overline{M}]\!]\rho'))$ and $P(J([\![\overline{M}]\!]\rho'))$.

12. Existence of acceptable predicates. To finish the main theorem, we need to show that in any environment model, there exists an acceptable predicate. We prove the existence of two acceptable predicates. The first uses induction on types; the second depends on the strong normalization theorem.

13. Proposition. Define Q as follows: Let $Q_\sigma(m) = \mathit{true}$ for ground types. At higher types, define $Q_{\alpha\to\beta}(m)$ to be true iff for all n such that $Q_\alpha(n)$ holds, we have

$$Q_\beta(m\bullet n)$$

$$(jm)(jn) = j(m\bullet n)$$

$$\text{and } mn = I(m\bullet n)$$

Then Q is an acceptable predicate.

Proof: The definition proceeded by induction on types. Property (1) in the definition of acceptability follows by induction on types as well. Property (2) follows *a fortiori*.

14. Theorem. Let R be the smallest predicate containing ix for all x, containing $J\overline{S}$ and $J\overline{K}$ of every type, and closed under $\bullet$. Then R is acceptable.

Proof (Sketch): Any element of R can be expressed as a term built up from combinations of ix, $J\overline{S}$, and $J\overline{K}$ under $\bullet$. We turn these terms into a rewriting system using the usual rules for S and K. We first show that R is acceptable when the range of the quantifiers in the definition of acceptability is restricted to the denotations of terms in normal form in the system. It follows that the usual rules for S and K are sound when applied applicatively, that is, when the subterms are in normal form. Therefore, by the Strong Normalization Theorem, any term, and hence any element of R, codesignates with a term in normal form and therefore the restriction of the quantifiers has no effect.

15. Conclusions. We have shown that at least in the case of the typed lambda calculus, we can explain the continuation transform using retractions and depending only on the principle of beta-conversion. Our development goes through as well if we redefine the continuation transformation to set

$$\overline{MN} = \lambda\kappa.\, \overline{N}(\lambda n.\, \overline{M}(\lambda m.\, mn\kappa))$$

where the operand is evaluated before the operator, or even to allow the algorithm to choose nondeterministically between the two. In that case we need to ensure that both versions of $\overline{S}$ satisfy the concrete invariant. The case of the call-by-name transformation, as given in [Plotkin 75], can also be treated by these methods.

The situation becomes more complicated if we study calculi in which strong normalization fails, such as the typed calculus with fixed-point operators. We are currently studying both this and the untyped case, but it is not clear as of this writing whether this approach extends to these cases. The retractions themselves are of some interest, and add another dimension to our understanding.

16. References

[Abelson & Sussman 84]
Abelson, H., and Sussman, G.J. *The Structure and Interpretation of Computer Programs*, MIT Press, Cambridge, MA, 1985.

[Hoare 72]
Hoare, C.A.R., "Proving Correctness of Data Representations," *Acta Informatica 1* (1972), 271–281.

[Meyer 82]
Meyer, A.R. "What Is a Model of the Lambda Calculus?" *Information and Control 52* (1982), 87–122.

[Plotkin 75]
Plotkin, G.D. "Call-by-Name, Call-by-Value and the λ-Calculus," *Theoret. Comp. Sci. 1* (1975) 125–159.

[Reynolds 74]
Reynolds, J.C. "On the Relation between Direct and Continuation Semantics," *Proc. 2nd Colloq. on Automata, Languages, and Programming* (Saarbrucken, 1974) Springer Lecture Notes in Computer Science, Vol. 14 (Berlin: Springer, 1974) 141–156.

[Sethi & Tang 80]
Sethi, R. and Tang, A. "Constructing Call-by-value Continuation Semantics," *J. ACM 27* (1980), 580–597.

[Stoy 81]
Stoy, J.E. "The Congruence of Two Programming Language Definitions," *Theoret. Comp. Sci. 13* (1981), 151–174.

[Strachey & Wadsworth 74]
Strachey, C. and Wadsworth, C.P. "Continuations: A Mathematical Semantics for Handling Full Jumps," Oxford University Computing Laboratory Technical Monograph PRG-11 (January, 1974).

[Wand 84]
Wand, M. "A Types-as-Sets Semantics for Milner-style Polymorphism," *Conf. Rec. 11th ACM Symp. on Principles of Programming Languages* (1984), 158–164.

Second-order logical relations
(Extended Abstract)

John C. Mitchell

AT&T Bell Laboratories
Murray Hill, New Jersey 07974

Albert R. Meyer

MIT Laboratory for Computer Science
Cambridge, MA 02139

Wednesday, 27 March 1985

ABSTRACT

Logical relations are a generalization of homomorphisms between models of typed lambda calculus. We define logical relations for second-order typed lambda calculus and use these relations to give a semantic characterization of second-order lambda definability. Logical relations are also used to state and prove a general representation independence theorem. Representation independence implies that the meanings of expressions do not depend on whether *true* is represented by 1 and *false* by 0, as long as all the functions that manipulate truth values are represented correctly.

1. Introduction

Logical relations have proved useful for demonstrating many properties of ordinary typed lambda calculus. These hereditarily-defined relations, which are similar to homomorphisms, are introduced in [Friedman 75, Plotkin 80, Statman 82, Tait 67]. Logical relations over models were used by Friedman [Friedman 75] to prove a completeness theorem over the full (set-theoretic) type hierarchy and in [Plotkin 80, Statman 82] to characterize the lambda-definable elements of models. Similar relations over terms themselves are used in [Statman 82, Tait 67] to prove syntactic results like the Church-Rosser and Strong Normalization Theorems. More recently, logical relations (along with other techniques) were used by Mulmuley to construct "fully-abstract" models of typed lambda calculus [Mulmuley 84]. The aim of this paper is towards a general theory of logical relations for second-order lambda calculus. The main results are a characterization of second-order lambda definability and a representation independence theorem.

The second-order lambda calculus, developed by Reynolds [Reynolds 74] and Girard [Girard 71], combines typed functions with polymorphic functions which take types as arguments. Some syntactic and operational aspects of the language are described in [Fortune, et. al. 83], while semantic models are discussed in [Bruce, Meyer and Mitchell 85, Bruce and Meyer 84, Mitchell 84c]. As described in [Mitchell and Plotkin 85], second-order lambda calculus may be viewed as having a general form of data abstraction, dual to polymorphism. The main difficulty in working with logical relations for second-order lambda calculus lies in the fact that the types of this calculus are not hierarchical. There does not seem to be any ordering of types which could be used to define logical relations inductively. We do present one technique for constructing relations and use this to prove the lambda definability and representation independence theorems. The construction uses rules for deducing membership in logical relations, and applies only to models which have "indeterminates" at all types.

Representation independence for second-order lambda calculus is of interest because many programming languages are based on this calculus. Intuitively, the purpose of a representation independence theorem is to show that certain implementation decisions do not effect the meanings of programs. Consequently, these decisions do not concern the language designer; they may be left to the taste and judgement of the compiler writer. Various representation independence, or "abstraction," theorems for second-order lambda calculus have been proposed by Reynolds, Donahue and Haynes [Donahue 79, Haynes 84, Reynolds 74, Reynolds 83]. Essentially, all of these theorems are slight generalizations of the statement,

> If two models $\mathcal{A}$ and $\mathcal{B}$ are related in a certain way, then the meaning $\mathcal{A}[\![M]\!]$ of any closed term M in $\mathcal{A}$ is related to the meaning $\mathcal{B}[\![M]\!]$ of M in $\mathcal{B}$ in the same certain way.

The pragmatic consequence of this sort of theorem is that if two programming language interpreters are related in this "certain way," then the result of executing any program using one interpreter will correspond to the result of executing the same program using the other interpreter. Thus the precise statement of the theorem describes the kind of implementation decisions that do not effect the meanings of programs.

Although several representation independence theorems have been proposed, none have been entirely satisfactory or general[1]. Using the model theory developed recently in [Bruce, Meyer and Mitchell 85, Bruce and Meyer 84, Mitchell 84c], we are able to generalize the definition of logical relation and the Fundamental Theorem of Logical Relations of [Statman 82] without much complication. Our "Fundamental Theorem of Second-Order Logical Relations" is a general representation independence theorem in the spirit of [Donahue 79, Haynes 84, Reynolds 74, Reynolds 83].

While the "Fundamental Theorem" describes a degree of representation independence in the second-order lambda calculus, there is no *a priori* reason to believe that it is the strongest representation independence theorem for the language. The theorem demonstrates that the meanings of programs are invariant under certain transformations on semantic interpretations, but does not say whether meanings are invariant under additional transformations as well. We explore the possibility of stronger representation independence theorems using the notion of *observational equivalence*. Intuitively, two models are observationally equivalent if we cannot tell them apart by looking at the meanings of closed terms of certain "observable" types. Representation independence is related to observational equivalence since we would like to leave any implementation decision that does not effect the observable behavior of programs up to the discretion of the implementer. Using logical relations, we are able to characterize observational equivalence precisely.

For ease of notation, we restrict our attention to binary logical relations. The entire development is easily generalized to relations of any arity. We also consider logical relations over models exclusively, although the theory of logical relations over terms themselves, or weaker structures that do not satisfy β-equivalence does not differ much. We describe the syntax of second-order lambda calculus in Section 2 and review models in Section 3. Logical relations are defined in Section 4, while Section 5 contains an inference systems that can be used to construct logical relations over certain kinds of models. We discuss representation independence in Section 6.

2. Second-Order Lambda Calculus

For convenience, we work with a version of the second-order lambda calculus which has type expressions based on the ordinary typed lambda calculus. This language, similar to PLEXP [McCracken 79], has a somewhat simpler model theory than the second-order lambda calculi of [Girard 71, Reynolds 74] and has the further advantage that the set of type constructors may be regarded as a parameter of the language definition. There are three classes of expressions in this variant, $\mathcal{S}\Lambda$, of second-order lambda calculus. They are *terms*, *constructionals*, and *kinds*. The typed terms of $\mathcal{S}\Lambda$ correspond to programming language expressions. Type expressions may include type constructors and type functionals, which we call *constructionals*. As in [MacQueen and Sethi 82, McCracken 79, Mitchell 84c], we associate a *kind* with each symbol that may appear in type expressions. The language consisting only of constructionals and kinds is essentially the ordinary typed lambda calculus. This allows us to refer to the typed lambda calculus literature for the semantics of constructionals.

2.1. Constructionals and Kinds

We use the constant T for the kind consisting of all types. The set of kinds is given by the grammar

$$\kappa ::= T \mid \kappa_1 \Rightarrow \kappa_2.$$

The kind $\kappa_1 \Rightarrow \kappa_2$ will be interpreted as a set of functions from κ_1 to κ_2. For example, functions from types to types will have kind $T \Rightarrow T$. We now define the set of expressions that have kinds. For lack of a better phrase, we call these expressions *constructionals*. Let $\mathcal{C}_{kind}$ be a set of constant symbols c^κ, each with a specified kind (which we write as a superscript when necessary) and let $\mathcal{V}_{kind}$ be a set of variables v^κ, each with a specified kind. We assume we have infinitely many variables of each kind. The constructionals over $\mathcal{C}_{kind}$ and $\mathcal{V}_{kind}$, and their kinds, are defined by the following derivation system

$$c^\kappa \in \kappa, \quad v^\kappa \in \kappa$$

$$\frac{\mu \in \kappa_1 \Rightarrow \kappa_2, \quad \nu \in \kappa_1}{\mu\nu \in \kappa_2}$$

1. A critique of the results of [Donahue 79, Reynolds 74, Reynolds 83] appears in [Haynes 84]. The representation independence theorem of [Haynes 84] repairs the lacunae of previous theorems, but applies only to a special class of models. Haynes uses a semantics requiring ordered domains and his semantics distinguishes primitive types from other types in a somewhat peculiar way.

$$\frac{\mu \in \kappa_2}{\lambda v^{\kappa_1}.\mu \in \kappa_1 \Rightarrow \kappa_2}$$

For example $(\lambda v^T.v^T)c^T$ is a constructional with kind T.

A special class of constructionals are the type expressions, the constructionals of kind T. Since we will often be concerned with type expressions rather than arbitrary constructionals, it will be useful to distinguish them by notational conventions. We adopt the conventions that

$r, s, t, \ldots$ denote type variables

$\rho, \sigma, \tau, \ldots$ denote type expressions.

As in the definition above, we will generally use μ and ν for constructionals. Two important constructional constants are the function-type constructor

$$\rightarrow \in T \Rightarrow (T \Rightarrow T)$$

and the polymorphic-type constructor

$$\forall \in (T \Rightarrow T) \Rightarrow T.$$

As usual, we write $\rightarrow$ as an infix operator, as in the type expression $\sigma \rightarrow \tau$, and write $\forall t.\sigma$ for $\forall(\lambda t.\sigma)$. We will always assume that $\mathscr{C}_{kind}$ includes the constants $\rightarrow$ and $\forall$.

We now define the terms of $\mathscr{S}\Lambda$ and their types. The terms will include variables and typed constants. Let $\mathscr{V}$ be a set of variables, which we will call *ordinary variables*, and let $\mathscr{C}_{typed}$ be a set of constants, each with a fixed, closed type. As in most typed programming languages, the type of an $\mathscr{S}\Lambda$ term will depend on the context in which it occurs. For each *type assignment* A mapping ordinary variables to type expressions, we define a set $\mathscr{S}\Lambda_A$ of terms that are well-typed in the context A. If x is a variable, σ a type expression and A a type assignment, then $A[\sigma/x]$ is a type assignment with $(A[\sigma/x])(y) = A(y)$ for any variable y different from x, and $(A[\sigma/x])(x) = \sigma$.

To be precise, we define a family of languages, one $\mathscr{S}\Lambda_A$ for each type assignment A, by defining a family of mutually recursive functions. Each function Type_A is defined by a set of deduction rules which may mention other Type_B functions. The deduction rule

$$\text{Type}_A(M)=\sigma, \ldots \vdash \text{Type}_A(N)=\tau$$

means that if the antecedents hold, then the value of Type_A at N is defined to be τ. The language $\mathscr{S}\Lambda_A$ is defined to be the domain of Type_A.

$$\text{Type}_A(c^\tau) = \tau$$

$$\text{Type}_A(x) = A(x) \text{ if x is in the domain of A}$$

$$\text{Type}_A(M)=\sigma\rightarrow\tau,\ \text{Type}_A(N)=\sigma \vdash \text{Type}_A(M\ N)=\tau,$$

$$\text{Type}_{A[\sigma/x]}(M) = \tau \ \vdash\ \text{Type}_A(\lambda x \in \sigma.M) = \sigma\rightarrow\tau,$$

$$\text{Type}_A(M) = \forall t.\sigma \ \vdash\ \text{Type}_A(M\ \tau) = [\tau/t]\sigma,$$

$$\text{Type}_A(M) = \tau \vdash \text{Type}_A(\lambda t.M) = \forall t.\tau,$$
provided t is not free in A(x) for x free in M

Free and bound variables are defined as usual, with λ binding ordinary or type variables in constructionals and terms. For example, x is bound in $\lambda x \in \sigma.M$, the type variable t is bound in $\lambda x \in \forall t.t.x$, and t is bound in $\lambda t.M$. If M is a term and t does not occur free in A(x) for any x free in M, then t is *bindable in* M *with respect to* A. We use $[\tau/t]\sigma$ to denote the result of substituting τ for free occurrences of t in σ.

Since the set of terms $\mathscr{S}\Lambda_A$ depends on $\mathscr{C}_{kind}$ and $\mathscr{C}_{typed}$, it is more accurate to write $\mathscr{S}\Lambda_A(\mathscr{C}_{kind}, \mathscr{C}_{typed})$ However, for simplicity of notation, we generally leave the sets of constants implicit. It is also convenient to leave the assignment A implicit when no confusion will arise. A term of $\mathscr{S}\Lambda$ is *closed* if it has no free ordinary variables. If M is closed, then $\text{Type}_A(M)$ does not depend on A and so we may write Type(M) for the type of M.

3. Semantics of $\mathcal{S}\Lambda$

We review the definition of $\mathcal{S}\Lambda$ model. The presentation is based on [Bruce, Meyer and Mitchell 85, Bruce and Meyer 84, Mitchell 84c]. Since terms do not appear in constructionals, the semantics of constructionals may be considered first, without reference to the meanings of terms.

3.1. Models for Constructionals

A *type structure* $\mathcal{T}$ for a set $\mathcal{C}_{kind}$ of constructional constants is a tuple

$$<\mathcal{U}, c_1^{\mathcal{T}}, c_2^{\mathcal{T}}, ...>,$$

where $\mathcal{U}$ is a family of sets $\{U_\kappa\}$ indexed by kinds with

$U_{\kappa_1 \Rightarrow \kappa_2}$ a set of functions from U_{κ_1} to U_{κ_2},

and the interpretation $c_i^{\mathcal{T}}$ of a constant $c_i \in \mathcal{C}_{kind}$ is an element of the appropriate U_κ. Since constructionals include all typed lambda expressions, $\mathcal{U}$ must be a model of $\mathcal{T}\Lambda$. This means that $\mathcal{U}$ must contain elements K_{κ_1, κ_2} and $S_{\kappa_1, \kappa_2, \kappa_3}$ at all appropriate kinds; cf. [Barendregt 81, Friedman 75, Henkin 50, Statman 82].

If a particular type structure $\mathcal{T}=<\mathcal{U},...>$ is a clear from context, we use closed kind expressions to refer to sets of $\mathcal{U}$. For example, T denotes the base set U_T of $\mathcal{U}$.

3.2. Higher-Order Lambda Frames and Models

A model of $\mathcal{S}\Lambda$ consists of an interpretation for constructionals, sets for interpreting typed terms, and a mapping from the interpretation for constructionals to the sets of meanings of terms. The collection of interpretations that makes up an $\mathcal{S}\Lambda$ model is called a *frame*, following [Henkin 50]. However, not all frames are actually models, since the definition of frame does not guarantee that every term has a meaning. Therefore, models are defined to be frames which are rich enough to allow all terms to be given meanings.

A *frame* $\mathcal{F}$ *for* $\mathcal{S}\Lambda(\mathcal{C}_{kind}, \mathcal{C}_{type})$ is a tuple

$$\mathcal{F}=<\mathcal{T}, \mathcal{D}, \{\Phi, \Psi, c^{\mathcal{F}}\}_{c \in \mathcal{C}_{typed}}>$$

satisfying conditions (i) through (v) below.

(i) $\mathcal{T} = <\mathcal{U}, c^{\mathcal{T}}, ...>$ is a type structure for $\mathcal{C}_{kind}$

(ii) $\mathcal{D}$ is a family of sets D_a indexed by elements of $T^{\mathcal{T}}$

(iii) For each $a,b \in T^{\mathcal{T}}$, we have a set $[D_a \to D_b]$ of functions from D_a to D_b with functions

$\Phi_{a,b} : D_{a\to b} \to [D_a \to D_b]$ and $\Psi_{a,b} : [D_a \to D_b] \to D_{a\to b}$

such that $\Phi_{a,b} \circ \Psi_{a,b}$ is the identity on $[D_a \to D_b]$.

(iv) For every $f \in [T \to T]^{\mathcal{T}}$, we have a subset

$[\Pi_{a \in T} D_{f(a)}] \subseteq \Pi_{a \in T} D_{f(a)}$ with functions

$\Phi_f : D_{\Pi f} \to [\Pi_{a \in T} D_{f(a)}]$ and $\Psi_f : [\Pi_{a \in T} D_{f(a)}] \to D_{\Pi f}$

such that $\Phi_f \circ \Psi_f$ is the identity on $[\Pi_{a \in T} D_{f(a)}]$.

(v) For every $c \in \mathcal{C}_{typed}$ there is a specified element $c^{\mathcal{F}}$ of the appropriate type.

Essentially, condition (iii) states that $D_{a\to b}$ must "represent" some set $[D_a \to D_b]$ of functions from D_a to D_b. Similarly, condition (iv) specifies that $D_{\forall f}$ must represent some subset $[\Pi_{a \in T} D_{f(a)}]$ of the product $\Pi_{a \in T} D_{f(a)}$. In a full "classical" model of $\mathcal{S}\Lambda$, we might expect $[D_a \to D_b]$ to include all functions from D_a to D_b, but this does not seem to be possible [Reynolds 84]. For simplicity, we will assume that all frames are *extensional*, i.e., each $\Phi_{a,b}$ and Φ_f is 1-1.

An $\mathcal{S}\Lambda$*-environment model* is an $\mathcal{S}\Lambda$-frame which is sufficiently rich to allow all terms of $\mathcal{S}\Lambda$ to be interpreted. More precisely, an $\mathcal{S}\Lambda$-frame $\mathcal{F}$ is an $\mathcal{S}\Lambda$*-environment model* if, for every environment η satisfying A (as defined below), the meaning function $[\![\bullet]\!]\eta$ specified below is a *total* function from $\mathcal{S}\Lambda_A$ to elements of $\mathcal{F}$.

Let A be a type assignment. Let η be an environment mapping $\mathcal{V}_{kind}$ to elements of the appropriate kinds, and $\mathcal{V}$ to elements of $\cup\mathcal{D}$. We say that η *satisfies* A, written $\eta\models A$, if

$$\eta(x) \in [\![A(x)]\!]\eta$$

for each variable $x\in dom(A)$.

If $\eta\models A$, then the meanings of expressions of $\mathcal{S}\Lambda_A$ are defined inductively as follows.

$$[\![x]\!]\eta = \eta(x)$$

$$[\![c]\!]\eta = c^{\mathcal{F}}$$

$$[\![MN]\!]\eta = (\Phi_{a,b}[\![M]\!]\eta)\, [\![N]\!]\eta,$$

where $Type_A(M)=\sigma\to\tau$ and $a=[\![\sigma]\!]\eta$, $b=[\![\tau]\!]\eta$,

$[\![\lambda x\in\sigma.M]\!]\eta = \Psi_{a,b}\, g$, where

$g(d) = [\![M]\!]\eta[d/x]$ for all $d\in D_a$ and

a, b are the meanings of σ and $Type_A(M)$ in η

$$[\![M\tau]\!]\eta = (\Phi_f\, [\![M]\!]\eta)\, [\![\tau]\!]\eta,$$

where $Type_A(M)=\forall t.\sigma$ and $f=[\![\lambda t.\sigma]\!]\eta$,

$[\![\Pi t.M]\!]\eta = \Psi_f\, g$, where

$g(a) = [\![M]\!]\eta[a/t]$ for all $a\in T$ and

$f \in [T \to T]$ is the function $[\![\lambda t.Type_A(M)]\!]\eta$

It is easy to check that the meanings of typed terms have the appropriate semantic types. Properties such as the Substitution Lemma are also easily verified. We often omit Φ's when they are clear from context. For example, if $d\in D_{a\to b}$ and $e\in D_a$, we write de for $\Phi_{a,b}(d)e$.

4. Logical Relations

Although logical relations are relations rather than functions, it is often useful to think of logical relations as homomorphisms between $\mathcal{S}\Lambda$ models. Often, we use a logical relation $\mathcal{R}$ over models $\mathcal{A}$ and $\mathcal{B}$ as a way of establishing a correspondence between $\mathcal{A}$ and $\mathcal{B}$. If $\mathcal{R}(a, b)$, then we think of b as "$\mathcal{B}$'s picture of $a\in\mathcal{A}$." The essential property of a logical relation $\mathcal{R}$ over $\mathcal{A}$ and $\mathcal{B}$ is that for functions f in $\mathcal{A}$ and g in $\mathcal{B}$ of appropriate types, $\mathcal{R}(f, g)$ is determined by whether $\mathcal{R}(f(a), g(b))$ holds for all related a, b of appropriate types. In the case that f and g are polymorphic elements, $\mathcal{R}(f, g)$ is determined by whether $\mathcal{R}(f(a), g(b))$ for all related types a from $\mathcal{A}$ and b from $\mathcal{B}$.

4.1. $\mathcal{T}\Lambda$ Logical Relations

We briefly review the properties of logical relations for ordinary typed lambda calculus. Since we will use $\mathcal{T}\Lambda$ logical relations as relations over type structures, our terminology will be slightly unusual.

Let

$$\mathcal{S} = <\mathcal{U}^{\mathcal{S}}, c^{\mathcal{S}}, \ldots> \qquad \mathcal{T} = <\mathcal{U}^{\mathcal{T}}, c^{\mathcal{T}}, \ldots>$$

be type structures for $\mathcal{C}_{kind}$. A $\mathcal{T}\Lambda$ *logical relation* $\mathcal{R}$ over $\mathcal{S}$ and $\mathcal{T}$ is a family $\{R_\kappa\}$ of relations such that

$R_\kappa \subseteq \kappa^{\mathcal{S}}\times\kappa^{\mathcal{T}}$ for each kind κ

$$<s, t>\in R_{\kappa_1\to\kappa_2} \text{ iff } \forall s_1\in\kappa^{\mathcal{S}}.\forall t_1\in\kappa^{\mathcal{T}}{}_{\cdot 1}<s_1, t_1>\in R_{\kappa_1} \supset <ss_1, tt_1>\in R_{\kappa_2}$$

We say that $\mathcal{R}$ *preserves* a constant c of kind κ if

$$<c^{\mathcal{S}}, c^{\mathcal{T}}>\in R_\kappa$$

and generally assume that a relation $\mathcal{R}$ preserves all constants from $\mathcal{C}_{kind}$. We will always assume that any logical relation preserves $\to$, $\forall\in\mathcal{C}_{kind}$. The basic property of logical relations, called the Fundamental Theorem of Logical Relations in [Statman 82], is

THEOREM 1. *(Fundamental Theorem of $\mathcal{T}\Lambda$ Logical Relations [Statman 82]) Let $\mathcal{R}$ be a constant-preserving logical relation over type structures $\mathcal{S}$, $\mathcal{T}$ and let η_s, η_t be environments for $\mathcal{S}$ and $\mathcal{T}$ such that for each variable v of kind κ we have $<\eta_s(v), \eta_t(v)> \in R_\kappa$. Then for any constructional μ of kind κ,*

$$<\mathcal{S}[\![\mu]\!]\eta_s, \mathcal{T}[\![\mu]\!]\eta_t> \in R_\kappa.$$

4.2. $\mathcal{S}\Lambda$ Logical Relations

A logical relation $\mathcal{R}$ over models $\mathcal{A}$ and $\mathcal{B}$ will consist of a $\mathcal{T}\Lambda$ logical relation over $\mathcal{T}^{\mathcal{A}}$ and $\mathcal{T}^{\mathcal{B}}$, together with a family of relations over $\mathcal{D}^{\mathcal{A}}$ and $\mathcal{D}^{\mathcal{B}}$. The relations on $\mathcal{D}^{\mathcal{A}}$ and $\mathcal{D}^{\mathcal{B}}$ will be indexed by pairs of related types $a \in T^{\mathcal{A}}$, $b \in T^{\mathcal{B}}$. More precisely, let

$$\mathcal{A} = <\mathcal{T}^{\mathcal{A}}, \mathcal{D}^{\mathcal{A}}, \{\Phi^{\mathcal{A}}, \Psi^{\mathcal{A}}, c^{\mathcal{A}} \ldots\}>$$

$$\mathcal{B} = <\mathcal{T}^{\mathcal{B}}, \mathcal{D}^{\mathcal{B}}, \{\Phi^{\mathcal{B}}, \Psi^{\mathcal{B}}, c^{\mathcal{B}} \ldots\}>$$

be models for $\mathcal{S}\Lambda(\mathcal{C}_{kind}, \mathcal{C}_{type})$. An $\mathcal{S}\Lambda$-*logical relation* over $\mathcal{A}$, $\mathcal{B}$ is a family $\mathcal{R}$ of relations

$$R_\kappa \subseteq \kappa^{\mathcal{A}} \times \kappa^{\mathcal{B}} \text{ for each kind } \kappa$$

$$R_{a,b} \subseteq D_a^{\mathcal{A}} \times D_b^{\mathcal{B}} \text{ for each } <a, b> \in R_T$$

such that

(LR.1) $\{R_\kappa\}$ is a $\mathcal{T}\Lambda$-logical relation over $\mathcal{T}^{\mathcal{A}}$, $\mathcal{T}^{\mathcal{B}}$,

(LR.2) For all $<a_1, b_1>, <a_2, b_2> \in R_T$ and $<c, d> \in D^{\mathcal{A}}_{a_1 \to a_2} \times D^{\mathcal{B}}_{b_1 \to b_2}$ we have

$$<c, d> \in R_{a_1 \to a_2,\, b_1 \to b_2} \text{ iff } \forall c', d'. <c', d'> \in R_{a_1, b_1} \supset <cc', dd'> \in R_{a_2, b_2}$$

(LR.3) For all $<f, g> \in R_{T \Rightarrow T}$ and $<c, d> \in D_{\forall f}^{\mathcal{A}} \times D_{\forall g}^{\mathcal{B}}$ we have

$$<c, d> \in R_{\forall f, \forall g} \text{ iff } \forall a, b. <a, b> \in R_T \supset <ca, db> \in R_{f(a), g(b)}$$

This definition applies to extensional models only. For models which may not be extensional, conditions (LR.2) and (LR.3) become more complicated. A logical relation $\mathcal{R}$ over models $\mathcal{A}$ and $\mathcal{B}$ for $\mathcal{S}\Lambda(\mathcal{C}_{kind}, \mathcal{C}_{type})$ *preserves* a constant $c \in \mathcal{C}_{type}$ if

$$<c^{\mathcal{A}}, c^{\mathcal{B}}> \in R_{a, b}, \text{ where } a = \mathcal{A}[\![\sigma]\!],\ b = \mathcal{B}[\![\sigma]\!], \text{ and } \sigma \text{ is the type of c.}$$

Note that by the Fundamental Theorem for $\mathcal{T}\Lambda$ Relations, the semantic types $a = \mathcal{A}[\![\sigma]\!]$ and $b = \mathcal{B}[\![\sigma]\!]$ of any constant c^σ must be related. Unless otherwise specified, we will assume that any relation $\mathcal{R}$ over models $\mathcal{A}$ and $\mathcal{B}$ for $\mathcal{S}\Lambda(\mathcal{C}_{kind}, \mathcal{C}_{type})$ preserves both $\mathcal{C}_{kind}$ and $\mathcal{C}_{type}$.

Let $\mathcal{R}$ be a logical relation over $\mathcal{S}\Lambda(\mathcal{C}_{kind}, \mathcal{C}_{type})$ models $\mathcal{A}$ and $\mathcal{B}$. If $\eta_{\mathcal{A}}$ and $\eta_{\mathcal{B}}$ are environments for $\mathcal{A}$ and $\mathcal{B}$, respectively, we say that $\eta_{\mathcal{A}}$ and $\eta_{\mathcal{B}}$ are *related environments with respect to type assignment* A if

$$\eta_{\mathcal{A}}, \eta_{\mathcal{B}} \models A$$

and for every variable x we have

$$<\eta_{\mathcal{A}}(x), \eta_{\mathcal{B}}(x)> \in R_{a, b},$$

where $a = \mathcal{A}[\![A(x)]\!]\eta_{\mathcal{A}}$ and $b = \mathcal{B}[\![A(x)]\!]\eta_{\mathcal{B}}$.

THEOREM 2. *(Fundamental Theorem of $\mathcal{S}\Lambda$ Logical Relations) Let $\mathcal{R}$ be a logical relation over $\mathcal{S}\Lambda(\mathcal{C}_{kind}, \mathcal{C}_{type})$ models $\mathcal{A}$ and $\mathcal{B}$ and let $\eta_{\mathcal{A}}$, $\eta_{\mathcal{B}}$ be related environments with respect to type assignment A. Assume that $\mathcal{R}$ preserves the constants of $\mathcal{S}\Lambda(\mathcal{C}_{kind}, \mathcal{C}_{type})$. Then for any term M of $\mathcal{S}\Lambda_A(\mathcal{C}_{kind}, \mathcal{C}_{type})$,*

$$<\mathcal{A}[\![M]\!]\eta_{\mathcal{A}}, \mathcal{B}[\![M]\!]\eta_{\mathcal{B}}> \in R_{a, b},$$

where $a = \mathcal{A}[\![Type_A(M)]\!]\eta_{\mathcal{A}}$ and $b = \mathcal{B}[\![Type_A(M)]\!]\eta_{\mathcal{B}}$.

5. Inference Rules and Lambda Definability

A set of inference rules for deducing membership in logical relations gives some insight into the structure of logical relations. In addition, the rules allow us to build logical relations over certain kinds of models by a "term" construction. The inference rules consist of a set of rules for $\mathcal{T}\Lambda$ logical relations and a set of rules for relations among terms. The system is sound and complete for deducing that pairs of terms are related over pairs of models.

5.1. Rules for $\mathcal{T}\Lambda$ Relations

We first consider rules for deducing membership in $\mathcal{T}\Lambda$ relations. Recall that every variable $v \in \mathcal{V}_{kind}$ and every constructional μ has a fixed kind that does not depend on context. An *atomic $\mathcal{T}\Lambda$ relational assertion* is a formula

$$R_\kappa\ \mu\ \nu,$$

where μ and ν are constructionals of kind κ. Intuitively, $R_\kappa\ \mu\ \nu$ means that "μ and ν denote related elements of kind κ." Generally, we will only be able to say that μ and ν are related after making some assumptions about the free variables of μ and ν. A *$\mathcal{T}\Lambda$ relational assertion* is a formula

$$S \supset R_\kappa\ \mu\ \nu,$$

where S is a set of atomic relational assertions R_κ x y, with x and y variables. We call S a *$\mathcal{T}\Lambda$ relational hypothesis.*

The definitions of satisfaction and validity for relational assertions are relatively straightforward. Let $\mathcal{R}$ be a $\mathcal{T}\Lambda$ relation over type structures $\mathcal{S}$ and $\mathcal{T}$, and let η_s, η_t be environments for $\mathcal{S}$ and $\mathcal{T}$, respectively. Then $\mathcal{R}, \eta_s, \eta_t$ *satisfy* the atomic assertion $R_\kappa\ \mu\ \nu$, written

$$\mathcal{R}, \eta_s, \eta_t \models R_\kappa\ \mu\ \nu,$$

if $<\mathcal{S}[\![\mu]\!]\eta_s, \mathcal{T}[\![\nu]\!]\eta_t> \in R_\kappa$. A relation and pair of environments satisfy a set S of atomic relational assertions if all elements of S are satisfied, and satisfy a non-atomic assertion

$$S \supset R_\kappa\ \mu\ \nu$$

if

$$\mathcal{R}, \eta_s, \eta_t \models S \text{ implies } \mathcal{R}, \eta_s, \eta_t \models R_\kappa\ \mu\ \nu.$$

As usual, a relation $\mathcal{R}$ satisfies an assertion if $\mathcal{R}$ and every pair of environments satisfy the assertion. Two type structures, $\mathcal{S}$ and $\mathcal{T}$ satisfy a relational assertion if every $\mathcal{R}$ over $\mathcal{S}$ and $\mathcal{T}$ satisfy the assertion. An assertion is valid if pair of type structures satisfy the assertion.

We also have semantic implication of relational assertions with respect to theories. If Th_1 and Th_2 are sets of equations between constructionals and $Th_{\mathcal{R}}$ is a set of relational assertions, then

$$Th_1, Th_2, Th_{\mathcal{R}} \models S \supset R_\kappa\ \mu\ \nu$$

if, for every $\mathcal{S} \models Th_1$, $\mathcal{T} \models Th_2$ and every relation $\mathcal{R}$ over $\mathcal{S}$ and $\mathcal{T}$ satisfying $Th_{\mathcal{R}}$,

$$\mathcal{R} \models S \supset R_\kappa\ \mu\ \nu.$$

The axioms and inference rules for deducing relational assertions from theories Th_1, Th_2 and $Th_{\mathcal{R}}$ are as follows.

$$R_{T \Rightarrow T \Rightarrow T} \to \to$$

$$R_{[T \Rightarrow T] \Rightarrow T} \forall\ \forall$$

$$S \cup \{R_\kappa\ u\ v\} \supset R_\kappa\ u\ v$$

$$\frac{S \supset R_{\gamma \Rightarrow \kappa}\ \mu_1\ \mu_2,\ S \supset R_\gamma\ \nu_1\ \nu_2}{S \supset R_\kappa\ \mu_1\nu_1\ \mu_2\nu_2}$$

$$\frac{S \cup \{R_\gamma\ u\ v\} \supset R_\kappa\ \mu_1\ \mu_2}{S \supset R_{\gamma \Rightarrow \kappa}\ \lambda u.\mu_1\ \lambda v.\mu_2}\text{, provided u, v not free in S}$$

$$\frac{S \supset R_\kappa\ \mu_1\ \mu_2,\ \mu_1 = \nu_1,\ \mu_2 = \nu_2}{S \supset R_\kappa\ \nu_1\ \nu_2}$$

The rules above are complete for inferences that do not involve assuming relational assertions as given. However, some additional rules are required for deductive completeness with respect to assumptions. One is a "structural" rule allowing redundant assertions to be added or removed from the hypotheses of an assertion, and the other is a substitution rule. A few preliminary definitions make the rules easier to write down. If S is a relational hypothesis and μ, ν a pair of constructionals, we write

$S|_{\mu,\nu}$ for $\{R_\kappa\ u\ v \in S \mid u \in FV(\mu)$ or $v \in FV(\nu)\}$.

If T is a relational hypothesis

$$B = \{R_{\kappa_1}\ u_1\ v_1, \ldots, R_{\kappa_k}\ u_k\ v_k\}$$

and α is a kind-preserving substitution of constructionals for variables, then we write

$$S \supset \alpha T$$

as an abbreviation for the set of relational assertions

$$S \supset \alpha(R_{\kappa_1}\ u_1\ v_1), \ldots, S \supset \alpha(R_{\kappa_k}\ u_k\ v_k).$$

The free variable and substitution rules are

$$\frac{S \supset R_\kappa\ \mu\ \nu}{T \supset R_\kappa\ \mu\ \nu} \quad S|_{\mu,\nu} \subseteq T|_{\mu,\nu},$$

$$\frac{S \supset \alpha T,\ T \supset R_\kappa\ \mu\ \nu}{S \supset \alpha(R_\kappa\ \mu\ \nu)}$$

We say $S \supset R_\kappa\ \mu\ \nu$ is *provable* from theories Th_1, Th_2 and $Th_{\mathcal{R}}$, written

$$Th_1, Th_2, Th_{\mathcal{R}} \vdash S \supset R_\kappa\ \mu\ \nu,$$

if $S \supset R_\kappa\ \mu\ \nu$ can be derived from these theories using the rules above and the usual inference rules for deducing equations between terms of typed lambda calculus.

LEMMA 1. *($\mathcal{T}\Lambda$ Soundness) If $Th_1, Th_2, Th_{\mathcal{R}} \vdash S \supset R_\kappa\ \mu\ \nu$ then $Th_1, Th_2, Th_{\mathcal{R}} \models S \supset R_\kappa\ \mu\ \nu$.*

LEMMA 2. *($\mathcal{T}\Lambda$ Completeness) If $Th_1, Th_2, Th_{\mathcal{R}} \models S \supset R_\kappa\ \mu\ \nu$ then $Th_1, Th_2, Th_{\mathcal{R}} \vdash S \supset R_\kappa\ \mu\ \nu$.*

5.2. Rules for $\mathcal{S}\Lambda$ Relations

An *atomic $\mathcal{S}\Lambda_A$-relational assertion* is a statement of the form

$$R\ \sigma\ \tau\ M\ N$$

where $Type_A(M)=\sigma$ and $Type_A(N)=\tau$. Intuitively, this assertion means "σ and τ are related types and M and N are related by $R_{\sigma,\tau}$." An *$\mathcal{S}\Lambda$-relational hypothesis* is a finite set of atomic $\mathcal{S}\Lambda$ relational assertions about variables. An *$\mathcal{S}\Lambda$-relational assertion* is a formula

$$S \supset R\ \sigma\ \tau\ M\ N,$$

where S is a pair $\langle S_{kind}, S_{type}\rangle$, with S_{kind} a $\mathcal{T}\Lambda$-relational hypothesis, S_{type} a $\mathcal{S}\Lambda$-relational hypothesis, and such that $S_{kind} \supset R_T\ \sigma\ \tau$ for every $R\ \sigma\ \tau\ x\ y$ in S_{type}. The definitions of satisfaction and validity for $\mathcal{S}\Lambda$-relational assertions are analogous to those for $\mathcal{T}\Lambda$-relational assertions. The axioms and rules of inference follow.

$$\langle S_{kind}, S_{type} \cup \{R\ \sigma\ \tau\ x\ y\}\rangle \supset R\ \sigma\ \tau\ x\ y, \text{ provided } A(x)=\sigma \text{ and } A(y)=\tau.$$

$$\frac{S \supset R\ \sigma_1{\to}\tau_1\ \sigma_2{\to}\tau_2\ M_1\ M_2,\ S \supset R\ \sigma_1\ \sigma_2\ N_1\ N_2}{S \supset R\ \tau_1\ \tau_2\ M_1N_1\ M_2N_2}$$

$$\frac{\langle S_{kind}, S_{type} \cup \{R\ \sigma_1\ \sigma_2\ x\ y\}\rangle \supset R\ \tau_1\ \tau_2\ M_1\ M_2}{\langle S_{kind}, S_{type}\rangle \supset R\ \sigma_1{\to}\tau_1\ \sigma_2{\to}\tau_2\ \lambda x{\in}\sigma_1.M_1\ \lambda y{\in}\sigma_2.M_2}\ \text{, provided x, y not free in } S_{type}$$

$$\frac{\langle S_{kind}, S_{type}\rangle \supset R\ \forall s.\sigma_1\ \forall t.\sigma_2\ M_1\ M_2,\ S_{kind} \supset R_T\ \sigma\ \tau}{\langle S_{kind}, S_{type}\rangle \supset R\ [\sigma/s]\sigma_1\ [\tau/t]\sigma_2\ M_1\sigma\ M_2\tau}$$

$$\frac{\langle S_{kind} \cup \{R_T\ s\ t\}, S_{type}\rangle \supset R_\sigma\ M_1\ M_2}{\langle S_{kind}, S_{type}\rangle \supset R\ \forall s.\sigma\ \forall t.\tau\ \lambda s.M_1\ \lambda t.M_2}$$

$$\frac{S \supset R\ \sigma\ \tau\ M_1\ M_2,\ M_1{=}N_1,\ M_2{=}N_2}{S \supset R\ \sigma\ \tau\ N_1\ N_2}$$

As with $\mathcal{T}\Lambda$ relations, we need "structural" and substitution rules. If S is a $\mathcal{S}\Lambda$ relational hypothesis and M, N a pair of terms, we write

$$S|_{M,N} \text{ for } \{R\ \sigma\ \tau\ x\ y \in S \mid x \in FV(M) \text{ or } y \in FV(N)\}.$$

We write $<S_{kind}, S_{type}>|_{M,N}$ for $<S_{kind}, S_{type}|_{M,N}>$. If T is a relational hypothesis

$$T = \{R\ \sigma_1\ \tau_1\ x_1\ y_1, \ldots, R\ \sigma_k\ \tau_k\ x_k\ y_k\}$$

and α is a substitution of constructionals for variables of the appropriate kinds and terms for ordinary variables of the appropriate types, we write

$$S \supset \alpha T$$

as an abbreviation for the set of relational assertions

$$S \supset \alpha(R\ \sigma_1\ \tau_1\ x_1\ y_1), \ldots, S \supset \alpha(R\ \sigma_k\ \tau_k\ x_k\ y_k).$$

The free variable and substitution rules are

$$\frac{S \supset R\ \sigma\ \tau\ M\ N}{T \supset R\ \sigma\ \tau\ M\ N} \quad S|_{M,N} \subseteq T|_{M,N},$$

$$\frac{S \supset \alpha T,\ T \supset R\ \sigma\ \tau\ M\ N}{S \supset \alpha(R\ \sigma\ \tau\ M\ N)}$$

An $\mathcal{S}\Lambda_A$-theory is a set of equations M=N between $\mathcal{S}\Lambda_A$ terms such that $Type_A(M)=Type_A(N)$. Due to some syntactic difficulties, we do not allow $\mathcal{S}\Lambda$-theories to contain equations between constructionals[2]. We say $S \supset R\ \sigma\ \tau$ M N is *provable* from $\mathcal{S}\Lambda$ theories Th_1 and Th_2, and a set of $\mathcal{S}\Lambda_A$-relational assertions $Th_{\mathcal{R}}$, written

$$Th_1, Th_2, Th_{\mathcal{R}} \vdash S \supset R\ \sigma\ \tau\ M\ N,$$

if $S \supset R\ \sigma\ \tau$ M N can be derived from these theories using the rules above and the inference rules for deducing equations between $\mathcal{S}\Lambda$-terms presented in [Bruce, Meyer and Mitchell 85, Mitchell 84c].

LEMMA 3. *($\mathcal{S}\Lambda$ Soundness) If $Th_1, Th_2, Th_{\mathcal{R}} \vdash S \supset R\ \sigma\ \tau\ M\ N$ then $Th_1, Th_2, Th_{\mathcal{R}} \models S \supset R\ \sigma\ \tau\ M\ N$.*

THEOREM 3. *($\mathcal{S}\Lambda$ Completeness) If $Th_1, Th_2, Th_{\mathcal{R}} \models S \supset R\ \sigma\ \tau\ M\ N$ then $Th_1, Th_2, Th_{\mathcal{R}} \vdash S \supset R\ \sigma\ \tau\ M\ N$.*
The completeness theorem is proved by constructing a relation $\mathcal{R}$ over models $\mathcal{A}$ and $\mathcal{B}$ for theories Th_1 and Th_2.

We can characterize the $\mathcal{S}\Lambda$ definable elements of a model $\mathcal{A}$ using unary logical relations over models with indeterminates added. A model $\mathcal{A}$ *has indeterminates* if $\mathcal{A}$ is isomorphic to the term model of some $\mathcal{S}\Lambda$ theory *Th*. For any model $\mathcal{A}$, $\mathcal{S}\Lambda(\mathcal{A})$ is the language with a constant symbol for each element of $\mathcal{A}$, i.e. each $a \in T^{\mathcal{A}}$, $f \in [T \to T]^{\mathcal{A}}$, ..., $d \in D^{\mathcal{A}}_a$. Given any model $\mathcal{A}$, we let $\mathcal{A}^*$ be the $\mathcal{S}\Lambda(\mathcal{A})$ term model for the theory $Th(\mathcal{A})$ consisting of all closed $\mathcal{S}\Lambda(\mathcal{A})$ equations (between terms of the same type) satisfied by $\mathcal{A}$. We can embed $\mathcal{A}$ into $\mathcal{A}^*$ by mapping each element of $\mathcal{A}$ to the equivalence class of the corresponding constant.

If $\mathcal{A}$ is a $\mathcal{S}\Lambda$ model, then $\mathcal{S}\Lambda_A(\mathcal{T}^{\mathcal{A}}, \mathcal{C}_{type})$ is the language with a constant for each element of $\mathcal{T}^{\mathcal{A}}$ and typed constants from $\mathcal{C}_{type}$. We omit $\mathcal{C}_{type}$ if this set is empty, writing $\mathcal{S}\Lambda_A(\mathcal{T}^{\mathcal{A}})$ for the language with constants for elements of $\mathcal{T}^{\mathcal{A}}$.

THEOREM 4. *($\mathcal{S}\Lambda$-Definability) Let $\mathcal{A}$ be a $\mathcal{S}\Lambda$-model and $d \in D^{\mathcal{A}}_a$. Then $d \in R_a$ for every unary logical relation over $\mathcal{A}^*$ satisfying $R_T a$ all $a \in T^{\mathcal{A}}$ iff there is some closed $\mathcal{S}\Lambda_A(\mathcal{T}^{\mathcal{A}})$ term M with $\mathcal{A}[\![M]\!]=d$.*

The $\mathcal{S}\Lambda$-Definability Theorem is a generalization of part (2) of the Characterization Theorem of [Statman 82]. An argument in [Statman 82] shows that the $\mathcal{T}\Lambda$ analog of this theorem fails if $\mathcal{A}^*$ is replaced by $\mathcal{A}$. The $\mathcal{S}\Lambda$-Definability Theorem is proved by observing that $Th_{\mathcal{R}} \models R\sigma d$ holds over $\mathcal{A}^*$ iff $Th(\mathcal{A}), Th_{\mathcal{R}} \vdash R\sigma d$. This allows us to use induction on the proof of $R\sigma d$.

2. The problem with constructional equations is that the set of well-formed terms depends on the set of equations. This is discussed briefly in [Mitchell 84c].

6. Representation Independence and Observational Equivalence

The Fundamental Theorem of Second-Order Logical Relations describes a representation independence property of the lambda calculus. In this section, we examine another notion of representation independence based on the observable behavior of programs. We characterize observational equivalence using logical relations and compare observational equivalence with the properties demonstrated by the Fundamental Theorem.

In general, programs differ from arbitrary expressions of a programming language in that programs do not have free variables and programs cannot produce values of arbitrary types. Programs must be closed expressions and must describe integer, string, boolean, or other simple output values. Thus we only observe the behavior of functions and polymorphic expressions by inserting them into closed expressions of some particularly simple types. This allows a degree of flexibility in the representation of functions and polymorphic expressions. Since a programmer cannot ask to have the value of a function printed out, an interpreter or compiler may use any representation for functions, as long as the functions have the correct observable behavior.

We will ignore the issue of truly correct behavior and focus on the the *observational equivalence* relation on interpretations of expressions. Informally, two models $\mathcal{A}$ and $\mathcal{B}$ for $\mathcal{S}\Lambda(\mathcal{C}_{kind}, \mathcal{C}_{type})$ are observationally equivalent if any program has the same meaning in $\mathcal{A}$ and $\mathcal{B}$. This requires that for all possible program types, $\mathcal{A}$ and $\mathcal{B}$ use the same interpretation. The main result of this section is a characterization of $\mathcal{S}\Lambda$ observational equivalence using logical relations.

We separate programs from other closed terms by choosing some set of "program types," the types that complete programs in the language may have. Let $\mathcal{A}$ and $\mathcal{B}$ be models for $\mathcal{S}\Lambda(\mathcal{C}_{kind}, \mathcal{C}_{type})$. Suppose that for closed type expressions $\sigma_1, \ldots, \sigma_n$ we have

$$D^{\mathcal{A}}_{\sigma_i} = D^{\mathcal{B}}_{\sigma_i}.$$

Then $\mathcal{A}$ and $\mathcal{B}$ are *observationally equivalent with respect to* $\sigma_1, \ldots, \sigma_n$ if, for all closed M of type σ_i, we have

$$\mathcal{A}[\![M]\!] = \mathcal{B}[\![M]\!].$$

We have the following characterization of observational equivalence.

THEOREM 5. *(Observational Equivalence) Let $\mathcal{A}$ and $\mathcal{B}$ be models for $\mathcal{S}\Lambda(\mathcal{C}_{kind}, \mathcal{C}_{type})$ and suppose that for closed type expressions $\sigma_1, \ldots, \sigma_n$ we have*

$$D^{\mathcal{A}}_{\sigma_i} = D^{\mathcal{B}}_{\sigma_i}.$$

Then $\mathcal{A}$ and $\mathcal{B}$ are observationally equivalent with respect to $\sigma_1, \ldots, \sigma_n$ iff there exist a logical relation $\mathcal{R}$ on $\mathcal{A}^*$ and $\mathcal{B}^*$ preserving all constants and such that each relation

$$H_i = R_{c_i^{\mathcal{A}}, c_i^{\mathcal{B}}} \cap D^{\mathcal{A}}_{\sigma_i} \times D^{\mathcal{B}}_{\sigma_i}$$

is the identity relation on $D^{\mathcal{A}}_{\sigma_i} \times D^{\mathcal{B}}_{\sigma_i}$.

In one direction, this theorem follows directly from the Fundamental Theorem of $\mathcal{S}\Lambda$-Logical Relations. The converse is proved using a construction based on the inference system described in Section 5.

7. Conclusion and Open Problems

Many properties of logical relations for ordinary typed lambda calculus $\mathcal{T}\Lambda$ generalize to second-order ($\mathcal{S}\Lambda$) logical relations without unexpected complication. In particular, logical relations may be used to characterize the definable elements of models and to express representation independence properties. A number of other facts about $\mathcal{T}\Lambda$ relations, described in [Statman 82], remain to be investigated.

One major difference between $\mathcal{T}\Lambda$ logical relations and $\mathcal{S}\Lambda$ logical relations is that $\mathcal{T}\Lambda$ logical relations are easily constructed by induction on types. In contrast, it seems difficult to prove the existence of $\mathcal{S}\Lambda$ logical relations in general. While the inference rules presented here apply to models with indeterminates, this is a very special class of models. An important open problem is to develop additional methods for constructing $\mathcal{S}\Lambda$ logical relations. We conjecture that there exist $\mathcal{S}\Lambda$ models without any nontrivial unary logical relations.

The representation independence properties we have discussed apply to the representation of functional and polymorphic types. A straightforward extension of $\mathcal{S}\Lambda$, described in [Mitchell and Plotkin 85], includes abstract data type declarations as well. In this extended language, a collection of types and operations may be packaged together. Since the type checking rules restrict the way that programs may make use of such packages, there is some degree of representation independence associated with abstract data types. We expect $\mathcal{S}\Lambda$ logical relations to provide a useful characterization of representation independence with abstract data type declarations.

It is interesting to note that the inference rules of Section 5 are remarkably similar to the type inference rules considered in, e.g., [Leivant 83a, MacQueen, Plotkin and Sethi 84, MacQueen and Sethi 82, McCracken 84, Mitchell 84b]. This suggests that there may be some interesting semantic connections between second-order lambda calculus and type inference systems based on this calculus, although this connection is not clear at present.

References

[Barendregt 81] Barendregt, H.P, *The Lambda Calculus: Its Syntax and Semantics*. North Holland 1981.

[Bruce and Meyer 84] Bruce, K. and Meyer, A., A Completeness Theorem for Second-Order Polymorphic Lambda Calculus. In *Proc. Int. Symp. on Semantics of Data Types, Sophia-Antipolis (France)* , 1984, pages 131-144..

[Bruce, Meyer and Mitchell 85] Bruce, K.B., Meyer, A.R. and Mitchell, J.C., The semantics of second-order lambda calculus. to appear

[Donahue 79] Donahue, J., On the semantics of data type. *SIAM J. Computing* 8 1979. pages 546-560

[Fortune, et. al. 83] Fortune, S., Leivant, D. and O'Donnel, M., The Expressiveness of Simple and Second Order Type Structures. *JACM* 30, 1 1983. pages 151-185

[Friedman 75] Friedman, H., Equality Between Functionals. In R. Parikh (ed.), *Logic Colloquium*, pages 22-37. Springer-Verlag 1975.

[Girard 71] Girard, J.-Y., Une extension de l'interpretation de Gödel à l'analyse, et son application à l'élimination des coupures dans l'analyse et la théorie des types. In Fenstad, J.E. (ed.), 2nd *Scandinavian Logic Symp.*, pages 63-92. North-Holland 1971.

[Haynes 84] Haynes, C.T., A Theory of Data Type Representation Independence. In *Int. Symp. on Semantics of Data Types* , Springer-Verlag , 1984, pages 157-176.

[Henkin 50] Henkin, L., Completeness in the Theory of Types. *Journal of Symbolic Logic* 15, 2 June 1950. pages 81-91

[Leivant 83a] Leivant, D., Polymorphic Type Inference. In *Proc. 10-th ACM Symp. on Principles of Programming Languages* , 1983, pages 88-98.

[MacQueen, Plotkin and Sethi 84] MacQueen, D., Plotkin, G and Sethi, R., An Ideal Model for Polymorphic Types. In *Proc. 11-th ACM Symp. on Principles of Prog. Lang* , January, 1984, pages 165-174.

[MacQueen and Sethi 82] MacQueen, D. and Sethi, R., A Semantic Model of Types for Applicative Languages. In *ACM Symp. on Lisp and Functional Programming* , 1982, pages 243-252..

[McCracken 79] McCracken, N., *An Investigation of a Programming Language with a Polymorphic Type Structure*. Syracuse Univ. 1979.

[McCracken 84] McCracken, N., The Typechecking of Programs with Implicit Type Structure. In *Proc. Int'l Symp. on Semantics of Data Types* , June, 1984, pages 301-316.

[Mitchell 84b] Mitchell, J.C., Type Inference and Type Containment. In *Proc. Int'l Symp. on Semantics of Data Types* , June, 1984, pages 257-278.

[Mitchell 84c] Mitchell, J.C., Semantic models for second-order lambda calculus. In *Proc. 25-th IEEE Symp. on Foundations of Computer Science* , 1984, pages 289-299.

[Mitchell and Plotkin 85] Mitchell, J.C. and Plotkin, G.D., Abstract types have existential types. In *Proc. 12-th ACM Symp. on Principles of Programming Languages* , January, 1985. pp. 37-51.

[Mulmuley 84] Mulmuley, K., A semantic characterization of full abstraction for typed lambda calculus. In *Proc. 25-th IEEE Symp. on Foundations of Computer Science* , 1984, pages 279-288.

[Plotkin 80] Plotkin, G.D., Lambda definability in the full type hierarchy. In *To H.B. Curry: Essays on Combinatory Logic, Lambda Calculus and Formalism*, pages 363-373. Academic Press 1980.

[Reynolds 74] Reynolds, J.C., Towards a Theory of Type Structure. In *Paris Colloq. on Programming* , Springer-Verlag , 1974, pages 408-425.

[Reynolds 83] Reynolds, J.C., Types, Abstraction, and Parametric Polymorphism. In *IFIP Congress* , 1983.

[Reynolds 84] Reynolds, J.C., Polymorphism is not Set-Theoretic. In *Int. Symp. on Semantics of Data Types* , Springer-Verlag , 1984, pages 145-156.

[Statman 82] Statman, R., Logical relations and the typed lambda calculus. (Manuscript.) To appear in Information and Control.

[Tait 67] Tait, W.W., Intensional interpretation of functionals of finite type. *J. Symbolic Logic* 32 1967. pages 198-212

Behavior: a Temporal Approach to Process Modeling

Van Nguyen, Alan Demers, and David Gries

Deptartment of Computer Science, Cornell University, Ithaca, New York 14853

Susan Owicki

Computer Systems Laboratory, Stanford University, Stanford, California 94305

Abstract

This paper describes an approach to modeling processes and networks of processes that communicate exclusively through message passing. A process is defined by its set of possible behaviors, where each behavior is an abstraction of some infinite execution sequence of the process. The resulting model of processes is simple and modular and facilitates information hiding. It can describe either synchronous or asynchronous networks. It supports recursively-defined networks and can characterize liveness properties such as progress of inputs and outputs, termination and deadlock. A sound and complete temporal proof system for processes is presented. It is compositional – a specification of a network is formed naturally from specifications of its component processes. A nontrivial example, comprising a specification and correctness proof for a recursive network, is given to demonstrate the usefulness of our techniques.

1. Introduction

A number of models have been proposed for processes [BA, P, Ho83, Mi, Br, HB]. None of these models handles both synchronous and asynchronous communication in a single framework. In addition, their modeling of liveness properties is generally unsatisfactory. The models that seem most promising, due to their simplicity and ability to hide information, are those based on traces. A *trace* is a finite sequence of communication events, which can be thought of as an abstraction of a process state in which all irrelevant internal details are hidden. Roughly, a trace represents the state reached by the process after some computation in which the events of the trace occur.

Liveness properties, such as progress and termination, are difficult to specify in trace-based models. Liveness properties can deal with complete, possibly infinite execution sequences of a process, while traces specify only finite prefixes of execution sequences. For example, a property like "eventually a message is sent on port *k*" may fail to hold of a particular infinite computation even though every finite prefix (hence every trace) of the computation is also a prefix of some other computation for which the property does hold. It is difficult to see how a model based on finite traces could be used to specify such a property.

This problem is related to the question of *continuity* of processes. A process, defined as a set of traces, is *continuous* if the least upper bound (lub) of any ascending chain of traces in the set also belongs to the set. Using the partial order "is a prefix of" on traces, nondeterministic processes are not continuous in general – the lub of an infinite ascending chain of traces may not represent a possible execution sequence, even though each trace in the chain does. We know of no simple model of processes with an appropriately defined partial ordering on traces that preserves continuity. Continuity is a desirable property, since it makes the analysis of the semantics more

This research supported by NSF under grants DCR-83-202-74 and DCR-83-123-19, and by NASA under contract NAGW419.

elegant. However, since there seems to be no natural way to achieve continuity, and we are able do without it, we see no reason to insist on having it.

In [NGO], to allow better specification of liveness properties, we introduce the notion of *behavior*. A behavior is an abstraction of an entire execution sequence in which irrelevant internal details are hidden. Here, we extend the notion of behavior to model termination, deadlock and recursive networks using either synchronous or asynchronous communication. The resulting model is simple and modular and facilitates information hiding.

Our model is well-suited for temporal reasoning about processes. Using it, we can define a temporal proof system that is *compositional*: a specification of a process is formed naturally from specifications of its component processes. Hoare-like proof systems for concurrent processes are compositional, but most temporal proof systems are not. We believe that this is a problem with the underlying models that have been chosen, and not with temporal logic itself. The models underlying most proof systems are *state-transition* models, in which a program is specified by a (binary) transition relation on the set of states. Such models are suitable for a Hoare-like proof system because the pre- and postconditions of the Hoare-like system correspond naturally to the initial and final states of the relation. For temporal proof systems, however, modeling processes by behaviors seems more appropriate. Our temporal proof system is compositional due to the modularity and information-hiding properties of the underlying model. It is a sound and relatively complete extension of the proof system in [NGO].

The remainder of the paper is organized as follows. Section 2 reviews the basic model and proof system from [NGO]. In each of the next two sections we add a new property or program construct to the model and present a sound and relatively complete temporal proof system for it: Section 3 treats termination and deadlock, and Section 4 treats recursively-defined networks. Section 5 is a nontrivial example, in which we apply our techniques to the specification and correctness proof of a recursive network. The final section is a conclusion and discussion of related work.

Because of space limitations, we consider in this paper only synchronous networks of processes. However, our model applies equally well to asynchronous systems. Our techniques can also be applied to sequential program constructs. By combining the models for concurrent and sequential processes, we can define a behavior model for a version of Hoare's CSP. Details can be found in [Ng].

2. The basic model and proof system

Our basic process model is that of [NGO]. The development here is more formal, however, to enable us to treat recursive and nonrecursive networks in a uniform way.

2.1. Processes and networks

Informally, a process has associated with it a finite number of distinctly-named input and output ports, as shown in Figure 1. Processes can be combined into networks, as shown in Figure 2, by linking some input ports of some processes to some output ports of *other* processes in a one-to-one manner. A network can itself be viewed as a process whose input and output ports are the unlinked ports of its component processes. Formally, a syntax to describe processes and networks is given by the following:

Definition 2.1.1: Assume for each $n, m \geq 0$ we are given a fixed set of zero or more *primitive process names* of *arity* (m, n). Assume also an infinite set of distinct *port names* $i_1, i_2, \ldots j_1, j_2, \ldots$ etc. A *primitive process* description is

$$P\ (i_1, \ldots, i_m\ ; j_1, \ldots, j_n)$$

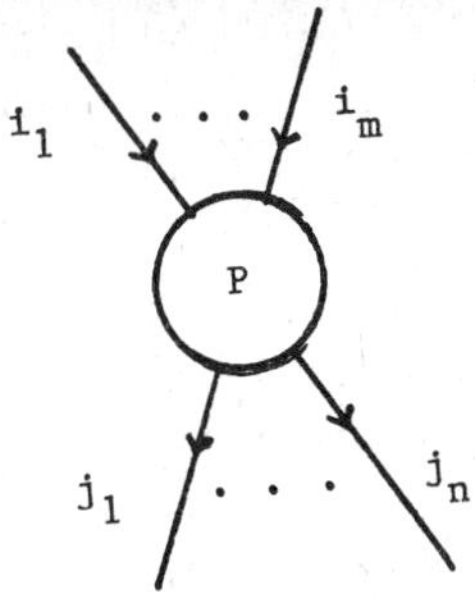

Figure 1 A (primitive) process

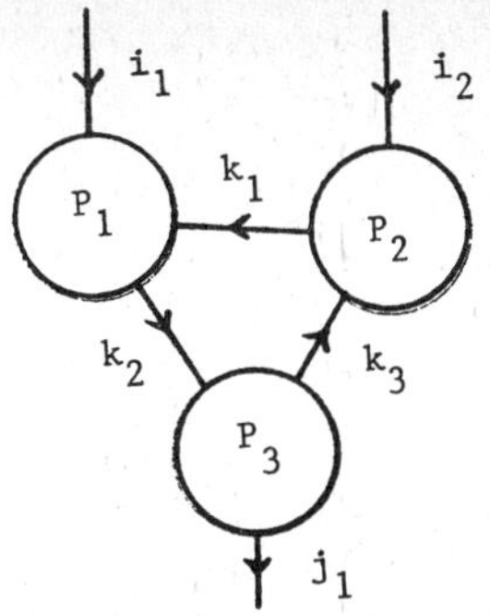

Figure 2 A network

where

- P is a primitive process name of arity (m, n); and
- $i_1, \ldots, i_m, j_1, \ldots, j_n$ are distinct port names.

Ports $i_1, \ldots, i_m$ are the *input ports* of the process; ports $j_1, \ldots, j_n$ are its *output ports*. □

The order of presentation of port names is significant. For example, processes $P(a, b; c, d)$ and $P(b, a; d, c)$ are in general different. However, we shall omit port names whenever they are clear from context.

Definition 2.1.2: A *network* description is either

- a primitive process description, or
- a *parallel composition*, of the form $\| (N_1, \ldots, N_k)$, where the *components*, $N_1, \ldots, N_k$, are network descriptions.

For primitive processes, input and output ports are defined above. For composite network $N = \| (N_1, \ldots, N_k)$, ports are defined inductively: k is an *input* (*output*) *port* of N iff k is an input (output) port of some component N_i. We also impose the following *unique port naming* requirement:

- The sets of input (output) port names of distinct components of N must be disjoint.

This requirement allows a name to occur (once) as both an input and output port; such a port is said to be *linked* in N. An *external* port of N is one that is not linked. □

Note that a primitive process is a (degenerate) network. We view a process or network as an active computing agent that receives and sends messages on its input and output ports. The semantics of a network is the set of all possible input/output behaviors that it can exhibit. This notion is developed formally in the next few definitions.

Definition 2.1.3: An *event* on port k is a pair (x, k) where x is a datum; (x, k) is said to *occur on* k. □

Definition 2.1.4: A *trace* on set S of ports is a finite sequence of events on ports in S. □

Definition 2.1.5: An *observation* on set I of input ports and set J of output ports is a triple (t, In, Out), where t is a trace on $I \cup J$, In is a function from I to $\{T, F\}$ and Out is a function from J to $\{T, F\}$. In (Out) is called an *input (output) communication function*. □

Definition 2.1.6: A *communication behavior* on I and J is an infinite sequence

$$\sigma = (t_1, In_1, Out_1), (t_2, In_2, Out_2), (t_3, In_3, Out_3), \ldots$$

of observations on I and J, such that

- t_1 is empty, and
- for all n, t_{n+1} equals t_n or is an extension of it, i.e. is t_n followed by some event (e, k). In the latter case, if $k \in I$ then $In_n(k) = T$, and if $k \in J$ then $Out_n(k) = T$. □

Intuitively, a communication behavior is the sequence of observations produced by some execution of a process or network as time progresses. The trace in an observation records the events that have happened at the ports up to some time; the communication functions indicate which ports are ready to communicate at that time.

A network is characterized by its set of communication behaviors. For technical reasons, we require the behaviors of a network to be closed under finite repetition, defined as follows:

Definition 2.1.7: A set B of behaviors is *closed under finite repetition* iff for any two behaviors σ and σ' the following condition holds: if σ' can be obtained from σ by repeating a (possibly infinite) number of observations, each finitely many times, then $\sigma \in B$ iff $\sigma' \in B$. Any set of behaviors has a *closure* (i.e. smallest superset closed) under finite repetition. □

We require the behaviors of a network to be closed under finite repetition because this allows our system to have the important non-interference property (see Lemma 2.2.4.1) and facilitates information hiding. Invariance under repetition of states is also discussed by Lamport in [L], where it is called "stuttering."

To give a formal semantics for networks, we assume the behaviors of primitive processes are given and define the behaviors of composite networks inductively from the behaviors of their components. Intuitively, a behavior of a network is a combination of behaviors of its components in which an event on an external port represents a message being passed between the network and its environment, while an event on a linked port represents a message being passed internally between two components. To formalize this, we define a restriction of a network behavior to one of its components as follows:

Definition 2.1.8: The *restriction* of trace t to a set S of ports is that subsequence of t containing exactly those events occurring on ports in S. The restriction of observation (t, In, Out) to input ports I and output ports J is observation $(t', In', Out',)$ where t' is the restriction of t to $I \cup J$, In' is the function obtained by restricting the domain of In to I, and Out' is the function obtained by restricting the domain of Out to J. The restriction of a communication behavior σ to I and J, denoted $\sigma|_{I,J}$, is defined similarly. We let $\sigma|_N$ denote the restriction of behavior σ to the input and output ports of network N. □

We can now give a formal semantics for networks:

Definition 2.1.9: For each primitive process $P(i_1, \ldots, i_m ; j_1, \ldots, j_n)$ let [[P]] be a given set of behaviors on the input and output ports of P. We require that [[P]] be closed under finite repetition, as defined above, and that [[P]] respect renaming of ports:

$$[[P(h_1, \ldots, h_m ; k_1, \ldots, k_n)]] = [[P(i_1, \ldots, i_m ; j_1, \ldots, j_n)]]\ [h_1, \ldots, k_n / i_1, \ldots, j_n]$$

where the notation $B[\ldots p_r \ldots / \ldots q_r \ldots]$ represents the result of simultaneous substitution of port names p_r for q_r in every observation of set B, provided no unlinked port becomes linked as a result of the substitution. Finally, we require that an enabled input port must be willing to accept any input value. That is, if $[[P]]$ contains behavior

$$\sigma = (t_1, In_1, Out_1), \ldots, (t_n, In_n, Out_n), \ldots$$

and $In_n(i) = T$ for some port i, then for any data value x $[[P]]$ must contain a behavior

$$\sigma' = (t_1, In_1, Out_1), \ldots, (t_n, In_n, Out_n), (t'_{n+1}, In'_{n+1}, Out'_{n+1}), (t'_{n+2}, In'_{n+2}, Out'_{n+2}), \ldots$$

such that $t'_{n+1} = t_n \cdot (x, i)$.

For composite networks $N = \| (N_1, ..., N_k)$, the meaning function [[.]] is defined inductively by

$$\sigma \in [[\, \|(N_1, ..., N_k)]] \quad \textit{iff} \quad \sigma|_{N_i} \in [[N_i]],\ 1 \le i \le k$$

where σ ranges over communication behaviors on the ports of N. □

A network can also be viewed as a process by "hiding" the internal structure represented by its linked ports. The input and output ports of such a process are just the external (i.e. unlinked) ports of the underlying network; its communication behaviors are the external communication behaviors of the network, defined as follows:

Definition 2.1.10: An *external communication behavior* of network N is any behavior of the form $\sigma|_K$, where $\sigma \in [[N]]$ and K is the set of external ports of N. □

In later sections we shall need the notion of a port being disabled by a process or network.

Definition 2.1.11: Let N be a network, and let $s = (t, In, Out)$ be an observation on some set of ports including all the ports of N. Port k is said to be *disabled* by N if k is an input (output) port of N and $In(k)$ ($Out(k)$) is F. Otherwise, k is said to be *enabled*. □

To prove liveness properties, we need to associate with each network a predicate on behaviors (e.g. justice, fairness), which we call a *liveness assumption*. If Ψ is the liveness assumption then a process is specified by its *Ψ-communication behaviors*, i.e. communication behaviors that satisfy Ψ. To ensure that the set of Ψ-communication behaviors of a process is closed under finite repetition, we require that Ψ itself be invariant under finite repetition, i.e. σ satisfies Ψ iff any τ obtained from σ by finite repetition of observations satisfies Ψ. The results of this paper all hold if communication behaviors are everywhere restricted to Ψ-communication behaviors.

2.2. The basic temporal proof system

We describe the basic temporal proof system in [NGO]. By the modularity and information-hiding facility of the model, the proof system is compositional. It is also sound and relatively complete.

2.2.1. Temporal logic and behaviors

We assume familiarity with temporal logic −see e.g. [MP81]− and make only the following comments. As usual, the temporal operators are: ○ (next), □ (always), ◇ (eventually), $\mathcal{U}$ (until), $\mathcal{N}$ (unless), etc. Following [MP81], we assume that the set of basic symbols in the language (individual constants and variables, proposition, predicate and function symbols) is partitioned into two subsets: global symbols and local symbols. The *global* symbols have a uniform interpretation and maintain their values or meanings from one state to another. Quantification is allowed over global variables only. The *local* symbols may assume different values in different states of the sequence. Unlike [MP81], we allow local function and predicate symbols in the assertion language.

A *model* (I, α, σ) for our language consists of a (global) interpretation I, a (global) assignment α and a sequence of states σ. The interpretation I specifies a nonempty domain D and assigns concrete elements, functions and predicates to the global individual constants, function and predicate symbols. The assignment α assigns a value to each global free variable. The sequence $\sigma = s_1, s_2, ...$ is an infinite sequence of states. Each state is an assignment of values to the local free individual variables, functions and predicate symbols. The truth value of a temporal formula or term with respect to a model is defined as in [MP81, NGO]. Intuitively,

(1) ○ w is true iff w is true in the next state of the sequence.

(2) □ w is true iff w is always true throughout the sequence.

(3) $\diamond w$ is true iff w is eventually true in the sequence.

(4) $w_1 \,\mathcal{U}\, w_2$ is true iff w_1 holds true continuously until w_2 becomes true.

(5) $w_1 \,\mathcal{N}\, w_2 = \Box w_1 \vee (w_1 \,\mathcal{U}\, w_2)$

Whenever w is true in a model, we say that the model *satisfies* w. For a set of axioms and theorems of temporal logic, see [MP81, MP83].

An observation s can be treated as a state by assigning to each (local) port variable k the sequence of values of events on k, to the local function symbols *In* and *Out* the corresponding communication functions of s and to the local predicate symbol $\ll$ the total ordering on the trace of s. Thus temporal formulas can be interpreted over behaviors. We write $\sigma \models R$ to mean behavior σ satisfies temporal assertion R. A complete description of the interpretation of temporal formulas over behaviors can be found in [NGO] or [Ng].

2.2.2. Network specifications

In the basic proof system and the variants of it described in this paper, a *specification* of a network N has the form

$<N>\ R$

where R is a temporal assertion in which

- the only local free variables are names of N's ports,
- the only local function symbols are *In* and *Out*,
- the only local predicate symbol is $\ll$ ($\ll$ is needed to axiomatize behaviors completely); and
- there is no occurrence of $In(k)$ ($Out(k)$) if k is an external output (input) port of N.

The interpretation of specification $<N>\ R$ is:

Every behavior of N satisfies R.

We prove in [NGO] that if the only free variables of R are the names of N's external ports the above interpretation is equivalent to:

Every external behavior of N satisfies R.

In this case $<N>\ R$ is called an *external* specification.

Finally, under liveness assumption Ψ, the interpretation becomes:

Every Ψ-behavior of P satisfies R.

Example: Suppose process $BUFF1$ iteratively reads input on port i and reproduces it on port j. A specification of $BUFF1$ is

$< BUFF1 >\ \ \Box (j \sqsubseteq i \wedge In(i) = \neg\, Out(j) = (|j| = |i|))$

2.2.3. Basic proof rules

There are three proof rules in the basic system:

Renaming rule:

$$\frac{<N>\ R}{< N[h_1 \ldots h_m / k_1 \ldots k_m] >\ R[h_1 \ldots h_m / k_1 \ldots k_m]}$$

where the notation $[h_1 \ldots h_m / k_1 \ldots k_m]$ indicates simultaneous substitution of port names, with the restriction that no unlinked port become linked as a result of the substitution.

Network formation rule:

$$\frac{<N_i> \ R_i, \ i = 1, \ldots, m}{<||(\ldots, N_i, \ldots)> \ \wedge_i R_i}$$

Note that the N_i must satisfy the unique port name requirement of Definition 2.1.9 in order for their parallel composition to be sensible.

Consequence rule:

$$\frac{<N> \ R, \ R \Rightarrow S}{<N> \ S}$$

where $R \Rightarrow S$ can be proved from the axioms and inference rules for temporal logic, the axioms and inference rules for the data domain and the axioms that characterize behaviors.

2.2.4. Soundness and completeness

Soundness and completeness are defined as follows.

Let L be a temporal assertion language whose only local function symbols are In, Out and whose only local predicate symbol is $\ll$. Let I be an interpretation whose domain D contains a set of elements (e.g. integers) and a set of sequences of these elements (e.g. sequences of integers). Global variables range over elements or sequences; local variables over sequences. Let $\{P_i\}$ be a set of *primitive* processes, from which networks of processes are to be formed.

Definition 2.2.4.1: A specification $<P> \ R$ is *precise* if: every behavior on P's port names is a behavior of P iff it satisfies R. □

Definition 2.2.4.2: With L, I, $\{P_i\}$ as above, define L to be *expressive relative to I* and $\{P_i\}$ if for every primitive process P_i there exists an assertion R_i such that $<P_i> \ R_i$ is a precise specification. We denote this by $I \in E(L, \{P_i\})$. □

Definition 2.2.4.3: A temporal proof system is *sound* if, for every $I \in E(L, \{P_i\})$, every specification $<P> \ R$ that is provable (with all the $<P_i> \ R_i$ as axioms, and the renaming rule, the network formation rule and the consequence rule as inference rules, together with a complete proof system for temporal logic and behaviors) is true (i.e. every behavior of P satisfies R under I). The proof system is *relatively complete* if, for every $I \in E(L, \{P_i\})$, every specification that is true is provable. □

Our definitions and results remain valid if "behavior" is everywhere replaced by "Ψ-behavior". This definition of soundness and relative completeness follows closely that for sequential programs (as in [A]).

The proof system of the previous section is shown to be sound and relatively complete in [NGO]. Because a process is specified by a single assertion, not by a pair of pre- and postconditions as in Hoare-logic, it is quite easy to prove completeness. In general, it is sufficient to prove a "non-interference" property and that the proof rules −except the consequence rule− preserve preciseness of specifications. The necessary non-interference property is given by the following:

Lemma 2.2.4.1: Let I and J be sets of port names, and let R be an assertion in which

- the only free variables are local (port) variables in $I \cup J$,
- there is no occurrence of $In(j)$ for $j \in J$, and
- there is no occurrence of $Out(i)$ for $i \in I$.

Then for any behaviors σ and τ,

$$\sigma\lfloor_{I,J} = \tau\lfloor_{I,J} \quad \text{implies} \quad \sigma \models R \text{ iff } \tau \models R$$

that is, satisfaction of R depends only on the interpretations of port variables occurring (free) in R. □

An analogous noninterference lemma holds for each of the variants of our model described below.

3. Termination and deadlock

The difficulty in modeling termination and deadlock is that these properties involve internal states of a process. For example, a network should not be considered terminated unless each of its component processes is terminated. To model termination and deadlock in the presence of information hiding, we add global bits of information to each communication behavior. These bits contain the essential abstraction of the information that would otherwise be lost when information is hidden.

3.1. Termination

To characterize *termination* of a network, we add to each behavior a termination bit, $t \in \{T, F\}$. Intuitively, $t = T$ means the network terminates; thus, if $t = T$ we require that the communication behavior "appear" terminated. Formally,

Definition 3.1.1: A *T−behavior* is a pair (t, σ), where $t \in \{T, F\}$ and σ is a communication behavior, such that if $t = T$ then σ is eventually constant, converging on an observation in which all ports of the network are disabled. □

The meaning of a network N is now a set $[[N]]_T$ of T-behaviors:

Definition 3.1.2: As in definition 2.1.9, assume $[[P]]_T$ is given for each primitive process P. For composite network $N = ||(N_1, \ldots, N_m)$, we define $[[N]]_T$ as follows:

A T-behavior (t, σ) is in $[[N]]_T$ iff there exist $(t_i, \sigma_i) \in [[N_i]]_T$ such that

- $t = \vee_i t_i$; and
- $\sigma\lfloor_{N_i} = \sigma_i$.

Thus a network communication behavior terminates iff each of its component communication behaviors terminates. □

To prove termination, we associate with each network component N a global variable $t_N \in \{T, F\}$. An assertion on N can have as free variables t_N and N's port names. The new proof system consists of renaming and consequence rules, obtained from the basic rules in the obvious way, together with the following new network formation rule:

Network formation rule (termination):

$$\frac{\langle N_i \rangle\, R_i, \quad i = 1, \ldots, n}{\langle ||_i N_i \rangle\, \exists t_{N_1} \ldots \exists t_{N_n} ((\wedge_i R_i) \wedge t_{||_i N_i} = \wedge_i t_{N_i})}$$

Lemma : The proof system is sound and relatively complete.

Proof:

Soundness:

Let $(t, \sigma) \in [[\|_i N_i]]_T$. Then, (t, σ) results from combining T-behaviors $(t_1, \sigma_1), \ldots, (t_n, \sigma_n)$, where $(t_i, \sigma_i) \in [[N_i]]_T$, $i = 1, \ldots, n$. Hence, (t_i, σ_i) satisfies R_i. Equivalently, σ_i satisfies $R_i[t_{N_i} \leftarrow t_i]$ (R_i with all free occurrences of t_{N_i} replaced by t_i). By the non-interference property, it follows that σ satisfies $\wedge_i R_i[t_{N_i} \leftarrow t_i]$. Thus, (t, σ) satisfies the specification of $\|_i N_i$ given in the proof rule, and the proof rule is sound.

Completeness:

We first prove that the proof rule preserves preciseness of specifications. Assume <N_i> R_i are precise. Let (t, σ) satisfy the specification of $\|_i N_i$ given in the proof rule. Then σ satisfies $\exists t_{N_1} \ldots \exists t_{N_n} (\wedge_i R_i \wedge t = \wedge_i t_{N_i})$. So σ satisfies $\wedge_i R_i[t_{N_i} \leftarrow t_i] \wedge t = \wedge_i t_i$ for some t_i, $i = 1, \ldots, n$. By the non-interference property, it follows that $\sigma(N_i)$ satisfies $R_i[t_{N_i} \leftarrow t_i]$. Equivalently, (t_i, σ_i) satisfies R_i. By preciseness of the specifications, $(t_i, \sigma_i) \in [[N_i]]_T$. Therefore, $(t, \sigma) \in [[\|_i N_i]]_T$. Conversely, if $(t, \sigma) \in [[\|_i N_i]]_T$, then it satisfies the specification of $\|_i N_i$ by soundness of the rule. Thus, the proof rule preserves preciseness.

Now, let <N> R be a specification that is true and let N be built from components $N_1, \ldots, N_n$ by network formation. From the network formation rule and precise specifications of N_i's we obtain a precise specification <N> S. So $S \Rightarrow R$ is satisfied by every pair (t, σ), where σ is a behavior on N's ports. Consider any (t', σ'). $(t', \sigma'|_N)$ satisfies $S \Rightarrow R$. Hence, $\sigma'|_N$ satisfies $S \Rightarrow R[t_P \leftarrow t']$. By the non-interference property, σ' satisfies it, too. So (t', σ') satisfies $S \Rightarrow R$. $S \Rightarrow R$ is satisfied by every pair (termination bit, behavior). Hence <N> R is provable from <N> S by the consequence rule, i.e. it is provable in the system. Therefore, the proof system is relatively complete. □

3.2. Deadlock

To characterize *deadlock*, we introduce the notion of waiting: a network is in a *wait state* if it cannot change state without a communication event taking place on one of its external ports. We now add two bits of information to each behavior. The wait bit, w, means that eventually the network reaches a wait state and remains in that state forever. The deadlocked bit, d, means that eventually the network becomes deadlocked, i.e. there exists a set D of components of the network such that

- Every member of D is in a wait state, and
- All the ports of D are disabled by members of D (i.e. members of D cannot communicate with one another and refuse to communicate with outsiders).

These conditions agree with the usual intuitive requirements for deadlock; however, see the discussion of "total deadlock" below. Formally:

Definition 3.2.1: A *D-behavior* is a triple (d, w, σ), where $d, w \in \{T, F\}$ and σ is a communication behavior, such that if $w = T$ then σ is eventually constant, converging on an observation in which all linked ports are disabled. □

We remark that the condition "all linked ports are disabled" in the above definition is essential to our intuitive notion of a wait state − a network in which some linked port is enabled cannot be in a wait state, since it can clearly change state (by sending a message on the enabled linked port) without an external communication event taking place.

The meaning of network N is now a set $[[N]]_D$ of D-behaviors:

Definition 3.2.2: As in definition 2.1.9, assume $[[P]]_D$ is given for each primitive process P. For composite network $N = \|(N_1, \ldots, N_m)$, we define $[[N]]_D$ as follows:

A D-behavior (d, w, σ) is in $[[N]]_D$ iff there exist $(d_i, w_i, \sigma_i) \in [[N_i]]$ such that

- $w = T$ iff $w_i = T$ for all i, and eventually all linked ports in N are disabled forever; and
- $d = T$ iff either $d_i = T$ for some i, or there exists a subset D of components of N such that

  (a) $w_i = T$ for each i such that $N_i \in D$; and

  (b) eventually all ports in D become disabled by members of D, and remain so forever. □

An interesting fact about this characterization of deadlock is that network formation is no longer associative. It is easy to construct four processes a, b, c and d such that

- $a \| b \| c \| d$ and $(a \| b) \| (c \| d)$ are deadlocked in our model because a and b get into deadlock.
- $(a \| c) \| (b \| d)$ is not deadlocked in our model – due to information-hiding, the separate identity of a and b is lost.

While surprising, this property is not technically a problem, and it is reasonable to take the view that the way processes are composed should affect our view of whether a system is deadlocked. There is, however, a different notion of deadlock, for which associativity is preserved: a network is ***totally deadlocked*** if *all* of its component processes get into deadlock – i.e., the set D in Definition 3.2.2 above consists of all the components of N. This is the notion of deadlock treated in [Br]. A complete discussion of total deadlock using our model appears in [Ng].

To prove deadlock (freedom), we associate with each process P global variables $d_P, t_P \in \{T, F\}$. It is clear how the renaming and consequence rules should be modified. The new network formation rule is

Network formation rule (deadlock):

$$\frac{\langle N_i \rangle\, R_i, \quad i = 1, \ldots, n}{\begin{array}{l}\langle \|_i N_i \rangle\;\; \exists d_{N_1} \ldots \exists d_{N_n} \exists w_{N_1} \ldots \exists w_{N_n} \\ \qquad ((\wedge_i R_i) \wedge w_{\|_i N_i} = ((\wedge_i w_{N_i}) \wedge \diamond \Box\, disabled(\|_i N_i)) \\ \qquad\qquad \wedge\, d_{\|_i N_i} = ((\vee_i d_{N_i}) \vee (\vee_{D \in \mathcal{A}} B_D)))\end{array}}$$

where $\mathcal{A}$ is the collection of all subsets of $\{N_1, \ldots, N_n\}$ with more than one member, and

$$B_D = ((\wedge_{N_i \in D} w_{N_i}) \;\wedge\; \diamond \Box\, inactive(D)))$$

where *disabled*(N) means that all linked ports of N are disabled, and *inactive*(D) means that all ports of members of D are disabled by members of D. It is clear how these formulas are expressed in temporal logic.

Theorem 3.2.1: The proof system is sound and relatively complete.

Proof:

The proof of soundness and completeness of this rule is similar to Theorem 3.1.1. Note, however, that in this case, $P_1 \| .. \| P_n$ is different from $(P_1 \| P_2) \| \cdots \| P_n$ in general, since associativity does not hold. The order in which processes are combined is important. Therefore, in the proofs, one needs to use induction on the structure of the network. □

4. Procedural and recursive networks

We now define procedural networks, in which certain components do not begin execution until they are activated by neighboring components. A restricted but useful class of infinite networks, in which only finitely many processes can be active at any time, can be defined using procedural networks. This leads naturally to the notion of recursive network, a useful abstraction that can model constructs of languages such as Concurrent Prolog [ST] and the parallel language of [KM].

4.1. Procedural networks and subroutine components

Informally, a procedural network is one in which certain components are designated as subroutines, and may not execute until activated externally. This restriction on the behaviors of subroutine components makes possible a simple definition of infinite procedural network, in which all but finitely many components are subroutines.

Definition 4.1.1: A *procedural network* description is either

- an (ordinary) network description; or
- a *procedural composition* of the form $\| (M_1, \ldots, M_m ; Q_1, Q_2, \ldots)$, in which each of finitely many *main* components $M_1, \ldots, M_m$ and each of perhaps infinitely many *subroutine* components $Q_1, Q_2, \ldots$ is a procedural network description.

For composite procedural network N, we impose the same unique port naming requirement as in Definition 2.1.9 for ordinary networks; i.e.,

- The sets of input (output) port names of distinct components of N must be disjoint.

The *input, output, linked* and *external* ports of N are also defined as for ordinary networks. Finally, we require that

- All ports of subroutine components of N must be linked in N.

That is, no subroutine component of N can be connected to an external port of N. □

Graphically, we represent a subroutine component of a procedural network by a double circle.

A procedural network may have infinitely many ports, though only finitely many of them can be external. The definitions of event, observation and behavior are not affected by this.

In a procedural network, each subroutine is initially inactive and may not begin executing without having been activated by some neighboring process attempting to communicate with it. To formalize this notion we define activation and execution of network components in terms of communication behaviors.

Definition 4.1.2: Let N be a procedural network, and let Q be a subroutine component of N. Let I and J respectively be the input and output ports of Q that are external to Q (recall that all ports of Q are internal to N by definition). Finally, let $s = (t, In, Out)$ be an observation of N. Then s is an *activation* of Q iff $(\vee_{i \in I} Out(i)) \vee (\vee_{j \in J} In(j))$ is true, i.e. if some neighbor of Q in N is ready to communicate with Q. □

Let ϵ denote the empty observation, i.e. the observation with an empty trace and In, Out equal to F everywhere in their domains. Technically, there are infinitely many different empty observations – one for each pair of domains for In and Out – but our use of a single symbol to denote them should not lead to confusion.

Definition 4.1.3: Let N be a procedural network. Then $[[N]]$ is a set of of behaviors on the ports of N defined as follows:

- if N is an ordinary network, then $[[N]]$ is given by Definition 2.1.9.
- if N is a composition $\| (M_1, \ldots, M_m ; Q_1, Q_2, \ldots)$, then a behavior $\sigma = s_1, s_2, \cdots$ is in $[[N]]$ iff for every main component M_i of N

$\sigma|_{M_i} \in [[M_i]]$,

and for every subroutine component Q_i of N, either

(a) for all $j > 0$,

(i) s_j does not activate Q_i, and

(ii) $s_j|_{Q_i} = \epsilon$;

that is, Q_i is never activated and never begins execution; or else

(b) there exist nonnegative integers $p < q$ such that

(i) s_p activates Q_i,

(ii) $s_j|_{Q_i} = \epsilon$ for all $j<q$, and

(iii) $(s_q, s_{q+1}, \dots)|_{Q_i} \in [[Q_i]]$;

that is, Q_i is activated and does not begin execution until some time after it is activated. □

Intuitively, the requirement in Definition 4.1.1 that all ports of subroutine processes must be linked ensures that each behavior of a procedural network uniquely determines whether its subroutine components are activated. The requirement that there be only finitely many main components ensures that, even in an infinite procedural network, only finitely many subroutine processes have been activated at any time. Note the implicit liveness assumption in this definition: once a subroutine is activated, it must eventually execute.

Because a procedural network may contain infinitely many components, a complete proof rule requires the use of infinitary logical operators. The network formation rule for procedural networks is as follows:

Procedural network formation rule:

$$\frac{\begin{array}{l} <M_i> R_i,\ 1 \le i \le m \\ <Q_j> S_j,\ 1 \le j \end{array}}{\begin{array}{l} < \|(M_1, \dots, M_m ; Q_1, Q_2, \dots) > \wedge_i R_i \wedge \\ \qquad \wedge_j (((\neg\, Q_j \textit{ is activated}) \wedge \textit{observation of } Q_j \textit{ is } \epsilon) \\ \qquad\qquad \mathcal{W}\ (Q_j \textit{ is activated} \wedge ((\textit{observation of } Q_j \textit{ is } \epsilon)\ \mathcal{U}\ S_j))) \end{array}}$$

The two phrases "Q_j is activated" and "observation of Q_j is ϵ" can easily be expressed in temporal logic.

The proof of soundness and completeness of the system with this proof rule is lengthy, and is omitted for lack of space. As usual, see [Ng] for details.

4.2. Recursive networks

Informally, a procedural network is *recursive* if some of its subroutine processes are designated as "recursive copies" of itself. To make the exposition clearer, we restrict ourselves to the case in which the recursive network has a single recursive copy and no other subroutine process. Relaxing this restriction is a tedious but straightforward exercise.

Definition 4.2.1: A recursive network description is

$$X(i_1, \dots, i_m ; j_1, \dots, j_n) = \|(N_1, \dots, N_t ; X(h_1, \dots, h_m ; k_1, \dots, k_n))$$

where $N_1, \dots, N_t$ are procedural network descriptions. □

See Figure 3 for an example. We shall define the behaviors of a recursive network to be the the behaviors of the infinite procedural network obtained by "unrolling" the recursive definition in a natural way. To define the unrolling operation requires a uniform method of obtaining new port names. For any port k, we define

- $k^0 = k$; and
- k^{r+1} is a new port name, distinct from h^s if $h \neq k$ or $s \neq r+1$.

We extend this notation to networks in the obvious way: N^r is the network obtained from N by replacing every (internal or external) port k of N by k^r.

Given recursive network description

$$X(i_1, \ldots, i_m\,; j_1, \ldots, j_n) = \|(N_1, \ldots, N_t\,; X(h_1, \ldots, h_m\,; k_1, \ldots, k_n))$$

as above, we define a sequence $G_r(X)$, $r = 1, 2, \ldots$ by:

$$G_r(X) = (\,\|\,(N_1, \ldots, N_t\,;\,))^r[h_1^{(r-1)} \ldots h_m^{(r-1)}\, k_1^{(r-1)} \ldots k_n^{(r-1)} / i_1^r \ldots i_m^r\, j_1^r \ldots j_n^r]$$

Intuitively, $G_{r+1}(X)$ is a uniquely renamed copy of the "body" of X, with its external ports linked to $G_r(X)$ in place of a recursive instance of X. An example appears in Figure 4.

The "completely unrolled" infinite procedural network for X is:

$$F(X) = \|\,(N_1, \ldots, N_t\,; G_1(X), G_2(X), \ldots\,)$$

Such a network is depicted in Figure 5. The behaviors of X are defined in terms of $F(X)$:

Definition 4.2.2: Let X and $F(X)$ be as above; then we define $[[X]] = [[F(X)]]$. □

The reader may find our unrolling process slightly unnatural. However, the "obvious" way to unroll a recursive definition would lead to an infinite procedural network in which the nesting of subroutine subnetworks was infinitely deep. Such a network would be inconvenient for technical reasons. Its equivalence to our "flattened"

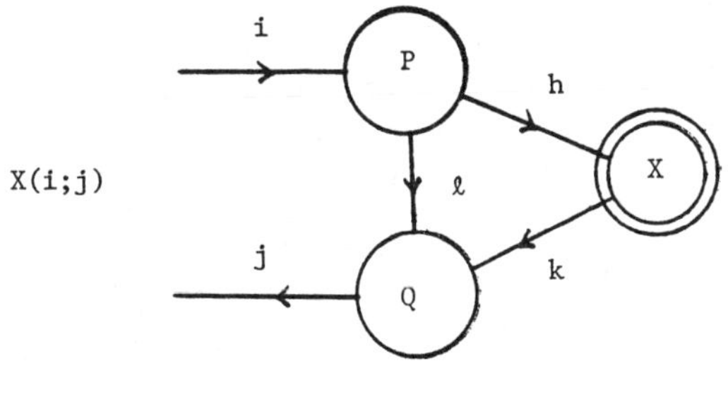

Figure 3 A recursive network

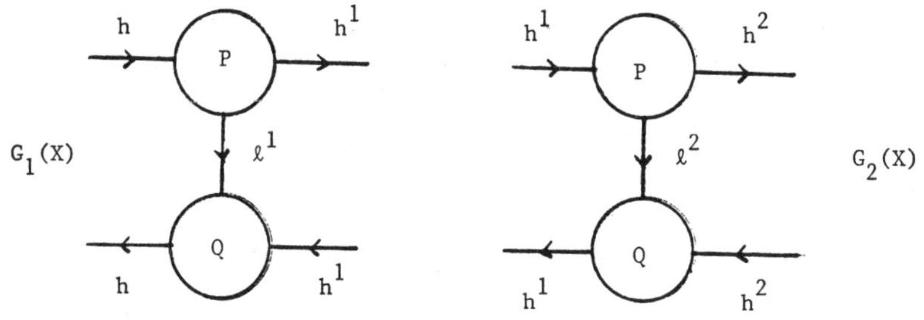

Figure 4 $G_1(X)$, $G_2(X)$

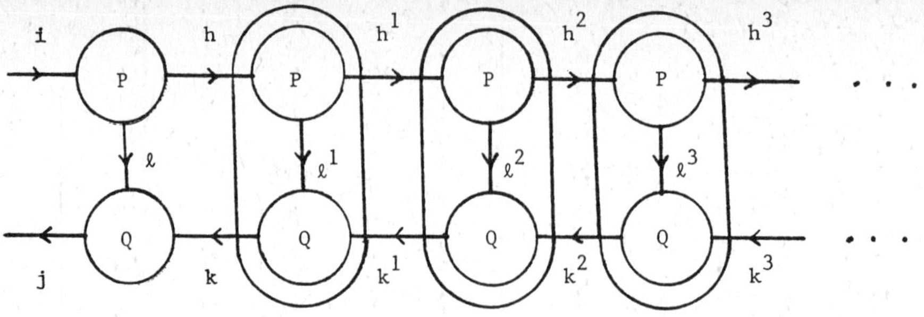

Figure 5 F(X)

network can be seen from the following:

Lemma 4.2.1: For procedural networks N_i, M_j and Q,

$$[[\ \| (M_1, \ldots, M_m ; \| (N_1, \ldots, N_n ; Q))\ ]]$$
$$= [[\ \| (M_1, \ldots, M_m ; \| (N_1, \ldots, N_n ;), Q)\ ]]$$

provided these compositions satisfy the requirements for unique port names.

Proof: A direct application of Definitions 4.2.2 and 4.1.3. Omitted for lack of space. □

This rule justifies our definition of $F(X)$, allowing us to devise a proof rule for recursive networks directely from the rule for procedural networks. The proof rule for recursive networks is:

Recursive network formation rule:

$$\frac{<\|(N_1, \ldots, N_t ;)> R}{\begin{array}{l} <X> R \wedge \\ \quad \bigwedge_n (((\neg\, G_n(X) \textit{ is activated}) \wedge \textit{observation of } G_n(X) \textit{ is } \epsilon) \\ \qquad\qquad \mathcal{N}\ (G_n(X) \textit{ is activated} \wedge ((\textit{observation of } G_n(X) \textit{ is } \epsilon)\ \mathcal{U}\ R'_n))) \end{array}}$$

where $<G_n(X)> R'_n$ is obtained from $<\|(N_1, \ldots, N_t ;)> R$ by a suitable application of the renaming rule.

Soundness and completeness of this rule follow directly from soundness and completeness of the rule for procedural networks, from which this rule was derived.

5. An example

Consider recursive network *PRIME* shown in Figure 6.

Process R produces the first input from i on j and then all the inputs from m on j. At the same time, R produces on l those inputs from i that are not divisible by the first input from i.

A formal specification for R is

$<R>\ \square S \wedge T$, where

$$S = j \sqsubseteq \textit{first}(i).m \wedge l \sqsubseteq \textit{div}(i^{(2)}, \textit{first}(i))$$
$$T = \square\,(In(i) \wedge In(m))$$
$$\wedge \diamond\ |\textit{first}(i).m| = n \Rightarrow (\diamond\ |j| = n \vee \square \diamond\ Out(j))$$
$$\wedge \diamond\ |\textit{div}(i^{(2)}, \textit{first}(i))| = n \Rightarrow (\diamond\ |l| = n \vee \square \diamond\ Out(l))$$

where $s^{(n)}$ denotes the n-truncated suffix of s, and $div(s, a)$ is the subsequence of s containing those elements that are not divisible by a.

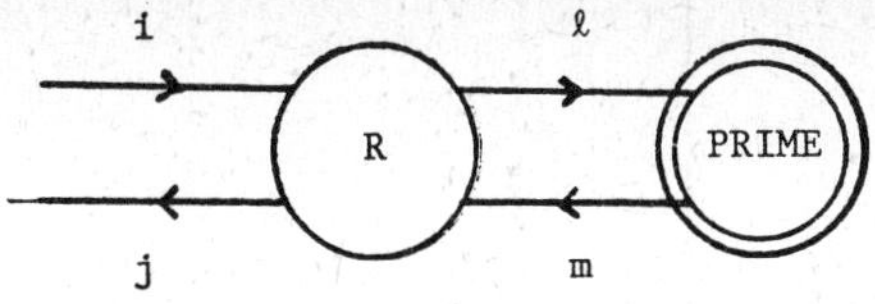

Figure 6

We want to prove

$$\langle PRIME\rangle\ \Box\, i \sqsubseteq ODDNUM \Rightarrow$$
$$(\Box\, j \sqsubseteq ODDPRIME \wedge (\diamond\, |prime(i)| = n \Rightarrow (\diamond\, |j| = n \vee \Box\diamond\, Out(j))))$$

where *ODDNUM* and *ODDPRIME* are the infinite ascending sequences of odd numbers and odd primes greater than 1, respectively, and $prime(i)$ is the sequence of primes in i.

By the renaming rule, we obtain

$$\langle G_n(PRIME)\rangle\ \Box\, S_n' \wedge T_n'$$

By the proof rule for recursive networks, we have

$$\langle PRIME\rangle\ \Box\, S \wedge T \wedge$$
$$\wedge_n((\neg G_n(PRIME) \textit{ is activated} \wedge \textit{observation of } G_n(PRIME) \textit{ is } \epsilon)$$
$$\mathcal{U}\ (G_n(PRIME) \textit{ is activated} \wedge (\textit{observation of } G_n(PRIME) \textit{ is } \epsilon\ \mathcal{U}\ (\Box\, S_n' \wedge T_n'))))$$

See Figure 7.

5.1. Safety

We first prove the safety specification

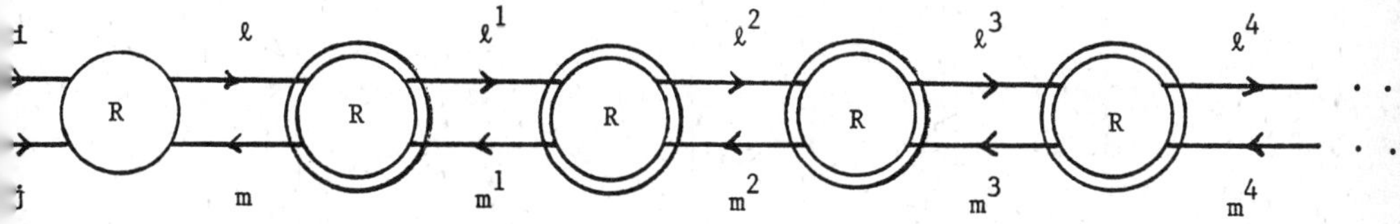

Figure 7

$$<PRIME> \ \square\, i \sqsubseteq ODDNUM \Rightarrow \square\, j \sqsubseteq ODDPRIME$$

From $<R> \ \square\, S$, by applying the proof rule for recursive networks and using the fact that S_n' is satisfied by the empty observation on $G_n(PRIME)$, we obtain

$$<PRIME> \ \square\, S \wedge \wedge_n \square\, S_n'$$

From

$$<G_1(PRIME)> \ \square\, (m \sqsubseteq first(l).m^1 \wedge l^1 \sqsubseteq div(l^{(2)}, first(l)))$$

$$<G_2(PRIME)> \ \square\, (m^1 \sqsubseteq first(l^1).m^2 \wedge l^2 \sqsubseteq div(l^{1^{(2)}}, first(l^1)))$$

...

It follows that *PRIME* satisfies at all times

$$\begin{aligned} j &\sqsubseteq first(i).m \\ &\sqsubseteq first(i).first(l).m^1 \\ &\sqsubseteq first(i).first(l).first(l^1).m^2 \end{aligned}$$

...

By induction, we obtain

$$\square\, (j \sqsubseteq first(i).first(l).first(l^1).first(l^2)...)$$

If $\square\, i \sqsubseteq ODDNUM$ then $first(i)$, $first(l)$ are the first two primes and $first(l^n)$ is the $(n+2)^{th}$ prime in i.

Hence

$$\square\, i \sqsubseteq ODDNUM \text{ implies } \square\, j \sqsubseteq ODDPRIME$$

5.2. Liveness

We take the liveness asumption to be that of *fairness*: if a linked port is enabled infinitely often then eventually communication must take place.

$$\square\, ((|k| = n \wedge \square \diamond (In(k) \wedge Out(k))) \Rightarrow \diamond\, |k| > n)$$

We now prove the liveness specification

$$\begin{aligned} &<PRIME> \ \square\, i \sqsubseteq ODDNUM \Rightarrow \\ &\qquad (\diamond\, |prime(i)| = n \Rightarrow (\diamond\, |j| = n \vee \square \diamond Out(j))) \end{aligned}$$

Since $<R> \ \square\, In(m)$, $G_1(PRIME)$ is activated as soon as R starts executing. Similarly, all the $G_n(PRIME)$ are activated eventually. Hence the original specification of *PRIME* can be simplified to

$$\begin{aligned} &<PRIME> \ \square\, S \wedge T \wedge \\ &\qquad \wedge_n \diamond (\square\, S_n' \wedge T_n') \end{aligned}$$

Assume $\square\, i \sqsubseteq ODDNUM$. By fairness assumption, from specification T we obtain

$$\diamond\, |div(i^{(2)}, first(i))| = n \Rightarrow \diamond\, |l| = n$$

Since $\square\, l \sqsubseteq div(i^{(2)}, first(i))$, it follows that

$$\diamond\, |prime(i^{(2)})| = n \Rightarrow \diamond\, |prime(l)| = n$$

By a similar argument

$$\diamond\, |prime(l^{(2)})| = n \Rightarrow \diamond\, |prime(l^1)| = n$$

...

Hence

$$\diamond\, |prime(i^{(2)})| = n \Rightarrow \diamond\, |l| = n \Rightarrow \diamond\, |l^1| = n - 1$$
$$\Rightarrow \cdots \Rightarrow \diamond\, |l^{n-1}| = 1$$
$$\Rightarrow \diamond\, |first(l).first(l^1)...first(l^{n-1}).m^n| = n$$

The fairness assumption and specifications $T_n{}'$ imply

$$\diamond\, |first(l).first(l^1)...first(l^{n-1}).m^n| = n \Rightarrow \diamond\, |first(l).first(l^1)...first(l^{n-2}).m^{n-1}| = n$$
$$\Rightarrow \cdots \Rightarrow \diamond\, |first(l).m^1| = n \Rightarrow \diamond\, |m| = n$$

Hence

$$\diamond\, |prime(i^{(2)})| = n \Rightarrow \diamond\, |m| = n$$

By this and specification T, we have for $n > 0$

$$\diamond\, |prime(i)| = n \Rightarrow \diamond\, |prime(i^{(2)})| = n - 1$$
$$\Rightarrow \diamond\, |m| = n - 1 \Rightarrow \diamond\, |first(i).m| = n$$
$$\Rightarrow (\diamond\, |j| = n \vee \Box \diamond\, Out(j))$$

The case $n = 0$ is trivial. Hence *PRIME* satisfies the required specification.

6. Discussion

We have presented a new technique for process modeling that uses the notion of behavior. This technique gives rise to a model of processes that is as simple as trace-based models [BA, Br, Ho83, P] but is more general and expressive. It is more suitable for temporal reasoning than state-transition models: a sound and complete temporal proof system based on the model is simpler than comparable proof systems based on state-transition models, e.g. [BKP, MP81, MP83].

References

[A] Apt, K.R., Ten years of Hoare's logic: a survey – Part 1, ACM TOPLAS, vol. 3, no. 4, Oct 1981, 431–483.

[BKP] Barringer, H., Kuiper, R. and Pnueli, A., Now you may compose temporal logic specifications, 16th ACM Symposium on the Theory of Computing, May 1984.

[BA] Brock, J.D. and Ackerman, W.B., Scenarios: a model of non-determinate computation, International Colloquium on Formalization of Programming Concepts, April 1981.

[Br] Brookes, S.D., A semantics and proof system for communicating processes, Lecture Notes in Computer Science, vol. 164, 1984, 68–85.

[Ha] Harel, D., First-order dynamic logic, Lecture Notes in Computer Science, vol. 68, 1979.

[HKP] Harel, D., Kozen, D. and Parikh, R., Process logic: expressiveness, decidability and completeness, JCSS vol. 25(1982), 144–170.

[HB] Hewitt, C. and Baker, H.G., Laws for communicating parallel processes, IFIP 77, 1977, 987–992.

[Ho78] Hoare, C.A.R., Communicating sequential processes, Communications of the ACM, vol. 21, no. 8, Aug 1978, 666–677.

[Ho83] Hoare, C.A.R., Notes on communicating sequential processes, Technical Monograph PRG−33, Programming Research Group, Oxford University Computing Laboratory, Aug 1983.

[KM] Kahn, G. and MacQueen, D.B., Coroutines and networks of parallel processes, IFIP 77, 1977, 993−998.

[L] Lamport, L., What good is temporal logic? Proceedings IFIP 1983, 657−668.

[MP81] Manna, Z. and Pnueli, A., Verification of concurrent programs, Part 1: The temporal framework, Technical report STAN−CS−81−836, Stanford University, June 1981.

[MP83] Manna, Z. and Pnueli, A., How to cook a temporal proof system for your pet language, 10th Annual ACM Symposium on Principles of Programming Languages, Jan 1983, 141−154.

[Mi] Milner, R., A calculus of communicating systems, Lecture Notes in Computer Science, vol. 92, 1980.

[Ng] Nguyen, V., A theory of processes, Ph.D. Thesis, Department of Computer Science, Cornell University (in preparation).

[NGO] Nguyen, V., Gries, D. and Owicki, S., A model and temporal proof system for networks of processes, 12th ACM Symposium on Principles of Programming Languages, Jan 1985, 121−131.

[P] Pratt, V., On the composition of processes, 9th ACM Symposium on Principles of Programming Languages, Jan 1982, 213−223.

[ST] Shapiro, E. and Takeuchi, A., Object-oriented programming in Concurrent Prolog, Journal of new generation computing, vol. 1, no. 1, 1983, 25−48.

EQUATIONAL LOGIC AS A PROGRAMMING LANGUAGE: ABSTRACT

Michael J. O'Donnell
Department of Electrical Engineering and Computer Science
The Johns Hopkins University
Baltimore, Maryland 21218

An experimental programming language interpreter was presented at the workshop. The interpreter, which runs under Berkeley UNIX 4.1 and 4.2, accepts as programs sets of abstract equations. The action of an equational program is to reduce input terms to *normal form* (a form with no instance of a left-hand-side of an equation). Instead of applying heuristics, the interpreter enforces restrictions on equational programs that allow efficient and logically complete strategies for reducing terms to normal form. Logical completeness requires outermost, or "lazy," evaluation instead of the conventional innermost evaluation of LISP. The demonstration explored equational programming through several examples.

Bibliography

Hoffmann, C. M., and O'Donnell, M. J., Programming with Equations, *ACM Transactions on Programming Languages and Systems,* 4:1, January 1982, pp. 83-112.

Hoffmann, C. M., and O'Donnell, M. J., Implementation of an Interpreter for Abstract Equations *10th Annual Symposium on Principles of Programming Languages* , 1984, pp. 111-120. Revised version, with R. Strandh, to appear in Software Practice and Experience.

O'Donnell, M. J., *Equational Logic as a Programming Language,* MIT Press, Cambridge, Massachusetts, 1985.

Distributed Processes and the Logic of Knowledge

(Preliminary Report)

Rohit Parikh[1] and R. Ramanujam[2]

Abstract: We establish a very natural connection between distributed processes and the logic of knowledge which promises to shed light on both areas.

Introduction: Interest in the logic of knowledge among computer scientists has recently taken a sharp upturn as evidenced by a number of recent publications [XW], [FHV], [HM], [Le], [Pa]. In particular the last three papers emphasise the possibility of a connection between the logic of knowledge and problems in distributed processing, for example between questions about Byzantine general problems and the possibility of attaining common knowledge under specified circumstances. In this paper we carry out a somewhat more systematic analysis, giving a definition of what it means for an individual process in a distributed system to know some fact and what axioms this knowledge obeys.

Philosophers have traditionally defined knowledge as justified true belief, at least until recently, when problems with this definition were pointed out by Gettier [G]. Nonetheless, a consensus remains that knowledge at least requires true belief and it is not clear what meaning we may give to the "beliefs" of an individual process in a distributed system.

Another problem for the logic of knowledge, at least as applied to humans, is that all prevalent logics of

---

1. Department of Computer Science, Brooklyn College and Mathematics Department, CUNY Graduate center. Research supported in part by NSF grant MCS83-04959 and a Faculty Research Assistance grant from the research foundation of CUNY.

2. Computer science group, Tata Institute of Fundamental Research, Homi Bhabha Road, Bombay 400005, India.

knowledge assume that the knowledge of any particular person is closed under logical inference. Humans are notorious, however, for failing to carry out all the logical inferences that are available to them. Thus any existing logic of knowledge as applied to humans is at best an approximation. A similar problem arises in public key cryptography since the public key together with the coded message do contain the decoded message as information, and the available logics are unable to adequately represent the fact that the cost of actually extracting this information is prohibitive. In other words, existing logics are able to represent a lack of knowledge, when this lack arises due to the absence of some necessary information; but they are unable to represent a lack of knowledge that arises when an inference which is possible, is not in fact carried out.

It will turn out, as we shall see below, that this problem does not arise with our definition and that individual processes do in fact know just what they ought to know. This is because the definition is purely information based and does not involve anything that could be called introspection.

The Basic Notions: In the following we assume that we have n processes $1 \le i \le n$ which may communicate with each other along binary channels, by broadcast, limited or global, or by setting variables to which more than one process may have access. The set I will be the set of all processes. We assume a global clock at the metalevel, i.e. that all events are partially ordered by a global (discrete) time, (two events may take place simultaneously) but we do not assume, except where explicitly stated, that the processes themselves have access to this or any other clock.

By a local history we shall mean the sequence of all (relevant) events, in the order of occurrence, internal events as well as messages sent and received, for some process i. In case there is a common clock, then the events will be time stamped, i.e. each element of the local history will be a pair (t,e) where e is the event and t is the instant of time at which the event takes place. Variables h,h' etc will range over local histories. By considering compound events we may assume that each process has at most one event happening at any moment of global time.

By a global history we shall mean a sequence of pairs (t, X) where t is the global time and X is some set of local events. As said before, we may assume that at most one event of some particular process i is in X. Variables H, H' etc will range over global histories.

We define a map Φ_i from global events to local events∪{null} as follows.

$\Phi_i(t, X)$ = null if there is no i-event in X.

otherwise

$\Phi_i(t, X)$ = the unique i-event in X, if there is no common clock,

= (t, e) when there is a common clock and e is the unique i-event in X.

Φ_i extends to a unique map (also called Φ_i) which preserves concatenation and whose domain is the set of global histories. If U is a subset of I then $\Phi_U(H)$ is the sequence $\langle\Phi_i(H): i\in U\rangle$. θ is Φ_I.

Clearly the map θ is one to one if there is a common clock or what amounts to the same thing, some event is happening at every individual process at every moment of global time. In the absence of a common clock, a weaker property may sometimes hold.

Call two global histories H, H' equivalent if the same sequence of events is obtained when the time stamps are erased.

Many properties of interest do not distinguish between equivalent histories. Examples are fairness (of various kinds) and deadlock freedom (provided, as is usually the case, that the boolean guards controlling parallelism do not depend explicitly on time, but only on the values of certain program variables.)

Then the map θ will be weakly one to one if θ(H)=θ(H') implies that H and H' are equivalent. An example where θ is weakly one to one but not one to one, would be a blind chess game played by correspondence, in which case the players need not possess a clock nor need they know the moves of the other player, but the game can be uniquely determined if the moves of the white and black players are given separately.

There is a map TL which forgets time stamps and converts global histories into timeless histories, i.e. sequences of sets of events. Evidently, H, H' are equivalent iff TL(H)=TL(H'). By a protocol we shall mean simply a set of possible global histories closed under the "prefix of" relation. (We shall write $H \leq H'$ to mean that H is a prefix of H'.) There may be some finite mechanism for ensuring that no history outside the protocol is actually ever possible and usually it is this mechanism that is called the protocol, but we shall prefer to work abstractly and hope that the reader will forgive this transgession. This decision is really analogous to the decision in mathematics to study sets rather than properties. To use another analogy, if the usual notion of a protocol corresponds to a grammar, then ours corresponds to the language generated by that grammar. If we are interested in fairness, then the protocol will consist only of fair histories. There is of course no finite mechanism to achieve exactly the fair histories.

A protocol P is **weakly one to one** if for all H, H' in P, $\theta(H)=\theta(H')$ implies TL(H)=TL(H'). It is **full** if $H \in P$ and TL(H')=TL(H) imply $H' \in P$. If a protocol is not weakly one to one, then there are likely to be questions about the current global history of the system which cannot be answered even by pooling the knowledge of all the systems. Problems that depend on such knowledge being available will then not be soluble.

We assume some language L whose formulas correspond to properties of individual global histories. Such properties may be, "the local variable x is now zero", "the variable y has never been zero" or protocol dependent properties like "this history has no proper extensions in the protocol". L will be assumed to have the classical boolean connectives. L will be **time-free**, if for all H, H' and $A \in L$, TL(H)=TL(H') and $H \models A$ implies $H' \models A$. L will be **separating** if for all H, H' with TL(H)$\neq$TL(H') there is an A in L such that $H \models A$ and $H' \models \neg A$.

We extend L to a language L^+ as follows.

(i) Every A in L is in L^+.

(ii) If A, B are in L^+, so are $\neg A$ and $A \vee B$.

(iii) If A is in L^+ and U is a set of processes, the $K_U(A)$ is in L^+.

(iv) If A is in L^+ then so are GA, FA, AUB.

We now define the relationship $H \models A$ for H in the protocol P and A in L^+ as follows.

(i) If $A \in L$ then the notion is supposedly given as part of the definition of L.

(ii) $H \models \neg A$ iff it is not the case that $H \models A$. Similarly for $A \vee B$.

(iii) $H \models K_U(A)$ iff for all H' with $\Phi_U(H) = \Phi_U(H')$, $H' \models A$.

(iv) $H \models GA$ iff all H' such that $H \leq H'$, $H' \models A$.

(v) $H \models FA$ iff for all maximal sequences $H_1, \ldots H_i, \ldots$ with $H = H_1$ and $H_i < H_{i+1}$ for all i, there is an i such that $H_i \models A$.

(vi) $H \models AUB$ iff for all maximal sequences $H_1, \ldots$ as above, there is an $i > 1$ such that $H_i \models B$ and for all j, $1 < j < i$, $H_j \models A$.

Note that the construct K_U does not represent common knowledge, but is in some sense dual. It is straightforward to show that $K_{\{1,2\}}$ cannot be expressed in terms of K_1 and K_2.

Intuitively $K_{\{1,2\}}(A)$ means, 1 and 2 together have enough information to deduce A.

Note that the connectives F and X (next) can be defined from U as follows. FA is trueUA where true can be any simple tautology. Similarly XA, (next A) can be defined as falseUA.

Note also that that knowledge is really dependent on three parameters. The individual i, the fact A, and finally, the protocol P. We do not assume that the protocol is known to the processes in any sense. Rather, it is background knowledge of the programmer. Thus for example, suppose the programmer knows that given the program, if gcd(x, y)=z if the boolean flag f is true, and that action α is safe if gcd(x, y)=z then he can perfectly well program a process to do α just in case f is true. The process does not need to know why f contains the right information, only the programmer needs to know that.

Finally, we point out that we have defined two global histories H. H' to be equivalent for i iff $\Phi_i(H)=\Phi_i(H')$. (similarly for a subset U of I) However, in practice a a more severe equivalence relation may be relevant. I.e. given the initial state s of a process and a local history h, there is a new state t depending only on s and h, let us call it t=h(s). Then one would really like to say that knowledge of i depends not on h, but only on h(s) and that if h(s)=h'(s) but h≠h', then the information that would distinguish between h and h', though i once had it, is now forgotten and not available to the program. It is clear that this is the right intuition for some applications, e.g. if i is a finite automaton, then the truth of theorems like the pumping lemma depends on the fact that i is awfully forgetful so that things that he knew at one time, are now gone from his memory.

The Basic Results:

Theorem 1: If L is time free and P is full, then L^+ is also time free. If, moreover, P is weakly one one, then $A \Leftrightarrow K_I(A)$ is valid in the model (holds for all histories). If L is separating and $A \Leftrightarrow K_I(A)$ is valid, then P is weakly one one.

Proof: Recall that H, H' are equvalent if TL(H)=TL(H'). We need to show that for all H, H' equivalent and all A in L^+, $H \models A$ iff $H' \models A$. This is obvious for elements of L and is preserved under the truth functional connectives. Now note that if H, H' are equivalent, and U is a subset of I, then $\Phi_U(H)=\Phi_U(H')$. Hence if for all H'' with $\Phi_U(H'')=\Phi_U(H)$ implies $H'' \models A$, then for all H'' with $\Phi_U(H'')=\Phi_U(H')$ also implies $H'' \models A$. I.e. $H' \models K_U(A)$ implies $H \models K_U(A)$ and vice versa. This settles the case for K_U.

To deal with the connectives G, F, and U we need the fullness of P. Suppose for example that H, H' are equivalent. Then if $H \models GA$ does not hold, then there is an H'' extending H such that $H'' \models \neg A$. But then there is an H''' which extends H' and such that TL(H''')=TL(H''). By fullness H''' is in P. Hence H' does not satisfy GA either. The other cases are similar.

It immediately follows that if P is weakly one to one, then A and $K_I(A)$ must be equivalent, for $\Phi_I(H)=\Phi_I(H')$ implies TL(H)=TL(H'). Thus if $H \models A$, then we must have $H \models K_I(A)$.

Conversely, if L is separating and P is not weakly one to one, then there are H. H' with $TL(H) \neq TL(H')$ but $\Phi_I(H) = \Phi_I(H')$. Now there is a formula A of L such that $H \vDash A$ and $H' \vDash \neg A$. Then $H \vDash \neg K_I(A)$ so that A and $K_I(A)$ are not equivalent. ∎

In the following theorem we consider only the connectives F, G, and X.

Theorem 2: The following axiom system is sound.

(i) Tautologies

(ii) $K_I(A) \Rightarrow A$

(iii) For $U \subseteq V$, $K_U(A) \Rightarrow K_V(A)$

(iv) $K_U(A) \Rightarrow \{K_U(A \Rightarrow B) \Rightarrow K_U(B)\}$

(v) $K_U(A) \Rightarrow K_U(K_U(A))$

(vi) $\neg K_U(A) \Rightarrow K_U(\neg K_U(A))$

(vii) $GA \Rightarrow (A \& GGA)$

(viii) $K_U(GA) \Rightarrow G(K_U(GA))$

(ix) $FA \& G(XA \Rightarrow A) \Rightarrow A$

(x) $FA \Leftrightarrow A \vee XFA$

Rules of inference

$$\frac{A \quad A \Rightarrow B}{B} \quad \text{(modus ponens)}$$

$$\frac{A \Rightarrow B}{K_U(A) \Rightarrow K_U(B)} \quad \text{(K-generalisation)}$$

(similarly for F and X which are both monotonic)

$$\frac{A \Rightarrow XA}{A \Rightarrow GA}$$

There cannot be a completeness result since the details of L are not known. L may. for instance, have quantifiers. We suspect that in case knowledge depends only on the current state of a process and not on its total history, and there are only finitely many states for each process, then the logic will be decidable by reduction to CTL* or SnS. See [ES], [HKP].

Proof: Most of the proofs are quite straightforward. Axioms (i) are obvious. Axioms (ii), (iv), (v) follows from the fact that the relation of being U-equivalent $\Phi_U(H)=\Phi_U(H')$ among histories is an equivalence relation and that if U is a subset of V, then V-equivalence implies U-equivalence. ∎

In the following theorem, we make an assumption about the protocol which is almost always realised in practice. Namely, that what a process i is about to do next depends only on its history h so far and not directly on the current state of any of the other processes. (Of course there may be an indirect dependence due to a prior communication between i and another process) We assume moreover that the relative speeds of the processes, though finite, are undetermined. Thus let $h_i \rightarrow h_i'$ mean that there are global histories H, H' with $H<H'$, $\Phi_i(H)=h_i$, $\Phi_i(H')=h_i'$ and h_i' is an immediate proper extenson of h_i. (H' need not be an immediate extension of H) Suppose now that we are in a state where the local hostory of i is h_i, $h_i \rightarrow h_i'$, h_j is the current local history of j and $h_j \rightarrow h_j'$. Then all of the next pairs of local histories are possible for i, j: (h_i, h_j'), (h_i', h_j) and (h_i', h_j'). I.e. one or both processes may go ahead to the next step. A similar remark will apply if more than two processes are involved.

Theorem 3: Let P be a protocol for several processes to share a critical section (CS). Safety and liveness properties of the protocol are related to the knowledge properties in the following way.

(i) The protocol is safe in the sense that two systems cannot simultaneously enter the CS iff no process attempts to enter the CS unless it "knows" that it is empty and that no other process is about to enter it.

(ii) If the protocol is safe and every process must terminate properly, then whenever the CS is empty and some process needs to enter it, then eventually it comes to know that the CS is empty.

Proof: (i) Suppose that the current global history is H, process i is about to enter the CS (i.e. h_i has an immediate extension where entering the CS was the last step) H' is any history i-equivalent to H, and H" is an immediate extension of H'. We must show that no other process can be in the CS in H' or H". For suppose some other process j was in the CS in H'. $\Phi_j(H')=h_j$ with j in CS and $\Phi_i(H')=\Phi_i(H)$ $=h_i$ (say) and h_i has an immediate extension h_i' where i has entered the CS. Then the pair (h_i', h_j) is in the protocol which was not safe after all. A similar argument applies if j was not in the CS but was about to enter it. Since H' was arbitrary with $\Phi_i(H')=\Phi_i(H)$, then process i knows that the CS is empty etc.

We also have to show that if every process knows, whenever it is about to enter the CS that it is safe to do so, then it is obvious that the protocol itself is safe, since no global history can have two processes in the CS simultaneously.

(ii) Suppose that process i needs to enter the CS, then since we know that eventually i must enter the CS, by part (i) eventually i must come to know that the CS is available. ∎

The theorem above shows that for a protocol to guarantee safety and liveness, it must provide for an exchange of information in a a systematic way so that the processes can acquire the knowledge that they need.

We illustrate by the following simple example.

Consider two processes 1 and 2 which share a CS. There is a boolean variable x which process 1 can set and which process 2 can read. Similarly with y and 1,2 interchanged. When the process 1 wants to enter the CS it proceeds as follows:

(i) Set x to a random value. If x=1 then goto (i).
(ii) test y. If y=0 then goto (i).
(iii) Enter the critical section.
(iv) Set x to 1.

The procedure for process 2 is dual.

We can show by informal arguments that the protocol is safe (and also live with probability 1). However, let us consider the safety from the point of view of knowledge.

Now suppose 1 is about to enter the CS. Then its local history h_1 ends with the steps x:=0; y=1?. If process 2 were in the CS or about to enter the CS then its history h_2 would end y:=0; x=1? or y:=0; x=1?; CS2. However, no global history H has the property that $\Phi_1(H)=h_1$ and $\Phi_2(H)=h_2$. Thus process 1 knows that the CS is empty and that 2 is not about to enter it.

Common Knowledge: Let E(A) denote $\bigwedge K_i(A): i\in I$. Note that E(A) is stronger than $K_i(A)$ whereas $K_I(A)$ is weaker. E(A) means, everyone knows A. Then C(A), A is common knowledge, stands for the infinite conjunction $E(A) \wedge E(E(A)) \wedge \ldots$. We can define $C_U(A)$ for any subset $U \subseteq I$ by replacing I by U in the definition above. Common knowledge has been investigated by both [HM] and [Le]. Our results do not always agree with those in [HM] but it canbe verified that ours do hold for the definition we have given.

Consider a stable statement A, i.e. one which implies GA. Then it is straightforward to show that if A ever becomes common knowledge, then it does so simultaneously. More specifically, let H be a minimal history such that $H \models C_U(A)$. Then unless H is the empty history, H is of the form H';(t,X) where X has an event from every process in U. Moreover, if $\Phi_i(H)=h_i$ where $i \in U$, then h_i is minimal such that for all H' with $\Phi_i(H')=h_i$, $H' \models C_U(A)$.

Note however that attaining common knowledge depends on the protocol P. One can attain more common knowledge in a "narrower" P than in a wider one.

Using the observation above we can derive the following somewhat paradoxical result. Suppose that A and B are two friends, A lives in New York, B in Boston. The mail from New York to Boston takes exactly four days. On November 1, A writes to B that he has a new apartment, giving his address, Though he does not date his letter, the date can be guessed when it arrives on November 5, and it can easily be verified that A's new address becomes common knowledge on that date.

There is then an improvement in the mail service, and mail starts arriving faster, taking either two or three days. On January 10, A writes to B again that he has a new dog. Let D be the proposition that A has a dog. It turns out that D will never become common knowledge!

The intuitive reason is as follows. suppose in fact that the letter arrives on January 13. On the 13th both A and B know D. However B does not know that A knows that B knows D. For if the letter was received on the 13th, it might have been mailed on the 11th, and then A could not be sure of receipt till the 14th. Thus on the 14th $K_B(K_A(K_B(D)))$ is true. However, even then, $K_B(K_A(K_B(K_A(K_B(D)))))$ does not yet hold. For if the letter was mailed on the 11th, true as far as B knows, it might have, from A's point of view, been received only on the 14th in which case B would have to allow for the possibility (in A's mind) that the letter might have been mailed on the 12th and so...

To see this formally, consider histories H_j defined as follows: H_1 is the actual history where the letter is mailed on January 10 and arrives on the 13th. For even numbers 2j, H_{2j} is the history where the letter is mailed on January 10+j and arrives on January 12+j, i.e. two days later. For odd numbers 2j+1, the history H_{2j+1} is that where the letter is mailed on January 10+j and arrives on January 13+j.

It is easily checked that $\Phi_1(H_{2j})=\Phi_1(H_{2j+1})$, and that $\Phi_2(H_{2j-1})=\Phi_2(H_{2j})$. After j days have passed, the formula $K_A(K_BK_A)^j(K_B(D))$ is not yet true, since the real history H_1 is linked to the history H_{2j+1} by a chain of length 2j, and in that history B has not yet heard about the dog!

If the letter does arrive by chance on the 12th, the situation does not change much since of course A does not know this and a similar argument applies. Similarly if B acknowledges receipt of the letter, provided he does not date his reply.

However, things are not too bad. The formula E(D) holds on the 13th, E(E(D)) on the 14th and so on. Hence the level of knowledge is rising as time passes even though there is no further communication. Now it was shown in [Pa], page 210 that if there is any formula B which does not have the construct C, and B is implied by C(D), then it is also implied by some $E^j(D)$ and hence will be true after a finite number of days.

We finally point out that the fact that D is (reasonably) persistent is relevant to the discussion. If A were to write "it is snowing today", then it does not make sense to say that that fact could be common knowledge, though the persistent propositions, "A has experienced snow" or "it snowed in New York on January 10" can of course be under suitable circumstances.

Conclusions: The results established here are only preliminary and the real purpose is to show that the connection has genuine possibilities. Obvious extensions of the current work include a completeness result corresponding to theorem 2 when the ground language L is simple; handling the probabilistic case where there is a probabilistic distribution on the protocol P; and finally, if some aspects of the structure of the system are hidden from some of the processes, then allowing for different processes to "imagine" different protocols P_i.

References

[ES] E. Emerson and A. Sistla, "Deciding Branching Time Logic", STOC 84 14-24.

[FHV] R. Fagin, J. Halpern and M. Vardi, "A Model Theoretic Analysis of Knowledge", IEEE-FOCS 1984, 268-278.

[G] E. Gettier "Is Justified True Belief Knowledge?", Analysis 1963, 121-123.

[Hi] J. Hintikka, Knowledge and Belief, Cornell University Press 1962.

[HM] J. Halpern and Y. Moses, "Knowledge and Common Knowledge in a Distributed Environment", ACM-PODC 1984, 50-61.

[HKP} D. Harel, D. Kozen and R. Parikh, "Process Logic: Expressiveness, Decidability, Completeness", JCSS 25 (1982) 144-170.

[Ho] C.A.R. Hoare, "Communicating Sequential Processes", CACM, 21 (1978) 666-677.

[Le] D. Lehmann, "Knowledge, Common Knowledge and Related Puzzles", ACM-PODC 1984, 62-67.

[MSHI] J. McCarthy, M. Sato, T. Hayashi, S. Igarashi, "On the Model Theory of Knowledge", Computer Science Technical Report, Stanford 1978.

[Pa] R. Parikh, "Logics of Knowledge, Games and Non-monotonic Logic", FST-TCS 1984. Springer LNCS #181, 202-222.

[S] M. Sato, "A Study of Kripke-type Models of some Modal Logics by Gentzen's sequential Method" Pub. Res. Inst. Math. Sci. Kyoto University, 1977.

[XW] M. Xiwen and G. Welde, "A Modal Logic of Knowledge", IJCAI 1983, 398-401.

Some Constructions for Order-Theoretic Models of Concurrency

Vaughan Pratt
Stanford University
Stanford, CA 94305

Abstract

We give "tight" and "loose" constructions suitable for specifying processes represented as sets of pomsets (partially ordered multisets). The tight construction is suitable for specifying "primitive" processes; it introduces the dual notions of concurrence and orthocurrence. The loose construction specifies a process in terms of a net of communicating subprocesses; it introduces the notion of a utilization embedding a process in a net.

1. Introduction

1.1. An Application

In September 1983 STL (Standard Telecommunications Laboratories Ltd) and SERC (Science and Engineering Research Council) jointly sponsored a workshop on the analysis of concurrent systems [DH]. The workshop was organized around ten problems for solution by the attendees. Each problem informally described a concurrent system to be formally specified.

The first problem was probably the easiest. For whatever reasons, it also attracted the lion's share of the attention. The formal solutions presented varied in length from seven axioms of one line each (Koymans-de Roever) to two pages. The following paragraph reproduces verbatim the statement of the problem.

The "channel" between endpoints "a" and "b" can pass messages in both directions simultaneously, until it receives a "disconnect" message from one end, after which it neither delivers nor accepts mesages at that end. It continues to deliver and accept messages at the other end until the "disconnect" message arrives, after which it can do nothing. The order of messages sent in a given direction is preserved.

Intuitively, the complexity of the presented solutions is out of proportion to the complexity of the concept of a two-way channel with disconnect. The "tight" construction of this paper yields a sufficiently short solution that we can conveniently preview it here:

$$(\Sigma^{*} \times TR \times \{C,D\}) \cap \sim\blacklozenge\delta$$

In English this reads "(Message sequence, Transmitted then Received, on channels C and D) no prior disconnect". It specifies essentially the same mathematical object that we required 13 lines of detail to specify in [Pr83] (our contribution to the workshop). A key construct here is the operation $\times$ of *ortho-currence* which provides the interpretation of the commas in the English.

1.2 The Significance of Pomsets

Strings arise naturally in modelling ongoing sequential computation, whether their elements correspond to states, state transitions, or message transmission-receipt events. Thinking of a string as a linearly ordered multiset, a mathematically natural generalization is to relax the linear order to a partial order. If the resulting objects are used for modelling computation, the meaning of incomparability between elements may be interpreted as concurrency of events.

We abbreviate partially ordered multiset to pomset.

The almost universal practice in modelling concurrency is to represent concurrency as choice of order in sequential computation. The two arguments supporting this approach are that partial orders are no more expressive than linear, and are not as convenient to work with.

We refute both these arguments. The first is correct for posets but not for pomsets, as demonstrated in [Gis] with the counterexample ab||ab, which in a linear model is indistinguishable from N(a,a,b,b) where N(1,2,3,4) schedules 1<3, 2<4, 1<4. The second is only true in that relatively little work has been done on partial orders for modelling computation. In fact the opposite seems to be the case - total orders turn out to be very inconvenient to work with for some basic concurrency applications, so much so that we speculate that this is one of the major reasons why the formal modelling of concurrency remains an arcane topic today.

In earlier papers [Pr82,Pr84] we showed how to derive event-order models as homomorphic images of real time models. For this to be possible the former must have a structure similar to that of the latter. Only partial orders on events meet this requirement.

In this paper we exhibit two dual operations and show various applications for them. We see these operations as being fundamental to concurrency. The only way we see to define them for a linearly ordered model is to define them for a partially ordered model and at the last step complete the partial orders to linear orders. The analog of this in astronomy would be to use Newtonian mechanics to derive the motions of the planets and at the last step convert all the results to epicycles.

1.3 Why Categories

Given "all" sets, ordered by inclusion, union and intersection are the operations of least upper and greatest lower bound respectively. This definition is popular, whether for its elegance, convenience, or algebraic flavor. It certainly makes it obvious that union and intersection are dual notions.

Another commonly encountered dual pair are disjoint union and Cartesian product. These too can be described as the operations of least upper and greatest lower bound, if we generalize from inclusions to all functions between sets and define "least upper bound" and "greatest lower bound" appropriately so that they continue to make sense, and are willing to settle for uniqueness up to isomorphism.

A category is a collection of objects such as these sets together with some morphisms between them such as inclusions or functions, viewed at the right distance for seeing the commonality of these definitions. At this distance least upper and greatest lower bounds on a set X of objects are coproducts and products respectively, while the upper and lower bounds, whether or not least or greatest, are the vertices of cones from or to X. (A minimal account of cones and products is provided for convenience as an appendix.)

In our case we want to define two basic operations of concurrency for pomsets that turn out to be coproducts and products in the category of pomsets with morphisms all pomset homomorphisms. Both the duality of these operations and their affinity with the important cases above are made clearly visible with a categorical treatment.

Winskel [W84a] describes a morphism of Petri nets, having in mind just these sorts of applications: defining coproducts and products. This is then extended [W84b] to a number of morphisms appropriate to various models of concurrency, whose relationships to each other are expressed via adjunctions. With luck there will turn out to be either a straightforward or an interesting connection between his morphisms and ours.

2. Definitions

2.1 Pomsets

The setting is order-theoretic models of concurrency. We take the central concept to be the pomset or partially ordered multiset. Informally, a pomset is to a string as a partial order is to a total order; a string is not a totally ordered set but rather a totally ordered multiset. Pomsets are intended to model *behaviors* (synonyms: trace, computations) of some process. The process itself is identified with the set of all its possible behaviors.

Pomsets may be defined in elementary language as labelled partial orders up to isomorphism. In the context of dealing with pomsets as objects of a category the obvious way (in hindsight) is to treat them as functors from a category of events to a category of actions. To keep the material reasonably accessible we do both here. More detailed elementary treatments may be found elsewhere [Gis,Pr84].

A *labelled partial order* (lpo) is a 4-tuple $(V,\Sigma,\mu,\leq)$ consisting of

(i) a set V of *events*,

(ii) an *alphabet* Σ of *actions*, e.g. the arrival of integer 3 at port Q, the transition of pin 13 of IC-7 to 4.5 volts, or the disappearance of the 14.3 MHz component of a signal,

(iii) a labelling function $\mu:E\rightarrow\Sigma$ assigning actions to events, each labelled event representing an *occurrence* of the action labelling it, with the same action possibly having multiple occurrences, and

(iv) a partial order $\leq$ on E, with the intended interpretation of $e\leq f$ being that e precedes f in time.

A *pomset* (partially ordered multiset) is then the isomorphism class of an lpo, denoted $[V,\Sigma,\mu,\leq]$. By taking lpo's up to isomorphism we confer on pomsets a degree of abstractness equivalent to that enjoyed by each of strings (regarded as finite linearly ordered labelled sets up to isomorphism), ordinals (regarded as well-ordered sets up to isomorphism), and cardinals (regarded as sets up to isomorphism).

(Cryptic remark: the reason isomorphism appears in our definition of pomsets but not in the usual definitions of string, ordinal, or cardinal, is that partial orders, unlike well-ordered sets, have nontrivial automorphisms. This complicates finding a canonical representative of the isomorphism class.)

No assumption is made about atomicity of events; in fact our tight construction of processes depends on events having structure.

2.2 Types of Pomsets

It will be convenient to regard all of the following structures as kinds of pomsets.

Multiset	Pomset with a minimal (i.e. empty) order
Tomset	Pomset with a maximal (i.e. total) order
String	Finite tomset
Poset	Pomset with an injective labelling
Set	Poset that is also a multiset
Atom	A singleton pomset (both a set and a string)
Unit	The empty pomset (hence the empty string, and empty set)

A *process* is a set of pomsets. Close analogs are binary relations, which are sets of pairs, and languages, which are sets of strings. In all cases the set structure can be regarded as modelling variety of one or another kind of behavior. A *language* is a process all of whose behaviors are strings. The language of a process is the set of strings in that process.

We write $\Sigma\dagger$ for the set of all finite pomsets with alphabet Σ, by analogy with Σ^* for the set of all strings with alphabet Σ, which happen to be all strings in $\Sigma\dagger$.

Implicit in this two-layered notion of process (sets of pomsets of events) is a two-sided distributivity axiom, that order may be distributed over choice, i.e. concatenation over union. This axiom is appropriate for partial correctness but not always for termination and deadlock. We impose this axiom on our notion of processes for now in the interest of understanding the basic pomset model better, with a minimum of distracting detail. Note that this is a limitation only of our notion of processes, not of the pomsets themselves.

2.3 Pomset Homomorphisms and the Category POM

We now wish to define homomorphism between pomsets, to facilitate the definitions of concurrence (disjoint union) and orthocurrence (direct product).

We take a pomset homomorphism to be a consistently-relabelling monotonic function between the underlying sets of the two pomsets. Consistent relabelling means that if two events have the same label so do their images under the homomorphism. Monotonicity is defined in the usual way with respect to the partial order.

The category POM consists of all pomsets together with all their homomorphisms.

We call coproduct and product (see appendix) in this category respectively *concurrence* and *orthocurrence.* Concurrence takes the disjoint union of pomsets while orthocurrence takes their direct product. Events accumulate under concurrence but combine orthogonally under orthocurrence, as will become clearer below. We write $p \| q$ for the concurrence of p and q ($p+q$ is a plausible alternative notation), and $p \times q$ for their orthocurrence.

If the string ab, a linearly ordered multiset and hence pomset, is thought of as two events a followed by b, then the concurrence of ab and cd contains four events, a followed by b, together with c followed by d, with no additional temporal relationships between ab and cd.

The orthocurrence of ab with cd contains four events, $\langle a,c\rangle$, $\langle a,d\rangle$, $\langle b,c\rangle$, and $\langle b,d\rangle$, with $\langle a,c\rangle \leq \langle a,d\rangle \leq \langle b,d\rangle$ and $\langle a,c\rangle \leq \langle b,c\rangle \leq \langle b,d\rangle$.

If we write **2** for the multiset {0,0} and 00 for the result of linearly ordering **2**, **2** and 00 both being pomsets, then $p \times \mathbf{2} = p \| p$ (ignoring the extra 0 on each label) whereas $p \times 00 = p.p$. This second operation is concatenation, in this case of p with itself. Like concurrence, the concatenation p.q is an "upper bound" on (the vertex of a cone from, see appendix) p and q. This makes it clear that concatenation is not the dual of concurrence but rather is a bound on {p,q} superior to $p \| q$ (since concurrence is the least upper bound) - indeed concatenation lies on the opposite side of concurrence from orthocurrence.

Between the concurrence and the concatenation of p and q lies a complete lattice of intermediate upper bounds on p and q, each consisting of p||q with some additional ordering information running from p to q, an arbitrary subset of the concatenation ordering in p.q. We will find some of these intermediate bounds of importance below.

All these intermediate bounds are representable as quotients of a concurrence, the quotients modifying only the order and otherwise constituting label-preserving bijections. We may call quotients of this form *serializations.*

3. The Tight Construction

3.1 The Cons Process

By way of motivation consider the Cons process. This process has two input ports A and B and one output port O. The first value output from O is the first value input from A; thereafter all outputs on O are taken in order from B. Further inputs on A are not accepted and therefore do not appear at all in the behaviors of Cons.

The typical behavior of this process can be diagrammed as in Figure 1.

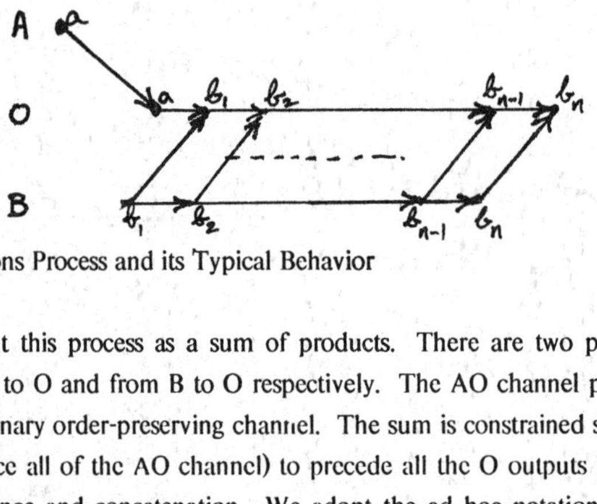

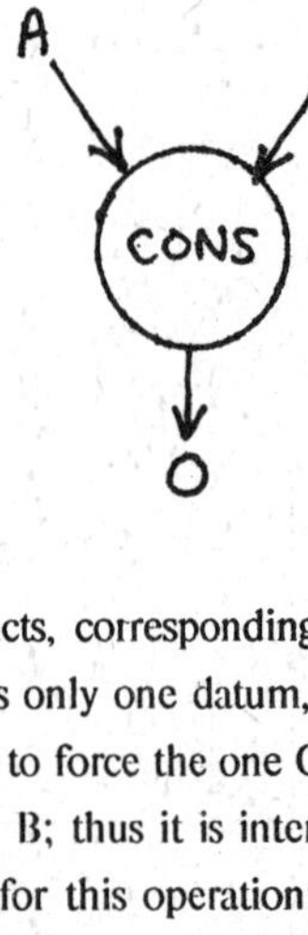

Figure 1. The Cons Process and its Typical Behavior

We may represent this process as a sum of products. There are two products, corresponding to two channels, from A to O and from B to O respectively. The AO channel passes only one datum, the BO channel is an ordinary order-preserving channel. The sum is constrained so as to force the one O output from A (and hence all of the AO channel) to precede all the O outputs from B; thus it is intermediate between concurrence and concatenation. We adopt the ad hoc notation $\bullet_O$ for this operation: $p_A{\bullet}_O q$ indicates partial concatenation in which the A component of p (say) precedes the O component of q. Omission of either subscript denotes no restriction, so $p{\bullet}q$ has its usual meaning.

Now consider the individual products. A channel is a set of behaviors, each which in turn is a sequence of message transitions. Such a sequence has two orthogonal components: a string σ of messages, and a string AO or BO consisting of a transmission action A or B followed by a receipt action O and constituting a "transition schema." The orthocurrence of σ with AO yields the pomset of Figure 2; BO is similar.

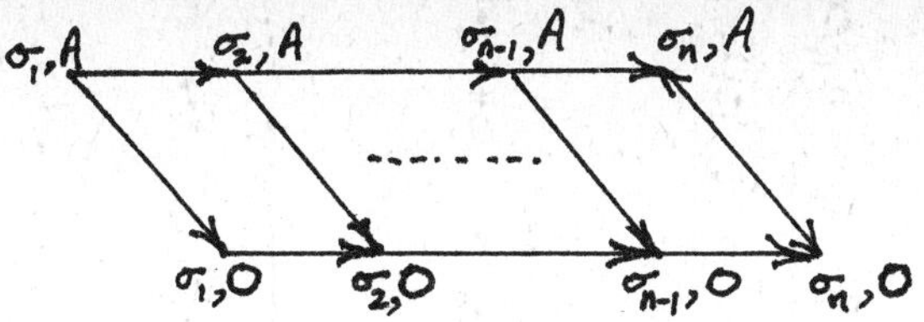

Figure 2. Orthocurrence of a Message String with the Transition Schema

Letting Σ^* denote the set of all message sequences, the set of all possible behaviors for the BO channel is then $\Sigma^* \times BO$ (with orthoccurrence being distributed over union).

We may now define the Cons process:

$$\text{Cons} \;=\; \Sigma \times AO \;\bullet_O\; \Sigma^* \times BO.$$

3.2 Related Processes

The dual of Cons is CarCdr, a process with one input I and two outputs A and B, which feeds its first input to A and the rest to B. Like Cons CarCdr is a sum of products. We leave it to the reader to interpret:

$$\text{CarCdr} \;=\; \Sigma \times IA \;{}_{I}\!\bullet\; \Sigma^* \times IB.$$

The duality of Cons and CarCdr is made quite clear from the formulas.

A somewhat different example is given by Merge, which has inputs A and B and output O and merges its two stream inputs arbitrarily. Similarly to Cons, Merge is a sum of two products, in this case $\Sigma^* \times AO$ and $\Sigma^* \times BO$. The sum however differs from that for Cons in that instead of specifying a particular order we impose the weaker requirement that the O channel merely be linearly ordered. Again adopting an ad hoc notation we write $[p]_A$ to indicate the set of all augmentations of the order of p in which the A component of p is linearly ordered, with omission of the subscript again denoting no restriction. This yields:

$$\text{Merge} \;=\; [\Sigma^* \times AO \;||\; \Sigma^* \times BO]_O$$

We might call the dual of Merge Spray. Spray has input I and outputs A and B, and sends each of its inputs to an arbitrarily chosen output. It is given by

$$\text{Spray} \;=\; [\Sigma^* \times IA \;||\; \Sigma^* \times IB]_I$$

A functional process F which computes the function f repeatedly has one input I and one output O, and for each input σ outputs $f(\sigma)$. It may be defined as

$$F = \varphi(\Sigma^* \times IO)$$

where φ is a pomset morphism which replaces each label $\langle\sigma,O\rangle$ with $\langle f(\sigma),O\rangle$ and leaves the rest of the pomset unchanged.

We take for our concluding example the two-way channel with disconnect described in our opening remarks, which was

$$(\Sigma^* \times TR \times \{C,D\}) \cap \sim\blacklozenge\delta$$

This has some features in common with the previous examples. However there are a couple of new ideas requiring explication here. We have remarked earlier that orthocurrence of p with a set such as {C,D} produces essentially the concurrence of p with itself, except that the events are marked with one of C or D according to which copy of p they are in. Hence this construction yields two concurrently operating one-way channels C and D. Each action in this system is a triple of the form <msg,type,channel> where type is T or R and channel is C or D, with <type,channel> providing the location of the action and msg its value.

The part about disconnection breaks newer ground. It is the one example in which temporal logic [Pn] is used. δ is a predicate on messages, and hence on actions and hence on events, defining which messages say to disconnect. $\blacklozenge$ (a solid diamond, Koymans-de Roever [DH]) is a temporal modality, an existential predicate transformer yielding predicates on events. $\blacklozenge$ projects out or smears its argument forwards in time. In our case it smears δ forwards so that it holds for any event f for which there exists an event $e<f$ satisfying $\delta(e)$; hence $\blacklozenge\delta$ asserts that a disconnect request has happened in the past. We wish to forbid or eliminate all such events, so we change the sign to yield $\sim\blacklozenge\delta$.

If we regard $\sim\blacklozenge\delta$ as the set of all processes all of whose events meet this condition then intersection with it forbids such events, an operation of a logical character. If we regard it as an operation on pomsets that shrinks them by removing unwanted events then application of it to each behavior in the process eliminates such events, an operation of an algebraic character. Either approach will work; in the formula above we used the former.

There is one detail in which the process named by this expression differs from the process named in [Pr83], namely that in the latter the events at each "endpoint" of the two-way channel were linearly ordered. The informal specification does not raise this as an issue, so the process named in our present solution is adequate. On the other hand one might object that our two channels are completely independent of each other. The linearization introduces at least a small degree of coupling. We may bring it into coincidence with the process named in our previous solution by use of the linearization operator $[p]_A$ introduced above. The two endpoints may then be incorporated into the solution by considering them as the names "a" for {TC,RD} (Transmit on C and Receive on D) and "b" for {TD,RC} respectively. This leads to our final solution:

$$[[\Sigma^* \times TR \times \{C,D\}]_{\{TC,RD\}}]_{\{TD,RC\}} \cap \tilde{\ } \blacklozenge \delta$$

These varied examples suggest that the notions of concurrence and orthocurrence, and associated serializations, may prove to be useful tools for the specification of processes.

4. The Loose Construction

In this section we give a construction of processes in terms of networks of constituent processes. In this manner of combining processes the constituent processes may be recognized merely by intercepting the flow of data along network channels. When wires implement channels the coupling can be adjusted merely by adjusting the connections of the wires. This seems to be a looser kind of coupling of processes than that of the last section, where the components of an assembled process were not identifiable merely by watching data flowing on channels, and where the coupling was of a more logical than physical character.

The general idea here is to define the notions of translation, projection, and utilization, each in terms of its predecessor, with translation being a particularly simple-minded notion. Then a net process may be defined as the intersection of utilizations of its constituent processes, and a process implemented by a net may be defined as a projection of a net process.

The main difference between this account of composition and that of [Pr84] is the explicit notion of a utilization as an operation determined solely by an insertion, with utilizations combining via intersection.

4.1 Substitutions

A pomset algebra is a collection of pomsets closed under the pomset-definable operations [Gis], described below. A *substitution* is an endomorphism of a pomset algebra that replaces each event e of a pomset by a pomset p, such that if $e \leq f$ ($f \leq e$) before the substitution then after the substitution $e' \leq f$ ($f \leq e'$) for every event e' in p, and such that the same pomset is substituted for events with the same label.

A substitution is determined by its behavior on atoms (singleton pomsets). As such it has the character of a homomorphism on a free algebra, which is determined by its behavior on generators. Pomset substitutions are the natural generalization of string homomorphisms.

The algebraic structure of strings is straightforward: they combine under the single binary operation of concatenation. It can be shown [Gis] that there is no corresponding finite set of operations for building all finite pomsets from atoms. However the pomsets themselves can be used to define an infinite set of operations using which all pomsets may be built from atoms, the *pomset-definable operations* [Gis]. Such an algebra is free, freely generated by its atoms, and substitution is a homomorphism on it. That is the sense in which substitution is a morphism of pomset algebras.

4.2 Translations

We shall refer to a function $f:\Sigma\rightarrow\Sigma'$ between two alphabets Σ and Σ' as a *translation*. This extends in the usual way to a length-preserving homomorphism of strings. In the same way it also extends to a size-and-structure preserving homomorphism of pomsets, as introduced in [Gis] and recounted below in the section on substitutions.

4.3 Insertion

Consider an alphabet of the form $C\times D$, where C is to be thought of as denoting a set of channels or locations and D a set of data or values. In this context an insertion is a data-preserving translation, one that affects only the location.

The example that gives rise to the name "insertion" is the insertion of a component (say an integrated circuit) into a net (say a printed circuit board). Each pin of the IC connects to some wire on the PC board. We assume two asymmetries: every pin connects to some wire, but not conversely, and a wire may short (connect) two pins but a pin may not short two wires (certainly true for socketed IC's, and more generally we may define "wire" to make it always true). It follows that the connection relation between pins and wires is actually a connection function mapping pins to wires. Not being injective corresponds to shorting pins, and not being surjective corresponds to some wires not being connected to any pin. (On the other hand, if insertion were a relation it would not compromise the development.)

An insertion is then a translation mapping (c,d) to (f(c),d) where f is a connection function.

4.4 Projection

A projection is the extension to a substitution of the inverse of a translation. The name is motivated by the case when the translation is an insertion, as will become apparent.

The inverse of a translation $t:\Sigma\rightarrow\Sigma'$ is $t^{-}:\Sigma'\rightarrow 2^{\Sigma}$, defined as usual as $t^{-}(\sigma') = \{\sigma | t(\sigma) = \sigma'\}$. In this context we take a set of actions to be a pomset that is a poset with the empty order; thus the inverse maps actions, i.e. atoms, to pomsets. This inverse t^{-} then extends homomorphically, as described above for substitutions, to a substitution t^{-+} from pomsets to pomsets.

The inverse of an insertion amounts to a coordinate transformation for actions, going from the net coordinates (wires) to the component coordinates (pins). In addition to renaming locations it takes care of whether a particular net action is relevant to this component, deleting it if not, and also whether it must occur simultaneously on more than one channel of the component, duplicating it if necessary. Duplicated events are unordered, which is as close as we can come in this model to saying that they occur simultaneously.

For example consider a component having channels C and D and a net having channels E and F. Insert the component into the net via the connection mapping C and D to E, thus connecting C and D together. Let the data domain be {0,1}. Then the inverse insertion maps action (E,1) to the set {(C,1),(D,1)} (meaning that event (E,1) can only occur in the net when events (C,1) and (D,1) both occur in the component) and action (F,1) to the empty set (meaning that this action is irrelevant to the component). More generally, if in a pomset (net behavior), (E,1) precedes (E,0) precedes (F,1), then the projection of that pomset onto the component has four events (C,1), (D,1), (C,0), (D,0), with each of the first two preceding each of the second two.

4.5 Utilization

A utilization is the union of the pointwise extension (to a function on processes) of the inverse of a projection. Let us take this one step at a time. Begin with $\pi:\Sigma'\dagger\rightarrow\Sigma\dagger$, a projection from pomsets to pomsets. Its inverse $\pi^{-}:\pi:\Sigma\dagger\rightarrow 2^{\Sigma\dagger}$ maps the pomset p to the set of those pomsets whose projection under π is p; we interpret that set as a process. For a process P, $\pi^{-}(P)$ is then a set $\{\pi^{-}(p)|p\in P\}$ of processes, the pointwise extension of π^{-} to a function from processes to sets of processes. Finally we write $\pi^{-\cup}(P)$ for $\cup\{\pi^{-}(p)|p\in P\}$, the union of that set.

The intended application for utilization is to embed a process's behavior into a net in such a way that, on the one hand the behavior contains information only about that process's behavior in terms of the topology of that net, yet on the other the behavior of the whole net reduces to the intersection of the utilizations of its components, as explained in the next section.

4.6 Composition

Given a family P_i of processes, each on an alphabet $C_i \times D$, and their associated connections $c_i:C_i\rightarrow C$ into a common net having connection set C, we may now express the process P consisting of the set of all possible behaviors of the net via the following formula.

$$P = \Pi_i(c_i \times I_D)^{-+-\cup}(P_i).$$

Each function $c_i \times I_D$ is the insertion induced by c_i, I_D being the identity function on D. The superscripts then promote each insertion to a utilization. Finally the product of the resulting processes is formed, the product operator being ordinary intersection for the case of processes as sets of behaviors.

This rule is very far-reaching. It can model composition of binary relations, composition of processes via arbitrary nets, connection via a bus or ethernet where messages may be broadcast by any process attached to the bus or ethernet to any other such process, and analog circuits such as a net of resistors. The rule handles these diverse systems by being defined independently of whether behaviors are discrete orders (as associated with conventional models of computation) or dense orders (as associated with analog circuitry), and also independently of "direction" of flow of data on channels.

In the case of resistive nets, Ohm's law shows up as a local property of the constituent resistors and Thevenin's Theorem (including the special cases in which series resistances sum and parallel resistances sum harmonically) shows up as a global property of the net. This is all accomplished using resistor behaviors each consisting just of two events (e,i,p) giving the voltage e and current i at each of two ports p = 0 and 1, with the sum over the ports of the i's vanishing and the sum of the e/i's being the resistance; utilization then does *all* the remaining work of predicting the behavior of an arbitrary net of resistors. We hope to get into more depth with analog processes in future papers.

4.7 Evolution of the Utilization-Intersection Approach

Our approach to process composition evolved in small steps from Gilles Kahn's original rule for composing processes. The steps are:

1. [K,KM] Define a component to be a continuous function from n-tuples of sequences to sequences. Continuity is defined relative to the prefix order on sequences. Define a net to be a system of equations each of the form x = f(y,...,z) where each variable x,y,z denotes a connection in the net and each equation a component. Express the behavior of the net as the least solution (under prefix ordering) to this system.

2. [BA] Instead of a total order on events within each channel, have a partial order on all events, permitting between-channel ordering as well. This is to extend Kahn composition to deal with nondeterministic processes, which Brock and Ackerman showed could not work merely by using relations on sequences instead of functions.

3. [Pr82] Introduce the pomset as the underlying abstraction for Brock-Ackerman semantics. Separate the Brock-Ackerman composition rule into two steps: composition of component behaviors to form the maximal net behavior whose restrictions to those components are those components, then restriction of that behavior to the external ports of the net, itself modelled as a component of the net. Take all solutions, not just the least.

4. [Pr84] Recast the above using only standard constructions: inverse, homomorphic extension, pointwise extension, union. Remove the distinction between input and output ports. Remove all finiteness and discreteness requirements to admit analog circuits.

5. [this paper] Introduce the concept of a utilization. Separate the rule for forming net behavior into utilizations followed by intersection.

Appendix - Pure Categories

The many categorically innocent readers seeking relief in a comprehensive text [ML] have the dual burden of extracting just the relevant material and massaging it to fit our viewpoint. We address this here by listing all the definitions we need for this and the next paper, slanted appropriately. These definitions are rather cryptic on their own and are best read in conjunction with [ML].

An edge-labelled graph, or *multigraph*, is one with a set of edges between any two vertices, as opposed to zero or one edges. A *free category* is an algebra consisting of all paths of some directed multigraph. This algebra has only one operation, path concatenation g;f. Paths determine their endpoints, whence to each object corresponds a distinct empty path and g;f is only defined if g starts where f ends. By convention vertices are called *objects*, paths *morphisms*, loops *endomorphisms*, concatenation *composition*, the empty path at b the *identity* 1_b, and the two endpoints of a path its *domain* and *codomain* respectively.

A *category* is a quotient (homomorphic image) of a free category. (This just means that some paths are collapsed together by an equivalence relation that is furthermore a congruence with respect to concatenation.) A *discrete* category has only identity morphisms. Two morphisms $f{:}a \to b$, $g{:}b \to a$ satisfying $g;f = 1_a$ and $f;g = 1_b$ are called *isomorphisms* and a and b are said to be *isomorphic*. An *automorphism* is both an isomorphism and an endomorphism. A *preorder* is a category with at most one morphism between any two objects (in each direction). A *clique* is a maximal preorder. A *poset* is a preorder with only trivial (identity) isomorphisms. (Contrast: cliques and posets have respectively a maximal and a minimal set of isomorphisms.)

A *functor* is a homomorphism between two categories (e.g. the aforementioned quotient). A *natural transformation* τ of functors $S,T{:}C \to B$ is a function τ which maps each object c in C to a morphism $\tau c{:}Sc \to Tc$ in B such that for each morphism $f{:}c \to c'$ in C, $Tf;\tau c = \tau c';Sf$ (a "commuting diagram" with corners Sc,Sc',Tc,Tc'). Natural transformations compose according to $(\tau;\sigma)c = \tau c;\sigma c$ to yield a natural transformation (!). Hence a collection of natural transformations closed under composition constitutes the morphisms of a category of functors.

An object is *initial* (*final*) in a category C when there is exactly one morphism in C from it to (to it from) each object in C. Initial (final) objects are isomorphic (!). "Initial object in a category" appropriately generalizes "least element in a poset."

Given a functor $F{:}C \to B$, define C^+ to be C augmented with a final object (and hence with the additional morphisms required to make it final). A *cone from* F is any functor $F^+{:}C^+ \to B$ extending F; its *vertex* is the image under F^+ of the final object of C^+. The *category of cones from* F has as objects those cones and as morphisms those natural transformations of cones which assign 1_{Fc} to each object c of C. "Category of cones from F" generalizes "poset of upper bounds on a subposet of a poset."

A *colimit* of F is the vertex of an initial object of the category of cones from F. A *coproduct* is a colimit of a functor with a discrete domain. The respective dual notions are *cone to* F, *limit*, and *product*.

Acknowledgments

I thank Jose Meseguer for helpful discussions and hints.

Bibliography

[B] Brauer, W., Net Theory and Applications, Springer-Verlag LNCS 84, 1980.

[BA] Brock, J.D. and W.B. Ackerman, Scenarios: A Model of Non-Determinate Computation. In LNCS 107: Formalization of Programming Concepts, J. Diaz and I. Ramos, Eds., Springer-Verlag, New York, 1981, 252-259.

[DH] Denvir, T., W. Harwood, M. Jackson, and M. Ray, **The Analysis of Concurrent Systems**, Proceedings of a Tutorial and Workshop, Cambridge University, Sept. 1983, LNCS, Springer-Verlag, to appear.

[Gis] Gischer, J., **Partial Orders and the Axiomatic Theory of Shuffle**, Ph.D. Thesis, Computer Science Dept., Stanford University, Dec. 1984.

[H] Hoare, C.A.R., Communicating Sequential Processes, CACM, 21, 8, 666-672, August, 1978,

[K] Kahn, G., The Semantics of a Simple Language for Parallel Programming, IFIP 74, North-Holland, Amsterdam, 1974.

[KM] Kahn, G. and D.B. MacQueen, Coroutines and Networks of Parallel Processes, IFIP 77, 993-998, North-Holland, Amsterdam, 1977.

[ML] Mac Lane, S., **Categories for the Working Mathematician**, Springer-Verlag, NY, 1971.

[M] Milner, R., **A Calculus of Communicating Behavior**, Springer-Verlag LNCS 92, 1980.

[Pn] Pnueli, A., The Temporal Logic of Programs, 18th IEEE Symposium on Foundations of Computer Science, 46-57. Oct. 1977.

[Pr82] Pratt, V.R., On the Composition of Processes, Proceedings of the Ninth Annual ACM Symposium on Principles of Programming Languages, Jan. 1982.

[Pr83] Pratt, V.R., Two-Way Channel with Disconnect, in [DH], section 3.1.3.

[Pr84] Pratt, V.R., The Pomset Model of Parallel Processes: Unifying the Temporal and the Spatial,

Proc. CMU/SERC Workshop on Logics of Programs, to appear in Springer Lecture Notes in Computer Science series, Pittsburgh, 1984.

[W84a] Winskel, G., A New Definition of Morphism on Petri Nets, Springer Lecture Notes in Computer Science, *166*, 1984.

[W84b] Winskel, G., Categories of Models for Concurrency, Technical Report no. 58, University of Cambridge, England, undated (rec'd Dec. 1984).

PROVING FAIRNESS OF SCHEDULERS

R Ramanujam, Kamal Lodaya

Computer Science Group
Tata Institute of Fundamental Research
Homi Bhabha Road, Bombay 400 005, India

Abstract

Considering explicit schedulers of nondeterministic programs, we propose a notion of cycles in infinite choice sequences and characterize fair sequences as being composed of cycles. We demonstrate that proof of fairness reduces to showing the existence of such cycles. Guarded commands are used to represent the scheduled actions and a proof technique is presented to discover conspiracies among them.

1. Introduction

Fairness is an issue of interest whenever we have choice. The execution of a nondeterministic program periodically requires choices to be made between several possible actions. These actions can be thought of as contenders for choice. We would expect that over an arbitrarily long period all contenders are chosen. Thus, if we have a scheduler which chooses among contenders, the scheduler is fair if every infinitely often enabled action is infinitely often chosen.

Such a definition would seem to imply that the scheduler has to be observed for an infinite period of time before we can determine whether it is fair or not. However, the scheduler itself can be abstracted as a program and its behaviour analyzed to determine fairness. Note that such an analysis of schedulers would be worthwhile *per se*, since we need to assume very little about the choice environment which presents the choice of actions to the scheduler.

While there have been many attempts to analyze fairness in the context of proving the total correctness of nondeterministic programs [Lehmann et al 81; Grumberg et al 81; Apt & Olderog 84], we confine our attention to explicit schedulers and choose to analyze them without looking into what actions they schedule. However, actions conspire against (or with) each other to limit possible choices and, in that sense, affect scheduler behaviour as well.

We consider the infinite choice sequences generated by a scheduler and propose a notion of cycles to characterize fair choice sequences. The idea is that the behaviour of a fair scheduler is in some sense periodic: when there are many contenders, all of them are chosen before considering more.

In the following sections, we begin by intuitively explaining our methodology and then proceed to formally discuss cyclic sequences. We then consider a specific choice environment, that of guarded commands, and use proof techniques from Hoare logic to discover conspiracies among actions.

2. Cycles

Let A be the (finite) set of possible actions in the system, indexed by the set {0..n}, so that A_i refers to the action in A indexed by i, $0 \le i \le n$. Presented with a subset E of A, the scheduler selects one action in E for execution. E is called the set of _enabled_ actions. Let us assume that once an action is chosen for execution, the execution of that action terminates in finite time, after which another set of enabled actions is presented to the scheduler.

The operation of the scheduler can be characterized by a _choice sequence_, which is an infinite sequence of tuples (E,a), where $E \subseteq A$ is a set of enabled actions and $a \in E$. In the examples in this section, we assume all actions {0..n} are continuously enabled.

Consider the following scheduler:

Example 2.1: Round-Robin Scheduler.

```
RR: i := 0;
    do true -> Execute action i;
               i := (i+1) mod (n+1)
    od
```

To each element of the choice sequence, add a set I which is intially equal to the set E of enabled actions. Whenever an action in I is chosen, it is removed from I; that is, I maintains the set of initially enabled actions which have not yet been chosen. We call I the *inherited choice set*.

The choice sequence and inherited choice set for the Round-Robin scheduler are as follows:

E	{0..n}	{0..n}	...	{0..n}	{0..n}
Chosen	0	1	...	n	0
I	{1..n}	{2..n}	...	{}	

A choice sequence in which the associated set I reduces from E to the empty set is called a cycle. The computation of the scheduler RR is the above cycle repeated *ad infinitum*, because after n+1 choices, i is reset to zero. Each action in E is enabled infinitely often, and is chosen once in the cycle. As the cycle repeats forever, all the actions are chosen infinitely often. Hence the scheduler is fair.

Example 2.2: k-Robin scheduler, k < n.

```
KR: i := 0;
    do true -> Execute action i;
               i := (i+1) mod (k+1)
    od
```

We can construct the choice sequence as follows:

E	{0..n}	{0..n}	...	{0..n}	{0..n}			...
Chosen	0	1	...	k	0			
I	{1..n}	{2..n}	...	{k+1..n}	{k+1..n}	...	{k+1..n}	...

Note that I never reduces to the empty set as no action in {k+1..n} is ever chosen. No cycle exists, and as each action in {k+1..n} is infinitely often enabled but never chosen, the scheduler is unfair. However, KR is fair for the subset {0..k} of E: if {0..k} were the only infinitely often enabled actions, it would be a fair scheduler.

So far we have had just one cycle in the choice sequence. It is quite possible to have more than one: in fact, in the next scheduler, there is an infinite number of cycles, each of finite length.

Example 2.3: Increasing-length-of-cycles scheduler.

```
ILC: LenCycle := 0;
     do true -> LenCycle := LenCycle+1; Counter := LenCycle;
                i := LenCycle mod (n+1);
                do Counter ≠ 0 -> Execute action i;
                                  Counter := Counter-1
                od
     od
```

As an illustration, let n be 1. The choice sequence is as follows:

E	{0,1}	{0,1}	{0,1}	{0,1}	{0,1}	{0,1}	{0,1}	...
Chosen	1	0	0	1	1	1	0	...
I1	{0}	{}						
I2		{1}	{1}	{}				
I3				{0}	{0}	{0}	{}	

3. Proving Fairness

We now proceed to formally analyze cycles. Let IOE be a set of infinitely often enabled actions. As a group of actions can be enabled infinitely often as a whole, each element of IOE is a set of actions; that is, IOE is a subset of P(A), the set of nonempty subsets of A.

Assume the scheduler is a program and the choice sequence C is an auxiliary variable. The scheduler program with auxiliary assignments in brackets has the following form:

```
SCH: [C := <>;]
     do true -> Find set of enabled actions E ⊆ A;
                Select i from E;
                [C := C concat (E,i);]
                Execute action i
     od
```

Note that execution of action i may change E in each iteration of the scheduler. SCH generates an infinite choice sequence as it executes for ever.

Def 3.0: ChoiceSequences = $\{\langle (E_1, a_1), (E_2, a_2), \ldots\rangle \mid E_i \subseteq A_i,\ a_i \in E_i, \text{ for all } i\}$

The n'th element of a choice sequence C is denoted C_n. If C_n is (E,a), C_n.Enabled refers to E and C_n.Chosen to a.

Def 3.1: $C.\text{Enabled} = \bigcup_{i=1,n} C_n.\text{Enabled}$

$C.\text{Chosen} = \bigcup_{i=1,n} C_n.\text{Chosen}$

Given a set I ⊆ A, a choice sequence encompassing I is one in which every action in I is chosen at least once. We call such a sequence an I-sequence, with the understanding that the given set I is associated with that sequence.

Def 3.2: Given I ⊆ A,

I-sequences = $\{C \mid C \in \text{ChoiceSequences and } I \subseteq C.\text{Enabled}\}$

We now introduce a notion of minimality.

Def 3.3: Given I ⊆ A,

Minimal I-sequences = $\{M \mid M \in \text{I-sequences}, \forall M' \text{ prefix } M.\ M' \text{ is not an I-sequence}\}$

Given I, a minimal I-sequence M has all actions in I chosen; further, M is minimal in the sense that the last action in M makes it an I-sequence. Hence this last action must be in I and must not be chosen earlier in M. Indeed, a minimal I-sequence captures the idea of a cycle introduced earlier: if we were to remove an action from I as soon as it is chosen, the set I would reduce to the empty set exactly with the last element of M. In fact, the only cycles we need to consider are minimal I-sequences where I is chosen infinitely often.

Def 3.4: Cycles = {M | M ∈ Minimal I-sequences, I ∈ IOE}

A cyclic sequence is obtained by infinite concatenation of cycles. Intuitively, a cyclic sequence is a choice sequence obtained by unrolling cycles. Note that there can be many different cycles and they may be of arbitrary length.

Def 3.5: CyclicSequences =

    {C = W concat C' | W is a concatenation of
                          minimal I-sequences over all I ∈ IOE,
                      C' ∈ CyclicSequences}

If we examine the scheduler SCH again, we note that the inherited choice set I can be introduced as follows: I is initialized to E outside the loop and as soon as action j is selected, j is removed from I. (Obviously, if j is not present in I, removal of j leaves I unchanged.) Hence, to find a cycle, we have to show that I reduces to the empty set. We first rewrite our scheduler as follows:

```
SCH': do true -> get I from IOE;
                 CP(I): begin
                   I' := I; C' := <>;
                   {Invariant: I ⊆ I' U C'.Chosen}
                   do I' ≠ {} -> Find set of enabled actions E;
                                 Select i from E;
                                 I' := I' - {i};
                                 C' := C' concat (E,i);
                                 Execute action i
                   od
                 end
```

{T = C'}

od

We say that CP(I) terminates with T if the auxiliary variable C' has the value T on termination.

Def 3.6: TerSeq = {T | CP(I) terminates with T for I ∈ IOE}

The following lemma states that if we prove termination of the program CP(I) for all I in IOE, we have found all cycles.

Lemma 3.7: TerSeq = Cycles.

Proof:

(TerSeq ⊆ Cycles)

Assume there exists some I in IOE such that CP(I) terminates with T. We must show that T is a minimal I-sequence. Since I ⊆ I' U C'.Chosen is the invariant and on termination I' = {}, I ⊆ T.Chosen and hence T is an I-sequence. T is also minimal, because, if for some prefix T' of T, I ⊆ T'.Chosen, CP(I) would terminate with T', contradicting our assumption.

(Cycles ⊆ TerSeq)

Let M be a minimal I-sequence for some I ∈ IOE, and let CP(I) terminate with T. All elements M_i in M such that M_i.Chosen ∈ I are in T since I ⊆ T.Chosen. All other elements of M also are members of sequences in ChoiceSequences, so we can find some execution of "Select i from E" and "Execute action i" generating these elements in the same order as M. In that case, T is the same as M and M ∈ TerSeq.

QED.

Def 3.8: FairSequences = {C | C ∈ ChoiceSequences and

$\forall a \in A.\ (\forall m. \exists n > m.\ a \in C_n.\text{Enabled})$

$\Longrightarrow (\forall m. \exists n > m.\ a = C_n.\text{Chosen})$

where m and n are natural numbers which index C.

The following theorem states that cyclic sequences are exactly the same as fair choice sequences. This leads to the main contribution of the paper, because once we prove the existence of cycles for all I in IOE, we have proved the scheduler to be fair.

Theorem 3.9: CyclicSequences = FairSequences.

Proof:

(CyclicSequences $\subseteq$ FairSequences)

A cyclic sequence is an infinite concatenation of minimal I-sequences (from some I in IOE), in each of which every action in I is chosen. Thus all actions in I are chosen infinitely often. Since this is proved for all I in IOE, all actions enabled infinitely often are also chosen infinitely often, and the choice sequence is fair.

(FairSequences $\subseteq$ CyclicSequences)

Consider a fair infinite choice sequence F. Let C be the sequence obtained from F by omitting all elements F_m for which F_m.Enabled is not in IOE; that is, F_m.Enabled occurs only finitely many times in F. Clearly, C is fair.

Further, F is a cyclic sequence if and only if C is. This is because, given I in IOE, in a cycle each action in I is chosen at least once. Any number of actions not in I can be chosen within the cycle. Hence, we only need to show that C $\in$ CyclicSequences.

Consider I in IOE. By the definition of fairness, if C is fair,

$$\forall a \in I.\ (\forall m. \exists n > m.\ a = C_n.\text{Chosen})$$

In particular, for all m, we can find the first n such that C_n has action a as the chosen action. That is,

$$\forall a \in I.\ (\forall m. \exists n > m.\ (a = C_n.\text{Chosen and } \forall k.\ m \leq k < n.\ a \neq C_k.\text{Chosen}))$$

Hence we can write C as M concat C', where M satisfies

$$\forall a \in I.\ \exists n. (a = M_n.\text{Chosen and } \forall k: k < n.\ a \neq M_k.\text{Chosen})$$

It can be easily shown that M is a cycle and since C' is also fair, and has elements from IOE, the same analysis applies -- that is, C' is in CyclicSequences and thus C $\in$ CyclicSequences.

QED.

4. Infinitely often enabled actions

We have all along assumed that the set IOE of infinitely often enabled actions is given. A pertinent question would be to ask how such a set can be found. Further, why is it worthwhile to analyze enabling at all?

Consider the following scheduler:

Example 4.0: Partial-to-j scheduler, $0 \leq j \leq n$.

```
PJ: i := 0;
    do j enabled     -> Execute action j
    □ j not enabled -> if i = j then i := (i+1) mod (n+1);
                       Execute action i;
                       i := (i+1) mod (n+1)
    od
```

Obviously, if j is continuously enabled and there is another action k which is infinitely often enabled, scheduler PJ is unfair to k. However, if j is infinitely often enabled as well as infinitely often disabled, PJ can be a fair scheduler. Thus, in different _choice environments_ (which determine enabling and disabling of actions), a scheduler may be fair or unfair.

In general, execution of an action may enable another action (adding it to E), disable an action (removing it from E), or ignore an action (neither adding nor removing it). This can in fact be generalized to sets of actions and we can analyze conspiracies among actions.

In order to study this problem, we consider a system which presents choices to the scheduler as a program in a programming language.

$$GC \equiv A_0 \; \Box \; A_1 \; \Box \; \dots \; \Box \; A_n,$$

where $A_i \equiv g_i \rightarrow S_i, \; 0 \le i \le n.$

We use $\wedge g_i$ to stand for $g_0 \wedge \dots \wedge g_n$,
$\vee g_i$ for $g_0 \vee \dots \vee g_n$,
and $\Box \; g_i \rightarrow S_i$ to denote $g_0 \rightarrow S_0 \; \Box \; \dots \; \Box \; g_n \rightarrow S_n$.

"$\Box$" is Dijkstra's nondeterministic selection operator; it is used to represent choice. The g_i's are called _guards_ and the A_i's (guarded) actions. A guard is enabled if it evaluates to true. We use X,Y,... to represent arbitrary conjunctions of guards. (If $X \equiv g_i \wedge g_j \wedge g_k$, X is enabled means that all three guards i,j and k are enabled.) For simplicity, we assume that each guarded action S_i is deterministic.

We use GC^m to stand for GC repeated m times (GC;...;GC m times). Since we require that the guards be enabled infinitely often, we ensure that $\vee g_i$ holds always, and that the guarded actions are all terminating. We now need to consider only finite, but unbounded repetitions of GC to determine infinitely often enabled actions. Thus, the base language for our proof system only has programs from GC^*, i.e. programs GC^m, for any $m \ge 0$.

Base language and proof system

Once the actions are given as programs, in order to show that each action terminates, we can use a logic of programs with total correctness assertions. A proof system can be used to show whether a guard is infinitely often enabled or not. Note that this is a semantic notion and cannot be analysed syntactically.

Language:

S ::= skip, v:=f, S1;S2, if b then S1 else S2 fi,
while b do S od

GC ::= $\Box \; g_i \rightarrow S_i$

RGC ::= GC^*

Proof rules are given in the usual form of correctness formulae {p} S {q} in a total correctness Hoare logic H. p and q are assertions from some suitably-defined assertion language. By H |- {p} S {q}, we mean that the correctness formula {p} S {q} can be derived using the axioms and inference rules in H. Validity is defined in terms of a model: by M |= {p} S {q}, we mean that the correctness triple is valid in the model M. We shall usually leave H and M implicit, but it should be noted that validity is implied only with respect to a specific model.

The language represented by the class S is that of while programs. [Apt 80] has given a sound and complete total correctness proof system for while programs, as follows:

<u>Proof system H0</u>:

Axiom 0: Skip.

```
{p} skip {p}
```

Axiom 1: Assignment.

```
{p[f/v]} v:=f {p}
```

Rule 2: Composition.

```
{p} S1 {q}, {q} S2 {r}
----------------------
     {p} S1;S2 {r}
```

Rule 3: If-then-else.

```
{p /\ g} S1 {q}, {p /\ ~g} S2 {q}
---------------------------------
{p} if g then S1 else S2 fi {q}
```

Rule 4: While. Let p(m) be an assertion with a free variable m which does not appear in S and ranges over natural numbers.

```
p(m+1) ==> g, {p(m+1)} S {p(m)}, p(0) ==> ~g
--------------------------------------------
      {∃m.p(m)} while g do S od {p(0)}
```

Rule 5: Consequence.

$$\frac{p \Longrightarrow p',\ \{p'\}\ S\ \{q'\},\ q' \Longrightarrow q}{\{p\}\ S\ \{q\}}$$

Proposition [Harel 79]. H0 is arithmetically sound and arithmetically complete.

We extend H0 to the proof system H1 by adding the following rule:

Rule 6: Box.

$$\frac{p \Longrightarrow \bigvee g_i,\ \{p \wedge g_i\}\ S_i\ \{q\},\ \text{for all } i}{\{p\}\ \Box\ g_i \rightarrow S_i\ \{q\}}$$

Proposition [Apt 84]. H1 is arithmetically sound and arithmetically complete.

Enabling and disabling

Having established the above framework, we can now represent the enabling and disabling of guards as correctness formulae within Hoare logic, and use the above proof rules to find the actions that are infinitely often enabled. We proceed as follows.

Let PI be a given invariant. That is, {PI} GC {PI} has been proved.

Def 4.1: Enabling.

i enables j $= \ \models \{PI \wedge g_i\}\ S_i\ \{PI \wedge g_j\}$

(X,i) enables j $= \ \models \{PI \wedge X\}\ S_i\ \{PI \wedge g_j\}$

(X,i) enables Y $= \forall j\!: Y \Longrightarrow g_j.$ (X,i) enables j

X enables Y $= \forall i\!: X \Longrightarrow g_i.$ (X,i) enables Y

Def 4.2: Eventual Enabling.

X eventually enables Y = X enables Y or
(for some Z, X enables Z and
Z eventually enables Y)

Lemma 4.3: X eventually enables Y

$$\text{iff } \exists m > 0.\ \models \{PI \wedge X\}\ GC^m\ \{PI \wedge Y\}$$

Proof: By expanding the definition and using the Sequencing rule.

Def 4.4: IOE = {X | X eventually enables X}

This curious definition is explained by the following lemma.

Lemma 4.5: For any X in IOE,

$$\forall m \geq 0.\ \exists n > m.\ \models \{PI \wedge X\}\ GC^n\ \{PI \wedge X\}$$

Proof: X eventually enables X. That is, X eventually enables X, which eventually enables X, which ... and so on. Using Lemma 4.3, the result can easily be seen.
QED.

Note that such a definition of IOE includes a set of infinitely often enabled actions as well as a set of infinitely often simultaneously enabled actions. For example, if we had only two guards g_i and g_j, IOE is {{i}, {j}} when i and j are infinitely often enabled by themselves, whereas IOE is {{i,j}} wnen they are infinitely often enabled as a group.

Now, if we can find out all those enabled actions which eventually enable themselves, we can generate IOE. However, this is not so easy.

Example 4.6:

```
GC:     g0: v ≤ 0          -> v := 40
     □  g1: 0 < v ≤ 30     -> v := v-1
     □  g2: 30 < v ≤ 40    -> v := v-1
     □  g3: v > 40         -> v := -v
```

Consider GC^* with PI $\equiv$ true. Showing that g_0 eventually enables itself requires careful analysis of the execution sequence of the program. We have to prove that g_0 does not enable itself, but enables g_2; g_2 eventually enables g_1 and g_1 eventually enables g_0.

We adopt the complementary notion of starting with all possible subsets of actions P(A) and removing from it all actions which will not eventually enable themselves. This complementary notion is the one of an action <u>disabling</u> another <u>forever</u>.

<u>Def 4.7</u>: Disabling.

$$\text{i disables j} \;=\; \models \{PI \wedge g_i\}\; S_i\; \{Pi \wedge \sim g_j\}$$

<u>Def 4.8</u>: Disabling Forever.

i disables j forever

$$= \forall m \geq 0.\; \models \{PI \wedge g_i\}\; S_i;GC^m\; \{PI \wedge \sim g_j\}$$

Next, we ensure that the complementarity that we require actually holds.

<u>Lemma 4.9</u>: For any i,j, exactly one of the conditions below may hold:
(i) i eventually enables j,
(ii) i disables j forever.

<u>Proof</u>: Using Lemma 4.3 and the completeness of the Box-rule, we can show that (i) leads to

$$(*) \qquad \text{For some } m \geq 0,\; \models \{PI \wedge g_i\}\; S_i;GC^m\; \{PI \wedge g_j\}.$$

On the other hand, by Def 4.8, (ii) yields

$$(**) \qquad \forall m \geq 0.\; \models \{PI \wedge g_i\}\; S_i;GC^m\; \{PI \wedge \sim g_j\}.$$

Clearly, (*) and (**) contradict each other. Further, for a given m > 0, at least one of

$$\models \{PI \wedge g_i\}\; S_i;GC^m\; \{PI \wedge g_j\}$$

and

$$\models \{PI \wedge g_i\}\; S_i;GC^m\; \{PI \wedge \sim g_j\}$$

must hold. Therefore, exactly one of (i) and (ii) must be true.
QED.

To be able to use the complementary notion, we need some simple way of showing that i disables j forever. The following theorem shows that we can find a condition q that is maintained invariant after the execution of S_i, such that j remains disabled all the time.

<u>Theorem 4.10</u>: For any i,j, i disables j forever iff
for some q such that $\models \{PI \wedge g_i\}\ S_i\ \{q\}$,
$\models \{q\}\ GC\ \{q\}$,
we have $q \Rightarrow PI \wedge \sim gj$.

<u>Proof</u>:
<==. Given q, using the Sequencing and Consequence rules, Def 4.8 can be easily satisfied.

==>. Assume the contrary. Then we have

(1) i disables j forever;
(2) $\models \{PI \wedge g_i\}\ S_i\ \{q\}$, $\{q\}\ GC\ \{q\}$;
(3) $\sim(q \Rightarrow PI \wedge \sim g_j)$, i.e. $q \wedge (\sim PI \vee g_j)$.

Using the Sequencing and Consequence rules in conjunction with (2), we can show that, for some m,

$$\{PI \wedge g_i\}\ S_i;GC^m\ \{q\}.$$

Since PI is invariant, (3) is true after $S_i;GC^m$ only if g_j holds, i.e.

For some m, $\models \{PI \wedge g_i\}\ S_i;GC^m\ \{PI \wedge g_j\}$

From Lemma 4.3, i eventually enables j. This contradicts (1) by Lemma 4.9.
QED.

<u>Example 4.11</u>:

GC: g_0: $v \leq 0$ -> v := 40
□ g_1: $0 < v \leq 30$ -> v := v-1
□ g_2: $30 < v \leq 40$ -> if v > 36 then v := v-1
else skip
□ g_3: $v = 31$ -> v := -v
□ g_4: $v > 40$ -> v := -v

Once again, we can use $PI \equiv true$. Clearly, 0 disables 0, 1, 3 and 4. In fact, if we use $q \equiv 36 \leq v \leq 40$ in Theorem 4.10, we can see that 0 disables all these guards forever.

Actually, if $Y \equiv \wedge j: \sim g_j$ such that i disables j forever, PI /\ Y will satisfy all the conditions for g. In this example,

$$PI \wedge Y = true \wedge \sim(v \leq 0) \wedge \sim(0 < v \leq 30) \wedge \sim(v = 31) \wedge \sim(v > 40)$$
$$\Longleftrightarrow 32 \leq v \leq 40$$

is also invariant after execution of v := 40.

To generate IOE, we proceed as follows: for any pair of actions i and j, check if i disables j. If it does, further check if i disables j forever. Now any set of actions containing i as well as j cannot be infinitely often enabled, so it will not be in IOE. Starting with P(A) and removing sets of actions in this way, we can obtain IOE.

Def 4.12: IDJ = $\{X \mid \exists i,j: X \Rightarrow (g_i \wedge g_j).$ i disables j forever$\}$

Theorem 4.13: IOE = P(A) - IDJ.

Proof: We know that IOE $\subseteq$ P(A). Consider the set P(A) - IOE. It will consist of all X such that X does not eventually enable X. By Lemma 4.9, X therefore disables X forever. This means that there is at least one j such that X ==> g_j and X disables j forever. That is, there exists an i such that X ==> g_i and i disables j forever. X must therefore belong to IDJ. Hence, IDJ = P(A) - IOE.
QED.

Hence by analyzing the guarded command program, we can find the set of infinitely often enabled actions and check that the scheduler is fair for them by proving the existence of cycles. Although we have used guarded commands and the proof system H1 to analyze enabling and disabling of guards, this is only to generate IOE; proving cycles can be performed independently. For a different choice environment (or even for the same one!), a different proof system can be employed to generate IOE.

5. Conclusion

The proof technique presented in the paper considers a scheduler in the abstract setting of a choice environment. Once the scheduler is proved to be fair, analysis of the system which generates these choices can exploit fairness assumptions. We show that though scheduler fairness can be proved without reference to the system in which it is embedded, it is useful to analyze enabling and disabling to discover conspiracies among actions. Thus, as fairness assumptions about the scheduler can be used to prove properties of the scheduled programs, assumptions about the behaviour of the program can be used in proofs of scheduler fairness.

Several papers [Lehmann et al 81; Grumberg et al 81; Apt & Olderog 83; Apt et al 84] have studied the issue of fair termination -- i.e., using fairness assumptions to prove the total correctness of nondeterministic programs. Our approach is complementary: we consider the scheduler explicitly and analyze its fairness, whereas these papers consider the source program and assuming fairness, prove properties such as its termination (by adding random assignments to the source program, or by associating well-founded orderings with actions).

[Lehmann & Rabin 81] discusses several fairness-related issues in the framework of the Dining Philosophers problem. [Mahadevan & Shyamasundar 82], in a similar setting, use a notion of conspiracy-freedom to give a proof rule for fairness in distributed systems. The idea of finding cycles can be applied to such situations, as well as to notions like k-fairness [Best 84]. Using cycles to prove fairness of schedulers is only one application of the more general paradigm of using cycles to prove properties of nonterminating programs. It should be possible for other properties to be proved in this manner.

Acknowledgements

It is our pleasure to acknowledge the help of Paritosh Pandya -- we thank him for the time and energy he devoted to debating various issues with us. We thank Mathai Joseph for encouragement and

P.S.Thiagarajan for insightful remarks. RR thanks Pierpaolo Degano of Pisa University for inspiring discussions on the subject of cycles.

References

K R Apt: Ten years of Hoare's logic: a survey -- Part I, ACM TOPLAS 3 (4) (Oct 1981) 431-483.

K R Apt: Ten years of Hoare logic: a survey -- Part II: Nondeterminism, TCS 28 (1/2) (1984) 83-109.

K R Apt, E-R Olderog: Proof rules and transformations dealing with fairness, SCP 3 (1) (1983) 65-100.

K R Apt, A Pnueli, J Stavi: Fair termination revisited -- with delay, TCS 33 (1) (1984) 65-84.

E Best: Fairness and conspiracy, IPL 18 (4) (1984) 215-220; Erratum, IPL 19 (3) (1984) 162.

O Grumberg, N Francez, J A Makowsky, W P de Roever: A proof rule for fair termination of guarded commands, Proc. Intl. Symp. Algorithmic languages (North-Holland, 1981) 339-416.

D Harel: First-order dynamic logic, LNCS 68 (Springer, 1979).

D Lehmann, A Pnueli, J Stavi: Impartiality, justice and fairness: the ethics of concurrent termination, Proc. 8th ICALP, Akko, LNCS 115 (Springer, 1981) 246-277.

D Lehmann, M O Rabin: On the advantages of free choice: a fully distributed symmetric solution to the dining philosophers' problem, Proc. 8th POPL, Williamsburg (ACM, 1981).

S Mahadevan, R K Shyamasundar: On the fairness of distributed programs, Proc. 2nd FST&TCS, Bangalore, (NCSDCT, TIFR, 1982) 171-191.

THE REASONING POWERS OF BURSTALL'S (MODAL LOGIC) AND PNUELI'S (TEMPORAL LOGIC) PROGRAM VERIFICATION METHODS

(An application of model theory)

I. Sain
Math. Inst. of the Hungar. Acad. of Sci.
Budapest 1364, PF.127, Hungary

In this paper we are looking into a problem originally raised in Burstall's pioneering paper [5] in 1974. This problem concerns the various celebrated program verification methods like Floyd's method, the so called Intermittent Assertion Method (which we shall call here Burstall's method), the Manna-Cooper method (see [22]), Pnueli's temporal logics of programs*/ etc. From now on, we shall refer to these (and similar) formal systems as "famous program verification methods". The original problem was twofold, see items (1), (2) below.

(1) Find explicit characterizations of the program verifying powers of the various famous program verification methods in terms of classical first order logic (many sorted logic is included for obvious reasons). Such a characterization should be simple and mathematically transparent.

(2) Compare the program verifying powers of the various famous methods.

These problems were reformulated later several times, see e.g. Richter-Szabo [17] , Németi [15] , or Pasztor [24,25] .

What are Burstall's reasons to ask these problems (1) and (2) ? A reason he gave in [5] was to obtain deeper insight into and "clarify the nature of (these methods and) special logics designed for reasoning about programs". A further reason was supplied during a discussion in Edinburgh (1974) which concerned the possible improvements of the program verifyer produced by Németi's group, see [1] . The conclusion of the debate (probably summarized by Pat Hayes) was that, in order to decide what kind of theorem-prover is needed to back up a system using a certain program verification method, one should know the amount of information implicitely contained in that particular method. In other words, the answer to Problem(1) above might be rather relevant for making decisions during the design and implementation process. (It is not at all obvious that the stronger method is the better, all depends

*/ Well, it wasn't around in 74 but it is so important now that we should not leave it off the list. Anyway, Burstall's original problem went through some transformations lately, see e.g. [15] .

on the concrete situation when the decision is made, e.g. if we do not want to use an extremely powerful theorem prover then a weaker method might be preferable.)

Herein we shall answer Problem(1) both within and without the framework suggested in [15]. This time, we shall concentrate on Burstall's and Pnueli's methods and on provability of partial correctness (but we shall consider and indicate the statuses of other ones, too).

What do we mean by writing that a part of our answer to these problems will be done in the framework of [15] ? Well, [15] made a rather concrete suggestion to attack (1) by suggesting to characterize all program verification methods in a single many-sorted (classical first order) logic called Nonstandard Dynamic Logic (NDL from now on) the main sorts of which were the time scale T and the data domain D .*/ The characterization of a fixed program verification method, say $\vdash^{F}$, consists of finding a set Ax of (first order) formulas of the many-sorted language NDL and proving that a program property is provable by $\vdash^{F}$ iff it follows from Ax in the framework of NDL. An example for such a characterization of Floyd's method $\vdash^{F}$ is Csirmaz's theorem saying that partial correctness of any program is Floyd provable iff it follows from the axiom system Iq of NDL (see [6] or [3] Thm 9). Iq is a restricted T-induction. More precisely, recall that T has a distinguished element $0 \in T$ and a nexttime function or successor $suc : T \longrightarrow T$. Now, for <u>any</u> formula $\gamma(z)$ of NDL, the full induction schema **Ind** postulates

$$(\gamma(0) \wedge (\forall z \in T)[\gamma(z) \rightarrow \gamma(suc\ z)]) \rightarrow (\forall z \in T)\gamma(z) .$$

Clearly this **Ind** is the strongest possible many-sorted induction on the time structure T . (Note that γ may contain statements about the data structure D and other things as well and not only statements about T .) Well, Iq$\subset$**Ind** is a rather restricted subset of **Ind** . The definition of Iq is rather clean: Iq postulates induction for exactly those formulas $\gamma(z)$ of NDL which contain no quantifier of sort T . A similar characterization of Burstall's modal logic method**/ $\vdash^{Bur}$ was attempted in [15] but the mathematical transparency of

*/ Before going into further details, we want to mention that Sec 4 of Richter-Szabo [17], and [25] are introductions to the NDL approach (and related ones) to Burstall's Problems (1),(2) quoted here, as well as to related problems. Those introductions are superior to the (NDL part of the) present one in several ways, e.g. they are broader in scope and are really easy to understand for the outsider. They are pleasant armchair readings even for those not familiar with logic.

**/ This method was independently discovered in [1] in 1974, too.

the characterization was less than that of Iq . Well, in [15] another set Imd of induction axioms was singled out with the property $Iq \subset Imd \subset \mathbf{Ind}$. It was proved then that Burstall's method is equivalent with Imd w.r.t. partial correctness, in symbols $\overset{Bur}{\vdash} \equiv_{\Box} (Imd\overset{N}{\vdash})$. To explain this notation, we note that the above characterization of Floyd's method ($\overset{F}{\vdash}$) in this notation reads as $\overset{F}{\vdash} \equiv_{\Box} (Iq\overset{N}{\vdash})$. (The subscript $\Box$ of the equivalence sign $\equiv$ refers to partial correctness, and in $(Ax\overset{N}{\vdash})$ the $\overset{N}{\vdash}$ part indicates that Ax is used in the framework of NDL. Occasionally we write Ax instead of $(Ax\overset{N}{\vdash})$ for simplicity.)

Here we try to improve the characterization $\overset{Bur}{\vdash} \equiv_{\Box} (Imd\overset{N}{\vdash})$ given in [15] in two directions:

(i) we try to be more careful in recalling Burstall's original method (to ensure faithfulness of the characterization, i.e. to ensure that what we characterize is really Burstall's method), and

(ii) we prove $\overset{Bur}{\vdash} \equiv_{\Box} (\mathbf{Ind}\overset{N}{\vdash})$ (to satisfy the requirement of simplicity of characterization in the formulation of Problem(1) above).

About (i), see Preliminaries of the present paper. Concerning (ii), there are further questions about characterization. Namely, M.E.Szabo [23] raised the problem of sharpness of a characterization. This question asks, roughly, what happens if we add (or remove) a few axioms from the set of axioms characterizing the method under investigation. For example, consider the single axiom Tsuc $(\forall z,z_1 \in T)(\text{ suc } z = \text{suc } z_1 \rightarrow z=z_1)$ saying that the nexttime (or successor) function is one-one on the time structure T . What happens if we add Tsuc to **Ind** ? Will then $\overset{Bur}{\vdash} \equiv_{\Box} (\mathbf{Ind}+Tsuc\overset{N}{\vdash})$ or $\overset{Bur}{\vdash} \equiv_{\Box} (Imd+Tsuc\overset{N}{\vdash})$ or $\overset{F}{\vdash} \equiv_{\Box} (Iq+Tsuc\overset{N}{\vdash})$ remain still true ? Well, the answer is no for the first one, and yes for the second two.

Let's make a small detour here. This answer might look like a contradiction since it implies $(Imd+Tsuc) \equiv_{\Box} Imd \equiv_{\Box} \mathbf{Ind} \not\equiv_{\Box} (\mathbf{Ind}+Tsuc)$. This is not a contradiction, because our equivalence $\equiv_{\Box}$ is only modulo provability of partial correctness statements (and not all formulas). (Actually, it would be meaningless to compare these systems from the point of view of provability of all formulas since Burstall's language may have fewer formulas than NDL.) Comparing axiom systems w.r.t. provability of special formulas is not new in logic at all, such are e.g. the equiconsistency investigations in set theory, where the set of special formulas is {FALSE} . The methodology of dealing with such situations already exists in logic (especially in set theory) and is built around the so called transfer principles. Borrowing from this area, we elaborated our own transfer principles (in this and related papers).

Let us return to the contrasting results Imd $\equiv_{\Box}$ (Imd+Tsuc) and **Ind** $\not\equiv_{\Box}$ (**Ind**+Tsuc). The second one has implications for Burstall's original method (in its original form). Namely, if we replace the modality sometime γ with "two times γ" then we can prove more programs correct. It remains an open problem to decide whether "three times γ" is even more powerful or not. About the first statement (the positive one) we shall prove something much stroger here. Namely we shall prove Imd $\equiv_{\Box}$ (Imd+Th($\langle\omega,0,suc,\leq,+,\cdot\rangle$) for time). To be able to appreciate this, we note that Pnueli's temporal logic of programs $\vdash^{Pnu}$ is much stronger than $\vdash^{Bur}$ (see[18,19]) and in [19] we prove that $\vdash^{Pnu}$ $\equiv_{\Box}$ (**Ind**+Time is linearly ordered$\vdash^{N}$). So, as far as responsiveness to additional time axioms goes, the gap between Imd and **Ind** is big. Coming back to the problem of characterizing $\vdash^{Bur}$, the above result means $\vdash^{Bur}$ $\equiv_{\Box}$ (Imd+Time is linearly ordered$\vdash^{N}$). A further axiom system I1 was suggested in [15] for the purpose of characterizing $\vdash^{Bur}$. Well, I1$\leq$**Ind** is induction on those formulas of NDL which contain at most one variable of sort time (T). Thus Iq$\subset$I1$\subset$**Ind**. The problem was raised in [15] whether I1 is equivalent with $\vdash^{Bur}$. We solve this problem affirmatively herein.

Summing up our characterization of Burstall's method, it says: $\vdash^{Bur}$ $\equiv_{\Box}$ **Ind** $\equiv_{\Box}$ I1 $\equiv_{\Box}$ Imd $\equiv_{\Box}$ (Imd+Time is linearly ordered) and $\vdash^{F}$ $<_{\Box}$ $\vdash^{Bur}$ $<_{\Box}$ (**Ind**+Tsuc$\vdash^{N}$).

Independently of the above outlined NDL approach, we also give a <u>direct</u> characterization of the program verifying power of Burstall's method $\vdash^{Bur}$. (See the results concerning the relational semantics $\models^{R}$ of $\vdash^{Bur}$, e.g. Thm 1a(ii), Lemma 1.1(ii), Lemma 2.1(ii).) This intends to be an answer to Problem(1) complementary to the NDL oriented answers. It intends to provide further insight into the nature of $\vdash^{Bur}$ and related temporal logic (and/or modal logic) based program verification methods. We do the same for Pnueli's $\vdash^{Pnu}$ as well.

<u>Concerning Problem(2)</u> quoted at the beginning of this introduction, we note the following: Most of the results here concerning (2) are indirect, via the lattice of program verification methods as described in [15]. However, several of the problems raised in [15] concerning the lattice of program verification methods are solved herein. Problem 1 therein (immediately after Figure 2) receives an affirmative answer (the proof of this solution is in [19]). The answers to problems raised on Figure 2 of [15] will be summed up in Appendix of the present paper.

A sharpening of the characterizations of $\models^{Bur}$ and Pnueli's temporal logic of programs is given in [21]. Many of the results there concern the Σ_n-fragments of these logics. (In the Σ_n-fragment of $\models^{Bur}$ we do not allow deeper nesting of the modality Sometime than n. For example, the formula Sometime($\varphi \wedge$ Sometime ψ) is not Σ_1 but only Σ_2 (well, it is Σ_2 only if Sometime does not occur in φ and ψ).) Cf. also [8].

All the investigations here are carried through for Floyd's method, too, and not only for Burstall's method $\models^{Bur}$ (cf. Remark 1). Moreover, herein we carry through the same investigations for Pnueli's future-enriched method $\models^{Pnu}$ as well.

PRELIMINARIES

In this paper we use the notation of [15], and additional notation introduced here. However, here we shall recall some definitions from [15], too.

Let $n \in \omega$, let A be an arbitrary set, and let $h^0, \ldots, h^{n-1}$ be functions with $Dom(h^0) = \ldots = Dom(h^{n-1}) = A$. Then
$\{h^0_i, h^1_i, \ldots, h^{n-1}_i : i \in A\} := \{h^j_i : j < n \text{ and } i \in A\}$.
E.g. $\{f_i, g_i : i < 2\} = \{f_0, f_1, g_0, g_1\}$.

Let γ be a formula and τ be a term. Then $\gamma(z/\tau)$ denotes the formula obtained from γ by replacing every free occurrence of z in γ by τ. Instead of $\gamma(z/\tau)$ we shall write $\gamma(\tau)$ if the context makes clear which variable is replaced by τ in γ. If $\tau_0, \ldots, \tau_{n-1}$ are terms and $\bar{z} \in {}^nZ$ then $\gamma(\bar{z}_i/\tau_i : i<n)$ denotes the formula obtained from γ such that for every $i<n$, we replace every free occurrence of $\bar{z}_i$ in γ by τ_i simultaneously.

Instead of z_0, x_0, y_0 we shall often write z, x, y resp.

$ext(y_i, z_j)$ will often be abbreviated as $y_i(z_j)$.

Throughout the paper, d denotes an arbitrary but fixed similarity type. Recall from [15] Def.1 that d is defined to be a pair $\langle d_0, d_1 \rangle$ where d_0 is a set (called the set of function symbols) and d_1 is a function $d_1 : Dom(d_1) \longrightarrow \omega$ such that $d_0 \subseteq Dom(d_1)$ and $(\forall r \in Dom(d_1))\, d_1(r) > 0$. Intuitively, the function d_1 correlates arities (natural numbers) to function and relation symbols contained in $Dom(d_1)$. We shall often write d(r) instead of $d_1(r)$. If d' is a similarity type such that $d'_1 \subseteq d_1$ and $d'_0 \cap Dom(d_1) \subseteq d_0$ then we say that d' is a sub-similarity type of d and we write (ambiguously) that $d' \subseteq d$.

Recall the definitions of $ind(\gamma, z_i)$ and **Ind** from [15] Def.14: Let $\gamma \in F_{td}$ and $i \in \omega$. Then

$$ind(\gamma, z_i) := [(\gamma(0) \wedge \forall z_i[\gamma \rightarrow \gamma(\text{suc } z_i)]) \rightarrow \forall z_i \gamma] .$$

$$\textbf{Ind} := \{ ind(\gamma, z_i) : \gamma \in F_{td} \text{ and } i \in \omega \} .$$

Note that **Ind** was denoted by Ia in [15].

Recall that the sets $Ict \subseteq Iq$ and I1 of induction axioms were defined in [15]Def.15. Recall from [15]Def.16 that the set of time-axioms Tord is defined as follows:

$$Tord := \{ z \leq z_1 \leq z_2 \rightarrow z \leq z_2,\ z \leq z_1 \leq z \rightarrow z_1 = z,\ z \leq z_1 \vee z_1 \leq z,\ 0 \leq z,$$
$$z \neq z_1 \leq z \leftrightarrow \text{suc } z_1 \leq z,\ 0 = z \vee \exists z_1(z = \text{suc } z_1) \} \subseteq F_t .$$

As we indicated in the introduction, in this paper we concentrate on two famous (endogenous) program verification methods <u>based on multimodal logics</u>. We denote them by $\vdash^{Bur}$ and $\vdash^{Pnu}$, and call them Burstall's method and Pnueli's method respectively. We shall define an additional method $\vdash^{Fum}$ (based on multimodal logic), which will turn out to be equivalent to $\vdash^{Pnu}$ modulo $\equiv_{\square}$.

<u>DEFINITION 0.1</u> (<u>Syntaxes</u> of the languages of $\vdash^{Bur}$, $\vdash^{Pnu}$, and $\vdash^{Fum}$)
Let d be an arbitrary but fixed similarity type.

<u>(i)</u> ([15]Def.18(i)) The set T_d^{mod} of <u>modal dynamic terms</u> of type d is defined to be the smallest set satisfying (1) and (2) below.

(1) $\{ x_i , y_i : i \in \omega \} \subseteq T_d^{mod}$.

(2) $\{ f(\tau_1, \ldots, \tau_k) : f \in d_0 , d_1(f) = k+1 , \{\tau_1, \ldots, \tau_k\} \subseteq T_d^{mod} \} \subseteq T_d^{mod}$.

<u>(ii)</u> The set F_d^{Fum} of modal formulas is defined to be the smallest set satisfying conditions (3) - (5) below.

(3) $\{ (\tau = \sigma) : \tau, \sigma \in T_d^{mod} \} \subseteq F_d^{Fum}$.

(4) $\{ R(\tau_1, \ldots, \tau_k) : R \in (Dom(d_1) \sim d_0) , d_1(R) = k , \{\tau_1, \ldots, \tau_k\} \subseteq T_d^{mod} \} \subseteq F_d^{Fum}$.

(5) $\{ Alw\gamma, Fst\gamma, Nxt\gamma, Afu\gamma, Apa\gamma, \exists x_i\gamma, \neg\gamma, (\gamma \wedge \delta) : i \in \omega , \gamma, \delta \in F_d^{Fum} \}$
$\subseteq F_d^{Fum}$.

<u>(iii)</u> The definitions of F_d^{Pnu} and F_d^{Bur} can be obtained from the definition of F_d^{Fum} by <u>omitting</u> Apa , and both Apa and Afu respectively, from condition (5) above, and by substituting F_d^{Fum} with F_d^{Pnu} and F_d^{Bur} resp. Thus $F_d^{Bur} \subset F_d^{Pnu} \subset F_d^{Fum}$. □□□

F_d^{Bur}, F_d^{Pnu}, and F_d^{Fum} are the sets of formulas used in methods $\models^{Bur}$, $\models^{Pnu}$, and $\models^{Fum}$ respectively. The modalities Alw, Fst, Nxt, Afu, Apa are called "Always", "First", "Next", "Always in the future", and "Always in the past" respectively. We shall also use the duals of Alw, Afu, Apa : Stm ("Sometime"), Sfu ("Sometime in the future"), and Spa ("Sometime in the past") are defined by $\mathrm{Stm}\,\gamma := \neg\mathrm{Alw}\neg\gamma$ etc.

<u>DEFINITION 0.2</u> <u>(i)</u> Let $\gamma \in F_d^{Fum}$. Then

$\mathrm{ind}^{Bur}(\gamma) := ([\mathrm{Fst}\,\gamma \wedge \mathrm{Alw}(\gamma \rightarrow \mathrm{Nxt}\,\gamma)] \rightarrow \mathrm{Alw}\,\gamma)$ and

$\mathrm{ind}^{Fum}(\gamma) := ([\gamma \wedge \mathrm{Afu}(\gamma \rightarrow \mathrm{Nxt}\,\gamma)] \rightarrow \mathrm{Afu}\,\gamma)$. Further we define

$\mathrm{Ind}_d^{Bur} := \{ \mathrm{ind}^{Bur}(\gamma) : \gamma \in F_d^{Bur} \}$,

$\mathrm{Ind}_d^{Pnu} := \{ \mathrm{ind}^{Fum}(\gamma) : \gamma \in F_d^{Pnu} \}$, and

$\mathrm{Ind}_d^{Fum} := \{ \mathrm{ind}^{Fum}(\gamma) : \gamma \in F_d^{Fum} \}$.

We shall usually omit the subscripts d from Ind_d^{Bur} etc.

<u>(ii)</u> We define 2 sets of modal axioms (Tfum was introduced in [15]):

$\mathrm{Tpnu} := \{\mathrm{Afu}\,\gamma \rightarrow \mathrm{Afu}\,\mathrm{Afu}\,\gamma,\ \mathrm{Afu}\,\gamma \rightarrow \mathrm{Nxt}\,\gamma,\ \mathrm{Fst}(\mathrm{Afu}\,\gamma \rightarrow \mathrm{Alw}\,\gamma) : \gamma \in F_d^{Pnu}\}$ and

$\mathrm{Tfum} := \{\mathrm{Fst}(\gamma \leftrightarrow \mathrm{Apa}\,\gamma),\ \gamma \rightarrow (\mathrm{Spa}\,\gamma \wedge \mathrm{Sfu}\,\gamma),\ (\mathrm{Apa}\,\gamma \wedge \mathrm{Afu}\,\gamma) \rightarrow \mathrm{Alw}\,\gamma,$
$\mathrm{Spa}\,\mathrm{Spa}\,\gamma \rightarrow \mathrm{Spa}\,\gamma,\ \mathrm{Nxt}\,\mathrm{Apa}\,\gamma \leftrightarrow (\mathrm{Nxt}\,\gamma \wedge \mathrm{Apa}\,\gamma) : \gamma \in F_d^{Fum}\}$. □□

By now, we are ready to define 3 distinguished temporal logics:

(I) language: F_d^{Bur}, logical axioms: Ind^{Bur}, inference system: that of multimodal logic;

(II) F_d^{Pnu}, (Ind^{Pnu}+Tpnu), same inference system as in (I);

(III) F_d^{Fum}, (Ind^{Fum}+Tfum), same inference system as in (I).

Logics (I) and (II) form the basis for Burstall's method (i.e. Intermittent Assertion Method) and Pnueli's method respectively.

To every program p and output condition ψ, all of these endogenous methods associate a rather natural temporal (or multimodal) formula $\mu(p,\psi)$ expressing the claim that whenever p terminates then ψ holds. We say that $\Box(p,\psi)$ is <u>Burstall-provable</u> (in symbols $\models^{Bur} \Box(p,\psi)$), if $\mu(p,\psi)$ is provable in logic (I). Similarly, $\models^{Pnu} \Box(p,\psi)$ iff $\mu(p,\psi)$ is provable in logic (II). $\models^{Fum}$ is exactly the same in logic (III). If we have a set of axioms $\mathrm{Th} \subseteq F_d$ about our data structures then $\mathrm{Th} \models^{Bur} \Box(p,\psi)$ is defined the natural way from the above. Similarly for $\models^{Pnu}$ and $\models^{Fum}$.

Recall the definition of the translation function $\text{fum} : F_d^{Fum} \longrightarrow DF_d$ from [15] Def.19, which translates the multimodal formulas defined above to dynamic formulas. This way, we provided F_d^{Fum} with a <u>semantics</u>. In [19] we prove that this semantics is equivalent with the usual Kripke-style semantics of F_d^{Fum}. Further the following equivalence theorem is proved in [19] for $\vdash^{Bur}$, $\vdash^{Pnu}$, and $\vdash^{Fum}$. (Roughly speaking, the theorem says that the translation fum is faithful.) Let $\text{Imd} := \{ \text{fum}(\gamma) : \gamma \in \text{Ind}^{Bur} \}$, $\text{Ipn} := \{ \text{fum}(\gamma) : \gamma \in \text{Ind}^{Pnu} \}$, $\text{Ifm} := \{ \text{fum}(\gamma) : \gamma \in \text{Ind}^{Fum} \}$, $\text{Tpn} := \{ \text{fum}(\gamma) : \gamma \in \text{Tpnu} \}$, $\text{Tfm} := \{ \text{fum}(\gamma) : \gamma \in \text{Tfum} \}$.

<u>THEOREM 0</u> (i) $\vdash^{Bur} \equiv_\Box (\text{Imd} \vdash^{N})$

(ii) $\vdash^{Pnu} \equiv_\Box (\text{Ipn+Tpn} \vdash^{N})$

(iii) $\vdash^{Fum} \equiv_\Box (\text{Ifm+Tfm} \vdash^{N})$ □□□

THE RESULTS

Our main theorem is the following:

<u>THEOREM 1</u>

(i) $\vdash^{Pnu} \equiv_\Box \vdash^{Fum} \equiv_\Box (\text{Ipn+Tpn} \vdash^{N}) \equiv_\Box (\mathbf{Ind}\text{+Tord} \vdash^{N})$

(ii) $\vdash^{Bur} \equiv_\Box (\text{Imd} \vdash^{N}) \equiv_\Box (\text{I1} \vdash^{N}) \equiv_\Box (\mathbf{Ind} \vdash^{N}) \equiv_\Box (\text{Imd+Tord} \vdash^{N})$

(iii) $\vdash^{F} \equiv_\Box (\text{Ict} \vdash^{N}) \equiv_\Box (\text{Iq} \vdash^{N}) \equiv_\Box (\text{Ict+Tord} \vdash^{N})$. □□□

Something seems to be funny about Thm 1. Namely, by [18,19] $\vdash^{Pnu} >_\Box \vdash^{Bur}$, hence by (i) and (ii), $(\mathbf{Ind}\text{+Tord}) >_\Box \mathbf{Ind}$ <u>but</u> $\mathbf{Ind} \equiv_\Box \text{Imd} \equiv_\Box (\text{Imd+Tord})$. The explanation is that $\equiv_\Box$ is not simple equivalence, but equivalence w.r.t. program verifying power.

<u>REMARK 1</u> <u>a)</u> Csirmaz [6] proved that $\text{Iq} \equiv_\Box (\text{Iq+Tord})$ and it is proved in Sain [18] that $\mathbf{Ind} <_\Box (\mathbf{Ind}\text{+Tsuc})$. (It is almost sure that $\text{I1} \equiv_\Box (\text{I1+Tord})$ but I had no time to check this.)

<u>b)</u> Thm 1(iii) has already been known, a proof can be found in [3] Thm 9, p.56 ($\vdash^{F} \equiv_\Box \text{Iq} \equiv_\Box (\text{Iq+Tord})$), Thm 12, p.111 ($\text{Ict} \equiv_\Box \text{Iq}$). Our new proof in [27] or [26], however, is a direct simple proof, while the original one used Csirmaz's completeness result on $\vdash^{F}$ ([7]) which had a very difficult proof and Csirmaz's result $(\text{Iq} \vdash^{N}) \equiv_\Box (\text{Iq+Tord} \vdash^{N})$ (see [6]) with a not too easy proof again. □□□

The kind of semantics, which we call "relational semantics", introduced in [7] will be of great use in the proof. In [7] Def.2.2 a kind of relational semantics ($\models^{r}$) is introduced to characterize Floyd's method $\vdash^{F}$ for proving correctness of programs. In the present paper we shall generalize that semantics to give other, similar semantical characterizations ($\models^{R}$ and $\models^{f}$) for Burstall's and Pnueli's modal methods $\vdash^{Bur}$ and $\vdash^{Pnu}$, respectively. The comparison of the three relational semantics ($\models^{r}$, $\models^{R}$, and $\models^{f}$) gives a semantical insight into the difference between the program proving methods $\vdash^{F}$, $\vdash^{Bur}$, and $\vdash^{Pnu}$. Now we turn to defining $\models^{r}$, $\models^{R}$, and $\models^{f}$.

<u>DEFINITION 1</u> (the similarity types $d\{m\}$ and $d[m]$)
Let d be an arbitrary similarity type and let $m\in\omega$.

<u>(i)</u> We extend d with an m-ary relation symbol R , with binary function symbols nex_i , with constant symbols inp_i $(i<m)$, and with a binary relation symbol $\preccurlyeq$. Assume that all the new symbols are different from each other and from the symbols in $Dom(d_1)$. We define

$$d\{m\} := \langle d_0 \cup \{nex_i, inp_i \ : \ i<m\} ,\ d_1 \cup \{\langle R,m\rangle, \langle\preccurlyeq,2\rangle, \langle nex_i,2\rangle, \langle inp_i,1\rangle \ : \ i<m\}\rangle \ , \quad \text{and}$$

$d[m] := \langle (d\{m\})_0 \ , \ (d\{m\})_1 \sim \{\langle\preccurlyeq,2\rangle\}\rangle$. That is, we obtain $d[m]$ from $d\{m\}$ by omitting $\preccurlyeq$ from $d\{m\}$. Thus $d\subset d[m]\subset d\{m\}$.

<u>(ii)</u> Let $\underline{\underline{D}}\in Mod_d$, $R\subseteq {}^mD$, $\overline{nex} : {}^mD \longrightarrow {}^mD$, $\overline{inp}\in {}^mD$, $\preccurlyeq\subseteq({}^2R)$. Then $\langle \underline{\underline{D}}, R, \overline{nex}, \overline{inp}, \preccurlyeq\rangle$ denotes the model of type $d\{m\}$ which we get (the natural way) from $\underline{\underline{D}}$, R, $\overline{nex}$, $\overline{inp}$, $\preccurlyeq$; analogously, $\langle \underline{\underline{D}}, R, \overline{nex}, \overline{inp}\rangle$ denotes the model of type $d[m]$ obtained from $\underline{\underline{D}}$, R, $\overline{nex}$, $\overline{inp}$ only. □□□

<u>DEFINITION 2</u> (indr, Iar, IaR, Iaf)
The induction concerning R, nex, inp : Let γ be a formula (i.e. a string of symbols) and let $\bar{x}\in {}^mX$ be a sequence of variables. Then

$indr(\gamma,\bar{x}) := (\gamma(inp) \wedge (\forall\bar{x}\in R)[\gamma \rightarrow \gamma(nex(\bar{x}))]) \rightarrow (\forall\bar{x}\in R)\gamma$, where $\gamma(inp) := \gamma(\bar{x}_i/inp_i \ : \ i<m)$, $(\forall\bar{x}\in R)\chi := (\forall\bar{x})(R(\bar{x}) \rightarrow \chi)$, and $\gamma(nex(\bar{x})) := \gamma(\bar{x}_i/nex_i(\bar{x}_i) \ : \ i<m)$.

The sets of induction formulas $Iar\subseteq F_{d[m]}$, $IaR\subseteq F_{d[m]}$, and $Iaf\subseteq F_{d\{m\}}$ are defined as follows:

$$Iar := \{ indr(\gamma,\bar{x}) \ : \ \gamma\in F_d \text{ and } \bar{x}\in {}^mX \} \ ,$$

$$IaR := \{ indr(\gamma,\bar{x}) \ : \ \gamma\in F_{d[m]} \text{ and } \bar{x}\in {}^mX \} \ ,$$

$$Iaf := \{ indr(\gamma,\bar{x}) \ : \ \gamma\in F_{d\{m\}} \text{ and } \bar{x}\in {}^mX \} \ .$$

□□□

Many examples for models of Iar , IaR , and Iaf are given in §5 of [27] and in [19].

DEFINITION 3 (the state-transition function $\bar{p}$ defined by a program p)
Let $p = \langle (i_o:u_o),\dots,(i_n:\mathrm{HALT})\rangle \in P_d$, $\bar{x} := \langle x_o,\dots,x_c\rangle$, and $\bar{x}' := \langle x_{c+1},\dots,x_{c+1+c}\rangle$. (Recall that c is the index of the control variable of p .) Then

$$\pi(p,\bar{x},\bar{x}') := \pi(\bar{x},\bar{x}') := \bigwedge\{(x_c=i_k \rightarrow \chi(i_k,u_k,\bar{x},\bar{x}')) \ : \ k<n\} \text{ , where}$$

$$\chi(i_k,u_k,\bar{x},\bar{x}') := \begin{cases} \bar{x}'_c=i_{k+1} \wedge \bar{x}'_w=\tau \wedge \bigwedge\{\bar{x}'_i=x_i \ : \ w\neq i<c\} \\ \qquad\qquad \text{if } u_k = \text{"}x_w \leftarrow \tau\text{"} \\ (\gamma \rightarrow \bar{x}'_c=v) \wedge (\neg\gamma \rightarrow \bar{x}'_c=i_{k+1}) \wedge \bigwedge\{\bar{x}'_i=x_i \ : \ i<c\} \\ \qquad\qquad \text{if } u_k = \text{"IF } \gamma \text{ GOTO } v\text{"} \\ \bar{x}'=\bar{x} \quad \text{if } k=n . \end{cases}$$

It can be checked that $\pi(p,\bar{x},\bar{x}')$ defines a function in every model $\underline{\underline{D}} \in \mathrm{Mod}_d$, that is $\underline{\underline{D}} \models (\forall\bar{x})(\exists!\bar{x}')\,\pi(p,\bar{x},\bar{x}')$. Therefore we write $\pi(p,\bar{x})=\bar{x}'$ instead of $\pi(p,\bar{x},\bar{x}')$ and moreover, we use $\pi(p,\bar{x})$ as a term. Most often we write $p(\bar{x})$ instead of $\pi(p,\bar{x})$, that is $p(\bar{x}) := \pi(p,\bar{x})$. Let $\underline{\underline{D}} \in \mathrm{Mod}_d$. Then
$\bar{p} := \bar{p}^{\underline{\underline{D}}} := \{\langle\bar{a},\bar{a}'\rangle \in {}^2({}^{\bar{c}+1}D) \ : \ \underline{\underline{D}} \models \pi(\bar{a},\bar{a}')\}$. That is,
$\bar{p} : {}^{c+1}D \longrightarrow {}^{c+1}D$ is the function defined by p in $\underline{\underline{D}}$. ◻◻◻

REMARK 2 a) We note that $\nu_k(p,z,\bar{y}) = \chi(i_k,u_k,\bar{y}(z),\bar{y}(z+1))$, where $\nu_k(p,z,\bar{y})$ is defined in [3] p.207.

b) Csirmaz's notion of a program (see [7] Def.2.1) is generalized from the formula $\pi(\bar{x},\bar{x}')$. Let us recall Csirmaz's notion of a program from [7]. Let $Th \subseteq F_d$, $m\in\omega$, $\bar{x} := \langle x_o,\dots,x_{m-1}\rangle$, $\bar{x}' := \langle x_m,\dots,x_{2m-1}\rangle$, and let $\gamma(\bar{x},\bar{x}') \in F_d$ be a formula with free variables $\{x_o,\dots,x_{2m-1}\}$. Then we say that γ is a program of Th , in symbols $\gamma \in P_d(m,Th)$, if $Th \models \forall\bar{x}\,\exists!\bar{x}'\,\gamma(\bar{x},\bar{x}')$.

By the above, clearly, if $p \in P_d$ then $\pi(\bar{x},\bar{x}') \in P_d(c+1,\emptyset)$. But there are definitely more programs in Csirmaz's sense than in the usual block-diagram sense. Everything what follows in this paper applies to Csirmaz's programs, too. ◻◻◻

DEFINITION 4 (the relational semantics $\overset{r}{\models}$, $\overset{R}{\models}$, and $\overset{f}{\models}$; $\overset{e}{\models}$)
Let d be a similarity type, $p \in P_d$, and $\underline{\underline{D}} \in \mathrm{Mod}_d$. Recall that p containes at most c variables i.e. $var(p) \subseteq \{x_i : i<c\}$, and x_c is the control variable of p . Recall that the label of the first command of p is i_o and that of the HALT command is i_n . Let $R \subseteq {}^{c+1}D$, $inp^- \in {}^cD$, $inp := inp^- \cup \{\langle c,i_o^D\rangle\}$, $\preccurlyeq\ \subseteq ({}^2R)$.

(i) We say that $\langle R,inp\rangle$ is a pre-relational trace of p in $\underline{\underline{D}}$, in symbols $\underline{\underline{D}} \overset{e}{\models} p[R,inp]$, if conditions (a), (b) below hold.

(a) $inp \in R$.

(b) $(\forall\bar{b} \in R)\ \bar{p}^D(\bar{b}) \in R$.

We say that $\langle R,inp,\preccurlyeq\rangle$ is a <u>pre-future-relational trace</u> of p in $\underline{\underline{D}}$, in symbols $\underline{\underline{D}} \models^{e} p[R,inp,\preccurlyeq]$, if conditions (a), (b) above, and (c) below hold.

(c) $\preccurlyeq$ is transitive, reflexive, and $(\forall \bar{b}\in R)[\bar{b}\neq \bar{p}^{D}(\bar{b}) \rightarrow \bar{b}\preccurlyeq \bar{p}^{D}(\bar{b})\not\preccurlyeq \bar{b}]$.

<u>(ii)</u> We say that $\langle R,inp\rangle$ is a <u>relational trace</u> (<u>strong relational trace</u>) of p in $\underline{\underline{D}}$, in symbols $\underline{\underline{D}} \models^{r} p[R,inp]$ ($\underline{\underline{D}} \models^{R} p[R,inp]$) if $\underline{\underline{D}} \models^{e} p[R,inp]$ and $\langle \underline{\underline{D}},R,p,inp\rangle \models Iar$ ($\langle \underline{\underline{D}},R,p,inp\rangle \models IaR$) . Analogously, we say that $\langle R,inp,\preccurlyeq\rangle$ is a <u>future-relational trace</u> of p in $\underline{\underline{D}}$, in symbols $\underline{\underline{D}} \models^{f} p[R,inp,\preccurlyeq]$, if $\underline{\underline{D}} \models^{e} p[R,inp,\preccurlyeq]$ and $\langle \underline{\underline{D}},R,p,inp,\preccurlyeq\rangle \models Iaf$. That is

$$\underline{\underline{D}} \models^{r} p[R,inp] \quad :\overset{df}{\Longleftrightarrow} \quad (\underline{\underline{D}} \models^{e} p[R,inp] \text{ and } \langle \underline{\underline{D}},R,p,inp\rangle \models Iar),$$

$$\underline{\underline{D}} \models^{R} p[R,inp] \quad :\overset{df}{\Longleftrightarrow} \quad (\underline{\underline{D}} \models^{e} p[R,inp] \text{ and } \langle \underline{\underline{D}},R,p,inp\rangle \models IaR),$$

$$\underline{\underline{D}} \models^{f} p[R,inp,\preccurlyeq] :\overset{df}{\Longleftrightarrow} (\underline{\underline{D}} \models^{e} p[R,inp,\preccurlyeq] \text{ and } \langle \underline{\underline{D}},R,p,inp,\preccurlyeq\rangle \models Iaf).$$

<u>(iii)</u> Let $\varphi,\psi\in F_d$ be such that all the free variables of φ and ψ occur in p . We say that p is <u>partially correct w.r.t. future-relational semantics</u> concerning input condition φ and output condition ψ in the model $\underline{\underline{D}}$, in symbols $\underline{\underline{D}} \models^{f} [\varphi \rightarrow \Box(p,\psi)]$, if for every $R\subseteq {}^{c+1}D$, $inp^{-}\in {}^{c}D$, $\preccurlyeq\ \subseteq ({}^{2}R)$ we have

$$(\underline{\underline{D}} \models^{f} p[R,inp,\preccurlyeq] \wedge \underline{\underline{D}} \models \varphi(inp)) \Longrightarrow [(\forall \bar{b}\in R)(\bar{p}^{D}(\bar{b})=\bar{b} \rightarrow \underline{\underline{D}} \models \psi(\bar{b}))]$$

where $\varphi(inp) := \varphi(x_i/inp_i : i<c)$, $\psi(\bar{b}) := \psi(x_i/\bar{b}_i : i<c)$.

We obtain the definitions of $\underline{\underline{D}} \models^{r} [\varphi \rightarrow \Box(p,\psi)]$ and $\underline{\underline{D}} \models^{R} [\varphi \rightarrow \Box(p,\psi)]$ by changing $\models^{f}$ in the above definition to $\models^{r}$ and $\models^{R}$ resp., and omitting $\preccurlyeq$.

<u>(iv)</u> The generalization to <u>arbitrary</u> $\varphi,\psi\in F_d$ (possibly having free variables not occurring in p) is straightforward. Namely, let $H := \omega\sim(c+1)$. Now $\underline{\underline{D}} \models^{f} [\varphi \rightarrow \Box(p,\psi)]$ is defined to hold if for every $k\in {}^{H}D$, $R\subseteq {}^{c+1}D$, $inp^{-}\in {}^{c}D$, $\preccurlyeq\ \subseteq ({}^{2}R)$ we have

$$(\underline{\underline{D}} \models^{f} p[R,inp,\preccurlyeq] \wedge \underline{\underline{D}} \models \varphi[q]) \Longrightarrow [(\forall \bar{b}\in R)(\bar{p}^{D}(\bar{b})=\bar{b} \rightarrow \underline{\underline{D}} \models \psi[g])]$$

where $q := inp \cup k$ and $g := (\bar{b}\restriction c) \cup \{\langle c,i_n^D\rangle\} \cup k$ i.e. $g := \langle \bar{b}_0,\ldots,\bar{b}_{c-1},i_n^D,k_{c+1},k_{c+2},\ldots\rangle$. Analogously to $\models^{r}$ and $\models^{R}$.

<u>(v)</u> Let $Th\subseteq F_d$ and $\varphi,\psi\in F_d$. We say that $Th \models^{w} [\varphi \rightarrow \Box(p,\psi)]$ iff $(\forall \underline{\underline{D}}\in Mod(Th))\ \underline{\underline{D}} \models^{w} [\varphi \rightarrow \Box(p,\psi)]$, where $w\in\{r,R,f\}$. ▭▭▭

<u>REMARK 3</u> <u>a)</u> In the above definition, inp could be eliminated e.g. by replacing inp everywhere by $R(\bar{x})\wedge \bar{x}_c=i_0$.

<u>b)</u> The above definition of $\models^{r}$ coincides with [7] Def.2.2.

<u>c)</u> Let us see, how correctness statements about usual blockdiagram programs are special cases of the above definition. Let $p\in P_d$

and φ, ψ be formulas with c free variables (and not with $c+1$ free variables). Let $\varphi'(\bar{x}) := (x_c = i_o \wedge \varphi(x_o,\dots,x_{c-1}))$ and $\psi'(\bar{x}) := (x_c = i_n \rightarrow \psi(x_o,\dots,x_{c-1}))$. Then we define
$\underline{\underline{D}} \overset{r}{\models} [\varphi \rightarrow \Box(p,\psi)] \;:\Longleftrightarrow\; \underline{\underline{D}} \overset{r}{\models} [\varphi' \rightarrow \Box(\,\pi(p,\bar{x},\bar{x}'),\, \psi')]$.

d) $\underline{\underline{D}} \overset{f}{\models} p[R,inp,\preccurlyeq]$ implies that $\preccurlyeq$ is a linear ordering on R with least element $\langle inp^-, i_o^D\rangle$ (and possibly with a greatest element). ◻◻◻

Next we show how to construct a relational trace from a trace and a trace from a relational trace.

DEFINITION 5 Let $s \in {}^A({}^B C)$ be a function. Then $\hat{s}$ denotes the function we get by "turning s with 90 degrees" (see Figure 1), i.e.
$\hat{s} := \Big\langle \langle s(a)b : a \in A\rangle : b \in B \Big\rangle \in {}^B({}^A C)$.
(Note that $s = \Big\langle \langle s(a)b : b \in B\rangle : a \in A \Big\rangle$.) ◻◻◻

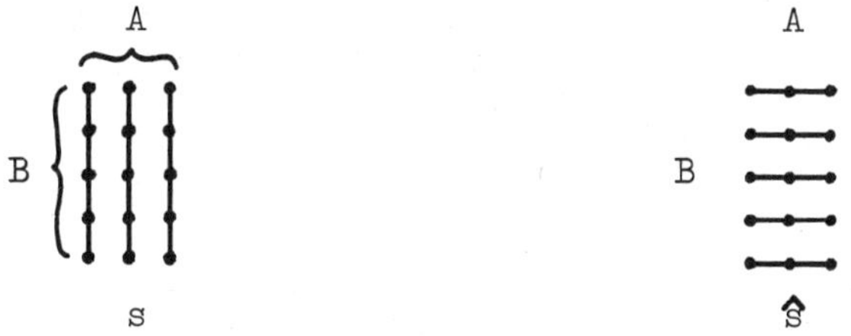

FIGURE 1

REMARK 4 Let s be a trace of a program. That is s correlates to the program variables their histories during the execution. Then $\hat{s}$ correlates the states to the time-points. (A history of a program variable is a function mapping the set T of time-points into the set D of data values. Let the program variables be $x_o,\dots,x_c$. Then a state of the program is a function mapping $c+1$ into D, that is it is an element of ${}^{c+1}D$. Now $s \in {}^{c+1}({}^T D)$ while $\hat{s} \in {}^T({}^{c+1}D)$.) Then $Rng\,\hat{s}$ can be conceived of as (the universe of) the state-space. ◻◻◻

STATEMENT 1: $\mathfrak{M} \models p[s] \;\Rightarrow\; \underline{\underline{D}} \overset{e}{\models} p[Rng\,\hat{s}, \hat{s}(0)]$.◻◻◻(See also Lemma 1.)

DEFINITION 6 Let $\underline{\underline{D}}^R := \langle \underline{\underline{D}}, R, nex, inp, \preccurlyeq\rangle \in Mod_{d\{m\}}$ be such that $\underline{\underline{D}}^R \models R(inp) \wedge (\forall \bar{x} \in R)\, R(nex(\bar{x}))$. We define $\mathfrak{M}(\underline{\underline{D}}^R) \in Mod_{td}$ as follows:
$\mathfrak{M}(\underline{\underline{D}}^R) := \Big\langle \langle R, nex, inp, \preccurlyeq\rangle, \underline{\underline{D}}, \{pj_i\restriction R : i<m\}, valueof \Big\rangle$, where
$pj_i\restriction R := \langle r_i : r \in R\rangle$, and $valueof(pj_i\restriction R, r) := r_i$ for $i<m$ and $r \in R$.◻◻◻

STATEMENT 2: $(\underline{\underline{D}} \overset{e}{\models} p[R,inp] \;\Rightarrow\; \mathfrak{M}(\langle \underline{\underline{D}}, R, p, inp\rangle) \models p[\langle pj_i\restriction R : i \leq c\rangle]$.
◻◻

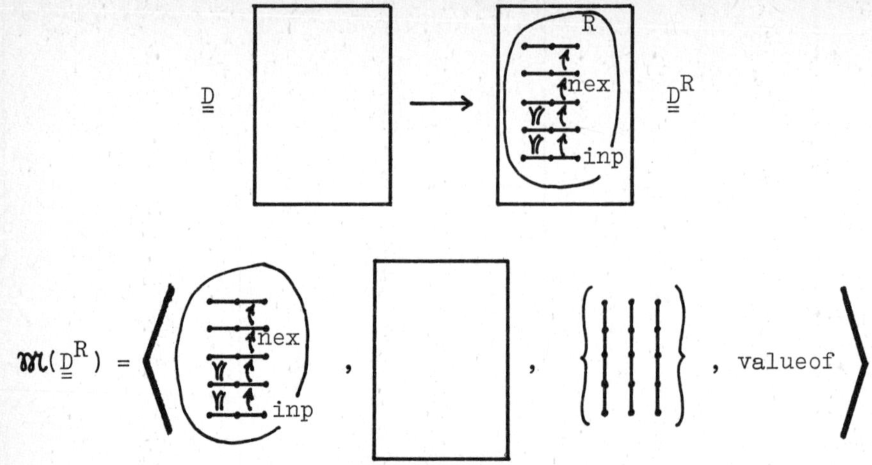

FIGURE 2

Instead of Thm 1, we shall prove the following stronger

THEOREM 1a

(i) $\overset{f}{\models} \equiv_{\Box} \overset{Pnu}{\models} \equiv_{\Box} \overset{Fum}{\models} \equiv_{\Box} (Ipn+Tpn\overset{N}{\vdash}) \equiv_{\Box} (\mathbf{Ind}+Tord\overset{N}{\vdash})$

(ii) $\overset{R}{\models} \equiv_{\Box} \overset{Bur}{\models} \equiv_{\Box} (Imd\overset{N}{\vdash}) \equiv_{\Box} (\mathbf{Ind}\overset{N}{\vdash}) \equiv_{\Box} (I1\overset{N}{\vdash}) \equiv_{\Box} (Imd+Tord\overset{N}{\vdash})$

(iii) $\overset{r}{\models} \equiv_{\Box} \overset{F}{\vdash} \equiv_{\Box} (Ict\overset{N}{\vdash}) \equiv_{\Box} (Iq\overset{N}{\vdash}) \equiv_{\Box} (Ict+Tord\overset{N}{\vdash})$. ◻◻◻

The proof of Thm 1a is based on the following 3 lemmas.

LEMMA 0 $\overset{r}{\models} \equiv_{\Box} \overset{F}{\vdash}$. ◻◻◻

LEMMA 1 Let $\mathfrak{M} \in Mod_{td}$, $p \in P_d$, and let $s \in {}^{c+1}I$ be a trace of p in $\mathfrak{M}$, i.e. $\mathfrak{M} \models p[s]$. Then (i) and (ii) below hold.

(i) $\mathfrak{M} \models Ict \Rightarrow \underline{\underline{D}} \overset{r}{\models} p[Rng\,\hat{s}, \hat{s}(0)]$.

(ii) $\mathfrak{M} \models Imd \Rightarrow \underline{\underline{D}} \overset{R}{\models} p[Rng\,\hat{s}, \hat{s}(0)]$.

Assume further that s terminates p in $\mathfrak{M}$. Let $\hat{s}(\leq) := \{ \langle s(b), s(b_1) \rangle : b \leq b_1 \in T \} \subseteq {}^2(Rng\,\hat{s})$. Then

(iii) $\mathfrak{M} \models (Ipn+Tpn) \Rightarrow \underline{\underline{D}} \overset{f}{\models} p[Rng\,\hat{s}, \hat{s}(0), \hat{s}(\leq)]$. ◻◻◻

LEMMA 2

(i) $\underline{\underline{D}} \overset{r}{\models} p[R, inp] \Rightarrow \mathfrak{M}(\langle \underline{\underline{D}}, R, \bar{p}, inp \rangle) \models Iq$.

(ii) $\underline{\underline{D}} \overset{R}{\models} p[R, inp] \Rightarrow \mathfrak{M}(\langle \underline{\underline{D}}, R, \bar{p}, inp \rangle) \models \mathbf{Ind}$.

(iii) $\underline{\underline{D}} \overset{f}{\models} p[R, inp, \preccurlyeq] \Rightarrow \mathfrak{M}(\langle \underline{\underline{D}}, R, \bar{p}, inp, \preccurlyeq \rangle) \models (\mathbf{Ind}+Tord)$. ◻◻◻

The converses if (i) and (ii) of Lemmas 1, 2 are also true (if $I=Rng\,s$), see Lemmas 1.1, 2.1 below. Instead of (i) and (ii) of Lemmas 1, 2, in [27] we prove (the stronger) Lemmas 1.1, 2.1 because they are interesting in themselves.

LEMMA 1.1 Let $\mathfrak{M} \in \mathrm{Mod}_{td}$, $m \in \omega$, and $s \in {}^{m}I$ be such that Rng s=I. Let $\hat{s}(suc) := \{\langle \hat{s}(z), \hat{s}(suc\ z)\rangle : z \in T\} \cup \{\langle \bar{a}, \bar{a}\rangle : \bar{a} \in ({}^{m}D \sim \mathrm{Rng}\,\hat{s})\}$. Assume that $\hat{s}(suc)$ is a function ($\hat{s}(suc) : {}^{m}D \longrightarrow {}^{m}D$). Then

(i) $\mathfrak{M} \models \mathrm{Ict} \iff \langle \underline{\underline{D}}, \mathrm{Rng}\,\hat{s}, \hat{s}(suc), \hat{s}(0)\rangle \models \mathrm{Iar}$.

(ii) $\mathfrak{M} \models \mathrm{Imd} \iff \langle \underline{\underline{D}}, \mathrm{Rng}\,\hat{s}, \hat{s}(suc), \hat{s}(0)\rangle \models \mathrm{IaR}$. ☐☐☐

REMARK 1.1 a) Lemma 1.1 gives an insight into the nature of Ict and Imd. It says explicitly that all what Imd and Ict can reflect about the time structure $\underline{\underline{T}}$ are properties of $\langle T, suc, 0\rangle$ projected by the intensions onto the data. (Imd can "speak about" the image of T in D as a whole, while Ict cannot.) This fact is reflected in Corollary 1.2 below.

b) Lemma 1.1 gives also a method for checking Imd and Ict in models: There is a well developed technique using ultraproducts to check **Ind** (see e.g. [15] proof of Thm 6). This technique can easily be modified to check Iq, $I\Sigma_1$, $I\Pi_1$ etc., or to check Iar, IaR (see the proof of Prop 30 in [21] and the examples in §3 of [27]). But it cannot be applied directly to Imd or Ict because in the latter the formulas have very special shapes. But the formulas in Iar and IaR are again of good form. Thus Lemma 1.1 makes available the well developed technique using ultraproducts for checking Ict and Imd. (We note that $|I|<\omega$ is not an essential constraint here since $\mathfrak{M} \models \mathrm{Ict} \iff (\forall I_0 \subseteq I)(|I_0|<\omega \rightarrow \mathfrak{M}{\restriction}I_0 \models \mathrm{Ict})$, where $\mathfrak{M}{\restriction}I_0 := \langle \underline{\underline{T}}, \underline{\underline{D}}, I_0, ext\rangle$). ☐☐☐

COROLLARY 1.2 (i) $(\mathrm{Ict} \overset{N}{\vdash}) \equiv_{\Box} (\mathrm{Ict}+\mathrm{Tord} \overset{N}{\vdash}) \equiv_{\Box} (\mathrm{Ict}+\mathrm{Tpa} \overset{N}{\vdash})$.

(ii) $(\mathrm{Imd} \overset{N}{\vdash}) \equiv_{\Box} (\mathrm{Imd}+\mathrm{Tord} \overset{N}{\vdash}) \equiv_{\Box} (\mathrm{Imd}+\mathrm{Tpa} \overset{N}{\vdash})$. ☐☐☐

In the proof of Lemma 1.1, in [27], we use the following

LEMMA 1.1.1 Assume the hypotheses of Lemma 1.1. Let $\mathfrak{M}^R := \langle \underline{\underline{T}}, \langle \underline{\underline{D}}, \mathrm{Rng}\,\hat{s}, \hat{s}(suc), \hat{s}(0)\rangle, I, ext\rangle \in \mathrm{Mod}_{td[m]}$. Then

$$\mathfrak{M} \models \mathrm{Imd} \iff \mathfrak{M}^R \models \mathrm{Imd} \iff \mathfrak{M}^R \models \mathrm{Ict}. \quad ☐☐☐$$

LEMMA 2.1 Let $\underline{\underline{D}}^R \in \mathrm{Mod}_{d[m]}$. Then (i) and (ii) below hold.

(i) Assume that nex is definable in the d-type reduct of $\underline{\underline{D}}^R$. Then

$$\underline{\underline{D}}^R \models \mathrm{Iar} \iff \mathfrak{M}(\underline{\underline{D}}^R) \models \mathrm{Iq} \iff \mathfrak{M}(\underline{\underline{D}}^R) \models \mathrm{Ict}.$$

(ii) $$\underline{\underline{D}}^R \models \mathrm{IaR} \iff \mathfrak{M}(\underline{\underline{D}}^R) \models \mathbf{Ind} \iff \mathfrak{M}(\underline{\underline{D}}^R) \models \mathrm{Imd}. \quad ☐☐☐$$

Lemmas 0-2.1 form the outline of the proof of Thm 1a. The detailed proof is in [27] and [19] (concerning $\overset{Bur}{\vdash}$, $\overset{F}{\vdash}$, and $\overset{Pnu}{\vdash}$ resp.).

REMARK 2.1 a) $\mathfrak{M} \models \mathrm{Iq} \iff \mathfrak{M} \models \mathrm{Ict}$ is true only for special models like $\mathfrak{M}(\underline{\underline{D}}^R)$. In §3 of [27], models $\mathfrak{M}, \mathfrak{N}$ are given for which $\mathfrak{M} \models \mathrm{Ict}$, $\mathfrak{M} \not\models \mathrm{Iq}$, and $\mathfrak{N} \models \mathrm{Imd}$, $\mathfrak{N} \not\models$ **Ind** .

b) The assumption in (i) of Lemma 2.1 cannot be omitted since without it $\underline{\underline{D}}^R \models \mathrm{Iar} \Rightarrow \mathfrak{M}(\underline{\underline{D}}^R) \models \mathrm{Iq}$ does not hold, for counterexample see Example 2 Corollary 3.3 in §3 of [27]. (The other implications hold without the assumption.)

c) The assumption in Lemma 2.1(i) that nex is definable in the d-type reduct of $\underline{\underline{D}}^R$, is not a strong one since our main concern is proving partial correctness statements and in those questions nex is always $\bar{p}$ with $p \in P_d$ thus nex is clearly definable by a formula of type d (see Def.3). □□□

REMARKS: Return to Burstall's Problem(1), concerning $\vdash^{\mathrm{Pnu}}$

a) There are several versions of $\vdash^{\mathrm{Pnu}}$ in the literature. In the definition of $\vdash^{\mathrm{Pnu}}$ here, we used all the 4 modalities Fst, Nxt, Stm, Sfu . This is not necessary, e.g. the "Nexttime System" $\vdash^{\mathrm{Pnt}}$ of Manna-Pnueli [13] uses only 2 of these 4 modalities: Nxt and Sfu (they denote them by σ and $\Diamond$ resp.). (Accordingly, the correctness of a program is expressed by a weaker statement in $\vdash^{\mathrm{Pnt}}$: instead of "Alw(terminates → correct)", $\vdash^{\mathrm{Pnt}}$ uses "Afu(terminates → correct)".) In [19] we prove that $\vdash^{\mathrm{Pnt}} \equiv_{\Box} \vdash^{\mathrm{Pnu}}$.

In the definition of $\vdash^{\mathrm{Pnu}}$ here, we used as few axioms as possible, namely in [19] we prove that none of the axioms can be omitted from Tpnu without loosing from the program verifying power of the method $\vdash^{\mathrm{Pnu}}$. In [19] we also show that one of the axioms of $\vdash^{\mathrm{Pnt}}$, as formulated in [13], is superfluous (namely, axiom (C3) follows from the rest).

b) Notice that the result $\vdash^{\mathrm{Pnu}} \equiv_{\Box} \vdash^{\mathrm{Fum}}$ (in Thm 1 herein) intuitively expresses that the program proving power does not increase if, besides being able to speak about future, we allow to speak about past as well. Actually, $\vdash^{\mathrm{Pnu}} \equiv_{\Box}$ (**Ind**+Tord$\vdash^{N}$) shows that we may throw in all the temporal modalities definable from linear ordering of time (e.g. "until") without increasing the program verifying power. (Multiplying time "lengths" or "durations" is an entirely different matter, as $\vdash^{\mathrm{Pnu}} <_{\Box}$ (**Ind**+Tpeano$\vdash^{N}$) on Figure 3 below shows.)

The induction principle $\mathrm{Ind}^{\mathrm{Pnu}}$ is very strong. It is much stronger than $\mathrm{Ind}^{\mathrm{Bur}}$ or our usual **Ind** . Is it perhaps this strength of $\mathrm{Ind}^{\mathrm{Pnu}}$ which is at the heart of the temporal logic $\vdash^{\mathrm{Pnu}}$? A positive answer would follow from observing that for every axiom system

Twhatever , whenever $(\mathbf{Ind}+\text{Twhatever}\vdash^{N}) \equiv_{\square} \vdash^{Pnu}$ then we have $(\mathbf{Ind}+\text{Twhatever}) \models \text{Ind}^{Pnu}$ (more precisely, $(\mathbf{Ind}+\text{Twhatever}) \models \text{Ipn}$). Is this true ? Well, in [19] we prove the opposite: there we define a rather weak set $\text{Tleo} \subset \text{Tord}$ of axioms for which $\mathbf{Ind}+\text{Tleo} \not\models \text{Ipn}$ but $(\mathbf{Ind}+\text{Tleo}\vdash^{N}) \equiv_{\square} \vdash^{Pnu}$. This shows that it is not the rather strong induction principle Ind^{Pnu} in $\vdash^{Pnu}$ which is responsible for its great program verifying power.

In a way, all the above indicated investigations of [19] form a kind of return to Burstall's Problem(1) as formulated in the present introduction. Namely, this problem is about explicit logical characterization and about obtaining insight into the nature of these logics of programs. Well, trying to figure out if e.g. Ind^{Pnu} is the source of the extra power, belongs to the quest for insight. Trying to replace Tord with Tleo and other axiom systems belongs to sharpening or refining the characterization $\vdash^{Pnu} \equiv_{\square} (\mathbf{Ind}+\text{Tord}\vdash^{N})$. Could we replace linear ordering in Tord with preordering ? Is transitivity needed in Tord ? Could we replace Tord with a well known stronger or weaker system ? These questions are investigated in [19]. □□□

A P P E N D I X

Figure 3 on next page is a recent version of the lattice of program verification methods published in [15]. The results new compared to Figure 2 of [15] are indicated with thick lines here. The new results are due to the present author except $I\Sigma_1 >_{\square} \text{Iq}$ and $I\Pi_1 <_{\square} \mathbf{Ind}$, which are due to L.Csirmaz, and $\mathbf{Ind}+\text{Tpres} <_{\square} \mathbf{Ind}+\text{Tpa}$ is a joint result with B.Biró.

R E F E R E N C E S

1. Andréka,H. Balogh,K. Lábadi,K. Németi,I. Tóth,P.: Plans to improve our program verifyer program. (In Hungarian). Working paper, NIM IGÜSZI, Dept. of Software Techniques, Budapest, 1974.
2. Andréka,H. Németi,I. Sain,I.: A complete first order logic. Preprint Math.Inst.Hung.Acad.Sci. 124 p.
3. Andréka,H. Németi,I. Sain,I.: A complete logic for reasoning about programs via nonstandard model theory, Parts I-II. Theoretical Computer Science 17 (1982), No.2 193-212, No.3 259-278.
4. Bowen,K.A.: Model theory for modal logic (Kripke models for modal predicate calculi). Synthese Library Vol 127, Reidel Publ. Co., 1979.

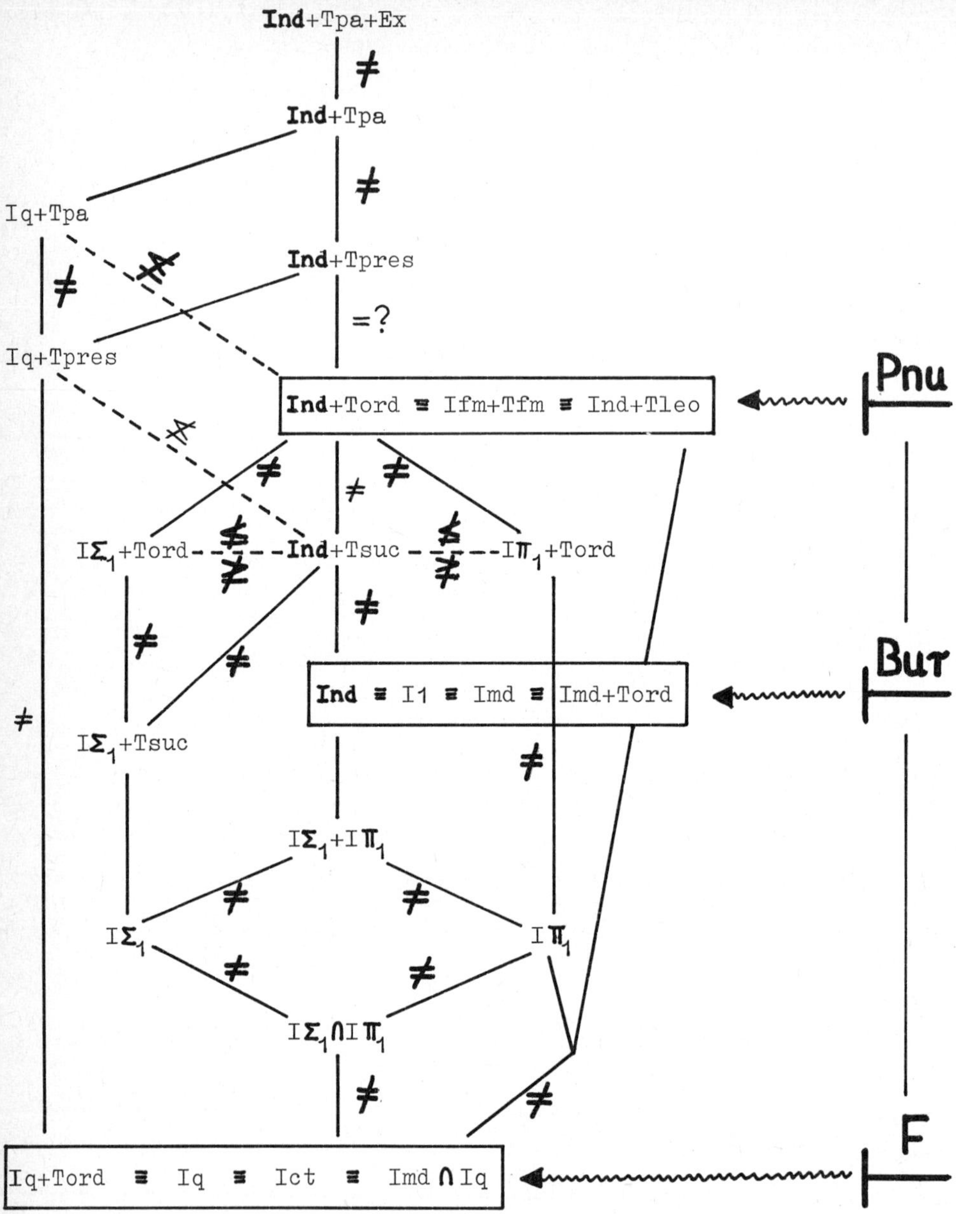
Ind+Tpa+Ex
Ind+Tpa
Iq+Tpa
Ind+Tpres
=?
Iq+Tpres
Ind+Tord ≡ Ifm+Tfm ≡ Ind+Tleo
Pnu
IΣ1+Tord
Ind+Tsuc
IΠ1+Tord
Ind ≡ I1 ≡ Imd ≡ Imd+Tord
BuT
IΣ1+Tsuc
IΣ1+IΠ1
IΣ1
IΠ1
IΣ1∩IΠ1
Iq+Tord ≡ Iq ≡ Ict ≡ Imd ∩ Iq
F

FIGURE 3

5. Burstall,R.M.: Program Proving as Hand Simulation with a Little Induction. IFIP Congress, Stockholm, August 3-10, 1974.

6. Csirmaz,L.: On the completeness of proving partial correctness. Acta Cybernetica, Tom 5, Fasc 2, Szeged, 1981, 181-190.

7. Csirmaz,L.: Programs and program verification in a general setting. Theoretical Computer Science 16 (1981) 199-210.

8. Csirmaz,L.: On the Strength of "Sometime" and "Always" in Program Verification. Information and Control, vol 57, Nos 2-3, 1983.

9. Gergely,T. Szőts,M.: On the incompleteness of proving partial correctness. Acta Cybernetica, Tom 4, Fasc 1, Szeged, 1978, 45-57.

10. Gergely,T. Ury,L.: Time models for programming logics. In: Mathematical Logic in Computer Science (Proc.Conf. Salgótarján 1978) Eds.: B.Dömölki, T.Gergely, Colloq.Math.Soc.J.Bolyai vol 26, North-Holland, 1981, 359-427.

13. Manna,Z. Pnueli,A.: The Modal Logic of Programs. Preprint CS81-12, June 1981.

14. Mirkowska,G.: Multimodal logics. Preprint, Institute of Math., Warsaw University.

15. Németi,I.: Nonstandard Dynamic Logic. In: Logics of Programs, Ed.: D.Kozen (Proc.Conf. New York 1981) Lecture Notes in Computer Science 131, Springer-Verlag, Berlin, 1982, 311-348.

16. Pnueli,A.: The Temporal Logic of Programs. Preprint Weitzmann Institute of Science, Dept. of Applied Math., May 1981.

17. Richter,M.M. Szabo,M.E.: Nonstandard Computation Theory. Preprint, Concordia University, Montreal, 1983.

18. Sain,I.: Successor axioms for time increase the program verifying power of full computational induction. Preprint No 23/1983, Math.Inst.Hung.Acad.Sci., Budapest, 1983.

19. Sain,I.: Model theoretic characterization of Pnueli's temporal program verification method. Manuscript, 1983.

21. Sain,I.: How to define the meaning of iteration ? and Sharpening the characterization of Pnueli's program verification method (Structured NDL Parts II-III). Preprint No 48/1984, Math.Inst. Hung.Acad.Sci., Budapest, 1984.

22. Sain,I.: Total correctness in nonstandard dynamic logic. Preprint No 8/1983, Math.Inst.Hung.Acad.Sci., Budapest, 1983.

23. Szabo,M.E.: Personal communication, 1981.

24. Pasztor,A.: Nonstandard Dynamic Logic to Prove Standard Properties of Programs. Carnegie-Mellon Univ., Dept. of Math., Research Report 84-3.

25. Pasztor,A.: Nonstandard Logics of Programs. Carnegie-Mellon Univ. Dept. of Math., Research Report, Dec. 1984.

26. Sain,I.: A simple proof for the completeness of Floyd's method. Theoretical Computer Science vol 35, 1985, to appear.

27. Sain,I.: The implicit information content of Burstall's (modal) program verification method. Preprint No 57/1984, Math.Inst.Hung. Acad.Sci., Budapest, 1984.

28. Biró,B. Sain,I.: Peano Arithmetic for the Time Scale of Nonstandard Logics of Programs. Preprint, 1985.

A partial correctness logic for procedures
(in an ALGOL-like language)

Kurt Sieber
Fachrichtung Informatik
Universität des Saarlandes
D-6600 Saarbrücken

Abstract:

We extend Hoare's logic by allowing quantifiers and other logical connectives to be used on the level of Hoare formulas. This leads to a logic in which partial correctness properties of procedures (and not only of statements) can be formulated adequately. In particular it is possible to argue about free procedures, i.e. procedures which are not bound by a declaration but only "specified" semantically. This property of our logic (and of the corresponding calculus) is important from both a practical and a theoretical point of view, namely:
- Formal proofs of programs can be written in the style of stepwise refinement.
- Procedures on parameter position can be handled adequately, so that some sophisticated programs can be verified, which are beyond the power of other calculi.

The logic as well as the calculus are similar to Reynolds' specification logic. But there are also some (essential) differences which will be pointed out in this paper.

1. Introduction

Developing a program by stepwise refinement means
- writing an abstract program that uses procedures which are not (yet) declared but only specified by semantical properties,
- independently writing declarations for these procedures, so that they satisfy their specifications.

If a program is developed in this style, then of course it should be proved in the same style. In a logic which allows such proofs, it must be possible

- to specify procedures, i.e. to describe them by purely semantical properties,
- to verify an abstract program starting from such specifications.

In order to understand the difficulties arising with this way of reasoning in Hoare's logic, consider the following example: Assume we want to express that a (parameterless) procedure P increases the value of a (global) variable x by 1. Apparently this can be realized by the Hoare formula

$$\{x = y\}\ P(\ )\ \{x = y + 1\} \tag{1}$$

(apart from the fact that Hoare formulas only describe partial correctness). Assume further that P is used in an abstract program and we want to conclude from (1), say

$$\{x = 1\}\ P(\ )\ \{x = 2\} \tag{2}$$

which is usually written as a so-called proof line

$$\{x = y\}\ P(\ )\ \{x = y + 1\} \supset \{x = 1\}\ P(\ )\ \{x = 2\}. \tag{*}$$

Then the question arises how to define the semantics of formulas like (*) (which is "intuitively valid"). It is well known that the naive approach - where arbitrary procedures can be inserted for P - fails: If P is declared by

P( ) = x := y + 1 or

P( ) : <u>if</u> x = y <u>then</u> x := x + 1 <u>else</u> x := x + 2 <u>fi</u>,

then - in both cases - the premise (1) is satisfied but the conclusion (2) is not.

The usual way out is to forbid the variable y to be accessed by the procedure P. This can be achieved by inspecting a context which contains all variables accessed by P (cf. [dBa 80], [Old 81]) or by distinguishing between program variables (occuring in the programs) and algebraic variables (occuring in the assertions only, cf. [Sie 81], [CGH 83]).

Here we propose a more "natural" solution: We distinguish between value identifiers (a, b, c, ...), variable identifiers (x, y, z, ...) and procedure identifiers (P, Q, R, ...) of various types. Quantifiers for all these identifiers are allowed and explicit dereferencing from variables to values is expressed by a symbol "cont". A quantified value identifier can then be used to reformulate our example (*):

$\forall c.\{cont(x) = c\}\ P(\ )\ \{cont(x) = c + 1\}$
$\quad\supset \{cont(x) = 1\}\ P(\ )\ \{cont(x) = 2\} \qquad (**)$

This formula is valid in the naive interpretation. The premise now really means that "for all values c" partial correctness holds with respect to cont(x) = c and cont(x) = c + 1, hence it holds in particular for the value 1. Note that the procedures declared by
P( ) : x := c + 1   or
P( ) : <u>if</u> x = c <u>then</u> x := cont(x) + 1 <u>else</u> x := cont(x) + 2 <u>fi</u>
don't satisfy the premise of (**).
(Of course this last argumentation was rather informal; it will be justified by the formal definition of our logic in section 3.)

So far, the use of quantifiers can be regarded as a matter of taste, because they can be replaced by variables which are not accessed by certain procedures. But it will turn out that - in connection with procedures on parameter position - quantifiers even increase the power of the calculus.

Semantically procedures with parameters are usually considered as functions of their parameters. In order to describe a function it is necessary to define its values <u>for all</u> arguments. From this point of view quantifiers are useful for all kinds of identifiers which may occur as parameters.
As an example consider the formula

$\forall c,x.\{cont(x) = c\}\ Q(x)\ \{cont(x) = c + 1\}$

which means that for each parameter x the procedure call Q(x) increases the value of x by 1. Hence it is satisfied if Q is declared by:

Q(y) :   y := cont(y) + 1   ,

but it fails for:

Q(y) :   y := cont(x) + 1   .

Finally the use of quantifiers for procedure identifiers can be illustrated with the aid of the formula

$\forall a,R.(\forall c.\{\underline{true}\}\ R(c)\ \{cont(x) = c + a\}$
$\quad\supset \forall b.\{cont(x) = b\}\ P(a,R)\ \{cont(x) = 2 * b + 1\})$

which will be used in section 4 to prove a (slight variant of a) program constructed by E. Olderog (cf. [Old 81]). The precise meaning of the formula is not important here, but note that it describes the effect of the procedure P under a certain <u>semantical</u> condition for the procedure parameter R. This property of the formula is essential, because in E. Olderog's program in each recursion a new procedure is declared and inserted on parameter position. "Classical" Hoare-like calculi which - like ours - use a first order oracle, fail in proving this program, because they require some syntactical "similarity" for the different procedures occuring on a certain parameter position (cf. [Old 81], [Old 83]). Hence it was only proved in calculi based on a higher order assertion language like those of [Old 84], [DaJ 83], in which semantical properties of procedure parameters are implicitely expressed with the aid of predicate variables. But even these calculi fail, when the complexity of the program is increased by additionally declaring a new variable in each recursion (cf. section 4), because they can deal with "simple side effects" only (a notion introduced in [Lan 83]).

We conclude with some remarks about related approaches (in which also quantifiers are used on the level of Hoare formulas).

(a) In [CGH 83] a calculus is presented, which only works for procedures without global variables. Nevertheless this paper contains some ideas about a completeness proof, which can possibly be applied to our calculus.

(b) The proof system of [Hal 83] again differs from ours by using a higher order assertion language (which is not even precisely defined!).

(c) The most similar approach is Reynolds' specification logic ([Rey 81], [Rey 82]).

But there is one essential difference: Reynolds considers call-by-name as the basic mechanism for parameter passing. As a consequence he only uses identifiers which stand for integer expressions or variable expressions (and not for integers or variables). If now e is such an identifier, then a formula like

$$\forall e.\ \{cont(x) = e\}\ P(\ )\ \{cont(x) = e + 1\}$$

does not have the "desired" meaning, because in particular e can be replaced by cont(x), which leads to

$$\{\underline{true}\}\ P(\ )\ \{\underline{false}\}.$$

Hence it is again necessary (like in usual Hoare logic) to impose a restriction on e, e.g. that the value of e does not depend on the value of x (called "non-interference" in specification logic). This means that one important advantage of using quantifiers - which was illustrated above with the formula (**) - has been lost in specification logic, and that difficulties with procedure parameters reappear (cf. section 11 in [Rey 82]).

On the other hand it should be mentioned that specification logic is of course much more general than our approach, e.g. type coercion is considered and higher order predicates are used.

2. The programming language

We consider a fully typed ALGOL-like language in which arbitrary nesting of blocks and (mutually recursive) procedure declarations is possible. Procedures may have value-parameters (call-by-value), var-parameters (call-by-reference) and procedure parameters of all types. But note that self application is impossible, because every procedure has its (finite) type. Sharing (between parameters or between parameters and global variables) is allowed without restrictions. Global variables and procedures are handled by the static scope rule.

We begin with syntactical definitions.

First a set Type of *types* τ is defined by:

$\tau ::= \underline{value} \mid \underline{var} \mid \underline{bool} \mid \underline{stat} \mid (\tau_1 \to \tau_2) \mid \tau_1 \times \ldots \times \tau_n$.

stat is intended to be the type of statements and parameterless procedures; hence the subsets Proctype of *procedure types* and Partype of *parameter types* are defined by:

proctype $::= \underline{stat} \mid (\text{partype}_1 \times \ldots \times \text{partype}_n \to \underline{stat})$

partype $::= \underline{value} \mid \underline{var} \mid$ proctype

For every parameter type τ a set Id_τ of *identifiers* id of type τ is given, in particular:

- $Id_{\underline{value}}$ is the set of *value identifiers* a, b, c ...,
- $Id_{\underline{var}}$ is the set of *variable identifiers* x, y, z ...,
- $\bigcup_{\tau \in \text{Proctype}} Id_\tau$ is the set of *procedure identifiers* P, Q, R...

Additionally a signature Ω is needed, containing *function symbols* f and *predicate symbols* pr of various arities.

On this basis the constructs C of the programming language (and the type of each construct C, denoted type(C)) can be defined as follows.

Terms t:

t ::= c | cont(x) | $f(t_1,\ldots,t_n)$ where n is the arity of f.
(Remember the meaning of "cont".)
type(t) = ((var → value) → value) for all terms t.

Formulas p(q,r,s):

p ::= x = y | $t_1 = t_2$ | ¬p' | $(p_1 \wedge p_2)$ | ∀c.p
| $pr(t_1,\ldots,t_n)$ where n is the arity of pr.

(x = y is intended to express sharing in contrast to cont(x) = cont(y); this is necessary, because formulas will be also used as assertions in Hoare formulas. The same argument applies to quantifiers, but note that they are restricted to value identifiers c.)

type(p) = ((var → value) → bool) for all formulas p.

Statements St:

St ::= x :=t | if p then St_1 else St_2 fi | $(St_1;St_2)$
| begin var x;St end | begin E;St end
| $Proc(par_1,\ldots,par_n)$ where $par_1,\ldots,par_n$ must be of "adequate" type.

(Of course the parantheses in $(St_1;St_2)$ are omitted if possible, otherwise they are replaced by "begin...end".)
type(St) = stat for all statements St.

Procedures Proc:

Proc ::= P | Pb
type(Proc) is inherited from P or Pb.

Parameters par:

par ::= x | t | Proc
Again the type is inherited.

Procedure bodies Pb:

Pb ::= St | λ $id_1,\ldots,id_n$.St where $id_1,\ldots,id_n$ are different.
In the first case type(Pb) = stat, in the second case
type(Pb) = $(\tau_1 \times\ldots\times \tau_n \rightarrow$ stat) where τ_i is the type of id_i.

Procedure declarations E:

E ::= $P_1 \Leftarrow Pb_1;\ldots P_m \Leftarrow Pb_m$ where $P_1,\ldots,P_m$ are different and $\mathrm{type}(P_i) = \mathrm{type}(Pb_i)$.

$\mathrm{type}(E) = \mathrm{type}(P_1) \times\ldots\times \mathrm{type}(P_m)$; $P_1,\ldots,P_m$ are called the procedure identifiers *declared* by E, the set (or the tuple) of these identifiers is denoted decl(E).

This concludes the syntactic definitions.
Note in particular that

- complete procedure bodies may occur in procedure calls (on "call position" as well as on parameter position),
- procedure declarations have the form
  $P \Leftarrow \underline{\lambda}\ id_1,\ldots,id_n.St$ instead of $P(id_1,\ldots,id_n) : St$.

These conventions are necessary for defining a substitution of procedure identifiers by procedure bodies.

The semantics of our language is defined in a purely denotational style, i.e. without any operational concepts like - say - the copy rules of [Old 81].

As usual the basis of the semantics definition is an interpretation $I = (D, I_o)$ where D is a nonempty set of *datas* ($\delta \in D$) and I_o assigns functions and predicates on D to the symbols of Ω. Additionally an infinite set Adr($\alpha \in$ Adr) of *addresses* (storage locations) is assumed to be available. A (total) function σ : Adr $\rightarrow$ D is then called a (storage) *state*, the set of all states is denoted Σ, and relations $\rho \subseteq \Sigma \times \Sigma$ are called (nondeterministic) *state transformations*.

The semantical domains are partial orders (po's) which do not necessarily contain bottom elements. Those which have one (denoted $\perp$) are called *strict* (due to [GTW^2 77]); those which are ordered by the equality are called *trivial*. If D and E are partial orders, then D $\times$ E denotes their cartesian product with the componentwise defined ordering and if additionally M is a set, then (M $\rightarrow$ E) denotes the set of functions from M to E with the argumentwise defined ordering.

With these notations a semantical domain D_τ is defined for each type τ, such that:

(i) $D_{\underline{value}} = D$,

(ii) $D_{\underline{var}} = Adr$,

(iii) $D_{\underline{bool}} = Bool = \{true, false\}$,

(each made into a trivial po by the equality);

(iv) $D_{\underline{stat}}$ is an "adequate" set of state transformations, containing in particular the empty set $\emptyset \subseteq \Sigma \times \Sigma$, (made into a strict po by the subset relation "$\subseteq$");

(v) $D_{\tau_1 \times \ldots \times \tau_n} = D_{\tau_1} \times \ldots \times D_{\tau_n}$,

(vi) $D_{(\tau_1 \to \tau_2)}$ is an "adequate" subset of $(D_{\tau_1} \to D_{\tau_2})$,

(each made into a po by the induced ordering).

Note that D_τ is strict for all procedure types τ, because $D_{\underline{stat}}$ is strict.

The precise definition of $D_{\underline{stat}}$ and $D_{(\tau_1 \to \tau_2)}$ is left open here. We only give some informal remarks:

The crucial point of the semantics definition is the connection of local variables with global (i.e. free) procedures. Consider e.g. the block

<u>begin</u> <u>var</u> x; P(x) <u>end</u>.

We want to define the semantics of the variable declaration by allocating to the identifier x a "new" address, which is not "global" for P, i.e. which is "not accessed by P itself". But in our purely denotational framework P is interpreted as a function $f \in D_{(\underline{var} \to \underline{stat})}$, hence it is necessary to define the set of addresses "accessed" by such a function, i.e. to define the notion of "access" on the <u>semantical</u> level. A precise solution of this problem can be found in [HMT 83], here we only want to present the main idea.

There are three kinds of access (of a procedure to a variable):

- access by <u>writing</u>: the contents of the variable is (possibly) changed by the (nondeterministic) procedure;
- access by <u>reading</u>: the initial contents of the variable has an influence on the output of the procedure;
- access by a <u>sharing effect</u>: This can be illustrated with the aid of an example. Let P be declared by

```
P ⇐ λy.begin y := cont(x) + 1;
       if cont(x) = cont(y) then y := 1 else y :=2 fi
    end.
```

Then there is neither a writing nor a reading access of P to x, but nevertheless x has a certain (semantical) influence on P: While the call P(x) sets its parameter x to 1, each other call P(y) sets its parameter y to 2.

It is not necessary to distinguish exactly between these three kinds of access, but we are only interested in the following notions and facts:
The set Glob(f) of *global addresses* of f contains all addresses which are accessed by f (by writing, reading or a sharing effect). The set Out(f) of *output addresses* of f only contains those elements of Glob(f) which are accessed by writing. The definition of each semantical domain D_τ ($\tau \in$ Proctype) guarantees that Glob(f) (and hence Out(f)) is finite for every $f \in D_\tau$. This makes it possible to select a "new" address in the semantics definition of variable declarations.

We want to present the most interesting clauses of this semantics definition . For this purpose we first need the following definition .
The set Env of *environments* ε is defined by

$$\mathrm{Env} = \prod_{\tau \in \mathrm{Partype}} (\mathrm{Id}_\tau \to D_\tau),$$

i.e. every environment ε is a family of mappings

$$\varepsilon_\tau : \mathrm{Id}_\tau \to D_\tau .$$

The *meaning* of each syntactical construct C of type τ is then defined as a function $M(C) : \mathrm{Env} \to D_\tau$.

Note in particular that (due to our definition of types):
- $M(t)(\varepsilon) : \Sigma \to D$ for every term t,
- $M(p)(\varepsilon) : \Sigma \to \mathrm{Bool}$ for every formula p,
- $M(St)(\varepsilon) \subseteq \Sigma \times \Sigma$ for every statement St.

The most interesting clauses of the definition of M are:

(i) block with variable declaration:
M(begin var x;St end)(ε)
$= \{(\sigma[\alpha/\delta], \sigma'[\alpha/\delta]) \mid (\sigma,\sigma') \in M(\lambda x.St)(\varepsilon)(\alpha)\}$ [1]

---

[1] As usual the variant $f[m/n]$ of a function $f : M \to N$ is defined by $f[m/n](m) = n$
$f[m/n](m') = f(m')$ for all $m' \neq m$.

where α is an arbitrary address, not occuring in $Glob(M(\underline{\lambda}x.St)(\varepsilon))$. Intuitively this definition means that α is a "new" address and that the block statement is executed in three steps:

- the initial contents δ of α is replaced by a random value $\sigma(\alpha)$,
- $M(\underline{\lambda}x.St)(\varepsilon)(\alpha) = M(St)(\varepsilon[x/\alpha])$ is executed (transforming σ to σ'),
- the initial contents δ of α is restaured.

This careful definition of the variable declaration semantics guarantees that

- the semantics is indeed independent of the particular choice of α,
- α is not accessed (in the sense explained above) by the state transformation M(begin var x;St end)(ε).

(ii) block with procedure declaration:

$$M(\underline{begin}\ E;St\ \underline{end})(\varepsilon) = M(St)(\varepsilon[\bar{P}/M(E)(\varepsilon)])$$
$$\text{where } \bar{P} = decl(E)$$

This definition says that the procedure declaration E is evaluated (to the least fixpoint of a functional, cf. next clause) "at declaration time" and that the resulting objects (of procedure type) are bound to the procedure identifiers $\bar{P}$ (in order to use them in a procedure call). This shows that our programming language works with static scope of variable and procedure identifiers.

(iii) procedure declaration:

Let E be the declaration $P_1 \Leftarrow Pb_1;\ldots;P_m \Leftarrow Pb_m$ and let τ_i be the type of P_i. Then $M(E)(\varepsilon)$ is defined as the least fixpoint of the function

$$\Phi_{E,\varepsilon} : D_{\tau_1} \times\ldots\times D_{\tau_m} \to D_{\tau_1} \times\ldots\times D_{\tau_m}$$
$$(\eta_1,\ldots,\eta_m) \mapsto (M(Pb_1)(\varepsilon[P_1/\eta_1] \ldots [P_m/\eta_m]),$$
$$\vdots$$
$$M(Pb_m)(\varepsilon[P_1/\eta_1] \ldots [P_m/\eta_m])).$$

Unfortunately our semantics does not fit into the classical framework of Scott's theory: A sequence of elements $f_n \in D_\tau$ ($\tau \in$ Proctype) for which every set $Glob(f_n)$ is finite, may have a least upper bound f with infinitely many global addresses. Hence the partial orders D_τ are not complete and - moreover - the semantics of the variable declaration leads to functions which are not continuous. These (technical but difficult) problems are discussed and solved in [HMT 83] by using a "refined" version of Scott's theory.

The connection between [HMT 83] and our approach is as follows: Our set Glob(f) corresponds to their "support of f", apart from one (small but serious) difference. We have <u>separately</u> defined a set Out(f) of output addresses, e.g. for each

$$f \in D_{(\underline{stat} \to \underline{stat})} : \mathrm{Out}(f) = \bigcup_{\rho \in D_{\underline{stat}}} (\mathrm{Out}(f(\rho)) \setminus \mathrm{Out}(\rho))$$

(i.e. α is called an output address of f if its contents is changed by a call $f(\rho)$ without the aid of ρ). In [HMT 83] this set is not defined and its finiteness is not required.

On the other hand this set plays an important role in our proof system, so that this difference of the two semantical approaches has serious consequences (cf. example (iv) of section 3, the definition of the formula strange($\underset{\sim}{x}$, P), the variable declaration axiom and example (ii) of section 4).

3. The logic

The basic objects of our partial correctness logic are (classical) Hoare formulas. Other formulas are constructed from them by two kinds of operators, namely

- the usual logical operators $\neg$, $\wedge$, $\forall$ ($\vee$, $\supset$, $\equiv$, $\exists$ are considered as abbreviations);
- a *substitution operator* <E> for every procedure declaration E.

More precisely we define the set of *generalized Hoare formulas* h by:

$h ::= \{p\}\ St\ \{q\} \mid \neg h' \mid (h_1 \wedge h_2) \mid \forall id.h' \mid \langle E\rangle h'$.

In order to define the semantics of these formulas, a formal definition of partial correctness is needed: A state transformation $\rho \subseteq \Sigma \times \Sigma$ is called *partially correct* with respect to the predicates $\pi, \pi' : \Sigma \to \mathrm{Bool}$, if $\pi(\sigma) = \mathrm{true}$ implies $\pi'(\sigma') = \mathrm{true}$ for all pairs $(\sigma,\sigma') \in \rho$.

Now a meaning $M(h) : \mathrm{Env} \rightharpoonup \mathrm{Bool}$ can be assigned to every generalized Hoare formula h by:

(i) $M(\{p\}\ St\ \{q\})(\varepsilon) = \mathrm{true}$
 $\Leftrightarrow M(St)(\varepsilon)$ is partially correct with respect to $M(p)(\varepsilon)$ and $M(q)(\varepsilon)$
 (remember that $M(p)(\varepsilon)$ and $M(q)(\varepsilon)$ are predicates);

(ii) $M(\neg h)(\varepsilon) = \mathrm{true} \quad \Leftrightarrow \quad M(h)(\varepsilon) = \mathrm{false}$;

(iii) $M(h_1 \wedge h_2)(\varepsilon) = \text{true} \Leftrightarrow M(h_1)(\varepsilon) = \text{true}$ and $M(h_2)(\varepsilon) = \text{true}$;

(iv) $M(\forall id.h)(\varepsilon) = \text{true} \Leftrightarrow M(h)(\varepsilon[id/\eta]) = \text{true}$ for all $\eta \in D_\tau$,
where τ is the type of id;

(v) $M(\langle E\rangle h)(\varepsilon) = \text{true} \Leftrightarrow M(h)(\varepsilon[\bar{P}/M(E)(\varepsilon)]) = \text{true}$,
where $\bar{P} = \text{decl}(E)$
(i.e. $\langle E\rangle h$ means that h is true "after" the declaration E).

Some comments are necessary:

- Note that in our logic the Hoare formulas are evaluated and combined (with the aid of logical operators) on the level of environments, and not (like in dynamic logic, cf. [Har 79]) on the level of states.
- Recall that M(h) (like all semantical definitions) depends on the underlying interpretation I of the signature Ω, i.e. (in a more precise notation) it is a function $M_I(h) : Env_I \to Bool$.

With this last notation we define: h is *valid* in I (notation: $\models_I h$) if $M_I(h)(\varepsilon) = \text{true}$ for all $\varepsilon \in Env_I$.

We now present some examples illustrating the use of our logic. It is assumed that the interpretation I assigns the usual meaning to the symbols 0, 1, ..., +, *, ... In all examples a detailed interpretation of the formulas is left to the reader.

(i) Let E be the declaration
$P \Leftarrow$ if cont(x) = c then x := cont(x)+1 else x := cont(x)+2 fi
and let h be the formula
$\{cont(x) = c\}\ P(\ )\ \{cont(x) = c + 1\}$.
Then $\models_I \langle E\rangle h$ holds, but $\langle E\rangle\forall c.h$ is not valid in I
(as already indicated in section 1).
On the other hand the declaration E' defined by
$P \Leftarrow x := cont(x) + 1$ yields $\models_I \langle E'\rangle\forall c.h$.

(ii) Let h be as in (i) and let h' be the formula
$\{cont(x) = 1\}\ P(\ )\ \{cont(x) = 2\}$.
Then $\forall c.h \supset h'$ is valid in I, but $h \supset h'$ is not.
This possibility of substituting (only) quantified identifiers indicates the predicate logical character of our formulas, which will also come out in the axioms and rules of the calculus (in section 4). Moreover - together with (i) - we get a first hint how to accomplish (formal) stepwise refinement proofs:
$\langle E'\rangle\forall c.h$ means that the procedure P declared by E' satisfies the semantical property $\forall c.h$. The formula $\forall c.h \supset h'$ says that this (ge-

neral) property implies the (special) instance h', which is possibly needed for the proof of an "abstract program" calling the procedure P. Hence it must be possible to conclude <E>h' from these two formulas; this will be accomplished by the "stepwise refinement axiom" of section 4.

(iii) The following example illustrates the use of quantified variable identifiers, which are particularly interesting in connection with sharing effects.
Let E be the declaration

```
P ⇐ λy. begin y := cont(x) + 1;
              if cont(x) = cont(y) then y := 1 else y := 2 fi
        end ,
```

let h be the formula {true} P(x) {cont(x) = 1}
and h' the formula {true} P(y) {cont(y) = 2}.
Then <E>h is valid in I (because of sharing), but <E>∀x.h is not. Moreover <E>h' is not valid in I, because it fails in the case of sharing, nor is <E>∀y.h'. A valid formula describing the non sharing case is:

<E>∀y. {¬y = x} P(y) {cont(y) = 2}.

Substituting x for y in this formula and applying the stepwise refinement lemma mentioned in example (ii) yields:

<E>{¬x = x} P(x) {cont(x) = 2},

which is valid in I (but meaningless).
This treatment of variable identifiers (which again shows the predicate logical character of our formulas) is possible, because variable identifiers stand for addresses and in particular different identifiers can denote the same address. In many other Hoare-like systems such an unrestricted substitution of variable identifiers is not allowed, because the underlying semantics is defined without the aid of addresses (cf. [Old 81]).

(iv) The last example illustrates the difficulties which can arise from the connection of local variables and global procedures.
Let St be the statement

```
begin var x; x := 1; begin E; P(R); R( ) end end
```

where E is the declaration R ⇐ y := cont(x).
We want to prove that $\models_I$ {true} St {cont(y) = 1}. The argumentation remains a bit informal because of our vague definition of the semantics.

First note that P is global w.r.t. St, hence it can be assumed that (the address assigned to) x is not accessed by (the function assigned to) P. As moreover R does not access x by writing (but only by reading), also P(R) cannot change the contents of x. Because x initially contains 1, this value is finally assigned to y by the call of R, and this proves the validity of the formula.

Note that the argumentation of example (iv) was only possible because the set of output addresses of P is defined separately (as mentioned at the end of section 2). If this is not the case (like in [HMT 83], [Hal 83]) then the validity of the above-mentioned formula is (at least) questionable.
Note moreover that this validity is not only a matter of taste. If St occurs within a procedure Q where a new procedure P is created in each recursion and inserted on parameter position of Q (like in example (iii) of section 4) then the formula might be a step in the proof of a "complete program" (without global procedures).

We conclude this section with some preparations for the calculus:
(i) First we need a definition of free (resp. bound) occurence and of substitution for the constructs C of our programming language and the formulas h of our logic. The binding mechanisms are: quantifiers, $\underline{\lambda}$-abstraction (i.e. formal parameters), variable declarations and procedure declarations. The sets free(C) and free(h) of identifiers which are not bound by one of these mechanisms are defined inductively, e.g.:

$$\text{free}(P_1 \Leftarrow Pb_1; \ldots ; P_m \Leftarrow Pb_m) = \bigcup_{i=1}^{m} \text{free}(Pb_i) \setminus \{P_1,\ldots,P_m\},$$

$$\text{free}(\underline{\text{begin}}\ E;St\ \underline{\text{end}}) = (\text{free}(E) \cup \text{free}(St)) \setminus \text{decl}(E).$$

Now it is possible to define a *substitution* of
- a value identifier c by a term t,
- a variable identifier x by a variable identifier y,
- a procedure identifier P by a procedure Proc of the same type.

The substitutions are defined "as usual", i.e. bound identifiers must be possibly renamed, in order to avoid new bindings.

The formulas which are obtained from h are denoted h_c^t, h_x^y and h_P^{Proc} respectively, similarly for constructs C.

As usual a *substitution theorem* holds:

- $M(h_c^t(\varepsilon) = M(h)(\varepsilon[c/\dot{M}(t)(\varepsilon)])$ if t is variable free,

- $M(h_x^y)(\varepsilon) = M(h)(\varepsilon[x/\varepsilon(y)])$,
- $M(h_P^{Proc})(\varepsilon) = M(h)(\varepsilon[P/M(Proc)(\varepsilon)])$.

Again everything generalizes the constructs C and to a simultaneous substitution of two or more identifiers.

The theorem shows that the substitution operator <E> can be considered as an abbreviation: If $decl(E) = \{P_1,\dots,P_m\}$, then <E>h is obtained from h by substituting for each P_i the procedure body

$$\underline{\lambda} id_1,\dots,id_n\text{: } \underline{\text{begin}}\ E;P_i(id_1,\dots,id_n)\ \underline{\text{end}}.$$

This will be the point of view in section 4.

(ii) For our variable declaration axiom we need a formula strange(x,P) such that

$$M(\text{strange}(x,P))(\varepsilon) = \text{true} \Leftrightarrow \varepsilon(x) \notin Out(\varepsilon(P))$$
(cf. section 2)

It can be defined by induction on the type of P.
For type (P) = stat it is the formula:
$\forall c.\{cont(x) = c\}\ P(\ )\ \{cont(x) = c\}$
and for type (P) = $(\tau_1\times\dots\times\tau_n \to \tau)$:

$$\forall id_1,\dots,id_n.\ (\bigwedge_{\tau_i \in Proctype} \text{strange}(x,id_i)$$
$$\supset \forall c.\{\bigwedge_{\tau_i=\underline{var}} \neg x = id_i \wedge cont(x)=c\}\ P(id_1,\dots,id_n)\{cont(x)=c\}).$$

Note that strange(x,P) is just an abbreviation for a generalized Hoare formula. The other authors who need a similar axiom or rule ([Hal 83], [Rey 82]) have introduced a new formula in order to express the (stronger) property $\varepsilon(x) \notin Glob(\varepsilon(P))$ (or a similar condition). We conjucture that our variable declaration axiom is still strong enough in spite of the weaker assumption.

(iii) In order to formulate the fixpoint induction principle we must characterize a subset of generalized Hoare formulas, which express admissible predicates (cf. [Man 74]). More precisely for every finite set $\{P_1,\dots,P_m\}$ of procedure identifiers a set of socalled *specifications* spec for $P_1,\dots,P_m$ is defined syntactically which all have two semantical properties:

For every environment ε
- $M(spec)(\varepsilon[P_1/\bot_1]\dots[P_m/\bot_m]) = \text{true}$ and
- the precidate Φ_ε defined by
$\Phi_\varepsilon(f_1,\dots,f_m) = M(spec)(\varepsilon[P_1/f_1]\dots[P_m/f_m]$

is admissible.

The precise syntactical definition is omitted here; a similar restriction is imposed on the formulas in Reynolds' axiom of recursion ([Rey 82]).

4. The proof system

Our proof system consists of three groups of axioms and rules.

I. *Logical* axioms and rules:

They are needed for "purely logical reasoning" on the level of generalized Hoare formulas.

(a) Tautology-rule:

$$\frac{h_1,\ldots,h_n}{h} \quad \text{if } (h_1 \wedge \ldots \wedge h_n) \supset h \quad \text{is a tautology.}$$

(b) Substitution-axioms:

(i) $\forall c.h \supset h^t_c$ if t is variable free.

(ii) $\forall x.h \supset h^y_x$

(iii) $\forall P.h \supset h^{Proc}_P$

(c) ($\forall$)-rule:

$$\frac{h \supset h'}{h \supset \forall id.h'} \quad \text{if } id \notin free(h).$$

II. Axioms and rules for *partial correctness*:

They are needed for manipulating the assertions p and q of a Hoare formula {p} St {q} without referring to the special structure of St.

(a) Invariance-axiom:

{p} St {p} if p does not contain the symbol "cont".

(b) ($\wedge$)-axiom:

$(\{p\}\ St\ \{q\} \wedge \{r\}\ St\ \{s\}) \supset \{p \wedge r\}\ St\ \{q \wedge s\}$

(c) ($\vee$)-axiom:

$(\{p\}\ St\ \{q\} \wedge \{r\}\ St\ \{s\}) \supset \{p \vee r\}\ St\ \{q \vee s\}$

(d) ($\forall$)-axiom:

$\forall c.\ \{p\}\ St\ \{q\} \supset \{\forall c.p\}\ St\ \{\forall c.q\}$ if $c \notin free(St)$

(e) ($\exists$)-axiom:

$\forall c.\{p\}\ St\ \{q\} \supset \{\exists c.p\}\ St\ \{\exists c.p\}$ if $c \notin free(St)$

(f) ($\supset$)-rule:

$$\frac{r \supset p\ ,\quad q \supset s}{\{p\}\ St\ \{q\} \supset \{r\}\ St\ \{s\}}$$

III. *Language specific* axioms and rules:
They are used to deal with the "operations" of the programming language like composition or recursion.

(a) (:=)-axioms:

(i) $\forall x,c.\{\underline{true}\}\ x := c\ \{cont(x) = c\}$

(ii) $\forall y,c.\ \{\neg y=x \wedge cont(y)=c\}\ x:=t\ \{cont(y)=c\}$

(b) (;)-axiom:

$(\{p\}\ St_1\ \{q\} \wedge \{q\}\ St_2\ \{r\}) \supset \{p\}\ St_1;St_2\ \{r\}$

(c) ($\underline{if}$)-axiom:

$(\{p\wedge r\}St_1\{q\} \wedge \{p\wedge\neg r\}St_2\{q\}) \supset \{p\}\ \underline{if}\ r\ \underline{then}\ St_1\ \underline{else}\ St_2\ \underline{fi}\ \{q\}$

(d) (PD)-axiom (for procedure declarations):

$\langle E\rangle\ \{p\}\ St\ \{q\} \supset \{p\}\ \underline{begin}\ E;St\ \underline{end}\ \{q\}$

(e) (VD)-axiom (for variable declarations):

$\forall x.((\bigwedge_{P\in free(St)} strange(x,P))\supset\{p\wedge\neg x=y_1\wedge\ldots\wedge\neg x=y_n\}\ St\ \{q\})$
$\supset \{p\}\ \underline{begin}\ \underline{var}\ x;St\ \underline{end}\ \{q\}$

if $x \notin free(p) \cup free(q) \cup \{y_1,\ldots,y_n\}$

(f) (FPI)-axiom (for fixpoint induction):

$\forall P_1,\ldots,P_m.(spec\supset spec^{Pb_1,\ldots,Pb_m}_{P_1,\ldots,P_m}) \supset \langle P_1 \Leftarrow Pb_1;\ldots;P_m \Leftarrow Pb_m\rangle spec$

if spec is a specification for $P_1,\ldots,P_m$ (cf. section 3).

(g) ($\underline{\lambda}$)-axiom:

$\{p\}\ St^{par_1,\ldots,par_n}_{id_1,\ldots,id_n}\ \{q\} \supset \{p\}\ \underline{\lambda}\ id_1,\ldots,id_n.St(par_1,\ldots,par_n)\ \{q\}$

if no par_i is a term which contains variables.

(h) call-by-value-axiom:

$\forall c.\{p \wedge t = c\}\ St\ \{q\} \supset \{p\}\ St^t_c\ \{q\}$

if $c \notin free(p) \cup free(t) \cup free(q)$
and St is an assignment or a procedure call without procedure bodies.

Instead of giving comments on the axioms and rules we want to illustrate their use with the aid of some examples. For this purpose we first present a derived axiom:

(SR)-axiom:

$$(\langle E\rangle spec \wedge \forall P_1,\ldots,P_m.(spec \supset h)) \supset \langle E\rangle h$$
$$\text{if } decl(E) = \{P_1,\ldots,P_m\}.$$

This axiom reflects the idea of stepwise refinement: If the formula h expresses partial correctness of an "abstract program", using the free procedure identifiers $P_1,\ldots,P_m$, then E<h> can be proved in two steps:

- h is proved under the assumption spec, which expresses certain semantical properties of the procedures;
- spec is proved for the procedures declared by E.

The derivation of this axiom is easy: Recall that the operator <E> is considered as a syntactical substitution; now apply the substitution axiom (iii) and the tautology rule.

We now present three derivations in the form of "derivation trees". We always concentrate on the most difficult "branches" of the tree; e.g. proofs for assignments are omitted at all. (Indeed proving the partial correctness of an assignment is tedious with the "pure" calculus; another derived axiom would be needed for reasonable derivations.)

We start with a procedure computing the factorial function (as a warming up example):

(i) Let E be the declaration $P \Leftarrow \underline{\lambda} x,a.St$ where St is the following statement:

$\underline{if}$ a = 0 $\underline{then}$ x := 1 $\underline{else}$ P(x,a-1); x := cont(x) * a $\underline{fi}$,

and let spec be the specification

$\forall x,a.\ \{\underline{true}\}\ P(x,a)\ \{cont(x) = a!\}$.

Then the (valid) formula <E>spec can be derived as follows

(1) <E>spec

↑----- (FPI)-axiom, (∀)-rule

(2) $spec \supset \forall x,a.\ \{\underline{true}\}\ \underline{\lambda} x,a.St(x,a)\ \{cont(x) = a!\}$

↑----- (∀)-rule, ($\underline{\lambda}$)-axiom

(3) $spec \supset \{\underline{true}\}\ St\ \{cont(x) = a!\}$

↑----- ($\underline{if}$)-axiom, (;)-axiom, tautology-rule

├─(4) $\{\underline{true} \wedge a = 0\}\ x := 1\ \{cont(x) = a!\}$

├─(5) $spec \supset \{\underline{true} \wedge \neg a=0\}\ P(x,a-1)\ \{cont(x)=(a-1)! \wedge \neg a=0\}$

└─(6) $\{cont(x)=(a-1)! \wedge \neg a=0\}\ x:= cont(x) * a\ \{cont(x)=a!\}$

We restrict our attention to the procedure call (5):

(5)

----- $(\wedge)$-axiom, tautology-rule

— (7) $spec \supset \{\underline{true}\}\ P(x,a-1)\ \{cont(x) = (a-1)!\}$

— (8) $\{\neg a=0\}\ P(x,a-1)\ \{\neg a=0\}$

(7) is an instance of the substitution axiom (i), and (8) is an instance of the invariance axiom. □

The second example illustrates the connection between global procedures and local variables. It was already considered from the semantical point of view in section 3.

(ii) Let St be the statement

$\underline{begin}\ \underline{var}\ x;\ x := 1;\ \underline{begin}\ E;\ P(R);\ R(\ )\ \underline{end}$

where E is the declaration $R \Leftarrow y := cont(x)$.

We want to prove $\{\underline{true}\}\ St\ \{cont(y) = 1\}$.

For this purpose we need the following specification spec for R:

$\forall c.\{cont(x)=c\}\ R(\ )\ \{cont(x)=c\} \wedge \forall b.\{cont(x)=b\}\ R(\ )\ \{cont(y)=b\}$

and the formula strange(x,P)

$\forall R.(\forall c.\{cont(x)=c\}R(\ )\{cont(x)=c\} \supset \forall c.\{cont(x)=c\}P(R)\{cont(x)=c\})$

Then we get the following derivation

(1) $\{\underline{true}\}\ St\ \{cont(y) = 1\}$

↑----- (VD)-axiom, $(\forall)$-rule

(2) $strange(x,P) \supset \{\underline{true}\}\ x:=1;\underline{begin}E;P(R);R(\ )\ \underline{end}\{cont(y)=1\}$

↑----- (;)-axiom, tautology rule

— (3) $\{\underline{true}\}x := 1\ \{cont(x) = 1\}$

— (4) $strange(x,P) \supset \{cont(x)=1\}\underline{begin}\ E;P(R);R(\ )\ \underline{end}\{cont(y)=1\}$

(3) is trivial.

(4)

↑----- (PD)-axiom

(5) strange(x,P)⊃<E>{cont(x)=1} P(R);R( ){cont(y)=1}

↑----- (SR)-lemma, $(\forall)$-rule, tautology rule

— (6) <E>spec

— (7) $strange(x,P) \supset (spec \supset \{cont(x)=1\}\ P(R);R(\ )\{cont(y)=1\})$

The derivation of (6) is routine, we concentrate on (7):

(7)

↑----- (;)-axiom, tautology rule

— (8) $(strange(x,p) \wedge spec) \supset \{cont(x)=1\}P(R)\{cont(x)=1\}$

— (9) $spec \supset \{cont(x) = 1\}\ R(\ )\ \{cont(y) = 1\}$

(8) and(9) can be derived with the aid of the tautology rule and the

substitution axioms. □

The last example is a (slight variant) of a procedure constructed by E. Olderog in order to illustrate the limits of his own calculus (in [Old 81]).

(iii) Let E be the declaration $P \Leftarrow Pb$,
where Pb is the procedure body
$\underline{\lambda}\ a,R.\ \underline{\text{begin}}\ Q \Leftarrow \underline{\lambda} c.R(c+1);St\ \underline{\text{end}}$
and St is the statement
$\underline{\text{if}}\ a < cont(x)\ \underline{\text{then}}\ P(a+1,Q)\ \underline{\text{else}}\ R(a+1)\ \underline{\text{fi}}$.

We want to prove $\langle E\rangle h$, where h is the formula
$\forall b.\{cont(x)=b\}\ P(0,\underline{\lambda} c.x:=c)\{cont(x)=2*b+1\}$.
For this purpose we choose the following specification spec for P:
$\forall a,R.(\forall c.\{\underline{true}\}\ R(c)\ \{cont(x) = c + a\}$
$\quad \supset \forall b.\{cont(x) = b \wedge a \le b\}\ P(a,R)\{cont(x) = 2 * b + 1\})$

Then we get the following derivation

(1) $\langle E\rangle h$
----- (SR)-axiom, ($\forall$)-rule
(2) $\langle E\rangle spec$
(3) $spec \supset h$

The derivation of (3) is relatively easy: The main step is the substitution of a by 0 and of R by $\underline{\lambda} c.x:=c$. We concentrate on (2):

(2) $\langle E\rangle spec$
----- (FPI)-axiom, ($\forall$)-rule
(4) $spec \supset (\forall c.\{\underline{true}\}\ R(c)\ \{cont(x) = c + a\}$
$\quad \supset \forall b.\{cont(x) = b \wedge a \le b\}\ Pb(a,R)\{cont(x) = 2*b+1\})$
----- tautology rule, ($\forall$)-rule, ($\underline{\lambda}$)-axiom
(5) $(spec \wedge \forall c.\{\underline{true}\}\ R(c)\ \{cont(x) = c + a\})$
$\quad \supset \{cont(x)=b\wedge a\le b\}\ \underline{\text{begin}}\ Q \Leftarrow \underline{\lambda} c.R(c+1);St\ \underline{\text{end}}\ \{cont(x) = 2*b+1\}$
----- (PD)-axiom, (SR)-axiom, ($\forall$)-rule
(6) $(spec \wedge \forall c.\ \{\underline{true}\}\ R(c)\ \{cont(x) = c + a\})$
$\quad \supset \langle Q \Leftarrow \underline{\lambda} c.\ R(c+1)\rangle\ \forall c.\ \{\underline{true}\}\ Q(c)\ \{cont(x) = c+a+1\}$
(7) $(spec \wedge \forall c.\{\underline{true}\}\ R(c)\ \{cont(x) = c + a\})$
$\quad \supset (\forall c.\ \{\underline{true}\}\ Q(c)\ \{cont(x) = c + a + 1\}$
$\qquad \supset \{cont(x) = b \wedge a \le b\}\ St\ \{cont(x)=2 * b + 1\})$

(6) is routine. As far as (7) is concerned, note that:
- spec together with the specification of Q is sufficient

to deal with the then-part of the statement St (where the main step is a substitution of R by Q and of a by a + 1)

- the specification of R is sufficient to deal with the else-part (because a = cont(x) = b in this case) □

As mentioned in the introduction, example (iii) has been proved with the aid of calculi using higher order oracles (in [Old 84], [DaJ 83]). In order to obtain a program which even exceeds the power of these calculi, just replace the declaration of Q by:

var y; Q ⇐ λc.begin y := c;R(cont(y)+1) end.

This does not change the semantics of P, and in our calculus the formula h of example (iii) can still be proved. (The variable declaration is just removed with the aid of the (VD)-axiom, the information strange(x,P) is not needed.)

But from a syntactical point of view the new program contains a "serious side effect", because y is global in the body of Q and local in the body of P (cf. [Lan 83]). Hence in each recursion a new procedure Q is generated (and inserted on parameter position), which has one additional global variable. This phenomenon does not fit into the framework of [Old 84] or [DaJ 83].

5. Conclusion

As usual the question arises now, if our proof system is sound and in some sense complete. The soundness can be proved without difficulties. Completeness - even relative completeness in the sense of [Coo 78] - cannot be expected for the partial correctness theory of the full programming language. This was proved in [Cla 79] by showing that for such a powerful language the divergence problem (i.e. the question if a program does not terminate for any input) is unsolvable even for finite interpretations. Hence we must look for less powerful sublanguages, in order to get completeness results.

Several adequate sublanguages can be found in [Old 81]: With our calculus we can simulate so-called standard proofs in E. Olderog's system $H(C_{60})$, provided that all procedures have finite mode (i.e. self application is not allowed). But of course this result does not exploit the power of our logic and calculus. A more interesting candidate for a sublanguage would be Clarke's L4 (cf. [Cla 79], [DaJ 83]), in which procedures with global variables are not allowed, a restriction which makes the divergence problem solvable for finite interpretations. A first hint how to obtain a completeness proof for a similar calculus can be found in [CGH 83], and we hope that their idea can be applied to our proof system.

In spite of this lack of reliable completeness results we hope that this paper has convinced the reader that our proof system is natural and powerful.

Acknowledgement: I am grateful to Ernst Olderog for his comments on an earlier version of this paper and to Albert Meyer for submitting my paper to this Workshop.

References:

[Cla 79] Clarke, E.M.: Programming language constructs for wich it is impossible to obtain good Hoare-like axioms. JACM 26, 129 - 147, 1979

[CGH 83] Clarke, E.M., German, S.M. and Halpern, J.Y.: Reasoning about procedures as parameters. Proc. of the CMU Workshop on Logics of Programs, LNCS 164, 206 - 220, 1983

[Coo 78] Cook, S.A.: Soundness and completeness of an axiom system for program verification. SIAM Journ. on Comp. 7, 70 - 90, 1978

[dBa 80] de Bakker, J.W.: Mathematical theory of program correctness. Prentice-Hall, 1980

[DaJ 83] Damm, W. and Josko, B.: A sound and relatively* complete Hoare-logic for a language with higher type procedures. Acta Informatica 20, 59 - 102, 1983

[$GTW^2 77$] Goguen, J.A., Thatcher, J.W., Wagner, E.G. and Wright, J.B.: Initial algebra semantics and continuous algebras. JACM 24, 68 - 95, 1977

[Hal 83] Halpern, J.Y.: A good Hoare axiom system for an ALGOL-like language. Proc. 11th POPL Conf., 262 - 271, 1983

[Har 79] Harel, D.: First order dynamic logic , LNCS 68, Springer-Verlag, 1979

[HMT 83] Halpern, J.Y., Meyer, A.R. and Trakhtenbrot, B.A.: The semantics of local storage, or what makes the free-list free? Proc. 11th POPL Conf., 245 - 257, 1983

[Lan 83] Langmaack, H.: Aspects of programs with finite modes. Proc. of the FCT-Conference, LNCS 158, 241 - 254, 1983

[Man 74] Manna, Z.: Mathematical theory of computation. McGraw-Hill, 1974

[Old 81] Olderog, E.R.: Sound and complete Hoare-like calculi based on copy rules. Acta Informatica 16, 161 - 197, 1981

[Old 83] Olderog, E.R.: A characterization of Hoare's logic for programs with PASCAL-like procedures. Proc. 15th ACM Symp. on Theory of Computing, 320 - 329, 1983

[Old 84] Olderog, E.R.: Correctness of programs with PASCAL-like procedures without global variables. TCS 30, 49 - 90, 1984

[Rey 81] Reynolds, J.C.: The craft of programming. Prentice-Hall International Series in Comp. Sc. 1981

[Rey 82] Reynolds, J.C.: Idealized ALGOL. Tools and notions for program construction. D. Néel ed., Cambridge University Press, 121 - 161, 1982

[Sie 81] Sieber, K.: A new Hoare-calculus for programs with recursive parameterless procedures. Bericht A 81/02, Universität Saarbrücken, 1981

A PROOF SYSTEM FOR DISTRIBUTED PROCESSES

A. E. K. Sobel and N. Soundararajan
Department of Computer and Information Science
The Ohio State University
Columbus, OH 43210

1. Introduction

The current paper defines a proof system for the language of Distributed Processes, henceforth called DP, given in Brinch Hansen [2]. An important aspect of our approach is that proofs of the individual processes of a program are completely isolated from each other. This allows us to consider an individual process without making assumptions about the behavior of the other processes. In fact, the most important idea underlying our work is that the individual processes of a concurrent program must be dealt with in isolation if we are to avoid getting lost in the complex interactions between the processes. Since the semantics of a construct is independent of the rest of the program, we have the flexibility to change any one construct without causing a change in the verification of the other processes in the program. Once we obtain the individual process proofs, we only need to combine the post-conditions of the processes in order to obtain the behavior of the entire program.

This aspect can be contrasted with the system in Gerth et. al.[3] where individual process proofs are closely related to each other. In their system, the properties of the individual processes are proved using assumptions about the behavior of the remaining processes in the program. Their parallel composition rule contains an "interference freedom test"[3] since this test is needed to substantiate these assumptions. The proof of interference freedom is often the most difficult part of the proof. Moreover, the interference freedom test requires the use of the complete proof outlines of each of the constructs within the program. Therefore, a modification to any construct would require the modification of potentially all the other processes defined within the program.

For these reasons, we feel that considering constructs entirely in isolation from the other processes leads to simpler proofs. This concept is also the motivation behind the development of the axiomatic semantics of CSP defined in [7,8,9].

2. The Language Distributed Processes

DP was proposed for real-time applications controlled by microcomputer networks with distributed storage. A DP program consists of a fixed number of sequential processes that are executed concurrently and exist forever. Each process can only access its own variables — there are no shared variables. A process may call the common procedures defined within the other processes. Processes are synchronized by means of nondeterministic statements called guarded regions.

2.1 Programs, Processes, & Procedures

If $P_1, P_2, \ldots, P_N$ denote N processes, a program is denoted as:

$$[P_1 || P_2 || \ldots || P_N]$$

A process is defined as follows:

Process name
Variables local to the process
Common Procedures
Process Initialization
Variables local to Process Initialization

Each process contains a number of variables that are accessible to all the procedures of the process. A procedure in one process may call a procedure in another process, but not a procedure within the same process. Each process also includes a process initialization section and the execution of a process begins with this section.

A procedure is defined as follows:

Proc name(input parameters#output parameters)
Variables local to procedure
Procedure body

There are two types of parameters: **in** and **out.** A procedure can be called by the process initialization of the process within which the procedure is defined (i.e. internal calls). It can also be called by any other procedures or process initializations that are defined within any of the other processes (i.e. external calls).

A process P can call the procedure R, defined within process Q, by the statement:

CALL Q.R(expressions#variables)

When a procedure call is accepted, a new incarnation of the called procedure is created for the calling process. Previous to the execution of the procedure R, the expression values of the call are assigned to the **in** parameters. When the execution of the procedure terminates, the **out** parameters are assigned to the variables listed within the call. An external request is regarded as an atomic action within the calling process. Using the previous example of a procedure call, the process P will be suspended until the process Q has completed the request. In the case of internal requests, the process initialization will be suspended until the called procedure has completed the request. Therefore, recursion will not be realized in the language.

A process is executed by executing the process initialization until it finishes, or until it reaches a synchronization statement where no synchronization condition is satisfied. In the latter case, the initialization is suspended and the process begins executing one of its procedures that has been called. If no call has been received as of yet, or the process initialization has finished, then the process waits for a procedure call. Therefore, the process never terminates. The process will execute a procedure call until the procedure finishes or until it reaches a synchronization statement where no synchronization condition is satisfied. The process will then either begin the execution of another procedure that has been called, or if one of these conditions is now satisfied, resume one of the synchronization statements that was previously suspended. This selection is made nondeterministically. The interleaving of the process initialization and external requests continues forever.

2.2 Nondeterminism

Nondeterminism can arise from the following statements which are called guarded commands and guarded regions. A guarded command causes the process to make an arbitrary choice between several statements based on the current state of the variables. The following two statements are used to define guarded commands.

$$\textbf{IF}\ b_1{:}S_1 | b_2{:}S_2 | \ldots | b_n{:}S_n\ \textbf{END}$$

An arbitrary selection is made anong those b_i that evaluate to **true** and the corresponding S_i is executed. If all the b_i's evaluate to **false**, a program exception will occur.

$$\textbf{DO}\ b_1{:}S_1 | b_2{:}S_2 | \ldots | b_n{:}S_n\ \textbf{END}$$

While any of the b_i evaluate to **true**, arbitrarly select one of them and execute the corresponding S_i. The execution of the **DO** statement terminates when all b_i evaluate to **false**.

A guarded region causes a process to wait until the state of the variables allows an arbitrary choice among several statements to be made. If the state of the variables makes this selection impossible, then the process will postpone the execution of the guarded region. The following two statements are used to define guarded regions.

WHEN $b_1:S_1|b_2:S_2|\ldots|b_n:S_n$ **END**

Wait until at least one b_i evaluates to **true**, arbitrarily select one of these b_i, and execute the corresponding S_i.

CYCLE $b_1:S_1|b_2:S_2|\ldots|b_n:S_n$ **END**

This is equivalent to the endless repetition of the **WHEN** statement.

3. The Proof System

3.1 An Introduction

Our proof system is centered around the interactions made between procedures, the process initializations, and the processes defined within a program. These interactions can be used to characterize the externally visible behavior of any construct. The semantics of any construct S is a simple formalization of what an external observer of S would see during the execution of S. Our assertions will refer to this sequence of interactions of the construct that we are verifying. Since we do not allow arbitrary assumptions, it will not be necessary to perform an interference freedom check as in [3].

In order to easily express the sequence of actions that are visible to an external observer, we will associate a sequence $h_{i,k}$ with each procedure Q_k of the process P_i. This sequence will record all interactions between $P_i.Q_k$ and external agents, any suspensions of $P_i.Q_k$, and any resumptions of $P_i.Q_k$. A similar sequence $h_{i,o}$ will be associated with the initialization statement of P_i. Similarly, we associate a sequence h_i with each process P_i that will record all interactions between P_i and external agents.

Because of the nature of DP, we had to modify the standard Hoare-logic of {p}S{q}. Since processes never terminate, we could trivially conclude {p}S{false} [4]. Therefore, we chose to use an invariant, instead of a postcondition, with the restriction that the invariant will be defined in terms of the sequence of interactions. The notation {p}S(r) will represent the following:

Given the precondition p, the interaction sequence h that corresponds to S will satisfy the invariant r during the execution of S.

The invariants of the procedures and process initialization will be combined to describe the behavior of the process, and ultimately these invariants will be combined to specify the program.

The proof system was constructed by examining what an observer would witness as he stood at different locations within the operating program. At the lowest level, the observer standing within a procedure would witness a single execution of the procedure. This single execution would include any suspensions or resumptions that occured during this execution. If that observer were to move directly outside the procedure but still only observe this procedure, he would witness the numerous procedure calls (both external and internal) to this procedure.

If the observer moved away from that procedure but still remained within the process, he would witness all the external and internal procedure calls made to this process and the order of execution of the procedures and process initialization. This order of execution will be dictated by the suspensions and resumptions of the procedures, the execution of the process initialization, and the accepted procedure calls. Lastly, if the observer moved directly outside the process, he would witness the external procedure calls move from the requesting process to the called process and back. He would not witness the order of execution of the procedures and process initialization defined within this process since these actions do not involve any external agents.

Using this methodology, the axioms will also describe the system at its lowest level, and then combine these results in order to describe the system at higher and higher levels until the program level is reached. The corresponding functions and predicates used in the proof system are contained in Appendix A.

3.2 <u>The Semantics</u>

3.2.1 <u>SKIP</u> Statement

$$\{p\}\ \textbf{Skip}\ \{p\}$$

3.2.2 Assignment Statement

$$\{p_e^x\}\ x:=e\ \{p\}$$

3.2.3 Body

$$\frac{\{p\}\ S\ \{q\}}{\{p\}\ \textbf{BEGIN}\ S\ \textbf{END}\ \{q\}}$$

3.2.4 Sequential Composition

$$\frac{\{p\}\ S_1\ \{q'\},\ \{q'\}\ S_2\ \{q\}}{\{p\}\ S_1;S_2\ \{q\}}$$

3.2.5 Consequence

$$\frac{p \text{ ==> } p',\ \{p'\}\ S\ \{q'\},\ q' \text{ ==> } q}{\{p\}\ S\ \{q\}}$$

3.2.6 Conjunction

$$\frac{\{p\}\ S\ \{q_1\},\ \{p\}\ S\ \{q_2\}}{\{p\}\ S\ \{q_1 \wedge q_2\}}$$

3.2.7 Disjunction

$$\frac{\{p_1\}\ S\ \{q\},\ \{p_2\}\ S\ \{q\}}{\{p_1 \vee p_2\}\ S\ \{q\}}$$

3.2.8 IF Statement

$$\frac{\{p \wedge b_j\}\ S_j\ \{q\},\ j=1,..,n}{\{p\}\ \mathbf{IF}\ b_1{:}S_1|\ldots|b_n{:}S_n\ \mathbf{END}\ \{q\}}$$

3.2.9 DO Statement

$$\frac{\{p \wedge b_j\}\ S_j\ \{p\},\ j=1,..,n}{\{p\}\ \mathbf{DO}\ b_1{:}S_1|\ldots|b_n{:}S_n\ \mathbf{END}\ \{p \wedge \neg b_1 \wedge\ldots\wedge \neg b_n\}}$$

3.2.10 External CALL Statement

$$\{\forall \mathbf{Y}.\, p^{\mathbf{Z},h_{i,k}}_{\mathbf{Y},h_{i,k}\hat{}\langle \mathrm{call\_to},i,k,l,j,\mathbf{X}\rangle\hat{}\langle \mathrm{return\_from},i,k,l,j,\mathbf{Y}\rangle}\}$$

$$\textbf{CALL}\ P_l.Q_j(\mathbf{X}\#\mathbf{Z})\ \{p\}$$

The effect of the statement **CALL** $P_l.Q_j$ within the procedure $P_i.Q_k$ is to extend the sequence $h_{i,k}$ by two elements: one corresponding to the call and the other to the return. In addition, the values of the variables returned by $P_l.Q_j$ will be assigned to the corresponding variables of $P_i.Q_k$.

The concatenation operation, "^", represents the addition of an element to the right end of a sequence. We add the element <call_to,i,k,l,j,**X**> to the sequence in order to indicate that control leaves $P_i.Q_k$ to call the procedure $P_l.Q_j$, and that the values of the variables **X** are the arguments associated with this call. The other element, <return_from,i,k,l,j,**Y**>, is added to the sequence to indicate that control returns to $P_i.Q_k$. The result values, **Y**, that are returned by the procedure are assigned to the corresponding argument variables Z. The universal quantifier ensures that we consider all possible result values that $P_l.Q_j$ could return.

3.2.11 Internal CALL Statement

$$p \Longrightarrow q'^{\,h_{i,0}}_{\,h_{i,0}\hat{}\langle \mathrm{call\_to},i,o,i,k,\mathbf{X},\mathbf{U}\rangle}$$

$$q' \Longrightarrow \forall \mathbf{Y},\mathbf{R}.\, q^{\mathbf{Z},h_{i,0}}_{\mathbf{Y},h_{i,0}\hat{}\langle \mathrm{return\_from},i,o,i,k,\mathbf{Y},\mathbf{R}\rangle}$$

$$\{p\}\ \textbf{CALL}\ P_i.Q_k(\mathbf{X}\#\mathbf{Z})\ \{q\}$$

Since the internal **CALL** causes the suspension of the execution of the process initialization, two elements are added to the corresponding sequence $h_{i,o}$. The first element records the current values of the process variables and the **in** parameters. When execution of the process initialization resumes, the second element records all possible process variable and **out** parameter values.

3.2.12 <u>WHEN</u> Statement

$$\{p \wedge b_j\}\ S_j\ \{q\},\ j=1,..,n$$

$$[p \wedge \bigwedge_{j}^{n} \neg b_j] \Longrightarrow \{\forall T.\, p'^{\;\bar{R},h_{i,k}}_{\;T,h_{i,k}\hat{}<suspend,i,k,\bar{R}>\hat{}<resume,i,k,T>}\}$$

$$\{p' \wedge b_j\}\ S_j\ \{q\},\ j=1,..,n$$

$$\{p\}\ \textbf{WHEN}\ b_1{:}S_1|\ldots|b_n{:}S_n\ \textbf{END}\ \{q\}$$

The first line considers the case when at least one of the b_j is satisfied; therefore, execution of the **WHEN** is not suspended. The second and third lines consider the case when a suspension occurs. The second line ensures that the proper elements have been concatenated to $h_{i,k}$, with $\bar{R}$ being the local variables of P_i, and T being the values of these variables after the execution of the **WHEN** is resumed. The universal quantifier ensures that we consider all possible values that these variables may have when the procedure resumes.

3.2.13 Procedure Rule

$$\forall Z,T.[\{h_{i,k}=<<call,i,k,Z,T>> \wedge \bar{X}=Z \wedge \bar{R}=T\} \Longrightarrow p]$$

$$\{p\}\ S\ \{q'\}$$

$$q' \Longrightarrow q^{\;h_{i,k}}_{\;h_{i,k}\hat{}<return,i,k,\bar{Y},\bar{R}>}$$

$$\{h_{i,k}=\epsilon\}\ \underline{\textbf{Proc}}\ Q_k(\bar{X}\#\bar{Y})\ \textbf{BEGIN}\ S\ \textbf{END}\ \{q\}$$

The first line ensures that when the execution of $P_i.Q_k$ begins, the appropriate element corresponding to the procedure call has been recorded as the first element in $h_{i,k}$. The values of $\bar{X}$, the **in** parameters, are Z; the values of $\bar{R}$, the local variables of P_i, are T. The quantifier reflects our ignorance of the values $P_i.Q_k$ will receive as input parameters or the values the common variables of P_i will have when the execution of $P_i.Q_k$ begins. The third line ensures that the element recording the return from $P_i.Q_k$ to the caller is concatenated to $h_{i,k}$. This element includes the output parameter values and the values of the local variables of P_i.

3.2.14 Externalize Procedure

$$\frac{\{h_{i,k}=\epsilon\}\ P_i.Q_k\ \{q\}}{\{h_{i,k}=\epsilon\}\ [P_i.Q_k]\ (\ \mathrm{CHECK}(h_{i,k}) \wedge \forall m \le \mathrm{NO\_CALLS}(h_{i,k}).\ [\ \exists h'_{i,k}.\ g(\mathrm{SUBSEQ}(m,\mathrm{SEQ}(h_i,k))) \sqsubseteq h'_{i,k} \wedge q^{h_{i,k}}_{h'_{i,k}}]\ )}$$

Once our observer moves outside the procedure but only observes this procedure, he will witness all the calls made to the procedure. The sequence $h_{i,k}$, as seen by this observer, will contain a record of the interactions of $P_i.Q_k$ during these various calls. Our rule should then give an invariant for the procedure that will ensure that each portion of $h_{i,k}$ corresponding to such a call satisfies the postcondition of $P_i.Q_k$. Some of these calls may be incomplete (due, perhaps, to suspensions of the procedure), and the record $h_{i,k}$ corresponding to such an incomplete call will not satisfy the postcondition of $P_i.Q_k$. It should be possible, however, to extend (possibly in more than one way) such incomplete records so that they will also satisfy the postcondition of $P_i.Q_j$.

CHECK performs a syntax check on $h_{i,k}$. The rest of the invariant ensures that the portion of $h_{i,k}$ corresponding to <u>each</u> call (hence the quantifier over m) can be extended in such a way that it will satisfy q, the postcondition of $P_i.Q_k$.

3.2.15 Process Initialization

The processes initialization statement may contain any of the statements that may appear in the procedures with the addition of the **CYCLE** statement.

3.2.16 <u>CYCLE</u> Statement

$$\frac{\begin{array}{l}\{p \wedge b_j\}\ S_j\ \{p\},\ j=1,..,n \\ [p \wedge \bigwedge_j^n \neg b_j] \Longrightarrow \{\forall T.p'^{\,R,h_{i,k}}_{\,T,h_{i,k}\hat{}<suspend,i,k,R>\hat{}<resume,i,k,T>}\} \\ \{p' \wedge b_j\}\ S_j\ \{p\},\ j=1,..,n\end{array}}{\{p\}\ \mathbf{CYCLE}\ b_1{:}S_1 | \ldots | b_n{:}S_n\ \mathbf{END}\ (\ r_{i,k}\ )}$$

The rule for the **CYCLE** statement is virtually identical to the **WHEN** rule except that it establishes an invariant rather than a postcondition. Also, the precondition to the **CYCLE** statement must be true after the execution of the selected S_j for each iteration of the **CYCLE** statement.

3.2.17 Process Rule

The verifications of the procedures and the process initialization statement of a process P_i will be combined using this rule in order to verify P_i.

$$\frac{\{h_{i,k}=\epsilon\}\ [P_i.Pr_k]\ (\ r_{i,k}\ ),\ k=1,..,m \qquad \{h_{i,int}=\epsilon\}\ PI_i\ (\ r_{i,int}\ )}{\{p_i\}\ P_i\ (\ r_{i,int}{}^{h_{i,int}}_{f_{int}(h_i)} \wedge [\forall j \le m. r_{i,j}{}^{h_{i,j}}_{SEQ(h_i,j)}] \wedge CONSIST(t_1,..,t_n,h_i)\ )}$$

As our observer examines the interactions that occur within a process, he will witness the execution of the various procedures and the process initialization. Therefore, we must verify that the sequence representing the interactions made by the process initialization that was taken from the process sequence h_i will satisfy the process initialization invariant $r_{i,int}$. We must also verify that the sequences representing the external actions of each procedure that are taken from the process sequence will satisfy their corresponding procedure invariant. Lastly, we must perform a consistency check, using the predicate **CONSIST**, on the process sequence h_i to ensure that this sequence represents a valid sequence of events for a process.

3.2.18 Externalize Process

$$\frac{\{p_i \wedge h_i=\epsilon\}\ P_i\ (\ r_i\ )}{\{p_i\}\ [P_i]\ (\ \exists h_i.(h_i^{ext}=STRIP(h_i)) \wedge r_i\ )}$$

When our observer moves outside of the process, he will witness the calls made to the procedures defined within the process and any calls made to any procedures external to this process but he will not witness the order of execution of the various procedures and the process initialization. Hence, the sequence h^{ext} that is seen by the observer should be obtained by **STRIP**ping these elements from a sequence h_i that satisfies the invariant r_i.

3.2.19 Parallel Composition

$$\frac{\{p_i\}\ [P_i]\ (\ r_i\ ),\ i=1,..,n}{\{p_1 \wedge \ldots \wedge p_n\}\ [\ [P_1]||\ldots||[P_n]\ ]\ (\ r_1 \wedge \ldots \wedge r_n \wedge \mathrm{COMPAT}(h_1^{ext},\ldots,h_n^{ext})\ )}$$

Lastly, we will combine the individual process invariants and perform a compatibility check using, the predicate **COMPAT**, on the externalized view of the process interaction sequences. We will assume that no external procedure calls from another program are made to any of the processes defined within this program. The compatibility check ensures that any action in which two processes participate is recorded on the two process sequences in a mutually consistent fashion.

4. An Example

4.1 The Program

In order to compare our system with an existing system, we will use the following parallel sort program taken from Gerth et. al.[3]. The program consists of the process $SORT_0$, the "user" process, and the processes $SORT_1,\ldots,SORT_n$ that implement the sort. The processes $SORT_1,\ldots,SORT_n$ maintain a sorted list of numbers given to them by $SORT_0$, with the smallest number being stored in $SORT_1$, the next smallest in $SORT_2$ ($SORT_1$'s immediate neighbor to the right), and so forth. This ordering is achieved by $SORT_1$ storing the smallest number and passing all other numbers to $SORT_2$, $SORT_2$ storing the second smallest number and passing all other numbers to $SORT_3$, and so forth. A process receives one of the remaining numbers from its successor after a number is output to its predecessor. The notation SORT[i] represents N-1 identical processes where SUCC refers to the next highest index of the processes. The Nth process requires slight modification since it does not have a successor.

```
Process SORT[i]
        HERE:SEQ[2] int; LEN,REST,TEMP: int;

Proc PUT(c:int)
        WHEN LEN=1 ∨ (LEN=0 ∧ REST=0):
                LEN+:=1;
                HERE[LEN]:=c;
        END
END
```

```
Proc GET(#v:int)
        WHEN LEN=1:
                v:=HERE[1];
                HERE:=[];
                LEN:=0;
        END
END
BEGIN
        HERE:=[];
        REST:=0;
        LEN:=0;
        CYCLE
                LEN=2:
                        IF HERE[1]≤HERE[2]:
                                TEMP:=HERE[2];
                                HERE:=[HERE[1]];
                        | HERE[1]>HERE[2]:
                                TEMP:=HERE[1];
                                HERE:=[HERE[2]];
                        END
                        CALL SORT[SUCC].PUT(TEMP);
                        REST+:=1;
                        LEN:=1;
                | LEN=0 /\ REST>0:
                        CALL SORT[SUCC].GET(TEMP);
                        REST-:=1;
                        HERE:=[TEMP];
                        LEN:=1;
        END
END
```

4.2 The Proof

The process $SORT_0$ will submit the list of numbers to be sorted to the process $SORT_1$ and remove this list from $SORT_1$. The following process invariant characterizes this behavior.

$$r_0: \forall k \leq \bar{h}_0.[\mathrm{TYPE}(h_0,k) \in \{\text{"Call\_to PUT}_1\text{"}, \text{"Call\_to GET}_1\text{"}, \text{"Return\_from PUT}_1\text{"}, \text{"Return\_from GET}_1\text{"}\} \wedge [\mathrm{NO\_OF}(h_0[1:k], \text{"Call\_to GET}_1\text{"}) \leq \mathrm{NO\_OF}(h_0[1:k], \text{"Call\_to PUT}_1\text{"})]]$$

Given the individual process invariants and r_0, the following program invariant can be determined. The program invariant illustrates that the numbers taken from $SORT_1$ are indeed in ascending order.

$$r: \forall k \leq \bar{h}_0.[\mathrm{TYPE}(h_0,k) = \text{"Return\_from GET}_1\text{"} \Rightarrow \mathrm{VAL}(h_0,k) = \mathrm{FIRST}(\mathrm{QUEUE}(h_0[1:k-1]))]$$

In order to verify the program invariant r, we must examine the relationship between the processes $SORT_i$ and $SORT_{i+1}$. This relationship has the following three properties. Once established, these properties will allow us to verify r.

(1) $\forall i.1 \leq i < n$

$$[\forall k \leq \bar{h}/i.[[NUM_i(h/i[1:k]) \geq 1 \wedge REST_i(h/i[1:k]) > 0] \implies \forall j.i<j \leq n.[MIN(HERE_i(h/i[1:k])) \leq MIN(HERE_j(h/j[1:k]))]]]$$

This first characteristic establishes that the smallest number associated with $SORT_i$ is less than or equal to any of the numbers associated with $SORT_{i+1}$ through $SORT_n$.

(2) $\forall i.1 \leq i < n$

$$[\forall k \leq \bar{h}/i[NUM_i(h/i[1:k]) \geq 1 \implies MIN(HERE_i(h/i[1:k]))=FIRST(LIST_i(h/i[1:k]))]]$$

The second characteristic illustrates the relationship between the sequence $HERE_i$ and the numbers passed to the process from its left and contained within the processes $SORT_i,..,SORT_n$.

(3) $\forall i.1 \leq i < n$

$$[\forall k \leq \bar{h}/i.[TYPE(h/i,k)=\text{"RETURN from } GET_{i+1}\text{"} \implies VAL(h/i,k)=FIRST(LIST_i(h/i[1:k-1]))]]$$

The third characteristic ensures the correspondence between the numbers passed from $SORT_{i+1}$ to $SORT_i$ and the numbers that were passed from $SORT_{i-1}$ to $SORT_i$. This characteristic follows almost directly from the previous one. It is not difficult to see that this last characteristic directly implies the program invariant r.

5. Conclusion

In this paper we have presented a proof system for DP which examines procedures and processes in isolation. We have illustrated the possibility of examining individual processes in complete isolation by banning any assumptions about the behavior of the other procedures and processes in the program. We feel that this methodology usually results in fairly simple proofs which can be envisioned given the previous example.

We used the concept of hierarchical decomposition in order to examine the different components of the program. This allowed us to verify a procedure by examining only one execution of the procedure. We then verified the multiple executions of a procedure, the process initialization, a process, and finally the entire program. As we examined higher and higher levels of the program, we combined the results from the previous level in order to draw conclusions about the next level.

The use of a variable to record the interaction sequence should not be confused with the notion of auxillary variables [1],[5]. It is our belief that this variable is used to record actual behavior; it is not a variable that has been added by the program prover. Our sequences should be considered as "hidden" variables which are updated by the statements that cause interaction between various components.

At first glance, our proof system appears to require extensive analysis at the parallel composition stage. This belief comes from the necessity of analyzing an infinite number of varying length communication sequences. The proof is simplified by performing an inductive proof on the length of each process interaction sequence. We believe that this proof is simpler than the cooperation check required in either [1], [3], or [5]. By not allowing assumptions to be made about the behavior of other processes, we pay a price in that our process invariants are usually weaker than the corresponding invariants of [3]. Despite this weakness, our system is (relatively) complete and a proof of (relative) completeness may be given along the lines of the proof in [8].

The methodology used to construct this proof system could easily be extended to higher and higher levels of parallelism. We stopped at the program level since DP could not support the definition of any higher program levels. It is our suggestion that DP be extended in order to support hierarchical decomposition. A process should be able to "call" another program without having to know the internal structure of the program. With this extention, the example could have been better written with the N sorting processes comprising one program, and a process of another program submitting a list of numbers to the sorting program and receiving the sorted list in return. The process should not need to be aware of the contents of the sorting program or how the sorting method is implemented in order to obtain a sorted list.

I. References

1. Apt, K.R., N. Francez, and W.P. de Roever. A Proof System for Communicating Sequential Processes. ACM TOPLAS, 2, 359-385, 1980.

2. Brinch Hansen, P. Distributed Processes: A Concurrent Programming Concept. CACM 21, 11, 934-941, 1978.

3. Gerth, Rob, W.P. de Roever, and Mary Roncken. Procedures and Concurrency: A Study in Proof. Proceedings of the 5th International Symposium on Programming. LNCS 137, 132-163, Springer Verlag, New York, 1982.

4. Hoare, C.A.R. An Axiomatic Basis for Computer Programming. CACM, 12, 10, 576-580,583, 1969.

5. Owicki, S.S., and D. Gries. An Axiomatic Proof Technique for Parallel Programs. ACTA Informatica, 6, 319-340, 1976.

6. Roncken, M., N. vanDiepen, M. Dramer, W.P. de Roever. A Proof System for Brinch Hansen's Distributed Processes. Technical Report RUU-CS-81-5, Department of Computer Science, University of Utrecht, 1981.

7. Soundararajan, N. Axiomatic Semantics of CSP. ACM TOPLAS, 6, 4, 647-662, 1984.

8. Soundararajan, N., O.J. Dahl. Partial Correctness Semantics for CSP. To appear in BIT.

9. Soundararajan, N. A Proof Technique for Parallel Programs. To appear in Theoretical Computer Science.

II. Appendix A

$\bar{h}$	The number of elements in the communication sequence h
ELEM(h,k)	The kth element from the left end of the sequence h
h[1:k]	<ELEM(h,1),ELEM(h,2),...,ELEM(h,k)>
TYPE(h,k)	The "type" of the kth element from the left of h. The possible types of elements used in this system are: {call_to, return_from, call, return, ICALL, IRETURN, CALL, RETURN, suspend, resume}.
VAL(h,k)	The values of the shared variables and the parameters in the kth element from the left of the sequence h
REST(h)	h' if h = ELEM(h,1) ^ h'
FIRST(h)	ELEM(h,1)
NO_CALLS(h)	The number of times an element of type "call" appears in the sequence h
CHECK(h)	$\forall k.2 \leq k \leq \bar{h}$.[TYPE(h,k)=call ==> TYPE(h,k-1)$\in${return,suspend}]
SEQ(h,k)	The sequence obtained by removing all elements from the sequence h that do not reference the procedure k
SUBSEQ(k,h)	The sequence obtained by removing all elements from the sequence h that do not reference the kth execution of the procedure

g(h) The sequence obtained by removing the incarnation numbers from the sequence h. This sequence represents an execution of a procedure.

$f_{int}(h)$ The sequence obtained by removing all elements from the sequence h that do not reference the process initialization

CONSIST(**T**,h) The values of the process variables observed by the process are the values that have been most recently assigned to them

STRIP(h) ϵ if $h=\epsilon$

ELEM(h,1)^STRIP(REST(h))
if ELEM(h,1)$\in${call_to,return_from,call,return}

STRIP(REST(h)) Otherwise

{The sequence obtained by removing the elements from the process sequence that an external observer would not see}

h/i The sequence obtained by omitting from the sequence h all elements that do not reference the process P_i

$COMPAT(h_1,h_2,\ldots,h_n) = \exists h.\ \forall i \leq n\ [h/i = h_i]$

NO_OF(h,t) The number of elements of TYPE t in the sequence h

$HERE_i(h)$ The sequence of numbers associated with $SORT_i$ that are from the list of numbers to be sorted. This sequence is of length 0,1, or 2.

$NUM_i(h)$ = NO_OF(h,"RETURN from PUT_i") + NO_OF(h,"RETURN from GET_{i+1}") -

NO_OF(h,"RETURN from GET_i") - NO_OF(h,"RETURN from PUT_{i+1}")

{The number of elements from the list of elements to be sorted that are contained in $SORT_i$}

$REST_i(h)$ = NO_OF(h,"RETURN from PUT_{i+1}") - NO_OF(h,"RETURN from GET_{i+1}")

{The number of elements from the list of elements to be sorted that are contained in the processes $SORT_{i+1},\ldots,SORT_n$}

QUEUE(h) A sorted list of the numbers that are contained in the processes $SORT_1,\ldots,SORT_n$

MIN(h) The smallest element in the sequence h

$LIST_i(h)$ A sorted list of the numbers that are contained in the processes $SORT_i,\ldots,SORT_n$

FIXPOINTS AND PROGRAM LOOPING: REDUCTIONS FROM THE PROPOSITIONAL MU-CALCULUS INTO PROPOSITIONAL DYNAMIC LOGICS OF LOOPING

Robert S. Streett
Computer Science Department
Boston University
Boston, MA 02215

ABSTRACT: The propositional mu-calculus is a propositional logic of programs which incorporates a least fixpoint operator and subsumes the Propositional Dynamic Logic of Fischer and Ladner, the infinite looping constructs of Streett and Sherman, and the Game Logic of Parikh. The propositional mu-calculus is strictly stronger in expressive power than any of these other logics. However, the mu-calculus satisfiability problem is polynomially reducible to the satisfiability problem for Propositional Dynamic Logic with Streett's looping construct. This result shows the connection between fixpoints and program looping, provides an alternative decision procedure for the mu-calculus, and rules out the possibility that the complexities of the two logics could be separated by new upper and lower bound results. We also give reductions from several weaker mu-calculi (including those investigated by Kozen, Vardi and Wolper) into variants of Propositional Dynamic Logic with weaker looping constructs (including Sherman's looping construct). The deterministic exponential time upper bounds obtained for these mu-calculi may also be obtained via these reductions.

1. Introduction

First-order logic is inadequate for formalizing reasoning about programs; concepts such as termination and totality require logics strictly more powerful than first-order (Kfoury and Park, 1975). The use of a least fixpoint operator as a remedy for these deficiencies has been investigated by Park (1970, 1976), Hitchcock and Park (1973), de Bakker and de Roever (1973), de Roever (1974), Emerson and Clarke (1980), and others. The resulting formal systems are often called mu-calculi and can express such important properties of sequential and parallel programs as termination, liveness, and freedom from deadlock and starvation.

Dynamic logic (Pratt, 1976; Harel, 1979) applies concepts from modal logic to a relational semantics of programs to yield systems for reasoning about the before-after behavior of programs. Analagous to the modal logic assertions $\diamond p$ (possibly p) and $\Box p$ (necessarily p) are the dynamic logic constructs $\langle A \rangle p$ and $[A]p$. If A is a program and p is an assertion about the state of a computation, then $\langle A \rangle p$ asserts that after executing A, p can be the case, and $[A]p$ asserts that after executing A, p must be the case.

Propositional Dynamic Logic (PDL) was first investigated by Fischer and Ladner (1979); Streett (1980, 1981) and Sherman (1984) have considered extension, *repeat-PDL* (originally called $PDL\Delta$) and *loop-PDL* respectively, which admit infinite looping or repeating constructs (*repeat-PDL* is strictly stronger in expressive power than *loop-PDL*, but *loop-PDL* appears to admit a quicker decision procedure). Propositional versions of the mu-calculus have been proposed by Pratt (1981) and Kozen (1982). Kozen's formulation subsumes *repeat-PDL* (and hence *loop-PDL*) as well as Parikh's Game Logic (1983a, 1983b).

Kozen and Parikh (1983) have shown that the satisfiability problem for the propositional mu-calculus can be reduced to the second-order theory of several successor functions (SnS). By results of Rabin (1969) this supplies a decision procedure for the propositional mu-calculus, but one which runs in non-elementary time, i.e., time not bounded by any fixed number of compositions of exponential functions. Meyer (1974) has shown that Rabin's algorithm for SnS cannot be substantially improved; SnS is inherently nonelementary.

Rabin's decision procedure for SnS involves finite automata on infinite trees (Rabin, 1969; Hossley and Rackoff, 1972). Streett (1980, 1981) has shown that the $PDL\Delta$ satisfiability problem can be directly reduced to an emptiness problem for such automata. Streett and Emerson (1984, 1985) have extended this technique to the full propositional mu-calculus. The original results yield triple exponential time decision procedures, but Vardi and Stockmeyer (1984) have recently established new automata theoretic results which lead to nondeterministic exponential time decision procedures. The best known lower bound for these logics is the deterministic exponential time bound established by Fischer and Ladner (1979) for PDL.

In this paper, we show that the mu-calculus satisfiability problem can be polynomially reduced to the satisfiabilifty problem for *repeat-PDL*, despite the fact that the mu-calculus is strictly stronger in expressive power than *repeat-PDL* (Niwinski, 1984). This result supplies an alternative decision procedure for the mu-calculus, as well as demonstrating that no new upper or lower bound results will separate *repeat-PDL* and the mu-calculus, i.e., it is not possible that *repeat-PDL* can be decided in deterministic exponential time while the mu-calculus requires nondeterminstic exponential time.

Kozen (1982) and Vardi and Wolper (1984) have obtained exponential time decision procedures for fragments of Kozen's mu-calculus. Both fragments can express all of *PDL*, but are not strong enough to capture all of *repeat-PDL*. We give a very natural definition of a still weaker fragment of the mu-calculus which is polynomially reducible to the *loop-PDL* investigated by Sherman (1984). We also introduce a new variant of *PDL*, *diverge-PDL*, which lies between *loop-PDL* and *repeat-PDL* in expressive power. We then show that the deterministic exponential time decision procedure obtained for *loop-PDL* extends to *diverge-PDL* and that the restricted mu-calculi of Kozen, Vardi, and Wolper are polynomially reducible to *diverge-PDL*. This result supplies an alternative proof of the upper bounds previously obtained for these mu-calculi.

2. Syntax and Semantics

DEFINITION 2.1. Given propositional letters $P, Q, R, \ldots$, and program letters $A, B, C, \ldots$, the formulas of the propositional mu-calculus are defined as follows:

(1) The propositional lettters $P, Q, R, \ldots$ are formulas,

(2) If p and q are formulas, then $\neg p$ and $p \vee q$ are formulas,

(3) If A is a program letter and p is a formula, then $\langle A\rangle p$ is a formula,

(4) If $f(Q)$ is a formula which is syntactically monotone in the propositional letter Q, i.e., all occurrences of Q lie under an even number of negations, then $\mu Q.f(Q)$ is a formula.

Formulas of the mu-calculus are interpreted in Kripke structures (borrowed from Kripke's semantics for modal logic (Kripke, 1963)), in which formulas are interpreted as sets of states and programs as binary relations on states.

DEFINITION 2.2. A Kripke structure is a triple $\langle U, \models, \rightarrow\rangle$, where U is a universe of states, $\models$ is a stisfaction relation between states and propositional letters, and $\rightarrow$ gives, for each program letter A, a binary relation $\xrightarrow{A}$ on states.

DEFINITION 2.3. A model is a Kripke structure with the satisfaction relation $\models$ extended to all formulas by means of the following rules.

(1) $x \models \neg p$ iff $x \not\models p$,

(2) $x \models p \vee q$ iff either $x \models p$ or $x \models q$,

(3) $x \models \langle A\rangle p$ iff for some state y, $x \xrightarrow{A} y$ and $y \models p$ (we will refer to formulas of this form as diamond formulas),

(4) $x \models \mu Q.f(Q)$ iff $x \in \bigcap\{S \subseteq U | S = \{y | y \models f(X)$ with X interpreted as $S\}\}$.

In a formula $\mu Q.f(Q)$, f denotes a monotone function on sets of states (monotonicity is ensured by the syntactic monotonicity of the formula $f(Q)$), and $\mu Q.f(Q)$ is interpreted as the least fixpoint of this function, i.e., the smallest set S of states such that $S = f(S)$.

EXAMPLE. The formula $\mu Q.P \vee \langle A\rangle Q$ is true x if there is a chain (possibly empty) of A edges leading from x to a state satisfying P. It is equivalent to the formula $\langle A^*\rangle P$ of *PDL*.

DEFINITION 2.4. The usual Boolean connectives are defined as abbreviations, as well as the following formulas:

(1) $[A]p \equiv \neg\langle A\rangle\neg p$ (we will refer to formulas of this form as box formulas) ,

(2) $\nu Q.f(Q) \equiv \neg\mu Q.\neg f(\neg Q)$.

The formula $\nu Q.f(Q)$ denotes the greatest fixpoint of the monotone function f.

EXAMPLE. The formula $\nu Q.\langle A\rangle Q$ is true at a state x if there is an infinite chain of A edges from x, and is therefore equivalent to the formula *repeat*(A) of *repeat-PDL* (originally written as ΔA when the logic was known as $PDL\Delta$).

EXAMPLE. The formula $\nu Q.\langle A\rangle Q \wedge \langle B\rangle Q$ is true at x if there is an infinite binary tree of A and B edges rooted at x.

Vardi and Wolper (1984) have investigated an extension of the mu-calculus which admits multiple fixpoints. Informally, an n-tuple of formulas $p_1, \ldots, p_n$ with n free variables denotes a function on n-tuples of sets of states. The least fixpoint of this function will be an n-tuple of sets of states; selecting a component of this n-tuple yields a single set of states, i.e., a suitable interpretation for a sentence.

DEFINITION 2.5. The mu-calculus of multiple fixpoints includes the following formulas: If $p_1, \ldots, p_n$ are formulas syntactically monotone in the free variables $X_1, \ldots, X_n$, then $\mu X_i(X_1, \ldots, X_n).(p_1, \ldots, p_n)$ is a formula (with semantics described informally above).

The programs of Propositional Dynamic Logic (PDL) are regular languages over the alphabet of atomic programs and tests. If p is a formula, the test $p?$ is a program whose edges consist of loops on states x satisfying p. Informally, $p?$ is equivalent to *if p then skip else abort*, i.e., it permits further computation if p is true, but blocks execution otherwise. If a is a PDL program, the formula $\langle a\rangle p$ is true at a state x when there is a computation of a leading from x to a state satisfying p. More formally, a computation of a from x to y is a chain of edges from x to y whose labels comprise a word in the regular language denoted by a. The logic *repeat-PDL* includes a formula *repeat*(a) for each program a which is true at x if a can be executed repeatedly ad infinitum from x, i.e., if there is an infinite chain of edges labelled with an infinite word from the ω-regular language a^ω.

Since regular languages can be represented either by regular expressions or by nondeterministic finite automata, there are two versions of PDL (and hence of *repeat-PDL*). The version using automata is sometimes called the Propositional Dynamic Logic of Flowcharts (Pratt, 1981; Harel and Sherman, 1983). These two variants are clearly equally expressive, but automata can be exponentially more succinct than regular expressions (Ehrenfeucht and Zeiger, 1976).

LEMMA 2.6. (Kozen, 1982) The propositional mu-calculus is at least as strong in expressive power as *repeat-PDL*.

Proof. The following rules show how to translate formulas of the regular expression version of *repeat-PDL* into equivalent mu-calculus formulas.

(1) $\langle a;b\rangle p \Rightarrow \langle a\rangle\langle b\rangle p$,

(2) $\langle a \cup b\rangle p \Rightarrow \langle a\rangle p \vee \langle b\rangle p$,

(3) $\langle a^*\rangle p \Rightarrow \mu Q.p \vee \langle a\rangle Q$,

(4) $\langle p?\rangle q \Rightarrow p \wedge q$,

(5) $repeat(a) \Rightarrow \nu Q.\langle a\rangle Q$.

The translation induced by the above rules involves an exponential blowup. This blowup can be avoided by using multiple fixpoints and rewriting rule (2) as follows:

(2′) $\langle a \cup b\rangle p \Rightarrow \mu Q(Q,R).(\langle a\rangle R \vee \langle b\rangle R,\ p)$.

Multiple fixpoints also permit a polynomial translation of the automata version of *repeat-PDL* into the mu-calculus (Vardi and Wolper, 1984).

EXAMPLE. The *repeat-PDL* formula $< (P?;A)^*;\neg P? > repeat(A \cup B; C)$ is equivalent to the mu-calculus formula $\mu Q.(\neg P \wedge (\nu R.\langle A\rangle R \vee \langle B\rangle\langle C\rangle R)) \vee (P \wedge \langle A\rangle Q)$.

The mu-calculus has recently been shown to be strictly stronger than *repeat-PDL*.

THEOREM 2.7. (Niwinski, 1984) The mu-calculus formula $\nu Q.(\langle A\rangle Q \wedge \langle B\rangle Q)$ is not expressible in *repeat-PDL*.

3. PRE-MODELS AND CHOICE FUNCTIONS

We can evaluate simple sentences in models by recursively evaluating subsentences. Thus to check whether or not $P \vee \langle A\rangle Q$ is true at a state x we either confirm that P is true at x or we look for an A edge leading to a state satisfying Q. In order to evaluate fixpoint sentences, we will need to confirm the fixpoint property, i.e., that $\mu Q.f(Q) \equiv f(\mu Q.f(Q))$ and $\nu Q.f(Q) \equiv f(\nu Q.f(Q))$. The following definition includes exactly those properties of a model which can be easily checked by recursive evaluation.

DEFINITION 3.1. A pre-model is a Kripke structure with a satisfaction relation $\models$ extended to all sentences under the following constraints.

(1) $x \models p$ iff $x \not\models \neg p$,

(2) $x \models p \vee q$ iff either $x \models p$ or $x \models q$,

(3) $x \models \langle A\rangle p$ iff there is some edge $x \xrightarrow{A} y$ such that $y \models p$,

(4) $x \models \mu Q.f(Q)$ iff $x \models f(\mu Q.f(Q))$.

A pre-model is almost a model, except that rule (4) permits $\mu Q.f(Q)$ to be interpreted as an arbitrary fixpoint (least, greatest, or intermediate).

EXAMPLE. Consider a Kripke structure with a single state x such that $x \xrightarrow{A} x$ and $x \models \neg P$. This structure can be extended to a pre-model in which $x \models \mu Q.P \vee \langle A \rangle Q$, $x \models P \vee \langle A \rangle(\mu Q.P \vee \langle A \rangle Q)$, and $x \models \langle A \rangle(\mu Q.P \vee \langle A \rangle Q)$. This pre-model will not, however, be a model.

Fixpoint sentences can generate nonterminating evaluation sequences. For example, occurrences of $\mu X.X$ and $\nu X.X$ merely trigger re-evaluation of themselves via the fixpoint property, while $\mu X.\langle A \rangle X$ and $\nu X.\langle A \rangle X$ can generate infinite sequences of reoccurrences along a chain of A edges. The presence or absence of nonterminating evaluations distinguishes least from greatest fixpoints (both of which share the fixpoint property). Least fixpoint sentences must have terminating evaluations, while nontermination is consistent with the semantics for greatest fixpoints (this explains why $\mu X.X \equiv \mathit{false}$ and $\nu X.X \equiv \mathit{true}$).

Disjunctions $p \vee q$ and existential program sentences $\langle A \rangle p$ introduce a complication; termination of the evaluation process depends on the choice of disjunct or edge used to satisfy such sentences. For example, the sentence $\mu X.P \vee X$ expands to $P \vee (\mu X.P \vee X)$; the disjunct P leads to termination, the disjunct $\mu X.P \vee X$ to nontermination. Consider the sentence $\mu Q.P \vee \langle A \rangle Q$, equivalent to the PDL sentence $\langle A^* \rangle P$, which is satisfied in a Kripke structure exactly when the sentence P is true somewhere along some path of A's. By the fixpoint property, $\mu Q.P \vee \langle A \rangle Q$ is equivalent to the disjunction $P \vee \langle A \rangle(\mu Q.P \vee \langle A \rangle Q)$. A terminating evaluation occurs if the A edges chosen to satisfy $\langle A \rangle(\mu Q.P \vee \langle A \rangle Q)$ eventually lead to a state where the disjunct P can be chosen. Consistently choosing to evaluate the disjunct $\langle A \rangle(\mu Q.P \vee \langle A \rangle Q)$ will lead to a nonterminating evaluation along an infinite A chain (since nonterminating evaluations are consistent with greatest fixpoints, this explains why $\nu X.P \vee \langle A \rangle X \equiv (\mu Q.P \vee \langle A \rangle Q) \vee (\nu X.\langle A \rangle X))$.

We shall consider pre-models supplied with a choice function responsible for guiding the evaluation of least fixpoint sentences towards termination.

DEFINITION 3.2. A choice function for a pre-model is a function which chooses, for every occurrence of a disjunction at a state, an occurrence of one of the disjuncts at that state, and for every occurrence of an existential program sentence $\langle A \rangle q$ at a state, an occurrence of q at an A-successor of that state.

DEFINITION 3.3. Any choice function over a pre-model determines a derivation relation between occurrences of sentences, defined by the following rules:

(1) A disjunction, $q \vee r$, derives the disjunct selected by the choice function.

(2) A conjunction, $q \wedge r$, derives both conjuncts.

(3) An existential program sentence, $\langle A \rangle q$, occurring at a state x, derives the occurrence of q selected by the choice function.

(4) A universal program sentence, $[A]q$, occurring at x derives occurrences of q at all A-successors of x,

(5) A mu-sentence, $\mu Q.f(Q)$, derives its fixpoint expansion $f(\mu Q.f(Q))$.

(6) A nu-sentence, $\nu Q.f(Q)$, derives its fixpoint expansion $f(\nu Q.f(Q))$.

We would like to say that a pre-model is in fact a model when there is no infinite derivation sequence which rederives a mu-sentence infinitely often. However, this claim is true only when restricted to derivations in which the given mu-sentence appears as a subsentence of every derivation step, hence the following definition.

DEFINITION 3.4. A least fixpoint sentence $\mu Q.f(Q)$ is regenerated from x to y if $\mu Q.f(Q)$ at x derives $\mu Q.f(Q)$ at y in such a way that $\mu Q.f(Q)$ is a subsentence of every derivation step.

EXAMPLE. The sentence $\mu Y.(\mu X.(P \vee \langle A\rangle(\mu Y.X \vee \langle B\rangle Y)) \vee \langle B\rangle Y)$ can be regenerated across a B-edge, but not across an A-edge. A derivation across an A-edge is possible, but requires $\mu X.P \vee \langle A\rangle(\mu Y.X \vee \langle B\rangle Y)$ as a derivation step.

EXAMPLE. The sentence $p = \mu Y.(\nu X.P \wedge \langle A\rangle(\mu Y.X \vee Y)) \vee \langle A\rangle Y)$ is true when there is an infinite chain of A edges along which P is infinitely often. Any model of this sentence will contain infinite derivation sequences rederiving p infinitely often, but the subsentence $q = \nu X.P \wedge \langle A\rangle(\mu Y.X \vee \langle A\rangle Y)$ must then occur infinitely often as a derivation step. It is possible to construct a choice function such that any regeneration sequence from p ultimately terminates at the choice q from the derived disjunction $q \vee \langle A\rangle p$.

DEFINITION 3.5. A choice function is well-founded when the regeneration relations for least fixpoint sentences are well-founded. A pre-model is well-founded if it has a well-founded choice function.

THEOREM 3.6. The models are exactly the well-founded pre-models.

Proof. Given a model, we can assign ordinal ranks to all sentences by transfinite induction. We can then construct a choice function which always selects the choice with least rank. It is then possible to show that the regeneration relations always decrease rank. The well-foundedness of the ordinals implies that the the regeneration relations are well-founded.

A Kripke structure can be extended to a model in only one way. Although a Kripke structure can be extended to possibly many different pre-models, two such pre-models must disagree on some least fixpoint sentence. It is then possible to construct an infinite regeneration chain in one of the pre-models. This shows that there is at most one well-founded pre-model based on a given Kripke structure. Since every model is a well-founded pre-model, the unique model determined by a Kripke structure is identical to the unique well-founded pre-model determined by a Kripke structure. Hence, every well-founded pre-model is a model.

4. THE REDUCTION

The main result of the paper is the following theorem.

THEOREM 4.1. The satisfiability problem for the propositional mu-calculus is polynomially reducible to the satisfiability problem for the automata version of *repeat-PDL*.

We will first demonstrate the reduction by applying it to a specific mu-calculus sentence $\mu Q.P \vee (\langle A\rangle Q \wedge [B]Q)$. This formula is true at x if there is a finite tree of A and B edges which is rooted at x, whose leaves all satisfy P, and whose interior nodes have at least one A edge and all the B edges from the full model.

We introduce a new propositional letter M intended to represent the least fixpoint sentence $\mu Q.P \vee (\langle A\rangle Q \wedge [B]Q)$; the derived *repeat-PDL* formula will be a formalization of the following assertion: M is true, M is a fixpoint of the function $\lambda X.P \vee (\langle A\rangle X \wedge [B]X)$, and there is a well-founded choice function.

Since $\mu Q.P \vee (\langle A\rangle Q \wedge [B]Q)$ contains only two program letters A and B, it suffices to use the program operator $[(A \cup B)^*]$ to propagte constraints to all the relevant states of a model.

The formula $M \equiv P \vee (\langle A\rangle M \wedge [B]M)$ asserts that M is a fixpoint, not necessarily the least fixpoint, of the function $\lambda X.P \vee (\langle A\rangle X \wedge [B]X)$.

To formally assert the existence of a choice function, we introduce two additional propositional letters D and E : D chooses between P and $\langle A\rangle M \wedge [B]M$, while E chooses an A-edge to satisfy $\langle A\rangle M$. Appropriate behavior is ensured by the following constraints:

(1) $(P \vee (\langle A\rangle M \wedge [B]M)) \wedge D \rightarrow P$,

(2) $(P \vee (\langle A\rangle M \wedge [B]M)) \wedge \neg D \rightarrow (\langle A\rangle M \wedge [B]M)$,

(3) $\langle A\rangle M \rightarrow \langle A\rangle E$,

(4) $E \rightarrow M$.

It remains to assert that the choice function determined by the letters D and E is well-founded. This is accomplished by constructing a program a which connects two states exactly when M is "regenerated" from one to the other. The *repeat-PDL* formula $\neg$*repeat*(a) will then assert that the regeneration relation is well-founded.

This program can be constructed as a finite automaton whose nodes are the subformulas of $P \vee (\langle A\rangle M \wedge [B]M)$. Edges connect formulas to their immediate subformulas. The disjunction $P \vee (\langle A\rangle M \wedge [B]M)$ has an edge to P labelled with $D?$ and an edge to $\langle A\rangle M \wedge [B]M$ labelled with $\neg D?$. The edges from the conjunction $\langle A\rangle M \wedge [B]M$ to its conjuncts are labelled by the empty string ϵ. The edge from the diamond formula $\langle A\rangle M$ to M is labelled with $A; E?$; the edge from the box formula $[B]M$ to M with B. The start state is $P \vee (\langle A\rangle M \wedge [B]M)$ and the final state is M. The program represented by this automaton can also be expressed as a regular expression: $\neg R?; (A; S? \cup B)$.

The desired translation of $\mu Q.P \vee (\langle A\rangle Q \wedge [B]Q)$ is then:

$$
\begin{aligned}
M \wedge [(A \cup B)^*]\Big(\quad & M \equiv (P \vee (\langle A\rangle M \wedge [B]M)) \wedge \neg \mathit{repeat}(\neg R?; (A; S? \cup B)) \\
\bigwedge \quad & ((P \vee (\langle A\rangle M \wedge [B]M)) \wedge D) \rightarrow P \\
\bigwedge \quad & ((P \vee (\langle A\rangle M \wedge [B]M)) \wedge \neg D) \rightarrow (\langle A\rangle M \wedge [B]M) \\
\bigwedge \quad & \langle A\rangle M \rightarrow \langle A\rangle E \\
\bigwedge \quad & E \rightarrow M \qquad\qquad \Big)
\end{aligned}
$$

A model of $\mu Q.P \vee (\langle A \rangle Q \wedge [B]Q)$ is a pre-model with a well-founded choice function. We can construct a model of the translated formula by making M equivalent to $\mu Q.P \vee (\langle A \rangle Q \wedge [B]Q)$ and by using the choice function to specify D and E. Conversely, a model of the the translated formula can be easily shown to be a model of $\mu Q.P \vee (\langle A \rangle Q \wedge [B]Q)$ at every state satisfying M.

In order to translate an arbitrary mu-calculus formula, we need to precisely define the set of sentences encountered during the recursive evaluation of a given sentence.

DEFINITION 4.2. The Fischer-Ladner closure of a sentence p is the smallest set $FL(p)$ of sentences satisfying the following constraints. We take the liberty of identifying $\neg\neg q$ with q.

(1) $p \in FL(p)$,

(2) if $\neg q \in FL(p)$ then $q \in FL(p)$,

(3) if $q \vee r \in FL(p)$ then $q, r \in FL(p)$,

(4) if $\langle A \rangle q \in FL(p)$ then $q \in FL(p)$,

(5) if $\mu Q.f(Q) \in FL(p)$ then $f(\mu Q.f(Q)) \in FL(p)$.

EXAMPLE. The Fischer-Ladner closure of the sentence $\mu X.[A]X$ contains only four sentences: $\mu X.[A]X$, $\nu X.\langle A \rangle X$, $[A]\mu X.[A]X$, and $\langle A \rangle(\nu X.\langle A \rangle X)$.

LEMMA 4.3. The cardinality of the Fischer-Ladner closure of a sentence p is linear in the length of p, i.e., $|FL(p)| = O(|p|)$.

Proof. A straightforward adaptation of the proof for PDL (Fischer and Ladner, 1979).

To demonstrate the general translation, let p be a fixed mu-calculus formula. Let the atomic programs appearing in p be $A_1, \ldots, A_l$. Let the least fixpoint formulas in $FL(p)$ be $\mu X_1.f_1(X_1), \ldots, \mu X_m.f_m(X_m)$. The greatest fixpoint sentences in $FL(p)$ can then be given as $\neg\mu X_i.f_i(X_i)$, for $1 \leq i \leq m$. Let the disjunctions in $FL(p)$ be $q_1 \vee r_1, \ldots, q_k \vee r_k$. Let the diamond formulas in $FL(p)$ be $\langle B_1 \rangle s_1, \ldots, \langle B_n \rangle s_n$.

Choose new propositional variables: $M_1, \ldots, M_m$ (these will be used to stand in for least fixpoint formulas), $D_1, \ldots, D_k$ (these will be used to choose between the parts of a disjunction), and $E_1, \ldots, E_n$ (these will be used to choose edges to satisfy existential program sentences). The negated variables $\neg M_i$, for $1 \leq i \leq m$, will stand in for the greatest fixpoint formulas. If $q \in FL(p)$, let q' be q with the largest fixpoint sentences appearing in q replaced by the appropriate M_i or $\neg M_i$.

For each least fixpoint subformula $\mu X_i.f_i(X_i)$, we construct a nondeterministic finite automaton a_i. The state space of a_i consists of the closure $FL(\mu X_i.f_i(X_i))$. The start state is $f_i(\mu X_i.f_i(X_i))$, and the final state is $\mu X_i.f_i(X_i)$. The automaton has the following edges:

(1) From each conjunction, edges to each conjunct labelled with the empty string ϵ,

(2) From each disjunction $q_j \vee r_j$, an edge to q_j labelled by $D_j?$, and an edge to r_j labelled by $\neg D_j?$,

(3) From each universal program sentence $[A]q$, an edge to q labelled with A,

(4) From each existential program sentence $\langle B_j \rangle s_j$, an edge to s_j labelled by $B_j; E_j?$,

(5) From each least fixpoint sentence $\mu X.f(X)$, except $\mu X_i.f_i(X_i)$, an edge labelled by ϵ to the fixpoint expansion $f(\mu X.f(X))$,

(6) From each greatest fixpoint sentence $\nu X.f(X)$, an edge labelled by ϵ to the fixpoint expansion $f(\nu X.f(X))$.

The translation of p is then:

$$
\begin{array}{lll}
p' \wedge [A_1 \cup \cdots \cup A_l]\big(& \bigwedge_{1 \le i \le m} & M_i \equiv f_i'(M_i) \wedge \neg repeat(a_i) \\
\wedge & \bigwedge_{1 \le i \le k} & ((q_i' \vee r_i') \wedge D_i) \rightarrow q_i' \\
\wedge & \bigwedge_{1 \le i \le k} & ((q_i' \vee r_i') \wedge \neg D_i) \rightarrow r_i' \\
\wedge & \bigwedge_{1 \le i \le n} & \langle B_i \rangle s_i' \rightarrow \langle B_i \rangle E_i \\
\wedge & \bigwedge_{1 \le i \le n} & E_i \rightarrow s_i' \qquad \big)
\end{array}
$$

5. Two More Reductions

Sherman (Harel and Sherman, 1983; Pnueli and Sherman, 1983; Sherman, 1984) has investigated a variant of *PDL* which includes a construct *loop*(a). If a is a program, *loop*(a) asserts that a contains an infinite computation. For each program a, let $L(a)$ denote the finite computations of a (defined in the usual manner as the language accepted by an automaton or described by a regular expression). Let $L^\omega(a)$ denote the infinite computations of a, defined for regular expressions as follows:

(1) $L^\omega(A) = \emptyset$,

(2) $L^\omega(p?) = \emptyset$,

(3) $L^\omega(a;b) = L^\omega(a) \cup L(a); L^\omega(b)$,

(4) $L^\omega(a \cup b) = L^\omega(a) \cup L^\omega(b)$,

(5) $L^\omega(a^*) = L(a)^\omega \cup L(a)^*; L^\omega(a)$.

The formula *loop*(a) is then true when there is an infinite chain of edges labelled with an infinite word from the ω-regular language $L^\omega(a)$. The constructs *repeat*(a) and *loop*(a^*) are related: *repeat*(a) clearly implies *loop*(a^*), but *loop*(a^*) could be true due to the behavior of a subprogram b^* of a. For example, the infinite chain b^ω satisfies *loop*$((b^*;a)^*)$ but not *repeat*$(b^*;a)$.

The *loop* construct can be defined inductively within *repeat-PDL* as follows:

(1) $loop(A) \equiv false$,

(2) $loop(p?) \equiv false$,

(3) $loop(a;b) \equiv loop(a) \vee \langle a \rangle loop(b)$,

(4) $loop(a \cup b) \equiv loop(a) \vee loop(b)$,

(5) $loop(a^*) \equiv repeat(a) \vee \langle a^* \rangle loop(a)$.

Harel and Sherman (1984) have shown that *loop-PDL* is strictly weaker in expressive power than *repeat-PDL*, and Pnueli and Sherman (1983) have shown that *loop-PDL* permits a deterministic exponential time decision procedure (the best known procedure for *repeat-PDL* runs in nondeterministic exponential time).

It is tempting to suppose that the reduction of this paper could be made to use the *loop* construct (as opposed to the full power of the *repeat* operator). A reduction from the mu-calculus into *loop-PDL* would, if succinct, give a new deterministic exponential time decision procedure for the mu-calculus. Below we show that the reduction is possible for a restricted sublogic of the mu-calculus in which interactions between least and greatest fixpoints are forbidden.

DEFINITION 5.1. A mu-calculus formula p is a restricted formula if whenever $\nu Y.g(Y)$ is a subformula of a subformula $\mu X.f(X)$ of p, then X does not appear free in $\nu Y.g(Y)$.

THEOREM 5.2. The restricted mu-calculus is polynomially reducible to the automata version of *loop-PDL*.

Proof. To appear in the full paper. •

This last theorem gives a deterministic exponential upper bound for the restricted mu-calculus. Vardi and Wolper (1984) have given a deterministic exponential time decision procedure for a larger fragment of the mu-calculus (their mu-calculus subsumes the fragment investigated by Kozen (1982)).

DEFINITION 5.3. Two occurrences of the formulas q, r are conjunctively related inside a third formula p if the smallest subformula of p containing both occurrences is a conjunction.

DEFINITION 5.4. A mu-calculus formula p is a Vardi-Wolper formula if whenever there is a subformula chain $\nu Y_1.g_1(Y_1,Y_2) \subset\subset \nu Y_2.g_2(Y_2,Y_3) \subset \nu Y_m.g_m(Y_m,X) \subset \mu X.f(X) \subset p$, then no occurrences of Y_1 and Y_2 are conjunctively related.

We now consider a variant of *PDL* which includes a construct $diverge(a)$. If a is a program, $diverge(a)$ asserts that there is an infinite computation which contains infinitely many finite a-computations as prefixes.

DEFINITION 5.5. The set, $L^\infty(a)$, of diverging computations of the program a is defined for regular expressions a as follows:

(1) $L^\infty(A) = \emptyset$,

(2) $L^\infty(p?) = \emptyset$,

(3) $L^\infty(a;b) = L(a); L^\infty(b)$,

(4) $L^\infty(a \cup b) = L^\infty(a) \cup L^\infty(b)$,

(5) $L^\infty(a^*) = L(a)^\omega \cup L(a)^*; L^\infty(a)$.

The formula *diverge*(a) is then true when there is an infinite chain of edges labelled with an infinite word of the ω-regular language $L^\infty(a)$. Clearly, *repeat*(a) implies *diverge*(a^*) which implies *loop*(a^*). The coverse implications are not true. Consider the program $a^*; b; c^*$. The infinite chain a^ω satisfies *loop*$((a^*; b; c^*)^*)$ but not *diverge*$((a^*; b; c^*)^*)$, and the infinite chain bc^ω satisfies *diverge*$((a^*; b; c^*)^*)$ but not *repeat*$(a^*; b; c^*)$.

THEOREM 5.6. The Vardi-Wolper mu-calculus is polynomially reducible to the automata version of *diverge-PDL*.

Proof. To appear in the full paper.

REFERENCES

DE BAKKER, J., AND DE ROEVER, W. P. (1973), A Calculus for Recursive Program Schemes, *First International Colloquium on Automata, Languages, and Programming*, 167–196.

DE ROEVER, W. P. (1974), *Recursive Program Schemes: Semantics and Proof Theory*, Ph.D. thesis, Free University, Amsterdam.

EHRENFEUCHT, A., AND ZEIGER, P. (1976), Complexity Measures for Regular Expressions, *Journal of Computer System Science* **12**, 134–146.

EMERSON, A. E., AND CLARKE, E. C. (1980), Characterizing Correctness Properties of Parallel Programs using Fixpoints, *Seventh International Colloquium on Automata, Languages and Programming*, 169–181.

FISCHER, M. J., AND LADNER, R. E. (1979), Propositional Dynamic Logic of Regular Programs, *Journal of Computer System Science* **18**, 194–211.

HAREL, D. (1979), *First Order Dynamic Logic, Springer-Verlag Lecture Notes in Computer Science* **68**.

HAREL, D., AND SHERMAN, R. (1984), Looping versus Repeating in Dynamic Logic, *Information and Control* **55**, 175–192, 1984.

HITCHCOCK, P., AND PARK, D. M. R. (1973), Induction Rules and Termination Proofs, *First International Colloquium on Automata, Languages, and Programming*, 225–251.

HOSSLEY, R., AND RACKOFF, C. W. (1972), The Emptiness Problem for Automata on Infinite Trees, *Thirteenth IEEE Symposium on Switching and Automata Theory*, 121–124.

KFOURY, A. J., AND PARK, D. M. R. (1975), On Termination of Program Schemes, *Information and Control* **29**, 243–251.

KOZEN, D. (1982), Results on the Propositional Mu-Calculus, *Ninth International Colloquium on Automata, Languages, and Programming*, 348–359.

KOZEN, D., AND PARIKH, R. J. (1983), A Decision Procedure for the Propositional Mu-Calculus, *Second Workshop on Logics of Programs.*

KRIPKE, S. A. (1963), Semantical Considerations on Modal Logics, *Acta Philosophica Fennica.*

MCNAUGHTON, R. (1966), Testing and Generating Infinite Sequences by a Finite Automaton, *Information and Control* **9**, 521–530.

MEYER, A. R. (1974), Weak Monadic Second Order Theory of Successor is not Elementary Recursive, *Boston Logic Colloquium, Springer-Verlag Lecture Notes in Mathematics* **453**.

NIWINSKI, D. (1984), The Propositional Mu-Calculus is More Expressive than the Propositional Dynamic Logic of Looping, unpublished manuscript.

PARIKH, R. J. (1979), A Decidability Result for a Second Order Process Logic, *Nineteenth IEEE Symposium on the Foundations of Computer Science*, 177–183.

PARIKH, R. J. (1983a), Cake Cutting, Dynamic Logic, Games, and Fairness, *Second Workshop on Logics of Programs.*

PARIKH, R. J. (1983b), Propositional Game Logic, *Twenty-third IEEE Symposium on the Foundations of Computer Science.*

PARK, D. M. R. (1970), Fixpoint Induction and Proof of Program Semantics, *Machine Intelligence* **5**, Edinburgh University Press.

PARK, D. M. R. (1976), Finiteness is Mu-Ineffable, *Theoretical Computer Science* **3**, 173–181.

PNUELI, A., AND SHERMAN, R. (1983),Propositional Dynamic Logic of Looping Flowcharts, Technical Report, Weizmann Institute of Science.

PRATT, V. R. (1976), Semantical Considerations on Floyd-Hoare Logic, *Seventeenth IEEE Symposium on Foundations of Computer Science*, 109–121.

PRATT, V. R. (1982), A Decidable Mu-Calculus: Preliminary Report, *Twenty-second IEEE Symposium on the Foundations of Computer Science*, 421–427.

RABIN, M. O. (1969), Decidability of Second Order Theories and Automata on Infinite Trees, *Transactions of the American Mathematical Society* **141**, 1–35.

SHERMAN, R. (1984), Variants of Propositional Dynamic Logic, Ph.D. thesis, Weizmann Institute of Science.

STREETT, R. S. (1980), A Propositional Dynamic Logic for Reasoning About Program Divergence, M.S. thesis, Massachusetts Institute of Technology.

STREETT, R. S. (1981), Propositional Dynamic Logic of Looping and Converse, MIT LCS Technical Report TR–**263**.

STREETT, R. S. (1982), Propositional Dynamic Logic of Looping and Converse is Elemantarily Decidable, *Information and Control* **54**, 121–141.

STREETT, R. S., AND EMERSON, E. A. (1984), The Propositional Mu-Calculus is Elementary, *Eleventh International Colloquium on Automata, Languages, and Programming, Springer-Verlag Lecture Notes in Computer Science* **172**, 465–472.

STREETT, R. S., AND EMERSON, E. A. (1985), An Automata Theoretic Decision Procedure for the Propositional Mu-Calculus, in preparation.

VARDI, M. Y., AND STOCKMEYER, L. (1984), Improved Upper and Lower Bounds for Modal Logics of Programs, unpublished paper.

VARDI, M., AND WOLPER, P (1984), Automata Theoretic Techniques for Modal Logics of Programs, *Sixteenth ACM Symposium on the Theory of Computing.*

Semantical Analysis of Specification Logic†

R.D. Tennent
Department of Computing and Information Science, Queen's University
Kingston, Canada K7L3N6.

Preliminary Report

Abstract A new interpretation of the specification logic of J.C. Reynolds as an intuitionistic theory is presented. The main features are a functorial treatment of storage structure due to Reynolds and Oles, and the use of a topos-theoretic construction to interpret specification formulas.

1. Introduction

In the beginning, C.A.R. Hoare[1] created a programming logic for *specification* formulas of the form $\{B_0\}\ C\ \{B_1\}$, where B_0 and B_1 are *assertions* (Boolean expressions) and C is a *command* (statement). And, Hoare's logic is *good* (for simple imperative programming languages without procedures). It is both *sound*[2] and, independently of how the vexed question of its *completeness* might be answered, *usable*: it shows how practical programs may be specified and verified in a rigorous and structured way.[3]

Many attempts have been made to extend Hoare's logic to languages with procedure mechanisms. The *specification logic* of J.C. Reynolds[4] is the only one of these whose usability has been clearly demonstrated.[3] The aim of the research described here is to do the same for its *soundness*.

Specification logic is essentially a many-sorted first-order theory, with Hoare triples as atomic formulas and conventional logical connectives, such as conjunction, implication, and quantification. There are some additional atomic formulas to permit expression of certain kinds of assumptions about free identifiers, such as *non-interference*. A fairly conventional semantics for specification logic is outlined in [3]; however, there are two problems with this interpretation.

---

†This research was supported by the Natural Sciences and Engineering Research Council of Canada, grant A8990.

The first difficulty is that commands are interpreted in an undesirably operational way: command meanings are functions from an initial state to the (possibly infinite) sequence of *all* states encountered during execution of the command. This seemed to be necessary in order to interpret non-interference specifications: $C \# E$ means that the value of expression E is invariant *throughout* the execution of command C.

The second difficulty with the conventional interpretation is that Section 11 of [4] points out that two axioms presented there, Strong Constancy and Leftside Non-interference Composition, are *invalid* relative to the interpretation in [3]. However, they are intuitively *true*, and furthermore, they seem to be very desirable or essential for verifying certain kinds of programs.

This paper describes a new approach to formalizing the semantics of specification logic. The rest of this introduction gives an informal (and somewhat over-simplified) presentation of the new model.

The first idea is adapted from the model of block structure described by Reynolds[5] and Oles:[6,7] the semantics of a phrase is a suitably-related *family* of environment-to-meaning functions for different sets of states. For example, the semantics of a command for any state-set X is a continuous function from environments appropriate for X to partial functions (or binary relations) on X. For a control structure such as $C_1;C_2$, the meaning for any state-set is expressed as a function of the meanings of the immediate constituents C_1 and C_2 for the *same* state-set. This ensures that "intermediate" states between the executions of C_1 and C_2 will also belong to that state-set, without requiring that these intermediate states be explicit in command meanings. A specification now becomes a predicate about state-sets as well as environments.

A satisfactory interpretation of $C \# E$ for any state-set X is then definable as follows. For any value v which E might have, let X_v be the subset of X for which the value of E is v; then $C \# E$ holds just if, for all v, any terminating execution of C in X whose initial state is in X_v, is also a terminating execution of C in X_v.

Consider now the axiom of Strong Constancy:[4]

$$C \# B \ \& \ (\{B\} \Rightarrow \{B_0\}\ C\ \{B_1\}) \Rightarrow \{B \textbf{ and } B_0\}\ C\ \{B \textbf{ and } B_1\}\,,$$

where C is a command, and B, B_0 and B_1 are assertions. Intuitively, if B holds before executing C and C does not interfere with B, then while reasoning about C it should be possible to assume that B holds. However, the static-assertion specification $\{B\}$ holds just if assertion B is true at *all* possible states, and not merely those that might be encountered while executing C. So the axiom is invalid according to the conventional interpretation given in [3]. There is a similar problem with the axiom scheme of Leftside Non-interference Composition.

The essence of the solution proposed here is to adopt a non-classical interpretation of specification implication, inspired by Kripke's[8-10] semantics for *intuitionistic* logics. The reason for interpreting specification logic as an intuitionistic theory is to take advantage of what McCarty[11] terms *axiomatic freedom*: "the recognition that intuitionistic logic allows axioms which are classically false but mathematically efficient to be consistent with powerful theories." (Intuitionists have quite different motivations.) Fortunately, all of the equivalences, axioms, and rules presented in [3,4] *are* intuitionistically acceptable.[1] Furthermore, Reynolds has shown (private communication) that if the classical but non-intuitionistic law of excluded middle were added to specification logic, then formulas asserting non-termination of compositions of simple assignment statements would be derivable. This shows that the only models possible for *classical* specification logic are trivial ones in which statements *never* terminate.

The new interpretation of the implication connective is essentially as follows: define $S_1 \Rightarrow S_2$ to be true for state-set X just if, for all $X' \subseteq X$, S_2 holds for X' whenever S_1 holds for X'. The quantification over restricted state-sets preserves the *monotonicity* of specification interpretation in the following sense: if any specification S holds for state-set X, then S holds for any $X' \subseteq X$.

To see how this new interpretation of the implication connective helps with Strong Constancy, let X' be the subset of state-set X for which B holds, and suppose that execution of C in X can map initial state x_0 to final state x_1, where x_0 satisfies both B and B_0. Then assumption $C \# B$ ensures that the execution from x_0 to x_1 can also take place in X', so that x_1 satisfies B. Furthermore, with the new interpretation of implication, assumption $\{B\} \Rightarrow \{B_0\}\, C\, \{B_1\}$ ensures that x_1 also satisfies B_1, because, by definition, B holds for all states in X'. This validates Strong Constancy.

Similarly, consider the following weak form of the axiom scheme of Leftside Non-interference Composition:[4]

$$C \# E \;\&\; (I \# E \Rightarrow \{B_0\}\, C\, \{B_1\}) \Rightarrow \{B_0\}\, C\, \{B_1\}\,,$$

where I is a free command identifier of command C, B_0 and B_1 are assertions, and E is an expression. Suppose again that execution of C in state-set X can map x_0 to x_1, where x_0 satisfies B_0. Let X' be the subset of X for which E has the same value as it does at x_0. Then assumption $C \# E$ ensures that the execution from x_0 to x_1 can also take place in X'. Now it does *not* in general follow from $C \# E$ that $I \# E$ in X; however, in X' execution of I cannot interfere with E, so that, using the new interpretation of implication, the second assumption ensures that x_1 satisfies B_1. The same approach may be used to validate the stronger form of the axiom given in [4] involving all of the command-like free identifiers of C.

[1] *Reductio ad absurdum* is not the correct name for rule R10 in [3].

2. Syntax

The abstract syntax of the basic language of specification logic is given in Table 1. The syntax has been simplified by avoiding coercions and conventional variables (but retaining *acceptors*, which are "write-only" variables).

Informally, a *data type*, τ, denotes a set of values appropriate for some kind of acceptor or expression, whereas a *phrase type*, θ or γ, denotes a set or poset of meanings appropriate for some kind of phrase. A *type assignment*, π, is a function from a finite set of identifiers, dom(π), to ordinary (i.e., computable) phrase types. The notation $[\pi \mid I:\theta]$ denotes the type assignment π' such that

$$\mathrm{dom}(\pi') = \mathrm{dom}(\pi) \cup \{I\},$$

$$\pi'(I') = \begin{cases} \theta & \text{if } I' = I \\ \pi(I') & \text{otherwise,} \end{cases}$$

and similarly for $[\pi \mid I_1:\theta_1 \mid \ldots \mid I_n:\theta_n]$. The same kind of notation will be used for extending environments.

The phrase-class name $<\gamma,\pi>$ denotes the set of well-formed phrases having type γ when the types of their free identifiers are given by π. Productions for expressions and acceptors (other than the "generic" ones for identifiers, applications and conditionals) and more complex control structures, such as conditionals, recursion and loops, are omitted. A "variable" declaration binds a pair of (distinct) identifiers to an acceptor meaning and an expression meaning, respectively.

The productions for specifications show that the specification language has been augmented by

(i) a constant **absurd**, which *never* holds (even for the null state-set, unlike the static-assertion specification {**false**} used for this purpose in [3,4]); and

(ii) an atomic formula for equivalence of phrases.

There should be no difficulty adding logical operators for disjunction and existential quantification, but there seems to be no reason to do so. (The negation of S is definable as $S \Rightarrow$ **absurd**.) The static-assertion form of specification, $\{B\}$, is omitted because it is definable as {**true**} **skip** $\{B\}$. The "good-variable" operator takes an (acceptor, expression) pair (rather than a variable) as its operand. Non-interference specifications involving acceptors and procedures are definable in terms of $C \#_\tau E$, as shown in Sections 5 and 6 of [4].

Metavariables

τ	data types
θ	ordinary phrase types
γ	general phrase types
π	type assignments
I	identifiers

Types

$\tau ::= \mathbf{Bool} \mid \ldots$	
$\theta ::= \tau\,\mathbf{exp}$	expressions
$\mid \tau\,\mathbf{acc}$	acceptors
$\mid \mathbf{comm}$	commands
$\mid \theta_1 \rightarrow \theta_2$	procedures
$\gamma ::= \theta$	
$\mid \mathbf{spec}$	specifications

Productions

$\langle \theta, [\pi \mid I:\theta] \rangle ::= I$	identifier
$\langle \theta_1 \rightarrow \theta_2, \pi \rangle ::= \lambda I:\theta_1 . \langle \theta_2, [\pi \mid I:\theta_1] \rangle$	procedural-abstraction
$\langle \theta_2, \pi \rangle ::= \langle \theta_1 \rightarrow \theta_2, \pi \rangle (\langle \theta_1, \pi \rangle)$	procedural-application
$\langle \mathbf{comm}, \pi \rangle ::= \mathbf{skip}$	null
$\mid \mathbf{new}\,(I_1, I_2) : \tau\ \mathbf{in}\ \langle \mathbf{comm}, [\pi \mid I_1 : \tau\,\mathbf{acc} \mid I_2 : \tau\,\mathbf{exp}] \rangle$	variable-declaration
$\mid \langle \tau\,\mathbf{acc}, \pi \rangle :=_\tau \langle \tau\,\mathbf{exp}, \pi \rangle$	assignment
$\mid \langle \mathbf{comm}, \pi \rangle ; \langle \mathbf{comm}, \pi \rangle$	sequencing
$\mid \ldots$	
$\langle \mathbf{spec}, \pi \rangle ::= \mathbf{absurd}$	absurdity
$\mid \langle \gamma, \pi \rangle \equiv_\gamma \langle \gamma, \pi \rangle$	equivalence
$\mid \langle \mathbf{spec}, \pi \rangle \Rightarrow \langle \mathbf{spec}, \pi \rangle$	implication
$\mid \langle \mathbf{spec}, \pi \rangle \,\&\, \langle \mathbf{spec}, \pi \rangle$	conjunction
$\mid (\forall I:\theta)\ \langle \mathbf{spec}, [\pi \mid I:\theta] \rangle$	universal-quantification
$\mid \{\langle \mathbf{Bool\,exp}, \pi \rangle\}\ \langle \mathbf{comm}, \pi \rangle\ \{\langle \mathbf{Bool\,exp}, \pi \rangle\}$	Hoare-triple
$\mid \langle \mathbf{comm}, \pi \rangle \#_\tau \langle \tau\,\mathbf{exp}, \pi \rangle$	non-interference
$\mid \mathbf{gv}_\tau(\langle \tau\,\mathbf{acc}, \pi \rangle, \langle \tau\,\mathbf{exp}, \pi \rangle)$	good-variable

Table 1. Abstract syntax.

3. Semantic Domains

Let V_τ denote the set of possible values for data type τ; for example, $V_{\mathbf{Bool}} = \{true, false\}$. Consider some state-set X. To interpret a non-interference specification, it must be possible (as discussed in the introduction) to *restrict* X to subsets $X' \subseteq X$, However, to interpret the declaration of a variable of some data type τ, it must also be possible to *expand* X to $X \times V_\tau$. It is not at present clear how to allow for both restrictions *and* expansions of state-sets. The approaches described in Reynolds[5] and Oles[6,7] are adequate for expansions, but do not allow for restrictions as well. In the rest of this preliminary report, variable declarations are not considered. A change of state-set from X to X' is modelled by an injective function $f \in X' \to X$ that specifies, for every state $x' \in X'$, which element of X it simulates; elements of X not in the image of f are "unreachable" when executing relative to X'. When $X' \subseteq X$, f is an insertion function.

A *predomain*[12] is a partially-ordered set in which every directed subset has a least upper bound, where a subset of a partially-ordered set is directed just if it has an upper bound for every pair of its elements. An ordinary set may be regarded as a predomain ordered by the identity relation. A *domain* (in roughly the sense of Scott[13]) is a predomain that has a least element. A function from one predomain to another is *continuous* just if it preserves least upper bounds of all directed subsets. The set of all continuous functions from predomain D_1 to predomain D_2, denoted $D_1 \to D_2$, is a predomain when ordered point-wise.

The *product* of predomains D_1 and D_2, denoted $D_1 \times D_2$, is the Cartesian product of the underlying sets, ordered component-wise. The product $f_1 \times f_2 \in D_1 \times D_2 \to E_1 \times E_2$ of continuous functions $f_1 \in D_1 \to E_1$ and $f_2 \in D_2 \to E_2$ is a continuous function defined by $f_1 \times f_2(d_1, d_2) = (f_1(d_1), f_2(d_2))$. These concepts may be generalized as follows: if D_i is a predomain for every i in some finite set S, then their product, denoted $\prod_{i \in S} D_i$, is the set of all functions f such that, for all $i \in S$, $f(i) \in D_i$, and is a predomain when ordered point-wise. Similarly, the product $\prod_{i \in S} f_i$ of continuous functions $f_i \in D_i \to E_i$ is a continuous function from $\prod_{i \in S} D_i$ to $\prod_{i \in S} E_i$; the definition is obvious.

Let $M_\gamma(X)$ denote the predomain of meanings for phrase type γ when X is the state-set. For the non-procedural ordinary phrase types of our language, the meaning predomains are as follows:

$$M_{\tau\,\mathbf{exp}}(X) = X \to V_\tau$$

$$M_{\tau\,\mathbf{acc}}(X) = V_\tau \to M_{\mathbf{comm}}(X)$$

$$M_{\mathbf{comm}}(X) = X \times X \to M_{\mathbf{spec}}(X)\,.$$

Note that expressions must always terminate (V_τ is a set), and cannot have side effects. If

$M_{\mathbf{spec}}(X)$ is thought of as a domain of truth-values, then the domain of meanings for commands provides what is essentially the "relational" semantics that allows for non-determinism but does not distinguish a command that *always* terminates from one that has the same possible effects but sometimes fails to terminate. This is acceptable for a logic of *partial* correctness.

Unexpectedly, the definition of $M_{\mathbf{spec}}(X)$ is somewhat more complicated. It might seem that the (constant) domain of the two truth values would be appropriate; however, this does not provide a suitable relation between the $M_{\mathbf{spec}}(X)$ for different X. Instead, the "truth values" needed are *collections of* injective *functions with co-domain* X. The collections record *which* of the possible ways of deriving new state-sets X' from X would satisfy a specification (not just whether or not they *all* do). Such a collection must satisfy a generalized form of the monotonicity property discussed in the introduction: if $f \in X' \to X$ is an element of such a collection, then so is $f \circ g$ for *all* state-set mappings g with co-domain X', where $\circ$ denotes function composition. A collection of functions with co-domain X satisfying this condition is termed a *sieve on* X.[14] For any X, the collection of *all* state-set mappings with co-domain X and the *null* collection are two sieves on X, and can be thought of as the analogues of *true* and *false*, respectively. Note that when id_X (the identity function on X) is in a sieve, so are *all* of the mappings to X.

$M_{\mathbf{spec}}(X)$ (more precisely, its underlying set) is then defined to be the set of all sieves on X. It becomes a predomain by adopting the rule that $W_1 \leq W_2$ if and only if $W_1 \supseteq W_2$, so that the analogues of *true* and *false* are the least and greatest sieves, respectively. This is appropriate for a logic of partial correctness, but has the consequence that the meaning of a command must be the *complement* of the usual relational semantics; that is, if $c \in M_{\mathbf{comm}}(X)$ and $x_0, x_1 \in X$, then $c(x_0, x_1)$ is the collection of all state-set mappings $f \in X' \to X$ for which there is *no* terminating execution of the command between states in X' that are mapped by f to x_0 and x_1, respectively.

The relations between the $M_\gamma(X)$ for different X must now be defined. For $f \in X' \to X$, let $M_\gamma(f) \in M_\gamma(X) \to M_\gamma(X')$ denote the continuous function that maps meanings appropriate for X to corresponding meanings appropriate for X'. For the non-procedural phrase types, these are defined as follows:

$$M_{\tau\,\mathbf{exp}}(f)(e \in M_{\tau\,\mathbf{exp}}(X)) = e \circ f$$

$$M_{\tau\,\mathbf{acc}}(f)(a \in M_{\tau\,\mathbf{acc}}(X)) = M_{\mathbf{comm}}(f) \circ a$$

$$M_{\mathbf{comm}}(f)(c \in M_{\mathbf{comm}}(X)) = M_{\mathbf{spec}}(f) \circ c \circ f \times f$$

$$M_{\mathbf{spec}}(f)(W \in M_{\mathbf{spec}}(X)) = \{g \in X'' \to X' \mid f \circ g \in W\}\ .$$

It is easy to verify that the collection of functions in the last of these equations *is* a sieve on

X' when W is a sieve on X.

As usual, *environments*[15] are used to give meanings to free identifiers of phrases. Let $\mathrm{Env}_\pi(X)$ denote the predomain of environments appropriate for type assignment π when X is the set of possible states; then

$$\mathrm{Env}_\pi(X) = \prod_{I \in \mathrm{dom}(\pi)} M_{\pi(I)}(X) .$$

Similarly, for type assignment π and state-set mapping $f \in X' \to X$, let $\mathrm{Env}_\pi(f) \in \mathrm{Env}_\pi(X) \to \mathrm{Env}_\pi(X')$ denote the continuous function mapping an environment appropriate for state-set X into the corresponding environment appropriate for X'; then

$$\mathrm{Env}_\pi(f) = \prod_{I \in \mathrm{dom}(\pi)} M_{\pi(I)}(f) .$$

It is easily verified that the M_γ and the Env_π defined above are *functors* from the category of state-sets and injective co-functions (denoted **X**), to the category of predomains and continuous functions (denoted **Pdom**):

$$\begin{array}{ccccc} X & \qquad & \mathrm{Env}_\pi(X) & \qquad & M_\gamma(X) \\ f \Big\uparrow & & \Big\downarrow \mathrm{Env}_\pi(f) & & \Big\downarrow M_\gamma(f) \\ X' & & \mathrm{Env}_\pi(X') & & M_\gamma(X') \end{array}$$

(See, for example, Goldblatt[14], for explanations of these category-theoretic concepts, and others to be used subsequently.) Procedural phrase types are treated by using the following

Theorem (Oles[6,7]): for any[2] category **C**, the category $\mathbf{C} \Rightarrow \mathbf{Pdom}$ of all functors from **C** to **Pdom** (with natural transformations as the morphisms) is *Cartesian-closed*. □

Hence, in $\mathbf{X} \Rightarrow \mathbf{Pdom}$ there is an *exponentiation* operation on the objects, which can also be written $\Rightarrow$, and $M_{\theta_1 \to \theta_2}$ is defined to be $M_{\theta_1} \Rightarrow M_{\theta_2}$.

4. Semantic Valuations

For any phrase P, let $[\![P]\!]X$ be the valuation of P appropriate for state-set X. For $S \in \langle \mathbf{spec}, \pi \rangle$, $[\![S]\!]X$ must be a function from $\mathrm{Env}_\pi(X)$ to $M_{\mathbf{spec}}(X)$. If $P \in \langle \theta, \pi \rangle$ for an *ordinary* phrase type θ, then $[\![P]\!]X$ must be a *continuous* function from $\mathrm{Env}_\pi(X)$ to $M_\theta(X)$. The semantic valuations for commands and specifications are defined in Table 2 and Table 3,

---

[2]Some might prefer that foundational proprieties be observed here by requiring **C** to be *small*; the state-set category **X** is small if the state-sets are restricted to whichever level of the Zermelo hierarchy would be required to accomodate a particular choice of data types.

Metavariables

$$E \in \langle \tau\,\mathbf{exp}, \pi \rangle$$
$$A \in \langle \tau\,\mathbf{acc}, \pi \rangle$$
$$C \in \langle \mathbf{comm}, \pi \rangle$$

$$u \in \mathrm{Env}_\pi(X)$$
$$x \in X$$

Semantic equations

$$[\![\mathbf{skip}]\!]Xu(x_0,x_1) = \{f \in X' \to X \mid \text{if } x_0 = fx_0' \text{ and } x_1 = fx_1', \text{ then } x_0' \neq x_1'\}$$

$$[\![A :=_\tau E]\!]Xu(x_0,x_1) = [\![A]\!]Xu([\![E]\!]Xux_0)(x_0,x_1)$$

$$[\![C_0 ; C_1]\!]Xu(x_0,x_1)$$
$$= \{f \in X' \to X \mid \text{if } x_0,x_1 \in f(X'), \text{ then, for all } x' \in X', f \in [\![C_0]\!]Xu(x_0,fx') \text{ or } f \in [\![C_1]\!]Xu(fx',x_1)\}$$

Table 2. Semantics of commands.

respectively, and, for any $u \in \mathrm{Env}_\pi(X)$ and $I \in \mathrm{dom}(\pi)$, $[\![I]\!]Xu = u(I)$. This leaves only procedural abstraction and application; the key fact[16-18] is that a typed lambda calculus may be interpreted in any Cartesian-closed category. See Reynolds[5] and Oles[6,7] for detailed discussions of procedures in this kind of framework.

In the equation for $C \#_\tau E$, the condition says that any terminating execution in X'' can *also* occur in the subset of X'' for which E has the value it has initially. The quantification over all functions g is needed to ensure that the collection of mappings is a sieve. For example, suppose that

(1) a (non-deterministic) command C_0 allows execution from state x_0 to both state x_1 and to state x_1',

(2) command C_1 allows execution to x_2 from both x_1 and x_1', and

(3) Boolean expression B is *true* for x_0, x_1, and x_2, but *false* for x_1'.

Now, consider whether $(C_0;C_1)\#_{\mathbf{Bool}} B$; there is an execution of the composite command from x_0 to x_2 that preserves the truth of B for the state-set $\{x_0,x_1,x_1',x_2\}$, but *not* if x_1 is excluded. The quantification prevents this non-monotonicity, and similarly in the equations for implication and universal quantification.

Metavariables

$$P \in \langle\gamma,\pi\rangle$$
$$E \in \langle\tau\,\mathbf{exp},\pi\rangle$$
$$B \in \langle\mathbf{Bool\ exp},\pi\rangle$$
$$A \in \langle\tau\,\mathbf{acc},\pi\rangle$$
$$C \in \langle\mathbf{comm},\pi\rangle$$
$$S \in \langle\mathbf{spec},\pi\rangle$$
$$S' \in \langle\mathbf{spec},[\pi\,|\,I:\theta]\rangle$$

$$u \in \mathrm{Env}_\pi(X)$$

Semantic equations

$$[\![\mathbf{absurd}]\!]Xu = \varnothing$$

$$[\![P_1 \equiv_\gamma P_2]\!]Xu = \{f \in X' \to X \mid M_\gamma(f)([\![P_1]\!]Xu) = M_\gamma(f)([\![P_2]\!]Xu)\}$$

$$[\![S_1 \Rightarrow S_2]\!]Xu = \{f \in X' \to X \mid \text{for all } g \in X'' \to X', \text{ if } f \circ g \in [\![S_1]\!]Xu \text{ then } f \circ g \in [\![S_2]\!]Xu\}$$

$$[\![S_1 \,\&\, S_2]\!]Xu = [\![S_1]\!]Xu \cap [\![S_2]\!]Xu$$

$$[\![(\forall I:\theta)S']\!]Xu = \{f \in X' \to X \mid \text{for all } g \in X'' \to X' \text{ and } m'' \in M_\theta(X''),\ \mathrm{id}_{X''} \in [\![S']\!]X''[\mathrm{Env}_\pi(f \circ g)(u) \mid I:m'']\ \}$$

$$[\![\{B_0\}\ C\ \{B_1\}]\!]Xu = \{f \in X' \to X \mid \text{for all } x_0,x_1 \in f(X'), \text{ if } [\![B_0]\!]Xux_0 \text{ and } f \notin [\![C]\!]Xu(x_0,x_1), \text{ then } [\![B_1]\!]Xux_1\}$$

$$\begin{aligned}
&[\![C \ \#_\tau E]\!]Xu \\
&= \{f \in X' \to X \mid \text{for all } g \in X'' \to X',\ x_0,x_1 \in (f \circ g)X'' \text{ and } v \in V_\tau, \\
&\qquad \text{if } x_0 \in (f \circ g)X_v \text{ and } (f \circ g) \notin [\![C]\!]Xu(x_0,x_1), \text{ then } x_1 \in (f \circ g)X_v \text{ and } (f \circ g \circ \mathrm{ins}_v) \notin [\![C]\!]Xu(x_0,x_1), \\
&\qquad\quad \text{where } \mathrm{ins}_v \text{ is the insertion function from } X_v = \{x'' \in X'' \mid [\![E]\!]Xu(f(gx'')) = v\} \text{ into } X''\ \}
\end{aligned}$$

$$[\![\mathbf{gv}_\tau(A,E)]\!]Xu = \{f \in X' \to X \mid \text{for all } x_0,x_1 \in f(X') \text{ and } v \in V_\tau,\ f \in [\![A]\!]Xuv(x_0,x_1) \text{ or } [\![E]\!]Xux_1 = v\}$$

Table 3. Semantics of specifications.

The following theorem shows that the semantics defined above has the essential property required by the method of Reynolds[5] and Oles:[6,7]

Theorem: for all $P \in \langle\gamma,\pi\rangle$ and state-set mappings $f \in X' \to X$,

$$[\![P]\!]X' \circ \mathrm{Env}_\pi(f) = M_\gamma(f) \circ [\![P]\!]X\ ;$$

that is, the rectangle in the following diagram commutes:

$$\begin{array}{ccccc} X & & \mathrm{Env}_\pi(X) & \xrightarrow{[\![P]\!]X} & M_\gamma(X) \\ \uparrow f & & \downarrow \mathrm{Env}_\pi(f) & & \downarrow M_\gamma(f) \\ X' & & \mathrm{Env}_\pi(X') & \xrightarrow[{[\![P]\!]X'}]{} & M_\gamma(X') \end{array}$$

Proof: a tedious but straightforward structural induction. □

Corollary: For all $P \in \langle\theta,\pi\rangle$ and $S \in \langle\mathbf{spec},\pi\rangle$,

(1) $[\![P]\!]$ is a natural transformation from Env_π to M_θ, and

(2) $[\![S]\!]$ is a natural transformation from $E \circ \mathrm{Env}_\pi$ to $E \circ M_{\mathbf{spec}}$, where E is the obvious embedding functor from **Pdom** to the category of predomains and *arbitrary* functions[3], and $\circ$ here denotes functorial composition. □

Expressions have not been considered, but in order to validate the assignment axiom it is necessary to assume that the value of an expression at some state is independent of the values of its free expression-like identifiers for any *other* state; that is, for $E \in \langle\tau\,\mathbf{exp},\pi\rangle$, state-set X, $u \in \mathrm{Env}_\pi(X)$, $x_0 \in X$,

$$[\![E]\!]Xux_0 = [\![E]\!]X[u \mid I : \lambda x \in X.u(I)x_0]x_0$$

for any expression identifier I, and similarly for other expression-like identifiers. This assumption only precludes bizarre interpretations in which sub-expressions are evaluated after "temporary" side-effects.

Finally, $S \in \langle\mathbf{spec},\pi\rangle$ is termed *universally valid for* π if and only if $\mathrm{id}_X \in [\![S]\!]Xu$ for all state-sets X and $u \in \mathrm{Env}_\pi(X)$.

5. Axiomatics and Soundness

The logical part of the formal system presented by Reynolds[4] is essentially many-sorted intuitionistic predicate logic with equality. (Occurrences of the static-assertion specification {**false**} should be replaced by the new constant **absurd** to allow for the null state-set.) The non-logical axioms and derived rules are discussed in considerable formal detail by Reynolds and will not be repeated here. Axioms involving the **explike** and **commlike** phrase types must be replaced by separate axioms for each of the relevant types, and axioms involving variables must be modified in obvious ways to suit our restricted language.

The main result is the following

---

[3]The latter category is a *topos*,[14] but **Pdom** is not.[7]

Theorem (soundness): for $S \in$ <**spec**,π>, S is universally valid for π whenever $S :: \pi$ is derivable. □

6. Concluding Remarks

Specification logic is an *Algol-like*[5] programming logic. It is (statically) typed. It avoids making explicit the low-level concept of "locations". It treats substitution, binding and scope correctly. It includes the (typed) lambda calculus as a sub-system. It requires expressions to be side-effect-free. It distinguishes between data types and phrase types: classical reasoning is allowed for assertions, but specifications require intuitionistic reasoning. It provides facilities such as quantification and non-interference specification uniformly for all relevant phrase types.

Finally, specification logic "obeys a stack discipline".[5] Of course, this operational description of the property is not appropriate to specifications. The general formulation is that every kind of phrase is interpreted relative to a "possible world" of allowed states, and these valuations satisfy a naturality condition ensuring suitable relations between the interpretations for *different* state-sets. This structure allows a stack implementation for ordinary phrase types, including higher-order procedures, and (intuitionistic) reasoning about state-sets, without making the state-sets explicit in the logical language.

In at least one respect, however, specification logic is not yet sufficiently Algol-like: non-terminating expressions should be possible. The intuitionistic "free" logic of Scott[19] might be applicable here, because it allows non-denoting terms in restricted contexts. It may be possible to generalize or simplify the logic in other ways. A *natural-deduction*[20] presentation of the formal system would simplify the manipulation of "assumptions", and might lead to a generalization of the tableau conventions of [3]. *Jumping* mechanisms, such as the "completers" of [5], would require a form of continuation semantics. The treatment of static-assertion and non-interference specifications would seem to be well-suited to the handling of *concurrency*. Finally, it would be interesting to explore the changes required to interpret a *total*-correctness variant of specification logic.

The most pressing open problem is to find a way to handle state-set expansions, as well as restrictions, in order to interpret variable declarations. In any case, it should be noted that the most important aspects of the interpretation developed in this paper are not sensitive to the structure of **X**, the state-set category. In particular, the treatments of $M_{\mathbf{spec}}$ and procedures are based on general category-theoretic constructions and the properties of **Pdom**.

Acknowledgements

The author is very grateful to John Reynolds for suggesting that Kripke semantics and the Reynolds-Oles approach to modelling block structure might be relevant to the interpretation of specification logic, and for many helpful discussions. A preliminary version of the material in the introductory section was presented to the 1983 meeting of IFIP Working Group 2.3, at Pont-à-Mousson, France.

References

(1) C.A.R. Hoare, "An axiomatic basis for computer programming", *Comm. ACM* **12** (10), pp. 576-580 and 583 (October 1969).

(2) C.A.R. Hoare and P.E. Lauer, "Consistent and complementary formal theories of the semantics of programming languages", *Acta Informatica* **3** (2), pp. 135-153 (1974).

(3) J.C. Reynolds, *The Craft of Programming*, Prentice-Hall International (1981).

(4) J.C. Reynolds, "Idealized Algol and its specification logic", in *Tools and Notions for Program Construction* (D. Néel, ed.), pp. 121-161, Cambridge University Press (1982); also: Report 1-81, School of Computer and Information Science, Syracuse University (July 1981).

(5) J.C. Reynolds, "The essence of Algol", in *Algorithmic Languages* (J.W. de Bakker and J.C. van Vliet, eds.), pp. 345-372, North-Holland (1981).

(6) F.J. Oles, "Type algebras, functor categories and block structure"; in *Algebraic Methods in Semantics* (M. Nivat and J.C. Reynolds, eds.), Proceedings of the Symposium on the Applications of Algebra to Language Definition and Compilation, June 1982, Fontainebleau, Cambridge University Press (1985).

(7) F.J. Oles, *A Category-Theoretic Approach to the Semantics of Programming Languages*, Ph.D. dissertation, Syracuse University (August 1982).

(8) S.A. Kripke, "Semantical analysis of intuitionistic logic I", in *Formal Systems and Recursive Functions* (J.N. Crossley and M.A.E. Dummett, eds.), pp. 92-130, North-Holland (1965).

(9) M. Dummett, *Elements of Intuitionism*, Oxford University Press (1977).

(10) D. van Dalen, *Logic and Structure*, 2nd edition, Springer-Verlag (1983).

(11) C. McCarty, "Information systems, continuity and realizability"; in *Logics of Programs, Proceedings 1983* (E. Clarke and D. Kozen, eds.). Lecture Notes in Computer Science, vol. 164, pp. 341-359, Springer-Verlag (1984). Also, Chapter 7 of *Realizability and Recursive Mathematics*, D.Phil. thesis, Oxford University, and technical report CMU-CS-84-131, Dept. of Computer Science, Carnegie-Mellon University (1984).

(12) J.C. Reynolds, "Semantics of the domain of flow diagrams", *J. ACM* **24** (3), pp. 484-503 (July 1977).

(13) D.S. Scott, "Domains for denotational semantics"; in *Automata, Languages and Programming* (M. Nielsen and E.M. Schmidt, eds.), Proceedings of the Ninth Colloquium, Aarhus, Denmark, July 1982, Lecture Notes in Computer Science, vol. 140, pp. 575-613, Springer-Verlag (1982).

(14) R. Goldblatt, *Topoi, The Categorial Analysis of Logic*, North-Holland (1979).

(15) P.J. Landin, "A λ-calculus approach", in *Advances in Programming and Nonnumerical Computation* (L. Fox, ed.), pp. 97-141, Pergamon Press (1966).

(16) J. Lambek, "From λ-calculus to Cartesian-closed categories"; in *To H.B. Curry, Essays in Combinatory Logic, Lambda Calculus and Formalism* (J.P. Seldin and J.R. Hindley, eds.), pp. 375-402, Academic Press (1980).

(17) D.S. Scott, "Relating theories of the λ-calculus"; in *To H.B. Curry, Essays in Combinatory Logic, Lambda Calculus and Formalism* (J.P. Seldin and J.R. Hindley, eds.), pp. 403-450, Academic Press (1980).

(18) G. Berry, *Some Syntactical and Categorical Constructions of Lambda-Calculus Models*, Report no. 80, INRIA, Rocquencourt, France (1981).

(19) D.S. Scott, "Identity and existence in intuitionistic logic"; in *Applications of Sheaf Theory to Algebra, Analysis and Topology* (M.P. Fourman, C.J. Mulvey and D.S. Scott, eds.), Lecture Notes in Mathematics, vol. 753, pp. 660-696, Springer-Verlag (1979).

(20) D. Prawitz, *Natural Deduction, A Proof-Theoretical Study*, Almquist and Wiksell, Stockholm (1965).

A simple programming language with data types: semantics and verification.*

(Extended Abstract)

Jerzy Tiuryn

Institute of Mathematics
University of Warsaw
Poland

Introduction

The aim of this paper is to provide a uniform framework for defining the semantics of deterministic while-programs equipped with auxiliary data types. The emphasis of this paper is on data type definitions and on proving partial correctness properties of programs which use these data types.

Many existing programming languages allow user-defined data types. Simula 67 uses the notion of a class (cf. [DMN 68]), Pascal uses records which correspond to sorts in our formalism, EUCLID uses the notion of a module (cf. [VR 78]). Data types of EUCLID are absolute data types in our formalism in the sense that bounds of the "subrange types" (i.e. sizes of objects) are typed constants which are computed upon entry to the scope. This feature is absent in Modula (cf. [EO 80]) and in Pascal. Modules of Modula and clusters of CLU (cf. [LS 77]) correspond to data types in our formalism. Also modules of OBJ2 (cf. [FG 85]) can be expressed as data types in our formalism.

Our view of data types essentially differs from other approaches based on type theory (cf. [M-L 73], [BL 84], [MP 85]). It represents data types as sets (i.e. as set-theoretical notions) with its theory to be interpreted in a well defined class of standard models for which we have a well tailored axiomatization.

---

*This research was supported in part by NSF Grant Number DCR-8402305 while the author was visiting the Computer Science Department of Washington State University, Pullman, WA.

There are only very few papers which discuss the issue of verification of programs which use auxiliary data types. In the pioneering work of C.A.R. Hoare [H 72] the case of the Simula 67 class concept is discussed and some extensions of it are mentioned. A formal proof system is only implicitly contained in the paper, there is no discussion of soundness or completeness. It is even not clear what syntactic constraints are put on assertions and therefore it is difficult to justify how adequate the language of assertions is. In [OC 75] D.C. Oppen and S.A. Cook consider quite a general class of data structures. They are essentially finite ordered graphs with nodes and arrows labeled by natural numbers, and the operations performed on the graphs are: "add a new node" and "move an arrow". (As we will see our approach is more general.) The assertion language is as expressive as the first-order language of Peano arithmetic. Completeness is proved assuming knowledge of all true assertions in the intended model (which contains together with the ground structure all finite graphs). We find this assumption unreasonbly strong. It prevents having truly effective proof systems for verification of programs over finite ground structures. In Section 4 of this paper we show that "knowing" only first-order theory of the ground structure suffices in many interesting cases. R.L. London, et. al. give proof rules for EUCLID in [LG 78]. All comments on [H 72] are fully applicable here except that the proof system is explicit.

We believe that the trade-off between expressiveness of a programming language and provable properties of programs is not well understood yet, especially if programs use data types. Therefore, as the first step in this research, we decided to concentrate on the simplest non-trivial control of while-programs but allow full generality of data types which the programs may use.

The data types expressible in our formalism constitute a very rich family of objects including arrays of all finite types, algebraic and binary stack, counters. We also show how nondeterminism and random assignments may be handled by a suitable data type (for that reason we allow a data type to have multi-valued operations). This formalism is strong enough to express the notion of a parameterized data type. Thus we are able to talk about such data types as a stack of arrays of binary stacks, etc.

Let L be a first-order language with equality. Our aim is to investigate partial correctness properties of programs in an L-structure $\underline{\underline{M}}$. In addition to the usual assignments and tests performed by a program p on elements of M, p can use auxiliary objects which come from the data type. Therefore, it should be quite obvious that we have to allow as assertions a richer class of formulas than the first-order formulas over L.

We assume in this approach that elements of any data type during any computation in an L-structure $\underline{\underline{M}}$ range over $M \cup HF_M$, where HF_M is the collection of all <u>hereditarily finite sets over M</u>. HF_M is the least collection of sets which satisfies the following conditions

(h1) the empty set, $\emptyset$, is in HF_M

(h2) for any $x \varepsilon HF_M$ and $y \varepsilon HF_M \cup M$, $x \cup \{y\} \varepsilon HF_M$.

The elements of M are called in this formalism ur-elements (cf. [B 75]). Let $L^* = L(\varepsilon, U)$ be an extension of L by a binary relation symbol ε (membership relation), and by a unary relation symbol U (expressing the property of being an ur-element).

Given an L-structure $\underline{\underline{M}}$ we define the L^*-structure $\underline{\underline{M}}^*$ as follows. The carrier of $\underline{\underline{M}}^*$ is $M^* = M \cup HF_M$. All L-operations are extended to M^* by setting the value $\emptyset$ whenever at least one argument is not in M. L-relations remain the same. ε is a relation in $M^* \times HF_M$ which interprets the membership relation. For $x \varepsilon M^*$, U(x) holds iff $x \varepsilon M$. L^*-structures of the above form will be called the <u>standard models.</u>

We are going to work with a formal proof system <u>Pr</u>, within which we shall provide the semantics for data type definitions, the (denotational) semantics of programs, and verification of programs. We introduce Pr in Section 1 by a set of postulates we want Pr to satisfy. As we indicate in the conclusion, KPU, the Kripke-Platek set theory with ur-elements can be shown to be the minimal natural axiomatization which fulfills our postulates. Throughout the paper we exhibit which postulates are used to establish the results.

The rest of the paper is organized as follows. Section 2 is devoted to data types. We discuss there data type definitions and their models. Due to space limitations we only mention the possibility to express in our formalism parameterized data types. Among all data types we further distinguish absolute data types as those which have the same meaning (up to isomorphism) in all models of Pr. The collection of absolute data types is still very rich as it includes algebraic arrays of all finite types, nondeterminism and random assignments. In Section 3 we define a programming language as a language of program schemes over a given data type signature plus a data type definition. We further provide a semantics for any programming language (this is done in the denotational style). We also show that the operational semantics is expressible in our language. It is a theorem of Pr that the operational semantics coincides with the denotational one. Section 4 is devoted to the verification of programs. We show that all rules of Hoare's proof system for while-programs are derivable in Pr. We also show that Pr is a relatively complete proof system for every programming language over absolute data types (a suitable notion of an assertion is defined in this section too).

Programming languages over absolute data types form a very interesting class with a lot of computational power. It can be shown that every such a programming language has the halting problem over finite interpretations elementarily decidable. Also a converse statements holds: every programming language whose the halting problem over finite interpretations is elementarily decidable can be translated into a programming language over an absolute data type.

1. A proof system Pr

We first introduce some syntactic notions.

1.1 Δ_o formulas (cf. [B 75]) are first-order formulas in L* in which all quantifiers are bounded, i.e. $x\varepsilon y\ldots$, or $x\varepsilon y\ldots$

1.2 Σ formulas form the least set of L* formulas which contains all Δ_o formulas and closed under conjunction, disjunction, bounded quantification and unbounded existential quantification.

1.3 If in the above definition existential quantification is replaced by universal quantification then we obtain the notion of a Π formula.

1.4 Postulates on Pr

(1.4.1) (effectiveness)

Pr is a recursive set of first-order sentences in L*. Derivations are performed in any complete first-order formalism.

(1.4.2) (fixing the ground structure)

$\underline{Pr} \vdash \forall x_o \ldots \forall x_n[U(x_o)\wedge\ldots\wedge U(x_{n-1})\wedge f(x_o,\ldots,x_{n-1})=x_n) \rightarrow U(x_n)]$,

for every n-ary operation symbol f of L.

$\underline{Pr} \vdash \forall x_o \ldots \forall x_n[((\neg U(x_o)\vee\ldots\vee\neg U(x_{n-1}))\wedge f(x_o,\ldots,x_{n-1})=x_n)$

$\rightarrow (\neg U(x_n)\wedge \forall y\varepsilon x_n\ y\neq y)]$

for every n-ary operation symbol f of L.

$\underline{Pr} \vdash \forall x_o \ldots \forall x_{n-1}(r(x_o,\ldots,x_{n-1}) \rightarrow (U(x_o)\wedge\ldots\wedge U(x_{n-1})))$,

for every n-ary relation symbol r of L.

$\underline{Pr} \vdash \forall x\,\forall y(x\varepsilon y \rightarrow \neg U(y))$.

(1.4.3) (fixed-points)

Let $\bar{x} = (x_o,\ldots x_{n-1})$, $\bar{y} = (y_o,\ldots,y_{k-1})$ be vectors of variables, and let R be an n-ary relation symbol not in L*. For every Σ formula $\phi(\bar{x},\bar{y},R)$ in the language $L^*\cup\{R\}$ there exists a Σ formula $I\phi(\bar{x},\bar{y})$ in L* such that (FP-1) and (FP-2) hold.

(FP-1) $\underline{Pr} \vdash \phi(\bar{x},\bar{y},\lambda\bar{x}.I\phi(\bar{x},\bar{y})) \leftrightarrow I\phi(\bar{x},\bar{y})$

(FP-2) For every L* formula $\Psi(\bar{x},\bar{y})$, if $\underline{Pr} \vdash (\phi(\bar{x},\bar{y},\lambda\bar{x}.\Psi(\bar{x},\bar{y})) \rightarrow \Psi(\bar{x},\bar{y}))$, then $\underline{Pr} \vdash (I\phi(\bar{x},\bar{y}) \rightarrow \Psi(\bar{x},\bar{y}))$.

Here $\phi(\ldots,\lambda\bar{x}\Psi(\bar{x},\bar{y}))$ denotes the result of simultaneously substituting Ψ for all occurrences of R in ϕ (applying the usual rule of renaming bounded variables), $\lambda\bar{x}\ldots$ indicates which variables of Ψ should be treated as those of R, and which play the role of parameters.

The above postulate does not say that $\phi(\bar{x},\bar{y},R)$ has the least fixed-point expressible by a Σ formula. It says that it has a fixed-point expressible by a Σ formula which is the least among all first-order expressible fixed-points.

(1.4.4) (initiality)

(I-1) Pr $\models \underline{\underline{M}}^*$ holds for every L-structure $\underline{\underline{M}}$.

(I-2) For every L*-structure $\underline{\underline{A}} = (A,\ldots,E,U)$, if Pr $\models \underline{\underline{A}}$, then there exists an L-structure $\underline{\underline{M}}$ and an embedding $i:M^* \to A$ such that i preserves all operation symbols of L; and for every $n\geq 1$, every n-ary relation symbol r of L*, and any $x_o,\ldots,x_{n-1}\varepsilon M^*$, $(x_o,\ldots,x_{n-1})\varepsilon r_{M^*}$ iff $(i(x_o),\ldots,i(x_{n-1}))\varepsilon r_{\underline{\underline{A}}}$.

We shall call $i(M^*)$ the standard part of $\underline{\underline{A}}$.

(1.4.5) (foundation)

$\exists x\Psi(x) \to \exists x(\Psi(x)\wedge \forall y\varepsilon x\neg\Psi(y/x))$,

for all L*-formulas $\Psi(x)$ in which y does not occur free.

(1.4.6) (extensionality)

$\forall x\ \forall y[(\neg U(x)\wedge\neg U(y)\wedge\ \forall z(z\varepsilon x \leftrightarrow z\varepsilon y)) \to x = y]$.

1.5 A Σ formula $\phi(\bar{x})$ is called a Δ formula (with respect to Pr) if there exists a Π formula $\Psi(\bar{x})$ such that

$$\text{Pr} \vdash \phi(\bar{x}) \leftrightarrow \Psi(\bar{x}).$$

2. Data types

We start with a special notation for many-sorted signatures.

2.1 Many-sorted signatures

We adopt a somewhat unusual definition of a many-sorted signature for reasons which will become obvious a little later.

Let L_{data} be a set of relation symbols of finite arities such that for every $n \geq 1$ there are uncountably many relation symbols in L_{data} of arity n. We assume that $L^* \cap L_{data} = \emptyset$.

A <u>many-sorted signature σ</u> is a pair $\sigma = ((s_\xi | \xi < \beta_1), (\sigma_\xi | \xi < \beta_2))$, where β_1, β_2 are countable ordinals, $s_\xi \varepsilon L_{data}$ is an unary relation symbol for $\xi < \beta_1, \sigma_\xi$ is a first order formula in L_{data} with equality for $\xi < \beta_2$, subject to the following conditions.

(2.1.1)

For every $\xi < \beta_2$ there exist $n \geq 1$, an n-ary relation symbol $r_\xi \varepsilon L_{data}$ and $\xi_o, \ldots, \xi_{n-1} < \beta_1)$ such that σ_ξ is in one of the following three forms:

(F) $\forall x_o \ldots \forall x_{n-2} [\exists ! x_{n-1} r_\xi (x_o, \ldots, x_{n-1}) \wedge$

$\forall x_{n-1} ((s_{\xi_o}(x_o) \wedge \ldots \wedge s_{\xi_{n-2}}(x_{n-2}) \wedge r_\xi (x_o, \ldots, x_{n-1})) \rightarrow s_{\xi_{n-1}}(x_{n-1}))]$

(R) $\forall x_o \ldots \forall x_{n-1} [r_\xi (x_o, \ldots, x_{n-1}) \rightarrow (s_{\xi_o}(x_o) \wedge \ldots \wedge s_{\xi_{n-1}}(x_{n-1}))]$

(MV) $\forall x_o \ldots \forall x_{n-2} [\exists x_{n-1} r_\xi (x_o, \ldots, x_{n-1}) \wedge \forall x_{n-1} ((s_{\xi_o}(x_o) \wedge \ldots$

$\wedge s_{\xi_{n-2}}(x_{n-2}) \wedge r_\xi (x_o, \ldots, x_{n-1})) \rightarrow s_{\xi_{n-1}}(x_{n-1}))]$.

(2.1.2) r_{ξ_1} and r_{ξ_2} are different symbols, for $\xi_1 \neq \xi_2$.

(2.1.3) s_{ξ_1} and s_{ξ_2} are different, for $\xi_1 < \beta_1, \xi_2 < \beta_2$.

The relation symbols S_ξ, for $\xi < \beta_1$, are called <u>sort symbols.</u> The relation symbols r_ξ, for $\xi < \beta_2$, which occur in the context (F), (R), (MV) are called <u>operation symbols</u>, <u>relation symbols</u>, and <u>multivalued operation symbols</u>, respectively. It is also clear what arities of the corresponding symbols are within σ.

Let $L(\sigma) = \{s_\xi | \xi < \beta_1\} \cup \{r_\xi | \xi < \beta_2\}$, and let $F(\sigma) = \{\sigma_\xi | \xi < \beta_2\}$.

<u>2.2 Data type definitions</u>

Let σ be a many-sorted signature. A <u>data type definition Γ</u> is an assignment to every $r \varepsilon L(\sigma)$, a Δ formula (in L^*) α_r having as many free variables as the arity of r is, subject to the following condition.

(2.2.1)

For every $\xi < \beta_2$, if $r_1, \ldots, r_k$ are all relation symbols which occur in σ_ξ, then $Pr \vdash \sigma_\xi (\alpha_{r_1}/r_1, \ldots, \alpha_{r_k}/r_k)$.

Given a model $\underline{\underline{A}}$ of $\underline{Pr}$ and a data type definition Γ, we can define a σ-structure $\Gamma(\underline{\underline{A}})$ as follows.

For $\xi<\beta_1$, the carrier of sort s_ξ is defined by

(2.2.2) $\Gamma(\underline{\underline{A}})_\xi = \{a\varepsilon A | \underline{\underline{A}} \models \alpha_{s_\xi}[a]\}$.

For $\xi<\beta_2$, if r_ξ is an operation symbol of arity $(s_{\xi_o},\ldots,s_{\xi_{n-2}},s_{\xi_{n-1}})$, then its interpretation is a function $f_\xi\colon \Gamma(\underline{\underline{A}})_{\xi_o} \times\ldots\times\Gamma(\underline{\underline{A}})_{\xi_{n-2}} \to \Gamma(\underline{\underline{A}})_{\xi_{n-1}}$ defined by

(2.2.3) $f_\xi(a_o,\ldots,a_{n-2}) = a_{n-1}$ iff $\underline{\underline{A}} \models \alpha_{r_\xi}[a_o/x_o,\ldots,a_{n-1}/x_{n-1}]$.

It follows from (2.1.1,F) and (2.2.1) that f_ξ is a function with domain and range as indicated above.

In a similar way we interpret relation and multivalued operation symbols in $\Gamma(A)$ (multivalued operations return as a value a nonempty set of elements of an appropriate sort).

The structure $\Gamma(\underline{\underline{A}})$ is called the <u>data type defined by Γ in $\underline{\underline{A}}$</u>. Let $\underline{\underline{B}}$ be the standard part of $\underline{\underline{A}}$. It easily follows from our definitions that $\Gamma(\underline{\underline{B}})$ is a σ-substructure of $\Gamma(\underline{\underline{A}})$. We call $\Gamma(\underline{\underline{B}})$ the <u>standard part</u> of $\Gamma(\underline{\underline{A}})$.

The next notion plays a crucial role for this paper. Γ is said to be <u>an absolute data type definition</u> if for every model $\underline{\underline{A}}$ of $\underline{Pr}$, $\Gamma(\underline{\underline{A}})$ is identical to its standard part. Thus, if Γ is an absolute data type definition, then for every L-structure $\underline{\underline{M}}$, Γ defines the same data type (up to isomorphism) in every model of $\underline{Pr}$ whose standard part is isomorphic to $\underline{\underline{M}}^*$.

We also remark that it follows from effectiveness of $\underline{Pr}$ that if $\underline{\underline{M}}$ is a computable L-structure, then $\Gamma(\underline{\underline{M}}^*)$ is a computable σ-structure for every data type definition over a many-sorted signature σ.

The next result characterizes absolute data type definitions. For $n\geq 0$ let $\mathrm{rank}(x)\leq n$ be the following Δ_o formula.

$\mathrm{rank}(x)\leq 0 \leftrightarrow U(x) \vee \forall y\varepsilon x\ y\neq y$

$\mathrm{rank}(x)\leq n+1 \leftrightarrow \forall y\varepsilon x\ \mathrm{rank}(y)\leq n$.

(2.2.4) Proposition

A data type definition Γ is absolute iff for every sort symbol s there exists $n \geq 0$ such that $Pr \vdash \forall x(\alpha_s(x) \rightarrow rank(x) \leq n)$.

Proof: A standard application of the compactness argument.

2.3 Examples of data type definitions

(2.3.1) (Ground data type $\underline{\underline{M}}$)

This data type has one sort and the same operation and relation symbols as L (though we have to use different names for them, let us say that s' corresponds to s in L). The definition of the sort is given by U(x). The definition of an n-ary function symbol f' (which is an n+1-ary relation symbol of L_{data}) is given by $f(x_o,\ldots,x_{n-1}) = x_n$. The definition of an n-ary relation symbol r' is given by $r(x_o,\ldots,x_{n-1})$.

All the above definitions are Δ_o formulas (and thus Δ formulas in every $\underline{Pr}$), and "fixing the ground structure" postulate (1.4.2) ensures that this is a right data type definition.

(2.3.2) (bounded nondeterminism)

This data type has one sort, one unary relation, and one multivalued operation of arity 0. The definitions are the following

sort: $x = \emptyset \vee x = \{\emptyset\}$

unary relation: $x = \emptyset$

multivalued constant: $x = \emptyset \vee x = \{\emptyset\}$

Observe that the above formulas can be clearly made into Δ_o formulas. A proof that this is a data type definition is obvious.

(2.3.3) (random assignment)

This data type has one sort and one multivalued constant.

sort: U(x)

multivalued constant: U(x)

By Proposition 2.2.4 we see that (2.3.1)-(2.3.3) are all absolute data type definitions. Below we give an example of a non-absolute data type.

(2.3.4) (counters)

This data type has one sort, two unary operations, one constant and one unary relation.

Let Nat(x) be the following formula.

$Ord(x) \wedge \neg Lim(x) \wedge \forall y \varepsilon x \neg Lim(y)$, where

$Ord(x) \leftrightarrow \neg U(x) \wedge \forall y \varepsilon x \forall z \varepsilon y (z \varepsilon x \wedge \forall v \varepsilon z \; v \varepsilon y)$ and

$Lim(x) \leftrightarrow Ord(x) \wedge x \neq \phi \wedge \forall y \varepsilon x \exists z \varepsilon x \; z = y \cup \{y\}$.

Define the sort of counters by Nat(x).

operation 1(x,y): $y = x \cup \{x\}$

operation 2(x,y): $(Nat(x) \wedge x \neq \emptyset \rightarrow x = y \cup \{y\}) \wedge$

$(\neg Nat(x) \vee x = \emptyset \rightarrow y = \emptyset)$.

Constant: $x = \emptyset$

unary relation: $x = \emptyset$

Again all the above definitions are Δ_o and we leave it for the reader to check that counters is a data type definition. The formula Nat(x) defines in every standard model the set of natural numbers (in sense of von Neuman). Operation 1 defines successors, Operation 2 defines predecessor, and $\emptyset$ is zero.

2.4 Parameterized data types

Due to lack of space we illustrate the concept of a parameterized data type with an example. We sketch the data type definition of arrays which use indecies from a set A and store values from a set B. Here A and B are parameters to be instantiated by a Δ formula with one free variable. More precisely, they are unary predicate symbols in L_{data}.

We denote this parameterized data type definition by Array(A,B). It has three sorts: A, B, and F(A,B). The latter sort has the Δ_o definition asserting that F(A,B) consists of all partial functions from A to B, i.e. $f \varepsilon F(A,B)$ iff "f is a function and $dom(f) \subseteq A$ and $range(f) \subseteq B$".

It has two operations

ap: $F(A,B) \times A \times B \rightarrow B$

$\underline{ins}$: $F(A,B) \times A \times B \rightarrow F(A,B)$

with the following Δ definitions

$\underline{ap}\ (f,a,b) = f(a)$, if $a \varepsilon dom(f)$

b, otherwise

$\underline{ins}\ (f,a,b) = f[a/b]$, if $a \varepsilon dom(f)$

$f \cup \{<a,b>\}$, otherwise

Here f[a/b] is the same function as f except that f[a/b](a) = b.

The signature has also one relation $D \subseteq F(A,B) \times A$ with the following Δ definition:

D(f,a) iff $a \varepsilon dom(f)$.

In order to make sure that Array(A,B) is a correct definition we have to show (in a routine way) that $\underline{Pr} \vdash$ "ap and ins are functions of the right arities" and "D is a relation of the right arity."

3. Programming Languages

Let σ be a fixed many-sorted signature. We are going to define a programming language over σ as an ordered pair, <language of program schemes, data type definition over σ>.

3.1 The language of program schemes, L_{ps}, over σ

(3.1.1) (typed variables)

Let K be the set of all sorts of σ. With every sort $s \varepsilon K$ a nonempty set of variables V_s is associated, so that for $s_1 \neq s_2$, $V_{s_1} \cap V_{s_2} = \emptyset$. Each set V_s may be either finite or countably infinite. Let $V_{ps} = \cup\{V_s | s \varepsilon K\}$. Elements of V_s are called the variables of sort s.

(3.1.2) (elementary assignments)

$x_o := x_1$, for any variables x_o, x_1 of the same sort.

$x_n := f(x_o, \ldots, x_{n-1})$, where f is either an operation symbol or a many-valued operation symbol in σ, and $x_o, \ldots, x_{n-1}, x_n$ are variables of appropriate sorts which match the aritity of f.

(3.1.3) (elementary tests)

These are Boolean combinations of $r(x_o,\ldots,x_n)$, where r is a relation symbol in σ and $x_o,\ldots,x_n \varepsilon V_{ps}$ are of appropriate sorts which match the arity of r.

(3.1.4) The language of program schemes over σ is the least set L_{ps} of expressions satisfying the following conditions:

(a) All elementary assignments are in L_{ps}

(b) If $p_1, p_2 \varepsilon L_{ps}$ and α is an elementary test, then the following expressions are in L_{ps}

$p_1;p_2$

if α then p_1 else p_2 fi

while α do p_1 od

3.2 Semantics of programming languages

Let PL = $\langle L_{ps},\Gamma\rangle$ be a programming language over σ. Let $V'_{ps} = \{x' \mid x \varepsilon V_{ps}\}$ be a disjoint copy of V_{ps}. For every $p \varepsilon L_{ps}$ and for every vector of variables $\bar{x} = (x_o,\ldots,x_n)$ in V_{ps} such that every variable of p occurs in $\bar{x}$ we construct by induction on the form of p a Σ formula in L*, $\phi_p(x,\bar{x}')$ which describes the input-output behaviour of p (here $\bar{x}' = (x'_o,\ldots,x'_n)$ is the vector of primed variables corresponding to x). This is a routine task. Δ definitions of Γ are used to handle elementary assignments and tests. The fixed-point postulate on Pr (1.4.3) is used to handle while-do construct. We call this semantics a denotational one.

3.3 The operational semantics

Let $p \varepsilon L_{ps}$ and let $\bar{x} = (x_o,\ldots,x_n)$ be variables in V_{ps} which contain all variables of p. We can label every occurence of an elementary assignment or test in p and those places in p which serve as halt statements. We omit the standard inductive definition of labeling of p. Let $T = \{0,\ldots,m-1\}$ be the set of labels for p, and let 0 be the label of the first instruction performed by p. Given a labeling of p, it clearly defines a Δ formula

$\underline{step}_p$ (x,v,x',v') which describes a one-step transition of p between the states <x,v> and <x',v'>, where v,v' range over labels.

Then the <u>operational semantics of p</u> is a Σ formula $Opr_p(x,x)$ defined below.

$Opr_p(x,x) \leftrightarrow \exists y \exists u[Nat(y) \wedge y>1 \wedge$ "u is a function with dom(u) = y" $\wedge$
$\forall z \varepsilon y$ "(u(z) is of the form $<<v_o,\ldots,v'_n>,\ell>$ for some $\ell \varepsilon T$, and $v_o,\ldots,v_n$)" $\wedge$
$u(0) = <x,0> \wedge u(y-1) = <x',\ell>$ for some $\ell \varepsilon T$, a label of a halt statement $\wedge$
$\forall z \varepsilon y-1$ $\underline{step}_p$ $(u(z)/(\bar{x},v),u(z+1)/(\bar{x}',v'))]$.

In the above definition Nat(y) is a Δ_o formula defined in (2.3.4).

<u>3.4 Proposition</u>

Let $p \varepsilon L_{ps}$. Then $\underline{Pr} \vdash \phi_p(\bar{x},\bar{x}') \leftrightarrow Opr_p(\bar{x},\bar{x}')$

<u>Proof</u>: The proof of ($\rightarrow$) is by induction on p (we use here the fixed-point postulate (FP-2)).

The proof of ($\leftarrow$) is by induction on p. In the induction step for while-do construct we show, using the axiom of foundation, that $Opr_p(\bar{x},\bar{x}')$ is the least fixed-point to the Σ formula defining while-do.

4. <u>Verification of programs</u>

Let PL = $<L_{ps},\Gamma>$ be a programming language. At the beginning we fix as a parameter a set <u>Assn</u> of formulas over L* which we call <u>assertions</u>. We only require at this point that all free variables of any assertion are in V_{ps}. Throughout this section we adopt the convention that if $x \varepsilon V_s$ is a variable of sort s, then x always ranges over the elements defined by $\alpha_s(x)$, the Γ definition of the sort s.

<u>A partial correctness formula</u> $\{\alpha\}p\{\beta\}$, where $\alpha,\beta \varepsilon \underline{Assn}$, $p \varepsilon L_{ps}$ is the sentence in L*

$\forall \bar{x}[\alpha(\bar{x}) \rightarrow \forall \bar{x}'(\phi_p(\bar{x},\bar{x}') \rightarrow \beta(\bar{x}'/\bar{x}))]$, where $\bar{x}$ is a vector of variables in V_{ps} containing all free variables of α, β and p.

For $p \varepsilon L_{ps}$, $\beta \varepsilon \underline{Assn}$ the <u>weakest precondition</u> of p w.r.t. β, $p\{\beta\}$, is the formula

$\forall\bar{x}'(\phi_p(\bar{x},\bar{x}') \to \beta(\bar{x}'/\bar{x}))$, where $\bar{x}$ is a vector of variables in V_{ps} containing all free variables of β and p.

The strongest postcondition of p w.r.t. β, $\{\beta\}p$, is the formula $\exists\bar{x}(\beta(\bar{x})\wedge\phi_p(\bar{x},\bar{x}'))$, where $\bar{x}$ satisfies the same assumption as above.

The next notion plays the same role as expressiveness of a structure (cf. [C 78]), though it is weaker than expressiveness and it is preserved under elementary equivalence (for suitable Assn).

An L-structure $\underline{\underline{M}}$ is strong for PL and Assn if for every $p\varepsilon L_{ps}$ and every $\beta\varepsilon$Assn there exists $\beta_p^*\varepsilon$Assn such that $\underline{\underline{M}}^* \models \forall\bar{x}(\beta_p^* \to p\{\beta\})$, and for every $\alpha\varepsilon$Assn and $q\varepsilon L_{ps}$, if $\underline{\underline{M}}^* \models \forall\bar{x}'[(\{\alpha\}q) \to (p\{\beta\})(\bar{x}'/\bar{x})]$, then $\underline{\underline{M}}^* \models \forall\bar{x}'[(\{\alpha\}q) \to \beta_p^*(\bar{x}'/\bar{x})]$.

Choosing assertions is a delicate point. We cannot take as assertions just first-order formulas in L since we want to be able to describe properties of auxiliary values used by a program (those come from the data type). Also, weaker assertions make that fewer are strong, restricting the class of structures where we can prove programs correct. On the other hand we cannot take too strong assertions since we could end up in a situation that fewer partial correctness formulas are provable for reasons not related to PL. This situation the reader may find in papers on program verification (cf. [C 78]), where the first-order properties of a structure are separated from reasoning about programs computing in that structure by assuming them as axioms in the proof system (the so-called "oracle" axiom). In our approach we also assume the first-order properties of an L-structure as given, but we want to avoid adding more specific axioms to Pr.

In order to define sufficiently strong assertions we first extent the syntactic notions introduced in (1.1)-(1.3).

Δ_o^e formulas form the least set of L* formulas which contains all atomic L* formulas and is closed under: $\neg, \wedge, \vee$, quantification over ur-elements, and bounded quantification $\forall x\varepsilon y$, $\exists x\varepsilon y$.

Σ^e formulas form the least set containing all Δ_o^e formulas and closed under: $\wedge$, $\vee$, quantification over ur-elements, bounded quantification, and existential quantification.

Π^e formulas are obtained from the above definition by replacing "existential" by "universal".

A Σ^e formula ϕ is called a Δ^e formula if there exists a Π^e formula ψ such that $\underline{Pr} \vdash \phi \leftrightarrow \Psi$.

Let Assn be all Δ^e formulas whose all free variables are in V_{ps}.

4.1 Proposition

(a) Let $\phi(\bar{x})$ be a Π^e formula and let $\underline{\underline{M}}_1$, $\underline{\underline{M}}_2$ be two L-structures which are elementarily equivalent. Then

$\underline{\underline{M}}_1^* \models \forall \bar{x}\phi(\bar{x})$ iff $\underline{\underline{M}}_2^* \models \forall \bar{x}\phi(\bar{x})$.

(b) Let $\phi(\bar{x})$ be a Σ^e formula, let $\underline{\underline{M}}$ be any L-structure and let $\underline{\underline{A}}$ be any model of $\underline{Pr}$ whose standard part is isomorphic to $\underline{\underline{M}}^*$. Then for every $a\varepsilon(M^*)^n$, if $\underline{\underline{M}}^* \models \phi[\bar{a}/\bar{x}]$, then $\underline{\underline{A}} \models \phi[\bar{a}/\bar{x}]$.

(c) For every programming language PL, the notion of a strong structure for PL and Assn is invariant under elementary equivalence.

Proof: (a) is proved by showing that for every Π^e formula $\phi(\bar{x})$ there exists a set of first order sentences X_ϕ in the language L such that for every L-structure $\underline{\underline{M}}$, $\underline{\underline{M}}^* \models \forall \bar{x}\phi(\bar{x})$ iff for all $\alpha\varepsilon X_\phi$, $\underline{\underline{M}} \models \alpha$.

(b) is proved by induction on ϕ.

(c) follows from (b) and the fact that the weakest preconditions are Π^e and the strong postconditions are Σ^e.

Now we can state the main result of this section.

4.2 Theorem

Let PL = $\langle L_{ps}, \Gamma\rangle$ be a programming language with absolute data type definition Γ.

(a) The standard model of arithmetic $\underline{\underline{N}}$ is strong for PL and Assn.

(b) Every finite L-structure is strong for PL and Assn.

(c) For every $p \in L_{ps}$, α, $\beta \in$ Assn and for every L-structure $\underline{M}$ strong for PL and Assn the following conditions are equivalent:

(c1) $\underline{M}^* \models \{\alpha\}p\{\beta\}$

(c2) Pr $Th(\underline{M}) \vdash \{\alpha\}p\{\beta\}$, where $Th(\underline{M})$ is the first-order theory of $\underline{M}$. (The sentences of $Th(\underline{M})$ are written in the language $L \cup \{U\}$ with all quantifiers restricted to range over U).

Proof: (a) and (b) hold for any set Assn, though for different reasons. In (a) and (b) the formula β_p^* of the definition of a strong structure can always be chosen to be Δ_o^e. (Here we use the assumption of absoluteness of PL.) In (a) we use the enormous possibilities of codding by first order formulas in $\underline{N}$. In (b), the data type defined by Γ in $\underline{M}^*$ has finite carriers and therefore every $p\{\beta\}$ can be replaced in $\underline{M}^*$ by a Δ_o^e formula.

For (c) we only sketch the proof of (c1) $\rightarrow$ (c2). The proof breaks into two steps. First we show that all Hoare's rules of inference for while-programs are derivable in Pr (here we again use the fixed-point postulate of Pr). Next we show that if $\underline{M}$ is strong, then we can get down with p to elementary assignments (this is a relatively standard argument).

In the second step of the proof we show that (c1) $\rightarrow$ (c2) holds for any elementary assignment p. Since $\{\alpha\}p\{\beta\}$ is a Π^e formula, by 4.1(a), it is true in every $\underline{M}_1^*$, where $\underline{M}_1$ is elementarily equivalent to $\underline{M}$.

Let $\underline{A}$ be any model of Pr $\cup$ $Th(\underline{M})$. The above observation together with the fact that Γ is absolute give, by 4.1(b), that $\underline{A} \models \{\alpha\}p\{\beta\}$. By the completeness of the first-order logic, (c2) follows.

5. Concluding remarks

We have shown that if Pr satisfies postulates (1.4.1)-(1.4.6), then (with a suitable set of assertions) Pr is a relatively complete proof system for partial correctness of any programming language with an absolute data type. It remains to be seen how far one can get with a proof system like Pr for programming languages over non-absolute data types. Since there are programming languages over natural non-absolute data types, with the halting problem over finite interpretations decidable--the above question seems to be very intriguing. On the other hand, absolute data types, as mentioned in the last paragraph of Introduction, provide a lot of computational power and give rise to a family of programming languages which is in a certain sense "complete" for all programming languages with elementarily decidable halting problem.

Finally, we would like to comment on the existence of an actual set of axioms Pr which satisfies postulates (1.4.1)-(1.4.6). If we add to (1.4.2), (1.4.5) the axioms asserting existence of a pair and of union, plus Δ_o-separation and Δ_o-collection (the last two schemes assert restricted principles for set construction), then the resulting system is exactly Kripke-Platek set theory with ur-elements (cf. [B 75], p. 11), which we abbreviate as KPU. Then KPU clearly satisfies (1.4.1) and (1.4.4). It also satisfies the fixed-point-postulate (1.4.3). This follows from a suitably modified version of Gandy's theorem (cf. [B 75], p. 208). The details of this modification and a proof will appear in the final version of the paper. Here we would like to stress that in general I_ϕ of (1.4.3) does not describe the least fixed-point of ϕ. It describes the least fixed-point in all admissible models (i.e. models with ε being well founded)--this is the essence of Gandy's theorem. However (1.4.3) asserts that I_ϕ describes a fixed-point which is the least among all which are fixed-order expressible. We claim that this is enough to build a denotational semantics.

One advantage of KPU as opposed to ZF is that it has clearly distinguishable standard models and in this respect it more resembles Peano Arithmetic. A possible objection, however, may be that these standard models have too few sets. To enrich the collection of sets in standard models we may add to KPU an axiom asserting that there exists a set of all ur-elements. The new theory, KPU^+ has still initial models HYP($\underline{\underline{M}}$) above every L-structure $\underline{\underline{M}}$ which may serve as new "standard" models. HYP($\underline{\underline{M}}$) has lots of interesting sets constructed from $\underline{\underline{M}}$, every set in HYP($\underline{\underline{M}}$) has a finite description, and the whole HYP($\underline{\underline{M}}$) may be viewed as a mini-universe for set theory. We believe that KPU^+ and HYP-construction can be used as an alternative tool to properly address the issue of polymorphism, higher order recursive procedures, and data types. This will be the subject for future research. On the other hand, the above modification is inessential from the point of view of proof theory since KPU^+ is interpretable into KPU (cf. [B 75], Thm. 5.5, p. 59). This last property shows another nice feature of KPU.

References

[B 75] Barwise, J. Admissible sets of Structures, Springer-Verlag, Berlin (1975).

[BL 84] R.M. Burstall and B. Lampson, "A kernel language for abstract data types and modules," Proc. of the International Symp. Semantics of Data Types, (G. Kah, D.B. MacQueen and G.D. Plotkin, eds.), Lecture Notes in Computer Science 173, Springer-Verlag (1984), pp. 1-50.

[C 78] S.A. Cook, "Soundness and completeness of an axiom system for program verification," SIAM J. Computing, 7 (1978), pp. 70-90.

[DMN 68] O.J. Dahl, B. Myhrhang, and K. Nygaard, "The Simula 67 common base language," Norwegian Computing Center, Oslo (1968).

[EO 80] G.W. Ernst and W.F. Ogden, "Specification of abastract data types in MODULA," ACM TOPLAS, Vol. 2, No. 4, (1980), pp. 522-543.

[FG 85] K. Futatsugi, J.A. Goguen, J.P. Jouannaud and J. Meseguer, "Principles of OBJ2," Proc. of the 12th Ann. ACM Symp. Principles of Programming Languages, (1985), pp. 52-56.

[H 72] C.A.R. Hoare, "Proof of correctness of data representation," Acta Informatica, 1 (1972), pp. 271-281.

[LS 77] B. Liskov, A. Snyder, R. Atkinson, and C. Schaffert, "Abstraction mechanisms in CLU," Communications ACM, 20 (1977), pp. 564-576.

[LG 78] R.L. London, J.V. Guttag, J.J. Horning, B.W. Lampson, J.G. Mitchell, and G.J. Popek, "Proof rules for the programming language EUCLID," Acta Informatica, 10 (1978), pp. 1-26.

[M-L 73] P. Martin-Lof, "An intuitionistic theory of types: predicative part," Logic Colloquium '73, (H.E. Rose and J.C. Shepherdson, eds.), North-Holland (1975), pp. 73-118.

[MP 85] J.C. Mitchell and G.D. Plotkin, "Abstract types have existential type," Proc. of the 12th Ann. ACM Symp. Principles of Programming Languages, (1985), pp. 37-51.

[OC 75] D.C. Oppen and S.A. Cook, "Proving assertions about programs that manipulate data structures," Proc. of the 7th Ann. ACM Symp. Theory of Computing, (1975), pp. 107-116.

[VR 78] T. Venema and J. des Rivieres, "Euclid and Pascal," SIGPLAN Notices, Vol. 13 (3), (1978), pp. 57-69.

COMPUTER AIDED REASONING

Andrzej Trybulec & Howard A. Blair

EECS U-157 University of Connecticut
Storrs, CT 06268

Abstract

We present a language intended to be a first step in approximating the language of mathematical papers, and a validator; that is, a program that checks the validity of arguments written in this language. The validator approximates the activity of a mathematician in certifying the structure and correctness of the mathematical argument. Both components together constitute a computer aided reasoning (CAR) system. Versions of the system, called MIZAR, have been in use for a decade for discrete mathematics instruction. We are concerned here with the features of the MIZAR language that that are used to diminish the gap between formal natural deduction and mathematical vernacular. The inference checking component of the validator can be easily changed. We demonstrate the influence on the way the expressive power of the language can be exploited by contrasting, for a fixed proposition, two proofs embodying the same idea but for which different checking modules have been used. The more powerful inference checker that we discuss incorporates the formalization of obviousness given by M. Davis.

1. Using Mizar

We begin this section with a short example of a correct MIZAR text that has been prepared with a conventional text editor. We have inserted explanatory comments that are set off by "==" at the beginnings of lines. This is the normal convention for comments in MIZAR. The following MIZAR text is an exercise proposed by Jerzy Los as a challenge to MIZAR's suitability: prove that if the union of two equivalence relations on a given set A is total, then at least one of them must be total. We mean here that a binary relation R on A is total iff R = the Cartesian square of A. We believe that after the following tabulation of MIZAR conventions the text will be readable at least by mathematicians.

environ	introduces the axiomatics
begin	introduces the proposition and its proof
for ... holds ...	stands for universal quantifier
ex ... st ...	stands for existential quantifier
then	the preceding proposition is used in the justification of the following one
thus	goal of the current proof or subproof
hence	combines "then" and "thus" (so "then thus" is not allowed)
thesis	what remains to be proved in the current proof or subproof at the point of occurrence of "thesis"

```
environ

== We introduce variables of sorts 'element' and 'equivrel'.  The
== elements are those of an implicit underlying set.
```

```
  let e,e1,e2,r0,r denote equivrel; let x,y,x1,y1,z,u,v denote
  element;

==  Relations are regarded as first-order individuals.  This view
==  entails the introduction of a first-order predicate for expressing
==  membership of pairs of elements in relations.

==  Axioms to be satisfied by equivalence relations:

  ref: for x,e holds in[e,x,x];
  sym: for x,y,e st in[e,x,y] holds in[e,y,x];
  trn: for x,y,z,e st in[e,x,y] & in[e,y,z] holds in[e,x,z];

==  The axiom for total relations.

  def1: for r holds total[r] iff (for x,y holds in[r,x,y]);

==  Definition of union of relations. Only equivalence relations need
==  to be united.

  def2: for e1,e2,e holds union[e1,e2,e] iff
          (for x,y holds (in[e1,x,y] or in[e2,x,y]) iff in[e,x,y])

begin

== The proposition to be proved:

  proposition: for r,e1,e2 st total[r] & union[e1,e2,r] holds
                                                total[e1] or total[e2]

proof
  let r,e1,e2 be equivrel such that total: total[r] and
                                     union: union[e1,e2,r];
  assume  not total[e1];

==  We therefore have to prove  total[e2].

  then consider x1,y1 being element such that 1: not in[e1,x1,y1]
                                                        by def1;
  2: for x,y holds in[r,x,y]                            by total,def1;
  then 3: in[r,x1,y1];
  4: for x,y holds (in[e1,x,y] or in[e2,x,y]) iff in[r,x,y]
                                                        by union,def2;
  then in[e1,x1,y1] or in[e2,x1,y1]                     by 3;
  then 5: in[e2,x1,y1]                                  by 1;

==  Establishes two elements x1,y1 such that  e2(x1,y1).

==  The idea of the proof is that since (e1 U e2) is total,

==  either [e1(x,y) and e1(y,z)] or [e2(x,y) and e2(y,z)] for any
==  triple x,y,z. So if any particular pair x,y can be placed in one
==  equivalence relation, then all triples must fall into that
==  equivalence relation.

    lemma: for u holds in[e2,u,y1]

==  Now show that every element must be e2-equivalent to y1 (and x1).

    proof
       let u be element;
       in[r,u,y1]                                       by 2;
```

```
        then 6: in[e1,u,y1] or in[e2,u,y1]                    by 4;
        in[r,x1,u]                                            by 2;
        then 7: in[e1,x1,u] or in[e2,x1,u]                    by 4;
       now
        assume  in[e1,u,y1];
        then in[e1,x1,u] implies in[e1,x1,y1]                 by trn;
        then in[e2,u,x1]                                      by sym,1,7;
        hence in[e2,u,y1]                                     by 5,trn;
       end;

 ==  Mizar will compute the conclusion of the preceding subproof
 ==  beginning with 'now' as
 ==           in[e1,u,y1] implies in[e2,u,y1]
 ==  A logical consequence of this and (6) is
              in[e2,u,y1]
 ==  which is what remains to be proved in the current (nested) proof
 ==  of the lemma, and that is the value of 'thesis'.

       hence thesis                                           by 6;
     end;

 ==  This completes the proof of the lemma.

    now let u,v be element;
        8: in[e2,u,y1]                                        by lemma;
        in[e2,v,y1]                                           by lemma;
        then in[e2,y1,v]                                      by sym;
        hence in[e2,u,v]                                      by 8,trn;
       end;
    hence total[e2]                                           by def1

 ==  Which was what was required to be proved.
 ==  We could have said 'thesis' instead of 'total[e2]' at this
 ==  last step.

 end
```

MIZAR checks texts submitted by the user; it does not create proofs by itself. When the text is correct MIZAR responds only "Thanks, O.K.". Otherwise error diagnostics are given. The burden is on the user to correct the text and then resubmit it to the system in a manner similar to submitting program sources to a compiler.

Both authors prepare MIZAR texts in an iterative fashion by first preparing proof skeletons. The practice is derived naturally enough from structured programming. Whatever its merits or demerits in principle, the result in fact is nearly always a more rapid, more elegantly structured proof than we obtain when we yield to the temptation of discarding this discipline in favor of a 'linearly' composed proof.

To conclude this section we present a printout of a partially developed proof. This was obtained from an implementation of MIZAR-MSE running under Unix on a Vax 780 at Computer Applications and Research Center of the University of Connecticut.

```
     proposition: for r,e1,e2 st total[r] & union[e1,e2,r] holds
                                                 total[e1] or total[e2]
     proof
       let r,e1,e2 be equivrel;
       assume total[r] & union[e1,e2,r]; then
        for x,y holds in[e1,x,y] or in[e2,x,y] by def2,def1;
****                                              *103
```

```
          assume total[e1];
****          *84
          then consider x1,y1 such
            1: not in[e1,x1,y1] & in[e2,x1,y1]
****        *36
                                                  by union,def1;

        lemma: for u holds in[e2,u,y1]
          proof let u be element;
           in[e1,u,y1] implies not in[e1,x1,u] by union,trn,1;
****                                                     *73   *73
          end;
****        *81

           hence thesis                      by def1,lemma,sym,lemma,trn;

        end

 s o r r y
 ---------
```

errors explanation

36 "that" is missing. (*1)

73 no sentence is designated by this label. the label was not used to label any of the previous sentences.

81 reasoning or proof is not concluded.

84 this assumption disagrees with the current thesis.

103 your inference is not accepted by the checker.

remarks

(*1) due to this error a portion of the text usually until "begin", "end", "environ", "now","proof" or semicolon has been skipped in the analysis.

2. Davis' Thesis

The inference checker is a disprover; it tries to refute the conjunction of the premises conjoined with the negation of the sentence to be justified. Temporarily treating universal sentences as primitives, a disjunctive normal form (DNF) is obtained from that conjunction. If the DNF is not empty, and if each disjunct contains at least one universal sentence, then for each disjunct one universal sentence is selected, and still treating the remaining universal sentences in that disjunct as primitives, unification is applied to try to refute that disjunct. If this fails, then another selection of a universal sentence is made and the process is repeated until each selection has been tried. The entire process is then repeated for each disjunct.

Some details are of course omitted. For example, we have not mentioned which DNF is constructed, or the problems arising from equality. In the first MIZAR text example, two constructions appear: "let ... " and "consider ... ". These constructions enable the use of universal generalization, and the choice rule (the so-called rule of existential instantiation), respectively.

Notwithstanding the appearance of the preceding MIZAR text, it is not essentially different from formal proofs in natural deduction systems. The checker is still simply too weak. Modulo the difficulty of checking sentential calculus tautologies, transforming proofs that are capable of being validated with MIZAR's basic checker into formal natural deduction proofs would be straightforward as the reader can observe.

The basic checker embodies a classical concept of obviousness (regarding logical consequence). In its somewhat modern formulation, within the predicate calculus, everything that follows from general to specific is obvious, and nothing else. [T84]. This concept arises in antiquity and is traditionally referred to as Aristotle's Dictum. Recently, Martin Davis put forward a more extensive formalization of obviousness. [D81].

> "THESIS: An inference is obvious precisely when a Herbrand proof of its correctness can be given involving no more than one substitution instance of each clause."

Under this thesis all sentential tautologies are obvious. This dismisses from consideration, quite properly in this context, the notions of quantitative complexity associated with structural complexity theory. In MIZAR it is permitted to have multiple copies of the premises (i.e. to repeat the premise's label several times after "by"). Davis' thesis permits multiple copies of the same clause to be present in the "given" premises. To conform to Davis' thesis in MIZAR it is necessary for the human user to function as an oracle by providing an upper bound on the number of times a particular premise needs to be used in a particular step. This conforms also to normal practice in presenting mathematical arguments. It is often said that "By two applications of theorem X we obtain ... ".

It may be necessary in using this checking module (which we call the Davis checker) to construct proofs that contain sentences to be justified that have the form

A or ... or A

since multiple copies of the sentence to be justified may be needed. Such occurrences indicate badly constructed proofs; it is perhaps better to retreat from the full power of the Davis checker when such constructions arise.

```
    proposition: for r,e1,e2 st total[r] & union[e1,e2,r] holds
                         total[e1] or total[e2]
    proof
      let r,e1,e2 be equivrel;
      assume total[r] & union[e1,e2,r]; then
      union: for x,y holds in[e1,x,y] or in[e2,x,y] by def2,def1;

==    Assuming e1 is not total, since (e1 U e2) is total there must be
==    a pair x1,y1 not related by e1 and therefore related by e2

      assume  not total[e1];
      then consider x1,y1 such
        that 1: not in[e1,x1,y1] and 2: in[e2,x1,y1]
                                  by union,def1;

==    For each u, assuming in[e1,u,y1], if we also had in[e1,x1,u]
==    then by transitivity we have a contradiction with 1, so in[e2,x1,u]
==    then by 2 we get in[e2,u,y1].
```

```
lemma: for u holds in[e2,u,y1]
  proof let u be element;
   in[e1,u,y1] implies in[e2,x1,u] by union,trn,1;
   hence in[e2,u,y1] by union,trn,sym,2;
  end;

  hence thesis                  by def1,lemma,sym,lemma,trn;

end
```

3. Miscellaneous

We conclude the paper with a brief report on the uses to which assorted versions of MIZAR have been put.

It has been used in teaching logic at Warsaw University for the past three years, and at the University of Alberta for the past year. At the University of Connecticut and at Washington State University, it is currently being used in teaching discrete mathematics for computer science.

Regarding mathematics research two interesting experiments are worth noting. In a version of MIZAR called MIZAR-HPF, fundamental axioms for a fragment of category theory were prepared and a series of exercises were scanned. The axiomatization strategy was carried through, in effect, by employing sorts for higher order objects. Davis' thesis was originally embodied in the basic inference checker of MIZAR-HPF. In MIZAR-2, a paper of Karol Borsuk, in Homotopy Theory, [B70] was thoroughly transcribed. This resulted in a text approximately twice the size, in lines/words, as the original text. The task of transcription for such a paper is rather similar to writing a detailed exegesis.

Mizar-2 has also been applied to proving properties of programs, using an approach based on the work of Burstall.

REFERENCES

[B70] Borsuk, Karol, On the homotopy types of some decomposition spaces, Bull.Acad.Pol.Sci., ser.math, astr. et phys. no.5, 18(1970)

[BTZ85] Byliński, Cz., Trybulec, A., Zukowski, S. MIZAR-HPF, Studies in Grammar, Logic, and Rhetorics V, Warsaw University. (to appear).

[dB70] de Bruijn, N.G., The mathematical language Automath, its usage and extensions, Lecture Notes in Mathematics, Springer Verlag, 125(1970)

[C82] Constable, R.L., An introduction to the PL/CV2 programming logic, Lecture Notes in Computer Science, Springer Verlag, 135(1982)

[D81] Davis, Martin, Obvious logical inferences, Proc. of IJCAI-81,Vancouver,BC, August 1981,530-531

[GMW79] Gordon, M., Milner, R., Wadsworth, C., Edinburgh LCF, Lecture Notes in Computer Science, Springer Verlag, 78(1980)

[MT85] Mostowski, Marcin; Trybulec, Zinaida, A certain experimental computer aided course of logic in Poland, Proc. of World Conference on Computers in Education, Norfolk, VA, July-August 1985, North Holland, (to appear).

[RuDr85] Rudnicki, Piotr; Drabent, Wlodzimierz, Proving properties of Pascal programs in Mizar-2, Acta Informatica, Springer Verlag, to appear.

[T84] Trybulec, A. On a System of Computer Aided Instruction of Logic, Bulletin of the Section of Logic. Polish Academy of Sciences, Warsaw-Lodz.

[TB85] Trybulec, A., & Blair, H. Computer Assisted Reasoning with MIZAR, Proceedings of the Ninth International Joint Conference on Artificial Intelligence, (to appear).

The Taming of Converse: Reasoning about Two-Way Computations

Moshe Y. Vardi†

Center for Study of Languages and Information, Stanford University

ABSTRACT

We consider variants of propositional dynamic logic (PDL) augmented with the *converse* construct. Intuitively, the converse α^- of a program α is a programs whose semantics is to run α backwards. While PDL consists of assertions about *weakest preconditions*, the *converse* construct enable us to make assertions about *strongest postconditions*. We investigate the interaction of *converse* with two constructs that deal with infinite computations: *loop* and *repeat*. We show that $converse-loop-PDL$ is decidable in exponential time, and $converse-repeat-PDL$ is decidable in nondeterministic exponential time.

1. Introduction

Propositional dynamic logic (PDL) [FL79], and its extensions (e.g., [HS83a], [Sh84], [St80]) are formal systems for reasoning about input/output and ongoing behavior of programs schemes. The basic constructs in these logics are assertions of the form $\langle\alpha\rangle q$, asserting that the program α can terminate in a state satisfying q, and assertions about the possibility of infinite computations, e.g., $loop(\alpha)$ [HS83a] or $repeat(\alpha)$ [St80].

The *converse* construct [Pr76] enables us to reverse our mode of reasoning. Intuitively, the converse of a program α, denoted α^-, is a program whose semantics is to run α backwards. Thus, if the assertion $\langle\alpha\rangle q$ is the weakest precondition for the program α to terminate in a state satisfying q, the assertion $\langle\alpha^-\rangle p$ is the strongest postcondition that holds after termination of α when started at a state satisfying p [dB80].

Intuitively, one would not expect the addition of *converse* to a logic L to change the properties of L in any significant way. Indeed, $converse-PDL$, the extension of PDL with *converse*, satisfies the same *small model property* as PDL [FL79], and the known decision procedures and completeness results for PDL extend without difficulty to $converse-PDL$ [Pa80, Pr79, Pr80].

This turns out, however, to be the exception rather then the rule. In variants of PDL, *converse* interacts with other constructs in a quite unpredictable way. For example, $converse-DPDL$, where atomic programs are required to be deterministic, does not have the *finite model property*. Indeed, the $converse-DPDL$ formula $P\wedge[a^{-*}]\langle a^-\rangle\neg P$ is not satisfiable in any finite model though it is satisfiable in an infinite model [Ha83]. The finite model property similarly fails for $converse-loop-PDL$ [St82]. The complications arising from the addition of *converse* seem also to make the decision problem much harder; the addition of *converse* to $repeat-PDL$ increases the running time of the decision procedure in [St82] quintuply exponentially (from $O(exp^3(n))$ to $O(exp^8(n))$).

In [VW84] it is shown that even though *converse* does make life harder, it does not make them as exorbitantly harder as it would seem from the results in [St82]. Specifically, it is shown there that validity for $converse-DPDL$ can be decided in time $O(exp(n^2))$ (the bound for $DPDL$ is $O(exp(n))$[BHP82]). The increase in the bound is due to a quadratic increase in the size of *closures* of formulas.

---

† Research supported by a gift from System Development Foundation. Address: CSLI, Ventura Hall, Stanford University, Stanford, CA 94305, USA.

In this paper we show that in general *converse* behaves in the manner suggested in [VW84] rather than in the manner suggested in [St82]. That is, it does makes life harder, but not too hard. We show this by proving two upper bounds. We prove that validity for *converse* $-$ *loop* $-$ *PDL* can be decided in time $O(exp(n^2))$ (the bound for *loop* $-$ *PDL* is $O(exp(n))$ [PS83]), and we prove that the validity for *converse* $-$ *repeat* $-$ *PDL* can be decided in nondeterministic time $O(exp(n^4))$ (the bound for *repeat* $-$ *PDL* is $O(exp(n^2))$ [VS85]. (Actually, we prove our results for extensions of *DPDL*, from which follow the results for extensions of *PDL*. No previous results about *converse* $-$ *loop* $-$ *DPDL* and *converse* $-$ *repeat* $-$ *DPDL* were known.) As in [VW84], the increase in the bounds is due to a quadratic increase in the size of closures of formulas.

We prove our bounds by the automata-theoretic approach suggested in [St80] and further developed in [VW84] and [VS85]. This approach is based on the fact that our logics have the *tree model property*. That is, models of these logics can be viewed as labeled graphs and these graphs can be unraveled into bounded-branching infinite tree-structured models. This suggest that decision procedures for program logics can be obtained by reducing satisfiability to the *emptiness problem* for certain classes of *tree automata*. The idea is to construct a tree automaton A_f for a given a formula f, such that A_f accepts exactly the tree models of f. Thus f is satisfiable if and only if A_f accepts some tree.

The reduction of satisfiability to emptiness for logic such as *DPDL* [VW84] or *repeat* $-$ *PDL* [St80,VS84] is relatively straightforward. This is not the case once *converse* is introduced. By their nature, tree automata are one-way devices, i.e., they scan the input in one direction. Computation of programs with *converse* are, on the other hand, two-way computations, and it is not clear how to check assertions about two-way computations by one-way automata. Indeed, to solve the decision problem for *converse* $-$ *repeat* $-$ *PDL*, Streett introduced two-way automata [St82]. The crux of his result is that two-way automata can be transfomed to equivalent one-way automata, but the transformation causes a quadruply exponential blow-up.

What we show in this paper is how to reduce satisfiability in the presence of *converse* to emptiness of one-way automata. The key to our reduction is the extension of the closure by assertions about cycling computations. Intuitively, *cycle*(α) holds in a state u if there is a computation of α that starts and terminates at u. We show that two-way computations can be viewed as one-way computations with cycles. Thus assertions about two-way computations can be checked by one-way automata.

2. *Converse* $-$ *DPDL*

We assume familiarity with *dynamic logic* [Pr76], with *propositional dynamic logic* (*PDL*) [FL79], and with *deterministic propositional dynamic logic* (*DPDL*) [BHP82]. We also assume familiarity with the necessary automata-theoretic background (see [VW84]). We will consider a variant of *DPDL*, in which programs are described by sequential automata rather than by regular expressions (c.f. [HS83b,Pr81]). This variant is called *ADPDL*. *ADPDL* is more succinct than *DPDL* and also has the advantage of fitting nicely with our automata-theoretic techniques. As the translation from regular expressions to automata is linear, our results for *ADPDL* apply easily to *DPDL*. In this section we describe Vardi and Wolper's approach to *converse* $-$ *ADPDL* [VW84]. In the sequel we extend this approach to *converse* $-$ *loop* $-$ *DPDL* and *converse* $-$ *repeat* $-$ *DPDL*.

Formulas of *converse* $-$ *ADPDL* are built from a set of atomic propositions *Prop* and a set *Prog* of atomic programs. The sets of *formulas*, *tests*, *backward programs*, and *programs* are defined inductively as follows:

- every proposition $p \in Prop$ is a formula.
- if f_1 and f_2 are formulas, then $\neg f_1$ and $f_1 \wedge f_2$ are formulas.
- If f is a formula, then $f?$ is a test.
- If a is an atomic program, then a^- is a backward program.
- if α is a program and f is a formula, then $\langle\alpha\rangle f$ is a formula

- If α is a sequential automaton over an alphabet Σ, where Σ is a finite set of atomic programs, backward programs, and tests, then α is a program. (A sequential automaton is a tuple (Σ,S,ρ,s,F), where Σ is a finite alphabet, S is a finite set of states, $\rho:S\times\Sigma\to 2^S$ is a nondeterministic transition function, $s\in S$ is the starting state, and $F\subseteq S$ is a set of accepting states.) A word w accepted by α is called an *execution sequence of* α.

Let $Prog'$ be the set of atomic and backward programs.

Converse $-$ $ADPDL$ formulas are interpreted over structures $M=(W,R,\Pi)$ where W is a set of states, $R:Prog\to 2^{W\times W}$ is a deterministic transition relation (for each state u and atomic program a there is at most one pair $(u,u')\in R(a)$), and $\Pi:W\to 2^{Prop}$ assigns truth values to the propositions in $Prop$ for each state in W. We now extend R to all programs and define satisfaction of a formula f in a state u of a structure M, denoted $M,u\models f$, inductively:

- $R(f?)=\{(u,u):M,u\models f\}$.
- $R(a^-)=\{(v,u):(u,v)\in R(a)\}$.
- $R(\alpha)=\{(u,u')$: there exists an execution sequence $w=w_1\cdots w_n$ of α and states $u_0,u_1,\ldots,u_n$ of W such that $u=u_0$, $u'=u_n$ and for all $1\leq i\leq n$ we have $(u_{i-1},u_i)\in R(w_i)\}$.
- For a proposition $p\in Prop$, $M,u\models p$ iff $p\in\Pi(u)$.
- $M,u\models f_1\wedge f_2$ iff $M,u\models f_1$ and $M,u\models f_2$.
- $M,u\models\neg f_1$ iff not $M,u\models f_1$.
- $M,u\models\langle\alpha\rangle f$ iff there exists a state u' such that $(u,u')\in R(\alpha)$ and $M,u'\models f$.

Note that only atomic programs are required to be deterministic, while non-atomic programs can be nondeterministic.

A formula f is *satisfiable* if there is a structure M and a state u in the structure such that $M,u\models f$. The *satisfiability problem* is to determine, given a formula f, whether f is satisfiable.

To use the automata-theoretic technique, we first have to prove that *converse* $-$ $ADPDL$ has the *tree model property*. A *tree structure* for a formula f is a structure $M=(W,R,\Pi)$ such that:

1) $W\subseteq[n]^*$, where n is bounded by the length of f and $W\neq\emptyset$.
2) $xi\in W$ only if $x\in W$.
3) $(x,y)\in R(a)$ for an atomic or a backward program a only if x is the predecessor or the successor of y and $(x,y)\notin R(b)$ for any other atomic or backward program b.

A tree structure $M=(W,R,\Pi)$ is a *tree model* for f if $M,\lambda\models f$ (note that since $W\neq\emptyset$, $\lambda\in W$).

Proposition 2.1: [VW84] *Converse* $-$ $ADPDL$ has the tree model property. ■

In tree models for $ADPDL$ eventualities are accomplished by "downward" paths. That is, if $\langle\alpha\rangle g$ is satisfied in a state x, then the sequence of states that leads to a state that satisfies g is of the form $x,xi_1,xi_1i_2,xi_1i_2i_3,\cdots$. Thus an automaton that checks for satisfaction of eventualities only needed to go down the tree (we view the trees as growing downwards). In the presence of the *converse* construct, however, eventualities may require "two-way paths". Indeed, in [St82] *two-way automata* are defined in order to deal with *converse*. Unfortunately, the way the emptiness problem is solved for these automata is to convert them to one-way automata with a fourfold exponential increase in the number of states.

To avoid this difficulty we extend the logic by adding formulas that deal with "cycling" computations. If α is a program, then $cycle(\alpha)$ is a formula. Let $M=(W,R,\Pi)$ and $u\in W$, then $M,u\models cycle(\alpha)$ if $(u,u)\in R(\alpha)$. That is, $cycle(\alpha)$ holds in the state u if there is a computation of α that starts and terminates at u. Note that we do not consider cycle formulas as formulas of *converse* $-$ $ADPDL$, but they will be helpful in the decision procedure, because they enable us to check eventualities using "one-way" automata. (It is interesting to note that the extended logic, i.e., the logic that contains also the cycle formulas, is undecidable [Da84]).

It is not clear yet how cycle formulas help us solve our problem. Furthermore, how are we going to check satisfaction of cycle formulas by one-way automata? The solution is to add *directed* cycle formulas, in which the direction of the computation is specified. The semantics of such formulas is defined only on tree structures. If α is a program, then both $cycle_d(\alpha)$ and $cycle_u(\alpha)$ are formulas. We call these formulas *directed cycle formulas*. Formulas of the first type are called *downward cycle formulas*, and formulas of the second type are called *upward cycle formulas*. We now define the semantics of these formulas.

Let $M=(W,R,\Pi)$ be a tree structure, and let $x \in W$. $M,x \models cycle_d(\alpha)$ if there are an execution sequence $w=w_1 \cdots w_m$, $m \geq 1$, accepted by α and nodes $x_0,x_1,\ldots,x_m$ of W such that

- $x=x_0$ and $x=x_m$,
- $(x_i,x_{i+1}) \in R(w_{i+1})$ for all $0 \leq i \leq m-1$, and either
  - $m=1$ (so w is a test), or
  - $m>1$ and x_i properly succeeds x for $1 \leq i \leq m-1$.

That is, $cycle_d(\alpha)$ is satisfied at x if there is an accepting computation that consists only of a test or if it is accomplished downwardly by a computation that does not go through x except at the beginning and at the end.

Let $M=(W,R,\Pi)$ be a tree structure, and let $x \in W$. $M,x \models cycle_u(\alpha)$ if there are an execution sequence $w=w_1 \cdots w_m$, $m \geq 1$, accepted by α and nodes $x_0,x_1,\ldots,x_m$ of W such that

- $x=x_0$ and $x=x_m$,
- $(x_i,x_{i+1}) \in R(w_{i+1})$ for all $0 \leq i \leq m-1$, and
- $x_1=x_{m-1}$ is the predecessor of x.

That is, $cycle_u(\alpha)$ is satisfied at x if it is accomplished upwardly. Note that $cycle_u(\alpha)$ can be satisfied at a node x even if the computation goes through x at some other points than its beginning and end. This implies that the definitions of downward cycle formulas and upward cycle formulas are not symmetric.

The relationship between the various *cycle* formulas is expressed in the following proposition. Let $\alpha=(\Sigma,S,\rho,s_0,F)$ be a program, and let $p,q \in S$. We denote by the program (Σ,S,ρ,p,F) by α_p, $(\Sigma,S,\rho,s,\{q\})$ by α^q, and $(\Sigma,S,\rho,p,\{q\})$ by α_p^q. As we shall see later, when dealing with cycle formulas it suffices to consider programs of the form α_p^q.

Proposition 2.2: [VW84] Let $M=(W,R,\Pi)$ be a tree structure, let $x \in W$, and let $\alpha=(\Sigma,S,\rho,s,\{t\})$ be a program. Then $M,x \models cycle(\alpha)$ if and only if there are states $s_{j_1},\ldots,s_{j_k}$ in S, where $1 \leq k \leq |S|$, such that $s_{j_1}=s$, $s_{j_k}=t$, and for all $1 \leq i \leq k-1$, if $p=s_{j_i}$ and $q=s_{j_{i+1}}$, then $M,x \models cycle_u(\alpha_p^q)$ or $M,x \models cycle_d(\alpha_p^q)$. ■

As with cycle formulas, we distinguish between downward and upward accomplishment of eventualities. We therefore introduce two new types of formulas, whose semantics is defined only on tree structures. If α is a program and g is a formula, then both $\langle\alpha\rangle_d g$ and $\langle\alpha\rangle_u g$ are formulas. We call these formulas *directed eventualities*. Formulas of the former type are called *downward eventualities*, and formulas of the latter type are called *upward eventualities*. We now define the semantics of directed eventualities.

Let $M=(W,R,\Pi)$ be a tree structure, and let $x \in W$. We have that $M,x \models \langle\alpha\rangle_d g$ if there are an execution sequence $w=w_1 \cdots w_m$, $m \geq 0$, accepted by α and nodes $x_0,x_1,\ldots,x_m$ of W such that:

- $x=x_0$,
- $(x_i,x_{i+1}) \in R(w_{i+1})$ for all $0 \leq i \leq m-1$,
- $M,x_m \models g$, and
- there is $0 \leq k \leq m$ such that $x_k=x$ and x_i properly succeeds x for all $k+1 \leq i \leq m$ (this is vacuously true if $k=m$).

Let $M=(W,R,\Pi)$ be a tree structure, and let $x \in W$. We have that $M,x \models \langle\alpha\rangle_u g$ if there are an execution sequence $w=w_1 \cdots w_m$, $m \geq 1$, accepted by α and nodes $x_0,x_1,\ldots,x_m$ of W such that:

- $x=x_0$,
- $(x_i,x_{i+1}) \in R(w_{i+1})$ for all $0 \leq i \leq m-1$,
- $M,x_m \models g$, and
- there is $0 \leq k \leq m$ such that x_k is the predecessor of x.

Note that an upward eventuality actually requires that the computation eventually goes upward, while a downward eventuality does not require that the computation eventually goes downward. Also note that an eventuality can be satisfied both upwards and downwards. The relationship between the various types of eventualities is expressed in the next proposition.

Proposition 2.3: [VW84] Let $M=(W,R,\Pi)$ be a tree structure, let $x \in W$, let α be a program, and let g be a formula. Then $M,x \models \langle\alpha\rangle g$ if and only if either $M,x \models \langle\alpha\rangle_d g$ or $M,x \models \langle\alpha\rangle_u g$. ■

We now define the *extended closure*, $ecl(f)$, of a *converse* $-$ *ADPDL* formula f (we identify a formula $\neg\neg g$ with g):

- $f \in ecl(f)$
- If $g_1 \wedge g_2 \in ecl(f)$ then $g_1, g_2 \in ecl(f)$.
- If $\neg g \in ecl(f)$ then $g \in ecl(f)$.
- If $g \in ecl(f)$ then $\neg g \in ecl(f)$.
- If $\langle\alpha\rangle g \in ecl(f)$ then $g \in ecl(f)$.
- If $\langle\alpha\rangle g \in ecl(f)$, where $\alpha=(\Sigma,S,\rho,s_0,F)$, then $g' \in ecl(f)$ for all $g'? \in \Sigma$
- If $\langle\alpha\rangle g \in ecl(f)$, where $\alpha=(\Sigma,S,\rho,s_0,F)$, then $\langle\alpha_s\rangle g, \langle\alpha_s\rangle_d g, \langle\alpha_s\rangle_u g \in ecl(f)$ for all $s \in S$.
- If $\langle\alpha\rangle g \in ecl(f)$, where $\alpha=(\Sigma,S,\rho,s_0,F)$, then $cycle(\alpha_s^t), cycle_d(\alpha_s^t), cycle_u(\alpha_s^t) \in ecl(f)$ for all $s,t \in S$.

It is not hard to verify that the size of $ecl(f)$ is at most quadratic in the length of f.

To establish a decision procedure for *ADPDL*, we reduce the satisfiability problem to the emptiness problem for Büchi automata. To this end we associate an infinite n-ary tree over $2^{cl(f) \cup Prog' \cup \{\perp\}}$ with the tree model $M'=(W',R',\Pi')$ constructed above in a natural way: every node in W' is labeled by the formulas in $ecl(f)$ that are satisfied at that node, and the other nodes are labeled by the special symbol $\perp$. We also label nodes by atomic programs, and the labeling is to be interpreted as follows: if a node x is labeled by atomic program b and the predecessor of x is y, then $(x,y) \in R(b)$. Note that a node cannot be labeled by more than one atomic program. Trees that correspond to tree models satisfy some special properties.

A Hintikka tree for a *converse* $-$ *ADPDL* formula f is an n-ary tree $T:[n]^* \rightarrow 2^{ecl(f) \cup Prog' \cup \{\perp\}}$ that satisfies the following *Hintikka conditions*:

1) $f \in T(\lambda)$,

   and for all $x \in [n]^*$:

2)

   2.1) $|T(x) \cap Prog'| \leq 1$,

   2.2) if y,z are two distinct successors of x, $a \in Prog$, and $a^- \in T(y)$, then $a^- \notin T(z)$,

   2.3) if y is a successor of x, $a \in Prog$, and $a \in T(x)$, then $a^- \notin T(y)$,

3)

3.1) either $T(x)=\{\bot\}$ or $\bot \notin T(x)$ and $g \in T(x)$ iff $\neg g \notin T(x)$,

3.2) $g_1 \wedge g_2 \in T(x)$ iff $g_1 \in T(x)$ and $g_2 \in T(x)$,

4) if $\alpha=(\Sigma,S,\rho,s,\{t\})$ is a program, then

4.1) $cycle(\alpha) \in T(x)$ if and only if there are states $s_0, \ldots, s_m$ in S, where $0 \leq m \leq |S|$, such that $s_0=s$, $s_m=t$, and for all $0 \leq i \leq m-1$ either $cycle_u(\alpha_{s_i}^{s_{i+1}}) \in T(x)$ or $cycle_d(\alpha_{s_i}^{s_{i+1}}) \in T(x)$,

4.2) if y is the predecessor of x, then $cycle_u(\alpha) \in T(x)$ if and only if there are states $p,q \in S$ and a $b \in Prog'$ such that

- $b \in T(x)$,
- $cycle(\alpha_p^q) \in T(y)$,
- $p \in \rho(s,b)$ and $t \in \rho(q,b^-)$,

4.3) $cycle_d(\alpha) \in T(x)$ if either there is a test $g?$ such that $g \in T(x)$ and $t \in \rho(g?,s)$, or there are states $s_1, \ldots, s_m$ in S, $1 \leq m \leq |S|$, a program $b \in Prog'$ and a successor y of x such that

- $b^- \in T(y)$,
- $cycle_d(\alpha_{s_i}^{s_{i+1}}) \in T(y)$ for all $1 \leq i \leq m-1$,
- $s_1 \in \rho(s,b)$ and $t \in \rho(s_m,b^-)$,

4.4) $cycle_d(\alpha) \in T(x)$ only if there is a finite subset $W' \subseteq [n]^*$ with $x \in W'$ and a mapping $\varphi: W' \rightarrow 2^{ecl(f)}$ such that $cycle_d(\alpha) \in \varphi(x)$, and if $y \in W'$ and $cycle_d(\alpha_p^q) \in \varphi(y)$, then either there is a test $g?$ such that $g \in T(y)$ and $p \in \rho(q,g?)$, or there are states $s_1, \ldots, s_m$ in S, $1 \leq m \leq |S|$, a program $b \in Prog'$ and a successor $z \in W'$ of y such that

- $b^- \in T(z)$,
- $cycle_d(\alpha_{s_i}^{s_{i+1}}) \in \varphi(z)$ for all $1 \leq i \leq m-1$,
- $s_1 \in \rho(p,b)$ and $q \in \rho(s_m,b^-)$.

5) if $\alpha=(\Sigma,S,\rho,s,F)$ is a program and g is a formula, then

5.1) $\langle\alpha\rangle g \in T(x)$ if and only if either $\langle\alpha\rangle_d g \in T(x)$ or $\langle\alpha\rangle_u g \in T(x)$.

5.2) if y is the predecessor of x, then $\langle\alpha\rangle_u g \in T(x)$ if and only if there are states $p,q \in S$ and a program $b \in Prog'$, such that

- $cycle(\alpha_s^p) \in T(x)$,
- $q \in \rho(p,b)$,
- $b \in T(x)$,
- $\langle\alpha_q\rangle g \in T(y)$,

5.3) $\langle\alpha\rangle_d g \in T(x)$ if either $cycle(\alpha) \in T(x)$ and $g \in T(x)$, or there are states $p,q \in S$, a program $b \in Prog'$, and a successor y of x, such that

- $cycle(\alpha_s^p) \in T(x)$,
- $q \in \rho(p,b)$,
- $b^- \in T(y)$,
- $\langle\alpha_q\rangle_d g \in T(y)$,

5.4) $\langle\alpha\rangle_d g \in T(x)$ only if there are nodes $x_0, \ldots, x_k$, states $s_0,t_0, \ldots, s_k,t_k$ of S, and programs $b_1, \ldots, b_k \in Prog'$ such that

- $x_0=x$, $s_0=s$, $t_k\in F$, and $s_{i+1}\in\rho(t_i,b_{i+1})$ for all $0\leq i\leq k-1$,
- x_{i+1} is a successor of x_i and $b_{i+1}^{-}\in T(x_{i+1})$ for all $0\leq i\leq k-1$,
- $cycle(\alpha_{s_i}^{t_i})\in T(x_i)$ for $0\leq i\leq k$,
- $g\in T(x_k)$.

Proposition 2.4: [VW84] A *converse* $-$ *ADPDL* formula f has a tree model if and only if it has a Hintikka tree. ■

It remains now to construct a Büchi tree automaton A_f that accepts precisely the Hintikka trees for f. This is described in [VW84]. A_f has $O(\exp(n^2))$ states, where n is the length of f. This yields a decision procedure whose running time is $O(\exp(n^2))$.

3. *Converse* $-$ *loop* $-$ *ADPDL*

Converse $-$ *ADPDL* is a logic to reason about input/output behavior of programs. This is not adequate for reasoning about the behavior of nonterminating programs such as operating systems. To this end we extend the logic by constructs that deal with infinite computations. One such construct is the *loop* construct [HS83a]. Intuitively, the formula $loop(\alpha)$ holds in a state if there is an infinite computation of α from that state. Sherman and Pnueli have shown that *loop* $-$ *PDL* is decidable in exponential time [PS83], and Vardi and Wolper have shown by automata-theoretic techniques that *loop* $-$ *DPDL* is also decidable in exponential time [VW84]. We now show how the automata-theoretic framework can be extended to *converse* $-$ *loop* $-$ *ADPDL*, for which no previous results were known.

Formally, we get *converse* $-$ *loop* $-$ *ADPDL* by extending the definition of of *converse* $-$ *ADPDL* by the following syntactic and semantic clauses.

- If α is a program, then $loop(\alpha)$ is a formula.
- $M,u\models loop(\alpha)$, where $\alpha=(\Sigma,S,\rho,s_0,F)$, iff there are an infinite word $w=w_1w_2\cdots$ over Σ, an infinite sequence $s_0,s_1,\cdots$ of states of S, and an infinite sequence $u_0,u_1,\cdots$ of nodes of W such that:
  - $u_0=u$, $s_0=s$ and
  - for all $i\geq 1$, $s_i\in\rho(s_{i-1},w_i)$ and $(u_{i-1},u_i)\in R(w_i)$.

Proposition 3.1: *Converse* $-$ *loop* $-$ *ADPDL* has the tree model property. ■

As with eventualities, we distinguish between downward and upward fulfillment of loop formulas. We introduce two new types of formulas, whose semantics is defined only on tree structures. If α is a program, then both $loop_d(\alpha)$ and $loop_u(\alpha)$ are formulas. We call these formulas *directed loop formulas*. Formulas of the former type are called *downward loop formulas*, and formulas of the latter type are called *upward loop formulas*. We now define the semantics of directed loop formulas.

Let $M=(W,R,\Pi)$ be a tree structure, and let $x\in W$. We have that $M,x\models loop_d(\alpha)$, where $\alpha=(\Sigma,S,\rho,s_0,F)$, iff there are an infinite word $w=w_1w_2\cdots$ over Σ, an infinite sequence $s_0,s_1,\cdots$ of states of S, and an infinite sequence $x_0,x_1,\cdots$ of nodes of W such that:

- $x_0=x$, $s_0=s$ and
- for all $i\geq 1$, $s_i\in\rho(s_{i-1},w_i)$ and $(x_{i-1},x_i)\in R(w_i)$.
- if there some $i\geq 0$ such that $x_i=x$ and $x_j\neq x$ for all $j>i$, then x_j properly succeeds x for all $j>i$.

Let $M=(W,R,\Pi)$ be a tree structure, and let $x\in W$. We have that $M,x\models loop_u(\alpha)$, where $\alpha=(\Sigma,S,\rho,s_0,F)$, iff there are an infinite word $w=w_1w_2\cdots$ over Σ, an infinite sequence $s_0,s_1,\cdots$ of states of S, and an infinite sequence $x_0,x_1,\cdots$ of nodes of W such that:

- $x_0=x$, $s_0=s$ and

- for all $i \geq 1$, $s_i \in \rho(s_{i-1}, w_i)$ and $(x_{i-1}, x_i) \in R(w_i)$.
- there is some $i \geq 1$ such that x_i is the predecessor of x.

Note that a downward loop formula actually requires that the computation eventually goes downward (unless it loops forever on the same state), while an upward eventuality does not require that the computation eventually goes upward. Also note that a loop formula can be satisfied both upwards and downwards. The relationship between the various types of loop formulas is expressed in the next proposition.

Proposition 3.2: [VW84] Let $M=(W,R,\Pi)$ be a tree structure, let $x \in W$, and let α be a program. Then $M,x \models loop(\alpha)$ if and only if either $M,x \models loop_d(\alpha)$ or $M,x \models loop_u(\alpha)$. ■

To deal with *loop* formulas, we extend the definition of the extended closure by the following clause:

- If $loop(\alpha) \in ecl(f)$, where $\alpha=(\Sigma,S,\rho,s_0,F)$, then $loop(\alpha_s), loop_d(\alpha_s), loop_u(\alpha_s) \in ecl(f)$ for all $s \in S$.

The size of $ecl(f)$ is of course still at most quadratic in the length of f.

We can now define Hintikka trees for $converse-loop-ADPDL$ formulas.

A Hintikka tree for a $converse-loop-ADPDL$ formula f is an n-ary tree $T:[n]^* \rightarrow 2^{ecl(f) \cup Prog' \cup \{\bot\}}$ that satisfies Hintikka conditions 1-5 and also

6) if $\alpha=(\Sigma,S,\rho,s,F)$ is a program then

   6.1) $loop(\alpha) \in T(x)$ if and only if either $loop_d(\alpha) \in T(x)$ or $loop_u(\alpha) \in T(x)$.

   6.2) if y is the predecessor of x, then $loop_u(\alpha) \in T(x)$ if and only if there are states $p,q \in S$ and an atomic program b, such that

   - $cycle(\alpha_s^p) \in T(x)$,
   - $q \in \rho(p,b)$,
   - $b \in T(x)$,
   - $loop(\alpha_q) \in T(y)$,

   6.3) if $loop_d(\alpha) \in T(x)$, where $\alpha=(\Sigma,S,\rho,s,F)$, then there exists a state $p \in S$ such that either

   a) $cycle(\alpha_s^p) \in T(x)$ and $cycle(\alpha_p^p) \in T(x)$, or

   b) there are a state $q \in S$, a program $b \in Prog'$, and successor y of x such that

   - $cycle(\alpha_s^p) \in T(x)$,
   - $q \in \rho(p,b)$,
   - $b^- \in T(y)$,
   - $loop_d(\alpha_q) \in T(y)$.

   6.4) if $\neg loop_d(\alpha) \in T(x)$ then, there is a finite subset $W' \subseteq [n]^*$ with $x \in W'$ and a mapping $\varphi: W' \rightarrow 2^{ecl(f)}$ such that $\neg loop_d(\alpha) \in \varphi(x)$, and if $y \in W'$ and $\neg loop(\alpha_p) \in \varphi(y)$, then

   - there is no state $p \in S$ such that $cycle(\alpha_s^p) \in T(y)$ and $cycle(\alpha_p^p) \in T(y)$,
   - if for some states $p,q \in S$, $b \in Prog'$, and z successor of y we have that
     - $cycle(\alpha_s^p)$,
     - $q \in \rho(p,b)$, and
     - $b^- \in T(z)$,

     then $z \in W'$ and $\neg loop_d(\alpha_q) \in T(z)$.

Proposition 3.3: A $converse-loop-ADPDL$ formula f has a tree model if and only if it has a Hintikka tree. ■

It remains now to construct a Büchi tree automaton A_f that accepts precisely the Hintikka trees for f. The method is that of [VW84]. A_f has $O(\exp(n^2))$ states, where n is the length of f. This yields a decision procedure whose running time is $O(\exp(n^2))$.

4. *Converse – repeat – ADPDL*

Another construct that deal with infinite computations is the *repeat* construct [St80] (*repeat* is denoted by Δ in [St80]). Intuitively, the formula $repeat(\alpha)$ is true in a state if there is a way to repeatedly execute α without stopping. It is known that the construct *repeat* is strictly more powerful than the construct *loop* [HS83a]. The addition of *repeat* to *PDL* seems to make the decision problem quite harder. The best known upper bound for *repeat* – (*D*)*PDL* is nondeterministic time $O(exp(n^2))$ [VS85]. We now show how to extend our technique to *converse – repeat – ADPDL* for which no previous results were known.

Formally, we get *converse – repeat – ADPDL* by extending the definition of *converse – ADPDL* by the following syntactic and semantic clauses:

- If α is a program, then $repeat(\alpha)$ is a formula.
- $M,u \models repeat(\alpha)$, where $\alpha=(\Sigma,S,\rho,s_0,F)$, iff there are an infinite sequence $w_1,w_2\cdots$ of execution sequences of α, and an infinite sequence $u_0,u_1,\cdots$ of nodes of W such that: $u_0=u$ and $(u_{i-1},u_i)\in R(w_i)$ for all $i\geq 1$.

Rather than deal with *converse – repeat – ADPDL*, we deal with an equivalent logic, *converse – Büchi – ADPDL*. The latter logic has infinite programs described by Büchi automata.

Formally, we get *converse – Büchi – ADPDL* by extending the definition of of *converse – ADPDL* by the following syntactic and semantic clauses.

- If α is a program, then $\langle\!\langle\alpha\rangle\!\rangle$ is a formula.
- $M,u \models \langle\!\langle\alpha\rangle\!\rangle$, where $\alpha=(\Sigma,S,\rho,s_0,F)$, iff there are an infinite word $w=w_1w_2\cdots$ over Σ, an infinite sequence $s_0,s_1,\cdots$ of states of S, and an infinite sequence $u_0,u_1,\cdots$ of nodes of W such that:
  - $u_0=u$ and $s_0=s$,
  - for some $s\in F$ we have $|\{i : s_i=s\}|\models\omega$ (i.e., some state in F occurs infinitely often in the sequence $s_0,s_1,\cdots$), and
  - for all $i\geq 1$, $s_i\in\rho(s_{i-1},w_i)$ and $(u_{i-1},u_i)\in R(w_i)$.

Note that the semantics of $\langle\!\langle\alpha\rangle\!\rangle$ is very closed to the semantics of $loop(\alpha)$; the only difference is the additional requirement that some state in F repeats infinitely often. This condition is essentially Büchi acceptance condition for automata on infinite words [Bu62].

Proposition 4.1. There is linear translation from *converse – repeat – ADPDL* to *converse – Büchi – ADPDL*. Namely, there is a logspace mapping γ such that if φ is a *converse – repeat – ADPDL* formula, then $\gamma(\varphi)$ is a *converse – Büchi – ADPDL* formula, $|\gamma(\varphi)|=O(|\varphi|)$, and φ is logically equivalent to $\gamma(\varphi)$. Similarly, there is quadratic translation from *converse – Büchi – ADPDL* to *converse – repeat – ADPDL*. ■

Thus it suffices to consider *converse – Büchi – ADPDL*.

Proposition 4.2: *Converse – Büchi – ADPDL* has the tree model property. ■

It turns out that cycle formulas, and even directed cycle formulas, are not sufficient to enable us to deal with tree models for *converse – Büchi – ADPDL* by one-way automata. What we need is to strengthen our cycle formulas in the following way. If $\alpha=(\Sigma,S,\rho,s,F)$ is a program, then $scycle(\alpha)$ is a formula. Let $M=(W,R,\Pi)$ and $u\in W$, then $M,u\models scycle(\alpha)$ if there are a sequence $s_0,\ldots,s_k$, of states in S, an execution sequence $w_1\cdots w_k$ of α, and a sequence $u_0,\ldots,u_k$ of nodes in W, $k\geq 1$, such that $s_0=s$, $u_0=u_k=u$, $s_i\in\rho(s_{i-1},w_i)$ and $(u_{i-1},u_i)\in R(w_i)$ for all $1\leq i\leq k$, and $s_i\in F$ for *some* $1\leq i\leq k$. That is, $scycle(\alpha)$ holds in the state u if there is a computation of α that starts and terminates at u and goes through a state in F.

We now can strengthen also directed cycle formulas in an analogous way. In fact the whole treatment of cycle formulas [VW84] can be strengthened in a straightforward way to deal with the requirement that the cycling computations go through designated states. To deal with <<>> formulas, we extend the definition of extended closure by the following clauses:

- If $\langle\!\langle\alpha\rangle\!\rangle g \in ecl(f)$, where $\alpha=(\Sigma,S,\rho,s_0,F)$, then $scycle(\alpha_s^t)$, $scycle_d(\alpha_s^t)$, $scycle_u(\alpha_s^t) \in ecl(f)$ for all $s,t \in S$.
- If $\langle\!\langle\alpha\rangle\!\rangle \in ecl(f)$, where $\alpha=(\Sigma,S,\rho,s_0,F)$, then $\langle\alpha^t\rangle\langle\!\langle\alpha_t\rangle\!\rangle \in ecl(f)$ for all $t \in S$.

It is not hard to verify that the size of $ecl(f)$ is still at most quadratic in the length of f.

We can now define Hintikka trees for $converse-B\ddot{u}chi-ADPDL$ formulas.

A Hintikka tree for a $converse-B\ddot{u}chi-ADPDL$ formula f is an n-ary tree $T:[n]^* \to 2^{ecl(f) \cup Prog' \cup \{\bot\}}$ that satisfies Hintikka conditions 1-5 and also

7) if $\alpha=(\Sigma,S,\rho,s,\{t\})$ is a program, then

7.1) $scycle(\alpha) \in T(x)$ if and only if there are states $s_0, \ldots, s_m$ in S, where $1 \le m \le |S|$, such that

- $s_0=s$, $s_m=t$,
- for all $0 \le i \le m-1$ either $cycle_u(\alpha_{s_i}^{s_{i+1}}) \in T(x)$ or $cycle_d(\alpha_{s_i}^{s_{i+1}}) \in T(x)$,
- for some $0 \le i \le m-1$ either $scycle_u(\alpha_{s_i}^{s_{i+1}}) \in T(x)$ or $scycle_d(\alpha_{s_i}^{s_{i+1}}) \in T(x)$,

7.2) if y is the predecessor of x, then $scycle_u(\alpha) \in T(x)$ if and only if there are states $p,q \in S$ and a program $b \in Prog'$ such that

- $b \in T(x)$,
- $cycle(\alpha_p^q) \in T(y)$, and if $p,q \notin F$ then $scycle(\alpha_p^q) \in T(y)$,
- $p \in \rho(s,b)$ and $t \in \rho(q,b^-)$,

7.3) $scycle_d(\alpha) \in T(x)$ if either there is a test $g?$ such that $g \in T(x)$ and $t \in \rho(g?,s) \cap F$, or there are states $s_1, \ldots, s_m$ in S, $1 \le m \le |S|$, a program $b \in Prog'$, and a successor y of x such that

- $b^- \in T(y)$,
- $cycle_d(\alpha_{s_i}^{s_{i+1}}) \in T(y)$ for all $1 \le i \le m-1$, and $scycle_d(\alpha_{s_i}^{s_{i+1}}) \in T(y)$ for some $1 \le i \le m-1$,
- $s_1 \in \rho(s,b)$ and $t \in \rho(s_m,b^-)$,

7.5) $scycle_d(\alpha) \in T(x)$ only if there is a finite subset $W' \subseteq [n]^*$ with $x \in W'$ and a mapping $\varphi: W' \to 2^{ecl(f)}$ such that $cycle_d(\alpha) \in \varphi(x)$, and if $y \in W'$ and $cycle_d(\alpha_p^q) \in \varphi(y)$, then either there is a test $g?$ such that $g \in T(y)$ and $p \in \rho(q,g?) \cap F$, or there are states $s_1, \ldots, s_m$ in S, $1 \le m \le |S|$, a program $b \in Prog'$ and a successor $z \in W'$ of y such that

- $b^- \in T(z)$,
- $cycle_d(\alpha_{s_i}^{s_{i+1}}) \in \varphi(z)$ for all $1 \le i \le m-1$, and $cycle_d(\alpha_{s_i}^{s_{i+1}}) \in \varphi(z)$ for some $1 \le i \le m-1$,
- $s_1 \in \rho(p,b)$ and $q \in \rho(s_m,b^-)$.

8) if $\alpha=(\Sigma,S,\rho,s,F)$ is a program then

8.1) $\langle\!\langle\alpha\rangle\!\rangle \in T(x)$ iff $\langle\alpha^t\rangle\langle\!\langle\alpha_t\rangle\!\rangle \in T(x)$ for some $t \in S$,

8.2) $\langle\!\langle\alpha\rangle\!\rangle \in T(x)$ if there there is a state $t \in S$ such that $cycle(\alpha_s^t) \in T(x)$ and $scycle(\alpha_t^t) \in T(x)$,

8.3) $\langle\!\langle\alpha\rangle\!\rangle \in T(x)$ if there are an infinite sequences $x_0,x_1,\cdots$ of nodes in $[n]^*$, infinite sequences $s_0,s_1,\cdots$ and $t_0,t_1,\ldots$ of states in S, and an infinite sequence $b_0,b_1,\cdots$ of programs in $Prog'$ such that

- $x_0 = x$ and x_{i+1} is a successor of x_i for all $i \geq 0$,
- $s_0 = s$, $cycle(\alpha_{s_i}^{t_i}) \in T(x_i)$, $s_{i+1} \in \rho(t_i, b_i)$, and $b_i^- \in T(x_{i+1})$ for all $i \geq 0$,
- there is a sequence $0 \leq i_0 < i_1, \cdots$ such that if $p = s_{i_j}$ and $q = t_{i_j}$ then $scycle(\alpha_p^q) \in T(x_{i_j})$ for all $j \geq 0$.

Theorem 4.3: A $converse - B\ddot{u}chi - ADPDL$ f has a tree model if and only if it has a Hintikka tree. ■

It seems that all that remains now is to construct a Büchi automaton that accepts precisely the Hintikka trees for f. Unfortunately, this is impossible (the impossibility follows from results by Rabin [Ra70].) The difficulty comes from condition 8.3, since, using the techniques of [VW84], it is not hard to construct a Büchi automaton that check the other conditions. Thus, rather than use Büchi automata to accept Hintikka trees for $converse - repeat - ADPDL$, we have to use the more powerful *hybrid* automata of Vardi and Stockmeyer [VS85].

A *hybrid* tree automaton H is a pair (A, B), where A is a Rabin tree automaton and B is a Büchi sequential automaton, both over the same alphabet Σ. H *accepts* a tree T if T is accepted by A and, for every infinite path P starting at λ, B rejects the infinite word $T(P)$. We need not concern ourselves here with Rabin automata; it suffices to say that every Büchi automaton can be viewed as a Rabin automaton. The key fact about hybrid automata, proven in [VS85], is that given a hybrid automata $H = (A, B)$, we can test whether H accepts some tree in nondeterministic time that is polynomial in the size of A and exponential ($O(2n^2)$) in the size of B.

To construct a hybrid automaton that accepts that Hintikka trees of f, we construct a Büchi tree automaton A_f that check all the conditions except for 8.3, and we construct a Büchi sequential automaton B_f that checks for *violations* of condition 8.3. The hybrid automaton $H_f = (A_f, B_f)$ accepts precisely the Hintikka trees of f. While A_f has $O(2^{n^2})$ states, B_f has only $O(n^2)$ states. This yields a decision procedure that runs in nondeterministic time $O(\exp(n^4))$.

References

[BHP82] M. Ben-Ari, J.Y. Halpern, A. Pnueli, "Deterministic Propositional Dynamic Logic: Finite Models, Complexity, and Completeness", *J. Computer and System Science,* 25(1982), pp. 402-417.

[Bu62] J.R. Büchi, "On a Decision Method in Restricted Second Order Arithmetic", *Proc. Int'l Congr. Logic, Method and Phil. Sci. 1960,* Stanford University Press, 1962, pp. 1-12.

[Da84] R. Danecki, *"Propositional Dynamic Logic with Strong Looping Predicate",* 1984.

[dB80] J. de Bakker, *Mathematical theory of program correctness*, Prentice hall, 1980.

[FL79] M.J. Fisher, R.E. Ladner, "Propositional Dynamic Logic of Regular Programs", *J. Computer and System Sciences,* 18(2), 1979, pp. 194-211.

[Ha83] J.Y. Halpern, private communication, 1983.

[HS83a] D. Harel, R. Sherman, "Looping vs. Repeating in Dynamic Logic", *Information and Control* 55(1982), pp. 175-192.

[HS83b] D. Harel, R. Sherman, "Propositional Dynamic Logic of Flowcharts", *Proc. Int. Conf. on Foundations of Computation Theory,* Lecture Notes in Computer Science, vol. 158, Springer-Verlag, Berlin, 1983, pp. 195-206.

[Pa80 Parikh, R.: A completeness result for PDL. *Symp. on Math. Foundations of Computer Science, Zakopane, 1978.*

[Pr76] V.R. Pratt, "Semantical Considerations on Floyd-Hoare Logic", *Proc. 17th IEEE Symp. on Foundations of Computer Science,* Houston, October 1976, pp. 109-121.

[Pr79] V.R. Pratt, "Models of Program Logics", *Proc. 20th IEEE Symp. on Foundation of Computer Science,* San Juan, 1979, pp. 115-122.

[Pr80] V.R. Pratt, "A Near-Optimal Method for Reasoning about Action", *J. Computer and Systems Sciences* 20(1980), pp. 231-254.

[Pr81] V.R. Pratt, "Using Graphs to understand PDL", *Proc. Workshop on Logics of Programs,* (D. Kozen, ed.), Yorktown-Heights, Lecture Notes in Computer Science, vol. 131, Springer-Verlag, Berlin, 1982, pp. 387-396.

[PS83] A. Pnueli, R. Sherman, *"Propositional Dynamic Logic of Looping Flowcharts",* Technical Report, Weizmann Institute, Rehovot, Israel, 1983.

[Ra70] M.O. Rabin, "Weakly Definable Relations and Special Automata", *Proc. Symp. Math. Logic and Foundations of Set Theory* (Y. Bar-Hillel, ed.), North-Holland, 1970, pp. 1-23.

[Sh84] R. Sherman, *"Variants of Propositional Dynamic Logic,"* Ph.D. Dissertation, The Weizmann Inst. of Science, 1984.

[St80] R.S. Streett, *"A Propositional Dynamic Logic for Reasoning about Program Divergence",* M.Sc. Thesis, MIT, 1980.

[St82] R.S. Streett, "Propositional Dynamic Logic of Looping and Converse is elementarily decidable", *Information and Control* 54(1982), pp. 121-141.

[VS85] M.Y. Vardi, L. Stockmeyer, "Improved Upper and Lower Bounds for Modal Logics of Programs", To appear in *Proc. 17th ACM Symp. on Theory of Computing,* Providence, May 1985.

[VW84] M. Y. Vardi, P. Wolper, "Automata Theoretic Techniques for Modal Logics of Programs", IBM Research Report, October 1984. A preliminary version appeared in *Proc. ACM Symp. on Theory of Computing,* Wahington, April 1984, pp. 446-456.